The McGraw-Hill College Handbook

An Alphabetical List of Correction Symbols

Numbers in parentheses indicate chapters and sections in *The McGraw-Hill College Handbook.*

ab	Incorrect abbreviation (31C–D)
act	Use active voice (15D)
ad	Misused adjective or adverb (9)
agr	Error in subject-verb agreement (6)
aud	Audience not clear (1D)
awk	Awkward sentence
bib	Bibliographic form incorrect (33C)
ca	Incorrect use of case (8H)
cap	Use a capital letter (30)
cit	Citation missing or in incorrect form (33I–L)
co	Coordination (13A)
corr	Make corrections indicated (1L)
cs	Comma splice (4)
d	Faulty diction (17)
dang	Dangling modifier (10A)
det	Use concrete details (1, 2E)
dev	Develop essay more fully (1E–H)
div	Word not divided correctly (29E)
draft	See sections on preparing drafts (1H–J)
emph	Inappropriate emphasis (15)
fig	Inappropriate figurative language (18)
frag	Sentence fragment (5)
gd	Good word or sentence
gl/gr *gl/us*	Refer to glossary of grammatical terms or to glossary of usage
gr	Error in grammar (3-11)
id	Incorrect idiom (17E)
ital	Underline to indicate italics (32)
k	Awkward construction
lc	Use a lowercase letter (30E)
lmt	Topic not sufficiently limited (1B)
log	Faulty logic (12)
misp (or mm)	Misplaced modifier (10B–E)
ms	Incorrect manuscript form (1K)
no cap	Capital letter not needed (30E)
no ∧,	Comma unnecessary (24P)
no ¶	New paragraph unnecessary (2)
n	Incorrect use of numbers (31A–B)
p	Punctuation error (23-28)
⊙	Period (23A)

?/	Question mark (23B)
!/	Exclamation point (23C)
∧,	Comma (24)
;/	Semicolon (25)
∨'	Apostrophe (26)
∨“\∨”	Quotation marks (27)
- ⊙ (\) [/] /	Dash, colon, parentheses, brackets, slash (28)
...	Ellipsis mark (28)
par, ¶	New paragraph needed (2)
¶ *coh*	Paragraph not coherent (2B)
¶ *dev*	Paragraph not developed (2C–D)
¶ *rev*	Paragraph needs revision (2E)
¶ *un*	Paragraph not unified (2A)
pass	Inappropriate passive voice (15D)
plan	Revise essay plan (1A–D)
pl	Error in plural use (29C)
pro	Error in pronoun use (8)
prf	Proofread (1J)
purp	Purpose unclear (1C)
red	Redundant (20E)
ref	Faulty pronoun reference (8)
rep	Needless repetition (20E)
rev	Revise (1I-1, 2E, 20A)
ro	Run-on sentence (4)
shift	Confusing shift (11)
sp	Spelling error (29)
sub	Subordination (13B)
sxl	Sexist language (21)
t	Error in verb tense (7)
thesis	Thesis unstated or unclear (1F)
trans	Transition required (2B, 5–6)
uc	Use a capital letter (30)
var	Vary sentence structure (16, App. A)
vb	Error in verb form (7)
wdy	Wordy (20)
ww	Wrong word (20)
∧	Something missing (19)
//	Faulty parallelism (14)
?	Unclear
◡	Close up space
#	Insert space

The McGraw-Hill College Handbook

Richard Marius
Harvard University

Harvey S. Wiener
The City University of New York
LaGuardia Community College

McGraw-Hill Book Company

New York St. Louis San Francisco Auckland Bogotá Hamburg Johannesburg London Madrid Mexico Montreal New Delhi Panama Paris São Paulo Singapore Sydney Tokyo Toronto

THE McGRAW-HILL COLLEGE HANDBOOK

1 2 3 4 5 6 7 8 9 0 KGPKGP 8 9 8 7 6 5 4

ISBN 0-07-040368-6

This book was set in Times Roman by Progressive Typographers, Inc.
The editors were Phillip A. Butcher, Emily G. Barrosse, Allan Forsyth, and David Dunham;
the designer was Merrill Haber;
the production supervisor was Joe Campanella.
Kingsport Press, Inc., was printer and binder.

Library of Congress Cataloging in Publication Data

Marius, Richard.
The McGraw-Hill college handbook.

Includes index.
1. English language—Grammar—1950- . 2. English language—Rhetoric. I. Wiener, Harvey S. II. McGraw-Hill Book Company. III. Title.
PE1112.M33 1985 808′.042 84-15402
ISBN 0-07-040368-6

Contents

PART THREE WRITING CLEAR AND EFFECTIVE SENTENCES

PART FOUR USING WORDS EFFECTIVELY

PART FIVE PUNCTUATION

Preface

To the teacher

A handbook is a tool for good writing, and we have tried to make this one sharp and efficient. We aimed for clear writing, accurate explanations that are easy to understand, and informative and engaging exercises.

We expect this book to be used in freshman composition classes and in other classes in writing, language, or literature offered in English departments. We value literature, long the staple of freshman writing courses, and so we draw many examples from it. But we believe that students should learn how to write for courses in all departments. Our book therefore uses examples from history, psychology, economics, physics, biology, business, engineering (to name a few), to illustrate our conviction that good writing exists in many fields. Indeed our society requires clear presentations of accurate information if people are to make sensible decisions. And no matter what form it takes—journal articles, books, speeches, newspaper reports, television scripts—most information comes to us, either directly or indirectly, through the medium of writing.

To emphasize this need for good writing in all fields, we have included a student research paper on a scientific topic in addition to a paper about a novelist's early years. Because a handbook should incorporate current standards, the scientific research paper uses the 1984 MLA style of referencing; while the literary paper illustrates the earlier (1977) MLA style.

We expect *The McGraw-Hill College Handbook* to serve as a guide for students throughout their college careers and in their personal and professional lives thereafter. For this reason, we have included an appendix on "Writing with Word Processors," even though these wonderful writing implements are just beginning to come into general use.

We also expect that students will enjoy reading this handbook even as they learn from it. We have tried to be serious without being solemn and challenging without being abstruse. Sometimes we have even tried to be humorous, but we have never intended to be condescending.

The McGraw-Hill College Handbook focuses as much on process as it does on product. Too often in the past handbooks have spent too much time showing students a correct writing product without telling them how to get there. We have worked hard on our chapters on process to give a realistic account of how writers write. Hardly any writer writes without studying the subject carefully beforehand and then writing several drafts on the way to publication. Students who follow our trail through process will arrive much more confidently at a piece of work that will make them proud of their efforts and their accomplishments.

We have also looked for a middle ground between the extreme positions about rules for writing. We have tried to be neither too rigid nor too flexible in our presentation and interpretation of the rules. We do not believe that writers are inspired to write by learning the rules first; people want to write because they have something to say. As they continue to write, most people want to know how to communicate more clearly and effectively. Therefore we have shown how good writers communicate with different audiences. We also observe that good writers sometimes break some of the "rules" of writing; but we make a distinction between those rules that can be broken now and then and those that cannot. We do not teach that the rules of writing are carved in granite; but neither do we teach that they are written in sand. Our philosophy is that writing is guided by principles rather than rules, and we have tried to state those principles clearly and to illustrate them by the work of good contemporary writers.

To the student

The best way to use this book is to keep it handy as a reference. From time to time, pick it up and browse through it at random. When your teacher refers you to a section of the handbook, study the section and do the exercises to fix the principles in your mind. By all means, read Chapters One and Two on the writing process before you begin writing your first paper.

The index at the back of the book and the plan of the text outlined on the inside back cover will help you locate information that deals with your special problems and your special interests. The correction symbols and the directory of special features on the inside front cover will help you find special sections quickly.

The ability to write well can give you both pleasure and power. You owe it to yourself to discover the joy of writing, the excitement of expressing your ideas, your feelings, your thoughts, your discoveries, your arguments, about everything from the daily events in your life to the demands of a perilous yet promising future. As you learn to write well, you will also discover that people are more likely to respect and accept your opinions, because you can express yourself in writing that engages and persuades your readers.

No handbook can make writing easy; good writing always takes hard work. But we hope that *The McGraw-Hill College Handbook* can make writing less difficult for you and can give you both guidance and pleasure along the way.

Acknowledgments

We are grateful to the many people who helped us with this book along the long way from its conception to publication. Teaching English composition is probably the most difficult job in any university. Perhaps it is the very difficulty of our profession that makes its members feel so strongly the sense of mutual obligation and respect that binds us all together. We have been the beneficiaries of those helpful sentiments from the many teachers in the field who have reviewed the manuscript of this book at its various stages, and we could not have done our work without their searching commentaries and their generous encouragement. These reviewers include:

Jay Balderson	Western Illinois University
John C. Bean	Montana State University
Kathleen L. Bell	University of Miami, Coral Gables
Richard H. Bullock	Northeastern University
Joseph J. Comprone	University of Louisville
Harry H. Crosby	Boston University
Robert M. Esch	University of Texas at El Paso
James A. Freeman	University of Massachusetts at Amherst
Dennis R. Gabriel	Cuyahoga Community College
Frank Hubbard	California State University, Sacramento
Lee A. Jacobus	University of Connecticut, Storrs
Russ Larson	Eastern Michigan University
Peter D. Lindblom	Miami-Dade Community College
Joe Lostracco	Austin Community College
Sheila J. McDonald	C.W. Post Center, LIU
Donald A. McQuade	Queens College, CUNY
Sharon Niederman	Metropolitan State, Denver
Jack B. Oruch	University of Kansas, Lawrence
Karen Reid	Midwestern State University
Kathleen W. Ritch	Santa Fe Community College, Gainesville
Annette T. Rottenberg	University of Massachusetts at Amherst
Donald C. Stewart	Kansas State University, Manhattan
John Stratton	University of Kansas, Little Rock
Margaret A. Strom	Eastern Maine Technical Institute
Sebastian J. Vasta	Camden Community College

We have worked with several McGraw-Hill editors along the way. Bill Talkington brought us together one night in New York and started us along the journey. As English editors in the College Division, Phil Butcher and Jim Dodd steadfastly supported the book's progress over the years. Cheryl Kupper edited with intelligence and thoroughness an earlier version of the manuscript, and Annette B. Hall carried the work on for a time.

Allan Forsyth finally came on to take the book firmly in hand and to guide it to a conclusion. He has read it all again and again, making myriads of suggestions in his strong, unmistakable handwriting, speaking to us sometimes almost daily on the telephone, encouraging us, sifting ideas, asking us to cut here and to add there, driving us to meet deadlines, and bringing five hard years of work to a good end. It is to his credit that after such labor, we all still like each other.

David Dunham and Joseph Campanella have shepherded the manuscript through the production process, somehow keeping the book on schedule while incorporating our last-minute efforts to correct and to improve it. Mel Haber's design has proved to be both practical and handsome.

Our thanks, too, to Seiji Yamada for allowing us to use elements of one of his term papers in Chapter 33.

To these people, and to all the others who have made contributions to this project, our gratitude. And to our families we give our loving thanks for being with us all the days.

Richard Marius
Harvey S. Wiener

PART ONE
The Writing Process

1

Planning, Developing, and Revising Papers

Although grammar, usage, and mechanics are important in writing courses, students usually must do a writing assignment before they do much else. Most instructors require a paper within the first class session or two. You may have to write in class on a topic such as your first reactions to college life, the chaos of registration, or the challenge of choosing a program of study. You may have to write outside of class on a topic such as a description of a room you know well, a scene you have observed, a person you have met recently, or your experience on a job. Or your instructor simply may tell you, "Write an essay on the topic of your choice."

To help you do that early assignment and others that will follow, the first part of this handbook describes the writing process. The term **writing process** includes all the related and overlapping tasks that writers perform in exploring, defining, and shaping a piece of work. From the time you *consider* writing something until the time you actually *produce* a final manuscript, you take several steps. You may be tempted to skip some of these steps in your rush to submit a paper, but you should resist that temptation. Most readers can tell when you have rushed through an assignment, and you will be disappointed in your own work when you try to cut corners.

The writing process involves thinking about a topic, recording ideas about it, thinking about the audience for the topic, and finally writing about it. Because different writers develop their topics in different ways, your own writing process need not follow a rigid order. But a finished piece of writing reflects a process of development that includes many steps, and the first of these usually involves a form of preparation called *prewriting.*

1A Use prewriting techniques to explore what you know, believe, or feel about a subject before you write about it.

Prewriting covers all the steps that writers take before they commit themselves to a specific subject. When you prewrite, you limber up. You think about your subject to jog loose ideas. You play with words and phrases,

following them where they take you without worrying about order or completeness. You see where your own impulses, thoughts, and interests lead before you investigate your topic rigorously. These suggestions for prewriting follow in no absolute sequence, but all of them will help you develop and record ideas.

1 Think about your subject.

Good writing for any assignment begins with thinking. Although this point may seem obvious, many students start writing an essay long before they have let their ideas on a topic sharpen and develop. As you consider a subject—either one that your instructor requires or one that you choose for yourself—take your own feelings seriously. You like some things about a subject; you dislike others. Ask yourself why you have these emotions about a subject, and you may have an idea for a paper. Some thinking is direct: you pursue an idea and try to develop it. Other thinking becomes random: you may be doing something unrelated to writing—jogging or riding a bike or rushing to class—when ideas about your subject pop into your mind. If you take time to think before you write, you can nurture inspiration, the sudden imaginative flash writers hope for that helps define, shape, or clarify a topic.

You should also think about your audience. Who is going to be interested in your paper? Who will read it? What do your readers know already about the topic? What can you tell your readers that they don't know? Or what thoughts do you have about a subject that your readers may not have had themselves? The best papers always tell readers something they do not already know or that they may not have thought of in just the way the writers think of the topic. That is one reason why honesty is so important in prewriting and writing. What do you really think about your subject? The chances are that if you are honest with yourself and with your readers, you will have an interesting and original paper.

2 Learn more about your topic by discussing it with knowledgeable people, by reading books, by exploring the media for information about it, and by talking it over with your friends.

Experienced writers expand their possibilities for developing a subject by developing every aspect of their daily experience, looking for ways to learn more about what they want to write about. They read popular magazines as well as serious books. They talk to experts. They think about their subject when they watch television or films with the hope of seeing something that may help them. They recall information and impressions from past experience. A student writing about sports may gather valuable insights from a roommate who hates exercise or from a teacher or a neighbor who jogs every morning at dawn. Someone writing about teenage drug abuse might read articles on the subject in a campus newspaper or a magazine, or watch a forum on drugs conducted on public television, or visit a local police station to inquire about crime and its relation to drugs. All these resources are easy to use, and they can stimulate thoughts for your writing topic.

3 Jot down ideas in an informal list.

List ideas about your subject without censoring anything, no matter how strange or inappropriate. Your list may grow over a couple of days as your thoughts develop and become more specific—one or two sentences or phrases scribbled in the morning, another few dashed off as you return from class. You may limit yourself to a list you can prepare in fifteen or twenty minutes at your desk. Try not to tighten up or be self-conscious. You are the only person who will see this list, and you can be loose or playful or even ridiculous in preparing it. Free association gives you access to ideas hidden in your mind. Although unformed, these ideas may come together later in coherent patterns.

A student who wanted to write about sports prepared the following list:

Sports

fun at sports

hard work and pain

Why do so many people work at sports when they know they can never excel at them?

exercise craze, jogging for fitness

swimming

bicycling—races involving middle-aged men

Jack Smith's delight at beating out other men in their fifties for a trophy that might have cost five dollars at a pawnshop

The running craze

Do joggers think they will stay young forever?

the pain in long-distance running

How people brag about suffering

women in sports

contact sports, a substitute for war?

Is bodybuilding a sport? What is the competitive value of swollen biceps?

Why do people believe they must buy expensive equipment for simple sports?

This list records many fragmentary ideas about sports. It combines serious thought, whimsy, and half-baked ideas. Examining the list, the writer decided to concentrate on jogging and to jot down ideas suggested by *that* topic.

Subject: Jogging

good for your heart, muscles, lungs

Some doctors say jogging harms the knees and ankles and hips.

enjoyment of open spaces, sound of leaves underfoot, feel of air in your face, sight of the sky and the clouds

shinsplints and other ailments (my torn Achilles tendon)

self-discipline to keep running every day

Are good running shoes important? Or will tennis shoes do?

marathons and how to enter them: Boston, New York, San Francisco

dangers to joggers: dogs, bicycles, cars, bad weather

Ramon's father assaulted by an angry homeowner when he jogged through a petunia bed

different kinds of joggers I have seen: couples, football players, men and women in their sixties and seventies, the people in neon running suits, my neighbor who jogs with his dog on a leash

the problems of running in different seasons

my first five-mile run and my astonishment at beating some people who looked stronger than I

running and the mind—learning that I don't like to sweat, getting a psychological high when I've been at it for a while, feeling good afterward, enjoying a shower, thinking better, sleeping well, feeling superior to my overweight friends

the crowds of joggers and the differences between the joggers who talk about running and those who merely run and keep silent

This informal list helps a writer define a limited topic and develop it in an essay. It also helps the writer become aware of what she knows about the topic and what she thinks about it. Successive revisions of the list will eliminate some points, expand others, and add some that are not now on it. Writing the list prepares you for the writing of the paper itself.

4 Ask yourself questions about your subject.

To stimulate ideas, writers frequently raise questions to themselves about a subject. For a paper on how television affects daily life, you might pose these questions: What role does television play in my life? In the lives of my family and friends? What programs do people on campus watch most, and how do those programs affect the way they think about other things? What effects does television have on people who watch it often: young children, the physically ill, or wives and husbands who are at home all day long? What positive effects does television have on people's lives? Does television make life more interesting for the poor? Are programs regulated adequately? Who makes decisions about programs on the various networks? How do ratings influence the variety of television offerings? How does the regulation of television fit the freedom of the press guaranteed by the First Amendment of the United States Constitution?

By making yourself ask questions like these, you can develop ideas for writing, and you may help yourself to determine the interests of your readers.

Another way to approach your subject is to apply the standard questions of journalists. Write the subject at the top of a page. Then, with ample space for your answers, write down as questions *who, what, where, when, why,* and *how.* Your answers to these and other questions may help you uncover other important aspects of a topic.

5 Write nonstop for a stated time period.

Filling up a page with your writing is a valuable way to overcome some of the nervousness that often grips people when they confront a writing task. The point in writing nonstop is to spin sentences uninterruptedly out of your head for five or ten minutes at a time, thus liberating any blocked ideas and ridding yourself of the feelings of dread that may come over you when you sit down to write.

Painful as it may be to keep your pen moving continuously, do not stop to look back at what you have written or to cross anything out. Do not stop to check spelling or grammar; in fact, do not stop writing *at all* until the time you have allotted for this exercise ends. If words do not come easily, it is all right to write "I can't think of anything to say" or to write again and again the last word you put down. Write whatever comes to mind without censoring or correcting. Writing nonstop forces you to *produce* and not to *edit.* When you are developing ideas on a topic, worrying about correctness can prevent your thoughts from flowing easily. Remember, you are the only person who will see this prose, and you should not trouble yourself about how it looks. When you look back over your page of sentences, you will probably find them worthy of further exploration.

A student responding to an assigned topic on the role of computers today produced a page of nonstop writing that included the following sample:

Nonstop Writing

Topic: Computers in the modern world

Computers. I love computers. But what can I say about them? I don't know what to write. I like keyboards. I like to look into the screen on my computer and see the letters and the numbers come up. What else? I don't know what to write. I love to make graphs. The other night I made a pie graph to show how many times the World Series has been won by every team in the big leagues. Boy, did the Yankees look fat, and did the Boston Red Sox look thin! People are buying computers more and more. They're expensive but well worth the cost because of the time they save. Even my kid sister is a whiz at her Apple. She even programs her own games. But when I started, I didn't know anything. They scared me to death. I walked into the terminal room at the Science Center and looked around at all those people bending over their keyboards, clicking away, looking like they knew what they were doing, like they were all important members of some big club or something, and they knew all the secrets, and I didn't know anything. The first time I tried to log in, I couldn't do it. I misspelled my own name, at least as far as the computer was concerned. I felt like a dumbbell. But now I sit in the terminal room at all hours of the night. Computers help me with my homework. How did people live without computers before now? What will computers do in the next decade? I heard about computers that respond to voice commands. It's so easy now. But it was hard to learn. Boy, was it hard to learn!

After rereading these sentences the writer might decide to explore his firsthand experiences in using a computer, the use of computers in presenting information visually or for saving time, societies with and without computers, computers in the future, or one of many other possible topics suggested here. The point is that by writing nonstop without editing, a writer can discover ideas to think about further and can investigate and refine them as the writing process continues.

6 Draw a subject tree.

A subject tree can encourage you to identify different branches of a subject and to see where they lead. Often, they lead to more and more specific ideas. Following one of these branches or comparing topics "growing" on two or more branches can provide you with a point of departure for your written essay.

The accompanying subject tree would help a writer branch out from a broad subject into several possible topics. Notice, for example, how the idea

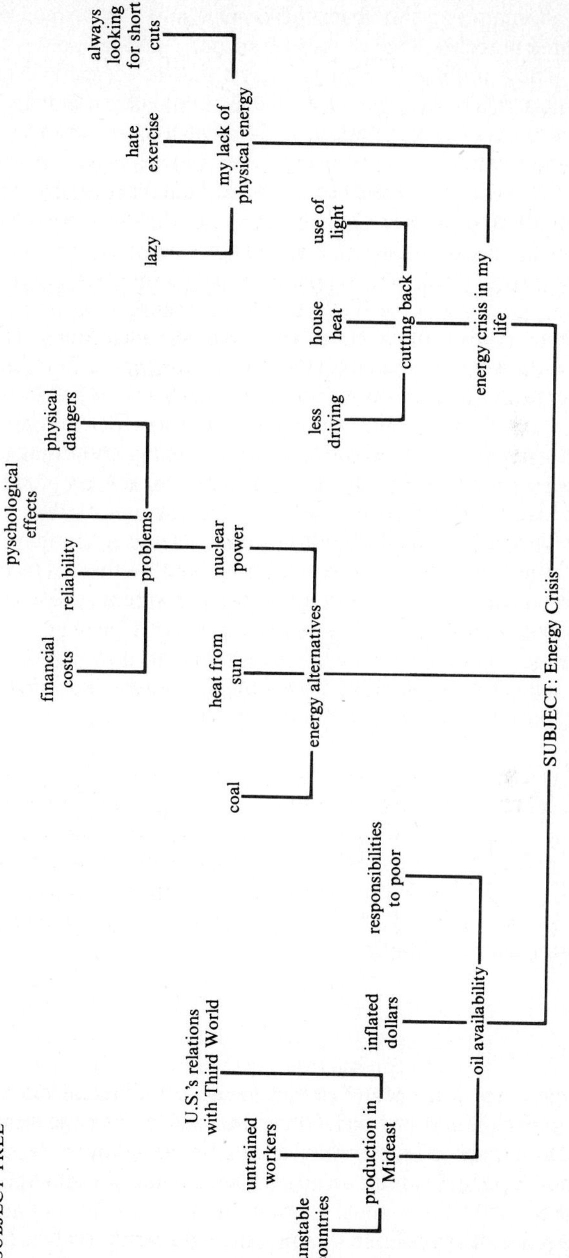
SUBJECT TREE
SUBJECT: Energy Crisis
oil availability
production in Mideast
unstable countries
untrained workers
U.S.'s relations with Third World
inflated dollars
responsibilities to poor
energy alternatives
coal
heat from sun
nuclear power
problems
financial costs
reliability
pyschological effects
physical dangers
energy crisis in my life
cutting back
less driving
house heat
use of light
my lack of physical energy
lazy
hate exercise
always looking for short cuts

of energy alternatives grows from the general subject "energy crisis" and leads to three branches. One of these branches, "nuclear power," suggests problems. These problems, in turn, suggest specific ideas for exploration: financial costs, reliability, psychological effects, and physical dangers. Note, too, how the branch "energy crisis in my life" can lead the writer to personalize the topic, even to alter it significantly. "My lack of physical energy" is not a common response to the topic "energy crisis," but that response could yield a creative and original paper.

7 Browse in the library or do research on your subject.

Reference books, other texts, and essays in magazines will suggest aspects of a subject that you have not thought of yourself. Several hours of browsing in the library and taking notes give many writers just the materials they need to develop a specific topic with confidence. You may also wish to interview people who know about your subject; many interesting papers do not depend on libraries. In any case, researching a subject broadens your understanding of it and provides important details you can draw on later.

Using these prewriting techniques individually or in combination, you can record the mixed impressions you have about a subject. Once you put some ideas on paper, you can start to narrow your topic into something you can manage in an essay.

Exercise 1.1 Use some of the prewriting techniques explained on pages 3–10 in exploring one or more of these general subjects:

1. fishing
2. America's volunteer army
3. alcohol
4. urban pollution
5. a college education
6. gun control
7. television
8. contact sports
9. advertising
10. pornography
11. teachers
12. outdoor life
13. religion
14. emotion
15. fads

1B Limit your subject.

Your instructor may assign a broad subject in class, or you may think that you want to write about a general subject you have chosen on your own. Yet if you try prewriting, you can see from your own materials that a subject as general as "sports," "television," or "the energy crisis" immediately suggests far too many possibilities to deal with in one paper. With a general subject, you may find it hard to resist writing generally—that is, off the top of your head—and few readers want to read such writing. To say something meaningful about a subject, you must first limit it. You can always find more of significance to say about a limited subject that you have sharply in focus than you can say about a broad, shapeless subject.

You may find it easier to develop a specific topic if you take a series of steps to limit it progressively:

Too broad	Still too broad	Less broad	Still less broad
sports	jogging	jogging for fitness	the effects of jogging on the heart
	winter sports	skiing	an experience I had skiing in Sun Valley
computers	how computers are becoming important in education	my experience with the computer	my experience in learning to use the computer
	computers and home use	the many computers available for use in the home	how to choose the right computer for your home and family
television	impact of TV	TV in our daily lives	good things TV does for us
	soap operas	comparison between *Days of Our Lives* and *Another World*	major themes in *Days of Our Lives* and *Another World*
Shakespeare	Shakespeare's later plays	Shakespeare's *The Tempest*	sound images in *The Tempest*
	performing in Shakespeare's plays	performing in *A Midsummer Night's Dream*	playing Bottom in a summer camp production of *A Midsummer Night's Dream*
the energy crisis	finding new sources of energy	solar energy	what solar energy can do for the single-family house
	how the energy crisis affects our lives	the energy crisis in my hometown	how group action led to a reduction in energy use in Allendale

Even topics in the column "Still less broad" may be further narrowed. Only the writer can decide just how much to limit the topic. That decision depends first on the physical demands of the task—minimum or maximum length, for example—and on a realistic view of the time that is available. And once you limit a topic, your ideas about it will expand. Record those ideas now too, and add them to your prewriting materials.

Exercise 1.2 Using the columns on page 11 as a model, limit in a series of steps any five topics from Exercise 1.1.

1C Decide upon the purpose of your paper, and pick the rhetorical approach that suits it best.

There are four long-established rhetorical categories—description, narration, exposition, and argumentation. Most types of writing fit into these categories. Description provides a picture of something; narration tells a story; exposition provides information and explains; argumentation debates opposing views and also may persuade opponents. Once you decide which of these modes best serves the purpose of your paper, you can use it to develop a theme appropriately.

Most college writing is *expository,* because it tries to inform a reader about a subject and to explain it. Of course, categories are never entirely exclusive of one another. Good narration always relies on description. Writers of exposition use description, narration, and argumentation to serve different purposes. To explain any point clearly, you will use various techniques, but one general rhetorical approach probably will fit any given subject especially well.

Think about the four basic categories as you plan your writing because they can help you clarify the purpose of your paper. The chart below shows how a writer might develop the same general subject along four distinct lines, once a specific purpose is established.

General Subject: Science in Our Lives

Category	Purpose
Description	To provide a picture of an industrial robot at work on an assembly line
	To describe the new observatory students built on the roof of a local high school
Narration	To tell the story of how soldiers from my hometown in Maine saved the day for the Union Army at the battle of Gettysburg
	To tell of the events leading to the discovery of radium

Exposition	To explain how laser beams are used in new surgical techniques
	To inform readers about new nonpoisonous methods of controlling gypsy moths
	To explain how an electron microscope works
	To explain the government's role in atomic research
Argumentation	To argue that government-sponsored health care is the best way to prevent high medical costs for Americans
	To persuade readers that nuclear power is no solution to America's energy problems
	To convince readers that chemical food preservatives pose dangers to the human body
	To persuade readers that gun control legislation will have little effect on the incidence of murder

A writer with a more limited topic in mind—hospital emergencies, say—also could use any of the four rhetorical categories according to the purpose of the paper.

Subject: Hospital Emergencies

Category	Purpose
Description	To describe the equipment in the emergency room of a nearby hospital
Narration	To tell how a victim of an automobile accident is treated in the hospital emergency room
Exposition	To explain why emergency-room doctors take certain steps when trying to save the life of a person badly injured in an automobile accident
Argumentation	To argue that hospitals should be located by law in many different parts of a city so that accident victims can be treated rapidly no matter where an accident occurs

You can see how easy it is to move from one of these categories to the others. You also can see that the final purpose of your paper will lead you to emphasize one of these categories above all the others. If your purpose is to present a convincing argument, you may want to keep description and exposition to a minimum. If you want to write a straight news story about an accident, you may not want to make any arguments at all. If you are explaining the various steps doctors take in treating an accident victim, you may find that telling the story of an actual accident is a distraction. The important thing is to keep your major purpose clearly in mind. Once your purpose is clear, it will be easy to choose the rhetorical category that best suits your aims in writing the paper.

1D Consider your intended audience.

Who is going to read your writing? You should not think of your audience only as the teacher who will correct your papers. You should write your paper to appeal to other people—your friends at school, for example, the other members of the class, or other people you know. Try to write in a way that will engage the attention of people you respect. Always remember that people in your audience have other things that they could be doing. Try to be so interesting and so clear that you can make them stop doing something else for the pleasure of reading what you write.

Try to anticipate what your readers expect, because their expectations will influence the way you shape your essay. You would write in one way about skating for an audience of college students, most of whom skate as well as you do. You would write another way for an audience of middle-aged English professors who have not skated for years. You would write one kind of paper about your childhood on a dairy farm for classmates who had grown up on similar farms. You would describe the same experience quite differently for people who think that milk and eggs come from the supermarket.

Sometimes instructors encourage experimentation by asking you to define the audience you have in mind for your paper. With a topic like skating, you might write for managers of roller rinks, for parents bent on teaching a seven-year-old how to roll to the rhythms of a popular melody, for skate manufacturers, or for potential buyers of expensive skating equipment. Each of these audiences demands different kinds of information.

As your most direct audience, your teacher may make certain requirements for the assignment. You should fulfill these requirements as well as you can by concentrating on what your teacher expects from each essay. But always try to think of your teacher not merely as the person who will mark up your paper but also as a reader who wants to be interested, who wants to know your honest reactions to a subject, and who wants to know why you have those reactions.

In much of the writing you will do after college, you will be trying to appeal to many different audiences. At work, your audiences may include your boss, those you supervise, the owners of the business, potential consumers, and the government agency that regulates what you do. For each different group of readers, the same subject demands different approaches in language, in form, in sentence structure, in tone and style, and in content.

1E Determine the kinds of details you need to make your points.

You must support your statements with specific information—that is, with details. In any essay, details vary, depending upon your purpose in writing and the sources of your ideas.

Source of detail	Kind of detail
Personal experience and observation	Concrete sensory images. Describe specific actions, colors, sights, sounds, smells, and tastes in order to re-create personal experience for a reader.
	Dialogues and indirect quotations. Reproduce the words people say in order to enliven a scene.
Books, periodicals, television, radio, films, interviews	Quotations, paraphrases, summaries. Support your points by quoting the words of authorities or by restating their ideas in your own words.
Statistics and cases	Use data (often from charts, graphs, and tables) to lend force to your assertions.

For a paper on laser surgery, a writer intent on capturing the drama in an operating room could turn to the language of the senses, recording the actions, colors, sounds, and smells that strike an observer and thus evoking the scene for someone else. You might read about an arm stretching for a bottle of plasma, the green cloth mask hiding the surgeon's mouth and nose, a nurse's half-suppressed cough, a whiff of an anesthetic. Another writer might take a historical approach, using books, journals, newspapers, material from television, and firsthand interviews. This writer might quote one of the developers of laser surgery, paraphrase a medical journal, summarize one or two successful and delicate operations, cite statements made in interviews with hospital personnel, or use statistics to summarize the history of eye surgery over the last twenty-five years.

These various kinds of details do not always exclude one another. A paper rooted in statistical or quoted detail also benefits from the concrete sensory images that engage readers.

It is impossible to say exactly where in the writing process your attention should turn to detail. Some writers begin to consider it only after they write a thesis sentence (see 1F), or as they write a rough draft (see 1H). Others think about detail earlier, as they formulate and refine their topic.

When you consider your chosen topic and the audience you have in mind, think about the kinds of details that will best suit your purpose and ask yourself where and how you will gather them. For most papers, you will find it helpful to ask yourself questions like these:

1. What experiences in my own life will help me make this topic interesting?
2. What have I read recently in books, newspapers, or magazines—or what can I read before I write—that will help me support my topic?
3. What have I heard on the radio or observed on television or in the movies that will help me support my topic?

4. What have I learned in recent conversations with friends, parents, relatives, teachers, and associates that will help me support my topic?
5. What do people in my audience know about my topic? What will interest them? What will bore them? What may even surprise them?

The answers you give to these questions will help you pinpoint sources of supporting details.

Exercise 1.3 Return to the topics you limited in Exercise 1.2 (or limit some new topics of your own choosing). For each, state your reason for writing about it, describe an intended audience, and suggest some probable sources of the kinds of details that you could use to develop the topic.

1F Think through the main idea of your composition, and formulate a thesis statement.

It is vital to define your main idea—the essential thing you want to say about your subject—before you plan and write your paper. This main idea serves to guide and control your presentation of the sentences and paragraphs that make up your finished composition. It is usually helpful to formulate your thesis as an argument: What is the most important thing I want my readers to believe about my subject? Do I want them to do something? If so, what do I want them to do?

Once you have narrowed the focus of your topic, construct a thesis statement. A **thesis statement** (or thesis) tells readers why they should read what you have written. It lets them know what to expect and lets them decide whether they want to go on with your work. It usually describes your position on the subject as well. How do you feel about the subject? If your subject is organic gardening, for example, your readers should know right away whether you believe in organic gardening or whether you are going to argue that it is a waste of time and money. Your thesis statement may also include the two or three major arguments you intend to use to support your proposition. The following limited topics at the left led writers to produce the thesis statements at the right.

Limited topic	Possible thesis statement
experiments with solar energy in major cities today	Three urban experiments with solar energy show mixed results and raise doubts about the sun as a source of energy for the future.
causes for the poisoning of the Green River	Industrial greed, strip mining, and the movement of people off the land and into the cities all contributed to the poisoning of the beautiful Green River.

In the first example, the thesis states the topic—experiments with solar energy in cities—and also makes the claim that those experiments suggest doubts about the practicality of harnessing the sun's energy. An essay built on such a thesis would have to win readers to that point of view. In the second example, too, the thesis states the topic and asserts something about it. Here, the claim is that the poisoning of the Green River occurred for three distinct reasons. Notice how this thesis statement previews the three explanations for the poisoning: industrial greed, strip mining, and the movement of people off the land and into the cities. In an essay on this topic, the writer would offer details and commentary to support these explanations.

Here are some more thesis statements that were produced for limited topics:

Limited topic	**Possible thesis statement**
the effects of jogging on the body	Despite its many advantages, jogging can cause serious physical problems.
dangers people face when they learn to ski	On a frozen hillside near Sun Valley, Idaho, one February morning I learned that not all grizzly bears hibernate in winter.
television commercials aimed at children	Television commercials aimed at children suggest that the advertised products bring pleasure, popularity, and family unity.
soap operas	*Days of Our Lives* and *Another World* present the theme of marriage and infidelity in absorbing and unrealistic ways.
sound images in Shakespeare's *The Tempest*	Sound images in *The Tempest* fall into patterns that reflect typical themes in Shakespeare's plays.
playing Bottom in a summer camp production of *A Midsummer Night's Dream*	A series of stage accidents, trousers that split in the third act, and a whole scene of garbled lines made my portrayal of Bottom last summer funnier than Shakespeare ever intended.
how group action led to a reduction in our use of energy in Allendale	With carefully scheduled car pools, curtailed shopping hours at Allendale Mall, and a successful campaign to install home insulation, group action led to a significant cut in energy consumption in Allendale.

Continued . . .

Limited topic	Possible thesis statement
how a student in State College can find a rewarding summer job	Although jobs in college towns are scarce every summer, students can find rewarding work if they are willing to do some things that homeowners will not do for themselves.
on-the-job training programs for future administrators in hospitals	Thanks to a new state program, trainees in hospital administration apply their skills under real hospital conditions and with the guidance of a skilled supervisor.
the value of IQ tests	Proponents point to the value of testing for intelligence, but some research has shown that the most creative people are not those with the highest IQ scores.

Preparing a thesis statement that makes an assertion about a limited topic takes considerable thought and effort. As you think about your subject, try posing a pertinent question about it—the answer could become your thesis. The rest of the paper then will offer details to support the answer you propose to the question.

Topic	Question	Thesis
Pittsburgh's unemployed steelworkers in the 1980s	What effect will unemployed steelworkers have on city government?	In the 1980s, Pittsburgh's unemployed steelworkers will increase their demands for services that the city cannot afford.

A strong thesis, developed early, permits you to control your material as it unfolds. It serves as a guide for your arguments and as a check on the details you include.

You may decide to change your position on your subject as you organize your paper and write your early drafts. You may also decide to revise your thesis statement slightly or even dramatically as you think about your topic. One writer developed this thesis statement for a paper about how he learned to use a computer:

I had a hard time learning how to use the computer.

As ideas for this topic took shape, and as the writer grouped and arranged details (see 1G), he felt that he needed to narrow his topic and be more specific. He revised his thesis to make it more direct and interesting.

When I learned to use the computer, my greatest mistake came just before I discovered that computers are not as smart as the people who use them.

After writing a rough draft and revising it, the writer finally decided on the following thesis statement for the essay (see page 46):

As it turned out, the computer is pretty stupid, and my first troubles came because I expected the computer to think.

Sharpening the main idea, clarifying sentence structure, selecting more precise words: these goals guide you as you revise a thesis statement for your essay.

Must you include a thesis statement in your finished themes? Most writers include a thesis statement because it puts the topic in focus for readers. Often the thesis appears as a single sentence in the introductory paragraph. A thesis certainly can take more than one sentence, and it can appear in a paragraph other than the first. Some writers begin with a general statement of their topic and introduce aspects of the thesis throughout the paper. Others *imply* a thesis statement, building their theme with such care that most readers can easily pick up the controlling idea. But most papers benefit when a thesis statement appears early.

If you decide not to state your thesis to your readers, then you must be sure you can state it to yourself. Producing it before you write your essay assures you that the ideas in the final theme will develop around a central point.

Exercise 1.4 For each of the limited topics that you worked on in Exercise 1.3, develop a thesis sentence. (Use the examples on pages 16–17 as models.)

Exercise 1.5 Discuss the thesis statements on pages 16–17. In each one, what special claim does the writer make about the topic? How would you improve the thesis statements?

1G To develop your paper, expand your informal written ideas, group them by subject, and organize these ideas in a rough outline.

As you write your thesis statement, you will probably think of more ideas related to your topic and ways to expand ideas you have already recorded. Do not hesitate to add these new ideas to your prewriting papers. It is important to include as many points as you can to help you write.

Next, examine all your prewriting papers and put together related thoughts. You can do this in many ways: cutting and pasting, drawing lines and arrows from one point to a related one, identifying ideas that belong together with a letter or a symbol in the margin. Some writers look at their lists or jottings produced in prewriting and recopy them into groups of connected thoughts.

As you read over your materials, look for some principle to guide you in clustering ideas. For instance, which points on one page depend on points you have made on other pages? If you tie together related ideas before you write, you can improve your chances for producing a clear and logical paper.

As you group your ideas, think about ways of organizing them. Of course there are many possible ways of arranging the thoughts you have grouped together. However, at this stage, most writers find it helpful to consider the following common methods for arranging information in an essay:

1. Chronological. A chronological arrangement simply deals with events as they occur in time. Narratives are usually chronological. The writer who tells about the grizzly bear in Sun Valley (page 17), for example, will probably begin with the first thing that happened and continue event by event to the end.

2. Spatial. You can choose a logical starting point and then move through space systematically. When you describe a house, for example, you might start at the front door, picture the living room, dining room, and kitchen as you move through them, and finally take your reader out the back door.

3. General to specific or specific to general. You may see a relation between a general point and some specific points that would support it. To group these related points together, you can move from a general statement to specific details, or you can arrange your points the other way around. A writer dealing with urban experiments in solar energy (page 16) could begin with a general statement about the difficulties of solar energy and then support that generalization with specific details about solar collectors. But such an essay could just as well describe the shortcomings of several kinds of solar collectors and then could conclude with the general statement that solar energy is expensive and unreliable.

4. By importance. Some points will seem less important than others in supporting an idea. Consider arranging your points so that the less important ones come first. When you write your essay, you can build dramatically to your major argument by treating minor ones along the way. Thus the student who recognizes themes in sound imagery in *The Tempest* (see page 17) could group ideas around each theme and then could arrange them so that the most important one comes last. The writer, of course, has to decide which ideas are more or less important than others.

These principles of organization should be especially useful to you during this early planning stage, though you may alter or abandon the sequence you have planned once you start to write.

When you put your ideas in sequence, you create a *rough outline* to expand and develop. Rough outlines are informal, private conveniences for the writer, and they follow no prescribed format. From prewriting material, one writer prepared this rough outline for a composition.

Rough Outline

Tentative thesis statement: I had a hard time learning how to use the computer.

Introduction—My first thoughts about the computer

1. First steps

Paying $50 to secretary who couldn't care less about teaching me anything. Fifteen minutes of instruction. passwords log-ons files going into the computer room Computer rooms are ugly places.

2. Getting started

Could not log on. Computer does not recognize my name!

Computer tells me, "No such account."

Frustration! I tried four times.

3. My problem

Typing in my name. I was using "Barkeley." The log-on word really "barkeley."

4. Computers are dumb

Like the wiring in a house. Plug in anything, but the house can't tell you what to plug in.

Computers the same way. They take whatever you plug in.

Takes a lot of patience to realize that.

5. Figuring it out

Need help from Ellen.

She couldn't remember my name! My log-on word "Barkeley." I typed it in with the capital B. Ellen used a little b.

Computer worked just fine. Log-ons and passwords usually have a small initial letter!

Computers are very easy to use.

Even kids are whizzes at computers.

Soon every elementary school will require computer training.

With a rough outline in hand, you can expand ideas further by adding points to the groups you have established. You can also write up a fully developed formal outline if a complex topic demands one (see 33H, section 1). Or you can start writing a rough draft, turning when necessary to your research notes or prewriting pages in order to construct and support your ideas with details.

As you develop the first draft of your paper, you probably will change your rough outline to include some new ideas. But before you even start writing, your outline can provide a first check on **unity** and **coherence.** A paper has unity when all the ideas pertain to the thesis statement and to each other. A paper is coherent when each idea flows logically into the next so that a reader can follow the progression from one point to another.

These two important features, unity and coherence, develop as you write successive drafts of your paper. But your outline can save time by helping you to unite your points and to connect them smoothly before you begin to write.

Checking his rough outline, for example, this writer began to see that he should tell his story chronologically. He could not log on—that is, reach his file in the computer—because he used a capital letter to spell his last name. The computer recognized his name only when the initial letter was in lowercase. But he did not understand his mistake until the terminal watcher showed him what to do. In its original place in the outline, idea 4 disrupted the coherent sequence of the events. Since the lesson he learned about computers was the most important part of the paper, he decided to put it last. The writer also discovered a lack of unity caused by the last three points under 5. They focused on the ease of computer use and on the future of computers for schools, but his thesis—"I had a hard time learning how to use the computer"—did not deal with those issues. To fix the lack of coherence shown by the outline, the writer decided to shift some ideas and eliminate others.

In short, a rough outline helps you see the shape and direction of your paper even before you write it. If you take the time to develop a clear and logical outline, you may save yourself from having to write several drafts of the entire paper.

Exercise 1.6 Examine the following rough outline. Do all the ideas pertain to the thesis statement and to each other, and do they flow logically from one to the other? What kind of research would the writer have to do to support the points he wants to make under 2? What might you eliminate from idea 3? Why? From idea 4? Why? How might you expand one of the points under 5? What would you recommend about idea 6? Might 7 serve as the basis for a conclusion?

Rough Outline

Tentative thesis statement: Television makes a valuable contribution in today's society.

1. Why people watch TV so much(?)

   convenient and easy to use

   less effort than reading

   habit

2. Television is inexpensive

   cost of buying a TV and using electricity for it vs. costs of other forms of entertainment

   watch TV at home

3. Television as excellent source of information

   up-to-date news as it happens—space shuttle, assassination attempts, war reporting, effects of poverty, corruption in government

   but facts often inaccurate because of required speed of reports to public

   personality often more important than substance

4. TV as entertainer

   comedy

   music, dancing, drama (all appeal to different tastes)

   programs often boring

   sports programming excellent

   TV makes science entertaining and interesting

5. Television teaches

   young children learn from *Sesame Street*

   all audiences learn from special documentaries

   travelogues and talk shows

6. Movies and books also make important contributions to education.
7. Expanding possibilities for television use
   in medicine
   in the home and the classroom

Exercise 1.7 Take one of the topics for which you developed a thesis sentence in Exercise 1.4 (or a limited topic of your own choice), and develop a rough outline.

1H Prepare the first draft of your composition.

With the results of your prewriting and your rough (or formal) outline close at hand, you are ready to start writing. Relax! Think of this first attempt at writing your paper as a kind of exploration. Don't try to produce more than a rough draft copy. The ideas that have come up in your prewriting and in constructing your outline will only begin to take shape as you develop statements and fill in details on your first draft.

Don't worry excessively about errors of fact, questionable spellings, or awkward constructions. Stopping to check the spelling of a word in your dictionary, for example, can derail your train of thought. And don't worry about being neat. At this stage, you should concentrate on producing a flow of ideas in language that is reasonable, clear, and readable. If you have problems, just mark those sticky points so that you can easily find them when you want to go back and work on them. To make room for additions and changes, leave wide margins. Some writers triple-space after each typewritten line or skip a line or two after each handwritten one so they can make a later improvement easily.

Don't worry about a title for your paper at this point. If you can think of one, fine. If not, develop your title *after* you write your first draft. Here is the first draft of the essay on learning how to use the computer. For this assignment early in the term, the instructor asked students to write about one of their most difficult moments in college.

? change beginning?

I had a hard time learning how to use the computer. I thought they were smart. ? I had seen lots of movies like "2001" and "Superman III" where computers started thinking for themselves and acting like real people with minds. So believe it or not, I was really scared when I sat down at the keyboard for the first time and looked into the empty screen at the Science Center. I thought something might reach out and grab me or something, and I was sure the computer was smarter than I was. That's why I got myself into my first trouble with the thing.

A fifteen-minute course had been given to me by a quick secretary who hardly looked up at me as my fifty-dollar check was taken by him and put into a cash drawer. Fifty bucks is a lot of money to a college student. He had a low, dull voice, and he explained about passwords. Naturally I had to have something easy to remember, so I decided to use my last name Barkeley as my log-on word, and this secretary whose indiffrence you wouldn't believe typed that name into the file. He had the longest fingers I've ever seen. Then he asked me for a password, and I chose "Chimichanga" which I had to spell for him of course. I chose such a dumb word just to wake him up, but he didn't give me the slightest acknowledgment. I figured I knew

something not right here

?

do something with this detail

?

dev 1H

what he was doing, but it was done very fast, and when I sat down in the terminal room before a keyboard and a small empty screen I was incredibly nervous, and maybe the most incredible thing of all is that my hands were trembling.

enlarge? So then I typed in the word Barkeley, and the computer said, "No such account." I like to of had a stroke! Impossible! What in blazes was wrong with this thing? Maybe I had spelled my name wrong. But I know how to spell my own name. Anyway, there it was, written out on the screen in green letters where I had put it. I could see that it was spelled right. So I tried again. So the computer said again, "No such account." I was stamping my feet by this time. I really was. I was incredibly frustrated. ? I had just forked over fifty bucks for my account, and I had just seen a secretary that looked like a robot set up my account on the computer terminal sitting there on his desk. Again I typed in "Barkeley." Again the computer said, "No such account," so I tried a fourth time and to add insult to injury, it hummed with annoyance and flashed "DISCONNECT."

So then I called over the terminal watcher, a terminal watcher is a student on duty in the terminal room ~~and she is~~ supposed to be experienced enough with computers to help you with all your problems. The terminal watcher on duty that afternoon was an attractive blonde named Ellen from my biology class and I didn't want her to think I'd made a mistake so I said, ? acting real cool, "Ellen, there's something wrong with my terminal. I can't get logged on, and I know I'm doing the right thing." She drifted over to my terminal and asked me for my log-on word and I told her that it was my last name, and she said, "What is your last name?" Cute! "Barkeley. You spell it B-a-r-k-e-l-e-y," maybe too informal I said, and she typed in "b-a-r-k-e-l-e-y" and the terminal said, "Password?" When I gave it to her I had to spell it again, and she raised an eyebrow, and I winced as she typed in my little joke with utter disgust. After she hit the return key, the terminal flashed, "This is active job one for you. You have fifty dollars in your account."

So off Ellen went, and I felt like an

~~incredible~~ fool. There I had been using a capital B to spell my name, and log-ons and passwords usually have small initial letters, and if the computer could think, it would of recognized the capital letter and let me log on. The computer is stupider than stupid. It will do just what you tell it to do.

oops!

change this

Now you can tell it some real complicated things, but you can't tell it how to think. It just won't do it. It can't. Like for instance an electrician can wire up your house so you can plug in a lamp or a radio into the same outlet. But if you plug in a lamp, the house can't decide it wants to have music and start playing the radio instead. You can wire up a computer the same way except that you use circuits in silicon chips rather than metal wires, and when you wire it to work when you plug in ''barkeley,'' it won't work when you try to use ''Barkeley.'' ~~So much for that.~~

So I don't think we have to worry that much about computers. In ''2001'' a computer named HAL kills some people and has to be killed himself. But HAL is just in the movies and not in real life.

Notice that the writer concentrated on recording his thoughts and did not worry about correctness. Obviously, many errors appear in these pages. The writer himself has marked some words and sentences that he wants to check during revision. Many ideas in this draft are unclear and far from their final shape. There are problems with language and with form. The vocabulary is often too informal ("cute," "real cool," and "fifty bucks," for instance). Some sentences lack the specific details a reader needs to understand the story. (What are log-ons and passwords?) Some words are repeated often without adding much to the paper ("incredible"). There are some sentences that are too long and some mistakes in grammar that are natural when someone is writing fast. But remember, this is only a first draft. Careful revision can change it into an acceptable essay.

Exercise 1.8 For an assignment in which the instructor asked the class to argue convincingly on a topic related to the media, one student produced this rough draft. (The rough outline for this essay appears in Exercise 1.6.) Read the draft, and then take notes so that you can discuss it in class. (If your instructor requires it, write a critique of the draft.) In your discussion notes, address these questions:

1. What is the thesis of the paper? Where does the writer state it?
2. How does the outline (pages 22–23) compare and contrast with the draft? What elements in the outline do not appear in the draft? What elements in the draft do not appear in the outline?
3. Which ideas in the draft seem particularly clear to you? Which seem unclear? Where is the language too informal? Where would you suggest more attention to unity and coherence (see page 22)?
4. What is your opinion of the introduction and of the conclusion? How would you improve each of these?
5. What errors would you point out for correction in the final draft?

Television

Many people have criticized television for its violence and its sensational treatment of events and lack of imagination in creating programs. They say that viewers turn on the set out of habit without thinking because it's so convenient and easy to use. All American households have at least one television, by turning the dial you get instant color and sound right in your own living room. Books may take effort, but with television you sit and you let things happen to you, your mind is really asleep. Critics call TV the vast wasteland, the land of violence, the land of the hard sell, the nightmare of middle America. Because many of these criticisms are right on. It's easy to ignore the valuable contribution television makes to our society. Television makes a positive contribution to the quality of life today.

In a time of inflation, the TV screen provides cheap entertainment. A good color set costs about $400 and lasts about ten years. That's $3.33 a month. The Consolidated Edison Company reports that a family using a color set for 4 hours a day burns electricity costing ten dollars and twenty cents a month, for about the cost of a night out for two at the movies a family of five can enjoy television programs seven nights a week. Every week!

The range of programs is incredible. Providing entertainment and current information for many different tastes and interests. On typical weekday evenings this year a viewer can choose a country and western variety show, a biography, an hour in a series about the Second World War, reruns of a 1950s comedy series with Lucille Ball, a baseball play-off, a talk show with Barbara Walters, and a documentary special on energy.

Cable television also provides varied shows so that people can now choose from many different kinds of artistic programs. In the past artistic programs rarely appeared on the commercial channels because they are unprofitable and do not appeal to audiences. Cable television relies on audience subscriptions and are not concerned about ratings. Cable stations can broadcast to special-interest groups. In large cities for example. You can have a full day's programs in a foreign language. So television entertains and gives us the news.

Television also teaches us there are programs like *Sesame Street* for children to teach language and math skills. Adults can learn how to cook or to garden on television. Also to decorate and repair a home and to exercise. There are television courses to take for college credit where networks and universities work together. The talk shows offer interesting opinions by experts and celebrities. People in the audience are exposed to different points of view. In addition, documentaries about travel teach us about different cultures, with wonderful photography they teach us through pictures more than most viewers would want to learn from books. The television science shows like *Nova* make science interesting and make it easier to understand than books can do, especially in an age of space exploring and all sorts of new things happening in medicine and the other sciences. Anyone with an open mind can come away from a day's TV watching with new ideas and unforgettable images of far off places.

Television makes an important contribution to our society. We are under so much pressure at school and on jobs, that television is a real wonder of pleasure technology but it is only one small product that will grow a lot over the years. Because people need to escape from pressure in their lives in order to live the best lives possible. This will encourage the media explosion like video tape recorders and video disk players for home use. Technology and pleasure will work together in a new machine age.

1I Revise your first draft and subsequent drafts for clarity and correctness. Give your draft to a friendly reader for comments and suggestions.

After you complete your first draft, take a long break. Put some time and distance between you and your paper to clear your mind.

When you return to your draft, be prepared to reread it carefully several times and to make changes in content, word choice, and sentence structure. As you revise, you will probably have to add details. You will undoubtedly have to change words, substituting more precise language for generalities that will puzzle the reader. You will want to shift sentences from one place to another, or to shorten or expand or combine them. Often you may find yourself reorganizing parts of your paper completely.

Think of a title for your paper. If you have a title already, look at it carefully and revise it, if necessary. It should suit your thesis and should engage the reader's attention without being too general, too long, or too cute.

Revised drafts can get messy. Whenever yours gets too messy to read easily, rewrite it as a new draft. Writing habits and skills vary, but most writers need to do at least two drafts; professional writers and good student writers nearly always do more.

When you have produced a readable draft, show it to someone whose opinion you trust. One of your classmates, your instructor, your roommate, or a family member may suggest new directions for your next draft. If someone reads your paper (or listens as you read it aloud), pay attention to any questions that person may pose about meaning, and make any changes needed to clarify your prose.

Pay careful attention to clarity as you revise. Many sentences will require radical changes to make your ideas easier to understand. Start by fixing the problems you marked in your first draft. Then address any questions readers may have raised. Thereafter, you should check every draft slowly and thoughtfully for errors. Mark your sentence boundaries clearly with periods or other end marks. Look out for troublesome verbs, vague pronoun references, and misspelled words.

The following checklist focuses on key elements to consider when you revise.

A. Revising ideas
   1. Is the thesis clear? (See 1F.)
   2. Does the paper speak consistently to the same audience? (See 1D.)
   3. Are there enough details to support your major points? (See 1E.)
   4. Does the paper show unity? Do all the ideas relate clearly to each other? (See 1G.)
   5. Is the paper coherent? Do ideas flow logically and smoothly from one to the other? (See 1G.)

6. Are ideas stated in precise language? (See 1E, 2C, and 18C.) Should any words be replaced by more accurate or appropriate ones?
7. Does each sentence state its information clearly? Is there sentence variety to hold the readers' interest? When read aloud, do the words sound right to the ear? (See Chapters 15 and 16.)
8. Are there unnecessary words that can be eliminated? (See 20A.)

B. Revising for essay structure

1. Does the introduction capture and hold the reader's interest?
2. Does the conclusion complete the ideas established and supported in the paper? (See 2D, section 2.)
3. Does the title engage the reader's attention?

C. Revising for correctness

1. Sentence completeness
   - **a.** Are periods and other end marks used to set off complete statements? (See 4A.)
   - **b.** Are there any run-on sentences that should be separated by end marks or combined with connecting words and suitable punctuation? (See 4E.)
   - **c.** Are there any sentence fragments that can be corrected by joining them to other sentences, by adding subjects or verbs, or both? (See 5A, sections 1–3.)
2. Sentence logic
   - **a.** Are parallel ideas expressed in parallel structures? (See Chapter 14.)
   - **b.** Have you corrected all of the needless shifts in tone or point of view? (See Chapter 11.)
   - **c.** Do modifiers stand near enough to the words they describe to avoid ambiguity? (See Chapter 10.)
   - **d.** Are the references to pronouns clear? (See 8A.)
   - **e.** Do subordinate sections relate correctly to main clauses? (See 13B, section 1.)
3. Verbs
   - **a.** Do subjects and verbs agree? (See Chapter 6.)
   - **b.** Are verb tenses correctly formed and consistent? (See Chapter 7.)
   - **c.** Have you corrected all unnecessary shifts in tense, mood, voice, number, or emphasis? (See Chapter 11.)
4. Punctuation and mechanics
   - **a.** Are punctuation marks clearly and firmly written? Do end marks, commas, colons, and semicolons serve the meaning of sentences? Are apostrophes placed to show possession and contractions? (See Chapters 23–28.)
   - **b.** Are quotation marks used in pairs to set off someone's exact words? (See 27A.)
   - **c.** Do italics, numbers, and symbols follow conventional uses? (See Chapters 31 and 32.)

d. Do capital letters follow the conventions of American English? (See Chapter 30.) Is the title of the theme correctly capitalized and punctuated?

e. Have troublesome words been checked in a dictionary for accurate spelling? (See Chapter 22.)

After the writer of the rough draft on computers (pages 24–28) rethought his paper entirely and made extensive changes, he produced this revised draft.

Computers Are Not So Smart

When I started
~~I had a hard time~~ learning how to use the

computer, ~~I thought they were smart,~~ I had seen

with
lots of movies ~~like "2001" and "Superman III"~~

that
~~where~~ computers started thinking for themselves

and acting like real people with minds. ~~So believe~~

~~it or not,~~ I was really scared when I sat down at

the keyboard for the first time and looked into

terminal
the ~~empty~~ screen at the Science Center. ~~I thought~~

~~something might reach out and grab me or~~

~~something, and~~ I was sure the computer was smarter

When I learned to use the computer, my greatest
than I was. ~~That's why I got myself into my first~~
mistake came just before I discovered that computers are not as smart as the people who use them.
~~trouble with the thing.~~
I felt that I had a good knowledge of how to work the computer because a
~~A~~ fifteen minute course had been given to me

and uncaring took
by a quick secretary who ~~hardly looked up at me~~

s to open an account. Computer
~~as~~ my fifty dollar ~~check was taken by him and put~~
time can be expensive!
~~into a cash drawer.~~ ~~Fifty bucks is a lot of money~~

~~to a student.~~ ~~He had a low, dull voice, and~~ In a monotone he explained about passwords. I had to use one word to log on, in other words, to call up my file, then I had to use another word to get into the file and start using it. Since my full name is David Hammond Barkeley, I picked the incredibly original super password of ~~Naturally I had to have something easy to remember so I decided to use my last name~~ "Barkeley," ~~to be my log-on word,~~ and ~~this~~ the secretary ~~whose indifference you wouldn't believe~~ typed that glorious name into the computer as the name for my account. ~~file. He had the longest~~ His long fingers ~~I've ever seen~~ raced across the letters of the keyboard.

Then he asked me for a password, and I chose "Chimichanga" to wake him up, and when ~~which I had to~~ I spelled it for him ~~of course. I chose such a dumb word just to wake him up, but~~ he didn't give ~~me~~ the slightest acknowledgment of my humor but just typed it in. I thought ~~I figured~~ I knew what he was doing, but it was done very fast, and when I sat down in the terminal room before a keyboard and a small empty screen I was incredibly nervous, and maybe the most incredible thing of all is that my hands were trembling.

So then I typed in the word Barkeley. The cold grey keys resisted my touch ever so slightly. And the ~~and the~~ computer said, "No such account." ~~I like to of had a stroke!~~ Impossible! What ~~in blazes~~ was wrong with this thing? Maybe I had spelled my name wrong. ~~But~~ I know how to spell my own name!

~~Anyway,~~ ~~t~~There it was, sprawled ~~written out on the screen~~ on the screen of the monitor where it went when I had typed it, and in green letters~~, where I had put it.~~ I could see that it was spelled right. ~~So~~ I tried again typing "Barkeley." ~~So~~ ~~t~~The computer said again, "No such account." I ~~was~~ stamp~~ing~~ed my f~~ee~~oot so angrily under the table. ~~by this time. I really was. I was incredibly frustrated.~~ I had just ~~forked over~~ paid fifty dollars ~~bucks~~ for ~~my~~ an account, and I had just seen a mindless secretary ~~that looked like a robot~~ set it up for me ~~my account~~ on the ~~computer~~ terminal sitting ~~there~~ on his desk. Again I typed in "Barkeley." Again the computer said, "No such account." After a fourth try the computer ~~and to add insult to injury, it~~ hummed with annoyance and flashed "DISCONNECT."

~~So then~~ With great frustration I called over the terminal watcher, a terminal watcher is a student on duty in the terminal room and ~~she is~~ supposed to be experienced enough with computers to help you with all your problems. The terminal watcher on duty that afternoon was an attractive blonde named Ellen from my biology class and I didn't want her to think I'd made a mistake so I said/

rev 1l

~~acting real cool,~~ in my coolest voice, "Ellen, there's something wrong with my terminal. I can't get logged on, and I know I'm doing the right thing." She drifted over to my terminal and asked me for my log-on word. ~~and~~ I told her that it was my last name. ~~and she said,~~ "What is your last name?" she said. "Boy, what an impression I made on her," I thought. ~~Cute!~~ "Barkeley," I said. "~~You~~ You spell it "B-a-r-k-e-l-e-y," I said. ~~and~~ She typed in "b-a-r-k-e-l-e-y." ~~and~~ The terminal immediately answered, ~~said,~~ "Password?" When I gave it to her I had to spell it again, and she raised an eyebrow, and asked me how to spell it, and I winced as she typed in my little joke with utter disgust. After she hit the return key, the terminal flashed, "This is active job one for you. You have fifty dollars in your account."

~~So off~~ As Ellen went off, ~~and~~ I felt like ~~an incredible~~ a fool. ~~There~~ I had been using a capital B to spell my name, and log-ons and passwords usually have a small initial letter~~s~~. ~~and~~ If the computer could think, it ~~would of~~ could've recognized the capital letter and let me log on. The computer is stupid~~er. than stupid~~. It will do *only* ~~just~~ what you tell it to do.

no ¶ ~~Now~~ *Y*~~y~~ou can tell it *to do* some ~~real~~ *pretty* complicated things*;* ~~,~~ but you can't tell it how to think. ~~It just won't do it. It cant. Like for instance~~ *A* ~~a~~n electrician can wire ~~up~~ your house so *that* you can plug in a lamp or a radio into the same outlet. But if you plug in a lamp, the house ~~can't~~ *cannot* decide *that* it ~~wants~~ *would rather* ~~to~~ have music *than light.* ~~and start playing the radio instead.~~ You can wire ~~up~~ a computer the same way except that you use circuits in silicone chips rather than metal wires, and when you wire it to work when you plug in ''barkeley,'' it won't work when you try to use ''Barkeley.'' ~~So much for that.~~

So I don't think we have to worry *much* ~~that much~~ about computers. In *the famous movie* ''2001'' a computer named HAL *starts thinking for itself and kills a lot of* ~~kills some~~ people and has to be killed*.* ~~himself.~~ But *such things are for* ~~HAL is just in~~ the movies*.* ~~and~~ *They are not going to happen* ~~not~~ in real life.

Note the extensive revisions in content and style that the writer has made to the draft appearing in 1H. He has continued to write in an informal style, but he has eliminated several slang expressions that might be offensive to some readers. For example, in the first draft he had said, "I had just forked over fifty bucks for my account." In the second draft he says, "I had just paid fifty dollars for an account." He has eliminated some sentences entirely: "I really was. I was incredibly frustrated." Where possible, he has shortened sentences. He has worked hard on his first paragraph, remembering his obligation to get to the point of his essay quickly. See how he works out his thesis in the first paragraph, concluding with the sentence "When I learned to use the computer, my greatest mistake came just before I discovered that computers are not as smart as the people who use them."

He has added some sentences that give visual images, such as "The cold gray keys resisted my touch ever so slightly." He has given us a definition of "terminal watcher." You will find many other changes as well. The writer is thinking as he revises, striving for both effect and economy.

But this draft is not his final draft. He continued to revise, sometimes making extensive changes, until he felt satisfied with his work. Comments from readers of early drafts guided some changes. His own careful deliberation guided others. The final copy that appears in 1L is a very different paper from the one you have just read here.

1J Proofread your paper for errors.

Both before and after you prepare your final copy, comb your paper for mechanical mistakes, and correct them. This step is called **proofreading.** Proofreading requires careful examination of each line on the page. Proofread your last rough draft before you turn it into your final draft, and proofread again as you prepare your final draft for submission. Hold a ruler or a blank sheet of paper beneath the line you are studying. Examine each sentence carefully for missing words and punctuation. Check each word carefully for missing or incorrect letters. Proofreading a paper from the last sentence to the first is another good technique; it helps you to focus on isolated units and to catch errors easily overlooked in the context of surrounding sentences. Some writers touch the point of a pencil to each syllable to help them read more slowly. It is always a good idea to read your paper slowly aloud to yourself.

1K Prepare the final copy carefully, setting it up according to accepted methods of manuscript preparation and using suitable materials.

Follow your instructor's guidelines for correct manuscript preparation in each course. The papers you submit for your instructor's evaluation must be clean and relatively free of handwritten corrections. But it is *always* better to write in a correction than to turn in clean pages that have misspelled words or other obvious errors.

Remember that your instructor must grade many papers, remaining alert and careful through them all, and messy papers enormously complicate that task. But sometimes you will find a mistake in a paper just as you are ready to hand it in and cannot copy it over. Always correct the mistake, but do so as neatly as you can.

General Manuscript Requirements

Margins

1. Leave margins of 1¼ or 1½ inches at the top, sides, and bottom of each page. Do not fold margins. You can mark off the four marginal areas with light pencil lines to keep your words from straying into them.
2. Indent all paragraphs.

Title

1. Center the title on the first page, 1½ inches below the top margin, or on the first line for handwritten copies.
2. Leave one line of space below the title.
3. Capitalize all *major* words in the title, including the first and last words, no matter what part of speech they are.
4. Prepositions of four or more letters require capitals.
5. Do *not* use a period at the end of the title; do not underline the title or enclose it in quotation marks. (The title of a book, an article, or a poem that appears within your title does need correct punctuation. See 27, section C, and 32, section A.)
6. A title on the cover page requires all-capital letters. If you use a cover page, use the title again at the top of the first page of your manuscript.

Cover page

The cover page usually includes your name, your class number, the submission date, and the professor's name. However, your instructor may have different requirements.

Format

1. Write on one side of each page only.
2. Number all pages consecutively, starting with page two of your composition. The first page is not numbered but is considered page one nonetheless. (Do not count the cover page or, if you submit one, the outline page.)
3. Use arabic numbers in the upper right hand corner or centered at the top of each page. Be consistent in whatever form of pagination you choose.

Typed Papers

1. Use 8½ × 11 unlined white bond paper, not onionskin paper and not the paper treated to allow corrections with pencil erasers. (Erasable paper smudges easily and often becomes unreadable.)

2. Use *only* black ribbon; if the type looks faded, change the ribbon.
3. Double-space between lines; indent paragraphs five spaces.
4. After periods, question marks, exclamation points, and colons, use two spaces; after commas and semicolons, use one space.
5. Do not use a space before or after a hyphen. To type a dash, use two consecutive hyphens without any spacing.
6. Make corrections with a typewriter eraser or with correction fluid. Do not strike over incorrect letters. For minor errors discovered after you have removed your pages from the typewriter, use a pen with blue or black ink.
7. Type should be clean enough to make clear, sharp letters.
8. Dot matrix printers used with word processors should have true descenders. That is, the tails on the letters *g*, *j*, *p*, *q*, and *y* should come down below the baseline for the rest of the type. (See Appendix A.)
9. Remember to leave adequate margins. (Left and right margins set at 10 and 70 are acceptable.)
10. In general, a manuscript prepared on a word processor is more readable if the right margin is *not* justified. Printers with proportional spacing may justify the right margin.

Handwritten Papers

1. Use 8½ × 11 paper with lines spaced about ⅜ inch apart. (For a clear layout, you can skip every other line.)
2. Use blue or black ink; write on one side only.
3. Indent the first line of each paragraph about an inch.
4. Make occasional corrections with an ink eraser or correction fluid, or draw a neat line through words you want to delete. Write in the new words above the deletions, using skipped lines and marginal space for additions.
5. Make your handwriting readable. Use firm, clear periods at the end of sentences, and leave space before the next sentence. Dot *i*'s and *j*'s directly above the letter. Avoid loops and curlicues, especially when you make capital letters. Make sure readers can distinguish between the *r* and the *n*, the *v* and the *u*, the *o* and the *a*, the *l* and the *t*, and the *e* and the *i*. Be careful to round off the letter *h* so it does not look like the letters *l* and *i*. Be sure to make the letters *m* and *n* so they do not look like the letter *u* combined with some other letter or standing alone.

Here is the first page of the final typed paper on computers. (The complete final copy appears along with the instructor's comments on pages 46–51.)

Exercise 1.9 Take a topic that you have been working on, and write a composition. Follow guidelines 1A through K as you write. Be sure to produce the following materials:

1. Prewriting
2. A limited topic

Computer Madness

When I started learning how to use the computer, I'd seen lots of movies with computers that started thinking for themselves and acting like superintelligent monsters. Thus, my hands shook when I sat down at the keyboard for the first time and looked into the vacant screen at the Science Center. As it turned out, the computer is pretty stupid, and my first troubles came because I expected the computer to think.

I felt that I knew pretty well how to use it because a 15-minute course had been given to me by a quick and indiffrent secretary in the computer office who took my fifty dollars to open an account. For a college student with a part-time job, computer time can be expensive. In a monotone he explained about passwords, I had to use one word to log on, in other words, to call up my file, and then I had to use another word to get

3. A statement of purpose for your paper, a description of the intended audience, and a description of the nature and sources of your supporting details
4. A thesis statement
5. An outline (As your instructor directs, prepare a rough outline or a more formal topic, sentence, or paragraph outline. See 33H, section 1.)
6. A first draft
7. A second draft and any subsequent drafts that may be necessary
8. A final draft

Exercise 1.10 Compare the rough draft of "Computer Madness" on pages 24–28 with the complete final draft on pages 46–50. Discuss the changes the writer made in each paragraph. Why do you think he made each of the changes? Where might you have made different changes? Where might you have left things as they were?

Exercise 1.11 Proofread the following introduction from a student's theme, and correct all the errors you find.

The Weight Room

I steped into the Greenpoint Y.M.C.A. ready to do battle the old gray building at Nassau Street and Metropolitan Ave. in Brooklyn was standing their daring me to teste my strength and skils in the weight room. When I aproached the registration desk. Mary Clyde, the tall, blue-eyed registrar, would ask, Can I see your card please"? I then would reach into my pocket. Pulling out my frayed brown wallet and show her my identification. I would than go down into the locker room and change from my street cloths into my gray gym shorts, dark blue sweat shirt, and jogging sneakers now I was properly dressed and readdy to enter the weight room its here I can not only improve my health and strength, but I can also release some of my anger and aggression.

Exercise 1.12 Read the following revised draft of "Television," submitted by the student writer for evaluation. Then, using the rough draft of the essay (pages 29–30) and the checklist for revisions (pages 31–33), evaluate the final copy in a discussion with the class. What significant changes did the writer make from one draft to the next? What further changes would you recommend?

Television

Many people have criticized television for its violence, its sensationalism, and its unimaginative programming. They say that viewers turn on the set out of habit because it is so convenient and easy to use and requires no thought or planning. All American households have at least one television set, and with the flick of a dial instant color and sound will flood the living room. Books take effort and concentration, but television viewers let things happen to them, their minds are kind of half asleep. Critics call TV the vast wasteland, the land of violence, the kingdom of the hard sell, the middle-American dream-nightmare. Because many of these criticisms are valid, it's easy to ignore the fact that television also improves considerably the quality of life today.

In an era of high inflation, the video screen provides inexpensive entertainment. A good color set costs about $400 and lasts about ten years. That's only $40.00 a year, $3.33 a month. The Consolidated Edison Company, an Eastern public utility, reports that using a color set daily for four hours burns electricity costing only 34 cents, $10.20 a month. Therefore, for a little more than the cost of a night out for two at the neighborhood movie house, a large family can enjoy television programs seven nights a week, every week!

At so little cost the range of programs is incredible. Providing entertainment and current information for many different tastes and interests. On typical evenings during the week a viewer can choose a country and western variety show, a film biography, an hour in a series about World War II, reruns of a 1950s comedy series with Lucille Ball, a baseball play-off, a talk show with Barbara Walters, and a documentary special on energy. The growth of cable television has added to these already varied programs so that viewers can now choose opera, classical or rock concerts, ballet, and dramas. In the past such "artistic" programs rarely appeared because they were thought of as unprofitable and unappealing. Relying upon audience subscriptions, and not concerned about the ratings war, cable stations can broadcast to small special-interest groups. In large cities Spanish-speaking viewers, for example, can have a full day's programs in their native language. So, as entertainer and news-giver for the average family, television has no equal.

But even more important than its entertainment value and its up-to-date reports, television improves our lives by teaching while it entertains. On most days it's easy to find many familiar programs designed specifically to teach. *Sesame Street,* for instance, develops language and mathematics skills in an amusing way for young children. For adults, programs on how to cook, plant and keep up a garden, decorate and repair a home, and exercise teach viewers important things. Universities and television stations sometimes cooperate to give courses where a student can watch a series of programs for college credit. The talk shows offer interesting opinions by experts and celebrities, so that people in the television audience are exposed to different points of view. And, to take another kind of program, documentaries teach about different cultures. Most people would never get to Easter Island, for example, but a television special on the ancient sculptured heads there brought that region to life. Many television science shows like *Nova* and others make science interesting and understandable. Jacques Cousteau takes viewers into the ocean world of whales, sponges, and speckled fish. He shows the battle for underwater survival, and entertains while he teaches more about the ocean with sound and pictures than most viewers would want to learn from books. Anyone with an open mind can come away from a day of television with new ideas and with unforgettable images of far off places.

By saving money for viewers, and entertaining and teaching them, television makes an important contribution to our society. In our high-pressured world where competition for grades, jobs, and money puts a strain on our lives, the video screen is a real wonder of technology. But it is only one small product in a field that will grow tremendously over the years. Because people need escape from the pressures of daily routines, this important need will encourage the media explosion. Home video tape recorders and video disk players for home use are, also, just the beginning. Technology and needs for pleasure work hand and hand, and will continue to stimulate each other as we move into a new machine age of entertainment and learning in the home.

1L Make the necessary changes and corrections after your instructor has commented on your paper.

When your instructor returns your graded paper, read it over carefully. Study the summary remarks that describe the strengths and weaknesses of your work. Examine the marginal notations, and be prepared to make revisions based on the commentary you find there.

You can learn to prevent errors next time around by correcting your mistakes and by responding to suggestions about style, form, and content.

Your instructor will probably grade your paper with a combination of comments, questions, and marking symbols. An alphabetical list of common correction symbols that are keyed to this handbook appears on the inside front cover of your book. If you see // in the margin of your paper, for example, the list on the inside cover tells you that // is a shorthand notation for *faulty parallelism* and that Chapter 14 explains the problem and how to correct it.

If your instructor writes chapter and section numbers only, check the inside back covers of this handbook for a quick guide to the plan of the text. If your instructor writes **2B** in the margin of your paper, for example, the plan on the inside back cover tells you that **2B** refers to *paragraph coherence.* After you read that section, you should understand the problem and some strategies for correcting it.

As you reread your paper, correct all the errors and make required revisions. If your instructor has raised any questions, answer them either by making changes in your composition or by writing a brief, direct response to the query. If you don't understand a particular comment or symbol, make an appointment to discuss the paper with your instructor.

Follow these guidelines for correcting graded papers.

Guidelines for Making Corrections on Evaluated Papers

1. Follow your instructor's guidelines for revisions. Some instructors read drafts and make comments *before* the work goes into final form. Others encourage full rewriting based on comments written on final drafts. Be sure to correct errors before you do complete revisions of graded papers.
2. Learn the symbol and comment system your instructor uses.
3. Make all corrections called for by marking symbols and comments. Use a pencil or a different color of ink to make corrections, so that your instructor can readily see what you have done.
4. As you make corrections, draw a line through the marginal symbol to help yourself keep track of what you have finished.
5. Write short corrections clearly, directly above the error noted by your instructor.
6. Rewrite any weak sentences in the margin (if there is room) or on the reverse side of the page. If you rewrite on the reverse side of the page, put an arrow in the margin to let your instructor know to turn the page over to see your revision.
7. Keep a record of your mistakes from theme to theme. Any writer tends to make errors in patterns, and if you keep a record of your errors, you will discover your own patterns. Then you can correct them more easily as you do further writing.

Here is the paper "Computer Madness," accompanied by commentary from the instructor, who used questions, marking symbols, and suggestions for revision. Your instructor may use various symbols, some taken from this book, others that are common abbreviations. Be sure that you understand the comments before you start to correct your paper.

rev 1L

Computer Madness

When I started learning how to use the computer, I'd seen lots of movies with computers that started thinking for themselves and acting like superintelligent monsters. Thus, my hands shook when I sat down at the keyboard for the first time and looked into the vacant screen at the Science Center. As it turned out, the computer is pretty stupid, and my first troubles came because I expected the computer to think.

I felt that I knew pretty well how to use it because a 15-minute course had been given to me by a quick and indiffrent secretary in the computer office who took my fifty dollars to open an account. For a college student with a part-time job, computer time can be expensive. In a monotone he explained about passwords, I had to use one word to log on, in other words, to call up my file, and then I had to use another word to get into the file and start using it. Since my name is David Barkeley, I picked the log-on word "Barkeley," and the secretary typed that name into the computer as the name for my account, his long fingers racing across the letters of the keyboard. I chose a password then, "Chimichanga"

emph Why passive voice?

sp

¶ un (see 2A2) How does expense suit the topic of the par.?

CS (see Ch. 4)

Good details here.

(just to wake him up), and he typed that in also without the slightest acknowledgment once I had spelled it for him. I thought I understood what he was doing, but it was done very fast, and when I sat down in the terminal room before a keyboard and a small empty screen, my headaches began.

emph 5 E and 5 D

Slowly, carefully, I typed in the word "Barkeley." The cold gray keys resisted my touch ever so slightly. And then the computer said, "No such account." Impossible! What was wrong with this thing? Maybe I had spelled my name wrong. I know how to spell my own name! There it was, sprawled out in green letters on the screen of the monitor where I'd typed it, and it was spelled right. I tried again, typing "Barkeley." The computer said, "No such account." Under the table I stamped my foot angrily. I'd just paid fifty dollars for my account, and I had just seen a mindless secretary set it up on the computer sitting on his desk. Again I typed in "Barkeley." Again the computer said, "No such account." After a fourth try the computer hummed with annoyance and flashed "DISCONNECT."

Good--double adverb opener

Again--clear sensory details really make the scene come alive for the reader.

With great frustration I called over the terminal watcher. A terminal watcher is a student

rev 1L

on duty in the terminal room and supposed to be // experienced enough with computers to help you with all your problems. The terminal watcher on duty that day was an attractive blonde named Ellen from my biology class. I did not want her to think I had made a mistake. So I said, in my coolest voice, "Ellen, there's something wrong with my terminal. I can't get logged on, and I know I'm doing the right thing." She drifted over to my terminal and asked me for my log-on word. I told her that it was my last name. "What is your last name? she said. Boy, what an impression I made on her, I thought. "Barkeley. You spell it B-a-r-k-e-l-e-y," I said. She typed in "b-a-r-k-e-l-e-y." The terminal immediately answered, "Password?" When I gave it to her, she raised an eyebrow, and I winced as she typed in my little joke with utter disgust. After she hit the return key, the terminal flashed, "This is active job one for you. You have fifty dollars in your account."

Why comma here? See 24Q.

You weave in actions and your own thoughts and feelings very naturally.

As Ellen turned and strolled away, I felt like a fool! I had been using a capital B to spell my name, and log-ons and passwords usually have a small initial letter. If the computer could think, it could've reconized [sp] the capital letter and let me log on. The computer is stupid. It will do)// [¶ Coh (see 2B5) a transition would help.] only what you tell it to do. You can tell it to do some pretty complicated things; but you can't tell it how to think. [This is the third or fourth time you've used *pretty* to mean *very*.] An electrician can wire your house so that you can plug a lamp or a radio into the same outlet. But if you plug in a lamp, the house cannot decide that it would rather have music than light. You can wire a computer the same way except that you use circuits in silicon chips rather than metal wires. And when you wire it to work when you plug in "barkeley," it will not work when you try to use "Barkeley." [Good point here]

At the present time many of our fears about [Wdy (20)] [¶ Coh (2B6) Clearer link to ¶ above?] modern technology are pretty unfounded. In the famous movie "2001," [ital.] a computer named HAL starts thinking for itself and kills a lot of people and has to be killed. But such things are for the movies. They are not going to happen in real life. Because computers cannot think. [frag (see Ch. 5)] People can, and they can do it with varying degrees of success at given moments. So I have learned to be patient not only with the computer but with myself the computer operator. When something goes wrong, I know I'm the one who made the mistake.

rev 1L

Technology doesn't cause errors. You have to have some intelligence before you can make mistakes, and the computer is completely stupid. If mistakes turn up, they're the mistakes of humans, not machines.

You have a breezy, narrative style that made me chuckle a couple of times. Your first paragraph sets the theme of your paper. We expect you to tell why you had trouble learning how to use the computer, and you do. I especially liked your analogy of making the computer work by plugging things into it the way we plug things into circuits at home. And I like the way you indicate that you have learned something about yourself as well as about computers.

Although your language is generally well suited to the informal nature of this essay, occasionally you are too informal -- "pretty," (to mean very), "a lot of," many contractions like "I'm," "I'd," and "doesn't" used inconsistently. In your next theme why don't you try for a slightly more formal tone? Also, try combining or eliminating some of the materials in pars. 1 and 2 for a more concise introduction. The last few sentences in your conclusion seem to be repeating themselves; can you sharpen the point there too? Occasionally unity and coherence are off (see comments in margin). Study sections 2 A, B, D in the handbook.

Exercise 1.13 Following the instructor's comments on the theme on pages 46–50, make corrections and any necessary revisions.

Exercise 1.14 When your instructor returns the essay you wrote for Exercise 1.9, follow the instructor's guidelines and make all necessary corrections and revisions.

2
Building Paragraphs

Because you have been writing paragraphs for a long time, these essential units of thought in a composition are familiar to you. But you can develop fresh insights into writing by analyzing the general characteristics of paragraphs, and these insights can help you improve the way you present and develop your thoughts on paper.

Although no absolute rules govern the building of good paragraphs, paragraphs do have a reason. They are unified, coherent, and complete elements that develop a main point—some controlling idea that a thoughtful reader can recognize. Like an essay itself, the paragraph has a beginning, a middle, and an end; it makes an assertion supported by substantial and clearly connected details; and it is a complete unit of expression, something that can stand alone and make sense.

Writers and teachers use the words *unified, coherent,* and *developed* or their noun equivalents—*unity, coherence,* and *development*—to describe paragraphs. **Unity** means that all sentences in the paragraph relate to a clearly identifiable main point. **Coherence** means that a logical plan underlies the organization of the paragraph, with sentences following each other smoothly and for apparent reason. **Development** means that adequate details support the ideas in the paragraph and that an appropriate structure or pattern helps establish the topic and what the writer says about it.

Unity, coherence, and development are not mutually exclusive terms. Building a unified paragraph depends on a coherent structure—logical connections between sentences, for example—and also upon well-developed details within a suitable plan. Also, the all-important central idea of a paragraph belongs in a treatment of coherence and of development as well as in a treatment of unity. In studying these terms, then, you should expect some overlapping. When you attempt to address one of the three qualities in your own writing, you should be addressing the other two as well.

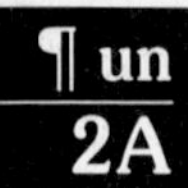

Paragraphs have several functions:

1. To separate a paper into manageable blocks of thought that readers can grasp one at a time
2. To provide progressive steps that carry readers through a paper
3. To help distinguish between the major ideas of a paper and to help group each major idea with the sentences that support it
4. To allow a writer to summarize parts of a paper or to shift from one part of a paper to another
5. To relieve the strain of continuous reading by breaking up the text into blocks of type on the page

A good paragraph usually has the following qualities:

1. The paragraph is built around one controlling idea, and every sentence in the paragraph supports or develops this controlling idea.
2. The controlling idea may be a general statement written into the paragraph itself, usually near the beginning, or the controlling idea may not be stated in the paragraph. If the controlling idea is not stated, it may easily be inferred from what is written in the paragraph.
3. A good paragraph has transitional words at the beginning that smoothly lead readers into the paragraph. Transitional words often appear at the close of the paragraph as well, to serve as a bridge to the next.
4. A paragraph is long enough to express a complete thought but not so long as to tax the reader.
5. A paragraph usually presents concrete details, actions, vivid statements, statistics, or direct quotations to support the controlling idea. Sometimes abstract statements support or develop paragraph ideas, especially when the paragraph deals with abstract thoughts rather than with objects or actions.

2A Build unified paragraphs.

To achieve unity you must make all sentences in a paragraph relate to and support some central idea.

1 Give each paragraph a controlling idea.

Every paragraph should have a controlling idea, a main point that all sentences support and clarify. Often a single sentence describes that main point somewhere in the paragraph, but in many paragraphs the major idea is implied, not stated.

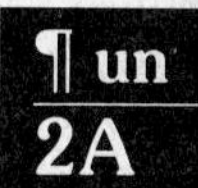

The sentence that states the main point of a paragraph is called the **topic sentence.** A topic sentence may limit and define the topic by presenting an opinion or an attitude about it. The topic sentence is often the first sentence in the paragraph.

Compare the following topic sentences:

1. My father spent the first years of his childhood in Chicago.
2. My father spent the first years of a hard childhood in Chicago.

[Both of these sentences make a general statement about a topic, the father's childhood, but no controlling assertion limits the topic in the first sentence. With limitless details from which to choose, an inexperienced writer may blur the focus of the paragraph and thereby lose the reader. However, the second sentence limits the topic to a dominant impression, the fact that the childhood was hard. Therefore, all supporting sentences in the paragraph should describe the difficulties in the father's childhood.]

See how the limited topic sentence works in the following paragraph:

> My father spent the first years of a hard childhood in Chicago. His father deserted the family, leaving a wife and five small children, of whom my father was the oldest. My father's mother had to take in washing and had to clean house for rich people on Michigan Avenue just to keep her family together. My father cleaned up yards for ten cents an hour when he was eleven. He got a paper route when he was twelve and had to crawl out of bed at five in the morning seven days a week, winter and summer, to deliver the papers before breakfast. He gave all the money he made to his mother for family expenses. Because they could not afford doctors, my father was left partly deaf by a childhood disease. Those were hard times, and he remembers every detail.

[Every sentence in the paragraph supports the general statement made in the topic sentence. Every detail illustrates the idea of a hard childhood to back up the general assertion made at the beginning.]

In the following paragraphs, the topic sentences make a generalization that limits and controls the topic.

> **Although smoking has been a popular habit for centuries, it has always had its enemies.** Some American Indians advised young braves not to smoke too much because tobacco would cut their wind in a hunt or a battle. King James I of England called smoking "a branch of the sin of drunkenness, which is the root of all sins." Ben Jonson, the playwright, said smoking was "good for nothing but to choke a man and fill him full of smoke and embers." Popular slang called cigarettes "coffin nails" long before the medical evidence on the harm from smoking was

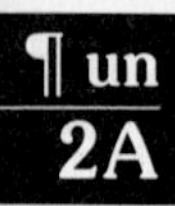

complete. Now every package of cigarettes and every advertisement for cigarettes must carry a warning from the Surgeon General that smoking is injurious to health.

[The first sentence announces the topic, asserting that smoking has always had enemies. Note how this topic sentence helps the writer limit and control the paragraph; every sentence in the paragraph supports the topic.]

> **What may be most discouraging about the corruption of sports is its widespread acceptance as the norm.** A dozen years ago, when blacks and campus radicals began questioning the sports establishment, athletes generally portrayed themselves as victims. Now many kids are admitting that they have tried to take the bribes and inducements on the sleazy terms with which they are offered. Their complaints are not so much that illegalities exist, but that they aren't getting their share of the goodies. That mentality only underscores the urgency of finding some way to turn the system back towards true educational goals.
>
> —*Newsweek*

[The topic sentence comes first; it provides an organizing framework for the sentences that follow. The topic sentence tells the reader why the writer has chosen these details to present and explains the reason for the rest of the paragraph.]

Many paragraphs do not begin with a summary topic sentence. Yet the most important sentence in setting the stage for the paragraph is always the first sentence, even though it may not tell you much about the topic. You may have to read the whole paragraph before you fully understand the first sentence. But if the paragraph holds together well, you will always be able to see how the first sentence announces the subject and how the rest of the paragraph develops the subject from the first sentence.

Sometimes the first sentence simply introduces the topic sentence for the paragraph. But the first sentence is still the essential sentence for catching and directing the reader's attention.

> The steam locomotive evokes nostalgia among many people who never rode a train pulled by one. **The nostalgia is better than the experience of the steam locomotive ever was.** The steam locomotive was a dirty, dangerous, and generally disagreeable companion to American life for well over a century. It spread filthy black smoke over large areas of every city it served, and it usually left a thick film of oily grime on the face of every passenger in the cars behind it. It started fires along the sides of the tracks in woods and fields. It was so heavy that it pounded rails until they broke, and when it crashed and turned over—as it frequently did—it poured lethal fire and steam on the engineer and the fireman in the cab. It had so many moving parts that it often broke down, stranding passengers for hours. And it was absurdly inefficient and costly to operate.

[The second sentence is the topic sentence. It tells you that the paragraph will describe the disadvantages of steam locomotives. But the first sentence leads into the topic, even though it does not tell you what the paragraph will say about steam locomotives. Everything else in the paragraph takes the lead from the first sentence.]

Sometimes the first sentence in the first paragraph of a longer work will begin the description of a scene. Several similar sentences will follow. Then the final sentence in this first paragraph will sum up the scene and will explain why it is important to the meaning that the paragraph expresses. Such scene-setting first paragraphs are often used to begin articles in popular magazines because they make readers want to know what is going to happen. Although the first sentence is not a topic sentence, it is still vitally important because it sets the stage for what follows:

> The bands are marching, the tailgates swinging open for the ritual of picnics and parties. The beverages are heady, the boosterism infectious, the old school colors vivid and bright. **This is college football, as the television slogan goes, a great way to spend an autumn afternoon.**
>
> —*Newsweek*

[The topic sentence comes last, uniting all the concrete details in the earlier sentences and explaining why the writer has put them in. But notice that the first sentence does introduce the topic, although it does not make a generalization about it.]

Often an introductory paragraph in an essay or an article simply tells a story. The first sentence begins with a striking detail, and the following sentences build on it. The reason for the story is reserved for a later paragraph. The role of the first sentence is to catch the interest of readers and to make them keep on reading.

> Dawn awoke the fleet to gale winds. These raked down from the northeast against the Gulf Stream current, stirring confused cross seas. Most of the passengers and soldiers aboard *Santa Margarita,* even the experienced sailors, were soon seasick.
>
> —EUGENE LYON

[The first sentence in this story from *National Geographic* puts us in the middle of a drama. The story of the shipwreck of the *Santa Margarita* in 1622 introduces the article that tells how divers found the wreck in 1980 and what they found in it.]

Paragraphs that start with details may appear in the middle of a piece of prose. The first sentence announces an interesting fact; other sentences build on that fact by adding others; then a final sentence in the paragraph explains the importance of these facts.

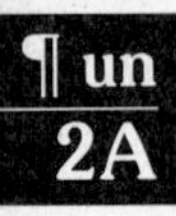

When a paragraph begins by stating the controlling idea in general terms, the second sentence often serves to limit the idea. In the following paragraph, the first sentence makes a general statement about how the police of Birmingham, Alabama, handled the arrest of civil rights demonstrators in the 1960s. Then the second sentence makes a limiting statement about the general subject introduced by the first. The rest of the paragraph flows from that more limiting statement to the topic sentence toward the end of the paragraph.

> It is true that they have been rather disciplined in their public handling of the demonstrators. In this sense they have been rather publicly "nonviolent." But for what purpose? To preserve the evil system of segregation. Over the last few years I have consistently preached that nonviolence demands that the means we use must be as pure as the ends we seek. So I have tried to make it clear that it is wrong to use immoral means to attain moral ends. But now I must affirm that it is just as wrong, or even more so, to use moral means to preserve immoral ends. **Maybe Mr. Connor and his policemen have been rather publicly nonviolent as Chief Prichett was in Albany, Georgia, but they have used the moral means of nonviolence to maintain the immoral end of flagrant racial injustice.** T. S. Eliot has said that there is no greater treason than to do the right deed for the wrong reason.
>
> —MARTIN LUTHER KING, JR.

Some paragraphs introduce the topic with a direct quotation that focuses attention on the information to come. But again, the general subject of the paragraph is signaled by the first sentence.

> **"Bullfighting is an animal inside me, and it is the one I cannot dominate—it dominates me," says the 43-year-old El Cordobes who returned to the bullring last year after a seven-year retirement.** By the end of the season El Cordobes was once again the most talked-about matador in the sport. But last month his comeback was interrupted, if not ended, by a serious goring.
>
> —*Newsweek*

[The first sentence announces that the rest of the paragraph is going to be about the bullfighter El Cordobes. It does not summarize the rest of the paragraph; the next two sentences are quite distinct. But all of them are related to the subject announced generally in the first sentence—El Cordobes the bullfighter.]

Some paragraphs introduce the topic by posing a question at the beginning. The rest of the paragraph offers some kind of response to the question. The response may be a firm answer, or it may suggest an answer or report an answer someone has given. In this paragraph, the biographer of William Carlos Williams reports on Williams' response to the question in the first sentence. (Ed is the poet's brother.)

> **But wasn't truth, after all, an act of intuitive faith, something that left poor logic far behind?** Truth, he told Ed that same month, was not something reasoned out but something intuitively grasped, something believed in. "Don't reason from feelings or rather don't reason at all," he told his brother. For he saw now that truth was not something arrived at by syllogisms and proofs, but something grasped by a quantum leap of faith. Truth was, after all, an intuitive insight into the essence of a thing, something radiantly perceived in a moment.
>
> —PAUL MARIANI

The sample paragraphs you have examined demonstrate the range of possibilities writers have developed for making their topics clear. The main idea in a paragraph may appear in a topic sentence that expresses a dominant impression about the topic. The topic sentence may be a general summary statement, or it may be a rather limited statement that the rest of the paragraph develops. The main idea may appear in the very first sentence of the paragraph, in the middle, or at the end—or the main idea may not be stated at all. Whether or not the topic is stated directly, it must be clear; both writer and reader should be able to state it easily for each paragraph. The first sentence always leads into the topic in some way.

Despite all these possibilities, when you write paragraphs about ideas, it is usually wise to state and limit your topic in your first sentence. Readers welcome clearly stated topics in paragraphs, and writers find it easier to keep to their main point by stating it right up front. And whether you use a general topic sentence or not, remember that the first sentence in every paragraph represents the writer's commitment to develop an idea presented there.

Exercise 2.1 Read and evaluate these topic sentences. Is the topic clearly stated? Is an opinion, an attitude, or a reaction expressed in some dominant impression about the topic? How would you improve any of these topic sentences that you find inadequate?

1. My cat Romona sits under the maple tree in our backyard.
2. The Atomic Energy Commission's Oak Ridge National Laboratory is located in a once isolated part of mountainous eastern Tennessee.
3. Airport security systems have been improved remarkably in the last decade.
4. Although many children do not attend school before the first grade, kindergarten offers a great advantage to five-year-olds.
5. In many states, new laws prevent anyone below nineteen from purchasing or drinking alcohol in public places.

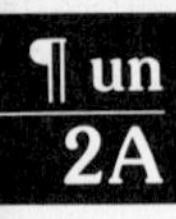

Exercise 2.2 For a paragraph on each of any five topics below, construct a topic sentence that states the topic and that offers an opinion about it, an attitude toward it, or a reaction to it.

1. Buying a used car
2. Seeking a job during a recession
3. Taking care of a chest cold
4. Advertisements children see on television
5. Improving grades in college
6. Baby-sitting
7. Doing housework
8. United States foreign policy in Latin America
9. Photography of people from close up
10. Illiteracy among high school students

Exercise 2.3 Take each of the following statements as the topic sentence for a paragraph, and write a paragraph of supporting sentences.

1. My neighborhood was a good [or bad] place to live when I was growing up.
2. If I am to like a piece of music, it has to have some special qualities.
3. Being able to write well offers several advantages.
4. Many Americans want to be physically fit, but the bodies of most of us are in woeful shape.

Exercise 2.4 State the topic of each of the following paragraphs in your own words. Then tell whether or not the writer states that topic in a topic sentence. Also, explain how the first sentence of the paragraph leads into the topic.

> To feed the seemingly insatiable appetite for news about *Star Wars,* Twentieth Century-Fox and Lucasfilm have mounted a promotional onslaught whose scope resembles a rock & roll world tour. Over the last few weeks, the film's stars have been hustled from Los Angeles to New York to Washington to London to Japan and then on to Australia to sit for literally hundreds of newspaper, radio, and television interviews. The effort is further supported by a multimillion-dollar ad campaign and a glut of aggressive merchandising schemes that include everything from a soundtrack album to a proposed Yoda doll, the gnomelike Jedi Master.
>
> —TIMOTHY WHITE

> There is a coarse and boisterous money-making fellow in the outskirts of our town, who is going to build a bank-wall under the hill along the edge of his meadow. The powers have put this into his head to keep him out of mischief, and he wishes me to spend three weeks digging there with him. The result will be that he will perhaps get some more money to hoard, and leave for his heirs to spend foolishly. If I do this, most will commend

me as an industrious and hard-working man; but if I choose to devote myself to certain labors which yield more real profit, though but little money, they may be inclined to look on me as an idler. Nevertheless, as I do not need the police of meaningless labor to regulate me, and do not see anything absolutely praiseworthy in this fellow's undertaking, any more than in many an enterprise of our own or foreign governments, however amusing it may be to him or them, I prefer to finish my education at a different school.

—HENRY DAVID THOREAU

If a husband and wife love one another, they do not think of divorcing; if a parent and child love one another, however, they must. So what my daughter was mourning, I suspect, was not only the displacement to "out there"—she knew, after all, that it was as inevitable as sunset—but the end of a marriage, a marriage whose break-up symbolizes that one has grown up. Some children are, of course, old at 10, and others are never young at all. My daughter has been very lucky, and so have I. She had her childhood; I had hers, too.

—MARY CANTWELL

2 Make all sentences in a paragraph support the main idea.

Every paragraph needs a logical structure based on the main point of the paragraph. The succession of sentences and the flow of ideas help bring that structure about. Any sentence that distracts readers from the main idea violates the architecture of the paragraph.

In the following paragraph, several sentences wander away from the main idea.

After vigorous exercise, the body enters a dangerous period that cooling off can help prevent. When you are swimming or running, a large blood supply from the heart brings your arms and legs the oxygen required for muscle activity. **The human heart works like a pump. When the right upper chamber of the heart (the auricle) fills with blood, blood pushes down into the right lower chamber (the ventricle). When this chamber fills, the strong muscles in its wall pump tired blood into an artery that speeds the blood to the lungs.** As you exercise, the muscles squeeze, and blood going back to the heart gets an added push as long as you move your limbs. But if you stop suddenly, all this extra blood stays there: your arm and leg muscles are no longer helping your heart pump the blood around. Blood that remains in the arms and legs is blood kept away from vital organs like the brain. But if you cool off, that is, slow down your activity gradually, you'll help bring your pulse rate and your body temperature down slowly, you'll help your muscles rid themselves of metabolic waste, and, most important, you'll keep the blood flowing normally throughout your body.

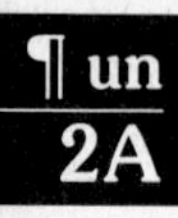

[The controlling idea of this paragraph may be stated like this: Stopping vigorous exercise suddenly can cause a strain on the heart and other body organs, but a gradual cooling off after activity can prevent serious problems. Now look again at the sentences that are in boldface. These details of how the heart operates may be interesting, but they distract the reader from the controlling idea of the paragraph. These sentences have no place here, although they might work well in another part of the paper. The paragraph is clearer and reads more smoothly with the distracting sentences removed.]

Check the sentences in your paragraph carefully against your main idea, and remove any sentences that do not support that main idea.

Exercise 2.5 Sentences that do not relate to the main idea have been added to these paragraphs written by professional writers. First, write out the main idea of each paragraph in your own words. Then rewrite the paragraph to eliminate any distracting sentences. Be prepared to explain why you removed these sentences.

> Obviously, in tough times, there is mounting pressure on publishers to collect payments earlier than in the past. Still, despite the booksellers' statements that publisher credit terms seem to be changing, the publishers insist that this new stringency does not mean a change of stated policy. Officially, payment to most publishers is due in 30 days; unofficially, the practice has been not to insist on payment until an overdue balance far exceeds the 30-day net terms. It is this application or enforcement of credit terms that booksellers report has changed in recent months. Some credit managers did acknowledge changes in the enforcement of credit policy.
>
> —Allene Symons

> What gives a word its connotative meanings are the associations we bring to the word. The word "home" for most of us conjures up images of comfort and security, a place more warm and personal than a house or a dwelling. To a person who's never had a home it may exist as an ideal in the back of his mind. To the person far from home it means roots. But to an orphan the word "home" may mean something else entirely: an institution, something artificial, something not really his, something to run away from. Orphans beyond infancy present serious problems to orphanages. Unless a child is under a year old, adopting couples do not think of the child as desirable. Thus orphan homes are filled with children and adolescents growing up without parents. Or think of "old people's home," "home for the blind," "home for unwed mothers." How does a grandmother feel when her children say to her, "Behave yourself, gran-gran, or we'll have to put you in a home"?
>
> —Thomas Whissen

Exercise 2.6 Explain how each sentence in the following paragraphs contributes to the main idea.

Psychophysicists who study food tastes have found four basic tastes: sweet, sour, salty, and bitter. There are wider variations in what people call sweet or bitter than in what they call sour or salty — variations we are only now beginning to understand. We have found, too, that there is not one but a number of receptor mechanisms in the mouth for bitterness, which may explain why people are sensitive to some bitter foods and not others. We have also discovered that certain substances can suppress one or more of the four tastes.

—LINDA BARTOSHUK

Some children dedicate themselves to being ridiculous, their behavior conjuring up memories of old Mack Sennett comedies and floppy-footed clowns. We have encountered a considerable number of these children in our counseling work over the last two decades. They are usually brought in for evaluation and treatment as "behavior problems"; they may be doing badly in school, be in conflict with everyone in the family, or have threatened to run away from home. Whatever the immediate difficulty, we have been impressed in each case with a theatrical clumsiness, a clownish awkwardness.

—SEYMOUR AND RHODA LEE FISHER

To begin with, there was the nature of the country. The front line, ours and the Fascists', lay in positions of immense natural strength, which as a rule could only be approached from one side. Provided a few trenches have been dug, such places cannot be taken by infantry, except in overwhelming numbers. In our own position or most of those round us a dozen men with two machine-guns could have held off a battalion. Perched on the hill-tops as we were, we should have made lovely marks for artillery; but there was no artillery. Sometimes I used to gaze round the landscape and long — oh how passionately! — for a couple of batteries of guns. One could have destroyed the enemy positions one after another as easily as smashing nuts with a hammer. But on our side the guns simply did not exist. The Fascists did occasionally manage to bring a gun or two from Zaragoza and fire a very few shells, so few that they never even found the range and the shells plunged harmlessly into the empty ravines. Against machine-guns and without artillery there are only three things you can do: dig yourself in at a safe distance — four hundred yards, say — advance across the open and be massacred, or make small-scale night-attacks that will not alter the general situation. Practically, the alternatives are stagnation or suicide.

—GEORGE ORWELL

2B Use a variety of methods to build coherent paragraphs.

In coherent paragraphs, units of thought follow each other logically. Writers use various methods to emphasize logical connections and to make ideas flow smoothly. As you use these methods, you must think carefully about the sequence of ideas you follow in each paragraph.

You can achieve coherence by carefully arranging the information in a paragraph. You can also achieve coherence by using pronouns, by repeating important words or phrases, by using parallel structures, and by using transitional words and expressions. These techniques rarely appear alone, and you should combine them to achieve paragraphs that hold together around a central theme or topic.

In the following sample, boldface print indicates some of the devices that lend coherence to the paragraph.

> Experience gained on the Santa Fe Trail was comparatively unimportant, and might be misleading. Conditions there were very different. The distance was only half as far, and the country was nearly all open and level. **Even more important,** as the expression "Santa Fe trade" indicates, that trail was used by traders, and not by **emigrants.** When the Oregon and California **emigrants** imitated the Santa Fe traders, **they** nearly always came to grief—as **in using big wagons, forming large companies,** and **organizing in military fashion.**
>
> **On the other hand,** the **emigrants** made use of a general backlog of experience with teams and wagons. Every **farmer** knew a good deal about that sort of thing, and **he** had probably made journeys of several hundred miles. What had to be faced, to get to California, were the new conditions—**the tenfold-long pull, the untamed Indians, the lack of supply points, the difficult country of deserts and mountains. But** in the handling of the wagon itself most of the men were already **proficient,** and this **proficiency** was essential to the success of the covered-wagon migration.
>
> —George R. Stewart

[In both paragraphs a logical plan controls the arrangement of information. Each paragraph starts with a generalization. Supporting elements appear in ascending order of importance, the most dramatic statement appearing last. The pronouns *they* and *he* in lines 9 and 15 link up with nouns stated earlier, *emigrants* and *farmer.* Repetition of the word *emigrants* in lines 7, 8, and 12 and the use of *proficient* and *proficiency* in line 21 advance the flow of ideas.

In lines 9–11, the writer uses a series of gerund phrases as objects of prepositions (see 3C, section 1). In lines 17–19 he uses a series of appositives (see 3B, section 2). In both cases the repeated grammatical structure adds coherence to the paragraphs. Finally, the use of the expressions *even more important* (line 5) and *on the other hand* (line 12) and the dramatic use of *but* to open a sentence (line 19) serve to clarify the relationship between ideas. These transitions connect the ideas smoothly.]

The section that follows will explain several devices for achieving coherence in your writing.

1 Arrange paragraph ideas according to a logical plan (see also 2A, section 2).

How you organize information in a paragraph is related to your main point and to what you want to say about it.

You can arrange information *spatially* by locating the reader somewhere in a scene and then moving through physical space—from back to front, from top to bottom, from left to right, or in some other logical way. A descriptive paragraph often follows a spatial plan:

Spatial Arrangement

> I walked out on the bridge and looked down at the lock. The canal flowed into the lock through a sprung wooden gate just under the bridge. It ran between two narrowly confining walls for about a hundred feet. Then, with a sudden boil and bubble, it broke against another gate, spilled through, and resumed its sluggish course. The walls of the lock were faced with big blocks of rust-red sandstone. Some of the stones were so huge that they could have been hoisted into place only with a block and tackle. It was beautiful stone, and it had been beautifully finished and fitted. Time had merely softened it. Here and there along the courses I could even make out the remains of a mason's mark. One device was quite distinct—a double-headed arrow. Another appeared to be two overlapping equilateral triangles. I went on across the bridge to the house. The windows were shuttered and boarded up, and the door was locked. No matter. It was enough just to stand and look at it. It was a lovely house, as beautifully made as the lock, and as firmly designed for function. It gave me a pang to think that there had once been a time when even a lock tender could have so handsome a house. A phoebe called from a sweet-gum tree in the dooryard. Far away, somewhere down by the river, a mourning dove gave an answering sigh. I looked at my watch. It was ten minutes after ten. I started up the towpath.
>
> —BERTON ROUECHÉ

[We look down from the bridge into the canal at the bottom of the lock, and then we examine the walls of the lock. Looking at the house, we then move to a tree in the dooryard and after that to a place far away down by the river. The scene unfolds through logical movement in space.]

Another way to present information in a paragraph is *chronologically.* In a chronological arrangement, events are organized sequentially through time; earlier incidents come before later ones. Narratives usually rely on a chronological organization of paragraphs.

Chronological Arrangement

> The sun rose slowly out of the hazy sea. We hiked through the great olive grove and by 7 we started our slow climb up the mountain. The trail wound back and forth, narrow, and twisting ever upward. We left the olive trees behind, and we entered a rocky world where a few poplars cast an occasional shade. By 10 o'clock the sun had burned the haze off the sea, and the heat grew as the sun climbed. We got thirsty but we had no water. By 11 we were drenched with sweat, and the heat made everything shimmer so that the tumbled rocks seemed to dance crazily in the uncertain air. By now we could see for miles down the island of Crete, and to the west the huge bulk of Mount Ida rose into the hot blue sky. By noon, when we were nearly crazy with thirst and fatigue we got to the top.

[The writer's intent here is to capture the experience as it happened. The description begins at the bottom of the mountain and follows the climbers upward as the sun climbs in the sky and the heat increases, hour by hour, until the parched climbers reach the mountaintop at high noon.]

Spatial and chronological arrangements often work together. For example, in the excerpt from Roueché (page 63), both chronological and spatial order contribute to the coherence of the paragraph.

You can arrange paragraph elements according to *importance,* starting with the least significant or least dramatic information and building to a climax with the most significant or most dramatic.

Order of Importance

> Shakespeare came to London at a fortunate time. If he had been born twenty years earlier, he would have arrived in London when underpaid hacks were turning out childish dramas about brown-paper dragons. If he had been born twenty years later, he would have arrived when the drama had begun to lose its hold on ordinary people and was succumbing to a kind of self-conscious cleverness. But his arrival in London coincided with a great wave of excitement and achievement in the theatre and he rode with it to its crest. William Shakespeare brought

great gifts to London, but the city was waiting with gifts of its own to offer him. The root of his genius was Shakespeare's own, but it was London that supplied him with the favoring weather.

—MARCHETTE CHUTE

[The fact that London's environment was perfectly suited to Shakespeare's genius is the most dramatic information in the paragraph and comes last.]

Paragraph elements may be arranged inductively or deductively. An **inductive** scheme provides instances to support a generalization that is made at the end of a paragraph. In other words, you present details, and then you draw some conclusion about them. In a **deductive** arrangement the generalization comes first, and the particular details succeed it in the paragraph.

Inductive Arrangement

We huddled together in the cool spring night, whispering in hoarse voices, thrumming with the excitement that vibrated through the crowd gathering in the parking lot outside the Ames train station. All the way home from Des Moines we had hugged each other, laughed, cried, and hugged each other again. When we passed through the small farming towns between Des Moines and Ames, we rolled down the windows of the Harbingers' station wagon and shouted down the quiet streets, "We beat Marshalltown in seven overtimes! We beat Marshalltown in seven overtimes!" It had a rhythmic beat, a chant we repeated to each other in unbelieving ecstasy. We beat Marshalltown in seven overtimes! For the first time in ten years, Ames High School had won the state basketball championship. Most of us sophomores felt nothing so important could ever happen to us again.

—SUSAN ALLEN TOTH

[The last sentence states the generalization that all the paragraph details support.]

Deductive Arrangement

Other scientific investigations also exerted considerable influence on present-day painters and sculptors. Inventions like the microscope and telescope, with their capacity to enlarge, isolate and probe, offer the artist provocative new worlds to explore. These instruments, which break up structures only to examine them more fully, demonstrate how details can be magnified and separated from the whole and operate as new experiences. Repeatedly, artists in recent years have exploited this idea, allowing one isolated symbol to represent an entire complex organism. Miró often needs merely part of a woman's body to describe all women, or Léger, one magnified letter of the alphabet to conjure up the numberless printed words that daily bombard us.

—KATHERINE KUH

[Supporting details about scientific inventions and their effect on artists follow the generalization stated in the first sentence.]

Information in the paragraph about childhood in Chicago (page 53) is also arranged deductively.

Exercise 2.7 Explain the method of arrangement used in each paragraph below.

> Then a strange blight crept over the area and everything began to change. Some evil spell had settled on the community: mysterious maladies swept the flocks of chickens; the cattle and sheep sickened and died. Everywhere was a shadow of death. The farmers spoke of much illness among their families. In the town the doctors had become more and more puzzled by new kinds of sickness appearing among their patients. There had been several sudden and unexplained deaths not only among adults but even among children, who would be stricken suddenly while at play and die within a few hours.
>
> —Rachel Carson

> The preacher preached a wonderful rhythmical sermon, all moans and shouts and lonely cries and dire pictures of hell, and then he sang a song about the ninety and nine safe in the fold, but one little lamb was left out in the cold. Then he said: "Won't you come? Won't you come to Jesus? Young lambs, won't you come?" And he held out his arms to all us young sinners there on the mourners' bench. And the little girls cried. And some of them jumped up and went to Jesus right away. But most of us just sat there.
>
> —Langston Hughes

> Once in a long while, four times so far for me, my mother brings out the metal tube that holds her medical diploma. On the tube are gold circles crossed with seven red lines each—"joy" ideographs in abstract. There are also little flowers that look like gears for a gold machine. According to the scraps of labels with Chinese and American addresses, stamps, and postmarks, the family airmailed the can from Hong Kong in 1950. It got crushed in the middle, and whoever tried to peel the labels off stopped because the red and gold paint came off too, leaving silver scratches that rust. Somebody tried to pry the end off before discovering that the tube pulls apart. When I open it, the smell of China flies out, a thousand-year-old bat flying heavy-headed out of the Chinese caverns where bats are as white as dust, a smell that comes from long ago, far back in the brain. Crates from Canton, Hong Kong, Singapore, and Taiwan have that smell too, only stronger because they are more recently come from the Chinese.
>
> —Maxine Hong Kingston

2 Use pronouns to link ideas.

Replacing nouns, pronouns help achieve coherence simply by their grammatical function (see 3B, section 3). Pronouns with antecedents refer the reader to a previously identified noun and help the writer to connect the ideas in a paragraph without having to mention the nouns again and again.

When you use pronouns, pay special attention to antecedents. Readers must always find it easy to determine which words pronouns are referring to.

> When a mother is afraid that **her** child will die when **it** has only a pimple or a slight cold we speak of anxiety, but if **she** is afraid when the child has a serious illness we call **her** reaction fear. If someone is afraid whenever **he** stands on a height or when **he** has to discuss a topic **he** knows well, we call **his** reaction anxiety; if someone is afraid when **he** loses **his** way high up in the mountains during a heavy thunderstorm we would speak of fear. Thus far we should have a simple and neat distinction; fear is a reaction that is proportionate to the danger one has to face, whereas anxiety is a disproportionate reaction to danger, or even a reaction to imaginary danger.
>
> —KAREN HORNEY

[The referent for each pronoun is clear, and the pronouns help to link the ideas together smoothly.]

3 Repeat important words or phrases to link ideas.

Repetition helps bind sentences together in a paragraph. By repeating key words you can help the reader follow your line of thought.

> We do not **choose** to be born. We do not **choose** our parents. We do not **choose** our historical epoch, or the country of our birth, or the immediate circumstances of our upbringing. We do not, most of us, **choose** to die; nor do we **choose** the time or conditions of our death. But within all this realm of choicelessness, we do **choose** how we shall live; courageously or in cowardice, honorably or dishonorably, with purpose or in drift. We **decide** what is important and what is trivial in life. We **decide** that what makes us significant is either what we do or what we refuse to do. But no matter how indifferent the universe may be to our choices and decisions, these choices and decisions are ours to make. We **decide.** We **choose.** And as we **decide** and **choose,** so are our lives formed. In the end, forming our own destiny is what ambition is about.
>
> —JOSEPH EPSTEIN

[The words **choose** and **decide** provide dramatic linkage of ideas, connecting thoughts smoothly while at the same time emphasizing the issue of choice as the writer sees it.]

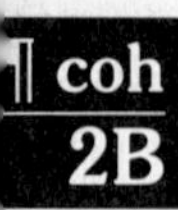

4 Use parallel structure to link ideas.

You can tie thought units together in your paragraphs by repeating grammatical or syntactical structures. In the paragraph below, parallelism dramatically links Macaulay's statements about Britain's King Charles I (1600–1649).

> We charge him with having broken his coronation oath; and we are told that he kept his marriage vow! We accuse him of having given up his people to the merciless inflictions of the most hot-headed and hard-hearted of prelates; and the defense is, that he took his little son on his knee and kissed him! We censure him for having violated the articles of the Petition of Right, after having, for good and valuable consideration, promised to observe them; and we are informed that he was accustomed to hear prayers at six o'clock in the morning! It is to such considerations as these, together with his Van Dyck dress, his handsome face, and his peaked beard, that he owes, we verily believe, most of his popularity with the present generation.
>
> —THOMAS BABINGTON MACAULAY

[The subject-verb-object structure opens each of the first three sentences: *we charge him, we accuse him, we censure him.* Also, a semicolon follows each attack on Charles and precedes each apology made by the opposition. The grammar and syntax of the sentences heighten the contrast between Macaulay's assertions and those of his opponents.]

In the paragraph by Joseph Epstein (page 67), grammatical and syntactical structures as well as key words are repeated.

5 Use appropriate transitional expressions to make your thoughts flow smoothly from sentence to sentence.

Transitional expressions may help you state with some exactness the relations between your ideas. The most obvious transitional expressions are words like *moreover, furthermore, and, but, or, nevertheless, then, still,* and *likewise.* These expressions look back to the thought just expressed and forward to the thought about to be expressed.

> Many couples who want to adopt a child run into frustrating difficulties. They may have a comfortable home and financial security. **And** they may be loving and generous people. **But** they may be too old for the standards set down by the adoption agency. **Or** they may discover that no children are available. **Then,** when a child is available, the couple may be charged an exorbitant fee. **Nevertheless,** couples who want to adopt a child usually persevere, **and** usually their determination pays off.

[The word *and* helps add a thought, whereas *but* and *or* point to contrasts. The word *then* states a relationship in time. *Nevertheless* contrasts previous ideas with the final ideas.]

In the list below, transitional expressions are organized by the function they perform. You should choose transitional expressions to signal specific relationships between thoughts.

Transitional Expressions

To signal spatial relations

above, adjacent to, against, alongside, around, at a distance from, at the, behind, below, beside, beyond, encircling, far off, forward, from the, in front of, in the rear, inside, near the back, near the end, nearby, next to, on, over, surrounding, there, through the, to the left, to the right, up front

To signal relations in time

afterward, at last, before, earlier, first, former, formerly, further, furthermore, immediately, in the first place, in the interval, in the meantime, in the next place, in the past, later on, latter, meanwhile, next, now, often, once, previously, second, simultaneously, sometime later, subsequently, suddenly, then, therefore, third, today, tomorrow, until now, when, years ago, yesterday

To add

again, also, and, and then, besides, further, furthermore, in addition, last, likewise, moreover, next, nor, too

To give examples or to intensify points

after all, as an example, certainly, for example, for instance, indeed, in fact, in truth, it is true, of course, specifically, that is

To show similarities

alike, in the same way, like, likewise, resembling, similarly

To show contrasts

after all, although, but, conversely, differ(s) from, difference, different, dissimilar, even though, granted, however, in contrast, in spite of, nevertheless, notwithstanding, on the contrary, on the other hand, otherwise, still, though, unalike, while this may be true, yet

To indicate cause and effect

accordingly, as a result, because, consequently, hence, since, then, therefore, thus

To conclude or summarize

finally, in brief, in conclusion, in other words, in short, in summary, that is, to summarize

Because well-constructed paragraphs will have their own dynamic coherence, you should use transitional expressions cautiously. The sentences in a good paragraph are linked together with clarity and logic so that transitional expressions are seldom needed. Sometimes readers are expected to make the linkages, mentally adding words like *for example, thus, however,* and *nevertheless* as they read. Also, you have already seen how linking devices other than transitional expressions can work in your paragraphs (see 2B, sections 1–4).

Even the punctuation in a sentence can serve as a connecting device. Notice how the dash and the colon in the two examples below link ideas without stating transitions directly (see also 28A and 28B).

> Some penny-arcade war machines were also busy—the familiar American sound of the thump and whine of miniature electronic holocausts.
>
> —GEORGE PLIMPTON

[The dash after *busy* links the thoughts. The writer might have written "and thus I heard" or some other transitional phrase in place of the dash, but the dash does the job very well, and no transitional expression is needed.]

> The controversies and rapid shifts in the linguists' camp have often prevented English teachers from asking the basic questions: What have we learned from English linguists *over the years?* What are the *lasting* contributions that linguists have made to the way we teach English? What are the aspects of the linguist's work that have proved most *stimulating* and *productive* in the classroom?
>
> —HANS GUTH

[The colon makes unnecessary a transitional expression like *for example;* it also makes unnecessary the repetition of key words such as *these basic questions are.* Either of these substitutions would have worked in the paragraph, but the colon alone works just as well.]

In using transitional expressions or other connecting devices, you must strike a balance between directness and subtlety. Lots of practice and guidance by friendly readers will develop your ear for appropriate linkages between sentences and paragraphs. But a steady repetition of *moreover, furthermore, nevertheless, but,* and so on, can easily bore your readers. If you can develop your thoughts without using obvious transitional expressions, you are more likely to write in a lively and readable style.

Exercise 2.8 Discuss the various techniques used to achieve coherence in the paragraphs below.

> Who are these men who defile the grassy borders of our roads and lanes, who pollute our ponds, who spoil the purity of our ocean beaches

with the empty vessels of their thirst? Who are the men who make these vessels in millions and then say, "Drink—and discard"? What society is this that can afford to cast away a million tons of metal and to make of wild and fruitful land a garbage heap?

What manner of men and women need thirty feet of steel and two hundred horsepower to take them, singly, to their small destinations? Who demand that what they eat is wrapped so that forests are cut down to make the paper that is thrown away, and what they smoke and chew is sealed so that the sealers can be tossed in gutters and caught in twigs and grass?

—MARYA MANNES

What could be more unpopular in an age of sexual equality than to insist that the psychological differences between men and women are as fundamental as their physical ones? Science writer Maggie Scarf, however, wonders what else could explain some lopsided statistics: for every man suffering from depression, there are two to six times as many women. Scarf studied case histories, observed women under treatment in psychiatric clinics and interviewed scores of others in her search for an answer. Now, in a powerful and disturbing book called "Unfinished Business: Pressure Points in the Lives of Women," she announces a conclusion that has aroused the ire of feminists—but may evoke the shock of recognition from many other women.

—*Newsweek*

The popular acceptance of the notion of Seven Healthy Life Habits, as a way of staying alive, says something important about today's public attitudes, or at least the attitudes in the public mind, about disease and dying. People have always wanted causes that are simple and easy to comprehend, and about which the individual can do something. If you believe that you can ward off the common causes of premature death—cancer, heart disease, and stroke, diseases whose pathogenesis we really do not understand—by jogging, hoping, and eating and sleeping regularly, these are good things to believe even if not necessarily true. Medicine has survived other periods of unifying theory, constructed to explain all of human disease, not always as benign in their effects as this one is likely to be. After all, if people can be induced to give up smoking, stop overdrinking and overeating, and take some sort of regular exercise, most of them are bound to feel the better for leading more orderly, regular lives, and many of them are surely going to look better.

—LEWIS THOMAS

6 Link ideas together from one paragraph to the next.

In an essay, coherence between paragraphs is just as important as coherence within paragraphs. Using the devices explained in the previous sections,

¶ coh
2B

you can help your readers follow the direction of your thought as you construct new paragraphs.

The opening sentence of a paragraph in the body of an essay usually looks back to information in the previous paragraph and forward to information about to be disclosed. Boldface print in the excerpts below indicates devices used to connect the ideas of consecutive paragraphs.

> When Africans first got to New York, or New Amsterdam as the Dutch called it, they lived in the farthest downtown portions of the city, near what is now called The Bowery. Later, they shifted, and were shifted, as their numbers grew, to the section known as Greenwich Village. The Civil War Draft Riots in 1863 accounted for the next move by New York's growing Negro population.
>
> **After this violence** (a few million dollars' worth of property was destroyed, and a Negro orphanage was burned to the ground) a great many Negroes moved across the river into Brooklyn. . . .
>
> —LeRoi Jones

[The words *after this violence* connect the ideas of the two paragraphs. *After* serves as a transitional expression indicating time, and *this* is a pronoun that refers to the Draft Riots named in the last sentence of the previous paragraph. Notice how the words *a great many Negroes moved across the river into Brooklyn* help establish the topic of the new paragraph.]

> Among those who now take a dim view of marijuana are Dr. Sidney Cohen, a drug expert at the University of California at Los Angeles, who once described marijuana as "a trivial weed," and Dr. Robert L. DuPont, former director of the National Institute on Drug Abuse, who had lobbied for marijuana's legalization.
>
> **According to these and other experts,** it is no longer possible to say that marijuana is an innocuous drug with few if any health effects aside from intoxication.
>
> —Jane E. Brody

[The words *according to these and other experts* connect the paragraphs by referring readers to the point developed in the previous paragraph. The rest of the opening sentence of the second paragraph states the major point to be developed in that paragraph.]

> If you just don't want to trim the shrubs, take the area they conceal into consideration when planning a lighting system for the house exterior. Of all the steps one can take to safeguard his home, perhaps the most effective is a good system of powerful **lights** strategically placed so that the entire property surrounding the house (particularly areas of thick plantings) is well illuminated.

Outdoor flood **light** fixtures are inexpensive and easily installed. It is preferable to have outdoor **lights** wired so they can be activated at once, either manually, or by an automatic detection device. . . .

—*Popular Mechanics*

[The nouns *light* and *lights* repeated in each of these paragraphs provide the transition from one paragraph to the next.]

In the body of an essay, the first sentence of a new paragraph usually provides the link to ideas in the preceding paragraph. Occasionally, however, the last sentence in a paragraph will link ideas by pointing ahead to the next paragraph.

Why is marking up a book indispensable to reading it? First, it keeps you awake. (And I don't mean merely conscious; I mean wide awake.) In the second place, reading, if it is active, is thinking, and thinking tends to express itself in words, spoken or written. The marked book is usually the thought-through book. Finally, writing helps you remember the thoughts you had, or the thoughts the author expressed. **Let me develop these three points.**

If reading is to accomplish anything more than passing time, it must be active. . . .

—Mortimer J. Adler

[The sentence in boldface print points the reader ahead to the next paragraph, and to the first of Adler's three points.]

To mark a dramatic shift in the direction of an essay, writers sometimes use a whole paragraph to bridge their thoughts from one part of the essay to the next. Such connecting paragraphs are always brief and appear only occasionally in long essays.

I have, I hope, cleared the ground for a dispassionate comparison of certain aspects of Shakespeare's technique in the Henry VI plays with his technique in the "romance" histories. Now, perhaps, some general remarks about the structure of the trilogy will be helpful.

—Paul Dean

[This short paragraph links two parts of an essay. The first sentence reminds readers of points made earlier; the second sentence states the purpose of paragraphs to follow.]

There is an expression called "the peak experience," a moment which, emotionally, can never again be equalled in your life. I had mine, that first day in the village of Juffure, in the back country in black West Africa.

—Alex Haley

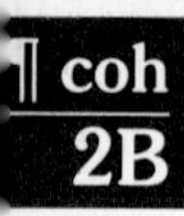

[This two-sentence paragraph provides a dramatic link for what is clearly a turning point in the essay.]

I am assured by our merchants that a boy or girl before twelve years old is no salable commodity; and even when they come to this age they will not yield above three pounds, or three pounds and half a crown at most on the Exchange; which cannot turn to account either to the parents or the kingdom, the charge of nutriment and rags having been at least four times that value.

I shall now therefore humbly propose my own thoughts, which I hope will not be liable to the least objection.

I have been assured by a very knowing American of my acquaintance in London, that a young healthy child well nursed is at a year old a most delicious, nourishing, and wholesome food, whether stewed, roasted, baked or broiled; and I make no doubt that it will equally serve in a fricassee or a ragout.

—JONATHAN SWIFT

[The short transitional paragraph dramatically links the paragraphs before and after and contributes to the shock Swift wants us to experience at his proposal.]

Exercise 2.9 Explain the various devices used to build coherence within and between paragraphs in the following selection from the start of a chapter in a college psychology text.

We civilized members of Western culture like to think of ourselves as rational beings who go about satisfying our motives in an intelligent way. To a certain extent we do that, but we are also emotional beings—more emotional than we often realize. Indeed, most of the affairs of everyday life are tinged with feeling and emotion. Joy and sorrow, excitement and disappointment, love and fear, attraction and repulsion, hope and dismay—all these and many more are feelings we often experience in the course of a week.

Life would be dreary without such feelings. They add color and spice to living; they are the sauce which adds pleasure and excitement to our lives. We anticipate our parties and dates with pleasure, we remember with a warm glow the satisfaction we got from giving a good speech, and we even recall with amusement the bitter disappointments of childhood. On the other hand, when our emotions are too intense and too easily aroused, they can easily get us into trouble. They can warp our judgment, turn friends into enemies, and make us as miserable as if we were sick with fever.

Just what is an emotion? There is no concise definition, because an emotion is many things at once. First of all, a definition would probably say something about the way we feel when we are emotional. Then it might mention the behavioral arousal that occurs in certain emotional states. It might also refer to the physiological, or bodily, basis of the emotions. Of course, a definition would most likely include the idea that emotions are expressed by language, facial expressions, and gestures. Finally, a definition of emotion would probably point out that some emotions—fear and anger, for example—are very much like motive states in that they drive behavior; in fact, the line between motives and emotions is sometimes thin indeed. This chapter will tell you something about all these aspects of emotion.

—CLIFFORD T. MORGAN, RICHARD A. KING, AND NANCY M. ROBINSON

2C Develop paragraphs in sufficient detail and within appropriate forms.

Well-developed paragraphs nearly always rely upon specific details. Such details provide evidence for your assertions, abstractions, and generalizations; they are concrete items of information that support your ideas. Choosing an appropriate form for your ideas and supporting details also contributes to paragraph development.

1 Use concrete sensory details, statistics, cases, examples, quotations, paraphrases, or summaries to support your points in a paragraph.

Details based on the senses are *concrete sensory details*—specific colors, actions, and sounds, and sensations of taste, touch, and smell. You build images, that is, word pictures, by faithfully reporting your sensory impressions. Contributing to the concreteness of an image is the use of highly specific words as opposed to more general or abstract ones. Words like *chair, oak,* and *Riviera Drive South,* for example, are more concrete than *furniture, tree,* and *street* (see page 78).

Sensory language is an essential quality of fiction, but it also adds life, clarity, and vividness to nonfiction prose, as you can see in this excerpt from George Orwell's essay, "Shooting an Elephant."

> I got up. The Burmans were already racing past me across the mud. It was obvious that the elephant would never rise again, but he was not dead. He was breathing very rhythmically with long rattling gasps, his great mound of a side painfully rising and falling. His mouth was wide open—I could see far down into caverns of pale pink throat. I waited a long time for him to die, but his breathing did not weaken. Finally I fired my two remaining shots into the spot where I thought his heart must be.

¶ dev 2C

> The thick blood welled out of him like red velvet, but still he did not die. His body did not even jerk when the shots hit him; the tortured breathing continued without a pause. He was dying, very slowly and in great agony, but in some world remote from me where not even a bullet could damage him further. I felt that I had got to put an end to that dreadful noise. It seemed dreadful to see the great beast lying there, powerless to move and yet powerless to die, and not even to be able to finish him. I sent back for my small rifle and poured shot after shot into his heart and down his throat. They seemed to make no impression. The tortured gasps continued as steadily as the ticking of a clock.
>
> —GEORGE ORWELL

[Specific colors, actions, and sounds—concrete sensory language—make an indelible impression on us here.]

Descriptive essays about people, places, or objects always rely upon sensory language. But even when your main purpose in writing is not to describe, sensory language can bring an idea to life for your readers.

Statistics and cases are the language of facts and figures, and you can use them effectively to support your topic. Statistics are numerical data; cases are specific instances involving real people and events. Notice how the numbers in the first paragraph and the dramatic use of a real instance in the second help the writer make his point forcefully.

> In 1969 there were 178,476 Indian students, ages five to eighteen, enrolled in public, Federal, private and mission schools. Approximately 12,000 children of this age group were not in school. Of the total in school, 119,000 were in public schools, 36,263 in boarding schools operated by the Bureau of Indian Affairs, 16,100 in Bureau day schools, 108 in Bureau hospital schools, and 4,089 in dormitories maintained by the Bureau for children attending public schools. The Bureau operated 77 boarding schools, 144 day schools, 2 hospital schools, and 18 dormitories. The number of Indian children being educated in public schools has steadily increased, aided by the financial assistance provided local school districts under the Johnson-O'Malley Act of 1934 (which provides financial support to fourteen states and four separate school districts with large Indian populations) and under Public Law 874 (which provided financial support, in cooperation with the Department of Health, Education, and Welfare, to aid federally affected areas). The closer relationship between state school systems and the Indian system has been welcomed by many Indian groups. Sixty-one tribes have established compulsory education regulations that conform with those of the states where they live.
>
> On the other hand, some more traditional Indian groups have rebelled at efforts to close down reservation schools. The attempt of the

¶ dev
2C

Bureau of Indian Affairs to close down, on July 1, 1968, a small grade-school at Tama, Iowa, created an instant reaction. Forty-five Mesquakie Indian children were attending school there on the reservation purchased by their ancestors, a separate body of the Sac tribe which, with the Fox, had a hundred years earlier been pushed out of Iowa into Kansas. The Mesquakie Indians, who had not been consulted about the closing of the school, promptly sought judicial relief. They got it in September 1968, in the Federal District Court at Cedar Rapids, when United States District Court Judge Edward J. McManus ordered the school reopened in the fall. The Mesquakie were able to call upon a numbeı of influential white friends in their attempt to retain their Indian school.The validity of integration into a white school system that is often both distant from and cold toward Indian values can be questioned, as the Mesquakie questioned it.

—WILCOMB E. WASHBURN

[The statistics are concrete numerical details about Indian students in 1969. The story of the Tama, Iowa, grade school supports the point that some groups rebelled at efforts to close schools on reservations.]

With quotations, paraphrases, and summaries, you can provide details drawn from expert testimony and resources of knowledge to support your assertions (see 33I). For example, notice how quickly Wilcomb Washburn summarizes such complex documents as the Johnson-O'Malley Act of 1934 and Public Law 874, giving his readers just enough details to support his theme.

Examples are specific illustrations that provide readers with support for your points.

Down South seemed like a dream when I was on the train going back to New York. I saw a lot of things down South that I never saw in my whole life before and most of them I didn't ever want to see again. I saw a great big old burly black man hit a pig in the head with the back of an ax. The pig screamed, oink-oinked a few times, lay down, and started kicking and bleeding . . . and died. When he was real little, I used to chase him, catch him, pick him up, and play catch with him. He was a greedy old pig, but I used to like him. One day when it was real cold, I ate a piece of that pig, and I still liked him. One day I saw Grandma kill a rattlesnake with a hoe. She chopped the snake's head off in the front yard, and I sat on the porch and watched the snake's body keep wiggling till it was nighttime. And I saw an old brown hound dog named Old Joe eat a rat one day, right out in the front yard. He caught the rat in the woodpile and started tearing him open. Old Joe was eating everything in the rat. He ate something that looked like the yellow part in an egg, and I didn't eat eggs for a long time after that. I saw a lady rat have a lot of little baby rats on a pile of tobacco leaves. She had to be a lady, because my

first-grade teacher told a girl that ladies don't cry about little things, and the rat had eleven little hairless pink rats, and she didn't even squeak about it.

—CLAUDE BROWN

[Four examples support the main point of this paragraph, the fact that the writer saw many gory things as a child down South.]

As you develop paragraphs in an essay, you will draw upon a variety of devices to support your points. Like Claude Brown, for instance, you may use concrete sensory details to make your supporting examples clear. Of course, not every point that you make in a paragraph can or should be supported by specific details. Especially in a long essay, a paragraph may build a series of generalizations or abstractions without providing supporting data. But every good writer knows that details are the substance of clear writing and that without them readers remain unconvinced about whatever the writer is trying to make them believe.

Exercise 2.10 Read the following selections, and identify the kinds of details the writers have used. Which details in each piece are the most vivid and convincing?

> During the 1970's the workforce expanded at an incredible annual rate of 2.3 per cent, nearly double the rate of increase during the 1960's. This was a direct result of the now famous Baby Boom of the late 1940's and early 1950's as well as of the sudden influx of women into the labor market. During the 1980's, some economists predict, the workforce will grow by only 1.1 per cent a year, thus making job opportunities more readily available (some even say that unemployment could be cut to 4 per cent by 1985).
>
> —JOHN W. WRIGHT

> When I first saw a water shrew swimming, I was most struck by a thing which I ought to have expected but did not; at the moment of diving, the little black and white beast appears to be made of silver. Like the plumage of ducks and grebes, but quite unlike the fur of most water mammals, such as seals, otters, beaver or coypus, the fur of the water shrew remains absolutely dry under water, that is to say, it retains a thick layer of air while the animal is below the surface. In the other mammals mentioned above, it is only the short, woolly undercoat that remains dry, the superficial hair tips becoming wet, wherefore the animal looks its natural color when underwater and is superficially wet when it emerges. I was already aware of the peculiar qualities of the waterproof fur of the shrew, and, had I given it a thought, I should have known that it would look, under water, exactly like the air-retaining fur on the underside of a water beetle or on the abdomen of a water spider. Nevertheless

the wonderful, transparent silver coat of the shrew was, to me, one of those delicious surprises that nature has in store for her admirers.

—KONRAD Z. LORENZ

2 Choose an appropriate form to develop your paragraphs.

No one can list every possible kind of paragraph, but the following examples offer several varieties for study and imitation.

Narration

Use narrative paragraphs to relate happenings in chronological order.

Banyan Street was the route Lucille Miller took home from the twenty-four-hour Mayfair Market on the night of October 7, 1964, a night when the moon was dark and the wind was blowing and she was out of milk, and Banyan Street was where, at about 12:20 A.M., her 1964 Volkswagen came to a sudden stop, caught fire, and began to burn. For an hour and fifteen minutes, Lucille Miller ran up and down Banyan Street calling for help, but no cars passed and no help came. At three o'clock that morning, when the fire had been put out and the California Highway Patrol officers were completing their report, Lucille Miller was still sobbing and incoherent, for her husband had been asleep in the Volkswagen. "What will I tell the children, when there's nothing left, nothing left in the casket," she cried to the friend who called to comfort her. "How can I tell them there's nothing left?"

—JOAN DIDION

[Covering a brief span of time, this narrative relates events in a clear sequence. Notice the use of detail that makes readers form pictures in their minds of what happened.]

Process Analysis

Use process analysis in paragraphs to explain how to do or how to make something.

The most effective way I know to improve your writing is to do freewriting exercises regularly. At least three times a week. They are sometimes called "automatic writing," "babbling," or "jabbering" exercises. The idea is simply to write for ten minutes (later on, perhaps fifteen or twenty). Don't stop for anything. Go quickly without rushing. Never stop to look back, to cross something out, to wonder how to spell something, to wonder what word or thought to use, or to think about what you are doing. If you can't think of a word or a spelling, just use a squiggle or else write, "I can't think of it." Just put down something. The easiest thing is just to put down whatever is in your mind. If you get stuck it's fine to write "I can't think what to say, I can't think what to say" as many

times as you want; or repeat the last word you wrote over and over again; or anything else. The only requirement is that you *never* stop.

—PETER ELBOW

[Any reader could duplicate this process because it follows a clear sequence.]

Comparison

Organize paragraphs by using comparisons that may include both similarities and differences.

You may make comparisons between conditions existing at two or more different times or between people, places, or things existing at the same time. But be sure that your comparisons are sensible. You can compare any two things with each other—a freight train with a short story, for example. Both have a beginning, a middle, and an end. But such meaningless comparison will not hold your readers.

The following paragraph compares a Russian tank, the T-34 of 1942, with earlier Russian tanks and also with the German tanks that the Russians encountered in World War II. Because the comparison involves weapons of two armies at war with each other, it is clearly a meaningful comparison.

> The new T-34s coming into action in 1942 had better guns and engines. And they retained the broad tracks that made them more mobile and more weatherworthy than German vehicles. In mud or snow they could—quite literally—run rings around the panzers. The turret of the earlier T-34 had been difficult to operate, and its large hatch was vulnerable to grenades and satchel charges; the hatch had been replaced by a smaller opening for the commander and a second one for the gunner. The rear overhang of the turret—a favorite place for the German tank-killer squads to plant their mines—was eliminated, and handrails were welded onto the rear deck so that infantrymen could be carried to counter enemy antitank teams.
>
> —JOHN SHAW

Classification

Use classification in paragraphs to put things or people into groups or lists.

Often you will want to divide a group of people or things into several parts so that your readers can see that there are different elements in a group that may, at first glance, seem to be without variation.

> People who understand high finance are of two kinds: those who have vast fortunes of their own and those who have nothing at all. To an actual millionaire a million pounds is something real and comprehensible. To the applied mathematician and the lecturer in economics (assuming both to be practically starving) a million pounds is at least as real

as a thousand, they having never possessed either sum. But the world is full of people who fall between these two categories, knowing nothing of millions but well accustomed to think in thousands, and it is of these that finance committees are mostly comprised. The result is a phenomenon that has often been observed but never yet investigated. It might be termed the Law of Triviality. Briefly stated, it means that the time spent on any item of the agenda will be in inverse proportion to the sum involved.

—C. NORTHCOTE PARKINSON

[The writer classifies people according to their understanding of finance.]

Causal Analysis

Organize paragraphs around an explanation of cause and effect when you want to explain why something happened or when you want to explain the results of some happening.

> Both the high levels of ultraviolet radiation and the globally dispersed radioactivity would cause genetic damage and mutations. Mutation of some pathogens would possibly lead to novel virulent strains that could cause disease epidemics both of crops and animals on a global scale. Moreover, in the target countries and those nearby where fallout radiation would be most intense, widespread destruction of plant and animal life could lead to major ecological imbalance, some species being far more radiosensitive than others. The changes would very likely be unfavorable to agriculture and animal husbandry. These imbalances could persist for one or more decades.

—HENRY KENDALL

[The writer analyzes the possible effects of nuclear war upon plant and animal life.]

Definition

Use paragraphs to define objects, concepts, ideas, terms, political movements, and anything else that may be important to something you write.

A useful definition first identifies something as a member of a class of similar things; then it states how it differs from everything else in its class.

Simple, concrete objects may often be identified in a single sentence if they require definition at all.

> A typewriter is a small, tabletop machine, operated by a keyboard, that allows a writer to produce writing on paper more quickly and more legibly than by handwriting.

[Once *typewriter* is set in a class of small, tabletop machines operated by a keyboard, it must be set off within its class by a description of its specific purpose *(allows a writer to produce writing on paper more quickly and more legibly than by handwriting)*.]

¶ dev 2C

Definitions of more abstract terms may require an entire paragraph or several paragraphs. Such paragraphs usually stand at the beginning of an essay so that writers may be sure their readers understand a term that is to be used throughout.

> We have a roster of diseases which medicine calls "idiopathic," meaning that we do not know what causes them. The list is much shorter than it used to be; a century ago, common infections like typhus fever and tuberculous meningitis were classed as idiopathic illnesses. Originally, when it first came into the language of medicine, the term had a different, highly theoretical meaning. It was assumed that most human diseases were intrinsic, due to inbuilt failures of one sort or another, things gone wrong with various internal humors. The word "idiopathic" was intended to mean, literally, a disease having its own origin, a primary disease without any external cause. The list of such disorders has become progressively shorter as medical science has advanced, especially within this century, and the meaning of the term has lost its doctrinal flavor; we use "idiopathic" now to indicate simply that the cause of a particular disease is unknown. Very likely, before we are finished with medical science, and with luck, we will have found that all varieties of disease are the result of one or another sort of meddling, and there will be no more idiopathic illness.
>
> —Lewis Thomas

[The paragraph defines *idiopathic* as a category of diseases and provides a brief history of the term up to its current usage.]

Writers frequently combine patterns. The paragraphs by Peter Elbow and Lewis Thomas, for example, use narrative techniques as well as process analysis and definition. The paragraph by C. Northcote Parkinson involves causal analysis as well as classification. When you write an essay, you should not feel bound to only one method of development.

Exercise 2.11 Identify the patterns used in each paragraph below.

> The figure that comes before me oftenest, out of the shadows of that vanished time, is that of Brown, of the steamer *Pennsylvania*—the man referred to in a former chapter, whose memory was so good and tiresome. He was a middle-aged, long, slim, bony, smooth-shaven, horse-faced, ignorant, stingy, malicious, snarling, fault-hunting, mote-magnifying tyrant. I early got the habit of coming on watch with dread at my heart. No matter how good a time I might have been having with the off-watch below, and no matter how high my spirits might be when I started aloft, my soul became lead in my body the moment I approached the pilot-house.

I still remember the first time I ever entered the presence of that man. The boat had backed out from St. Louis and was "straightening down." I ascended to the pilot-house in high feather, and very proud to be semi-officially a member of the executive family of so fast and famous a boat. Brown was at the wheel. I paused in the middle of the room, all fixed to make my bow, but Brown did not look around. I thought he took a furtive glance at me out of the corner of his eye, but as not even this notice was repeated, I judged I had been mistaken. By this time he was picking his way among some dangerous "breaks" abreast the wood-yards; therefore it would not be proper to interrupt him; so I stepped softly to the high bench and took a seat.

—MARK TWAIN

People react strongly and variously to being queued. Russians line themselves up without being told. Moscow theater audiences file out, last row first, like school children marching out of assemblies. In America, on the contrary, theatrical performances break up like the Arctic ice in springtime. Commuters and the constitutionally impatient gather themselves for a dash up the aisle, while the rest of the audience is still applauding. Fidgeters and people who can't bear having anyone ahead of them sidle across rows to emergency exits, while placid souls who seem to enjoy the presence of others drift happily up the aisle with the crowd. In Moscow, the theater is emptied faster. In New York, you can get out fast if you're willing to work at it.

—CAROLINE BIRD

The phonograph cartridge—the little device at the tip of the tone arm—is where the music really starts. It's the gateway by which music enters the sound system. As the originator of the audio signal, it holds a strategic position. If it doesn't read out the sound correctly from the record groove, the music gets distorted at the source. No matter how good your amplifier or your speakers, they cannot correct the faults introduced at the start by an inferior cartridge.

—HANS FANTEL

Exactly what happens when GNP falls or lags? The pace of business activity slows down. There is less demand for consumer goods and services, less demand for plant and equipment and other business items. Some businesses fire people; other businesses hire fewer new workers. Because our labor force is steadily growing as our population swells, even a small decrease in the willingness to take on new workers spells a sharp rise in unemployment for certain groups, such as young people. When a recession really deepens, as in 1980, it is not just the young who cannot find work, but experienced workers find themselves thrown out of work.

—ROBERT HEILBRONER AND LESTER THUROW

Exercise 2.12 Identify the paragraph form you would use to develop these topics. (Choose from narration, process analysis, comparison, classification, causal analysis, and definition.)

1. The meaning of genius
2. An embarrassing or humorous moment
3. Types of teachers
4. How to make a model car
5. American democracy and ancient Greek democracy
6. Why teenagers drop out of school
7. How a home video recorder works
8. What happened to the film industry after the introduction of the "talkies"

Exercise 2.13 Use the topics below to practice writing paragraphs according to the method listed by each number. Follow your teacher's instructions.

1. *Narration: (a)* going fishing, *(b)* your first dance, *(c)* Saturday morning, *(d)* getting lost, *(e)* a drive in the country, *(f)* a historical event
2. *Process analysis: (a)* baking an apple pie, *(b)* how to operate a food processor, *(c)* how a light bulb works, *(d)* how to study for a final, *(e)* throwing a curve ball, *(f)* getting from where you live to school
3. *Comparison: (a)* a book and a film based on the book, *(b)* a pet dog and a pet cat, *(c)* two college courses, *(d)* downhill skiing and cross-country skiing, *(e)* rowing and canoeing, *(f)* large automobiles and compact cars, *(g)* German war aims in 1914 and in 1939, *(h)* Richard Nixon and Ronald Reagan
4. *Classification: (a)* jobs for college graduates, *(b)* clothing styles today, *(c)* kinds of television watchers, *(d)* planets in the solar system, *(e)* popular movies, *(f)* members of the U.S. House of Representatives and members of the U.S. Senate
5. *Causal analysis: (a)* the effects of a nuclear war, *(b)* why some children have trouble learning to write, *(c)* why alcoholism is on the rise among teenagers, *(d)* how high unemployment rates affect teenagers, *(e)* why reading skills have declined over the last ten years
6. *Definition: (a)* democracy, *(b)* fascism, *(c)* religion, *(d)* women's rights, *(e)* rock music, *(f)* jazz, *(g)* spectator sports, *(h)* low-fat diet

3 Write paragraphs of appropriate length.

There are no absolute rules for the length of a paragraph. Writers for newspapers and magazines often favor short paragraphs of a few sentences, totaling one hundred words or so. Many professional essayists prefer paragraphs that fill a half page or a full page of typeset print. The paragraph by Orwell on pages 75–76—certainly not his longest—has fourteen sentences and over two hundred words. Paragraphs of three hundred to six hundred words are common, especially in academic writing.

Remember, a new paragraph signals a change of subject. Therefore, it is important to make each paragraph long enough so that readers can absorb and remember its subject. In a typical short college essay, the introductory paragraphs will be roughly the same length but generally will be shorter than most body paragraphs (see 2D, section 1).

In constructing paragraphs for the body of your essay, it is a good idea to strike a balance between short and long paragraphs. Variety makes for easier reading. However, students often produce paragraphs that are too brief. Your model should be Orwell more than *Time* or *Newsweek,* because a paragraph that lacks sufficient detail is a paragraph that leaves readers unconvinced.

A good, general rule is to have an indentation on each typed page, but a great deal of personal judgment is involved in deciding on paragraph length. Depending on the writer's taste, on the audience for the piece, and on the length of the rest of the essay, the selection below could appear as one, two, or even three paragraphs as shown by the ¶ symbol.

> The 1938 edition of Casner and Gabriel has a new title, *The Rise of American Democracy,* and is said to be a complete reworking of the original volume. It has a new rationale. In their foreword, the authors say that democracy is now being challenged by other forms of government, including "swift-striking dictatorships," and that we therefore have to ask, "What does the word, *democracy,* mean?" The book never quite gets around to answering this question, but its focus is more political than that of the first edition, and its tone more urgent. ¶ The story of the knight in the first chapter has been condensed, and the American scenery of birds, squirrels, and leafy boughs has largely disappeared. The Indians are now said to have practiced democracy, not religion; they are no longer "deeply religious." Jacob Riis is still around, but the United States government has become a much more positive actor in social reform. Whereas a mid-thirties edition seems to judge some of President Franklin Roosevelt's legislation to have been unconstitutional, this one simply credits him with having helped the country out of the Depression. ¶ In foreign policy, too, the government has taken a positive role: it "helps" the Allies in the First World War and "promotes" world peace thereafter, within the limits of its isolationist position. In the last part of the book, "American Democracy Faces a Confused World," the text maintains that Americans now have new ideals, including a balanced economy, Social Security, and well-being for all citizens. But it ends, rather ominously, "The struggle still goes on. It was never more intense than in our day. The outcome will depend upon the intelligence and alertness of this generation and of future generations."
>
> —FRANCES FITZGERALD

2D Construct opening and closing paragraphs that suit your thesis and that hold your readers' attention.

The opening and closing paragraphs of an essay are essential in drawing attention to your main point and in keeping your readers' interest to the end.

1 Construct opening paragraphs that seize the attention of readers as you introduce your subject.

Your opening paragraph is vital; it must win over the reader who is trying to decide whether to read your work. Your opening paragraph sets the tone for everything else in your essay, thereby announcing not only your subject but also the audience you seek to interest in it.

Some audiences expect your opening paragraph to outline everything you intend to do in your essay. Descriptions of scientific experiments almost always start with such an outline, called an **abstract** in scientific circles. But if you are writing about some personal topic or about something you wish to explain or report, your first paragraph usually gives only an inviting glimpse of what lies in store for the reader.

Note how the opening paragraphs that follow introduce a subject and set the tone for the piece.

> It is usually heartening to see an art revived, especially when you have forgotten how much pleasure it affords. The art of buck passing, for instance. It popped to life in New York a couple of weeks ago when Bruce Caputo, a candidate for the U.S. Senate, was caught as having described himself as a Viet Nam-era draftee and Army lieutenant. Mr. Caputo was neither. Yet when confronted with the fact that he had falsified his credentials in *Who's Who in American Politics,* he rose to the occasion as Michelangelo once rose to the ceiling: "To the extent that I or somebody on my staff was less than careful, we made a mistake." Thus in a single sentence he was able to identify the lie as carelessness and to imply that if anyone at all was responsible (a question he opens), it was probably an underling. Mr. Caputo is small potatoes, but his comment is buck passing at a very high level. When you see a performance like his, you see how intricate the art can get.
>
> —Roger Rosenblatt

[The subject of the essay in *Time* is introduced in an informal, humorous tone. The subject is to be "buck passing," evading responsibility, and how people do it. Like many informal essays, this one begins with a light-hearted story.]

> Spring is a glorious time to be in the Kansas Flint Hills, especially if the rains have been plentiful. The bluestem grasses have lost their winter

gray and brown in favor of a deep rich green, a color that will soon fade with the coming of the hot summer sun. Even if spring is brief, as it is in some years, it is sufficient. The clean sweet smells carried on the gentle warm breeze blowing up from the southwest carry a freshness that the nostrils have not sensed since the Indian summer days of fall. "The hills," as the local cattlemen call the land, have none of the flaming beauty of the forested New England mountains or the majesty of the Rocky Mountains. Rather, the gentle contour of the rolling carpet of grass stretching from horizon to horizon is soft and restfully inviting. It is peaceful because the hand of man is little in evidence. Most of the Flint Hills are still virgin prairie, much as they were a century or more ago when the Indian's cattle—buffalo—grazed on the tall grasses. Today the white man's cattle have replaced the shaggy monsters of the past.

—DAVID DARY

[This is the opening paragraph of a book called *Cowboy Culture,* an account of the way cowboys lived on the western plains in the nineteenth century. Notice that it is more formal than the opening paragraph of the magazine article in the earlier example. It is a descriptive paragraph that leads rather slowly into the theme of cattle raising, which itself serves to introduce the main theme of the book, the story of the men who raised the cattle and took them to market.]

I spent several days and nights in mid-September with my ailing pig, and I feel driven to account for this stretch of time, more particularly since the pig died at last, and I lived, and things might easily have gone the other way round and none left to do the accounting. Even now, so close to the event, I cannot recall the hours sharply and am not ready to say whether death came on the third night or the fourth night. This uncertainty afflicts me with a sense of personal deterioration; if I were in decent health I would know how many nights I had sat up with a pig.

—E. B. WHITE

[This paragraph introduces a personal-experience narrative. It sets a tone of sadness and lets readers know that the essay is going to be about the death of a pig, an unusual subject but one that may interest them because it has so moved the writer.]

In the following introduction, the writer tells readers just what to expect in the essay. Introductory paragraphs that summarize the paper to follow are especially popular among science writers.

In this paper I shall consider several educational issues growing out of A. R. Jensen's paper, "How Much Can We Boost IQ and Scholastic Achievement?" (Jensen, 1969.) The first deals with the question of how education should adjust to the incontestable fact that approximately half the children in our schools are and always will be below average in IQ.

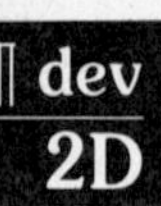

Following this, I take up some of the more moot points of the "Jensen controversy"—what does heritability tell us about teachability? What are the prospects for reducing the spread of individual differences in intelligence? And what are the educational implications of possible hereditary differences in intelligence associated with social class and race?—ending with some implications that these issues have for educational research.

—CARL BEREITER

[The assumption behind such an introduction is that people who will read this essay already have a strong interest in the topic. But most writers cannot assume that such an interest already exists, so they must woo readers and persuade them to read on by writing an attractive and energetic beginning.]

2 Write concluding paragraphs that complete your essay without summarizing it.

If you write a scientific or academic paper, you may be expected to summarize everything you have said at the end of the paper. However, there are more imaginative ways to conclude an essay. In fact, many professional writers make it a rule never to end a story or an essay with a summary.

A good concluding paragraph will complete the paper logically and clearly, without assuming a preachy tone, as the following concluding paragraphs show.

> Finally and fundamentally, you must be the kind of person capable of passing the buck in the first place. This is an art, after all. For Harry Truman, the buck stopped somewhere. For the true buck passer it never stops, but is constantly being turned over in his fingers, heads and tails, waiting for the moment of accusation when it may be gracefully flipped to a patsy. When a run-of-the-mill culprit says, "I did it because I was overtired," he implies that he is essentially a better person than his particular action indicates. But by adding the punishment of others to a mess of one's own making, the buck passer reveals that he is actually worse than his actions. Such people are rare, which may be why society reserves special positions for them: generals, senators, presidents, and kings.

—ROGER ROSENBLATT

[Compare this concluding paragraph with the first paragraph of the same essay on page 88. Notice that the word *finally* announces that this will be the last point made in the essay. The paragraph takes up again the idea of buck passing as an *art,* an idea expressed in the opening paragraph. The concluding paragraph repeats some of the thoughts of the first paragraph but adds a new element—the idea that passing the buck means blaming one's own actions on someone else who will then be punished. And notice how the concluding sentence gives us a surprising and novel perspective.]

As the sixteenth century was ending, the ranching industry was firmly established in the New World. It had spread northward on two fronts, one up the western and one up the eastern slope of the majestic Sierra Madre. It had swept more than a thousand miles from where it began southwest of Mexico City less than a century before. And the *vaquero* had become an integral part of the spreading cattle-related culture that emphasized the mounted horseman.

—DAVID DARY

[This paragraph concludes the chapter begun by the introductory paragraph you read on pages 86–87. Notice that just as the first paragraph speaks of cattle, so does the last, in the phrase *cattle-related culture.* The last sentence speaks of the *vaquero,* the Spanish word for "cowboy," and the chapter itself has discussed the development of cattle ranching on the plains by the first white settlers, who were Spanish.]

> The news of the death of my pig traveled fast and far, and I received many expressions of sympathy from friends and neighbors, for no one took the event lightly, and the premature expiration of a pig is, I soon discovered, a departure which the community marks solemnly to its calendar, a sorrow in which it feels fully involved. I have written this account in penitence and in grief, as a man who failed to raise his pig, and to explain my deviation from the classic course of so many raised pigs. The grave in the woods is unmarked, but Fred can direct the mourner to it unerringly and with immense good will, and I know he and I shall often revisit it, singly and together, in seasons of reflection and despair, on flagless memorial days of our own choosing.
>
> —E. B. WHITE

[The death of the pig mentioned in the first paragraph of White's article (page 87) is mentioned again in this last paragraph. He concludes with a mention of the grave—something we might expect when the essay has been about a death.]

Exercise 2.14 Take any popular magazine that you enjoy reading, and look at all the articles in it, carefully comparing the first and the last paragraphs of each article. What relation do you see between the two paragraphs even before you read the article? Discuss in class or with friends interested in writing the connection between each first and last paragraph that you survey.

Exercise 2.15 Take one of your own essays, and compare the first and last paragraphs. What similarities do you note between them?

Exercise 2.16 Write several first paragraphs for articles or essays that you might want to write. Try to make them interesting and appealing, and see if you can make them introduce your subject without revealing everything about it.

2E Revise a loose paragraph for unity, coherence, and development.

As you revise the rough draft of your essay, make sure that your paragraphs are unified, coherent, and well developed. You may want to add elements, eliminate elements, or subordinate one element to another. Because the controlling idea of your paragraph should guide any changes you make, start by rereading your paragraph carefully to determine the controlling idea that you want to express. A paragraph like the one that follows requires revision in an essay.

Loose Construction

> Wood-burning stoves are helping many Americans beat the huge inflation of oil prices. Wood is still readily available in some parts of the United States. Many states set off parts of their state forests where residents can cut designated trees at no charge. The technology of wood stoves has improved so that they are very safe. Unfortunately, they are sometimes bulky and ugly and take up too much space in small rooms. Sometimes they make rooms too hot. Many homeowners who have gone to wood stoves for heat report savings of hundreds of dollars each year over the former price of heating their houses with oil.

[In this paragraph, the controlling idea is clearly stated in the first sentence. Everything else in the paragraph should relate to the idea that wood stoves save money. The issues of availability and safety, though important, do not suit the topic of this paragraph. Similarly, the sentences about the disadvantages of wood stoves have no place in this paragraph about costs and detract from its unity. The sentence about the technology of wood stoves belongs in a paragraph about costs because technology has made wood stoves more efficient, that is, cheaper to operate. Smoother connections between sentences would make the paragraph more coherent, and the paragraph would benefit from added details about the availability of wood and about the efficiency of wood stoves.]

This paragraph has been revised as follows with the above points in mind.

Paragraph Revised for Unity, Coherence, and Development

Wood-burning stoves are helping many Americans beat the huge inflation of oil prices. Although the cost of oil, gas, and coal has skyrocketed, wood is still a cheap fuel in some parts of the United States. A cord of wood, a stack measuring 4 × 4 × 8 feet, costs just over a hundred dollars but goes a long way in a typical heating season. In fact, many states like Massachusetts and Montana set off parts of their state forests where residents can cut designated trees at no charge. It is no surprise on a warm summer morning to see dozens of families sawing trees and loading vans or pickup trucks with logs for use as a winter fuel. Not only can wood be obtained cheaply, but also the technology of wood stoves has improved; the new models are far more efficient than in previous years. Now a family can heat a house with a wood stove with a minimum of waste or expense. A good airtight wood stove heats a room far more efficiently than a conventional fireplace or a Franklin stove. Many homeowners who have turned to wood stoves for heat report savings of hundreds of dollars each year over the price of heating their houses with oil.

[All sentences now support the idea of costs involved with wood-burning stoves. The writer has added details: she names two states that make forests available for wood users, and she provides a lively image to imply the popularity of such programs. An example about efficiency adds substance to the paragraph, too. Transitional expressions like *in fact, but also,* and *now* connect ideas smoothly.]

Exercise 2.17 Revise the following paragraphs for unity, coherence, and development.

The blizzard began early in the morning of February 6. The snow began falling before dawn. The flakes were small and hard. The snow itself was very thick. By nine o'clock, six inches of white covered the streets, and commuting traffic was reduced to a crawl. None of this affected me, since the schools were closed, and I stayed home, warm and cozy by the fire. I read the morning newspaper and kept refilling the coffee mug that sat beside me on a glass-topped table. By ten-thirty, the streets were impassable, and motorists were abandoning their cars. By noon the offices in the city that had opened despite the storm were closing and sending workers home. At three o'clock the mayor declared a state of emergency and asked schools and churches and synagogues to give shelter to people stranded by the storm. By six o'clock, the city was locked in the enchantment of a profound silence. Two feet of snow lay on the ground, and more was falling from the low, heavy clouds.

Just after World War II a "portable radio" was a large, rectangular box with tubes, a heavy, expensive battery, and a handle on top that allowed the radio to be lifted out of the trunk of the car and carried a short distance to the beach or to a picnic table. No one would have thought of carrying a portable radio on a long hike in the mountains or for any distance at all. People used the portable radio to listen to the news, soap operas, jazz music, sports, and singing commercials. But with the invention of the transistor, the portable radio has become the daily companion of millions, truly portable, a small object that can be tucked into a shirt pocket or hooked onto a belt and carried anywhere.

PART TWO
Writing Correct Sentences

3
Sentence Grammar

Grammar includes two things:

1. Grammar is a collection of patterns that make sense in sentences, patterns that permit communication through language.
2. Grammar is the language we use to talk about such patterns.

The first definition of grammar is much more important than the second. We use grammar all the time as a set of patterns that make sense. Most of us use grammar well enough to make language do what we want it to do—communicate. We know the patterns of the English sentence, and we use them every day.

The word *patterns* is essential. We react to sentences as patterns. They happen to be patterns that evolved over several hundred years of the development of the English language, and they are not always logical. But many familiar patterns that we encounter in daily life are not logical. Think of the pattern of a stop sign, for example. If instead of using white letters on a red octagon we had used blue letters on a gold, diamond-shaped sign for many years, that would be the controlling pattern for all stop signs. But somebody decided that stop signs should have the pattern we now recognize, and we cannot change it just because some people believe that blue and gold are prettier colors than red and white.

The patterns of the English sentence are much the same. We are used to them. We cannot change them on whim. We learned these patterns from others, usually from our parents, and we discovered early in life that they work.

We probably started by giving something a name that got results. "Milk!" we shouted, and somebody gave us milk. A little later we said, "Give me milk." Still later we said, "Will you please give me some milk?" or "I like milk." These are complicated sentences for children, and no child can talk about them with a grammarian. But a child can make them work.

gr

As we grow older, we learn how to fit all kinds of thoughts into the basic sentence patterns. If you hear somebody say "I picked up the telephone," you know what the speaker means. The pattern is familiar. But if somebody says "Picked I the telephone up," you run it through your mind again. What is this person trying to say? The pattern is not right. People don't say "Drove I the car this morning to work" or "Stood bravely he resisting the last until." If you wrestle around in your mind with these sentences, you can probably make sense of them. But you wouldn't want to do much of this wrestling because it is difficult and gets in the way of reading or listening. The patterns are not right, and we dislike the surprise these unfamiliar patterns give us.

The sense of pattern is so strong in us that we can frequently understand a sentence even when some of the words are a mystery. If somebody says "Give me the phlumpis on the table," we hear the pattern, recognize it as a request or a command, and look on the table to see what the phlumpis is. The pattern tells us to do something, and we do it. The pattern is grammar in action.

There are only a few basic sentence patterns, although as you will see in 3A, section 2, you can make many changes in the basic form of any sentence. The most common pattern is the sentence that tells us that something does something to something else.

The man next door kills ants by spraying them with window cleaner. [This is a simple pattern. The man next door acts on the ants. It may seem odd to kill ants with window cleaner, but you read the sentence and know that the man next door does it. You can imagine him pumping away with his bottle of window cleaner aimed at the ants.]

You can substitute nonsense words in a pattern and still have an idea of what the sentence means.

The aardcam next door grinks ants by cooming them with dab. [Despite your confusion here, you know that something called an *aardcam* is the actor in this sentence. You know that *grinks* expresses the main act and that *cooming* expresses a helping act to the main act. And *dab* is some kind of tool, some instrument, used in this action. You know that something is doing something to the ants because you recognize a basic pattern of the English sentence.]

There are other patterns, of course, including the one that tells us that something acts but that nothing receives the action.

The telephone is ringing.

The telephone is not doing anything to anybody. It's just ringing. Many sentences follow this same pattern.

gr

The thermometer exploded.

The grass grows.

The child cries.

She will arrive tomorrow.

Another pattern describes something. The actor in the sentence is simply existing in a certain way. The only action in the statement is this existence.

The telephone is black.

The man was old and feeble but still witty and interesting.

[In the first sentence, you recognize from the pattern that the writer wants to make a statement about a telephone. The telephone isn't doing anything to anybody; it isn't doing anything at all in this sentence except existing as something black. And the man in the next sentence isn't doing anything. He is described. He was old and feeble but still witty and interesting.]

Another pattern tells that something is acted upon. When you read such a sentence, you expect to discover that from the viewpoint of the writer, the recipient of the action is the most important object or person in the sentence.

My brother was hit by a wheelbarrow on his way to work.

Obviously, the most important person in this sentence is the recipient of the action—*my brother. My brother* didn't act. He was acted upon. We recognize this pattern and understand its importance because we know that the normal pattern of expressing action in a sentence is different. Usually the actor is important and goes first. When the recipient of the action goes first, we are alerted to expect an unusual emphasis.

The basic patterns help sentences *make sense.* That is what the word *sentence* means—a group of words that make sense. They make sense because they conform to patterns we recognize. All of us can understand the sense of the following statements:

It rained last night.

The book on the shelf was old and dusty.

Bill Rodgers has won three Boston Marathons.

The baseball strike began in June and ended in August.

She wrote three books before she was thirty years old.

gr

Our knowledge of patterns tells us when we don't have a sentence. When we don't have a sentence, we don't have a pattern. We are not fooled by the words pretending to be sentences below. Each group looks like a sentence at first glance, but it is not.

The book opening.

Took the game away.

The music to come.

Each group begins with a capital letter and ends with a period—just like a sentence. But by itself, not one group makes sense. None of the groups has a sentence pattern. In each case we have to add some words to make a pattern—and thus a sentence. We may have to add several words.

When he entered the room, he saw *the book opening* under the single, small, bright light on the desk, but everything else was so dark that for a moment he did not see the silent, almost perfectly still man in gray who sat reading there.

John brought his Monopoly set but got angry when he went bankrupt, and *took the game away.*

The music to come will be even worse than what we have heard already.

To talk intelligently about these patterns and the various changes and expansions that can be performed with them, you do need to know grammatical terms like *subject, verb, participle, direct object, indirect object,* and many others. The rest of this chapter will introduce the most basic terms to you. Still, you do not need to know grammatical language to recognize that something is wrong with an incomplete pattern, a group of words that doesn't make sense.

Exercise 3.1 Some of the word groups below are sentences, and some are not. Mark each sentence with an **S**. Use an **X** to indicate incomplete sentences.

1. Steps in the hall.
2. Driving along the river's edge and watching the jays flapping in the water.
3. She spoke.
4. After an introductory course you should learn more about computer programming.
5. Attempted a new explanation of the origin of the universe.
6. With a sly, cold smile.
7. Prices rose, but supplies remained plentiful.
8. When the senator reached the lectern, applause shook the auditorium.
9. When nothing else will help.
10. Scratching at the window, the cat begged to be let in.

gr 3A

Exercise 3.2 Make sentences by adding as many words as necessary to the following incomplete patterns.

Example:

Incomplete pattern: the long stairway.

Complete pattern: He got his exercise every morning by climbing *the long stairway.*

1. ran away yesterday
2. the green, green grass of home
3. waiting for the 12:05
4. the air in the tire
5. taken while running
6. bouncing along the grass
7. the icy waters
8. at the station we
9. give me some small
10. explained the crash

3A Learn the basic structure of the English sentence.

Most sentences name something and then make some statement about the thing named. The part of the sentence that names is called the **subject.** The part of the sentence that makes a statement about the subject is called the **predicate.**

gr 3A

Subject	Predicate
The sun	is copper and gold.
Liberty	prevails.
Our love	will never die.
Charlie	is allergic to cigarette smoke.
Sarah Corwin	writes poetry.
None of the students in our history class	remembered to submit a rough draft of the essay along with the final draft.
The Giants	were beaten by their own mistakes.
My car	was stolen last night.

All the sentences above name something and then make an assertion about it. Each sentence tells you that the subject does something or that something is done to the subject or that the subject exists in a certain way. Questions, of course, do not make statements, but sentences that are questions always name a subject and always ask something about it.

Will liberty prevail?

Were the Giants beaten by their own mistakes?

Is Charlie allergic to cigarette smoke?

Sentences that give commands or make requests often imply the subject. If the subject is implied, it is always the person spoken to, and you can supply the subject with the word *you.* The word *you,* then, is the subject of a command or request that does not specifically name some other subject.

[You] Get me the medicine.

[You] Pass the potatoes.

Here are two distinguishing marks of any sentence:

1. The boundaries of the sentence are clearly marked off by a capital letter at the beginning and a period, a question mark, or an exclamation point at the end.
2. Within these boundaries, every sentence contains at least one *subject* and at least one *predicate* that fit together to give a command, ask a question, or make a statement.

All sentences have a subject and a predicate and tell one of three things:

1. The subject does [or did do or will do] something.
2. Something is done to the subject.
3. The subject exists in some state or condition.

gr
3A

The subject and the words that describe it often are called the **complete subject.** In the complete subject, the word (or words) serving as the focus of the sentence, with all the describing words removed, may be called the **simple subject.** Grammarians are not always consistent with their labeling system, however; the word *subject* can be used for either the complete subject or the simple subject. The simple subject may be a thing, a person, a place, an action, an idea, a name, or anything else that the sentence identifies. The subject exists in the sentence so that a statement can be made about it.

In the following sentences, the complete subjects are underlined once, and the simple subjects are in boldface:

The quick brown **fox** jumps over the lazy dog.

Rice won the game with a home run in the last of the ninth.

The **tree** in the yard is an oak.

Sometimes a subject is **compound;** that is, a conjunction such as *and* or *but* (see page 125) connects two or more words that serve as subjects of the sentence.

Original **thinking** and bold **actions** have distinguished her legal career. [Two subjects, *thinking* and *actions,* are joined by the conjunction *and.* The subject is compound.]

The predicate asserts something about the subject. The predicate, together with all the words that help it make a statement about the subject, is often called the **complete predicate.** In the complete predicate, the word (or words) that reports or states conditions, with all describing words removed, is called the **simple predicate** or the **verb.** Here, too, there is some overlap in terminology. *Predicate* can be used for the complete predicate and the simple predicate, and *verb* can be used instead of *predicate.*

In the following sentences, the complete predicates are underlined, and the simple predicates (the verbs) are in boldface.

The quick brown fox **jumps** over the lazy dog.

The tree in the yard **is** an oak.

Original thinking and bold actions **have distinguished** her legal career.

Like subjects, predicates also may be compound. In a compound predicate, two or more verbs are joined by a conjunction:

Rice **won** the game with a home run in the ninth and **lifted** his total to 38 homers this year.
[Two verbs, *won* and *lifted,* are joined by the conjunction *and.* The predicate is compound.]

gr
3A

Sometimes a verb combines with an *auxiliary verb* (also called a *helping verb*) to form a verb of more than one word. Such a verb is called a **verb phrase.** The verb phrases are in italics in the sentences below.

Original thinking and bold actions *have distinguished* her legal career.

Gold *was discovered* in California in 1848.

He *might have seen* that film before.

The old library *would have been sold* at auction if not for her generous contribution to save it.

1 Learn to recognize subjects and predicates.

Being able to locate subjects and predicates in your own sentences helps you check on their logic, clarity, and correctness. One way to find the two sentence components is to look at what the sentence says and to ask two questions about its meaning:

1. Who or what is the sentence about? *(subject)*
2. What statement is the sentence making about the subject? *(predicate)*

Consider this sentence:

Some harmless snakes imitate poisonous snakes in color and behavior.

Questions	Answers
1. Who or what is the sentence about?	Some harmless snakes *(subject)*
2. What statement is the sentence making about the subject?	imitate poisonous snakes in color and behavior *(predicate)*

Simple Predicates

Perhaps the best way to find these basic sentence components is to start by looking for the verb (the simple *predicate*).

If you know that verbs express action or state of being, you might be able to identify the verbs by finding the action words or the words that show existence (see 3B, section 1). But it is even easier to find verbs if you remember that they can change their form according to the different ways they may be used in a sentence. Because verbs change their forms to show time or *tense* (see 3B, section 1), you can locate verbs easily by forcing such a change in a sentence. If you use a word like *yesterday, today,* or *tomorrow* at the start of a sentence whose verb you are trying to identify, the word that changes will be the verb. Only the verb will change in the sentence.

My dog runs away.

Yesterday my dog *ran* away.

[*Runs* changed to *ran; runs,* therefore, is the verb in the original sentence.]

Mr. Smith goes to Washington.

Tomorrow Mr. Smith *will go* to Washington.

[The word *goes* changed to *will go; goes* is the verb in the original sentence.]

Another way to locate verbs is to memorize the verbs that serve as auxiliaries, that is, helpers, to other verbs. These auxiliaries are always verbs and never anything else. They often signal the presence of another part of the verb phrase close by in the sentence, or they serve alone as verbs in sentences (see page 185). Some common helping verbs are *am, is, are, was, were, shall, will, could, would, have, has, had, do, does, did, be, been, might, can, may,* and *must.*

A good way to test a word you think is a verb is to use *I, he, she, it, you, we,* or *they* before the word. If you make sense with this combination, the word you are testing is a verb.

Word	Test	Verb
try	I try She tries	yes
olive	I olive (?) They olive (?)	no
laughingly	They laughingly (?)	no
laugh	She laughs They laugh	yes
laughing	She laughing (?) I laughing (?)	no

See 3B, section 1, for further information about verbs.

gr
3A

Finding and Testing Verbs

1. Use *yesterday, today,* or *tomorrow* at the start of the sentence. The word that changes is a verb:

   He spoke softly
   Tomorrow he will speak softly.
2. Learn a list of the most familiar helping verbs.
3. Use *I, he, she, it, you, we,* or *they* before the word you think is a verb.

swim	I swim	verb
thing	I thing	not a verb

Simple Subjects

Once you find the verb, you can find the subject easily. Just put the verb in a question asking *who* or *what* does the action of the verb. Say the word *who* or *what;* then say the verb. The answer to the question you will have stated is the subject of the sentence. Note how the questions work for the following sentences; verbs and verb phrases are in boldface.

We **have been working** all night.
[*Who* has been working all night? *We* is the subject of the sentence.]

Trout fishing **is** a popular sport in northern New England.
[*What* is a popular sport in northern New England? Trout fishing. *Trout fishing* is the subject of the sentence.]

Napoleon **invaded** Russia in 1812.
[*Who* invaded Russia in 1812? *Napoleon* is the subject of the sentence.]

He **was looking** for his lost credit cards.
[*Who* was looking for his lost credit cards? *He* is the subject.]

Generally, subjects of verbs are nouns or pronouns (see 3B, sections 2 and 3). However, other words may on occasion also serve as subjects.

Exercise 3.3 Locate the subjects and verbs in the following sentences. First, draw a dividing line between the complete subject and the complete predicate. Then underline the simple subject and the verb (simple predicate).

Example: A tired gray moth, paralyzed by the light,/fluttered at the candle flame.

1. The battered little boat with the ragged sails limped into port after the storm.
2. My neighbor paved his driveway.
3. His back was injured in the fall.

4. She should have finished the job.
5. The lamps along the street were glowing in the dusk.
6. More bicycles were sold in America last year than cars.
7. The wind rattled the autumn leaves in the trees along the road.
8. A chill, red sunset streaked the brown fields and bare trees.
9. Most crows look alike.
10. The fans of the two teams were fighting each other in the stands while the teams battled each other on the field.

Other Predicate Parts

Although the controlling word in the predicate is always the verb, complete predicates also include objects, complements, and various words called modifiers that help describe other elements.

Direct object

The **direct object** tells who or what receives the action done by the subject. Not every sentence has a direct object, but many verbs require a direct object to complete their meaning. Such verbs are called **transitive verbs.**

If there is a direct object in a sentence, a subject is doing something to it. You can begin to think about direct objects by imagining sentences that express a vigorous action. Direct objects are underscored; verbs are in italics.

He *hit* the <u>nail</u> on the head.

She *painted* my <u>portrait</u>.

Erasmus *wrote* a <u>letter</u> almost every day.

But some direct objects receive action that is not so vigorous.

The children *crossed* the <u>street</u>.

She *saw* <u>him</u> at the beach.

We *heard* the <u>voice</u> in the distance.

In every example above, the italicized verb is *transitive.*

A verb that does *not* carry action over to a direct object is an **intransitive verb.** An intransitive verb may report action, but it is not action on or against anything. In the following sentences, the verbs are intransitive:

The ship *sank.*

The boiler *exploded.*

Millions of Americans *jog* every day.

In looking for direct objects in sentences, ask *what* or *whom* after the verb. The answer to the question will be the direct object.

The children crossed the street.
[Crossed *what?* Crossed the *street.* The word *street* is the direct object.]

She saw him at the beach.
[Saw *whom?* Saw *him.* The direct object is *him.*]

gr 3A

Indirect object

Many times a verb will report an action on a direct object and will tell you *for whom* or *for what* the action is done. Someone may say, "The singer sang me a song." The direct object is *song,* which receives the action of the verb *sang.* Sang what? Sang a *song.* But the reason for the action is expressed by *me,* and *me* is the indirect object. If you ask *to whom* (or *to what*) or *for whom* (or *for what*), you can find indirect objects.

Clarence ordered *me* a hamburger.
[Clarence ordered a hamburger *for whom?* The answer is for *me. Me* is the indirect object.]

I wrote *Bessie* a letter.
[I wrote a letter *to whom?* The answer is to *Bessie. Bessie* is the indirect object.]

The pageant gave *us* pride in America.

Ask *the teacher* your question.

Jack told *George* the whole story.

Direct objects and indirect objects, like subjects, are generally nouns or pronouns, or they are word groups that act like nouns or pronouns (see 3C, sections 1 and 2).

Complements

Complements complete descriptions of subjects and objects. **Subject complements** are located on the other side of the verb from the subject and help complete the description of the subject. The verb that joins a subject and its complement is called a **linking verb.** A linking verb does not express an action on an object; it links or joins a subject to some further description of itself not included in the subject.

The most common linking verbs include *is, are, was,* and *were,* but there are many others. Look at the subject complements after the linking verbs in the following sentences.

My father is *a welder.*
[*Welder* completes the meaning of the subject by identifying the father. The subject and its complement are linked by the verb *is.*]

America looked *good* to me after my long absence.

[*Good* completes the meaning of the subject, *America,* by describing it. The verb *looked* links the subject and the subject complement.]

The university was *a large and frightening place.*

Aunt Melissa was *old, wise, and stingy.*

Arthur became *alarmed.*

Object complements come immediately after direct objects and help complete the description of the action on the direct object by the verb. Object complements are always nouns or adjectives (see 3B, sections 2, 4), and they are never separated from the direct object by a comma.

Sue named her son *Paul.*

We painted our house *white.*

She called me *an idiot.*

My brother drove me *crazy.*

Complements may be nouns, pronouns, or adjectives (see 3B, sections 2–4).

Exercise 3.4 In the following sentences, identify direct objects (d.o.), indirect objects (i.d.o.), subject complements (s.c.), and object complements (o.c.).

1. General Lee ordered General Longstreet into battle.
2. Tell him the news so that he will feel good.
3. W. E. B. Du Bois told Americans a hard truth about how whites treated blacks.
4. The house remained unpainted, shabby, and deserted.
5. She thought me foolish for my obsession with automobiles.
6. The soup smelled rich and spicy.
7. Teddy Roosevelt made Americans angry and proud at the same time.
8. Her "revolver" was really a cigarette lighter.
9. They gave us the wrong directions.
10. We ate the biscuits whole.
11. He brings her her lunch each day on an old wooden tray.
12. They shut the door tight.
13. They felt bad because of what they had said.
14. Mike Hartman looked happy.
15. Allan told me that the project was almost finished.

gr 3A

2 Learn to recognize the grammatical structure of familiar sentence patterns.

You have already seen how important sentence patterns are in our language system. Knowing the structure of the familiar patterns can help you analyze sentences to see how they work grammatically. Also, you can see how well your own sentences conform to the patterns and to variations of those patterns. The chart below illustrates the structure of the most typical sentence patterns.

Pattern one:	**Subject**	**+ Verb**		
	We	laughed.		
	The trees	blossomed.		
	The house	was destroyed.		
Pattern two:	**Subject**	**+ Verb**	**+ Direct object**	
	She	drew up	the plans.	
	The old man	wrote	the speech.	
	The baseball	broke	the glass.	
Pattern three:	**Subject**	**+ Verb**	**+ Subject complement**	
	The house	was	large and cold.	
	He	appeared	busy.	
	It	looked	good.	
	The child	became	restless.	
	His sister	was	a reporter.	
Pattern four:	**Subject**	**+ Verb**	**+ Direct object**	**+ Object complement**
	They	called	Lindbergh	a daredevil.
	He	named	his son	John.
Pattern five:	**Subject**	**+ Verb**	**+ Indirect object**	**+ Direct object**
	They	sent	us	the package.
	Smoking	gives	my son	a headache.

The basic patterns of sentences can be rearranged in many different ways as long as you remember the importance of the different kinds of verbs in the patterns and the relations between the parts of the sentence.

Subject complement	**+ Verb**	**+ Subject**
Fair	lie	the fields of England.
Direct object	**+ Subject**	**+ Verb**
These bones	he	removed earlier today.

Exercise 3.5 Identify the structural patterns of these sentences.

Example:
Six people laughed.
Subject + verb

1. The president grew ill.
2. She frightened the bird.
3. Inez brought him chicken soup.
4. Thick and gray was the fog on the meadow at dawn.
5. There were good reasons for his absence.
6. The movie left me cold.
7. My friend was hit by a car this morning.
8. She always told me the truth.
9. She painted the mural slowly.
10. He broke the gears.

Exercise 3.6 Write one original sentence for each of the five sentence patterns you examined in 3A, section 2.

3B Learn the traditional eight parts of speech.

The eight parts of speech are *verbs, nouns, pronouns, adjectives, adverbs, conjunctions, prepositions,* and *interjections.*

When we say that each word in English can be classified as a *part of speech,* we mean that it can do some things in a sentence but cannot do other things. Words are like actors, able to play some roles but not others. For example, an eighty-year-old man cannot play Peter Pan and convince his audience, but he can play King Lear or the grandfather in a television soap opera. Similarly, every word plays at least one part of speech, and some words can play several parts, just as some actors can play several roles. For example, the word *act* can be a noun or a verb. If you say "The second *act* is beginning," *act* is a noun. If you say "We *act* as if we know what we are doing," *act* is a verb.

But although a word may play two or even three parts of speech, no word can play all the parts. You will puzzle people if you say "Her dog was much more *act* than mine." In this sentence, *act* tries to play the part of an adjective, and it cannot do the job. But you can add *-ive* to *act* and get the word *active,* which is an adjective and a different part of speech from *act.* Then you can say easily "Her dog was much more *active* than mine."

You can classify words according to the function they perform in sentences. *Subject, predicate,* and *direct object* are classifications based on function. Or you can classify words according to their part of speech. *Noun, verb,* and *pronoun* are examples of classifications based on parts of speech. In the following sentence, compare the two systems of classification.

gr 3B

	This	book	tells	us	stories	of	Roosevelt's	youth.
Function	modifier	subject	predicate	indirect object	direct object	preposition	modifier	object of preposition
Part of speech	adjective	noun	verb	pronoun	noun	preposition	adjective	noun

Exercise 3.7 Fill in the blanks in the following sentences with any words that make sense. The word in parentheses at the end of each sentence tells you the part of speech of the word that will go in the blank. But don't worry about the names. Look at them and go on. The exercise will prove that you have a feel for the parts of speech even if you don't readily come up with the names for them.

1. The __________ crawled up in the tree and killed the mockingbird. (noun)
2. Our teacher told __________ not to write in our textbook. (pronoun)
3. We __________ the house last night. (verb)
4. The leaves on the __________ in the yard are turning red. (noun)
5. John Lennon and __________ other Beatles made a revolution in music. (article)
6. The dog sleeps __________ in the shade. (adverb)
7. We painted the car __________. (adjective)
8. Come __________ the library tomorrow morning for the book. (preposition)
9. Judy __________ the page out of the magazine. (verb)
10. He kept __________ father's picture on his desk. (pronoun)
11. She __________ told me it was true. (reflexive pronoun)
12. Americans drink a __________ large quantity of milk each year. (adverb)
13. Children walk __________ to school in the morning. (adverb)
14. Alcohol is one of the __________ dangerous common drugs. (adverb)
15. "__________," he cried. "That hurt!" (interjection)
16. Bert, Jill, __________ Paul were always good friends. (conjunction)
17. He wanted me to stay, __________ I had to go. (conjunction)
18. Our arrival was delayed __________ we had a flat tire. (conjunction)
19. The __________ he found in his driveway was stolen. (noun)
20. The buffalo __________ the wide green plains of the West. (verb)
21. The __________ problem on page two was the only one I could not solve. (adjective)
22. She confessed that __________ had lied when she told me the story. (pronoun)

23. The __________ bicycle is much more complicated than its ancestors. (adjective)
24. Muggings __________ take place in broad daylight. (adverb)
25. The __________ at the end of the house glowed green in the night. (noun)

1 Verbs

Verbs are words that report an action, a condition, or a happening or that express a state of being. Verbs are the controlling words in complete predicates, but they themselves are controlled by subjects in *person* and *number*. Verbs also show whether the action of a sentence is taking place now, took place in the past, or will take place in the future.

The form of the verb changes according to the *person* of the subject and whether the subject is singular or plural. Study the following chart.

	Singular	Plural
First person:	I read	We read
Second person:	You read	You read
Third person:	She read**s**	They read
First person:	I loosen	We loosen
Second person:	You loosen	You loosen
Third person:	It loosen**s**	They loosen
First person:	I build	We build
Second person:	You build	You build
Third person:	He build**s**	They build

All the verbs in the chart are in the present tense. Notice that the only change that takes place is in the third person singular: a final *-s* is added to the common form of the verb.

The verb must agree with the subject in person in the present tense and in other tenses where helping verbs are necessary.

Helping Verbs and Verb Phrases

In a verb phrase, that is, a verb combined with an auxiliary verb, we call the final word the **main verb.** (The word *auxiliary* means "to help by adding on.") The main verb carries the primary meaning of the verb phrase. In the following sentences the verb phrases are underlined; **HV** appears over each helping verb; and **MV** appears over each main verb.

HV HV MV ... **HV MV**
The train will have left before we can get to the station.

HV HV MV ... **HV MV**
He had been walking for hours before he was found.

HV HV MV
We could have lived in Nebraska.

HV MV
He is bicycling down from Vermont.

gr
3B

HV MV
They will be in town before the end of the month.

HV MV
Contrary to your opinion, he does not have any imagination.

HV HV MV
Cy Young has always been considered one of the best pitchers in baseball history.

Sometimes words that are not part of the verb phrase come between the helping verb and the main verb, as in the last two sentences above. Neither *not* nor *always* is a verb. They are both adverbs (see 3B, section 4). Sometimes helping verbs come in clusters. Common helping verb clusters are *used to, are going, might be able to, could have, have to, ought to,* and *about to.*

English is rich in helping verbs. See how helping verbs change the sense of the main verb *play* in the following sentences.

They *are playing* chess right now.

I *used to play* chess.

I *am going to play* chess again tomorrow.

People *should play* chess in quiet places.

Contrary to your doubts, I *do play* chess well.

They *were about to play* chess again when the building collapsed.

Sometimes particles are added to verbs. **Particles** are short words that never change their form no matter how the main verb changes. They sometimes look like other parts of speech, but they always go with the verb to add a meaning to the verb that the verb does not have by itself. Look at how a change in particles changes the meaning of the verb *made* in the following sentences.

Harry made *up* with Adam.

She made *off* with the loot.

They made *out* their income-tax form.

The captain made *good* on his promise.

They made *over* the basement into a playroom.

The crowd made *way* for the parade.

Sometimes other words come between the verb and its particle.

When I got to New York, I *looked* Jack and Molly *up* in the Bronx.
He *looked* the word *up* in the dictionary.
They *put* me *up* in the spare room during my visit.
His enemies *made* Roscoe *out* to be a liar.

gr 3B

Time of Verbs
Verbs have three simple times.

Present: She works every day.

Past: She worked yesterday.

Future: She will work tomorrow.

You can form the simple past tense of most verbs by adding a final *-ed* to the common form of the present or a simple *-d* if the common form of the present ends in *-e*.

Present: I *save* some money every month.
The dogs in our neighborhood *bark* at night.

Past: I *saved* a thousand dollars last year.
My dog *barked* all night long at the back door.

But a great many verbs in English are irregular. That is, the simple past tense is very different from the common form of the present.

Present: We *grow* tomatoes every year on our back porch.
I *run* four miles a day.

Past: We *grew* corn back in Iowa.
Coe *ran* the mile in three minutes and forty-six seconds in August 1981.

The future tense of verbs is always formed by adding *shall* or *will* to the common form of the present.

Present: I often *read* in bed.

Future: I *will read* you a story before bedtime.

See Chapter 7 for a full discussion of verb tenses.

Exercise 3.8 Underline the verb phrases in the following sentences. Write **HV** over the helping verbs and **MV** over the main verbs.

1. Nomads in Arabia are wearing sunglasses.
2. Has he wrecked the Jeep?
3. Fees are rising at universities.
4. She ought to be here any minute.
5. He was sent out for pizza.
6. We cut up old clothes and made them into bandages.
7. They used up all the typewriter ribbons.
8. He was burned up because he could not find a parking place.
9. More people are moving to California every day.
10. The wounded passengers were carried away on stretchers.
11. I could never explain the accident to Chen.
12. There were three cats howling on the fence at 2:00 A.M.
13. The rock singers could have been hurt by their screaming and rioting fans.
14. Mr. Tang might have stayed with us more than a year had his wife and child not remained in China.
15. Carla should simply have refused the offer.
16. Can you find out their names and addresses?

2 Nouns

Nouns are the names we use for people, places, animals, things, ideas, actions, states of existence, colors, and so forth. In sentences, nouns serve as subjects, objects, and complements.

Common nouns namc things ordinary cnough not to be capitalized unless they begin a sentence. Common nouns include the following words and thousands more:

profession, color, man, beauty, democracy, philosophy, rope, students, cattle, libraries, justice, music, geometry, synagogue, cars, glove, showcases, horses, women, proficiency

Proper nouns name things special or individual enough to be capitalized any time they are used. Proper nouns include the following:

Germany, Department of Education, Greek Orthodox, Helen, Ms. Howard, General Dynamics, Belmont, Tennessee, Amtrak, Donald Stone, Frenchman

Compound nouns consist of two or more words that function as a unit. They include words like *heartache, mother-in-law, International Business Machines,* and *world view.* Compound nouns may also be proper nouns—*Federal Bureau of Investigation, Suez Canal.* And they may be common nouns—*father-in-law, great-grandmother.*

Sometimes you can recognize a noun by its ending. Words that end in *-ty, -tion, -sion, -or, -ism, -ist, -ment, -ness, -ship, -ture, -ance,* and *-ence* are usually nouns. But be careful! Some words with these endings may also be used as verbs:

Jackson made *mention* of you in his letter. (noun)

I hope you will *mention* me to him. (verb)

One of the best tests for a noun is to see if you can put the article *a, an,* or *the* before it and still make sense in your sentence. For example, you can say "He promised he would *mention* me to his boss," but you can't make sense by saying "He promised he would *the mention* me to his boss." So you know that *mention* is not playing the part of a noun in this sentence. But you can say "He told me he would make *a mention* of me to his boss." Here *mention* is playing the part of a noun.

Nouns also have singulars and plurals. You usually form the plural by adding *-s* or *-es* (see 29C, sections 1 and 2).

Singular	Plural
nest	nests
dog	dogs
street	streets
bush	bushes

You can form the possessive of nouns by adding *-'s* or *'* to show ownership or a special relation.

girl	girl's
girls	girls'
insect	insect's
insects	insects'

These qualities of plurality and possession can help you identify nouns in sentences. If you can make a word plural or can make it show possession, you have a noun.

gr 3B

Three Tests for Nouns

1. Use *a, an,* or *the* before the word.

Word	Test	A noun?
book	the book	Yes
injure	an injure	No

2. Make the word plural.

Word	Test	A noun?
egg	eggs	Yes
soon	soons	No

3. Make the word show possession.

Word	Test	A noun?
child	the child's blanket	Yes
criticize	criticize's	No

Nouns function typically as subjects, objects, and complements as well as in other sentence positions. When a noun (and any words that modify it) follows another noun to describe or to add information about the first noun, we call such a construction an **appositive.**

The speaker, *an experienced lawyer,* aroused the crowd with his passion and determination.

[The noun *lawyer* and its modifiers *an* and *experienced* appear after the word *speaker* to add information about the subject. The word group *an experienced lawyer* is in apposition to the word *speaker.*]

Look also for nouns in direct address (see 24, section K) and in absolute constructions (see 3C, section 1).

Exercise 3.9 In the following paragraph, circle all the nouns.

The Sahara's dryness begins at the Equator. There in the rainy tropics hot air rises and sheds its moisture as it cools. The cooled air begins to subside and warm up again between 15 and 30 north latitude. The subsiding air is too dry for clouds and rain to form. This subtropical high-pressure belt parches the earth from the Sahara through the Middle East and into northwestern India and Pakistan. It helps create the American deserts. A similar belt south of the Equator leads to the arid sands of the Kalahari and Namid Deserts as well as the deserts of Peru, Chile, and Australia's barren outback.

—Rick Gore

3 Pronouns

Like nouns, pronouns serve as subjects, objects, and complements in sentences.

There are different kinds of pronouns, and we use them for different purposes.

Some pronouns stand for nouns and help us avoid the monotony of repeating the same noun over and over again. We say, "I see the train coming; it will be here in a minute, and after it stops and some passengers get off and others get on, it will go on toward Chicago." Without pronouns we would have to say, "Dick Wagner sees the train coming; the train will be here in a minute, and after the train stops and some passengers get off and passengers different from the passengers getting off get on, the train will go on toward Chicago." Such a sentence would be unbearably clumsy and confusing, and pronouns help us avoid such things. However, you must always be sure to let your readers know what nouns your pronouns stand for. (The word to which a pronoun refers is its **antecedent.**) Pronouns that lack a clear reference lead to great confusion. If you do not present a clear reference in your pronouns, you create a situation for your readers that is a little like making them shop in a supermarket where someone has torn all the labels off the cans.

Personal pronouns are pronouns referring to a person or to people. Personal pronouns include *I, you, he, she, it, we,* and *they.* (Personal pronouns may be classified according to case as *subjective* or *objective* or *possessive* pronouns. See 8H.)

Definite pronouns stand for nouns that appear before the pronoun:

Here is my old typewriter. I have used *it* for thirty years.

[The pronoun is *it*, which refers to the noun *typewriter. Typewriter* is the *antecedent* of the pronoun, the word that comes before the pronoun and gives it meaning.]

Indefinite pronouns do not require an antecedent. They let us make statements about one member of a group when we are unable to name which one we mean. They do have a reference, but the reference to an indefinite pronoun usually comes in a word, phrase, or clause *after* the pronoun in the sentence.

Everybody in the room heard the explosion.

Anything you do to help will be appreciated.

[*Everybody* in the first sentence above receives its meaning from the following phrase, *in the room. Anything* receives its meaning from the following clause, *you do to help.*]

Reflexive pronouns refer to the noun or pronoun that is the subject of the sentence. Reflexive pronouns can serve as direct or indirect objects to show that a subject is doing action to itself.

She allowed *herself* no rest.

He sold *himself* into the slavery of law school.

gr 3B

Intensive pronouns are a variety of reflexive pronouns. Intensive pronouns add a special emphasis to nouns and other pronouns.

I *myself* have often made that mistake.

President Harding *himself* played poker and drank whiskey in the White House during Prohibition.

Intensive and reflexive pronouns have the same form; they always end in *-self.*

Demonstrative pronouns point out nouns or other pronouns that come after them.

That is the book I want.

These are my friends.

Are *those* the ones you meant?

Relative pronouns join word groups containing a subject and verb (clause) to nouns or pronouns that the word groups describe. Some relative pronouns change their form depending upon their use in a sentence (see Chapter 8).

He was the man **who** *would be king.*

[The words *who would be king* describe the man by telling which man is meant. *Who* is a relative pronoun.]

The tools **that** I lost in the burglary cost me a fortune to replace.

The physician **whom** you requested has been suspended for malpractice.

Possessive pronouns show possession or special relations.

She was *my* aunt.

Our door is always unlocked.

Their cat eats turnips.

The fault was *ours,* and the worst mistake was *mine.*

Interrogative pronouns (*who, which,* and *what*) introduce questions:

What courses are you taking?

Who spoke first?

Which of the wrenches is mine?

Here are the most common pronouns:

I, me, mine, myself, yourself, yourselves, we, our, ours, ourselves, you, yours, he, she, it, they, himself, herself, itself, themselves, his, hers, its, them, their, theirs, one, ones, oneself, everybody, anybody, anyone, everyone, that, which, who, whom, these, those, whoever, whichever, whomever

For a fuller discussion of pronouns, see Chapter 8.

Exercise 3.10 Circle the pronouns in the following paragraph:

Until 1972, Bob Light, then 30, and his wife Lee, 28, lived a rather ordinary suburban life in Upper Saddle River, New Jersey, one of those plush redwood-deck-and-blacktop-driveway places outside of New York City. He worked for his father in a successful textile machinery plant, she did freelance work, together they raised two children, and much of their free time they spent in the chic nightspots of New York—all the stuff of statistical tables and Hollywood movies. Then, that year, they sold their split-level house and moved to a 25-acre farm just outside the tiny village of Plainfield, Vermont.

—Kirkpatrick Sale

Exercise 3.11 Fill in the blanks with any pronouns that make sense.

1. ________ always wanted to put a small motor on ________ hang glider.
2. ________ house is on the street next to ________ school.
3. ________ who can square dance is welcome.
4. The President ________ promised to attend the party.
5. ________ is in charge here?
6. ________ error did he make?
7. The mechanic told me ________ was wrong.
8. ________ of the cars belongs to him?
9. The responsibility for giving the order was ________, and I forgot.
10. "The most important principle in dancing," ________ said, "is to think of the music and not ________ feet."
11. The gift ________ counted most was ________ will.

gr
3B

12. He pointed to __________ broken rocks over there and said __________ were the cause of the shipwreck.
13. Divers __________ go down deep in the ocean must be careful to avoid nitrogen poisoning in their blood when __________ rise to the surface again.
14. The potato, __________ came originally from the New World, became a primary food in Ireland, __________ was a poor country.
15. We built the house __________ and saved thousands of dollars, but the effort cost __________ hundreds of hours of __________ time.
16. __________ in the stadium could have won the lottery.
17. __________ who plays baseball well is not necessarily a superior athlete.
18. You can take __________ one you want.
19. __________ house burned to the ground before __________ saw the fire.
20. Tell __________ that __________ must feed and water __________ parakeet every day.

4 Adjectives, Articles, and Adverbs

Adjectives and adverbs add qualities to other words. They describe these words more fully. Sometimes we say that adjectives and adverbs *modify* other words; that is, they change, expand, limit, or otherwise help describe the words to which they relate. You can sometimes recognize adjectives and adverbs because they have comparative or superlative forms, that is forms that indicate degree. Take the adjective *large,* for example:

Positive: She owned a *large* boat.

Comparative: Her boat was *larger* than mine.

Superlative: She owned the *largest* boat on the lake.
[One object is *large;* between two, one is *larger;* among three or more, one is *largest.*]

And here is the adverb *strongly:*

Positive: My teachers *strongly* advised me to go to college.

Comparative: My depressed finances inspired me *more strongly* to get a job.

Superlative: It was the *most strongly* built tree house I had seen.

Adjectives modify nouns and pronouns. That is, they help describe nouns and pronouns in a sentence, giving these words qualities that they do not have by themselves. See how different adjectives change the meanings in the following sentences:

The fans booed the *helpless* coach.

The fans booed the *happy* coach.

The fans booed the *angry* coach.

Adjectives may be located immediately before or immediately after the words they modify, although they usually come before.

gr 3B

The *tired, thirsty,* and *impatient* horse threw its rider and ran away.

The horse, *tired, thirsty,* and *impatient,* threw its rider and ran away.

An adjective modifying the subject of a sentence sometimes appears on the opposite side of a linking verb from the subject.

The horse looked *tired, thirsty,* and *impatient.*

My friend was *late,* and I was *worried.*

In describing nouns, adjectives answer a number of questions: Which one? What kind? How many? What size? What color? What condition? Whose?

Which one?	*that* diner, *the* eggs
What kind?	*dead* leaves, *useful* idea
How many?	*six* children, *few* grapes, *many* apologies
What size?	*tall* building, *enormous* mountains
What color?	*red* lips, *brown* fields, *pale* skin
What condition?	*sick* people, *happy* nation
Whose?	*my* coat, *their* house

A Test for Adjectives

Ask *Which one? What kind? How many? What size? What color? What condition? Whose?* A word that answers one of those questions to describe a noun, a pronoun, or some other noun substitute is an adjective. (A noun substitute is usually a pronoun, but it may be a gerund, a noun clause, an infinitive, or a phrase. See definitions in the Glossary of Grammatical Terms.)

One (**How many?**) *small* (**What size?**) child lingered on the *empty* (**What condition?**) playground while the *hard* (**What kind?**) rain beat down on the (**Which one?**) *black* (**What color?**) pavement.

The articles *a, an,* and *the* function as adjectives, but they lack the power of description that we find in other adjectives.

The articles *a* and *an* are indefinite and singular; they call attention to one of several things without being particular about which one.

gr 3B

He sent me *a* card every Christmas.
[There are many different cards; he sent me one every Christmas. The sentence does not say which of the many he sent.]

Richard III cried, "*A* horse, *a* horse, my kingdom for *a* horse!"
[Any horse would do; the king did not have any special horse in mind.]

The article *a* appears before words that begin with a consonant sound. The article *an* is set before words that begin with a vowel sound.

a dish, a rose, a year, an apple, an entreaty, a war, an ideal, an out, an itch, an umbrella, an order, an artist

Many English words that begin with the vowel *u* sound as if they begin with the consonant *y*; these words are preceded by *a*:

a university, a union, a united country

A few English words that begin with the consonant *h* have a vowel sound and are preceded by *an*:

an hour, an honest man

The article *the* is used with both singular and plural nouns. It always denotes a definite noun. It always means "this and not any other." Often the difference between using *a* or *an* and using *the* depends on the writer's idea of how specific the following noun is.

He came down off *the* mountain and found *the* road.
[The writer has a particular mountain and a particular road in mind, and no other mountain and no other road will do.]

He came down off *a* mountain and found *a* road.
[The use of the indefinite *a* seems to show that the writer does not know or care what mountain the man descended or what road he found. Something else about the sentence is much more important to the writer than naming the mountain or locating the road.]

Adverbs add shades of meaning to words or sentence elements that cannot be modified by adjectives.

Since adjectives can only modify nouns, pronouns, and other noun substitutes (see 9A), adverbs are left to modify anything else in the sentence that can be modified. They most commonly modify verbs, adjectives, and other adverbs, but they can sometimes modify prepositions, phrases, clauses, and even whole sentences (see 9B and 9C).

Adverbs answer several questions. Study each of the sentences below. The question the adverb answers is in parentheses at the end of the sentence. The adverbs are in italics.

He *cheerfully* gave up the prize. (How?)

Sometimes I wonder what she means. (How often?)

I *intensely* dislike having to look for a parking place. (To what degree?)

In California we visited Disneyland and then turned *homeward.* (Where?)

Yesterday I took my last examination of my freshman year. (When?)

A Test for Adverbs

Ask *How? How often? To what degree? Where? When?* A word that answers one of these questions to describe a verb, an adjective, or another adverb is an adverb.

Afterward	she stood	*there*	*very*	*quietly.*
When?		**Where?**	**To what degree?**	**How?**

Adverbs may modify by affirmation:

He will *surely* call home before he leaves.

They may also modify by negation. *Not* is always an adverb.

They shall *not* pass.

We will *never* see anyone like her again.

Many adverbs end in *-ly,* and you can make adverbs of most adjectives simply by adding *-ly* to the adjective form.

Adjective	Adverb
large	largely
crude	crudely
beautiful	beautifully

But beware! A great many words that may function as adverbs do not end in *-ly:*

often, sometimes, then, when, anywhere, anyplace, somewhere, somehow, somewhat, yesterday, Sunday, before, behind, ahead, seldom

And many *adjectives* end in *-ly.* Here are just a few examples:

costly, stately, lowly, homely, measly, gentlemanly

In addition to their roles as modifiers, some adverbs also can serve to connect ideas logically between clauses. These are the **conjunctive adverbs,** words and phrases like *accordingly, consequently, hence, however, indeed, meanwhile, moreover, nevertheless, on the other hand,* and *therefore.* (See 4E.)

A squall hit the marina suddenly; *therefore* none of the boats left the dock.

Most students completed their investigation of lymphocytes by the assigned date. *However,* Simon and Teri requested another week to write up the results.

The book was bad; the film, *on the other hand,* was surprisingly good.

Unlike *coordinating conjunctions* (see 2B, section 5), conjunctive adverbs do not provide correct grammatical links between clauses. That is, if you use one of the conjunctive adverbs between clauses, you must also use a semicolon or a period. This makes it easy to tell a conjunctive adverb from a coordinating conjunction. Conjunctive adverbs may shift positions within a clause:

The book was bad; *on the other hand,* the film was surprisingly good.

The book was bad; the film was surprisingly good, *on the other hand.*

The best test for an adverb is to find what it modifies and then to ask yourself the adverb questions. If it does not modify a noun, a pronoun, or some other noun substitute, a modifier has to be an adverb. If it does modify a noun, a pronoun, or some other noun substitute, it cannot be an adverb.

Exercise 3.12 In the following sentences, underline the adverbs and draw a circle around the adjectives.

1. He walked the dog happily down the moonlit street, unaware that hostile eyes were watching him from a darkened window in a house everyone thought was empty.

2. Solar heat offers much promise to homeowners who want to save money in the long run, but in the short run solar heat is very expensive because the costs of both the equipment and installation are great.
3. They came Sunday after church and stayed until supper, sitting happily in the backyard, speaking now and then, but mostly remaining silent.
4. Handbooks are valuable instruments for sharpening your knowledge of grammar and writing, but they cannot serve you well unless you write often and want to write better.
5. I learned to appreciate the beauty of Hebrew by hearing our cantor sing during the Sabbath services on Friday nights, but I went for years and never understood exactly what the songs meant because I did not know the language.

5 Conjunctions

Conjunctions join elements within a sentence. These elements may be words, or they may be groups of words like clauses or phrases (see 3C, sections 1 and 2).

Coordinating conjunctions (or, simply, **coordinators**) join elements of equal weight or function. The common coordinating conjunctions are *and, but, or, for,* and *nor.* Some writers now include *yet* and *so* among the coordinating conjunctions.

He was tired *and* happy.

The town was small *but* pretty.

The road was steep, rough, *and* winding.

They must be tired, *for* they have climbed all day long.

You may take the green *or* the red.

He would not leave the table, *nor* would he stop talking.

Correlative conjunctions—that is, conjunctions used in pairs—also connect sentence elements of equal value. The familiar correlatives are *both . . . and, either . . . or, neither . . . nor, not only . . . but also,* and *whether . . . or.*

Neither the doctor *nor* the nurse believed the patient's story.

The year 1927 was *not only* the year Lindbergh flew solo nonstop across the Atlantic *but also* the year Babe Ruth hit 60 home runs.

Subordinating conjunctions (or **subordinators**) join dependent or subordinate sections of a sentence to independent sections or to other dependent sections (see 3C, section 2). The common subordinating conjunctions are *after, although, as, because, before, if, once, rather than, since, that, unless, until, when, whenever, where, wherever,* and *while.* There are several others.

The stylus will not track records *if* there is not enough weight on it.

Although the desert may look barren and dead, a vigorous life goes on there.

He always wore a hat *when* he went out in the sun.

Stories about divorce are common on television and in the movies *because* so many Americans have been divorced.

For the use of coordinators and subordinators to improve your writing style, see Chapter 13.

gr
3B

6 Prepositions

Prepositions show the relation between a word that comes after the preposition—the object—and another word in the sentence. Objects of prepositions are nouns or pronouns.

Suburban yards now provide **homes** *for* ***wildlife*** that once **lived** only *in* the ***country.***

[The preposition *for* relates the object *wildlife* to the noun *homes;* the preposition *in* relates the object *country* to the verb *lived.*]

The preposition, its noun, and any modifiers attached to the noun make up a prepositional phrase. Prepositional phrases act as adjectives or adverbs, and the function of prepositions is to bring the strength of nouns and pronouns to modify other words in the sentence.

Here are the common prepositions:

about	beyond	on
above	by	over
across	despite	since
after	down	through
against	during	to
along	except	toward
amid	excluding	under
among	following	underneath
as	from	until
at	in	up
before	including	upon
behind	inside	via
below	into	with
beneath	like	within
beside	near	without
between	of	

Some prepositions consist of more than one word:

according to	except for	instead of
along with	in addition to	on account of
apart from	in case of	up to
as to	in front of	with regard to
because of	in place of	with reference to
by means of	in regard to	
by way of	in spite of	

gr 3B

Prepositions usually precede their objects, but sometimes, especially in questions, they do not. Grammarians still debate whether or not prepositions should end a sentence, but most writers favoring an informal style will use a preposition to end a sentence now and then.

Which principles does he live by?
[Compare: By which principles does he live? This choice is more formal.]

His frequent crying is hard to put up *with.*
[The idiom *to put up with* ends with a preposition and sounds more natural here. You could rewrite the sentence: *It is hard to put up with his frequent crying.* Or: *I find it hard to put up with his frequent crying.* But what you gain in formality (the preposition no longer ends the sentence), you lose in emphasis. *His frequent crying* is the most important information in the sentence and belongs first.]

Notice that many words used as prepositions can also be used as other parts of speech, particularly as adverbs or as subordinating conjunctions.

He came *after* the elephant.
[The preposition *after* introduces a prepositional phrase with an adverbial sense modifying the verb *came.*]

Jill came tumbling *after.*
[Here, *after* is a simple adverb.]

After Jack broke his crown, Jill fell down too.
[*After* is a subordinating conjunction.]

7 Interjections

Interjections are forceful expressions, usually written with an exclamation point, though mild ones may be set off with commas.

Hot dog! Wow!

Ouch! Hooray!

Always remember that the same word may be used for several different parts of speech in different sentences or in different parts of the same sentence. How the word is used will determine what part of speech it plays.

gr
3B

The *light* drizzle foretold heavy rain. (adjective)

The *light* glowed across the dark water. (noun)

As you *light* the candle, say a prayer. (verb)

The cobra glides *outside.* (adverb)

The child was on the *outside.* (noun)

The mongoose was *outside* the house. (preposition)

When will he come home? (adverb)

He will come *when* he gets ready. (conjunction)

They decided the where and the *when* immediately. (noun)

Exercise 3.13 Identify the part of speech of each word in the following sentences.

1. The truck crashed through the railing.
2. She used a pen when she wrote.
3. The kite flew steadily in the steady wind out of the west.
4. He commuted to the university from his home by roller skates.
5. She drinks six cups of coffee daily.
6. The divers from the submarine came up under the aircraft carrier and planted their bombs on the keel.
7. Coal mines are dangerous to your health.
8. He discovered oil in his filling station.
9. "Ouch!" she shouted. "That hurt."
10. Although they loved tobacco, they hated cigarettes.
11. He was often angry because he did not believe in himself.
12. When her father was dying, she refused to let anyone speak of death, and so he died without being able to talk about what was happening to him.

Exercise 3.14 Write original sentences in which you use each word as various parts of speech as indicated. Use a dictionary if you need assistance.

1. Use *jump* as a noun, a verb, and an adjective.
2. Use *beyond* as an adverb, a preposition, and a noun.
3. Use *after* as an adverb, a preposition, and a conjunction.
4. Use *book* as a noun, a verb, and an adjective.

3C Learn the difference between phrases and clauses.

A **phrase** is a group of related words without a subject and a predicate. All phrases can play the role of a part of speech—usually a verb, an adjective, an adverb, or a noun.

They *were watching* the game. (verb phrase)

The child ran *into the house.* (prepositional phrase acting as an adverb)

Looking backward, he ran into the door. (participial phrase acting as an adjective)

To open a small business, you need lots of capital. (infinitive phrase acting as an adverb)

Digging for ruins takes patience. (gerund phrase acting as a noun)

He *might have been able* to survive if he had sat down at once when he knew he was lost and had started a fire. (verb phrase)

Cars with *huge tail fins and huge engines* were symbols of optimism in the early 1960s. (prepositional phrase acting as an adjective).

A **clause** is a group of related words containing both a subject and a predicate in a grammatical union with one another. Clauses may be *independent* or *dependent.* An independent clause can usually stand by itself as a complete sentence. A dependent, or subordinate, clause often cannot stand by itself because it is introduced by a subordinating conjunction or a relative pronoun, and therefore the clause alone does not make sense. But the main test for a dependent clause is to see if it serves as a part of speech in another clause. An independent clause does not serve as a part of speech in another clause.

She ran in the marathon *because she wanted to test herself.*
[The independent clause, **She ran in the marathon,** can stand by itself as a complete sentence. The dependent clause, *because she wanted to test herself,* cannot stand by itself. The independent clause does not serve as a part of speech for another clause. The dependent clause serves as an adverb modifying the verb *ran* in the independent clause.]

She said *she felt exhausted after fifteen miles.*
[The independent clause, **She said,** cannot stand by itself as a complete sentence. But it is an independent clause because it does not serve as a part of speech for another clause. The dependent clause, *she felt exhausted after fifteen miles,* can stand by itself as a complete sentence. But it is a dependent clause because it serves as a noun and a direct object for another clause. *What* did she say? She said she felt exhausted after fifteen miles.]

They took *what they could find.*

[The independent clause is **They took.** The dependent clause, *what they could find,* serves as a noun and the direct object for the independent clause.

When we had done everything possible, **we left the wounded to the enemy.**

gr 3C [The independent clause is **we left the wounded to the enemy.** The dependent clause is *When we had done everything possible.* It serves as an adverb modifying the verb *left*]

With clauses and phrases we can make careful distinctions in our thoughts, and we can give our sentences a pleasing variety. We use clauses and phrases to separate the more important things we want to say from the less important.

Exercise 3.15 In the following sentences, tell whether the italicized words make a phrase or a clause. A clause may include phrases; so you should judge each group of italicized words as a whole.

Example: *When he was a pilot on the Mississippi River in his youth,* Samuel Clemens learned the lore of the people along its banks.

[The italicized words as a whole make a clause with the subject *he* and the verb *was.* The clause contains two phrases, *on the Mississippi River* and *in his youth.* But they are part of the italicized clause.]

1. *Before she set out on the Appalachian Trail,* she had to buy a good backpack.
2. The circus used to set up on a vacant lot *outside of town.*
3. Although Americans feel nostalgic *about trains,* they don't ride them very much.
4. *When knighthood was in flower,* life was bloody and short.
5. While he took classes every weeknight at the university, *he worked every day in a factory.*
6. *I don't know* why she quit her job.
7. Truck drivers spend days and sometimes weeks *away from their families.*
8. Henry Wadsworth Longfellow is buried in Mount Auburn Cemetery *in Cambridge.*
9. In college football, the running game is more important *than it is in the pros.*
10. Soccer is a coming sport in the United States *because it is much cheaper and safer to play than high school football.*

1 Learn the basic kinds of phrases and their uses.

Prepositional Phrases

Prepositional phrases always begin with a preposition and end with a noun or pronoun that serves as the object of a preposition. Prepositional phrases generally function as adjectives or adverbs.

gr 3C

The tree *in the yard* is an oak.
[The prepositional phrase *in the yard* is an adjective modifying the noun *tree.*]

He arrived *before breakfast.*
[The prepositional phrase is an adverb modifying the verb *arrived.*]

To identify an adjective prepositional phrase or an adverb prepositional phrase, use the same tests that you used for simple adjectives and adverbs. If the prepositional phrase answers one of the adjective questions—Which one? What kind? How many? What size? What color? What condition?—it acts as an adjective. If the prepositional phrase answers one of the adverb questions—How? How often? To what degree? Where? When?—it acts as an adverb. Because phrases (and clauses) that function as adverbs often tell *why,* be sure to add *Why?* to your list of questions.

The book *about North American snakes* sold well *because of its outstanding photographs.*
[Which book? The book about North American snakes. The phrase is an adjective modifying the noun subject *book.* Sold well why? Because of its outstanding photographs. The phrase is an adverb modifying the verb *sold.*]

Without prepositions and prepositional phrases, we could not express many simple thoughts. The prepositional phrases in the following sentences are in italics.

He walked *on the grass.*

She sat *at the desk.*

[In both sentences the prepositional phrase functions as an adverb modifying the verb. The prepositional phrase *on the grass* in the first sentence answers the adverb question *Where?* Where did he walk? No adverb in English can answer the question so that you know he walked *on the grass.* The same is true of the adverb question *Where?* in the second sentence. You can't say "She deskly sat." But you can say "She sat *at the desk.*"]

Similarly, when prepositional phrases are used as adjectives, they may relate a noun to the rest of the sentence in a way not possible for any adjective.

The road *over the mountain* was safer than the one *in the valley.*

If you say "The mountain road was safer than the valley road," you might not express the meaning you want, especially if you mean the road that crosses the mountain and not the one that runs along the mountain crests. But some prepositional phrases are almost exactly interchangeable with adjectives or adverbs.

Adjective:	He lived in the *corner* house.
Prepositional Phrase:	He lived in the house *on the corner.*
Adverb:	The child read the ancient map easily.
Prepositional Phrase:	The child read the ancient map with ease.

Verbal Phrases

Verbals are words formed from verbs, but they do not function as verbs in sentences. There are three kinds of verbals—infinitives, participles, and gerunds. Verbals can stand alone as parts of speech, or they can have words attached to them that make a verbal phrase.

Infinitives and infinitive phrases

The infinitive of any verb except the verb *to be* is formed by putting the infinitive marker *to* before the common form of the verb in the first person present tense.

Verb:	go	**Infinitive:**	to go
Verb:	make	**Infinitive:**	to make

Infinitives and infinitive phrases function as nouns, adjectives, and adverbs. Here, too, the tests for adjectives and adverbs come in handy.

To get his novel published was his greatest ambition.
[The infinitive phrase functions as a noun, the subject of the sentence.]

He made many efforts *to get his novel published.*
[The infinitive phrase functions as an adjective modifying the noun *efforts.* Which efforts? The efforts *to get his novel published.*]

He laughed *to show his happiness.*
[The infinitive phrase functions as an adverb modifying the verb *laughed.* Laughed why? *To show his happiness.*]

Participles and participial phrases

The present participle of verbs is formed by adding *-ing* to the common present form of the verb. The past participle is usually made by adding *-ed* to the common present form of the verb, but past participles are frequently irregular. Participial phrases modify nouns and pronouns and serve as adjectives.

Driving across town, the chauffeur watched the other cars carefully.
[The present participial phrase modifies *chauffeur* and serves as an adjective.]

Flattered by the invitation, we decided to go to the wedding.
[The past participial phrase modifies *we* and serves as an adjective.]

Drawn to the highway by the lights, the deer stood in the road, unable to move.
[The past participial phrase modifies *deer* and serves as an adjective.]

Gerunds and gerund phrases

The **gerund** is simply the present participle used as a noun. The gerund phrase includes any words and phrases attached to the gerund so that the whole serves as a noun.

Walking is one of life's great pleasures.
[The gerund is the subject of the verb *is.*]

Walking swiftly an hour a day will keep you fit.
[The gerund phrase is the subject of the verb phrase *will keep.*]

He worked hard at his *typing.*
[The gerund is the object of the preposition *at.*]

He worked hard at *typing the paper.*]
[The gerund phrase is the object of the preposition *at.*]

Absolute Phrases

An absolute phrase is made by attaching a noun or a pronoun to a participle without the helping verbs that would make the participle part of a verb phrase.

Her body falling nearly a hundred miles an hour, she pulled the rip cord, and the parachute opened with a heavy jerk.

The storm came suddenly, *the clouds boiling across the sky* and *the wind howling fiercely in the trees.*

The absolute phrase modifies the whole sentence in which it appears. That is, absolute phrases do not modify any particular words or word groups in the way that participial phrases do.

Falling nearly a hundred miles an hour, she pulled the rip cord, and the parachute opened with a heavy jerk.

[By removing the noun *body* and its modifier *her,* we turn the absolute phrase into an adjective participial phrase modifying *she.*]

gr 3C

Exercise 3.16 Identify the italicized phrases in the following sentences. Tell what kind of phrase each one is and how it is used in the sentence.

1. The sheriff entered the saloon, *his hands hovering over the guns on his hips, his eyes darting around the room.*
2. He hoped *to arrive safely.*
3. He wrote out his view of the problem *to see it better.*
4. *To see a movie* in the 1930s was to escape from the depression.
5. *Opening the door softly,* he entered the room *in the dark.*
6. *Bicycling across the country* is becoming a popular way to spend the summer.
7. *Whispered softly and urgently,* the message was passed down the line.
8. *Wounded and bleeding from the wreck,* the two passengers climbed up the bank.
9. *Over the oaks and the poplars* an osprey rose *to his nest in the tallest pine.*
10. *His heart pounding, his legs tiring,* he raced for the finish line.

2 Learn the basic kinds of clauses and their uses.

Unlike phrases, clauses have subjects and predicates. Clauses may be independent or dependent. Sometimes we call independent clauses **main clauses** and dependent clauses **subordinate clauses.**

An independent clause can usually stand on its own as a complete sentence. A dependent clause cannot. A dependent clause always acts as a part of speech for another clause; an independent clause never serves as a part of speech for another clause.

He swam across the lake after the sun set.

[The independent clause, *He swam across the lake,* can stand grammatically as a complete sentence. The dependent clause, *after the sun set,* does not make complete sentence sense by itself. It must be connected to an independent clause.]

He claimed that he swam across the lake after the sun set.

[*He claimed* is an independent clause, but *claimed* is a transitive verb and must take a direct object. So *He claimed* cannot stand alone as a sentence. It is an independent clause because it does not play the role of a part of speech for another clause. The dependent clause *that he swam across the lake* serves as a noun that acts as the direct object of the verb *claimed.* The dependent clause *after the sun set* serves as an adverb for the verb *swam* in the previous dependent clause.]

A practical way to recognize dependent clauses is to see if they are introduced by a subordinating word or group of words. Some subordinators are subordinating conjunctions:

after, although, as, because, before, if, once, since, that, thought, till, unless, until, when, whenever, where, wherever, while, as if, as soon as, as though, even after, even if, even though, even when, for as much as, in order that, in that, so that, sooner than

Some subordinators are relative pronouns:

what, which, who, whoever, whom, whomever, whose

The subordinators *that* and *which* often are left out of sentences before dependent clauses. In the following sentences, the dependent clauses are in italics, and the subordinator has been omitted.

Many poor people in Latin America believe *they can gain dignity only by revolution.*

She said *she would enroll in evening school and work during the day.*

We thought *the Astros might win the pennant this year.*

Dependent clauses always act as nouns, adjectives, or adverbs for another clause.

Noun Clauses

Noun clauses act as subjects, objects, and complements.

That English is a flexible language is one of its glories.
[The noun clause serves as the subject of the verb *is.*]

He told me *that English is a flexible language.*
[Here the noun clause is the direct object of the verb *told.*]

His response was *that no response was necessary.*
[The noun clause is the subject complement of the linking verb *was.*]

Adjective Clauses

Adjective clauses modify nouns or pronouns, and relative pronouns often are used to connect them to the words they modify.

The contestant *whom he most wanted to beat* was his father.
[The adjective clause modifies the noun *contestant.* Which contestant? The contestant *whom he most wanted to beat.*]

gr
3C

The two boys *who looked so much alike* were not related.
[The adjective clause modifies the noun *boys.*]

Yard sales, *which have become common in America,* bring the excitement of a fair to modern suburbia.
[The adjective clause modifies the noun *sales.*]

The book *that she wrote about travel in Greece* was more popular than her novels.
[The adjective clause modifies the noun *book.*]

Adverbial Clauses

Adverbial clauses serve as adverbs, usually modifying the verb in another clause. Adverbial clauses are often introduced by the subordinators *after, when, before, because, although, if, though, whenever, where,* and *wherever,* as well as by many others.

After we had talked for an hour, he began to look at his watch.
[The adverbial clause modifies the verb *began.* Began when? *After we had talked for an hour.*]

If you learn to type, writing will be less of a chore.
[The adverbial clause modifies the verb phrase *will be.*]

Although he loved to cook, he hated to clean up the kitchen afterward.
[The adverbial clause modifies the verb *hated.*]

He reacted as swiftly *as he could under the circumstances.*
[The adverbial clause modifies the adverb *swiftly.*]

The desert was more yellow *than he remembered.*
[The adverbial clause modifies the adjective *yellow.*]

Exercise 3.17 Identify the dependent clauses italicized in the following sentences. Tell whether each serves as an adjective, an adverb, or a noun.

1. The bicycle, *which was invented before the automobile,* may take a major role in suburban commuting.
2. She told me *that she would drive.*
3. *That Alaska is more than twice as big as Texas* does not make Texans humble.
4. *Because medieval cities were made of wooden houses packed close together,* fires were common.
5. *If you want to learn to play a musical instrument,* be prepared to practice.
6. Doctors in the nineteenth century frequently recommended brandy, *which they thought of as a medicine,* to people with various ailments.

3D Learn to identify sentences as simple, compound, complex, or compound-complex.

Review the following distinctions.

1 The simple sentence

A simple sentence contains only one clause, and that clause is an independent clause, able to stand alone grammatically. A simple sentence may have several phrases; it may have a compound subject or a compound verb, or both a compound subject and a compound verb (see 3A, section 1). The following are simple sentences.

> Most Republicans in our town voted for the current mayor.
>
> The bloodhound is the oldest breed of dog.

[Each sentence is simple; it contains only one independent clause and no dependent clause.]

> He staked out a plot of ground high in the mountains and built his own house.

[The verbs *staked* and *built* make a compound predicate for the subject *he*, but the sentence has only one independent clause and no dependent clauses.]

> Both historians and novelists re-create a world of people and events.

[This sentence has a compound subject.]

> Singing, brawling, shouting, laughing, crying, and clapping at every play, the fans turned out every night, hungry for a pennant.

[Despite its numerous phrases, this sentence has only one independent clause; so it is a simple sentence.]

2 The compound sentence

A compound sentence contains two or more independent clauses, usually joined by a comma and a coordinating conjunction, but no dependent clause. Sometimes the independent clauses are joined by a semicolon, a dash, or a colon. The following are compound sentences.

> The sun blasted the earth, and the plants withered and died.
>
> He asked directions at the end of every street—but he never listened to them.
>
> The trees on the ridge behind our house begin to change in September: the oaks start to redden; the maples pass from green to orange; the pines take on a somber green.

A compound sentence may consist of a number of independent clauses joined in a series by commas, with a conjunction before the last clause.

They searched the want ads, she visited real estate agents, he drove through neighborhoods looking for for-sale signs, and they finally found a spacious old house.

3 The complex sentence

A complex sentence contains one independent clause and one or more dependent clauses. In the following sentences, the independent clause is in regular type, and the dependent clause is in boldface type.

He consulted the dictionary **because he did not know how to pronounce the word.**

She asked people **if they approved of what the speaker said.**

Although football players are reputed to be the most powerful athletes in team sports, the winners of the World Series beat the winners of the Superbowl in a tug-of-war on network television one year.

4 The compound-complex sentence

A compound-complex sentence contains two or more independent clauses and at least one dependent clause. In the following sentences, boldface type indicates dependent clauses, and regular type indicates independent clauses.

She discovered a new world in historical fiction, but she read so much and so often **that she left little time for anything else.**

Although Carrie Nation may seem ridiculous in retrospect, her belief **that God had called her to destroy saloons by violence if necessary** was widely applauded in her time, and she influenced the thinking of many Americans in the prohibition movement.

After Abraham Lincoln was killed, an angry and bewildered government could not determine **how many people were part of the plot,** and **since John Wilkes Booth, the assassin, was himself soon shot and killed,** he could not clarify the mystery, **which remains to this day.**

Exercise 3.18 Classify the following sentences as simple (S), complex (CX), compound (CD), or compound-complex (CC).

1. The winter of 1542 was marked by tempestuous weather throughout the British Isles: in the north, on the borders of Scotland and England, there

were heavy snowfalls in December and frost so savage that by January the ships were frozen into the harbor at Newcastle.

—ANTONIA FRASER

2. The female belted kingfisher, distinguished by a rusty band across her breast, lays six to eight pure white eggs on a bed of sand or regurgitated fish bones.

—ALEXANDER WETMORE

gr 3D

3. Prints, with woodblocks as the oldest form, began life humbly, not as works of art but as substitutes for drawings or paintings when multiples of a single image were needed, probably as long ago as the fifth century A.D. in China.

—JOHN CANADAY

4. Although America has some fine native cherries, some of the very best wild cherries to be found came originally from seedlings of cultivated varieties, and the birds have been the chief agents of scattering the seeds.

—EUELL GIBBONS

5. The notion of the painter as a sort of boon companion to the hangman is carried on by Leonardo, who was fond of attending executions, perhaps to study the muscular contortions of the hanged.

—MARY MCCARTHY

6. Once a month I would ride ten miles down the wretched mountain road to Winchester, go to confession, hear mass, and take communion.

—WILLIAM ALEXANDER PERCY

7. Huey had found another issue that would help to move him along the path to the governorship.

—T. HARRY WILLIAMS

8. When he had eaten seven bananas, Mr. Biswas was sick, whereupon Soanie, silently crying, carried him to the back verandah.

—V. S. NAIPAUL

9. The people who developed the English language were more interested in making distinctions between boats than they were in the differences between colors and feelings, not to speak of tastes and smells.

—WALTER KAUFMANN

10. Inside the tough-talking, hard-jogging man of 40 who is identified largely by his work, there is a boy trying not to cry, "Time is running out."

—GAIL SHEEHY

Exercise 3.19 Combine the following groups of sentences into complex, compound, or compound-complex sentences. You may have to add conjunctions or relative pronouns, and sometimes you may want to subtract some words. See how many combinations you can work out from each group.

gr
3D

1. A pitcher can throw a baseball more than ninety miles an hour. Batters may be severely injured if they are hit. Every batter must wear a helmet at the plate.
2. Ultralight planes now swoop down valleys and soar over mountains. They are hardly more than hang gliders with engines. The engines are small. The ultralights may fly at thirty to forty miles per hour.
3. Orson Welles terrified America with his radio presentation of *War of the Worlds* in 1938. Hitler was moving Europe toward war. Radio programs were regularly interrupted with news bulletins. Welles made the program sound like a news broadcast. He made people think that Earth was being invaded from Mars.
4. The Mississippi Delta has some of the richest farmland in the world. It grows more cotton than any comparable area on earth. It was not settled until after the Civil War. Mosquitoes gave people in the Delta yellow fever.
5. Almost a million accountants presently work in the United States. The profession is still growing. Positions will increase by 30 percent over the next ten years. This information has been reported by the Bureau of Labor Statistics.

4
Correcting Run-ons and Comma Splices

Run-on errors occur when two independent clauses run together. **Comma splices** occur when two independent clauses are linked by a comma. Appropriate punctuation and conjunctions can correct these common sentence errors.

In the example below, you can see both of these errors.

> Fuel emissions at Yosemite National Park can disrupt the delicate ecological balance, [A] authorities have acted firmly against pollution [B] they have banned the automobile in Yosemite Valley.

[(A) *Comma splice:* Only a comma marks the point of contact between two independent clauses here (see 3C). Commas alone are too weak to mark off independent clauses. (B) *Run-on sentence:* The end of one independent clause is not marked off by any punctuation.]

There are many ways to join or separate independent clauses.

4A Use a period or some other suitable end mark to set off independent clauses from one another.

A period at the end of an independent clause, followed by a capital letter, will give you two distinct sentences.

> Fuel emissions at Yosemite National Park can disrupt the delicate ecological balance. Authorities have acted firmly against pollution. They have banned the automobile in Yosemite Valley.

You may sometimes use a question mark or an exclamation point to separate the clauses.

Run-on Sentence

Are liberal arts graduates desirable employees in business many corporations report their strong interest in women and men with humanities backgrounds.

ro/cs
4A

Corrected

Are liberal arts graduates desirable employees in business? Many corporations report their strong interest in women and men with humanities backgrounds.

Comma Splice

I made it, I passed the bar exam, I can be a lawyer!

Corrected

I made it! I passed the bar exam! I can be a lawyer!

[A question mark corrects the run-on error after *business* in the first example; the exclamation point replaces the commas and corrects the comma splices in the second example.]

Exercise 4.1 The items below contain one or more run-on errors or comma splices. Correct them by creating complete sentences separated by appropriate end punctuation and, where necessary, appropriate capitalization.

1. Many states outlaw the sale of fireworks, every year they cause many children to lose their hands and eyes.
2. Despite the rise in fares, short ocean voyages continue to draw vacationers from all over America now "cruises to nowhere" have grown in popularity.
3. The art of welding is necessary to modern industry welding is an art that requires much care and patience.
4. How can noise ordinances protect urban dwellers against loud portable radios cradled like babies in the arms of strolling adolescents the police seem reluctant to arrest young offenders, since a loud radio is not a violent crime.
5. When my mother first started working, I had to make some sudden adjustments, I had to deal with an unexpected feeling of abandonment the first time I came home from grade school to an empty house and realized that Mom was not there to greet me and that everything seemed still and dead.
6. I stepped out onto the road with care, expecting a joke, and kicked the abandoned purse gently, it jingled.

ro/cs 4C

4B Use a comma to join two independent clauses only when it comes before a coordinating conjunction — *and, but, or, nor, for, yet,* or *so.*

A comma alone is not strong enough to mark off one independent clause from another (see 3D). Notice how conjunctions serve correctly in the following examples.

> Fuel emissions at Yosemite National Park can disrupt the delicate ecological balance, so authorities have acted firmly against pollution.

[The comma and the conjunction *so* coordinate the independent clauses, giving us a compound sentence.]

Comma Splice

> Cortez first introduced chocolate to Europe, the Spaniards later added sugar for sweetening.

[The comma after *Europe* incorrectly splices two independent clauses together.]

Corrected

> Cortez first introduced chocolate to Europe, and the Spaniards later added sugar for sweetening.

[The conjunction *and* added after the comma correctly joins two independent clauses in a compound sentence.]

Comma Splice

> Shakespeare's *Macbeth* is a morality play, it shows that some crimes are punished not only by society but also by the guilt criminals feel about their crimes.

Corrected

> Shakespeare's *Macbeth* is a morality play, for it shows that some crimes are punished not only by society but also by the guilt criminals feel about their crimes.

[The comma and the conjunction *for* correctly link the independent clauses.]

4C Use a semicolon between two independent clauses when those clauses are closely related in meaning, form, or both. (See 25A.)

When the ideas in two independent clauses are closely related, semicolons help stress the connection in meaning. The first word after a semicolon begins with a lowercase letter unless the word is a proper noun. When a conjunctive adverb such as *also, however,* or *therefore* or a transitional expression such as *for example* or *on the contrary* (see 4E) appears between two independent clauses, you can separate them both with a semicolon. Remember, however, that the period is a more usual mark of separation than a semicolon. When you use a period, you of course have two sentences; if you use the semicolon, you have one sentence.

ro/cs
4C

> Federal authorities in Yosemite National Park have acted firmly against pollution; they have banned the automobile in Yosemite Valley.

[By connecting the independent clauses, the semicolon stresses the point that the second clause is a consequence of the first.]

Comma Splice

> A good researcher may not know all the facts, however, she should know where to find them.

[The word *however* is not a coordinating conjunction, and the comma before or after it cannot set off the independent clauses.]

Corrected

> A good researcher may not know all the facts; however, she should know where to find them.

[The semicolon before *however* corrects the comma splice.]

Run-on Sentence

> Young children often watch television unsupervised as a result, they can see violence, fear, and danger in their own living rooms.

[The expression *as a result* cannot join the clauses sufficiently.]

Corrected

> Young children often watch television unsupervised; as a result, they can see violence, fear, and danger in their own living rooms.

[The semicolon joins the two clauses and helps emphasize the close relation between them that *as a result* suggests.]

In each example above, a period followed by a capitalized first letter would correct the run-on error or the comma splice by turning the two independent clauses into two distinct sentences.

Occasionally a writer will use both a semicolon and a conjunction to mark off independent clauses (see 25A).

> Nothing could be more racy, straightforward, and alive than the prose of Shakespeare; but it must be remembered that this was dialogue written to be spoken.
>
> —W. Somerset Maugham

[Both the semicolon and the coordinating conjunction *but* join the independent clauses appropriately; but instead of using the semicolon, the author could have used a comma before *but*.]

When independent clauses are short and closely related in structure and meaning, some writers occasionally join them with a comma to achieve a special effect.

> The sense fails in two ways. Sometimes it gives no information, sometimes it gives false information.
>
> —FRANCIS BACON

> You fly in with the goods, you fly out with the lucky.
>
> —JOHN LE CARRÉ

[The writers use commas to stress the close joining of the thoughts in the two independent clauses. A semicolon after *information* or after *goods* would have the same effect as the comma. A period, or a coordinating conjunction and a comma, would also connect the clauses correctly, but the writer would sacrifice the closeness of thought that the comma helps to establish.]

Exercise 4.2 Correct run-on errors and comma splices in the following sentences. Use either a coordinating conjunction and a comma or a semicolon, but be sure that your corrections yield logical sentences. Mark any correct sentences *C*.

1. The snow started falling at five o'clock then the wind began to blow hard from the north.
2. The best way to keep warm in icy weather is to wear layers of clothing moreover wool is much warmer than cotton.
3. She saw the cat spring through the air onto the bluebird she yelled.
4. Fewer jobs are open for teachers every year, yet many college students major in education to obtain teaching certificates.
5. The heavy black clouds meant rain, they came on swiftly with thunder and lightning.
6. Metro-Goldwyn-Mayer worked hard to make Tarzan's yell sound like that of a real animal, in the 1930s sound-effects specialists recorded and studied, among others, the cries of a hyena, the growls of a dog, and the wail of a mother camel whose young had been taken away.
7. The head on some old engines was nothing more than a cast-iron lid, cast iron was strong and heavy, just right to contain the explosions going on thousands of times a minute in the cylinders.
8. Cross-country skiing is cheaper than downhill skiing you can outfit two people with cross-country equipment for the price of outfitting one person with everything needed for downhill skiing.
9. Cramming for exams rarely helps, nevertheless many students stay up until dawn studying on the night before a big test.
10. Do not send cash or a check now simply phone in your order with a credit card number.

4D Use subordination occasionally to correct a sentence with independent clauses that are incorrectly joined with a comma splice or that are run together.

ro/cs 4D

Comma Splice

Fuel emissions at Yosemite National Park can disrupt the delicate ecological balance of the region, authorities there have acted firmly against automobiles.

Corrected by Subordination

Because fuel emissions at Yosemite National Park can disrupt the delicate ecological balance of the region, authorities there have acted firmly against automobiles.

[The subordinator *because* links the major thoughts in these clauses firmly by making the first clause dependent on the second.]

Run-on Sentence

Authorities have acted firmly against pollution_they have banned the automobile in Yosemite Valley.

Corrected by Subordination

Authorities who have banned the automobile in Yosemite Valley have acted firmly against pollution.

[Here the relative pronoun *who* (see 3B, section 3) subordinates the clause following it, making that clause an adjective modifying the noun *authorities.*]

Acting firmly against pollution, authorities have banned the automobile in Yosemite Valley.

[The writer has changed one of the clauses into a participial phrase, *acting firmly against pollution.* The phrase serves as an adjective modifying *authorities.*]

Exercise 4.3 Use an appropriate method of subordination to correct run-on errors and comma splices below. Mark any correct sentences *C.*

1. Learning to read lips is not easy young children can adapt to this preferred method of teaching language to the deaf more easily than older people can.
2. At Bourda Market in Georgetown, Guyana, daybreak stirs a rush of activity, vendors set up their wares for the 6:30 A.M. opening.
3. Play, which allows a child's free expression, helps early childhood education. However, children must keep some real control over the situation if play is to encourage real learning.
4. Different careers and different ambitions often separate childhood friends, they share only memories after a while and do not share any common experiences in the present.

5. The Super Bowl in January has now become an unofficial national holiday, people who hardly follow professional football during the regular season gather at parties before huge color television sets, eating and drinking and enjoying each other and sometimes watching the game.

Exercise 4.4 Correct the run-on errors and comma splices in Exercise 4.1 (page 142), this time by joining complete thoughts either through coordination (see 4B and 4C) or through subordination (see 4D).

4E Become alert to words, phrases, and punctuation that may cause run-on errors or comma splices.

Certain conjunctive adverbs (see 3B, section 4), transitional expressions (see 2B, section 5), or subject pronouns (see 3B, section 3) at the beginning of a sentence can mislead you into producing a run-on error or a comma splice. If you look for such words in your writing, you can proofread more carefully for comma splices and run-ons.

Conjunctive adverbs in this category include words such as *accordingly, also, anyway, as a result, besides, consequently, finally, furthermore, hence, however, incidentally, indeed, instead, likewise, meanwhile, moreover, nevertheless, nonetheless, now, otherwise, still, suddenly, then, therefore,* and *thus.*

Comma Splice

The price of gold varies greatly every year, nevertheless, speculators purchase precious metals in large quantities and hope always for a price rise.

[A comma before *nevertheless* incorrectly marks the boundary between the two independent clauses.]

Corrected

The price of gold varies greatly every year; nevertheless, speculators purchase precious metals in large quantities and hope always for a price rise.

[A semicolon correctly joins the two clauses before the conjunctive adverb (see 25B). A period and a capital letter would also separate the two clauses appropriately by converting them into two sentences.]

Run-on Sentence

Salt air corrodes metal easily_therefore, automobiles in coastal regions require frequent washing even in cold weather.

[*Therefore* neither links nor separates the clauses adequately.]

Corrected

Salt air corrodes metal easily. Therefore, automobiles in coastal regions require frequent washing even in cold weather.

[The period before *therefore* and the capital letter correct the run-on error and create two complete sentences. A comma and the conjunction *and,* or a semicolon alone, would work just as well here.]

ro/cs
4E

Some of the transitional expressions that may lead to comma splice or run-on errors are the following: *after all, after a while, as a result, at any rate, at the same time, for example, for instance, in addition, in fact, in other words, in particular, in the first place, on the contrary,* and *on the other hand.*

Comma Splice

Richard Rogers's music continues to delight audiences everywhere, in fact, revivals of *Oklahoma, Carousel,* and *The King and I* pack theaters every year.

[The transitional expression *in fact* made this writer believe that the two independent clauses are correctly joined. But *in fact* is not a coordinating conjunction, and a comma is not strong enough to help the expression connect the two clauses.]

Corrected

Richard Rogers's music continues to delight audiences everywhere. In fact, revivals of *Oklahoma, Carousel,* and *The King and I* pack theaters every year.

[A period after *everywhere* followed by a capital letter establishes the boundaries of the two sentences.]

Run-on Sentence

Americans continue their love affair with the automobile‸at the same time they are more successful than ever before in restricting its use.

[The transitional phrase *at the same time* does not serve to bind the two independent clauses together grammatically.]

Corrected

Americans continue their love affair with the automobile, but at the same time they are more successful than ever before in restricting its use.

[The coordinator *but* joins the two clauses correctly.]

The subject pronouns that may lead to comma splices and run-on sentences are the following: *I, you, he, she, it, we, they,* and *who.*

Comma Splice

Disneyland is fun for everyone, I think I enjoyed it as much as my ten-year-old niece did.

[The comma does not adequately set off the two independent clauses.]

Corrected

Disneyland is fun for everyone; I think I enjoyed it as much as my ten-year-old niece did.

[The semicolon coordinates the two independent clauses correctly. A period placed where the semicolon is would make two complete sentences.]

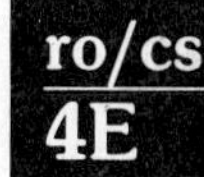

Run-on Sentence

The weather disappointed Vermont vacationers_they wanted snow in January, not warm, sunny skies.

[The subject pronoun *they,* despite its close connection to the noun *vacationers,* its antecedent in the previous clause, cannot join the two clauses grammatically.]

Corrected

The weather disappointed Vermont vacationers because they wanted snow in January, not warm, sunny skies.

[The addition of the word *because* connects the two clauses by subordinating the second one.]

In divided quotations or in consecutive sentences within a quotation, be sure to punctuate complete sentences correctly.

In a dialogue, commas are not sufficient to set off independent clauses.

Comma Splice

"Speak up, amigo," Juanita said, "I can't hear you."

[Commas frequently precede quotations (see 24J), but in constructions like this one, we have two distinct sentences, and the punctuation should show that fact. One sentence ends after *said;* another begins with the word *I.*]

Corrected

"Speak up, amigo," Juanita said. "I can't hear you."

[The period separates the two sentences correctly.]

Run-on Sentence

Finally he shrugged and said, "You don't love me_you never have loved me!"

[Although only one person speaks the words within the quotation marks, the sentence boundaries must be properly marked.]

Corrected

Finally he shrugged and said, "You don't love me! You never have loved me!"

[An exclamation point keeps the independent clauses apart and stresses the emotion of the speaker. You could use a period or a semicolon instead of the exclamation point; the semicolon would not be followed by a capital letter.]

ro/cs 4F

Exercise 4.5 Use the word in brackets correctly in the sentence that follows. Correct the punctuation and capitalization where necessary.

1. [they] The use of copying machines has replaced note-taking for many students ________ simply photograph text pages instead of taking notes on their readings.
2. [however] His car skidded and struck the telephone pole ________, he was not hurt.
3. [however] He said ________ that the car would never run again.
4. [it] The dulcimer has a soft, sweet tone ________ was long ago replaced by the guitar in bluegrass music.
5. [I] "Not I," she replied with a scowl "________ never liked him."
6. [on the contrary] He expected his lawyer to plead his case vigorously to the jury ________, she said only, "I think this man ought to be put away for life."

4F Examine drafts of your papers carefully for run-on errors and comma splices.

If you have trouble with run-on errors and comma splices, spend extra time trying to locate and correct them in your papers. If you read over your drafts with an eye to avoiding these errors, you can locate them before you produce a final draft.

1 Read your papers aloud slowly.

When you read aloud slowly, your ear probably will pick out the independent clauses. They will sound like complete sentences, and you are likely to pause for breath at the end of each one. When your voice clearly stops and drops, look for a period or a semicolon at that point.

2 Before you write your final draft, count your sentences.

Number your sentences all the way through the draft of your paper. Then see if you have separated them properly with the right punctuation and capitalization. Too few sentences on several pages of a draft may signal run-on errors.

3 Read your papers backward from the last sentence to the first.

When you use this technique, you can consider each sentence as a separate unit of meaning apart from the surrounding sentences. Each sentence appears as a complete statement on its own, and implied connections, such as those made through transitional phrases, adverbs, and pronouns, cannot trap you into making errors. You must read very carefully, being sure that each group of words you read aloud forms a complete sentence or a complete independent clause.

4 Watch for the words and phrases that often cause run-on errors or comma splices at sentence junctures. (See 4E.)

Subject pronouns, transitional expressions, and conjunctive adverbs frequently appear at sentence junctures. Words and phrases in these groups can trap you into writing run-on errors and comma splices, and by looking especially for those words and phrases when you read over your drafts, you can often locate and correct your mistakes.

Checklist: How to Correct Run-on Errors and Comma Splices

1. Use a period, a question mark, or an exclamation point.
2. Use *and, but, or, nor, for, yet,* or *so,* preceded by a comma.
3. Use a semicolon to coordinate closely related ideas in consecutive independent clauses.
4. Use subordination to relate some ideas that might otherwise be expressed in independent clauses.

Exercise 4.6 In each item below, underline the sentence element that gave rise to the run-on error or the comma splice. Correct the errors by using any of the methods explained in this chapter.

1. The deputy mayor enjoys speaking to civic groups, for example, she addressed the Kiwanis Club, the Young Republican Club, and the Daughters of the American Revolution all on one Sunday last month.
2. A hush fell over the crowd then a small man with an empty sleeve on his coat and a hideously scarred face got out of his seat and hobbled to the platform.
3. Public transportation is quick and safe on the other hand it does not offer the flexibility and privacy of travel by car.
4. Sidesaddles allowed women to ride horseback modestly in an age of long, thick skirts, however, such saddles were extremely dangerous because they did not allow women to grip the horse with their legs.
5. A two-cycle gasoline engine is excellent for lawn mowers and for boats using an outboard motor it is not good for larger machines because its lubrication is uneven at the higher temperatures larger machines generate.
6. "Many parents feel guilty about putting their young children in day-care centers," Mr. Carmichael said, "the children themselves usually seem to enjoy the experience."

Exercise 4.7 Correct the run-on errors and comma splices in the following passage. Do not change any correct sentences. Study the checklist on page 151.

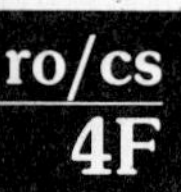

(1) During my early childhood, there were two rules I hated in our house, mother enforced them too rigidly. **(2)** The first was the rule against talking in the bedroom after she turned the lights out, I can vividly remember whispering in the dark to my sister Lisa as we exchanged secrets before going to sleep in our bedroom. **(3)** I had always thought that nighttime was ideal for chatting and giggling, consequently, I went over everything I had done during the day, we planned things to do tomorrow. **(4)** "Do I hear talking in there?" my mother would shout, "I'd better not!" **(5)** We would laugh our pillows only partly muffled our giggling. **(6)** We stayed quiet for a while then, minutes later, the talking resumed. **(7)** Why mother insisted on enforcing this rule remains a mystery the second annoying rule I hated was that we were not supposed to eat in the living room. **(8)** I remember watching television one evening I was sprawled out on the sofa with my eyes glued to the tube after a while I heard mother's voice. **(9)** "Dinner's ready," she called, "everyone to the table." **(10)** While I hurriedly filled my plate, the telephone rang, and Mom turned to answer it, then I sneaked out of the kitchen and back to the living room and the television set, "Linda," I heard, "I've told you not to eat in the living room." **(11)** The next thing I knew Mom came walking into the living room with the pruning shears she used on her roses in the garden, unplugged the electric cord on the TV, and cut off the plug with her shears, consequently nobody watched television until we got a new cord for our set. **(12)** By that time everybody had color TV however I never did find out if Gilligan and all the others escaped from Gilligan's Island, somebody said they did.

5
Correcting Sentence Fragments

End marks—periods, question marks, or exclamation points—separate grammatical units that are complete sentences. To be complete grammatically, a sentence needs both a subject and a predicate. A grammatically incomplete unit starting with a capital letter and closing with an end mark is called a **sentence fragment.**

In the following sentence fragments, the writer incorrectly makes an incomplete word group look like a sentence by using a capital letter for the first word and by placing a period after the last.

Through lively interviews and dramatic scenes.

And tried the hot tamales.

Watching ducks on the lake.

If they have empty home lives.

Who by that time had begun to get over their guilt feelings about Vietnam.

You can easily spot sentence fragments when they appear in isolation as these fragments do. But when a fragment is buried in surrounding sentences, you may have trouble seeing it and correcting it.

(A) Television brings current events to life. **(B)** *Through lively interviews and dramatic scenes.* **(C)** Newscasts flood our homes with interesting people and far-off places.

[As a prepositional phrase (see 3C, section 1), the fragment—(B)—contains neither a subject nor a predicate. The writer assumed that the subject and verb in (A), *television brings,* or in (C), *newscasts flood,* could serve (B) as well. Standing alone as it does, however, (B) is a fragment.]

(A) We visited a new Mexican restaurant downtown. **(B)** *And tried the hot tamales.* **(C)** They burned my mouth for a week.

[The fragment—(B)—is the second part of a compound predicate begun in (A). (See 3A.) The writer is trying to say we *visited* and *tried.* Without its own subject, though, (B) is a fragment.]

(A) On Sundays in May at Marjorie Post Park everyone relaxes. **(B)** *Watching ducks on the lake.* **(C)** Men and women sit everywhere beneath the flowering dogwoods and chat idly in the afternoon sun.

frag

[Although the *participial phrase*—(B)—contains a word that looks like a verb, the present participle *watching* cannot serve as a complete verb without the aid of an auxiliary, or helping, verb (see 3B, section 1, and 7A). In addition, (B) has no subject, although the writer probably believed the subject in (A), *everyone,* or the subject in (C), *men and women,* would serve. But because it contains neither its own subject nor its own predicate, (B) is a fragment.]

(A) Unhappy teenagers can become runaways. **(B)** *If they have empty home lives.* **(C)** Escape at any cost may be attractive, even if it means being broke and alone.

[Fragment (B) has a subject and a predicate, but the subordinator *if* at the beginning makes the clause dependent on another clause, which is not present in the group of words here begun by a capital letter and ended by a period. Dependent clause (B) could be attached to the sentence before it—(A)—or to the sentence after it—(C). But as it stands, (B) is a fragment—perhaps because the writer had some trouble deciding whether to tack it on at the end of the previous sentence or to put it at the beginning of the next sentence.]

(A) The capture of the American embassy in Iran by fanatical "students" angered Americans. **(B)** *Who by that time had begun to get over their guilt feelings about Vietnam.* **(C)** And the taking of American hostages created a new surge of patriotism across the United States.

[Unit (B) is a *relative clause,* which must be embedded in a complete sentence. The writer intends the relative clause to modify the noun *Americans* in (A). But to take part in a grammatically complete sentence, a relative clause must be attached to an independent clause that it modifies.]

Exercise 5.1 Identify the fragments and the complete sentences below. Explain your choices.

1. Without any funds from the federal government or from foundations.
2. Who found the lost keys.
3. Supported by heavy steel cables.
4. Driving through the California desert with the temperature at 114 degrees.
5. Johnny Cash sings many songs about prisons and prisoners, their loneliness and their hardships.

6. Since she spoke to the child's mother.
7. That woman holds two jobs.
8. Country music wailing with pain and loss.
9. A woman who holds two jobs.
10. Country music wails with pain and loss.
11. To learn a foreign language.
12. She wanted to learn a foreign language.
13. Because he cried and played the guitar woefully.
14. Fans at the Grand Ole Opry disliked him because he cried and played the guitar woefully and dressed in a tuxedo for his appearances.

Exercise 5.2 Identify the complete sentences and the fragment or fragments in each selection below, and explain your choices.

1. Alcohol can damage heart muscle tissue in a condition called *alcoholic cardiomyopathy.* Which can be fatal. Especially to people who cannot leave alcohol alone.
2. The United States Constitution gives three basic duties to Congress. Enacting laws, representing the people, and limiting the power of the executive branch.
3. Videodiscs and tapes have increased in popularity. As a result of this exciting new technology. Many more people can buy or rent their favorite movies. Seeing them without commercial interruptions on their own TV sets at home.
4. Human beings develop intellectually in leaps from one stage to another say some important theorists in psychology. Such as Erik Erikson and Jean Piaget.
5. Working for the government sometimes requires great personal sacrifice, but the rewards of public service are great. By hard work and careful attention to detail, a government worker can do much good for the society at large.

5A Correct sentence fragments by making them into complete sentences.

No handbook can give a complete set of rules for converting sentence fragments into sentences, but the following examples show some typical problems and some ways to remedy them.

frag
5A

1 Join the fragment to the sentence that comes before it.

Fragment

Television brings current events to life. Through lively interviews and dramatic scenes.

Corrected

Television brings current events to life through lively interviews and dramatic scenes.

[The prepositional phrase *through lively interviews and dramatic scenes* completes the meaning of the independent clause; the independent clause and the prepositional phrase can be easily joined in a complete sentence.]

Fragment

(A) Jean Rhys's *Good Morning, Midnight* is a novel about Sasha Jansen. **(B)** A lonely woman in Paris. **(C)** She searches desperately for escape from a dismal past.

[As an appositive (see 3B, section 2), the fragment—(B)—depends for its meaning on sentence (A) or (C). However, lacking a subject, a verb, and a clear meaning on its own, (B) as it stands is incomplete.]

Corrected

Jean Rhys's *Good Morning, Midnight* is a novel about Sasha Jansen, a lonely woman in Paris.

[The appositive is joined to the previous independent clause by a comma.]

Fragment

We visited a Mexican restaurant downtown. And tried the hot tamales.

Corrected

We visited a Mexican restaurant downtown and tried the hot tamales.

[The verbs *visited* and *tried* make a compound predicate for the subject *We.* The fragment *and tried the hot tamales* is easily joined to the sentence before it.]

Fragment

On Sundays in May at Marjorie Post Park everyone can relax. Watching ducks on the lake.

Corrected

On Sundays in May at Marjorie Post Park everyone can relax, watching ducks on the lake.

[The participial phrase *watching ducks on the lake* can be attached to the previous sentence; the phrase becomes a free modifier (see 3C, section 1).]

Fragment

Unhappy teenagers can become runaways. If they have empty home lives.

Corrected

Unhappy teenagers can become runaways if they have empty home lives.

[The subordinate clause *if they have empty homes lives* cannot stand by itself, but it can be joined to the independent clause preceding it.]

frag 5A

Fragment

The song "John Henry" tells the story of a man trying to save his job against a machine. An effort that killed him.

Corrected

The song "John Henry" tells the story of a man trying to save his job against a machine—an effort that killed him.

[The dash joins the fragment to the previous sentence, and the fragment becomes an appositive. The dash adds emphasis to the appositive.]

2 Correct a fragment by adding it to the beginning of the sentence that follows the fragment.

Fragment

Watching ducks glide across the lake. Men and women sit everywhere beneath the flowering dogwoods and talk softly under the afternoon sun.

Corrected

Watching ducks glide across the lake, men and women sit everywhere beneath the flowering dogwoods and talk softly under the afternoon sun.

[The fragment *watching ducks glide across the lake* is joined to the sentence after it and becomes a participial phrase modifying the subject *men and women.*]

Fragment

If they have empty home lives. Escape at any cost may be attractive to some teenagers, even if it means being broke and alone.

Corrected

If they have empty home lives, escape at any cost may be attractive to some teenagers, even if it means being broke and alone.

[The fragment *if they have empty home lives* becomes, in the corrected version, an adverbial clause opening the sentence and modifying the verb phrase *may be.*]

Fragment

(A) William L. Shirer wanted to travel the country beyond Iowa. **(B)** To see firsthand the people in the rest of Middle America. **(C)** He joined a tent crew for a road company of speakers, artists, and musicians.

[Although the subject and predicate in (A), *William L. Shirer wanted,* or in (C), *he joined,* may seem logically to serve in (B) to make it stand as a complete sentence, the fragment demands its own subject and predicate. The verbal unit in (B) is an *infinitive phrase* (see 3C, section 1).]

frag 5A

Corrected

William L. Shirer wanted to travel the country beyond Iowa. To see firsthand the people in the rest of Middle America, he joined a tent crew for a road company of speakers, artists, and musicians.

[The infinitive phrase now opens the sentence that comes after it.]

Fragment

(A) My mother and I sound alike. **(B)** Whenever I answer the telephone. **(C)** Her friends mistake me for her.

[As a subordinate clause, the fragment, (B), despite its close relation in meaning to neighboring sentences, cannot stand as a grammatically complete unit. The fragment does contain a subject and a verb, but the subordinator *whenever* makes a connection to an independent clause necessary (see 3C, section 2).]

Corrected

My mother and I sound alike. Whenever I answer the telephone, her friends mistake me for her.

[The subordinate clause now opens the second sentence.]

Your intended meaning determines whether you connect a fragment to the sentence before or to the sentence after. Sometimes neither one of these options will produce a sentence that makes sense and pleases stylistically.

3 Correct a fragment by adding or removing words to convert it into a complete sentence or by changing the wording of the fragment itself.

Fragment

On Sundays in May at Marjorie Post Park everyone can relax. Watching ducks on the lake.

Corrected

On Sundays in May at Marjorie Post Park everyone can relax. *Children enjoy* watching ducks on the lake.

[*Children,* a subject, and *enjoy,* a verb, have been added to the fragment to make a complete sentence and to change the emphasis somewhat.]

OR

On Sundays in May at Marjorie Post Park everyone can relax. *Children watch* ducks on the lake.

[Now the participle *watching* has been changed to a simple verb, *watch,* in the present tense, and a subject, *children,* has been added.]

Fragment

Old Mr. Warren is outdoors this afternoon. *Working in his rose garden.*

Corrected by Adding Words

Old Mr. Warren is outdoors this afternoon. Unlike all the young people who have fled to the beach, he is working in his rose garden.

Fragment

He wrote to his mother every day. *Which no one could understand.*

Corrected by Adding Words

He wrote to his mother every day. This was a devotion which no one could understand.

Fragment

Although she worked at a tiresome job driving a cab all day long, she studied long hours at night. *Because she wanted with all her heart to become an architect.*

Corrected by Eliminating a Word

Although she worked at a tiresome job driving a cab all day long, she studied long hours at night. She wanted with all her heart to become an architect.

Exercise 5.3 Return to Exercise 5.1 on pages 154–155. Correct each fragment by using any one of the techniques explained in 5A. That is, create a complete sentence by adding a subject, a verb, or both; by changing participles or infinitives into verbs; or by removing subordinators and making whatever other changes sentence logic requires. Be sure that your new sentences make sense.

Exercise 5.4 Find the fourteen fragments in the following selection. Correct each one by adding it to an adjacent sentence, by adding words to it, or by removing words from it. Be sure that each sentence has a subject and a predicate.

We knew him as heavyweight boxing champion of the world. A joking, mocking, happy showman. He wrote poems about his foes. Bad poems. But they made people laugh. Pay attention. He bragged on himself in a sport. Where the athletes supposed to be humble. Not telling the world how good they are. But he was good. Maybe the best fighter in boxing history. Now he no longer heavyweight champion. He writes no more poems. On television speaks slowly. Hesitates. Looks puzzled and hurt. Fighting kills the brain of people who take too many blows to the head. He not now what he used to be. No one cheers for him anymore. His glory gone with the wind. People who made money off him gone too. They took all he gave them. And went away.

Exercise 5.5 Find the thirteen fragments in the following selection. Correct each one by adding it to an adjacent sentence, by adding words to it, or by removing words from it.

Looking weak and red above the housetops to the southwest. The sun seemed to sink wearily toward the horizon at the end of a January day. The red liquid in the thermometer just outside my window standing at zero degrees. Snow piled deep in the street. The world looking shut up and very still. There was not a cloud in the sky. As the sun sank out of sight. The color of the sky turned slowly dark. Looking like a dome of ice. The world was a giant igloo. Remembering summer. We thought we were remembering dreams. Because it seemed impossible that we had ever walked in these streets with our bare feet. Or in our shirtsleeves without layers and layers of warm clothing. That we had sat in Fenway Park in the open air at night, sipping cold drinks and watching the Red Sox play baseball. Summer a myth. A lost world. It seemed something that never was. Something that would never come again.

5B Learn to recognize the words and phrases at sentence beginnings that can trap writers into producing fragments.

When you use present and past participles, infinitives, or certain adverbs, connectives, and subordinators as sentence openers, you may trap yourself into producing an incomplete sentence. If you check carefully when you proofread for words in these groups at the beginnings of your sentences, you may spot unwanted fragments.

Present participles are verb forms ending in *-ing,* such as *singing, running, speaking, trying, shouting, working,* and *flying* (see 3C, section 1, and 7A).

Fragment

Running wildly in the hills. The stallion looked untamed and beautiful and somehow ghostly.

Corrected

Running wildly in the hills, the stallion looked untamed and beautiful and somehow ghostly.

[The sentence opening, a participial phrase, is joined to a complete sentence and modifies the subject, *stallion.*]

Past participles are verb forms ending in *-ed, t, d,* or *-n,* such as *dressed, faded, hurt,* and *driven* (see 3C, section 1, and 7A).

Fragment

The toast popped up. *Burned black as coal.* It looked like a piece of volcanic rock.

Corrected

The toast popped up, burned black as coal.

[The participial phrase *burned black as coal* is a fragment that in the corrected version becomes a modifier describing the subject, *toast.*]

Corrected

The toast popped up. Burned black as coal, it looked like a piece of volcanic rock.

[In this version, the fragment has been added on to the beginning of the next sentence so that it becomes a modifier describing the pronoun *it.*]

Corrected

The toast popped up. It was burned black as coal.

[In this version, the subject *it* and the helping verb *was* have been added to the beginning of the fragment to convert it into a complete sentence.]

Infinitives are verb forms introduced by the word *to,* which is called the **infinitive marker** (see 3C, section 1). Infinitives include such forms as *to play, to scream, to study,* and *to eat.* Like participles and participial phrases, they express action vividly and sometimes seem so strong that writers may think them capable of standing alone as sentences.

Fragment

The mayor spoke forcefully. *To convince her audience of the need for tax reform.*

Corrected

The mayor spoke forcefully to convince her audience of the need for tax reform.

[The infinitive phrase contains the purpose of the mayor's speech. But it must be joined grammatically to the preceding sentence if it is to be a part of a complete statement.]

Corrected

The mayor spoke forcefully. She worked hard to convince her audience of the need for tax reform.

frag 5B

[Here words including a subject, *she,* and a verb, *worked,* are added to the beginning of the fragment to convert it into a complete sentence.]

Adverbs, subordinators, and connecting words and phrases that often begin fragments include *also, as well as, especially, for example, for instance, just, like, mainly,* and *such as.* In speaking we often use fragments along with adverbs and connecting words, but when we write, we must be sure that adverbs and connecting words or phrases lead into complete sentences. Otherwise our readers will be confused.

Fragment

An individual spectrum exists for each element. *For example, hydrogen.* It has a red, a blue-green, and a green line.

Corrected

An individual spectrum exists for each element. For example, hydrogen has a red, a blue-green, and a green line.

[In the corrected version, the fragment joins the independent clause that follows it. The word *hydrogen* replaces the original subject, *It*, which is deleted.]

Fragment

Vegetarians should supplement their diets with high-protein foods. *Like wheat germ and bean curd.*

Corrected

Vegetarians should supplement their diets with high-protein foods like wheat germ and bean curd.

[The fragment joins the complete sentence that precedes it.]

Subordinators that may lead writers into making sentence fragments include subordinating conjunctions, such as *as long as, after, although, as, as if, as soon as, because, before, wherever, once, while, how, provided, if, since, so that, though, unless, until, when, where,* and *whether,* and relative pronouns, such as *what, which, who, whoever, whose, whom, whomever, whatever,* and *that* (see 3B, sections 3 and 5).

Fragment

The University Government Association gives students a voice in making policy. *Because they too should influence the university administration in matters of academic, social, and cultural welfare.*

Corrected

The University Government Association gives students a voice in making policy because they too should influence the university administration in matters of academic, social, and cultural welfare.

[In the corrected version, the subordinate clause is added to the end of the complete sentence in the first version.]

Fragment

In Astoria in the late 1800s, an important community figure was August Frederick Geipel. *Whose saloon on Newton Road was a social center for German families in Queens.*

Corrected

In Astoria in the late 1800s, an important community figure was August Frederick Geipel, whose saloon on Newton Road was a social center for German families in Queens.

[In the corrected version, the relative clause introduced by *whose* is joined to the independent clause to make a complex sentence (see 3D, section 3).]

Fragment

Every winter morning he exercised by jogging behind his two pet hounds. *That ran ahead of him, barking and panting, and looking almost terrifying.*

Corrected

Every winter morning he exercised by jogging behind his two pet hounds that ran ahead of him, barking and panting, and looking almost terrifying.

[The word *that,* normally a demonstrative pronoun (see 3B, section 3), may serve as the subject of its own independent clause: "*That* was exactly what she wanted." In the fragment above, however, *that* is a relative pronoun. The clause it introduces is an adjective modifying *hounds.* As you see in the corrected version, the relative clause is now connected grammatically to an independent clause.]

Participles, infinitives, connectives, and *subordinators* make strong sentence openers, but you must give those words special attention at sentence beginnings to avoid fragments.

5C Examine drafts carefully for sentence fragments.

Check papers for incomplete sentences by following these suggestions:

frag
5C

1 Read your sentences aloud, or get a friend to read them aloud to you.

Distinguish between the pause that a speaker may make for emphasis and the grammatical pause marked off by a period, a question mark, an exclamation point, or a semicolon.

2 Read your paper backward, from the last sentence to the first, or have a friend read the paper aloud in that way to you.

You may then judge the completeness of each sentence unit apart from the context. Stop after you read each sentence and ask, Is it complete? Does it make a complete statement or ask a complete question?

3 Check for subjects and predicates.

Every complete sentence must have at least one subject and one predicate (see 3A).

4 Look with particular care at sentences that begin with present and past participles, connective words and phrases, and subordinators. (See 5B.)

Checklist: How to Correct a Sentence Fragment

According to sentence logic and to your own stylistic tastes, take one of these steps:

1. Connect the fragment to the sentence *before* or *after*, making the choice that makes more sense.
2. Add a new subject, a new verb, or both, and add any other words that will help you make the fragment into a complete sentence.
3. Remove any words that keep the fragment from being a complete sentence.
4. Make a present or past participle into a verb by adding a helping verb such as *am, is, are, was,* or *were* before the participle or by changing the participle into a correct verb form.
5. When necessary, add a subject to the fragment to convert it into a complete sentence.

Fragment

Running away
[present participle]

Corrected

She is *running* away.

OR

She *runs* away.

Fragment

Flown above the city.
[past participle]

Corrected

The tiny aircraft *has flown* above the city.

OR

The tiny aircraft *flew* above the city.

6. Change an infinitive to a verb by removing *to* and by using the correct form of the verb. Or you can sometimes use *like, likes, want, wants, plan, plans, try, tries, am, is,* or *are* before the infinitive. Sometimes you will have to add a subject to fragments using an infinitive.

Fragment

To watch the sun rise over San Francisco Bay.

Corrected

He *watches* the sun rise over San Francisco Bay.

OR

He likes to watch the sun rise over San Francisco Bay.

OR

We are to watch the sun rise over San Francisco Bay.

7. Make any necessary changes in the wording of the fragment to convert it into a complete sentence.

5D Recognize acceptable uses of sentence fragments.

Although most formal writing requires complete sentences, sentence fragments occasionally can achieve some special effects. Writers of fiction regularly use fragments to record dialogue, since when we speak, we often use incomplete sentences. However, the context always makes the meaning of the fragment clear.

frag 5D

Jean leaned back, her hands clasped round a knee, looking at the water below them. "I came to a decision last night, Dan." It was unexpected, and he glanced at her. *"Yes?"* She shrugged. *"Nothing momentous.* But I think I'll definitely try for a teacher training course when I get home. *If I can find a place."*

—JOHN FOWLES

I had a sudden mad impulse to pack my bags and get away from both of them. Maybe it wasn't a question of choosing between them but just of escaping both entirely. *Released in my own custody. Stop this nonsense of running from one man to the next. Stand on my own two feet for once.*

—ERICA JONG

Fragments may appear in nonfiction, especially when the writer is striving for an informal, conversational effect.

But such was Autry's impact that even the action-all-the-way Cowboys had to have somebody in their films who could sing a few cowboy songs while the hero stood around listening and tapping his foot. Charles Starrett was good enough not to need any yodelers slowing up his action. But you couldn't buck the fashion. Anyway, Dick Weston did not exactly stop the show. *And never would if he went on calling himself Dick Weston.* The name was definitely not a bell ringer. *No matter how many times you said it.* It would never do for the Cowboy-Hero being groomed to challenge Gene Autry. It made him sound like a newsboy. It was too blah. They decided to call him Roy Rogers at Republic. *And gave him his own horse to sing to.*

—JAMES HORWITZ

Questions and exclamations often have impact when written as fragments. To call attention to an idea, writers can use fragments effectively.

American culture? Wealth is visible, and so, now, is poverty. Both have become intimidating clichés. *But the rest?*

—PETER SCHRAG

The broadcaster is casually describing a routine landing of the giant gas bag. Suddenly he sees something. *A flash of flame!* An instant later the whole thing explodes.

—JOHN HOUSEMAN

Whatever economic sanctions can achieve will be duly tested. A semblance of Western resolve has been temporarily achieved. *At a considerable price.*

—*The New York Times*

Although they can be acceptable, as these examples show, fragments are still rare in the expository writing you will do in college. Use them carefully, and do not use them often. In writing for your courses, when you write a fragment, you may even want to mark it as such with an asterisk and a note at the bottom of the page. This will assure your teacher that you have made a deliberate choice and not an accidental mistake.

Exercise 5.6 In each selection, correct each fragment by adding it to the sentence that comes before or after or by changing it into an independent sentence. Write *C* by the number of any selection that is correct as it stands.

1. In 1980, the Supreme Court ruled that scientists could patent bacteria made in laboratories. An important decision that has made profitable genetic engineering possible.
2. In and around Boston, the sixty-eight institutions of higher learning draw both full-time and part-time students, numbering more than 150,000. Of these over 60 percent come from states other than Massachusetts.
3. When I approached him after school for extra help with my algebra. He replied that he had already given me enough time. That I should try to find a tutor. Who could explain things slowly and carefully.
4. Although styles change quickly, the jeans phenomenon looks as if it is here to stay. Worn all over the world, jeans are especially popular with teenagers. But adults wear them, too, sometimes with jackets and neckties.
5. Abigail Adams championed women's rights. Writing about new legislation to her husband John early in the history of the United States. She said, "I desire you would remember the ladies and be more generous and favorable to them than your ancestors." A strong remark, considering the times.
6. Some garden pests may be controlled by means other than chemicals. To keep cutworms from destroying broccoli and cauliflower. A twelve-inch cardboard collar around each plant helps prevent damage.

Exercise 5.7 Return to Exercise 5.2 on page 155. Correct each fragment. Do not change correct sentences.

Exercise 5.8 Using these fragments, construct complete sentences. You may add anything you want to make the sentences complete.

1. Breaking away from the pack.
2. The coiled snake under my bed.
3. A woman of enormous strength and speed.
4. When I had discovered myself walking in my sleep.
5. If he should die before Saturday.
6. Ruined nevertheless.
7. For example, the personal computer and the typewriter.

frag
5D

Exercise 5.9 Identify the fragments in the following passages. Then explain why you think each writer used a fragment instead of a complete sentence. If you wanted to avoid the fragment, what would you do?

1. Mr. Fitzgerald and his wife, Kathy Fitzgerald, realized that if their hopes for filming the script were to be realized, they would need more help. Which they got in the form of Tom Shaw, a well known production manager and old friend of John Huston, who left a big-budget Barbra Streisand picture to take charge of *Wise Blood.*

   —LINDA CHARLTON

2. But how many women can name marriage itself as a source of our turbulence? More often than not, we were the ones who most wanted to get married. Besides, if not marriage, what *do* we want? Divorce? That is too fearsome.

   —NANCY FRIDAY

3. Milan is quite an attractive little city. A nice cathedral, *The Last Supper,* a very glamorous train station built by Mussolini, La Scala, and many other enjoyable sights.

   —FRAN LEBOWITZ

4. There have been three views about the purpose of art. First that it aims simply at imitation; second that it should influence human conduct; and third that it should produce a kind of exalted happiness.

   —KENNETH CLARK

5. Style is not the man, yet its presence or absence is part of the man. *Which part?* Not so easily pinned down, to take a trope from tailoring, yet the clothes a man chooses or disdains, are important facets of him.

   —JOSEPH EPSTEIN (ARISTIDES)

6
Subject and Verb Agreement

When a verb is singular, its subject must be singular; when a verb is plural, its subject must be plural. When a subject is in the first, second, or third person, the verb must match it (see 3B, section 1). This matching in number and person of subjects and verbs is called **agreement.**

In the present tense, the presence of the —*s* suffix at the end of a subject or verb usually indicates a plural subject or a singular verb.

Our dog sleeps in the basement.
[Third person singular subject, *dog;* third person singular verb, *sleeps*]

Our dogs sleep in the basement.
[Third person plural subject, *dogs;* third person plural verb, *sleep*]

The suffix —*s* (or —*es*) on a noun subject generally means that the subject is plural. The absence of the suffix —*s* (or —*es*) on a noun subject generally means that the subject is singular.

The suffix —*s* (or —*es*) on a present-tense verb usually tells you that the verb is singular. The absence of the suffix —*s* (or —*es*) on a verb usually tells you that the verb is plural.

Singular noun subjects, which usually *do not* end in —*s*, accompany singular verbs, which usually *do* end in —*s*.

Agreement: Singular Noun Subject; Singular Verb, Third Person, Present Tense

Our dog sleeps.

Singular subject; no -*s* ending

Singular verb; -*s* ending

An *orchid* costs too much.

The *house* needs paint.

The *day* goes by quickly.

[The absence of the suffix —*s* (or —*es*) after *orchid, house,* and *day* shows that all these noun subjects are singular. The suffix —*s* on *costs* and *needs* and the suffix —*es* on *goes* show that all these verbs in the third person are singular.]

agr 6A

Plural noun subjects, which usually *do* end in —*s* (or —*es*), accompany plural verbs, which usually *do not* end in —*s*.

Agreement: Plural Noun Subject; Plural Verb, Third Person, Present Tense

Dogs sleep.

Plural subject; -*s* ending

Plural verb; no -*s* ending

Orchids *cost* too much.

The houses *need* paint.

The days *go* quickly.

[The —*s* suffix on *orchids, houses,* and *days* shows that these subjects are all plural. The absence of the —*s* (or —*es*) suffix on the verbs shows that they are all plural.]

6A Use singular verbs with singular noun subjects that end in —s.

The letter —*s* at the end of a word is not always a suffix denoting the plural form. Some singular nouns end in —*s*, and they, too, must match singular verb forms.

Glass	breaks.
[Singular subject ending in —*s*]	[Singular verb ending in —*s*]

Moss grows.

Fungus spreads.

6B Use plural verbs with plural noun subjects that do not end in –*s*.

Some nouns do not use the suffix –*s* for the plural form (see 29C, section 7). But no matter what the form is, a plural subject requires a plural verb.

Children [Plural subject without an –*s* ending]	giggle. [Plural verb]
Men	guffaw.
Alumni	contribute.

6C Use singular verbs for the singular pronoun subjects *he, she,* and *it*.

The third person singular pronouns *he, she,* and *it,* like the nouns they replace, require singular verbs.

She [Singular pronoun in the third person]	raises [Singular verb ending in –*s*]	tomatoes.

He keeps the cat away.

It eats all the seedlings.

6D The pronouns *I* and *you* always take present tense forms that look plural, except for forms of *to be*.

Even though the pronoun *I* is singular, it always takes the present tense without a singular –*s* ending.

I *applaud.*

I *dream.*

I *write.*

I *cry.*

The pronoun *you* functions both as a singular and a plural. Only the verb form without the singular –*s* works correctly with *you,* whether *you* is singular or plural.

agr 6E

You *live.*

You *laugh.*

You *love.*

[In each case, *you* may refer to just one person or to several people. However, the verb form remains the same for singular or plural, and this verb form is without the suffix –*s*.]

I *am.*

You *are.*

She *is.*

[The words in italics are all forms of the verb *to be.*]

6E Use plural verbs for plural pronoun subjects.

They	applaud.
[Plural pronoun]	[Plural verb; no –*s* ending]

They leap to their feet.

They shout "Bravo!"

We sneer at their bad taste.

Exercise 6.1 In the sentences below, subjects are underlined once, and verbs are underlined twice. If subjects and verbs are singular, make them plural; if they are plural, make them singular. You may need to change other words as well. Follow the example.

Example:

A field mouse takes cover in the house when the temperature drops.
Field mice take cover in the house when temperatures drop.

1. The horses gallop swiftly over the plains.
2. A city provides many interesting things for people to do.
3. Cigarette smokers run a high risk of getting certain diseases.
4. I drive her to class on Mondays, but on Thursdays she insists on taking the bus.
5. Terror stalks some neighborhoods; people face the possibility of violence every day.

6. Warm desert winds carry sand along the streets of Yuma and sting the eyes of people on the burning sidewalks.
7. He urges a balanced budget, although they want the government to pay for large social programs.
8. A direct-drive turntable costs more than a belt-drive, but my friends swear that belt-drives are just as good.

agr 6F

6F Use a plural verb when *and* joins more than one subject.

Pepper **and** garlic flavor the soup.

The word *and* joins two singular subjects, giving the sentence a plural subject

Plural verb; no *-s* ending

Greed and arrogance *disgust* most people.

Queenie and Clarence *work* on cars.

When subjects joined by *and* suggest a single idea, they may take a singular verb, but such uses are rare.

The tenor and star of the show is out with the flu.

Two subjects are joined by *and,* but both nouns refer to the same person, and so the whole subject is grammatically singular.

Singular verb

> Honest criticism and sensitive appreciation is directed not upon the poet but upon the poetry.
>
> —T. S. Eliot

[Eliot thought that "Honest criticism and sensitive appreciation" made one entity, that they were merely parts of the same approach to poetry, so he used the singular verb *is* in this sentence. But his usage here illustrates a danger, since to most people it is confusing. Most authorities would have been pleased if he had chosen to write "Honest criticism and sensitive appreciation are directed not upon the poet but upon the poetry."]

The words *each* and *every* preceding singular subjects that are joined by *and* require a singular verb for the whole subject, even though the subject may sound plural.

In the Nittany Mountains, each dawn and dusk fills the sky with soft, pink light.

Compound subject, preceded by *each* — Singular verb

agr 6G

When every window and every door *shuts* out drafts, your furnace will burn less oil.

In the rare instances when *each* follows subjects joined by *and,* you may choose either a singular or a plural verb, whichever sounds better to you.

In the Nittany Mountains, dawn and dusk each *fill* (or *fills*) the sky with soft, pink light.

6G For the verb *to be,* observe the rules of agreement in both the present and past tense. (See 7A, section 5.)

In the present tense, the various forms of *to be* are irregular and require selective use with subjects.

am: Use with the pronoun *I.*

When *I* **am** tired, I cannot think.

is: Use with all singular noun subjects and with singular pronoun subjects other than *I* and *you.*

The *door* **is rattling.**
Martha **is** late again.
He **is serving** tables.
It **is** dawn, and still *she* **is studying.**

are: Use with plural noun subjects, with plural pronoun subjects, and with the pronoun *you,* whether it is singular or plural.

The *waves* **are racing** to the shore.
They **are gardening;** *we* **are resting.**
When *you* **are finished,** you can go.

As you have seen, rules of agreement pertain to verbs in the present tense. In the simple past tense both singular and plural verbs use the same form for all subjects—except for the verb *to be,* which has two past tense forms, *was* and *were. Was* is singular, and *were* is plural.

was: Use with all singular noun subjects and with all singular pronoun subjects other than *you.*

The *ball* **was** high.

He **was** merely pink, but *I* **was** lobster-red.

were: Use with all plural noun subjects, with plural pronoun subjects, and with the pronoun *you,* whether it is singular or plural.

As *you* **were reading,** the *children* **were planning** their little surprise.

The *refugees* **were standing** patiently in line.

The rules of agreement also pertain to the present perfect tense (see 7A, section 2). In the present perfect tense, the helping verb *has* is singular, and the helping verb *have* may be either singular or plural.

I **have biked** across the country twice.
[The single subject *I* takes the helping verb *have* to form the present perfect tense of the verb *bike.*]

He **has** often **complained** about his back.
[*He,* a singular pronoun, takes the singular helping verb *has* in the present perfect tense.]

They **have been** out all night.
[*They* is a plural pronoun and takes the plural form *have* to form the present perfect tense of the verb *to be.*]

6H Take care to make your verbs and subjects agree when misleading words or phrases come between them.

Large *amounts* of money *go* to national defense.
[Although a singular noun, *money,* stands close to the verb *go,* the true subject of the verb is the plural noun *amounts,* and that subject requires a plural verb. The verb *go* is plural because its subject, *amounts,* is plural. The singular noun *money* is the object of the preposition *of* and is not the subject of the sentence.]

One *error* in a column of figures *throws* computations off by thousands.
[Although it stands right before the verb *throws,* the plural noun *figures* is the object of the preposition *of.* The subject, *error,* is singular; it requires a singular verb.]

Words such as *in addition to, as well as, along with, plus, including,* and *together with* do not affect the number of the subject. They usually serve as prepositions introducing the object of a preposition, which can never be the subject of a verb. (See 3C, section 1.)

A baseball *game* between the Philadelphia Athletics and the St. Louis Browns, along with my recollections of the bright colors of the grass and the uniforms and the excitement of the crowd, *makes* one of my happiest childhood memories.

[The singular subject, *game,* takes a singular verb, *makes,* and the combination of subject and verb is not affected by the extended prepositional phrase *along with my recollections of the bright colors of the grass and the uniforms and the excitement of the crowd.*]

agr
6I

Although such a sentence may be grammatically correct, it may still be awkward, and you should revise awkward sentences whether they are grammatically correct or not.

One of my happiest childhood memories is of a baseball game between the Philadelphia Athletics and the St. Louis Browns. I can still see the bright colors of the grass and the uniforms, and I can still feel the excitement of the crowd.

The *Marx Brothers,* including Groucho, still *make* audiences laugh in *A Night at the Opera,* filmed half a century ago.

[The plural subject, *Marx Brothers,* requires a plural verb, *make;* the phrase *including Groucho* does not influence the number of the verb.]

6I When words such as *or, either . . . or,* and *neither . . . nor* connect singular subjects, use singular verbs.

A simple fungus *infection or a rash* between the toes **is** often extremely painful.

Either running or swimming **improves** the heart's performance significantly.

When a subject with *or* or *nor* contains both a singular and a plural part, the verb agrees with the nearest part of the subject.

Either fine art or old coins **make** a good hedge against inflation.

[The verb *make* is plural because its closest subject, *coins,* is plural.]

Neither *Jack Miller* nor his friends *the Stanleys* **like** beer.

[The verb *like* is plural because it follows the plural noun *Stanleys.*]

Either old coins or fine art **makes** a good hedge against inflation.

[In this example, the verb *makes* is singular because it follows the singular noun *art.*]

Neither *the Stanleys* nor their friend *Jack Miller* **likes** beer.

Combined singular and plural subjects often sound awkward, and you should consider revising them to make compound subjects that may be expressed easily by a plural verb.

Awkward

Either the lilacs or the magnolia tree is responsible for the sweet smell that now hangs on the night air.

Improved

Either the lilacs or the magnolia blossoms are responsible for the sweet smell that hangs on the night air.

Old coins and fine art make a good hedge against inflation.

Both the Stanleys and their friend Jack Miller dislike beer.

6J With singular indefinite pronouns such as *anybody, anyone, anything, each, either, everybody, everyone, neither, nobody, none, no one,* and *one,* use singular verbs; the more ambiguous indefinite pronouns such as *all, any, more, most,* and *some* take singular or plural verbs, depending on their meaning in a particular sentence.

Everyone **is** on strike.

Nobody **likes** a losing team.

Use singular verbs with singular indefinite pronouns even when a prepositional phrase with a plural noun comes between the pronoun subject and the verb.

Everyone in all the departments **is** on strike.

Nobody among ardent fans **likes** a losing team.

[In both these examples, the presence of a plural noun as the object of a preposition between the subject and the verb has no influence on the choice of the verb; *everyone* and *nobody* are singular pronoun subjects; they take singular verbs.]

Some speakers sometimes slip into using verbs that agree with nearby nouns instead of indefinite pronoun subjects. The error may not be noticed in speaking, but it may disrupt a reader's concentration if it turns up in writing.

Hurried Speech

One of the shops *close* at five o'clock.

Written

One of the shops *closes* at five o'clock.

The more ambiguous indefinite pronouns such as *all, any, more, most,* and *some* take singular or plural verbs depending on whether their meaning is singular or plural in a particular sentence.

agr 6K

After the blizzard, workers made a huge pile of snow in the park. *Is* **any** of the snow left?

[The pile of snow is singular; *any,* in referring to it, takes a singular verb.]

Frank Sinatra once had thousands of young admirers who fainted when he sang. *Are* **any** of them still around?

[The noun *admirers* is plural; *any,* in referring to them, is also plural and takes a plural verb.]

She listens carefully to the children because *some* of them **have** mature ideas.

[*Children* is plural; *some,* a pronoun referring to the plural pronoun *them,* the antecedent of *children,* takes a plural verb, *have.*]

He made a cake last night; *some* of it **is** still on the table.

[*Cake* is singular; *some,* referring to it, is singular, too, and takes the singular verb *is.*]

The pronoun *none* has been a subject of much debate among writers. Strict grammarians point out that *none* means "no one" and should always take a singular verb:

None of my students **is** here yet.

But many writers make the same distinction with *none* that they make with *any.* When *none* refers to a plural noun, some writers use a plural verb. When *none* refers to a singular noun, these writers use a singular verb.

None of my students **are** here yet.

[Since *none* refers to the plural **students,** the verb *are* is plural.]

I read his *novel* and discovered that *none* of it **was** any good.

[Since *none* refers to the singular *novel,* it takes the singular verb *was.*]

6K Make verbs agree with their subjects when you invert the normal sentence order.

Below the waves **lurks** a great white *shark.*

[*Shark* is the subject of the sentence, although it comes after the verb *lurks.* As the object of the preposition *below,* the noun *waves* does not influence the verb.]

Beside the brook **grow** *tulips* in a profusion of color.

6L When verbs follow *there* or *here* at the beginning of a sentence, make sure that the subject that follows the verb agrees with it.

agr 6N

Here **lie** the *ruins* of a once-thriving civilization.
[The subject, *ruins,* is plural; its verb, *lie,* is also plural.]

There **are** five broken *pencils* on the desk.

There **is** a heavy glass *door* at the end of the corridor.

6M When the relative pronouns *who, that,* and *which* appear as subjects, use a verb that agrees with the antecedent.

Readers learn about new products from advertisements *that* sometimes **mislead** by making fantastic claims.
[The antecedent of *that* is *advertisements,* a plural noun; the verb *mislead* must also be plural.]

Chow Leung is one of those physicians *who* **work** compulsively.
[The antecedent for *who* is the plural noun *physicians; who* is plural and takes a plural verb, *work.* Even though the word *one* is singular, it does not influence agreement here.]

The word *only* placed before *one* can make a verb singular, even when the relative pronoun that later refers to it seems to have a plural antecedent.

The Glass Menagerie is the only one of Tennessee Williams's plays *that* **experiments** with slide photography.
[The word *only* establishes a singular context in the sentence, and because of that singular context, *that* refers to *one,* not to *plays.* No play by Tennessee Williams other than this one experiments with slide photography.]

6N Use linking verbs that agree with their subjects, not with complements of the subjects.

Scholarship and study **are** her passion.
[The plural subject, *scholarship and study,* takes a plural verb, *are.* The complement, *her passion,* is singular, but it does not affect the verb.]

Her *passion* **is** scholarship and study.
[The singular subject, *passion,* takes a singular verb, *is.* The verb is unaffected by the plural complement, *scholarship and study.*]

If such sentences sound awkward, you can revise them to make them smoother.

agr
60

Her passions are scholarship and study.

She loves scholarship and study.

60 Use singular verbs with most collective nouns that stand for or suggest a unit.

Such nouns have singular forms, although they have plural meanings. Words such as *army, audience, class, committee, majority, minority, team,* and so on, take singular verbs because the words stand for a single body acting as a unit.

This *class* **meets** too early.

An *army* **needs** good leadership and a good cause.

The parking *committee* **issues** permits to students.

The football *team* **travels** to East Lansing tomorrow.

Sometimes writers may emphasize the individual actions of separate members over the unity of a group by using a plural verb.

A *number* of the members **were** opposed to the majority report.
[The singular noun *number* here takes a plural verb, *were.*]

However, many writers would revise such a sentence to make it sound less awkward.

Some of the members **were** opposed to the majority report.
[The pronoun *some* becomes plural because it refers to the plural noun *members* and takes the plural verb *were.*]

A *number* of the members **opposed** the majority report.
[The singular *number* now takes the verb *opposed* in the simple past tense. Using the simple past is a convenient way to avoid awkwardness in making subjects and verbs agree, since the simple past is the same for both singular and plural.]

Some plural nouns that specify quantities require singular verbs because the nouns suggest a single unit.

Ten minutes **is** not enough time to see the Acropolis.

A hundred *dollars* **is** not much to pay for a bike these days.

[In these examples, a plural noun is taken as a single unit and takes a singular verb.]

6P Use singular verbs for those noun subjects that appear plural in form but are singular in meaning.

Gulliver's Travels **is** both a fantastic narrative and a serious satire on the human condition.

[Although plural in form (shown by the *–s* ending on the word *Travels*), the title takes a singular verb, since the subject is the title of a single book.]

Words like *mathematics, politics, athletics, ethics, kudos, pediatrics,* and many others are plural in form but nearly always take a singular verb.

Politics **is** both a science and an art.

Mathematics **is** difficult for many people.

[In both examples, the noun subject may be plural in form, but the meaning of each is singular. Hence a singular verb is required.]

Exercise 6.2 Change the infinitives shown in brackets into the correct forms of the *present tense* verb.

[to do]	**1.** The two books about health care for the senior citizen ________ not provide enough data.
[to like]	**2.** Neither she nor I ________ horror movies.
[to have]	**3.** Each of the children ________ to do some of the housework.
[to win]	**4.** The battery-powered car regularly ________ praise from environmentalists.
[to require]	**5.** Economics ________ careful study both for governments and for people planning to buy a new house or car.
[to give]	**6.** She is the only one of the trustees who ________ any consideration to what faculty members and students want.
[to be]	**7.** A pen and pencil ________ all you need.

[to recommend] **8.** Our group unanimously ________ an end to parking fees.

[to need] **9.** Each man and woman on the boat ________ a life jacket.

[to stand] **10.** Beyond the elms ________ a small cabin.

agr
6P

Exercise 6.3 Circle the appropriate form of the verb in each sentence below.

1. There (is, are) the primaries and the convention to endure before a candidate in either party (claim, claims) victory.
2. C. P. Snow's book *The Two Cultures* (was, were) a controversial statement on how little scientists and humanists understand each other.
3. Ten dollars (is, are) too much to pay for lunch.
4. Either the physician or the nurse (was, were) checking the chart.
5. Although she (has, have) a set of antique dueling pistols that (earn, earns) praise for beauty, neither she nor her father (has, have) ever fired a shot.
6. Here (is, are) the pianist and the flautist surrounded by a cheering orchestra that (love, loves) their outrageous mistakes.
7. Black bean soup topped with chopped onions (makes, make) a nourishing lunch, but some people (hate, hates) it.
8. Along the river bank (was, were) a child and a dog playing in the grass and sometimes in the dangerous water.
9. One of the supervisors who (was, were) not promoted felt that there (were, was) too few opportunities for advancement in the office where all the bosses (was, were) men; therefore, she, as well as her best friend, (is, are) looking for another job.
10. None of the jurors (seem, seems) prejudiced against the defendant.

7
The Forms of Verbs

Verbs can take a variety of forms, depending on the ways you use them. Learn how to make the various verb forms work for you.

7A Learn the principal parts of verbs and their uses in showing verb tenses.

Tense means "time," and verb tenses show the time of the action described by the verb. To form tenses correctly, you must know the *principal parts* of the verb. The principal parts are the *present* form, the *past* form, and the *past participle.*

The *present* form (the *infinitive* form without the infinitive marker *to*) is listed alphabetically in the dictionary; it is often called the **dictionary form.**

Dictionary forms: sing, dance, delight, slice

Infinitive forms: to sing, to dance, to delight, to slice

The *past* form for most verbs is made by adding the suffix *-d* or *-ed* to the dictionary form of the verb.

I ask**ed**, you play**ed**, he dance**d**, she slice**d**, we calculate**d**, they open**ed**

The *past participle* also is usually formed by adding *-d* or *-ed* to the dictionary form of the verb. But unlike the past form, the past participle always requires a helping verb to make the complete verb in a verb phrase.

(The past participle form is sometimes used as a *verbal;* see 3C, section 1.) *Helping,* or *auxiliary, verbs* are made from the verbs *to be* and *to have.*

In the following sentences, the past participle is in italics:

I should have *predicted* that result.

We were *finished* by noon.

He had *planted* his garden before he left for work.

vb 7A

The *present participle* is an essential verb form, but since it is always formed by adding the suffix *-ing* to the dictionary form, it is not usually listed among the principal parts. (See 29B, section 6, for spelling changes in adding *-ing* to some verbs.) Remember that the *gerund* has the same form as the present participle, but gerunds are always used as nouns. Here are some present participles:

singing, dancing, delighting, slicing

A further note: The verb *do* in its various forms helps other verbs to make emphatic statements, to ask questions, or to make negations.

Present emphatic:	I do work!
Present question:	Do I work?
Present negation:	I do not work.

1 Learn the verb forms for the three simple tenses.

The *simple tenses* for any verb are the *present, past,* and *future.*

The *simple present* for most verbs is the *dictionary form,* which is also called the **present stem.** To form the third person singular from the simple present, you usually add *-s* or *-es* to the present stem.

I run	we run
you run	you run
he run**s**	they run
I go	we go
you go	you go
she go**es**	they go
I join	we join
you join	you join
it join**s**	they join

The simple past is formed in regular verbs by adding *-d* or *-ed* to the present stem. The simple past does not change form.

I escaped	we escaped
you escaped	you escaped
he escaped	they escaped

Sometimes the simple past is irregular. Irregular verbs may not form the simple past tense with *-d* or *-ed.*

I ran	we ran
you ran	you ran
she ran	they ran

The simple future is made with the helping verbs *shall* and *will.*

I shall go	we shall go
you will go	you will go
she will go	they will go

Traditional grammar holds that *shall* should be used for the first person, *will* for the second and third person. In practice, this distinction is usually ignored; most people write "I will be twenty-five years old on my next birthday."

Helping verbs help form tenses. The common helping verbs are *have, has, had, am, is, are, was, were, be, being, been, do, does, did, shall, will, should, would, can, may, might, must,* and *could.* Helpers may also be groups of words like *have to, ought to, used to, is going to,* and *is about to.*

2 Learn the verb forms for the three perfect tenses.

In addition to the simple present, past, and future, verbs have three perfect tenses—the *present perfect,* the *past perfect,* and the *future perfect.* In grammar, the word *perfect* means that an act reported by one verb will be completed before an act reported by another verb. For that reason, a verb in the *perfect tense* should always be thought of as paired with another verb, either expressed or understood.

In the *present perfect* tense, the action of the verb started in the past. The present perfect is formed by using the helping verb *has* or *have* with the past participle.

I *have worked* hard for this diploma.
[The sentence means that the work you began in the past has just ended. The writer *implies* this compound sentence: I have worked hard for this diploma, but now my work is ended.]

I *have worked* all my life.
[The sentence means that the act of working began in the past and continues into the present. The writer implies this compound sentence: I have worked all my life, and I am still working now.]

She *has loved* architecture for many years, and now she *takes* architecture courses in night school.

[The interest in architecture began in the past, and it continues into the present; as a result, she takes architecture courses in night school.]

vb 7A

The *past perfect* tense reports an action completed before another action took place. The past perfect is also formed with the past participle, but it uses the helping verb *had.*

I *had worked* twenty years before I saved any money.

[The act of working twenty years had been completed before the act of saving took place.]

They thought they *had considered* all the dangers when they decided on the attack.

[The act of considering all the dangers had been completed before the act of deciding took place.]

Michelangelo *had painted* the ceiling of the Sistine Chapel and *had become* the most famous artist in Italy before he painted the great scene of the Last Judgment on the chapel's wall.

[The acts of painting the ceiling and becoming a famous artist had been completed before the act of painting the great scene took place.]

Often, as in the present perfect, use of the past perfect implies another act which is not stated in the sentence.

He *had told* me that he would quit if I yelled at him. I yelled at him, and he quit.

[The past perfect *had told* describes an action completed before the verbs *yelled* and *quit* in the next sentence.]

Abraham Lincoln *had dreamed* that he found the White House draped in black and that someone *had told* him that the President was dead.

[The past perfect implies the obvious fact that Lincoln *had dreamed* and that someone in his dream *had told* him of the President's death before he was assassinated and the dream came true.]

The *future perfect* tense reports an act that will be completed by some specific time in the future. It is formed by the helping verb *shall* or *will* added to *have* or *has* and the past participle.

I *shall have worked* fifty years when I retire.
[The working for fifty years will be completed at retirement.]

He *will have lived* with me ten years next March.
[It is not yet March, but when March comes, his ten years of living with me will be past. He may go on living with me, but that particular period of ten years will be finished.]

They *will have accepted* my invention by then.
[They have not yet accepted my invention, but when that future time comes, they will have done so.]

3 Learn the progressive form of the verb.

The progressive form of the verb is made with the present participle and a helping verb that is a form of *to be.* The progressive form is used with all tenses to show that an action continues during the time that the sentence describes, whether that time is past, present, or future.

Present progressive:	I am working.
Past progressive:	I was working.
Future progressive:	They will be working.
Present perfect progressive:	She has been working.
Past perfect progressive:	We had been working.
Future perfect progressive:	They will have been working.

Study the following progressive forms:

I *am working* on a new book.
[The action of working is in progress throughout the time of the sentence.]

I *was working* in the kitchen when the house caught fire.
[The action of working was going on during the beginning of the fire.]

They *will be working* in the garage tomorrow afternoon.
[The action of working will be going on throughout the afternoon.]

4 Learn how the various tenses of verbs show different divisions of time and different levels of force.

Present

Baseball *draws* millions of spectators every year.
[The statement expresses a habitual act, something that happens every year.]

Michael *is playing* outside.

[The time of the sentence is the present, and all during the time that the sentence describes, the act of playing goes on.]

John *does love* his friends.

[The statement is emphatic. Someone may have asked, "Does John love his friends?" The reply states emphatically that he does.]

vb 7A

Do you *remember* the St. Louis Browns?

[Use *do* or *does* to ask a question in the present tense.]

Past

The Orioles *won* the 1983 World Series.

[The sentence describes an action completed at a definite time in the past.]

The cars *were pouring* out of the city on Labor Day weekend.

[The past progressive shows that the action took place over the entire period of time described by the sentence.]

He *has worked* for the university for twenty years.

[The present perfect implies action begun in the past and continuing to the present.]

Robert E. Lee *had served* honorably in the U.S. Army before Virginia left the Union.

[The action took place before the definite time of the action described by the simple past tense *left* in the second clause.]

Ted Williams *did play* brilliantly in Boston despite the hostility of sportswriters who continually insulted him.

[The emphatic verb phrase *did play* contrasts with the negative *hostility.* The emphatic use of the verb often is a reply to some negative statement: He did not play well. Yes, he *did play* well!]

Did glaciers *contract* in the nineteenth century?

[*Did contract* is the verb phrase. By beginning the sentence with *did,* the writer asks a question.]

Future

The university *will build* a new library.

[The verb phrase *will build* expresses a future time without reference to its duration.]

I *shall have finished* by the time he arrives.

[The future perfect reports an action that will be completed by a definite time in the future.]

Next week I *fly* to Tucson.

[The present form is used with an adverbial phrase that puts the action in the future.]

He *is* to be sentenced Friday afternoon.

[The present tense is used with an infinitive phrase and an adverbial phrase to indicate action in the future.]

They *will be playing* all afternoon.

[The future progressive form indicates action that will go on throughout the time of the sentence.]

5 Learn the principal parts of the most common irregular verbs.

Although most verbs form their principal parts quite regularly, many of the most frequently used verbs are irregular. That is, their past tense and their past participle are not formed simply by adding *-ed.* The only way to master these irregular verbs is to memorize them.

The most important irregular verb is *to be,* often used as a helping verb. It is the only English verb that does not use the infinitive as the basic form for the present tense. Study the following forms:

To Be

	Singular	Plural
Present:	I am you are she is	we are you are they are
Past:	I was you were it was	we were you were they were
Past perfect:	I had been you had been he had been	we had been you had been they had been

If you are unsure of the principal parts of a verb, always look in a dictionary. If the verb is regular, a dictionary will list only the present form, and you will know that both the past and the past participle are formed by adding *-d* or *-ed.* If the verb is irregular, a dictionary will give the forms of the principal parts.

The following is a list of the principal parts of the most common irregular verbs. (Some verbs in this list are not irregular but are included because they confuse many people.) Read through it, and use it later on as a reference. Notice that some irregular verbs have more than one form for the past or the past participle.

vb
7A

Present stem	Past stem	Past participle
awake	awoke	awoke/awakened
become	became	become
begin	began	begun
blow	blew	blown
break	broke	broken
bring	brought	brought
burst	burst	burst
choose	chose	chosen
cling	clung	clung
come	came	come
dive	dove/dived	dived
do	did	done
draw	drew	drawn
drink	drank	drunk
drive	drove	driven
eat	ate	eaten
fall	fell	fallen
fly	flew	flown
forget	forgot	forgotten/forgot
forgive	forgave	forgiven
freeze	froze	frozen
get	got	gotten/got
give	gave	given
go	went	gone
grow	grew	grown
hang (things)	hung	hung
hang (people)	hanged	hanged
know	knew	known
lay (to put)	laid	laid
lie (to recline)	lay	lain
lose	lost	lost
pay	paid	paid
ride	rode	ridden
rise	rose	risen
say	said	said
see	saw	seen
set	set	set
shake	shook	shaken
shine	shone/shined	shone/shined
show	showed	shown
sing	sang	sung
sink	sank	sunk
sit	sat	sat
speak	spoke	spoken
spin	spun	spun
spit	spat/spit	spat/spit
steal	stole	stolen
strive	strove/strived	striven/strived

Present stem	Past stem	Past participle
swear	swore	sworn
swim	swam	swum
swing	swung	swung
take	took	taken
tear	tore	torn
tread	trod	trod/trodden
wake	woke	waked/woke/wakened
wear	wore	worn
weave	wove	woven
wring	wrung	wrung
write	wrote	written

Exercise 7.1 In the following sentences, supply the correct form of the verb that appears in parentheses at the end of the sentence.

Example: The book had __been published__ before he knew anything about it. (publish)

1. The plane __________ before we can get to the airport. (go)
2. He will __________ the house by the time we get back from our vacation. (paint)
3. He __________ while we were singing in the living room. (cook)
4. They had often __________ together in the same place where the shark attacked. (swim)
5. On the western frontier, horse thieves were sometimes __________ without a trial. (hang)
6. Every day she comes down to the ocean and __________ out to sea. (look)
7. Macbeth was __________ from a great victory when he met the three witches. (return)
8. She __________ for you at this very moment. (search)
9. Johnson, whom you see over there at his desk, has __________ in this office for twenty years. (work)
10. He __________ to escape from his job whenever he can. (like)

7B Review the various uses of the simple present tense.

The *simple present* has several uses:

It makes an unemphatic statement about something happening or a condition existing right now.

The earth *revolves* around the sun.

The car *passes* in the street.

vb
7C

It expresses habitual or continuous or characteristic action.

Porters *carry* things.

Dentists *fill* teeth and sometimes *pull* them.

Rocky McKnuckle *fights* with everybody.

The organization of his government always *seems* more important to an incoming president than the organization of his White House.
—THEODORE H. WHITE

It expresses a command or a warning.

Watch your step!

Periodicals *are* not to be taken out of the room.

It reports the content of literature, documents, movies, musical compositions, objects of art, or anything else that supposedly comes alive in the present each time it is experienced by an audience.

Macbeth *is driven* by ambition, and he *is haunted* by ghosts.

E. B. White *advises* writers to prefer the standard to the offbeat.

The Parthenon in Athens *embodies* grace, beauty, and calm.

In *Casablanca* Humphrey Bogart *plays* the role of a nightclub owner who *has* the chance to save the husband of his former lover, Ingrid Bergman.

Occasionally some writers use the present tense to describe historical action on the theory that history happens to us again each time we read about it.

Russia at the beginning of 1917 *is* bloody, famished, and weary.

[Note that this historical present is awkward to sustain in English; in general, you should avoid it. A wise rule is to write about the past in the past tense.]

7C Always observe the correct sequence of tenses.

If you have more than one verb in a sentence, you must be sure that the time of the verbs flows logically from one to the next. This means that past, present, and future actions must appear in sequences in a logical order.

While I *am writing,* I *like* to listen to the radio.

[Two actions take place at the same time—the present. Both are reported in verbs using the present tense.]

He *says* that Hamlet *felt* only self-pity.
[The action of saying appears in the present; it is a comment on something that happened in the past.]

Dickens *was* already famous when he *made* his first trip to America.
[The two verbs both report past action; both are in the simple past.]

The child *was crossing* the street when I *saw* the car bearing down on her.
[The past progressive is used with the simple past, the action *crossing* continuing to the definite point when I *saw.*]

He *had been* in Vietnam for a year when he *began* to write his book.
[The past perfect *had been* indicates an action in the past that continued before the action expressed in the simple past tense *began.*]

When I *get up,* he *will have been gone* for hours.
[A future time is indicated by the adverb *when* and the present *get up.* The future perfect *will have been gone* indicates an action that will be completed before the action of getting up takes place.]

vb
7C

Ordinarily, a past tense in the first clause of a sentence cannot be followed by the simple present, the present perfect, or a future tense.

Illogical
Sir Walter Scott *wrote* many novels because he *is* always in debt and *needs* to make money.

Illogical
Sir Walter Scott *wrote* many novels because he *has been* in debt and *has needed* to make money.

Illogical
Sir Walter Scott *wrote* many novels because he *will be* in debt, and he *will need* to make money.

Logical
Sir Walter Scott *wrote* many novels because he *was* always in debt and *needed* to make money.

However, you may use the present tense or the future tense in the second clause if it expresses a general truth always in force and follows a first clause containing a verb such as *say, tell, report, agree, promise,* and so on.

They *agreed* that relations between the sexes *are* difficult now.
[The subjects in these sentences commented in the past that some statement is always valid.]

He *says* that he *will pay* the bill next month.
[The present tense in the first clause is followed by a future tense.]

He *says* that he *has paid* the bill already.
[The present is followed by the present perfect, indicating an action with effects that continue to the present.]

He *says* that he *paid* the bill last month.
[A simple present is followed by a simple past.]

vb 7D

He *says* that he *had paid* the bill long before anyone *complained.*
[A simple present is followed by a past perfect. The past perfect indicates action completed before the action of the verb *complained* began.]

Exercise 7.2 Fill in the blanks with any verb that makes sense. Use the tense given in parentheses.

Example: After John __had been dancing__ for three hours, he realized that the band had stopped playing. (past perfect progressive)

1. He __________ to New York five times and plans to go again. (present perfect)
2. Tomorrow __________ the first day of the rest of my life. (future)
3. Ralph __________ in the bank when the robbery took place. (past perfect)
4. Hitchcock always __________ in his own movies. (present)
5. Canadian geese __________ continually while they fly. (present)
6. She __________ while she listened to the radio. (past progressive)

Exercise 7.3 Fill in the blanks with a logical tense of the verb given in parentheses.

1. They were going out the door when she __________. (call)
2. You will __________ home by the time you get this letter. (arrive)
3. They had been __________ for about an hour when the fire broke out in the boat. (sail)
4. Winter will have come and __________ by the time you come home from the army. (go)
5. They __________ supper right now. (eat)
6. The rain __________ since Sunday morning, but on Tuesday it stopped. (fall)

7D Use the mood of the verb that accurately expresses your meaning.

The **mood** of a verb expresses the attitude of the writer by showing the way in which an association is made. Verbs have three moods—the *indicative,* the *subjunctive,* and the *imperative.*

The **indicative** is used for simple statements of fact or for asking questions about fact. It is by far the most common mood of verbs in English. The **subjunctive** conveys a wish, a desire, or a demand in the third person, or else it makes a statement the writer thinks is contrary to fact. The **imperative** conveys a command or request in the second person.

Indicative

The tide *came* in at six o'clock and *swept* almost to the foundation of our house.

[The indicative mood is used because this sentence makes a statement of fact not doubted by the writer.]

Indicative

Can he *be* serious?

[The indicative is used because the question is asked with the expectation of a simple statement of fact as an answer. Questions are always in the indicative mood.]

Subjunctive

He requested that his son *use* the money to go to college.

[The verb *use* is in the subjunctive because it reports an action that is desired but not certain to take place. We don't know if the son will honor the request or not. Notice that here, in the third person singular, the subjunctive form leaves off the customary final *-s* of the indicative. If the subject of the verb *use* were in the plural, the verb would be the same as if it were in the indicative; we would have to understand a subjunctive sense that is not shown by the grammatical form.]

He requested that his sons and daughters *use* the money to go to college.

He asked that they never *forget* him.

For most verbs, the subjunctive form differs from the indicative only in the third person singular.

Although the subjunctive is not widely used in modern English, it is still alive in some common expressions:

She will finish her job, *come* hell or high water.

[The form *come* in the third person singular is subjunctive.]

All people should enjoy equal opportunity, *be* they rich or poor.

[The form *be* is subjunctive.]

Use the subjunctive in a clause beginning with *if* when the clause makes a statement contrary to fact:

If only I *were* in Paris tonight!

[I am not in Paris, alas! So the *were* in the *if* clause is in the subjunctive mood.]

With the verb *to be,* the present subjunctive is formed by using the form *were* for the first, second, and third persons, singular and plural.

vb
7D

If the moon *were* full on that night, he could have seen the murder as it happened.

[The subjunctive *were* tells us that the moon was not full on the fateful night; the indicative mood with *was* would tell us that the statement may be true.]

Were she my daughter, I would not permit her to date that member of the motorcycle gang.

[She is not my daughter; therefore, the subjunctive *were* is used as the verb.]

Use the subjunctive in clauses beginning with *that* after verbs that give orders or advice or express wishes or make requests.

He wishes that she *were* here.

She asked that he *draw* up a marriage contract before the wedding.

Sam suggested that Bill *get* a good night's sleep before the exam.

[In all three of these examples, a request is embodied in a *that* clause. Since no one can tell whether a request will be honored or not, the verb in each *that* clause is in the subjunctive, indicating uncertainty.]

Should and *had* may also express the subjunctive:

Should he step on a rattlesnake, his boots will protect him.

[He has not stepped on a rattlesnake; it is uncertain that he will ever step on a rattlesnake. But if he should, his boots will protect him. *Should* indicates a subjunctive mood.]

Had he taken my advice, he would not have bought stock in a dance hall.

[*Had,* the subjunctive, indicates a condition contrary to fact; he did not take my advice, and he did buy stock in a dance hall.]

I wish he *had* won the tournament.

[The *had* after the verb *wish* expresses a condition contrary to fact; he did not win the tournament.]

Be sure that when you use the word *had* as a past subjunctive, you do not confuse it with the conditional. Do not say "I wish we *would have* won the tournament." Say "I wish we *had* won the tournament."

Use the subjunctive in some commands or wishes expressed in the third person singular.

May the Good Lord *bless* and *keep* you.

Let there *be* light.

Grammar *be* hanged!

Imperative

The *imperative mood* is a particular kind of subjunctive. The imperative is used only to express commands in the second person, singular or plural, and the form of the verb is the same as the indicative. In the imperative sentence, the *subject* of the verb is always *you,* but the *you* is usually understood, not written out:

Pass the bread.

Drive me to the airport, please.

Leave the room!

He begged her, "*Become* an engineer!"

Sometimes the *you* is written for extra emphasis:

You give me my letter this instant!

Exercise 7.4 Identify the mood of the verbs in italics in the following sentences. Over each italicized verb, write **I** for indicative, **S** for subjunctive, or **IM** for imperative.

1. If she *was* awake, she must have heard the noise.
2. Prisoners in solitary confinement sometimes *dream* of enormous meals.
3. He said that Japan *has* one of the lowest crime rates in the world.
4. If Carlton Fisk *were* still *playing* for Boston, the Red Sox might not be so blue.
5. *Had* you *been* here, we might not have quarreled.
6. Please *send* me some postage stamps from the Vatican.
7. He asked that his father *stop* writing letters to the newspaper.
8. If he *used* a ballpoint pen, he could make six copies at once.
9. He asked that his friends neither *explain* him nor *excuse* him to others.
10. Should she *remember* me in her will, I would be astonished.

7E Learn the difference between the active voice and the passive voice. Use verbs in the active voice in most sentences; use verbs in the passive voice sparingly and only for good reason.

The voice of a transitive verb tells us whether the subject is the actor in the sentence or is acted upon. (A transitive verb carries action from an agent to an object. A transitive verb can take a direct object; an intransitive verb does not take a direct object. See 3A, section 1.)

When transitive verbs are in the *active voice,* the subject does the acting. When transitive verbs are in the *passive voice,* the subject is acted upon by an agent that is implied, or an agent that is expressed in a prepositional phrase. (Intransitive verbs cannot be passive. You can say "My brother *brooded* too much," but you cannot say "My brother *was brooded.*") In the passive voice, the transitive verb phrase includes some form of the verb *to be.*

vb
7E

Active: She *mailed* the letter.

Passive: The letter *was mailed* by her.

Active: John *washed* the dishes.

Passive: The dishes *were washed* by John.

Readers usually want to know the agent of an action; that is, they want to know *who* or *what* does the acting.

Active: **He** made the bed.

Passive: The bed was made **by him.**
[The agent of the action here is identified by boldface.]

Since the passive often fails to identify the agent of an action, it may be a means of evading responsibility.

Passive: The Mustangs lost because a tackle *was missed* on the punt return.

Active: The Mustangs lost because Al Tennyson *missed* a tackle on the punt return.

Use the passive only when the recipient of the action in the sentence is much more important to your statement than the doer of the action.

My car *was stolen* last night.
[*Who* stole your car is not important to this statement; you don't know who did it. The important thing in the sentence is that your car was stolen. So the verb phrase *was stolen* can be in the passive voice.]

After her heart attack, she *was taken* to the hospital in an ambulance.
[*Who* took her to the hospital is unimportant to this statement; the important fact is that she was taken.]

In scientific and technical writing, researchers generally use the passive voice throughout a report on an experiment so that they can keep the focus on the experiment rather than on the experimenters.

Passive: When the bacteria *were isolated,* they *were treated* carefully with nicotine and *were observed* to stop reproducing.

Active: When we *isolated* the bacteria, we *treated* them carefully with nicotine. They *stopped* reproducing.

A clear and direct writing style draws upon verbs in the active voice. Unless you have a special reason for using the passive, choose the active voice.

Exercise 7.5 Rewrite the following sentences to put the passive verbs in the active voice.

1. The paintings on the wall of my kitchen were done by my daughter.
2. The song "9 to 5" was written by Dolly Parton.
3. The movie *Citizen Kane* was made by Orson Welles, was the recipient of many awards, but was not viewed by Welles himself for years afterward.
4. In the 1950s, color was used by filmmakers to compete with television, where all the programs were still being shown in black and white.
5. The house was painted by Mr. Johnson last summer.
6. Poland was invaded by the Germans on September 1, 1939.
7. Our grass was cut by a neighborhood girl.
8. The home run was hit by Carlton Fisk in the bottom of the twelfth inning to win the game.
9. Disney's *Pinocchio* was being viewed by the fourth-grade children in the museum projection room.
10. The grass was watered despite the heavy rains last week.

Exercise 7.6 The following sentences were all written by professional writers. Analyze each verb to see whether it is in the active or the passive voice. Tell why the passive is used when you do find it.

1. Some birds can be identified by color alone.

   —Roger Tory Peterson
2. The radio was silenced, and all that could be heard was the echo of the Mayor's voice.

   —Mark Helprin
3. If you are bitten and the dog gets away, make every effort to find the dog and its owner.

   —Richard Ballantine

4. At this point, a doctor was summoned; a formal pronouncement of death was made; and Big Jim's carcass was dragged, feet first, and for the last time, through the front door of his saloon.

—JOE MCGINNISS

5. Many statesmen feel that weapons are in themselves evil, and that they should be eliminated, as you would crush a snake.

—E. B. WHITE

6. There was much justification for these prophecies. By the time I was nine years old, I had been hit by a bus, thrown into the Harlem River (intentionally), hit by a car, severely beaten with a chain. And I had set the house on fire.

—CLAUDE BROWN

7. The landscape too is dramatic, both in Israel and Jordan, which together make up the country of the Bible. Seeing it at first hand, one realizes that it was no accident that God was invented and two religions originated here.

—BARBARA TUCHMAN

7F Use the infinitive form of the verb to complete the sense of other verbs, to serve as a noun, and to form the basis of some phrases.

The word *to*, sometimes called the **infinitive marker,** is placed before the verb to identify the infinitive form.

The **present infinitive** describes action that takes place at the same time as the action in the verb the infinitive completes:

He *wants* to go. [present]

He *wanted* to go. [past]

He *will want* to go. [future]

The *present infinitive* uses the infinitive marker *to* along with the simple present tense of the verb:

to write, to dance, to play, to sing

The **present perfect infinitive** uses the infinitive marker *to*, the verb *have,* and a past participle:

to have written, to have danced, to have sung, to have swum, to have run

The *present perfect infinitive* describes action prior to the action of the verb whose sense is completed by the infinitive. The present perfect infinitive often follows verb phrases that include *should* or *would.*

I would like *to have seen* her face when she found the duck in her bathtub.

[The *liking* takes place in the present and is expressed in the verb phrase *would like.* The phrase *would like* implies that the action expressed in the infinitive *to have seen* did not take place. This wished-for seeing would have happened before the time of the verb phrase *would like.*]

Sometimes we say things like this:

I wanted to have finished this paper before you arrived.

[This usage is not incorrect, but it is unnecessarily wordy. We can say "I wanted to finish this paper before you arrived," and the present infinitive with the simple past tense would be enough to show that the finishing should have taken place before you arrived. If you wished to emphasize the *wanting* rather than the *finishing,* you would change the word order and say "Before you arrived, I wanted to finish this paper, but now that you are here, I don't want to finish it."]

An **infinitive phrase** includes the infinitive and the words that complete its meaning:

Her attempt *to bicycle through a New York subway tunnel* was frustrated by an express train.

[The infinitive *to bicycle* is modified by the prepositional phrase *through a New York subway tunnel.* In effect the prepositional phrase acts as an adverb modifying the infinitive, but the infinitive and its modifying prepositional phrase together make an *infinitive phrase.*]

To take such an immense journey required courage and money.

[The infinitive phrase in this sentence is the subject of the verb *required.* The infinitive here has an object, *journey,* but the object is also part of the phrase, and all the words in the phrase make up the subject of the sentence.]

Infinitives and infinitive phrases most often serve as nouns, but they can also be used as adjectives and adverbs.

To dance was his whole reason for living.

[Noun, subject of the sentence]

Her only aim was *to dodge his flying feet.*

[Noun, subject complement]

He also wanted *to sing.*

[Noun, direct object of the verb *wanted*]

She was not a woman *to take chances.*

[Adjective; the infinitive phrase modifies the noun *woman.*]

vb
7F

Infinitives and infinitive phrases may serve as adverbs when they answer the question *Why?* and modify the main verb.

He studied *to improve his voice.*
[The infinitive phrase tells why he studied, modifying the verb *studied* and thus acting as an adverb.]

Sometimes the infinitive marker is omitted before the verb, especially after verbs like *hear, help, let, see,* and *watch.* Study the following examples.

She heard him *come* in.
[The verbal *come* is an infinitive here, and the pronoun *him* serves as the subject of the infinitive. But by the conventions of English, we don't say "She heard him to come in." We omit the infinitive marker *to.*]

They watched the ship *sail* out to sea.
[The verbal *sail* is an infinitive here with the infinitive marker *to* omitted. Compare: "They expected the ship *to sail* out to sea."]

She made him *treat* her with respect.
[The verbal *treat* is an infinitive with the infinitive marker *to* omitted. Compare: "She asked him *to treat* her with respect."]

In general, *avoid split infinitives.* A **split infinitive** has one or more words awkwardly placed between the infinitive marker *to* and the verb form.

Split Infinitive
He loved *to loudly sing.*
[The adverb *loudly* splits the infinitive *to sing.*]

Better
He loved *to sing* loudly.

Some writers believe that split infinitives are acceptable:

> The government was little altered as Mr. Bush touched down at Andrews Air Force Base at 6:30 p.m. *to gracefully assume* the duties but not the powers of the Presidency. [italics added]
>
> —*Time*

The rule against split infinitives is not absolute; some writers split infinitives, and others do not. But the words used to split infinitives can usually go outside the infinitive, or they can be omitted altogether.

Split Infinitive

He told me to *really* try to do better.

[The adverb *really* is a weak intensifier that seldom adds anything to a sentence. It can be left out without harm.]

Better

He told me to try to do better.

vb 7F

In general, related elements in a sentence should be kept as close together as possible to avoid confusion. When you split an infinitive with a long phrase, you violate this principle by moving the infinitive marker away from its related element, the verb form of the infinitive.

Split: He intended *to carefully and completely revise* his paper.

Better: He intended *to revise* his paper carefully and completely.
[Note that the revision places the adverbs after the noun that follows the infinitive. English idiom favors this positioning. We don't write, "She ran ten miles a day thoroughly to condition herself for the marathon"; we say, "She ran ten miles a day to condition herself thoroughly for the marathon."

Exercise 7.7 Fill in the blank in each of the following sentences with the proper form of the infinitive of the verb in parentheses at the end of the sentence.

1. He asked her __________ his plane at 7:07 P.M. (meet)
2. I promise __________ your plane tomorrow. (meet)
3. He would have preferred __________ his education before he bought a car. (complete)
4. We often heard him __________ late at night in his shower. (sing)
5. She was not one __________ for opportunity to knock. (wait)

Exercise 7.8 Rewrite the following sentences to eliminate split infinitives.

1. She claimed to truly mean her promise to work hard.
2. They intended to speedily complete the job.
3. The pilot wanted to safely and happily complete the trip.
4. The United States Football League vowed to strictly refuse to sign college football players before they had played in their senior year.

7G Beware of common errors in the use of verbs.

vb 7G

1 Avoid confusing the simple past and the past participle in irregular verbs. When it is part of a predicate, the past participle always needs a helping verb.

Faulty

I *seen* her last night at the movie.

[The past participle of the irregular verb *see* is *seen;* the simple past tense is *saw.*]

Correct

I *saw* her last night at the movie.

Faulty

We *taken* our books with us to camp.

[The past participle *taken* cannot serve as the simple past tense of the irregular verb *take.*]

Correct

We *took* our books with us to camp.

[The principal parts of *take* are *take, took,* and *taken.* The simple past *took* is used without a helping verb.]

Correct

We *had taken* our books with us to camp, and we were glad.

[Here the helping verb *had* combines with the past participle *taken* to make a correct verb phrase.]

Faulty

I *done* the job myself.

[The principal parts of the verb *do* are *do, did,* and *done.* The past participle *done* must be used with a helping verb, or it must be changed to the simple past *did.*]

Correct

I *did* the job myself.

[The simple past *did* does not require a helping verb.]

Correct

I *have done* the job myself.

[The helping verb *have* with the past participle *done* makes the present perfect tense.]

2 Recognize irregular verbs, and avoid the error of trying to make them regular.

Faulty

The artist *drawed* the portrait in an hour.

[Ordinarily the suffix *-ed* makes the simple past. But the irregular verb *draw* forms the simple past by becoming *drew.*]

Correct

The artist *drew* the portrait in an hour.

Faulty

We *payed* for everything we got.

[The simple past of the verb *pay* is not *payed* but *paid.*]

Correct

We *paid* for everything we got.

3 Keep the distinction between *lay* and *lie*.

To lay means "to put down" or "to place." *To lie* means "to recline." *To lie* is an intransitive verb and cannot take a direct object.

I *lie* down to sleep every night at eleven o'clock.

To lay is a transitive verb and must always take a direct object.

I *lay* my books aside each evening to watch television.

The words *lay* and *lie* are often confused because they are both irregular verbs, and the past tense of *lie* is *lay.*

I *lie* down to sleep each night at eleven.

[The verb *lie* is in the present tense.]

Last night I *lay* down at eleven.

[The past tense of *lie* is *lay.*]

Yesterday I *laid* the keys on the table so he would find them when he came in.

[The past tense of *lay* is *laid.*]

We had *lain* there an hour when the clock struck midnight.

[The past participle of *lie* is *lain.*]

Although he could not find them, I had *laid* the keys on the table before I went to bed last night.

[The past participle of *lay* is *laid.*]

vb 7G

4 Keep the distinction between *sit* and *set*.

Sit is an intransitive verb and cannot take a direct object.

We all *sit* down.

[No direct object]

Set is a transitive verb and must always take a direct object when it means "to place."

We *set* the vase in the window when we want to signal our friends to come over.

[The direct object is *vase.*]

The principal parts of *sit* are *sit, sat,* and *sat.*

You sit to eat.
You sat all during yesterday's parade.
You have sat there an hour without speaking.

The principal parts of *set* are *set, set,* and *set.*

You set tables beautifully for your parties.
You set the clock last night before you went to bed.
You have set my teeth on edge with your horrifying tale.

5 Avoid illogical shifts in tense.

Illogical

The car *roared* down the street out of control, *hit* a tree, *bounced* over the sidewalk, and *comes* crashing into my living room.

[The first three verbs—*roared, hit,* and *bounced*—are in the simple past tense. The shift to *comes,* a present tense, is illogical and confusing.]

Revised

The car *roared* down the street out of control, *hit* a tree, *bounced* over the sidewalk, and *came* crashing into my living room.

Exercise 7.9 Correct the errors in the following sentences. If a sentence is correct as it stands, place a check mark beside the number.

1. He come home last night and find the dog sick.
2. They taken the kickoff and get to work and have a touchdown in five minutes of the first quarter.

3. She worked hard and done a good job.
4. After a long day it's always good to lay down.
5. He lay his pants over the back of the chair last night and go right to sleep and don't wake up until this morning at ten o'clock.
6. Last year she lay the book on top of the chest, and she forget all about it until the library notice come yesterday.
7. I stood as long as I could, but finally I had to set down and taken a load off my poor feet.
8. Joey went down the slope first with a big whoosh, and then Helen go flying after him, and then here come Herman skiing like a windmill with his big feet sailing up in the air and his poles flying off, and he shouting like a fool, "Look at me!"

8
Pronoun Problems

We use pronouns to avoid awkwardness, to simplify style, and to express certain ideas clearly. (See 3B, section 3, on identifying pronouns.)

Pronouns take the place of nouns in sentences. In the following sentence, if we had to repeat the noun *house* every time we wrote about the idea *house,* we would have awkward and unwieldy prose.

Awkward

The house stood on a shady street, and the house looked large and comfortable as if the house was perfectly suited for a large family and for two sets of grandparents who might visit the house for long periods.

[The pronoun *it* simplifies this sentence immediately.]

Better

The house stood on a shady street, and it looked large and comfortable as if it was perfectly suited for a large family and for two sets of grandparents who might visit it for long periods.

We could not express some ideas without pronouns. Many sentences require first-person pronouns (*I, we, our,* and *ours*) or second-person pronouns (*you, your,* and *yours*), and no other words can serve in their place.

By themselves, pronouns are indefinite words; therefore, most pronouns require an antecedent to give them content and meaning. The **antecedent** is the word that the pronoun substitutes for. The antecedent usually appears earlier in the same sentence or in the same passage.

The *snow* fell all day long, and by nightfall, *it* was three feet deep.

[The noun *snow* is an antecedent; the pronoun *it* looks back to *snow* so that in this sentence *snow* and *it* mean the same thing.]

Some pronouns are indefinite and take their meaning not from an antecedent but from the sentences where they are located.

Anybody who wants to see the Placido Domingo concert should get a ticket two months in advance.

[*Anybody* standing by itself would have almost no meaning at all; it receives meaning from the sentence and especially from the clause *who wants to see the Placido Domingo concert.* Nouns such as *John, house, garden, car,* and *dog* have a fairly clear meaning by themselves. An indefinite pronoun must have a sentence to give it meaning.]

Some pronouns are **reflexive.** They end in *-self,* and they add emphasis to the noun or pronoun they follow.

John *himself* admitted his error.

The legal battle about who owned the field went on for years while the field *itself* grew up like a jungle.

No matter how you may judge my actions, you *yourself* would have done the same thing in my situation.

I hurt *myself.*

[All these reflexive pronouns stress their antecedents.]

8A Make certain that pronouns refer clearly to their antecedents. Keep pronouns as close to their antecedents as possible.

Pronouns that do not refer clearly to their antecedents or that are widely separated from them may confuse your readers. Often the only way to remedy a confusing reference of pronouns to their antecedents is to rewrite the sentence.

Weak

Albert was with Beauregard when he got the news that his cigars had arrived.

[Did Beauregard get the news, or did Albert? Did the cigars belong to Beauregard, or did they belong to Albert?]

Improved

Albert's cigars arrived, and while he was with Beauregard, Albert got the news that they had come.

[Now the sentence is clear. The cigars belong to Albert, and he got the news of their arrival while he was with Beauregard. Readers would almost certainly understand another version: While *he* was with Beauregard, Albert got the news that *his* cigars had arrived. Although the pronoun *his* could refer grammatically to either Beauregard or Albert, nearly all readers would assume that the two pronouns, *he* and *his,* had the same antecedent.]

Weak

The engine stopped, and McHale thought of the mechanic in the last small town on the highway amid the torrid, dusty summer of West Texas with its long and blinding stretches of treeless land burned brown by the sun, waterless and desolate, *who* had told him *it* was in excellent condition despite the strange noise *it* was making.

pro 8A

[The relative clause beginning with *who* is a long way from its antecedent, *mechanic,* and the two instances of the pronoun *it* are even farther from their antecedent, *engine.* Readers may be confused by the pronoun references.]

Improved

The engine stopped, and McHale thought of the mechanic *who* had told him *it* was in excellent condition despite the strange noise *it* was making. That mechanic was now far behind him in the last small town on the highway amid the torrid, dusty summer of West Texas with its long and blinding stretches of treeless land burned brown by the sun, a land waterless and desolate.

[A thorough revision yields two sentences instead of one and places the pronouns much closer to the antecedents to which they refer.]

Avoid the use of *they* and *it* as indefinite pronouns in constructions such as *they say* and *it says.* Such constructions may be both awkward and unclear.

Vague: They say that the heat wave will break tomorrow.

Better: The weather forecast is that the heat wave will break tomorrow.

Vague: They say he dyes his hair.

Better: His former wife says he dyes his hair.

[The improvement in both examples is to make the source of the information clear.]

Vague: It says in the paper that we can expect a higher rate of inflation next year.

Better: A front-page article in today's paper says we can expect a higher rate of inflation next year.

[The improved example is somewhat longer, and the source of the information is presented early in the sentence.]

8B Make pronouns agree in number with their antecedents.

Singular antecedents require singular pronouns.

> The *house* was dark and gloomy, and *it* sat in a grove of tall cedars that made *it* seem darker still.

Plural antecedents require plural pronouns.

> The *cars* swept by on the highway, all of *them* doing more than 55 miles per hour.

[In the first sentence, *house,* a singular noun, requires a singular pronoun, *it;* in the second, the plural *cars* requires a plural pronoun, *them.*]

> *Roosevelt* and *Churchill* found radio a perfect medium for *their* speaking talents.

[The antecedents are compound—that is, joined by a coordinating conjunction. A compound antecedent is plural and takes a plural pronoun—in this example, *their.*]

Use a singular pronoun when all the parts of a compound antecedent are singular and the parts are joined by *or* or *nor.*

> Either *Ted* or *John* will take *his* car.
>
> Neither *Judy* nor *Linda* will lend you *her* horn.

[But if Ted and John own one car in partnership, you should write, "Either Ted or John will take *their* car." And if Judy and Linda own only one horn between them, you should write, "Neither Judy nor Linda will lend you *their* horn."]

Sometimes you must revise a sentence entirely because a single pronoun will not do.

> Neither *Patricia* nor *John* would let me borrow *his* lawn mower.

[Since we assume that Patricia is a woman and that John is a man, the pronoun *his* will not do unless Patricia has some control over John's lawn mower. The simplest way out of the problem would be to eliminate the pronoun: Neither Patricia nor John would let me borrow *a* lawn mower. Or you could write this sentence: John would not lend me his lawn mower, and Patricia would not lend me hers.]

When referring to collective nouns such as *team, family, audience, majority, minority, committee, group, government, flock, herd,* and many others, Americans usually use the singular pronoun.

The *team* won *its* victory gratefully.

In elections, the *majority* has *its* way.

The *committee* disbanded when *it* finished *its* business.

pro 8B

However, if the members of the group indicated by a collective noun are being considered as individuals, a plural pronoun is appropriate.

The hard-rock *band* broke up and began fighting among *themselves* when *their* leader was converted to Mozart.

[Although *band* is singular, the intent of the sentence is to stress the individuals in the group. Here *themselves* and *their*—both plural pronouns—are used to refer to the noun *band.*]

In British English, collective nouns usually take plural pronouns and plural verbs. In books first published in Great Britain or the Commonwealth, you often find sentences like these:

The cricket *team* quit playing when *they* discovered that *their* spectators had fallen into a profound sleep.

The government *refuse* to comment when *they* are asked about the prospects for peace in Poland.

Traditional writing textbooks direct you to use masculine singular pronouns to refer to nouns and pronouns of unknown gender.

Any *teacher* must sometimes despair at the indifference of *his* students.

Everybody can have what *he* wants to eat.

However, many people object that using the masculine pronoun when the gender of the noun is unknown or nonspecific creates sexist language. Chapter 21 explores the problem of sexist language and describes various remedies for it.

Exercise 8.1 Rewrite the following sentences to correct errors in pronoun reference. If you find no error in a sentence, put a check by it. You may rewrite a sentence to keep some pronouns, or you may eliminate the pronouns altogether.

1. The ship sailed under the Golden Gate Bridge as it put out to sea.
2. The painter complained to her model that she was too pale.
3. Blodgett met Whitney as he was returning from the swim meet.
4. It says in the menu that the special is fried eggplant.

5. The traveler bought a melon from the peasant as he stood in the shade on the road below Lamia, the city on the hill.
6. Anyone who loses their token will have to buy a new one if they want to ride the subway.
7. Neither Lewis nor Alfred brought their toothbrush.
8. If one wears polyester shirts, he will be much hotter in summer and much colder in winter than with cotton shirts, but he can enjoy them for years.
9. The golf team used the indoor tennis courts when they practiced in winter.
10. Neither Ellen nor Mike rode her bicycle to school that day, although they usually rode in together every morning.
11. They say that a penny saved is a penny earned, but they never considered how much you can spend when you try to save money at a half-price sale.
12. The control group was tested to see if they remembered the economics lecture as well as they remembered the soap opera.

8C Avoid making broad references with the pronouns *this, that, they, it, which,* and *such.*

Some writers occasionally use one of these pronouns to refer not to a specific antecedent but to the general idea expressed by the whole clause or sentence.

> The members of Political Writers for a Democratic Society did not constitute a pack. They were too confident, competitive, proud, and self-sufficient for *that.*
>
> —TIMOTHY CROUSE

[The pronoun *that* has as its antecedent the idea expressed in the first sentence, that the members of the organization called Political Writers for a Democratic Society did not constitute a pack.]

> Babe Ruth, playing for the Boston Braves, hit three balls out of Forbes Field in Pittsburgh on May 25, 1935. *They* were his last home runs.

[*They,* the subject of the second sentence, has as its antecedent the entire action of the first sentence rather than any one noun within that sentence.]

But broad reference with pronouns is often awkward or misleading.

Weak

> Andy Warhol once made a movie of a man sleeping for a whole night, *which* was a tiresome experience.

[Was the movie tiresome to watch? Or was making the movie the tiresome experience?]

Improved

Andy Warhol once made a tiresome movie of a man sleeping for a whole night.

Improved

Andy Warhol once went through the tiresome experience of making a movie of a man sleeping for a whole night.

Weak

That car gets good gas mileage and yet is so flimsy that it breaks up in the slightest accident. *This* ought to be a consideration to anyone thinking of buying it, but *this* is not likely when people live in a world like *this* where inflation is rampant.

[Writers sometimes use the demonstrative pronoun *this* far too frequently and far too broadly.]

Improved

That car gets good gas mileage and yet is so flimsy that it breaks up in the slightest accident. Anyone thinking of buying it ought to consider its safety record, but safety may not come to mind in today's world where inflation is rampant.

[Replacing the pronoun *this* with specific nouns and revising these sentences helps to clarify the meaning.]

8D Learn the difference between the expletive *it* and the pronoun *it*.

The pronoun *it* always has an antecedent; the expletive *it* serves as a grammatical subject when the real subject is placed after the verb or is understood.

Pronoun *it*

When a barn burned in rural America, *it* often took with *it* a year's hard work for a farm family.

[*It,* used twice in this sentence, has the noun *barn* as an antecedent.]

Expletive *it*

When a barn burned, *it* was difficult for a farm family to recover from the loss.

[The *it* does not have an antecedent but serves as the grammatical subject for the independent clause that it begins. The sentence could read, "When a barn burned, to recover from the loss was difficult for a farm family." But such a sentence, although correct grammatically, does not conform to customary English usage, and it sounds awkward compared with the sentence with the expletive *it*.]

Expletive *it*

It will be a pretty day tomorrow.

[The sentence could read, "Tomorrow will be a pretty day," but American usage often favors the expletive *it*.]

Expletive *it*

It is hot now.

[The subject is understood to be *the temperature* (*the temperature* is hot now) or *the day* (*the day* is hot now). But the expletive *it*, without an antecedent, is favored in common usage.]

Try to avoid using the expletive *it* and the pronoun *it* one after the other.

Weak

What will happen to the kite? If *it* is windy, *it* will fly.

Improved

What will happen to the kite? It will fly if the wind blows.

8E When you address your readers, use the pronoun *you* only when you are writing in an informal tone; use the pronoun *one* when you write more formally.

> The book's no good to *you* now. Neither is scientific reason. *You* don't need any scientific experiments to find out what's wrong.
>
> —ROBERT M. PIRSIG

[In his book *Zen and the Art of Motorcycle Maintenance,* Pirsig announces that he will talk with the reader throughout as though in a discussion. So the tone is informal, and he frequently uses the pronoun *you.*]

> One might have supposed that Abraham Lincoln's Gettysburg Address was disappointing because it was so short.

[Here the tone is more formal, and the pronoun *one* does the service that the pronoun *you* might perform in a less formal piece.]

8F Let the tone and intention of your essay determine whether you will use the pronouns *I*, *my*, *me*, and *mine*.

Many writing teachers tell students to avoid using pronouns in the first person singular. The intention of these teachers is to prevent student writers from calling attention to themselves and getting in the way of the subject they should be writing about. Readers do not like to feel that the author is intruding unnecessarily into a piece of writing.

pro 8F

Intrusive

For the first few minutes I saw Carew whack screamers down the right-field line, and I saw him frown at this unwanted consistency. I think Carew is a handsome man, but I don't mean that in the conventional sense. I think that the most arresting features on his face are a tiny turned-up nose and a mouth that in my opinion is a mile wide, and I believe it can exaggerate the mildest emotion. When he smiles, I believe the light can be seen as far away as Newport Beach. When he's downcast, I'd say there's an eclipse of the sun.

This kind of writing would quickly become tedious to all of us if it went on very long. Here is the way a writer for *Sports Illustrated* wrote about Rod Carew, first baseman for the California Angels baseball team:

> For the first few minutes Carew whacked screamers down the rightfield line, frowning at this unwanted consistency. Carew is a handsome man, but not in the conventional sense. The most arresting features on his face are a tiny turned-up nose and a mile-wide mouth that can exaggerate the mildest emotion. When he smiles, the light can be seen as far away as Newport Beach. When he's downcast, there's an eclipse of the sun.
>
> —RON FIMRITE

[Fimrite is writing informally, but he is not writing about himself and his opinions; he is directing our attention to Rod Carew. We know that the opinions expressed here are Fimrite's because he wrote the article. He does not have to use the expression *I think.* We know what he thinks without the personal pronoun.]

The first person singular pronouns are appropriate when you are writing about some experience of yours that is the center of your prose.

> From all available evidence no black man had ever set foot in this tiny Swiss village before I came. I was told before arriving that I would probably be a "sight" for the village; I took this to mean that people of my complexion were rarely seen in Switzerland, and also that city people are always something of a "sight" outside of the city. It did not occur to me—possibly because I am an American—that there could be people anywhere who had never seen a Negro.
>
> —JAMES BALDWIN

The first person singular pronouns are also acceptable when you are weighing two contradictory opinions and want to let readers know which side you are on.

Many scientists believe that the universe will end in a general collapse in which all matter falls back to a central mass, which will eventually explode again in a "big bang" like that which has created the universe we know. Others believe that the stars will continue forever to fly apart from each other in space and that the universe will end in the solitary deaths of all those stars scattered at an infinite distance from one another. I am inclined to accept the second view.

[The writer knows that much debate surrounds this issue; she expresses her own opinion at the last, and the effect of the use of the first person here is to admit of some doubt.]

The first person singular pronouns can be used in other kinds of writing, but you should always at least experiment with not using the first person. Avoiding the first person can help you avoid wordiness, but when you believe you must use it, you may do so with a good conscience. No rule of English holds that you should always avoid saying *I*, *me*, *my*, and *mine*.

8G Avoid the unnecessary placing of a pronoun after a noun.

Some Americans tend to use a pronoun immediately after the noun to give the noun special emphasis. In this regional style of speech, these pronouns play the part of reflexive pronouns. In writing they should be avoided.

Redundant

Harry Truman *he* played the piano.

Improved

Harry Truman played the piano.

[The noun *Harry Truman* is sufficient; the pronoun *he* is unnecessary.]

Improved

Harry Truman *himself* played the piano.

[Here a true reflexive pronoun, *himself,* adds emphasis to the noun *Harry Truman.*]

Redundant

The newspapers *they* admitted that advertising sometimes influences their editorial policy.

Improved

The newspapers admitted that advertising sometimes influences their editorial policy.

[The pronoun *they* is not needed in the sentence.]

Improved

The newspapers *themselves* admitted that advertising sometimes influences their editorial policy.

[The true reflexive pronoun *themselves* may add emphasis to the noun *newspapers.*]

pro
8G

Exercise 8.2 Rewrite the following sentences to eliminate pronoun errors. If a sentence is correct, put a check beside it.

1. He liked to read in the bathtub in the summer and to regulate the water temperature with his toes and to keep the door shut and locked, which was inconvenient for others in the family, since the house had only one bathroom.
2. The movie *Apocalypse Now* was based partly on a novel by Joseph Conrad. It is likely that it suffered because Marlon Brando was so fat in it that it was hard to take him seriously. It looked as if he himself had not taken the movie seriously, and despite the money spent on promoting it, it is clear that it failed to meet expectations about it.
3. The movies *Godfather* and *Godfather II* made millions of dollars, which proves that crime does pay if it is possible to make it exciting on film.
4. The house it was small and cramped for a family of four, and my mother and father, they loved each other, and they made the house seem as big as all creation.
5. The readers of this page will forgive this writer perhaps if he indulges himself in a personal recollection of hearing Hank Williams sing at the Grand Ole Opry in Nashville.
6. I have read that World War I began in 1914. It seems to me that I remember that the Germans invaded Belgium to get to France, and I think that then the British came in to defend Belgium, which, as I recall, was neutral.
7. This time she promised to write the essay, and this was said to be acceptable by the teacher, who said that after this all her work had to be turned in on time and that this was completely reasonable in a class where late papers created a lot of work for the teacher.
8. You can see from the statistical evidence that smoking cigarettes is dangerous to your health.
9. Oil has become so expensive that it is natural that Americans should reduce their use of it, but it remains to be seen whether they can eliminate it as a major item in their budgets.
10. As for wood, it is a good fuel, but it is inconvenient for most people, and its smoke may be dangerous to health.
11. He had a bad temper, and that was one reason why he had so few friends.
12. It is to be expected that it will be cold in winter, and yet in this winter it was said of the temperature that it was much warmer than it had been before in all the history of the weather bureau.

8H Use the proper cases for pronouns.

Pronouns often show *case* by their forms. **Case** refers to the grammatical relation of a pronoun to other words in the sentence. English has only three cases—the *subjective* (sometimes called the *nominative*), the *possessive* (sometimes called the *genitive*), and the *objective* (sometimes called the *accusative*).

Indefinite pronouns (*anybody, everybody:* See 3B, section 3), the pronoun *it*, and the pronoun *you* change their forms only for the *possessive* case. We speak of *anybody's* guess, *its* color, and *your* writing. The pronouns *I, we, he, she, they,* and *who* change forms in each of the three cases.

Subjective Case

Pronouns in the *subjective case* act as subjects or as subject complements.

He and *I* read books all summer long.

She was the candidate *who I* thought deserved the victory.

[The pronouns in italics serve as the subjects of the clauses where they appear.]

It could have been *anyone.*

Mark's best friends were *she* and *I.*

[The pronouns in italics are subject complements.]

Possessive Case

Pronouns in the *possessive case* show ownership or a special relation.

Their cat climbed up on *his* roof and ate *our* bird.

Her critics were louder than *her* admirers.

My uncle was *my* only relative *whose* tastes were like *mine.*

The decision was *theirs* to make after we had made *ours.*

[The pronouns in italics are in the possessive case. See 3B, section 3, for a list of possessive pronouns.]

Objective Case

Pronouns in the *objective case* are indirect objects, direct objects, objects of prepositions, or the subjects or objects of infinitives.

The company gave *her* a contract to design the building.

[indirect object]

Marlow told *them* his story.

[indirect object]

The team chose *me*.
[direct object]

The mouse ate *them*.
[direct object]

pro 8H

Just between *you* and *me*, I thought the play was terrible.
[objects of a preposition]

Who among *them* could possibly object?
[object of a preposition]

They believed *him* to be better qualified.
[subject of an infinitive]

They wanted *her* to be their friend.
[subject of an infinitive]

He expected *them* to wait for the late movie.
[subject of an infinitive]

She asked him to call *her* that evening.
[object of an infinitive]

1 A pronoun that is the subject of a dependent clause is always in the subjective case, even when the dependent clause serves as the object for another clause

He promised the prize to *whoever* made the best grades.
[Despite its position after the preposition *to*, the pronoun *whoever* is in the subjective case because it is the subject of the verb *made* in its own clause. The entire clause *whoever made the best grades* serves as the object of the preposition *to*.]

She was the writer *who* I thought deserved to win the Pulitzer Prize.
[Not *whom* I thought: The pronoun *who* is the subject of the verb *deserved*. The words *I thought* form a separate, parenthetical clause.]

2 Pronouns that serve as objects of prepositions, direct objects, and indirect objects must be in the objective case.

It was a secret between you and *me*.
[*Me* is correct because it is the object of the preposition *between*. The subjective form *I* cannot be the object of a preposition. Thus, *between you and I* is incorrect.]

The old man pushed David and *her* aside and then hobbled down the stairs.
[The pronoun *her* is in the objective case because it is the object of the verb *pushed*.]

She gave the driver and *me* quite a lecture on road safety and courtesy. [As an indirect object of the verb *gave, me* is in the objective case.]

Who's kicking *whom?*
[Some people do write "Who's kicking *who,*" but this usage is sometimes considered illiterate, and writers should use it with caution.]

3 In appositive constructions where a noun follows a pronoun, use the case for the pronoun that you would use if the noun were not present.

He gave the test to *us* students.
[You could say, "He gave the test to *us.*" The pronoun *us* is the object of the preposition *to* and must be in the objective case. Adding the noun *students* does not change the case of the pronoun.]

We students said that the test was too hard.
[You could say, "*We* said that the test was too hard." Adding the noun *students* does not change the pronoun *we.*]

4 Use the correct case of the pronoun after *than* and *as*, which often serve as conjunctions introducing implied clauses.

We do not need to write out some clauses because we understand the idea that follows a pronoun at the end of a sentence. The case of the pronoun depends on the way the pronoun is used in the *implied clause,* the clause we would make if we carried out the obvious thought suggested by the pronoun. (Sometimes implied clauses are called **elliptical clauses.** *Elliptical* comes from *ellipsis,* which means "something left out.")

I always thought that I was smarter than *he.*
[If we filled in the implied clause at the end of this sentence, we would have an awkward but perfectly grammatical construction. "I always thought that I was smarter than *he was smart.*" The pronoun *he* must be in the subjective case because it is the subject of this implied clause.]

Odetta likes George more than *I.*

Odetta likes George more than *me.*
[In the first sentence, Odetta likes George more than *I like George.* In the second sentence, Odetta likes George more than *she likes me.* Notice how the difference in case changes the meaning of these two sentences.]

pro 8H

5 Use the objective case for pronouns that are the subjects or the objects of infinitives.

They thought *her* to be an excellent choice for department head.
[The pronoun *her* is the subject of the infinitive *to be* and must be in the objective case. The subject of the infinitive acts through the infinitive verb. You could change the sentence to read, "They thought that she would be an excellent choice for department head."]

Lincoln decided to consult Johnson and *him.*
[The pronoun *him* receives the action of the infinitive verb *consult* and is therefore the object of the infinitive and must be in the objective case.]

6 Use the possessive case before gerunds. Use the subjective or objective case with present participles used as adjectives.

A gerund is an *-ing* verb form used as a noun. (See 3C, section 1.)

His returning the punt ninety-six yards for a touchdown spoiled the bets made by the gamblers.
[*His,* the possessive pronoun, puts the main emphasis on the act of returning the punt. Compare: "His ninety-six-yard punt return spoiled the bets made by the gamblers."]

He, returning the punt ninety-six yards for a touchdown, spoiled the bets made by the gamblers.
[In this example, the phrase *returning the punt* includes the present participle *returning.* This form of the verb *return* is acting as an adjective. The emphasis of the sentence is on the person rather than on the act. This emphasis becomes clearer if we rewrite the sentence: "Returning the punt ninety-six yards for a touchdown, he spoiled the bets made by the gamblers."]

They remembered him laughing as he said goodbye.
[The objective case *him* is used with the present participle *laughing,* which is used as an adjective to modify *him.*]

7 In compound and appositive constructions, use pronouns that agree in case with the nouns or pronouns with which they are paired.

Compound

He and Sebastian del Cano sailed around the world.
[Not *him* and Sebastian del Cano. The pronoun and the proper noun together form the subject of the sentence. So the pronoun must be in the subjective case.)

Appositive

The captain chose two crew members, *her* and *me*, to attempt the rescue.

[Not *she* and *I*. The appositive pronouns must correspond to the noun *members,* which in this sentence is the direct object. The pronouns must be in the objective case, too.]

Appositive

The last crew members on board, *she* and *I*, were given the first watch. [The pronouns *she* and *I* are appositives to the noun *members,* which serves as the subject of the verb *were given.* The pronouns must be in the subjective case.]

Exercise 8.3 Circle the correct pronoun within the parentheses in the following sentences.

1. He wrote the book for Nini, for (she, her) of the quick quip.
2. Of all the English kings, Henry VIII was the one (who, whom) I think was most cruel.
3. Between her and (I, me) little difference could be seen.
4. I had no objection to (she, her) walking across the country.
5. The candidates seemed to most Americans, including (I, me), to represent a choice between foolishness and stupidity.
6. Just between you and (I, me), I have to say that Hawley was to blame.
7. Jackson is the sculptor (who, whom) I believe to be worthy of the Sting Memorial Award.
8. Clark Gable played the same role again and again for (whoever, whomever) directed him.
9. Unfortunately, he built (we, us) a solar house in the shade of Mt. Tom.
10. Eisenhower was the President for (who, whom) the college was named.
11. Smog hurts (we, us) biking commuters.
12. (We, Us) writers must work long and hard for a good style.
13. She asked (we, us) to tell (he, him) that (she, her) was flying to Las Vegas that night.
14. (His, He) greasing his hair made him look like an Elvis fan from the 1950s.
15. Two cooks, Geoffrey and (I, me), were chosen to explain the food poisoning to the health department.

9 Adjective and Adverb Modifiers

Adjectives and adverbs are describing words. Because they qualify in some way the meaning of other words, we say they *modify* other parts of speech.

Adjectives tell us what kind or how many. They include words such as *big, little, beautiful, red, sunny, crazy,* and *important.* We speak of the *big* house, or the *little* farm, or a *beautiful* day, or the *red* tulip, or the *sunny* weather, or the *crazy* joke, or the *important* plans.

Adverbs tell us where, when, why, and how. They include words such as *quickly, yesterday, beautifully, crazily,* and *rightly.* We say that the dog came *quickly,* or that she was sad *yesterday,* or that the dancing couples spun *crazily* around the room, or that he was *rightly* indignant about being ignored.

Some words can be both adverbs and adjectives and can have the same form in both instances. We speak of *fast* cars, and we say that someone can run *fast.* But most adverbs are formed by adding *-ly* to the end of the adjective form of the word. So we say "He weaves *beautiful* rugs" when we want to emphasize that the rugs are beautiful, but we say "He weaves *beautifully*" when we want to emphasize the techniques he uses as he weaves.

Adjectives modify nouns and pronouns; they do not modify anything else. Adverbs modify verbs (including verb phrases), adjectives, other adverbs, and sometimes whole sentences.

9A Use adjectives to modify nouns or pronouns.

You can identify adjectives by locating words that answer one or more of these questions about nouns or pronouns: *Which one? How many? What color? What size? What kind?*

The adjectives in the following sentences are in italics.

She was a *brilliant* architect and a *good* person.
[The adjective *brilliant* tells us what kind of architect, and the adjective *good* tells what kind of person.]

The road was *long, hard,* and *twisting.*
[These adjectives, coming after the verb, serve as subject complements and tell what kind of road.]

The *red* Buick belonged to my aunt.
[The adjective *red* tells what color Buick and distinguishes it from other Buicks by telling us which one.]

The *six large* men were brothers.
[The adjective *six* tells how many; the adjective *large* tells what size the men were. The combination of adjectives tells us which ones.]

Writing is always *difficult.*
[The adjective *difficult* tells us what kind and modifies the subject *writing,* which is a gerund.]

The *American hockey* team beat the Russians in the Olympics of 1980.
[The adjectives *American* and *hockey* tell what kind of team.]

You may use adjectives before or after the noun or pronoun they modify.

The building, *ugly* and *tall,* burned down last night.

The *tall, ugly* building burned down last night.

The *old* car, *battered* and *rusty,* finally died.

Present and past participles of verbs often serve as adjectives.

Running hard, the bank robber fired back over his shoulder at the police.
[*Running,* the present participle, modifies the subject, *robber.*]

The trip was both *exhausting* and *rewarding.*
[The present participles modify the subject, *trip.*]

The *gathering* night was *filled* with stars.
[The present participle, *gathering,* and the past participle, *filled,* both modify the subject, *night.*]

Buried alive for days, he survived to tell about the earthquake.
[*Buried,* the past participle, modifies the subject, *he.*]

Tired and *discouraged,* she dropped out of the marathon.
[The past participles modify the subject, *she.*]

ad
9A

A noun can be used as an adjective.

Cigarette smoking harms your lungs.

The *energy* crisis is not helped by people who drive six miles for a six-pack.

The *Marshall* Plan helped rebuild Europe after World War II.

Adjectives can serve as nouns.

The *unemployed* are not always the *lazy* and the *inept.*

[All the italicized words are normally adjectives. But the sentence clearly means that the words modify an understood noun, *people* or *persons,* which can be left out, turning the adjectives into nouns.]

1 Use adjectives after linking verbs to modify the subject of the sentence.

A linking verb always links a subject with an adjective or a noun that adds to the description of the subject.

Charles was *fast* and *reliable.*

[Both adjectives modify the subject, *Charles.*]

The road became *difficult.*

[The adjective modifies the subject, *road.*]

2 Avoid using nouns as adjectives if an adjectival form conveys the same meaning or if a revision of the sentence makes the meaning clearer.

Bureaucratic jargon often uses many nouns as adjectives when perfectly good adjectives are available.

Jargon

An *opposition education* theory holds that children learn Latin best under strict *discipline* conditions.

Better

An opposing educational theory holds that children learn Latin best under strict disciplinary conditions.

Exercise 9.1 Draw a line under the adjectives in the following paragraphs.

The man in those pictures is the same man who was fascinated by Italian grand opera. I have never known just what my father saw in the spectacle, but he has told me that he would take my mother to the Opera House every Friday night—if he had enough money for orchestra seats. ("Why go to sit in the balcony?") On Sundays he'd don Italian silk scarves and a camel's hair coat to take his new wife to the polo matches in Golden Gate Park. But one weekend my father stopped going to the opera and polo matches. He would blame the change in his life on one job—a warehouse job, working for a large corporation which today advertises its products with the smiling faces of children. "They made me an old man before my time," he'd say to me many years later. Afterward, jobs got easier and cleaner. Eventually, in middle age, he got a job making false teeth. But his youth was spent at the warehouse. "Everything changed," his wife remembers. The dapper young man in the old photographs yielded to the man I saw after dinner: haggard, asleep on the sofa.

—RICHARD RODRIGUEZ

I fought him for three days. I beat him one day, and he beat me the next day. On the third day, we fought three fights. I had a black eye, and he had a bloody lip. He had a bloody nose, and I had a bloody nose. By the end of the day, we had become good friends. Somebody took us to the candy store and bought us ice-cream cones.

—CLAUDE BROWN

ad
9B

Exercise 9.2

1. Write a sentence in which the adjective *gigantic* appears before a noun subject and the adjectives *frightening* and *dreamy* appear as subject complements.
2. Write a sentence in which the adjective *happy* is used in a phrase immediately after the noun or pronoun that it modifies.
3. Write a sentence in which the adjective *young* is used as a noun.
4. Write a sentence in which the adjective *unwilling* is used to modify the subject.
5. Write a sentence in which the noun *baseball* is used as an adjective.

9B Use adverbs to modify verbs, adjectives, and other adverbs.

The child ran *quickly* into the house.
[The adverb *quickly* modifies the verb *ran.*]

The game was *hotly* contested.
[The adverb *hotly* modifies the adjective *contested.*]

He spoke *more* slowly at the end than at the beginning.
[The adverb *more* modifies the adverb *slowly.*]

ad 9B

1 Use adverbs to answer the questions *When? Where? How? How often? How much? To what degree?* and *Why?*

Yesterday she was in Chicago.
[*Yesterday,* an adverb, modifies the verb *was* and answers the question *when?*]

The lamp is right *there.*
[The adverb *there* modifies the verb *is* and answers the question *where?*]

He came *painfully* to the door.
[The adverb *painfully* modifies the verb *came* and tells *how* he came to the door.]

She *seldom* comes to visit any more.
[The adverb *seldom* modifies the verb *comes* and answers the question *how often?*]

We were *greatly* relieved to receive your letter.
[The adverb *greatly* modifies the adjective *relieved* and tells *how much* we were relieved.]

She was *completely* surprised at the results.
[The adverb *completely* modifies the adjective *surprised* and tells *to what degree* she was surprised.]

Dickens mixed humor and pathos better than any other English writer after Shakespeare; *consequently* he is still read by millions.
[The adverb *consequently* tells why Dickens is read.]

Most adverbs are formed by adding *-ly* to the adjective form, but adverbs may also end in *-wise, -where,* or *-ward.* And many adverbs lack any special ending. Among these are *anew, soon, never, ever, almost, already, well, very, often, rather, yesterday,* and *tomorrow.*

The surest way to recognize adverbs is not by looking at their endings but by understanding how they work in a sentence.

Exercise 9.3 Fill in the blanks in the following sentences with adverbs that make sense.

1. She waited __________ at the airport for the team to make its way __________ home.
2. Lincoln was __________ witty, but he was also __________ sad.

3. __________ the sun was shining when I got up, and a great blue heron flew __________ over the waters of the lake.
4. Doctors have __________ accused boxing of being responsible for serious brain injuries among fighters.
5. She was __________ careful after the accident.
6. We believe that manual dexterity helps __________ in developing the brain.
7. The gasoline was __________ gone when we __________ came to the service station.

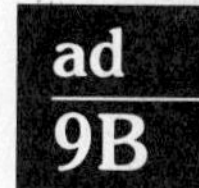

2 Use adverbs correctly as transitional expressions to carry readers smoothly from the ideas of one sentence or paragraph to the ideas of another.

Adverbs may help you tie your thoughts together from one part of your paper to another. Such transitional adverbs include *accordingly, also, anyway, besides, consequently, finally, furthermore, hence, however, incidentally, indeed, instead, likewise, meanwhile, moreover, nevertheless, next, nonetheless, otherwise, still, then, thereafter, therefore,* and *thus.*

These transitional adverbs can introduce sentences, but they cannot be used as conjunctions. Misuse of such transitional adverbs leads to the error called a comma splice (see 4E).

Comma Splice

The Appalachian region is rugged and mountainous, moreover, it is covered with forests and rich in coal.

Standard

The Appalachian region is rugged and mountainous. Moreover, it is covered with forests and rich in coal.

[In the standard version, the writer has made two sentences. The transitional adverb begins the second sentence.]

Standard

The Appalachian region is rugged and mountainous, and, moreover, it is covered with forests and rich in coal.

[In this version, the coordinating conjunction *and* has been inserted after the first independent clause and before the transitional adverb *moreover.*]

Standard

The Appalachian region is rugged and mountainous; moreover, it is covered with forests and rich in coal.

[A semicolon has been inserted before the transitional adverb *moreover,* replacing the comma.]

9C Be cautious when you use adverbs to modify whole sentences.

Sometimes adverbs may seem to modify whole sentences.

ad
9C

> *Unfortunately,* the *Quiz Kids* lost its popularity as an afternoon game show.
>
> *Presumably,* the climber was killed in an avalanche three years ago, although his body was never found.

Some authorities maintain that these adverbs modify the entire sentence, while others insist that these adverbs modify only the verbs in the clauses where they appear. In either case, the meaning of these sentences is clear. But other adverbs are much more ambiguous when they are used to modify full sentences. In common speech people often say things like this: "Hopefully, I will ride my bike to San Francisco." Grammatically, the sentence means that the speaker plans to pedal to San Francisco, feeling hopeful all along the way. Yet the speaker probably means that she hopes she will be able to bike to San Francisco.

This confusion leads many people to reject the use of *hopefully* to mean "I hope" or "they hope" or "she hopes."

> *Hopefully* he will change his job before this one gives him an ulcer.

[Who is doing the hoping? Is it the person who speaks the sentence or the person who is the subject of the sentence? The adverb *hopefully* does not tell us clearly. But if we say, "My children and I hope that my husband will change his job before this one gives him an ulcer," the source of the hope is clear.]

Similar confusions occur when other adverbs are used to modify whole sentences:

> *Briefly,* he was the source of the trouble.

[Does this sentence mean that the writer wishes to say briefly that the subject *he* was the source of the trouble? Or does it mean that *he* was briefly the source of the trouble and that he then changed and was no longer such a source?]

> *Happily,* the mad dog fell dead before it could bite anybody.

[Grammatically, this sentence means that the mad dog fell dead very happily before it could bite anybody. The writer probably means that people on the street were happy that the mad dog fell dead before it could bite one of them. Why not write that?]

It is better to revise such sentences to avoid confusion and the air of loose construction that such use of adverbs conveys.

To put it briefly, I think he was the source of the trouble.

The mad dog fell dead before it could bite anybody.
[Readers do not need to be told that this was a fortunate occurrence.]

9D Do not use adjectives when adverbs are clearly called for.

In common speech we sometimes use adjectival forms in an adverbial way; in writing, this colloquial usage should be avoided.

Nonstandard

He hit that one *real good,* Howard.
[Both *real* and *good* are adjectives, but they are used here as adverbs, *real* modifying *good* and *good* modifying the verb *hit.*]

Nonstandard

She *sure* made me work hard for my grade.
[The adjective *sure* here tries to do the work of an adverb modifying the verb *made.*]

Both these nonstandard usages can be revised simply by changing the improperly used adjectives to adverbs. Thus, "He hit that one *really well,* Howard," and "She *surely* made me work hard for my grade" would substitute correctly for the nonstandard sentences above. But a better solution is to rethink the sentences to make them stronger. Improperly used adjectives are often a sign of a general vagueness of thought, and you can make better sentences by being more concrete.

He hit that one to the warning track, Howard.

She made me write a five-page paper every week.

9E Use adverbs and adjectives correctly with verbs of sense and with certain other linking verbs.

Verbs of sense (*smell, taste, feel,* and so on) can be linking or nonlinking. You must decide whether the modifier after a verb of sense serves the verb or the subject. Study the following examples:

Adverb

The dog smelled *badly.*

[The adverb *badly* modifies the verb *smelled* and tells us that the dog had lost its sense of smell and could not track anything.]

ad 9F

Adjective

The dog smelled *bad.*

[The dog needed a bath. Mentally you can say, "The dog smelled as if he had been in something bad."]

Adverb

I felt *badly.*

[My sense of touch was bad, perhaps because my fingers were numb.]

Adjective

I felt *bad* because she heard me say that her baby looked like a baboon. [Mentally in this expression the person is saying, "I felt that I was bad because she heard me make such a terrible remark." A similar expression would be this: "I felt *guilty* because she heard me make that remark." You would not say, "I felt *guiltily* because I hurt her feelings."]

Adverb

He looked *calmly* to the crowd.

[The adverb modifies *looked* and describes the way that he swept his eyes over the crowd, perhaps waiting for some new response from them.]

Adjective

He looked *calm* to the crowd.

[The adjective shows the opinion of the crowd; the people in it thought he was calm.]

9F Learn the words that have the same spelling in the adjectival and adverbial forms.

As you know, not every adverb is formed by tacking *-ly* onto the end of an adjective. In standard English, many adverbs do not require the *-ly,* and some words have the same form whether they are used as adjectives or adverbs. When you are in doubt, consult your dictionary (see 22B, section 2).

Adjective	Adverb
fast	fast
hard	hard
only	only
right	right or rightly
straight	straight

Exercise 9.4 In each of the following sentences, locate the words misused as adjectives and put the proper adverbs in their place or vice versa. You may simplify the sentence by eliminating the misused adjective or adverb.

1. I felt badly because he took my advice about the horse race and lost all his money.
2. He did terrific on the exam, and I sure was unhappy about his success.
3. John felt real good because he ran so fast in the race.
4. McDonald looked greedy at the fried chicken on his neighbor's plate and decided he would go to Kentucky real fast.
5. She sat still while the poisonous snake twined silent in the arbor just over her head, but her heart beat hard, and she was real scared.
6. She thought she had done good in the lacrosse game, and hopefully she would make the team.
7. Briefly, the speech went on for three hours, and I don't remember a word of it.
8. Interestingly, he turned out to be a bore, although he was supposed to be a fine writer.
9. Hopefully they would never see her again.

ad 9G

Exercise 9.5 Fill in the blanks in the sentences below with any adverb that makes sense. Avoid the easy choices of *very, well,* and *badly.*

1. As the rains grew heavier, the houses were __________ damaged by the flood.
2. The procession wound __________ through the narrow streets and across the square, where the police had __________ blocked off traffic.
3. One by one the graduates walked __________ across the stage, shook hands __________ with the college president, received their diplomas, and stood __________ for a moment while relatives snapped their pictures.
4. She ate __________, saying that diets might help some but that eating __________ did her much more good.
5. Jokes are __________ funny because we do not expect the punch line.

9G Learn to use correctly the three degrees of adjectives and adverbs — the positive, the comparative, and the superlative.

Adjectives and adverbs are often used to compare. Usually an *-er* or an *-est* ending on the word or the use of *more* or *most* along with the word indicates degrees of amount or quality.

The simplest form of the adjective or the adverb is the *positive* degree, the form of an adjective or adverb used when no comparison is involved. This is the form you find in the dictionary.

ad 9G

Positive

The dog ran *quickly* out of the house.

[The running of the dog is not being compared with anything else, so the adverb *quickly* is used in the positive degree.]

Positive

The dog was *quick.*

[A simple statement is being made about the dog; the dog is not being compared with anything else, so the adjective *quick* is used in the positive degree.]

In the *comparative degree,* two things are being compared. For many adjectives the comparative degree is formed by adding the suffix *-er,* but the comparative degree can also be formed by using the secondary adverb *more* or *less.* For most adverbs the comparative is also formed by using the adverb *more* or *less.*

Comparative

The dog was *quicker* than the rabbit.

[The adjective *quicker* is used to make a comparison between the dog and the rabbit.]

Comparative

The dog was *more quick* than the rabbit.

[Here again, two things are being compared, but the writer has chosen to use the adverb *more* rather than the suffix *-er* to form the comparative of the adjective *quick.*]

Comparative

The dog ran *more quickly* than the rabbit.

[Here the adverb *more* modifies the adverb *quickly* to form the comparative of *quickly.*]

Comparative

The rabbit ran *less quickly* than the dog.

[Here the adverb *less* modifies the adverb *quickly* to form the comparative of *quickly.*]

Use the *superlative degree* for both adjectives and adverbs when you compare more than two things. The superlative degree of adjectives may be formed by adding the suffix *-est* to the positive form. It also may be formed by using the adverb *most* or *least* with the positive form. The superlative degree of adverbs is formed by using the adverb *most* or *least* with the positive form.

Superlative

She was the *happiest* of the three women.

[More than two women are being compared, so the superlative degree is used. The superlative degree, *happiest,* is formed by adding *-est* to the end of the adjective *happy.* (For the change from *y* to *i,* see 29B, section 5.)]

Superlative

George was the *most gloomy* person I ever knew.

[The superlative of the adjective *gloomy* is here formed by using the adverb *most* with the positive form of the adjective.]

Superlative

They sang *most happily* when they had eaten well.

[The superlative degree of the adverb *happily* is formed by using the adverb *most.*]

1 Do not use the superlative for only two things or units.

Not: Of the two brothers, John was *quickest.*

But: Of the two brothers, John was *quicker.*

2 Learn the forms of the adjectives and adverbs that are irregular in the comparative and the superlative.

Positive	Comparative	Superlative
bad	worse	worst
good	better	best
little	less	least
many/much	more	most
far	farther	farthest

3 Do not use the comparative and superlative degrees with absolute adjectives.

Absolutes are words that in themselves mean something complete or ideal, words like *unique, infinite, impossible, perfect, round, square, destroyed,* and *demolished.*

If something is *unique,* it is the only one of its kind. So we cannot say, "Her dresses were *more unique* than his neckties." Something is either unique or it is not. We should not say, "The answer to your question is *more impossible* than you think." Something is either possible or impossible; it cannot be *more* or *less* impossible.

ad
9G

4 Avoid using the superlative when you are not making a comparison with anything.

Dracula is the *scariest* movie!
[The scariest movie ever filmed? The scariest movie you have ever seen? The scariest movie ever shown in town?]

In common speech, we frequently use expressions like *scariest movie* or *silliest thing* when we are not in fact comparing the movie or the thing with anything else. In writing, such expressions lack the vocal emphasis we can give them when we speak. They become merely wordy and imprecise, taking up space without conveying any meaning.

5 Avoid adding an unnecessary adverb to the superlative degree of adjectives.

Not: She was the *very* brightest person in the room.

But: She was the brightest person in the room.
[The superlative degree of an adjective ending in *-est* does not take a supporting adverb.]

Not: The interstate was the *most* shortest way to Nashville

But: The interstate was the shortest way to Nashville.

6 Avoid making illogical comparisons with adjectives and adverbs.

Illogical comparisons occur when writers leave out some necessary words.

Illogical

The story of the *Titanic* is more interesting than the story of any disaster at sea.

[This comparison makes it seem that the story of the *Titanic* is one thing and that *the story of any disaster at sea* is something different. In fact the story of the *Titanic* is about a disaster at sea. Is the story of the *Titanic* more interesting than itself? The sentence is illogical.]

Logical

The story of the *Titanic* is the most interesting of all the stories of disasters at sea.

[Here the superlative degree quickly identifies the story of the *Titanic* as one about a disaster at sea and announces that in comparison with all the others, it is the most interesting.]

Illogical

Building houses with brick is harder than lumber.

[What is being compared here? Is the *act* of building harder than the *thing* we call lumber? The comparison is illogical because acts are different from things and cannot be compared in a sentence like the one above.]

Logical

Building houses with brick is harder than *building* them with lumber.

[Now it is clear that the comparison is between two acts of building, not between an act and a thing.]

Illogical

Mr. Lincoln's speech was shorter than Mr. Everett.

[In this sentence, one might suppose that Mr. Everett was six feet tall but that Mr. Lincoln's speech was only five feet.]

Logical

Mr. Lincoln's speech was shorter *than that* of Mr. Everett.

[Now it is clear that Mr. Lincoln's speech is being compared with Mr. Everett's speech and not with Mr. Everett himself.]

7 Avoid overusing adjectives.

Using too many adjectives in any one sentence will weaken the force of a statement. Strong writers put an adjective before a noun or pronoun only when the adjective is truly needed. They rarely put as many as three adjectives before a noun unless they need to create some special effect or unless one of the adjectives is a number.

Study the following paragraphs. The adjectives are in boldface.

> I had imagined Siberia as having been filled up by waves of settlers, much as the **American** West. But what impressed me most on that **train** trip was the sparseness of humanity and the **enormous** emptiness of the land. Cities would suddenly loom up without the warning of suburbs and then, after we stopped briefly, would vanish just as suddenly. The **petty** barter from ship-to-shore marked the progress of our voyage across the continent. The **dining** car left Moscow well stocked with **fresh** apples, oranges, cucumbers, **chocolate** candy and **other little** delicacies. At the **early** stops, townfolk would rush to purchase these goodies from the **dining car** staff leaning out doors and windows. But later, as supplies ran **low** and the menu became more **restricted,** the trade shifted the **other** way.
>
> —Hedrick Smith

ad
9G

The jet has radically altered the rate at which **Western** technology and culture have spread. When a **ten thousand foot** runway is constructed in some hitherto **remote** spot, life in that area will begin to change at once—probably faster than at **any** time since it was last invaded in war. And because the **modern** traveler demands as far as possible the comfort and lifestyle of his home, it becomes increasingly **difficult** to wake up in a hotel anywhere in the world and know, instantly, where you are. **Local** customs and the **physical** shape of the environment are changed to meet the requirements of visitors. The rate at which this is happening has increased with the construction of **widebody** jets, each capable of carrying nearly **four hundred** people. As the standard of living in the West has risen steadily since the end of the **last world** war, with a **consequent** increase in **disposable** income, the numbers of people **able** to afford holidays by air has risen too. Because the **new** jets operate more efficiently than their predecessors, costs have fallen and this has acted as a **further** stimulus to travel.

—JAMES BURKE

In the first paragraph, in 131 words we find only fifteen adjectives. In the second paragraph, we have 190 words and only eighteen adjectives (the numbers are counted as one adjective each, although each number in this selection has two words). Different writers will, of course, use adjectives at different rates. But it will help you limit your own use of adjectives if you study examples of writing you like to read and notice how economical good writers are in their use of adjectives.

Exercise 9.6 In the following sentences, use any adjectives you choose to fill in the blanks. But whatever adjective you write in must be in the proper degree—positive, comparative, or superlative. Be adventurous. Avoid common adjectives like *good* and *bad.*

1. President Franklin D. Roosevelt was a ________ man than many presidents who served before him.
2. Rhode Island is the ________ of all the states.
3. Lassie is a ________ actor than John Travolta.
4. Steam radiators are ________.
5. Percy owned the ________ leather vest in his motorcycle gang.
6. Rock records are generally the ________ of all records sold.
7. Rain is generally ________ than snow or ice.
8. The president of the university is ________ than the faculty.
9. The sea is ________ than the desert.
10. Dick Tracy was ________ than Batman.

Exercise 9.7 Choose a piece of nonfiction writing that you enjoy, such as an article in a popular magazine like *Sports Illustrated, Time, Newsweek, Popular Mechanics,* or *Rolling Stone.* Answer the following questions about the article you choose.

1. In three consecutive paragraphs chosen at random, what is the total number of nouns?
2. How many nouns have adjectives before them?
3. How many nouns have more than one adjective before them?
4. What is the total number of adjectives in these paragraphs?
5. How many times do you find two or more consecutive adjectives of more than one syllable in sentences taken from your randomly selected paragraphs?
6. What adjectives can be left out without injury to the clarity or to the tone of the piece?
7. What conclusions can you make about the use of adjectives by professional writers?

Exercise 9.8 Take any paper written by you or another student in the class, and ask the same questions you asked in Exercise 9.7.

Exercise 9.9 Eliminate as many adjectives as you can in the following paragraph:

> The old, bent, gray man stood still and thoughtful on the crowded edge of the crowded, busy, narrow street and looked down to the tall, lighted, brick building which loomed up in the thick, damp, gray mist of the early, chill, autumn, overcast, threatening night. He felt in the deep, warm, dark pocket of his new, wool, black, tweed overcoat for the hard, blue, loaded, automatic pistol and checked the tiny, metal safety catch on the lethal, heavy, criminal weapon. The important, threatening, dangerous gun was there, ready, waiting, eager to be fired.

10 Misplaced Sentence Parts

In English, clarity depends on the word order within sentences. We expect most adjectives and adjectival clauses and phrases to come either immediately before or immediately after the words they modify unless they are subject complements, joined to the words they modify by linking verbs (see 3A, section 1, pages 102–107). For example, it is common to find sentences like this one:

The quick, brown fox jumps over the **lazy** dog.
[The adjectives, in boldface, come immediately before the nouns they modify.]

And it is common to find sentences like this one:

The beggar, **sad** and **old,** held out his hand to me.
[The adjectives *sad* and *old* come immediately after the noun they modify.]

But adverbs and adverbial phrases are often separated by other words from the words or phrases they modify. We say "They began their job **yesterday,**" and we know without thinking much about it that the adverb *yesterday* modifies the verb *began,* although the words *their job* come between the verb and its modifier. It is not customary in English to say "They began yesterday their job." And we also write sentences like this one: "**When she was young,** she played softball every **Saturday.**" The adverbial clause *When she was young* modifies the verb *played,* and so does the adverb *Saturday.* But both the clause and the simple adverb are separated from the verb by other words.

So the trick in English is to know when you can separate modifiers from the words or phrases they modify and when you cannot. And in general you can separate adverbs and adverbials from the words they modify more easily than you can separate adjectives from the words they modify.

Yet even adverbs and adverbial phrases can be misplaced. In general, for example, an adverbial phrase modifies the nearest verb. It may be separated from that verb by other words, but English idiom makes us expect to join adverbs and adverbials to the nearest possible verb. When another verb gets in the way, our sentences get into trouble, as in the following sentences from one of the humorous squibs in *The New Yorker:*

> Wednesday morning, Lee's oldest son Mike signed a national letter of intent with Indiana University to play football for the Hoosiers in the family kitchen at 3838 Ashland Drive in West Lafayette.

[The writer intended to make the adverbial prepositional phrase *in the family kitchen* modify the verb *signed.* But since it is nearer to the infinitive phrase *to play football,* it seems to modify that phrase, giving the impression that Mike is going to be running for touchdowns over the kitchen sink.]

> During the lecture, Johanson will describe the discovery of a band of the new species of hominids who appeared to have been killed simultaneously by some disaster with color slides.

[The writer has intended to make the prepositional phrase *with color slides* modify the verb phrase *will describe.* But it is nearer to and appears to describe the noun *disaster* and seems to be an adjectival phrase.]

The lesson of errors like these should be to remind you to keep the related parts of a sentence as close to each other as you can. Otherwise you may create confusion for your readers.

10A Avoid dangling or misplaced participles.

Introductory participles and participial phrases must modify the grammatical subject of the sentence. Participles that do not modify the grammatical subject are called **dangling** or **misplaced** participles. A *dangling* participle lacks a noun to modify.

Dangling

> After drying up the Turkish and Asian poppy supplies, Mexico became a prime supplier of Mexican Brown heroin.
>
> —*Boston Globe, New England Magazine*

[As written, the sentence means that Mexico somehow dried up the Turkish and Asian poppy supplies and took over these parts of the drug trade itself, as if the Mexican government intended such a course of events. But this was not the sense of the article at all. The participial phrase *after drying up the Turkish and Asian poppy supplies* modifies nothing in the rest of the sentence. The writer has used a participle when we should have another form: "After Turkish and Asian poppy supplies dried up, Mexico became a prime supplier of a heroin called 'Mexican Brown.'"]

A *misplaced* participle occurs in a sentence containing a noun that the participle should modify. But since the participle is misplaced, it modifies the wrong noun instead.

Misplaced

dang 10A

Born in 1812, the novel commonly called *The Pickwick Papers* made Charles Dickens famous by the age of 25.

[*Born in 1812,* the past participle, should modify *Charles Dickens.* Instead it seems to modify the noun *novel* so that the book appears to have been born in 1812.]

As noted above, the only way to correct dangling and misplaced modifiers is to make a complete revision of the sentence.

Born in 1812, Charles Dickens became famous at the age of 25 when he published the novel commonly called *The Pickwick Papers.*

[The sentence has been rewritten to make *Charles Dickens* the grammatical subject, modified by the introductory participial phrase *born in 1812.*]

Dangling

Having studied small-engine repair in night school, fixing the lawn mower was easy.

[The subject of the sentence is the gerund *fixing.* But the *fixing* cannot have studied small-engine repair in night school. The writer had a subject in mind when he started the sentence but forgot it when he wrote the rest, so there is nothing in the second part of the sentence for the introductory phrase to modify.]

Revised

Having studied small-engine repair in night school, Jane found that fixing the lawn mower was easy.

[The introductory phrase now modifies the subject, *Jane.*]

Revised

After Jane studied small-engine repair in night school, fixing the lawn mower was easy.

[The opening has been changed to an adverbial clause.]

Dangling

Driving along Route 10, the sun shone in Carmela's face.

[This sentence says that the sun was driving along Route 10.]

Revised

Driving along Route 10, Carmela found the sun shining in her face.

[Now it is clearly Carmela who was driving along Route 10. The sentence has been revised to place a correct subject after the modifying participle at the beginning.]

Revised

When Carmela drove along Route 10, the sun shone in her face.

[The introductory phrase has been rewritten so that the sentence now begins with a clause.]

dang 10A

Dangling

Using elaborate charts and graphs, the audience understood the plan.

[The sentence says that the audience used the charts and graphs to understand the plan.]

Revised

Using elaborate charts and graphs, the mayor explained the plan to the audience.

[The added noun *mayor* becomes the subject of the rewritten sentence, and the introductory participial phrase now modifies the subject correctly.]

Revised

Because the mayor used elaborate charts and graphs, the audience understood the plan.

[Now the sentence begins with an introductory clause that serves as an adverb modifying the verb *understood.*]

Although dangling participles usually come at the beginning of a sentence, they can come at the end.

Dangling

The work was hard, sweating over hot machinery, bending in cramped spaces, sometimes mashing his fingers, skinning his knees, twisting heavy wrenches, and getting home late and exhausted every night.

[The writer has attached a series of participial phrases to the end of the sentence. Such participial phrases at the end of the sentence, often called **free modifiers,** should modify the subject of the sentence. But these modifiers cannot modify the subject, *work.*]

Revised

He worked hard, sweating over hot machinery, bending in cramped spaces, sometimes mashing his fingers, skinning his knees, twisting heavy wrenches, and getting home late and exhausted every night.

[Now all the participial phrases modify the subject, *he.*]

Note: Avoid confusing absolute phrases with dangling participles. Absolute phrases contain both a noun and a present or past participle (see 3C, section 1). They stand by themselves in sentences and do not modify single words, although they add to the meaning of the sentence as a whole.

dang 10A

Absolute Phrases

Intercollegiate athletic programs have become big business, their coaches paid more than presidents, their teams far better known than professors, their revenues contributing more to the general fund than tuition.

[The absolute constructions are *their coaches paid more than presidents, their teams far better known than professors,* and *their revenues contributing more to the general fund than tuition.* Each of these absolutes names something, and each concludes with a participle that modifies what is named.]

He remembered the old days in the now-abandoned railroad station, the steam locomotives puffing in and out, the newspaper boys shouting the headlines, passengers climbing down and looking around for taxis, a hum of activity filling the air.

[This sentence includes a string of absolute phrases, each naming something with a noun, then modifying the noun with a present participial phrase. The absolute phrases do not dangle.]

Usage note

Informal usage frequently accepts the following forms that combine an introductory participle with the expletive *it* (see 8D), especially when the participle expresses a habitual or general action.

Walking in the country at dawn, it is easy to see many different kinds of birds.

[The statement is general, expressing something that would be done by anyone. Many writers and editors would prefer this revision: "Walking in the country at dawn is an easy way to see many different kinds of birds."]

When beginning a new exercise program, it is good to have a complete physical examination by a doctor.

[The statement is general, and to many writers it seems preferable to an informal statement like this one: "When you begin a new exercise program, you should have a complete physical examination by a doctor." Or a formal statement like this one: "When one begins a new exercise program, one should have a complete physical examination by a doctor." But many other writers—perhaps a majority—would revise the sentence to read like this: "Anyone who begins a new exercise program should have a complete physical examination by a doctor."]

Exercise 10.1 Rewrite any of the following sentences that have dangling or misplaced participles. If a sentence does not have a dangling or misplaced participle, put a check beside it. If a sentence contains an absolute, write an A beside it.

1. Daydreaming about his new job, the doorbell startled him.
2. Working hard through the night, the job was finished by daybreak.
3. Everything went off exactly as planned, the false Arab sheik sitting in costume on a sofa, the congressmen led in one by one, the bribes offered, the congressmen making excuses for themselves to have reasons for taking the money, the FBI moving at last to put them under arrest.
4. Riding hard through the night, Paul Revere spread the alarm through Middlesex County to the sleeping town of Lexington.
5. Backed into a corner and hurt, the bell barely saved him.
6. Walking along the street, the city seemed calm.
7. Using a word processor, he was able to revise his paper in a couple of hours and turn in the finished product the next day, every error corrected and some sentences rewritten in a much more effective style.
8. Having played hard, the loss was bitter.
9. Taking the ship from New York, the trip was now under way.
10. Having been aged in an oak barrel for twelve years, he discovered that the wine was exactly to his taste.
11. The marathon was difficult, running up hills, knowing his shoes were inferior, sweating hard, thirsting for water.
12. They enjoyed the meal, talking, laughing, telling old stories, and drinking too much.
13. Having cleaned up the house, the garage was next on the list.
14. Looking up, the long V-shaped flock of geese could be seen by everyone in the valley.
15. Turning the car down the valley road, he could see the long shadows cast by the stark white moon, the houses shut up against the night, and the road itself running like a stripe painted across the earth and disappearing into the dark in the distance.

10B Avoid the misplaced prepositional phrase that modifies the wrong element in the sentence.

Prepositional phrases used as adjectives seldom give trouble. We use them commonly in speech, and these speech habits transfer readily to writing.

The book *on the table* belongs to me.

[The prepositional phrase *on the table* is used as an adjective modifying the noun *book.*]

We lived in a house *near the school.*

[The prepositional phrase *near the school* is used as an adjective modifying the noun *house.*]

Prepositional phrases used as adverbs are harder to place in sentences, and sometimes writers are led astray by their adverbial phrases.

misp 10B

Misplaced

He saw the first dive-bombers approaching from the bridge of the battleship.

[The misplaced prepositional phrase *from the bridge* makes it seem that the dive-bombers were approaching from the bridge of the battleship.]

Revised

From the bridge of the battleship, he saw the first dive-bombers approaching.

[*From the bridge* now clearly modifies the verb *saw.*]

Misplaced

The German chancellor was introduced to Americans on television.

[The position of the prepositional phrase *on television* functions as an adjective modifying the noun *Americans.*]

Revised

The German chancellor was introduced on television to Americans.

[Now the position of the prepositional phrase makes it function as an adverb modifying the verb phrase *was introduced.*]

Misplaced

He ran the ten-kilometer race from the shopping mall through the center of town to the finish line by the monument in his bare feet.

[The misplaced adverbial prepositional phrase *in his bare feet* might make a rapid reader think that the monument was in his bare feet.]

Revised

In his bare feet he ran the ten-kilometer race from the shopping mall through the center of town to the finish line by the monument.

[*In his bare feet* is now close enough to the verb *ran* to avoid confusion.]

Revised

From the shopping mall, through the center of town to the finish line by the monument, he ran the ten-kilometer race in his bare feet.

[This version preserves the sentence emphasis that the writer wanted in the first draft of the sentence, keeping the surprising phrase *in his bare feet* until the end.]

10C Avoid the misplaced clause that modifies the wrong sentence element.

Misplaced

Professor Peebles taught the course on the English novel that most students dropped after three weeks.

[Did they drop the course or the novel?]

misp 10C

Revised

Professor Peebles taught the course on the English novel, a course most students dropped after three weeks.

[The repetition of the word *course* before the adjectival clause makes the modification clear. Students dropped the course, not the novel.]

Revised

After three weeks, most students dropped Professor Peebles' course on the English novel.

[This version is a more thorough revision, and the need for a dependent clause has disappeared. The extent of such a revision will depend on the writer's view of what is most important in the sentence, a view that will be decided by the context of the sentence.]

Misplaced

For five years Dixon worked all day as an accountant to support her family and after supper went to night school to study law, which was hard, but finally she got her degree.

[Was law hard, or was her schedule hard?]

Revised

For five years Dixon worked all day as an accountant to support her family and after supper went to night school to study law. It was a hard schedule, but she finally got her degree.

Revised

For five years Dixon worked all day as an accountant to support her family and after supper went to night school to study law. Law was a hard field, but she finally got her degree.

[In both revisions, a long original sentence has been broken into two shorter ones. When you have trouble with modification, you can often clarify your thought by using two sentences instead of one.]

Exercise 10.2 Rewrite the following sentences to correct errors in modification.

1. Marco Polo traveled overland to China with his father and his uncle to visit the Mongol Empire, which was very dangerous.

2. He stood in the middle of the room and shouted at everyone in his pajamas.
3. He bought a digital watch at the jewelry shop which ran on tiny batteries.
4. She wrote the outline of her book on the wall in the kitchen with a black crayon.
5. When she was a little girl, she used to lie awake at night wishing that she had a horse in her bedroom.
6. The boat lost its sail in the hard wind which was made of canvas.

10D Avoid the confusing adverb or adverbial phrase that seems to modify both the element that comes immediately before it and the element that comes immediately after it.

Place your adverbs so that they modify only one sentence element.

Confusing

To read a good book *completely* satisfies her.

[Does reading a book satisfy her completely? Or must she read the book completely to be satisfied?]

Revised

She is completely satisfied when she reads a good book.

Revised

She is satisfied when she reads a good book completely.

Confusing

Changing gears *continually* gives mental exercise to people who ride bicycles.

[Does the writer mean that continually changing gears provides mental exercise or that changing gears gives mental exercise continually?]

Revised

Continually changing gears gives mental exercise to people who ride bicycles.

Revised

Changing gears gives continual mental exercise to people who ride bicycles.

[Notice that in the second revision, *continual* is an adjective. In the first revision, merely changing the position of *continually* clarifies the meaning of the sentence.]

Exercise 10.3 Rewrite the following sentences to eliminate the confusion of adverbs that may modify two elements in a sentence.

1. The car starting easily made this the best day of my trip.
2. People who disliked long hair very much liked having ten-dollar bills with long-haired Alexander Hamilton's picture on the front.
3. A scholar who studies often goes to sleep over her books.
4. People who love to criticize books sometimes do not write books themselves.
5. She woke up suddenly pushing off the covers.

10E As a rule, place one-word modifiers that define degree, extent, or limitation before the words or phrases that they modify.

These modifiers include words like *merely, completely, fully, perfectly, hardly, nearly, almost, even, just, simply, scarcely,* and *only.*

Note the differences in meaning in the following sentences:

The *almost* exhausted man finished the marathon.

The exhausted man *almost* finished the marathon.

The *completely* restored antique cars paraded proudly through the admiring town.

The restored antique cars paraded proudly through the *completely* admiring town.

In speaking, we sometimes put limiting modifiers in illogical places, but the sense of what we say is clear from the tone of our voice, our gestures, or the general context. In writing, lack of logic in misplaced modifiers can cause confusion.

Confusing

He *only* had one bad habit, but it *just* was enough to keep him in trouble. [The *only* in the sentence seems to modify the verb *had,* and the *just* modifies the adjective *enough.*]

Revised

He had only one bad habit, but it was just enough to keep him in trouble.

Confusing

They were all *nearly* about to graduate, but they wouldn't *even* send one invitation because all of them decided *almost* that the commencement speaker would insult the intelligence of the audience.

[The adverb *nearly* seems to modify *about,* but the phrase *about to graduate* and *nearly* say something similar; *even* seems to modify *send,* and *almost* seems to modify the entire dependent clause that comes after it. The sentence is difficult to understand.]

Revised

They were nearly all about to graduate, but they wouldn't send even one invitation because all of them decided that the commencement speaker would insult the intelligence of the audience.

Exercise 10.4 Use each of the modifiers below in at least two sentences.

only, even, just, scarcely, almost, nearly

11
Confusing Shifts

To keep your sentences clear and harmonious, you must be consistent in your use of verbs and nouns. You should avoid jarring shifts in point of view and sudden outbursts of emotion.

11A Be consistent in your verb tenses.

Inconsistent

Every day the parking lot *fills* up by eight in the morning, and commuting students arriving after that *could* not find parking places.

[The verb *fills* is in the present indicative tense; the verb *could* is in the past tense.]

Consistent

The parking lot *fills* up by eight in the morning, and commuting students arriving after that *can*not find parking places.

[Both verbs are now in the present tense.]

When you write about the content of any piece of literature, you usually use the present tense. Be careful not to shift out of the present tense when you have decided to use it for such a purpose. Take this care not only within sentences but from one sentence to another. Be especially careful when you quote a passage that is in the past tense. Do not shift your description of the passage into the past tense if you have been using the present. Here is an example:

> David Copperfield *observes* other people with a fine and sympathetic eye. He *describes* villains such as Mr. Murdstone and improbable heroes

such as Mr. Micawber with unforgettable sharpness of detail. But David Copperfield *was* not himself an especially interesting person.

[The unexpected shift from present to past tense in the third sentence will jar readers.]

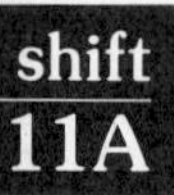

Avoid the temptation to fall into inconsistent tenses when you are telling an exciting story. Sometimes the events you are relating become vividly present to you as you speak or write, and you slip into the present tense. Such an inconsistency may be acceptable in conversation, but it confuses readers.

Inconsistent

The wind *was howling* and *blowing* a hundred miles an hour when suddenly there *is* a big crash, and a tree *falls* into Rocky's living room.

[The writer begins with the past progressive, or imperfect, tense (*was howling . . . blowing*) and in the excitement of describing a falling tree shifts the tense to the present (*is* and *falls*).]

Consistent

The wind *was howling* and *blowing* a hundred miles an hour when suddenly there *was* a big crash, and a tree *fell* into Rocky's living room.

Inconsistency may creep into your writing when you combine present perfect and past perfect tenses with present and past tenses of verbs.

Inconsistent

She *has admired* many strange buildings at the university, but she *thought* that the Science Center *looked* completely out of place.

Consistent

She *has admired* many strange buildings at the university, but she *thinks* that the Science Center *looks* completely out of place.

[The present perfect tense *has admired* leads readers from a point in the past to the present and assumes that the activity described still goes on. So in making successive clauses you must be sure that you take into account the continuing action of the first clause. The thought expressed in the consistent sentence is like this: She has admired and still admires in the present many strange buildings at the university, but she thinks now in the present that the Science Center looks completely out of place.]

Consistent

She *admired* many strange buildings at the university, but she *thought* that the Science Center *looked* completely out of place.

[The simple past in the first clause names an action considered finished at some point in past time. The second clause can also use a simple past verb for an action which, like the action in the first verb, is considered past.]

Verbs in successive clauses do not have to be in the same tense, but they should follow each other in tenses that make good grammatical sense and say what the writer wants them to say.

The present tense may be followed by another present tense:

> Dogs *bark* to show that they *are interested* in something, or to show that they *are* afraid, or to announce that someone—perhaps another dog—*is invading* their territory.

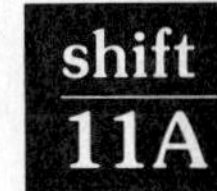

The present tense may be followed by a past tense:

> Michaelson *says* that transistors *made* stereo systems cheaper but *reduced* the fidelity of sound created by vacuum tubes.

The present can be used with the present perfect:

> Quality control in the American automobile industry *is* a long-standing problem that *has made* millions of Americans think that Japanese cars are better.

The present can be used with the future tense:

> We *predict* that word processors *will replace* electric typewriters in most offices by the end of this decade.

The present tense should not be used with the past perfect tense unless a suitable tense follows the past perfect.

Inconsistent

She *swears* that she *had registered* her car properly.

Consistent

She *swears* that she *had registered* her car properly before she *received* a ticket for having an improper license plate.

[In the consistent version, the past perfect comes before a clause that uses the simple past tense in its verb. The past perfect reports action that was finished in the past *before* some other past action occurred.]

If you are not going to follow the past perfect with a clause using a verb in the past tense, change the past perfect tense to a more suitable form.

Consistent
She *swears* that she *registered* her car properly.

The simple past can be followed by another simple past:

shift 11B

College football *was* so violent early in this century that President Theodore Roosevelt *threatened* to abolish it.

The simple past can be used with the imperfect:

Everyone *was* eager to know if she *was going* to enter the fifty-mile road race.

The simple past can be used with the future:

They *told* me that the tire shipment *will arrive* next week.

The simple past should not be used with the present perfect, although in informal speech we sometimes do use the two tenses together.

Informal
She *reported* that she *has been running* nine miles every morning.

Formal
She *reports* that she *runs* nine miles every morning.

Formal
She *reported* that she *had been running* nine miles every morning.

11B Be consistent in the mood of your verbs.

Mood is a change in a verb that shows the way in which an assertion is made in a sentence (see 7D). The indicative mood makes simple statements or asks simple questions. The conditional mood makes statements that would be true if something else were true. The subjunctive mood is now used rarely in English (see 7D), but when it is used, it often makes conditional statements known to be contrary to fact. (If I *were* in Rome on Easter morning, I would hear thousands of church bells. I am not in Rome on Easter morning, and I may not be there when Easter comes; so I use the subjunctive mood in the clause *if I were.*)

Inconsistent shifts from the indicative to the conditional or from the conditional to the indicative often cause trouble.

Inconsistent

He *will go* to night school and *would take* a course in hotel management. [The indicative *will go* seems to be about to make a statement, a simple report that someone is going to night school. But the conditional *would take* makes us think that this is not a simple report at all but that some uncertainty is involved. Maybe he is not going to night school. The conditional makes us expect a clause beginning with *if.*]

Consistent

If he *could go* to night school, he *would take* a course in hotel management.

[Now the conditional verb *could go* in the first clause makes us expect another conditional verb, *would take,* in the next clause. We have the uncertainty of his going to night school clearly stated.]

Inconsistent

If he *goes* to night school, he *would take* a course in hotel management. [Here the inconsistency arises because the indicative verb *goes* seems to start the sentence by making a simple statement to answer the question "What will he do if he goes to night school?" But the change in mood with the conditional verb *would take* in the next clause brings in an unnecessary confusion. We know that it is not certain that he will go to night school. The *if* tells us that. But if he does go to night school, is there any uncertainty about what he will take? The conditional mood in the verb *would take* indicates that there is, but we are not told why.]

Consistent

He *would go* to night school, and he *would take* a course in hotel management, if he *could get out* of jail.

[Here the conditional mood used throughout in the verbs makes everything about this sentence seem uncertain. The use of the conditional implies that none of these acts is likely to happen. He is probably not going to get out of jail, and he is probably not going to go to night school and take a course in hotel management.]

Consistent

He *will go* to night school and *will take* a course in hotel management if he *gets out* of jail.

[The mood throughout is indicative—and more optimistic. The sentence makes a simple statement of fact, telling what he will do if he gets out of jail. No uncertainty is involved in the verbs preceding the *if* clause, although the conjunction *if* does imply that he may not get out of jail. Yet the indicative mood shows that he has a good chance of getting out of jail, since it implies much less uncertainty than the conditional mood.]

Inconsistent

If he *were* absent, he *will fail* the course.

[The subjunctive *were* indicates a statement contrary to fact. He is not absent, but if he were, something would happen. But then the indicative *will fail* indicates a simple report of fact. The mood is inconsistent with the subjunctive that comes before it.]

shift 11B

Consistent

If he *is* absent, he *will fail* the course.

[Now we have a simple statement. We do not know if he is absent or not. But if he is absent, he will fail the course. The indicative is used in both verbs.]

Consistent

If he *were* absent, he *would fail* the course.

[The subjunctive *were* indicates a conditional statement contrary to fact. He is not absent. It is followed by a conditional verb in the following clause, *would fail.* The conditional makes the sentence mean that if he were absent, he would fail the course, but he is not absent, and he will not fail the course.]

You can see here the value of the moods of verbs; without these various moods, we would have a hard time saying some things.

Exercise 11.1 Correct the confusing shifts in the following sentences. If a sentence is correct as it stands, put a check by the number.

1. Hamlet has been in school in Wittenberg, and he came home to find his father dead and his mother married to his father's brother.
2. Mercutio has to die in *Romeo and Juliet,* or else he would have carried the play off from the two young lovers, who are not nearly as interesting as he was.
3. The band hit a sour note, and the drum major gets sore at the tuba section.
4. Parents who often get drunk embarrassed their children.
5. King James I, who died in 1625, had never taken a bath in his adult life, and those who prepared him for burial have to scour his underwear off his body.
6. If you travel abroad this summer, we would have enjoyed going with you.
7. She would design the building if she knows calculus.
8. If I were in Paris right now, I can hear the sounds of the streets.
9. If the queen will stop wearing those big, round hats, her people would think better of her taste.
10. She has been to automobile-mechanics school before she set up her business.

11C Use the same voice for verbs in closely related clauses and sentences.

The voice of a transitive verb is either active or passive. In clauses with active verbs, the subject does the acting; in clauses with passive verbs, the subject is acted upon (see 7E). Inconsistency in voice sometimes arises from a writer's desire to use variety in sentence forms. But when the actor remains the same in successive clauses, you should not change voice.

Inconsistent

> The Impressionist painters *hated* black. Violet, green, blue, pink, and red *were favored* by them.

[The actor in the successive sentences is the same—the Impressionist painters. But the voices of the verbs are inconsistent because *hated* is active and *were favored* is passive. The writer has bought variety at the expense of reader confusion.]

Consistent

> The Impressionist painters *hated* black. They *favored* violet, green, blue, pink, and red.

[Now both verbs in the successive sentences are in the active voice.]

Note that it is easy to go from a linking verb of simple description in the active voice to a verb in the passive voice in the next clause.

> Today American Indians *are* often poor, uneducated, and unhealthy. They *have been isolated* from the rest of the country, *deprived* of the benefits of the land which was taken away from them by force, and *forgotten* by the people who robbed them.

[The passive verbs *have been isolated, deprived,* and *forgotten* follow naturally after the simple descriptive sentence *Today American Indians are often poor, uneducated, and unhealthy,* which has a simple linking verb, *is*. The shift in voice is unobtrusive.]

You should avoid a sudden shift in voice from clause to clause or sentence to sentence when you are writing about the same actor or agent. Your readers may expect a shift if you move from one agent to another. They will not expect a shift when you are telling of the actions of the same agent in successive clauses.

Inconsistent

> The bulldozer clanked into the woods and bit into the ground. The trees and the earth were ripped up.

Consistent

The bulldozer clanked into the woods, bit into the ground, and ripped up the trees and the earth.

Consistent

McNabb *rode* his motorcycle through the plate-glass window and *was taken* to the hospital as soon as the ambulance could get there.

[Here you could say, "McNabb *rode* his motorcycle through the plate-glass window, and the ambulance driver *took* him to the hospital as soon as possible." But by changing to the passive voice with the verb *was taken,* the writer keeps attention on McNabb, the most interesting person in the action here reported.]

11D Be consistent in the person and number of your nouns and pronouns and in the way you address your reader.

In speaking and writing in an informal tone, we often use the pronoun *you* instead of the more formal pronoun *one* (see 8E).

If *you* smoke cigarettes, *you* run a high risk of getting lung cancer.

Problems arise when you mix the informal *you* with the formal *one.*

If *one* smokes cigarettes, *you* run a high risk of getting lung cancer.

Here the pronoun *one* is inconsistent with the pronoun *you,* and the sentence must be revised. A more formal statement is this:

If *one* smokes cigarettes, *one* runs a high risk of getting lung cancer.

OR:

Anyone who smokes cigarettes runs a high risk of getting lung cancer.

OR:

People who smoke cigarettes run a high risk of getting lung cancer.

If you address your reader directly as *you,* you may write in the third person from time to time. But you cannot shift from the third person to the second person or from the second person to the third person in the same sentence.

Consistent

You will always find good writing to be hard work. *Good writers* never think that their craft is easy.

[*You,* in the first sentence, addresses the reader directly. *Good writers,* the third-person subject in the second sentence, begins a statement consistent with the direct address in the first sentence. In effect, the reader is being addressed in both sentences and feels no discomfort with the shift from the second person to the third person.]

Inconsistent

People flying across the country nowadays discover that *you* can get many different fares to the same destination.

[The shift in the same sentence from the third-person *people* to the second-person *you* is confusing.]

Make your pronouns agree with their antecedents, but try to avoid sexist language (see 8B, section 1).

Inconsistent

Anyone who rides a bicycle every day will discover that *they* develop some muscles not developed in jogging.

[*Anyone* is an indefinite singular pronoun; the pronoun *they* is plural. Although in informal usage the pronoun *they* is used for the antecedent *anyone,* the usage is still not accepted by many editors, who hold that a pronoun must agree with its antecedent in number.]

Consistent

People who ride bicycles every day will discover that *they* develop some muscles not developed in jogging.

Consistent

Anyone who rides a bicycle every day will discover that *she* develops some muscles not developed in jogging.

Consistent

Anyone who rides a bicycle every day will discover that *he* develops some muscles not developed in jogging.

Consistent

Anyone who rides a bicycle every day will discover that *he* or *she* develops some muscles not developed in jogging.

You can make a much more sweeping revision:

Bike riders do not exercise some of the muscles used in jogging and usually discover that they get sore quickly when they try to run around the neighborhood at night.

11E Avoid jarring shifts in point of view.

shift
11E

Inconsistent

He sat idly in his seat and looked down at the land pouring beneath the low-flying plane like some immense sea whose waters reached to the sky. The green of the forest enchanted him. Everything was primitive and nearly unspoiled. Here and there a house stood in a solitary clearing that, from above, looked like a raft afloat on the great ocean of green. He saw it for a moment, and then it was whisked away behind him. *In the houses, people were sitting down to supper, unfolding napkins, looking expectantly at the head of the table where the father gravely bowed his head to say grace.*

[The point of view, quickly established, is of someone in an airplane looking down on the land passing underneath. But in the last sentence we shift to a scene that such a traveler cannot see. A reader must go back to look for what is missing because the shift is jarring. The last sentence can be easily fixed to match the point of view established in the rest of the passage.]

He could imagine that in the houses people were sitting down to supper, unfolding napkins, looking expectantly at the head of the table where the father gravely bowed his head to say grace.

Exercise 11.2 Rewrite the following sentences to eliminate confusing shifts. If a sentence is correct as it stands, put a check beside it.

1. American landscape painters of the nineteenth century viewed the American wilderness as the handiwork of God; signs of God's work were seen by them in lakes, mountains, and prairies.

2. Government paperwork costs forty billion dollars a year, and government accountants are working to trim those costs—and making more paperwork as they do so; you can see the problem.

3. If anyone carries a pack on your back while they ride a bicycle up a mountain in the summer, be prepared to be hot and tired.

4. People who take a lot of pictures sometimes find that you get tired carrying a camera, and they often stop taking pictures all at once, the way some people stop smoking.

5. Anyone who writes a long letter of complaint is frustrated when they get a form letter in return.

6. Everybody who uses the library has to be responsible for the damage they may do to books.

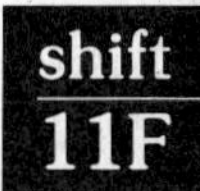

7. Some of the new sun-screening lotions offer relief to people who sunburn easily—unless you happen to be allergic to the chemical agent in such lotions.

8. My Uncle Charley always brought his queen out on the third move when he played chess—something you'll have to admit was pretty stupid.

9. Ralph Waldo Emerson shocked people in the nineteenth century because he seemed so radical. You could be sure that a conservative school like Yale would not let him speak there.

10. Captain Ahab in *Moby Dick* was a figure for all those people so obsessed with the wrongs that they had suffered that they finally destroyed themselves in their quest for vengeance.

Exercise 11.3 Rewrite the following paragraph to correct the confusing shift.

In Thomas More's book *Utopia,* which is the name for an island supposedly located off the coast of the new world, the people of his commonwealth wear unbleached wool, eat together in great halls, punish adultery with death when one is convicted twice of the offense, and allow husbands and wives to inspect each other naked before they are married so one will not be deceived by the other. The Utopians had no individuality. They tried as hard as they could to eliminate passion. More made no mention of any artists among them.

11F Avoid sudden outbursts of emotion in your writing.

You may have strong feelings about a subject, and having discussed some of the issues in an essay, you may be tempted to conclude with a highly emotional ending so readers will know where you stand. Excessive emotionalism in writing is almost always a mistake. Most readers dismiss the opinions of a ranter, and if you rant in your writing, few people will take your thoughts seriously. You may embarrass even those people who agree with you because you present their opinions in such an irrational way. Sarcasm is one of the most objectionable devices in writing because it implies that the writer is a hateful person. Readers want to like the writer of the prose they read; otherwise they will not enjoy spending time in his or her company. Few readers like to spend time with an angry or overwrought or sarcastic person. They will almost inevitably dislike the prose that comes from such a person—or that seems to come from such a person.

Consider these two paragraphs on the military draft:

> The armed forces of the United States need brave men and women who stand ready to save this precious country from all the bloodthirsty rats ready to gnaw us to bloody pieces if we let our guard down for a minute. The President has brought back the military draft, and wouldn't you know it? All the long-haired, dirty, cowardly college punks are protesting their feeble brains out. They don't want to go to the army! Not those vermin! They're too good to go to the army and die for their country! All they're good for is sitting around smoking dope and shacking up with each other and putting fertilizer on their hair so it will grow longer. Once in a while they crack a book so they can seem intellectual and better than everybody else. They want to live in the country like worms in a pig, and they want somebody else to do their fighting and their dying for them. Well, let me tell you something: Red-blooded true Americans aren't going to resist the draft.

[For the overwhelming majority of readers—even those who support the military draft—the frantic and ugly tone of this paragraph would be repulsive. It could only please those people already in support of the draft and unreasonably angry with those who do not believe in conscription. It could not convince anybody who does not already believe the writer's point of view.]

> The military draft has raised protests among America's young people, especially among college students. They do not remember the Vietnamese war, but they are convinced that the war was useless and that many Americans died uselessly in it. They think that the draft opens the way for similar wars, and they do not want to fight in them. But even among college students, few believe that the country could long survive without military force. Not many people like to be in the army, and

although more Americans are killed on the highways every year than died in the entire war in Vietnam, most of us would rather be at home dodging cars than in the jungle dodging bullets. But it can be argued that the best way to avoid war is to be strong, and the draft is not the same as a declaration of war. It is rather a statement that we will defend our vital interests, and it does not push aside the fervent hope of Americans, both in and out of the army, that we never have to fight. The volunteer army has put the burden of military service on the poor and the ignorant. The American tradition of fair play makes many leaders think that military burdens should be borne by all who receive the benefits of safety that the military provides. And the desire for an able and efficient army makes these same leaders believe that sophisticated military technology cannot be left in the hands of the most poorly educated people in our society. The solution to these problems is the military draft.

[By making his point rationally and calmly, the writer wins readers to his point of view and forces even opponents to think of arguments to counter the arguments here. They cannot merely dismiss his thoughts as the ravings of a lunatic. They must argue with him if they are to maintain their position.]

Exercise 11.4 Write a short, argumentative paragraph on a controversial subject, one for which you have deep feelings. Convey your point of view without undue emotion and with full respect for those who may disagree with you.

Now do the best you can to make arguments for the opposite point of view. Write a paragraph that might convince you to reconsider your own opinions, one that would treat you—an opponent—with the respect that might win you over.

Exercise 11.5 The following passage is excessively overwrought. Rewrite it, using understatement, to convey the sense of the text.

Lord Crenshaw strode mightily into the room, his bushy eyebrows looking like forests waving in the mightiest of all God's storms, his cold blue eyes flashing like bolts of lightning as he looked around at the assembled guests. Philippa felt her heart go bang in her chest with a wild emotion, wilder than anything she had ever felt before, wild as the incandescent lava that bursts from a volcano and pours down the mountainside, burning up all the reserve and all the hesitation that she might have felt. This was the famous Lord Crenshaw, dauntless leader of Wellington's right at Waterloo, the bold, brave man who flung his great arms skyward and shouted at his troops to hold fast while all around his gallant head the bullets whizzed and whirled, the thunderhead of a hero whose voice sounded like ten thousand organs booming through ten thousand cathedrals. People nodded gravely to him, knowing his reputation for sudden anger, for the outburst that could lead to the duel at sunrise that had more than once snuffed out the tender flower of a young life before it could grow and flourish and become a mighty tree. As he entered the room, a silence like that of Judgment Day itself fell over everyone, and it seemed that the world held its breath while he walked to the buffet and thundered a command to the trembling waiter there. "Give me a ham sandwich," he said. "And hold the pickles."

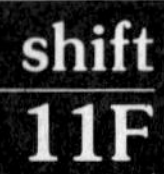

PART THREE
Writing Clear and Effective Sentences

12 Establishing Sentence Logic
13 Coordinating and Subordinating Ideas
14 Parallelism
15 Emphasis
16 Variety

12 Establishing Sentence Logic

Every sentence should make a statement that may be easily understood by readers. Short, simple sentences offer little difficulty:

> The world came to life at dawn.
>
> Jack graduated from high school last year.
>
> Many young people work for years to break into a career in acting.

Such sentences clearly answer all or some of the five journalistic questions: Who? Where? What? When? and Why? *What* came to life? The world. *What* happened? The world came to life. *When?* At dawn. *Who* graduated from high school? Jack. *What* did Jack do? Jack graduated from high school. *When?* Last year. *Who* works? Many young people. *When?* For years. *Why?* To break into a career in acting.

When we read any sentence, we are looking for answers to some of these questions. Any sentence must give us some of the answers if it is to be comprehensible. Even when your sentences are long and complicated, you must be sure that they are giving clear answers to the questions readers bring to your writing. To be sure that a sentence is clear and logical, ask yourself which of the five W questions the sentence answers.

> To ride a horse into battle would have been to come to the field already prepared for flight, and such was against the Saxon battle ethic, which decreed that if a man's lord died on the field, he could not leave it alive.
>
> —James Burke

[What questions does this sentence answer? The most important is *Why? Why* did Saxon warriors not fight on horseback? Because the horse offered a chance for flight, and flight was impossible in the Saxon battle ethic. *Who* is this sentence about? The Saxon warrior who came to the fight under the leadership of a lord. *What* are we talking about? Riding a horse into battle—or, more particularly, the custom of not riding a horse into battle.]

Few sentences will answer all five W questions, but every sentence must answer one or more of them. If your sentence does not answer at least one of those questions, or if it gives a confusing or ambiguous answer, you should rewrite it. How many of the five W questions does the following sentence answer?

> Every day meteorites plunge to Earth and add at least a quarter of a ton to our planet's mass.
>
> —ROY A. GALLANT

[*What?* Meteorites. *What happens?* They plunge to earth and add at least a quarter of a ton to our planet's mass. *When?* Every day.]

In a clear sentence, we quickly see the interrelations of the questions the sentence answers. We quickly feel uncomfortable when the elements of a sentence do not combine logically to answer questions that seem related.

> Born in Lincoln, Nebraska, my mother always loved potato chips.

[The *who* of this sentence is the subject, *my mother.* The *what* of the sentence is that she always loved potato chips. And the *where* of the sentence is Lincoln, Nebraska, where *my mother* was born. But what is the relation between these questions? Does being born in Lincoln, Nebraska, make people love potato chips? The writer may make some connection between the *where* and the *what* later on in sentences that follow this one. But as it stands, the sentence consists of two unrelated ideas. It answers questions in a confusing way.]

> Clarence, who learned how to type when he was fifteen years old, had a ruddy complexion.

[The sentence tells us *who:* Clarence. But it gives us two seemingly unrelated answers to the question *What?* Clarence learned how to type when he was fifteen years old, and he had a ruddy complexion. What do these answers have to do with each other?]

When you ask someone a direct question, you expect a coherent reply. When someone gives you several unrelated answers to the question, you are confused. You want a clear, logical, and economical answer. You want to understand as quickly as you can. Your sentences, answering questions for your readers, should give those answers as efficiently as possible.

12A Prune away irrelevant details.

Unnecessary information may confuse your readers by blurring the central thought of your sentence. Everything in a sentence must support the central statement. In casual conversation you might say something like this:

> Clifford Jenkins, whose brother runs a restaurant near the stadium, took the opening kickoff and ran it back 103 yards for a touchdown.

But in writing that must be more orderly and focused, you must stick to your major statement and eliminate confusing details.

> Clifford Jenkins, a substitute running back, took the opening kickoff and ran it back 103 yards for a touchdown.

In the rapid writing of a first draft, you may throw in irrelevant details as you try to put down everything you know about a topic. When you revise, cut out these details so that everything in each of your sentences will contribute to the major statement you wish to make in it.

First Draft

> *The Adventures of Huckleberry Finn,* by Mark Twain, who lectured widely in the United States and Great Britain, received only one review when it was published in 1883.

Revised

> *The Adventures of Huckleberry Finn,* by Mark Twain, received only one review when it was published in 1883.

Often you can revise a sentence so that all the details you throw into your first draft can be made to support the major purpose of the sentence:

> Although Mark Twain lectured widely in the United States and Great Britain and was well known to the public, *The Adventures of Huckleberry Finn* received only one review when it was published in 1883.

[In the version above, the principal questions answered by the sentence are, What happened? and When did it happen? *The Adventures of Huckleberry Finn* received only one review when it was published in 1883. *Although Mark Twain lectured widely in the United States and Great Britain and was well known to the public,* the introductory clause, helps expand the statement.]

Don't cram your sentences with too many ideas. When you have several important ideas to communicate, put them in different sentences so that your readers can absorb your thoughts in manageable statements.

Mixed Ideas

The First World War began on July 28, 1914, when the Austrians, whose army was huge but badly commanded and badly supplied, attacked the city of Belgrade in what was then called Serbia.

[Although there might seem to be a connection between the beginning of the First World War and the size, command, and supplies of the Austrian army, that connection should not be made in this sentence. The main idea is not the condition of the Austrian army but how the war began.]

Revised

The First World War began on July 28, 1914, when the Austrians attacked the city of Belgrade in what was then called Serbia. The Austrian army was huge, badly commanded, and badly supplied, but the Serbians were no match for it by themselves, and so they had to call on the Russians for help. The Austrians thereupon called on the Germans for help against the Russians, and the Germans decided to defeat the French first and then give all their attention to fighting Russia. Suddenly all Europe was in conflict.

Often when you create a sentence with mixed ideas in a first draft, you can revise by making a separate sentence for each idea. Sometimes you may be tempted to throw in unnecessary information to show readers how much you know. Then you must revise by eliminating the unnecessary information altogether.

Mixed Ideas

Small computers, which have become a new source of trade rivalry between the United States and Japan, most often have at their heart a tiny silicon chip, which may contain thousands of circuits capable of millions of different combinations.

[The major statement in this sentence concerns the tiny silicon chip at the heart of small computers. The information about the place of the computer in trade rivalry between the United States and Japan may belong in another sentence later on in the paper, but it blurs the focus of the main statement in this sentence.]

Revised

Small computers most often have at their heart a tiny silicon chip, which may contain thousands of circuits capable of millions of different combinations.

Exercise 12.1 Rewrite the following sentences to clarify the main statement in each of them. You may want to revise to make two sentences if you want to give play to two related main statements.

1. My mother, who always hated to wash windows, worked on newspapers for twenty years in places as diverse as Beaumont, Texas, and Montgomery, Alabama.
2. Notoriously hard to spell, the English language has spread all over the world largely because of the power and influence of the United States and the British Empire and Commonwealth.
3. Scurvy, a disease once common among sailors who spent many weeks at sea, can be prevented by eating citrus fruits, which grow in warm climates.
4. Born in 1809, Abraham Lincoln was the only American President forced to wage a civil war.
5. If Lincoln had not sent ships to supply the federal garrison at Ft. Sumter, thus starting the Civil War, the British might have recognized the Confederacy as an independent nation so that they might ensure a steady supply of southern cotton to British textile mills, which by 1861 were using steam engines.
6. The greatest center for making glass in the Middle Ages was Venice in Italy, which is today endangered by flooding.
7. Terrorism is one of the frightening symbols of modern society because it is violent, bloody, and merciless and often completely anonymous, since the terrorists sometimes do not know and do not care who their victims are, but they know that a bomb exploding in an airport or a bullet tearing through the body of a police officer will get publicity, which they think will make them look important in the eyes of the world, and they think that if they are important, they may be able to get their way.

12B Organize the elements of your sentences to give the greatest emphasis to the most important parts of your statements.

The most emphatic places in a sentence are at the beginning and at the end. Think about your sentences enough to have a clear idea about those elements that you most want to emphasize.

Weak and Illogical

When you are looking for a good book, try *The Adventures of Huckleberry Finn,* which you will find to be a great one.

Better

The Adventures of Huckleberry Finn is one of the greatest books in American literature.

Weak and Illogical

He opposed Russian tyranny in Poland and Czechoslovakia very strongly. However, he did not want nuclear war, which would be a calamity, as everyone would agree.

[The illogic in this sentence comes from the weakness of the language that reports such important thoughts. Serious thoughts should have an emphatic place in the sentence that reports them.]

Better

Although he strongly opposed Russian tyranny in Poland and Czechoslovakia, he did not want the calamity of nuclear war.

log 12C

12C Clearly establish cause and effect in your sentences.

Be logical when you attribute an effect to a cause, and avoid statements that imply causal relations that you do not intend.

English syntax often helps make statements about cause and effect. The most obvious example is the sentence that uses the word *because* to introduce a dependent clause.

The experiment failed *because* the lab technicians had not cleaned the instruments.

The car would not start *because* the battery was dead.

Words like *for, since,* and *so* also make causal relations.

Since his doctor told him to stop drinking coffee, he says he feels much better.

He felt sad and lonely, *for* no one in the dorm seemed to like him.

She worked hard, *so* she could graduate in three years.

Often adverbs like *when, after,* and *before* imply cause-and-effect relations.

When they had biked for four hours, they began to get hungry.

[The use of the clause introduced by *when* implies that their biking for four hours caused them to get hungry.]

After Scarlett saw how much Ashley grieved for Melanie, she realized that he had always been devoted to his wife.

[The use of the clause introduced by *after* implies that Scarlett's awareness that Ashley had always been devoted to his wife came because she saw how much Ashley grieved for Melanie.]

Sometimes putting two ideas close together in a sentence implies a cause-and-effect relation.

She had a great talent for design, and she did well in architecture.
[Putting the two statements together implies that one helps cause the other. You could make the causal relation more explicit: *Because* she had a great talent for design, she did well in architecture.]

Jack bought a videodisc player, and he and his children started watching movies at home every night.
[The cause of Jack's watching movies at home with his children was that he bought a videodisc player.]

log
12C

Confusion may arise when a writer puts two ideas together so that readers think some cause-and-effect relation exists between them when in fact the writer intends no such thing.

In 1950, the most popular song in America was "Tennessee Waltz," and the United States went to war in Korea.
[Was the popularity of "Tennessee Waltz" the cause of the Korean war? A reader may think that the writer means just that. The thought needs filling out to clarify the writer's point, that two different things were happening at the same time, not that one was the cause of the other.]

In 1950, when the most popular song in America was the slow, dreamy "Tennessee Waltz," the United States went to war in Korea, and a peaceful dream ended for thousands of young men.

Confusion may also result from the joining of a dependent clause to an independent clause.

After he saw the movie *Casablanca,* my friend Bert had a heart attack.
[Did the movie *Casablanca* have anything to do with the heart attack? Probably not. But a rapid reader might think that it did. Again, one solution is to fill out the thought so that readers will not think you imply a cause-and-effect relation.]

My friend Bert had a heart attack last week as he was leaving a movie house. He had just seen the film *Casablanca,* and he looked to be in perfect health.

Some words establish negative relations. These include words like *but, although,* and *however.* Often we wish to make a statement that, we know, sets up certain expectations in the minds of readers. But we wish to tell them that these expectations are not fulfilled. We say this:

Although seat belts save lives in automobile accidents, most motorists refuse to wear them.

[*Although* begins a clause that makes a statement about seat belts saving lives. The statement makes us expect motorists to wear them because we think people should be interested in saving their lives. But the second statement, *most motorists refuse to wear them,* contradicts the expectation caused by the first statement.]

Here are some other examples of statements that raise expectations that are in fact not fulfilled.

log 12C

I love David Bowie's music; when he gave his concert here in town, *however,* I was sick and could not go.

The triathlon, a race where contestants swim, bike, and run, has become one of America's most rapidly growing sports. *But* many people still think triathloners are crazy.

Words like *but, however,* and *although* tell us that we might expect some relation of cause and effect but that in fact that relation does not exist. Use these words only when you suppose that your readers may have an expectation that you wish to contradict. Confusion results when the writer uses one of these words to join two statements that seem unrelated.

Although I like to read, television is exciting.

[The first statement, *I like to read,* does not have any clear relation to the second statement, *television is exciting.* What does liking to read have to do with exciting television? The writer meant to say something else.]

Although I like to read, it is easier for me to watch an exciting television show in the evening.

[Now the relation is clear. When I say that *I like to read,* you may expect me to say that I read every evening. But I contradict that statement by saying that it is easier to watch television instead.]

Be sure to establish clear relations between statements joined by *although, however, but,* and other such words. Simply adding some information can show readers how you relate the statements in your own mind.

Although my Aunt Anastasia was old, I loved to hear her stories about her childhood in Greece.

[Does the writer mean that she is surprised to discover that old people are interesting?]

Although my Aunt Anastasia was old and spoke slowly in a soft voice I could barely hear, I sat for hours by her chair straining to hear what she said because I loved to hear her stories about her childhood in Greece.

[Now we have enough information to understand the *although* that begins the sentence, and the sentence logic is plain.]

Be careful to make clauses beginning with *if* and *when* show a clear causal relation to the rest of the sentence. Sometimes writers will say this:

If you see that movie, it is great.

[The implication here is that if you do not see the movie, it is not great. The writer means to say something else.]

If you see that movie, you will agree that it is great.

[Now the clause beginning with *if* has a clear causal connection to the rest of the sentence: *you will agree that it is great.*]

Some writers may say this:

When you see the Grand Canyon for the first time, all the photographs cannot show how grand it is.

They mean to say this:

When you see the Grand Canyon for the first time, you will also see that all the photographs cannot show how grand it is.

Be sure that you do not imply a cause-and-effect relation between two statements when none exists.

Exercise 12.2 Where necessary, rewrite the following sentences to eliminate faulty patterns of cause and effect. Add information when necessary to establish sentence logic.

1. Personal computers were unknown twenty years ago, and Elvis Presley was in his prime.
2. Aspirin is a potent pain reliever, although some doctors believe that too much aspirin may damage the kidneys.
3. After we had got off the plane in Cleveland, the Russians shot down the Korean jetliner over Sakhalin Island.
4. If you read Shakespeare, he speaks to all human conditions and to all personality types.
5. When you go to college, many teachers love to write books and to talk to students about research.
6. Although seat belts save lives, my friend Jack was severely injured when he was thrown out of his car when it hit a curb and the door flew open.

7. I wrote three drafts of my paper, but writing is very difficult.
8. Athens, Greece, is the most polluted city in Europe these days, and the Acropolis draws millions of tourists every year.
9. If you visit New York, hotels there are very expensive.
10. Although the Natural History Museum has a great collection of dinosaur bones, those giant reptiles flourished for millions of years on the earth.

log 12D

12D Limit generalizations. Avoid sweeping statements that assert too much on too little evidence.

Whenever you are tempted to say that all members of a group share some quality, or when you start to use words such as *always* and *never,* be sure your statement is limited enough to be true.

Faulty Generalization

Students nowadays lack dedication and seriousness, and they never read anything worthwhile.

Better

Some students nowadays lack dedication and seriousness, and they seldom read anything but the sports pages.

Faulty Generalization

Football coaches always think that they are symbols of real Americanism because they are emotional, hardworking, and dedicated to winning.

Better

Many fans believe that football coaches are symbols of real Americanism because they are emotional, hardworking, and dedicated to winning.

Faulty Generalization

There never has been another play as good as *Macbeth.*

Better

Macbeth is the best play I have ever seen.

Faulty Generalization

The Germans have always been authoritarian and militaristic, but all the French want is love and wine and good food.

Better

The Germans have a reputation for being authoritarian and militaristic, and the French have a reputation for being preoccupied with love and wine and good food. Neither reputation is entirely deserved.

Exercise 12.3 Rewrite the following sentences to qualify sweeping generalizations. Don't be afraid to change words if the changes help you improve the sentences.

Example

Sweeping Generalization

The critics tell us that Faulkner's story "A Rose for Emily" is not one of his better works; it is too melodramatic.

Limited Generalization

Some critics tell us that Faulkner's story "A Rose for Emily" is not one of his better works because, they say, it is too melodramatic.

1. In Detroit the other day, the driver of one car shot another driver who dented his fender. This kind of thing happens because people in big cities carry pistols in the glove compartments of their cars.
2. My cousin Charles could not get anybody to speak English when he asked directions in downtown Paris. The French all hate the Americans except when they want us to help them in war.
3. Members of the crime syndicates are always photographed smoking cigars, and the cigar has long been regarded as a symbol of success by everyone who thinks about such things.
4. Colstrop's necktie was found at the scene of the murder along with his wristwatch, his notebook, and a pair of his trousers; so he was the killer, and the police have arrested him.
5. Picasso's fame has spread all over the world, and any painting of his is worth thousands of dollars. My Aunt Matilda stood in line for three hours to see an exhibit of his work, and anyone who would not do the same does not truly love art.

12E Avoid mixed images.

Carelessness in using colorful, figurative language can confuse readers (see 18). This is especially likely to happen when we rely on familiar, overworked expressions, called **clichés.** Here are some common clichés:

She climbed the ladder of success.

She nipped his ambitions in the bud.

They kept their noses to the grindstone.

He was willing to launch out into the deep.

Often writers who use clichés or excessively colorful language do not think about the literal meaning of the words, and they mix images.

People in every walk of life can climb the ladder of success by launching out into the deep and keeping their noses to the grindstone. [If we think of these images at all, we are going to be confused. Is there a ladder on the boat that is going to launch out into the deep, and how are we going to climb that ladder if we must haul a grindstone up with us?]

log 12E

He took off like a rocket in his new job and came up smelling like a rose. [Can you imagine a rocket that smells like a rose?]

She was busy as a bee, and in the end her drawings sold like hotcakes. [It is hard to imagine a bee that would make hotcakes.]

Exercise 12.4 Rewrite the following sentences to eliminate the mixed images. You may wish to change a cliché altogether and write a simple, declarative sentence.

Example

Mixed Images

My opponents wish to put their heads in the sand and ride roughshod over those who point to the skeletons in their closets.

Revised

My opponents wish to hide from reality and try to suppress anyone who calls attention to their faults.

1. She burned the midnight oil until the crack of dawn.
2. He insisted on passing the buck, and so he nipped his chance for success in the bud.
3. We've all got to put our shoulders to the wheel if we expect to pave our way to the finals.
4. They took the primrose path and came up smelling like a rose.
5. My opinions ran off him like water off a duck's back, and he remained rooted in silly ideas that helped carry him down the broad way that leads to destruction.
6. Because she believed in calling a spade a spade, she sometimes acted like a bull in a china shop when we had committee meetings, and many people wanted to avoid her like the plague.

12F When you define a word, use other concrete words. Do not define the word by repeating it or by using one of its cognates.

Repetitious Definition

A grammar book teaches you grammar.

[If you don't know what grammar is, this definition will not help you; if you do know what grammar is, you do not need the definition.]

Better

A grammar book explains the system of rules about word endings and word arrangements that allow a language to communicate.

log 12F

Repetitious

A floppy disk is a disk used in a computer.

Better

A floppy disk is a small, flat, circular sheet of magnetized plastic that looks a little like a 45 rpm phonograph record. It is used in personal computers to store information much as tape is used in cassette recorders.

Words should not be defined by their cognates. **Cognates** are words that come from the same root. *Grammar* and *grammatical* are cognates.

Repetitious

A community is a group with communal interests that communicates within itself.

Better

A community is a group that shares similar ceremonies, goals, habits, and patterns of work as well as information about its members.

Repetitious

Students of ancient history study antiquities.

Better

Students of ancient history explore the art, artifacts, and literature of the period that began with the invention of writing about three thousand years before Christ and ended with the fall of the Roman Empire in the West.

Avoid definitions that use the words *is when.*

Awkward and Unclear

Fascism is when you have a dictator who wears a uniform and controls everybody with the secret police and won't allow freedom of the press or of assembly.

Better

Fascism is usually characterized by a military dictator who rules the state with the help of a secret police force and does not allow freedom of the press or of assembly.

log 12F

Exercise 12.5 Rewrite the following sentences to give proper definitions. Use the dictionary when necessary (see 22B, section 3).

1. An accident is when you have something happen by chance that is unexpected and usually harmful, although you can have lucky accidents.
2. A traffic jam is when you have too much traffic to move on the streets.
3. Inflation is when you have inflated prices.
4. A bicycle built for two is for two people.
5. A quarterback is a back on a football team.
6. A poet is a man or a woman who writes poems.
7. The English House of Commons is the representative body of the commoners in Great Britain.
8. Oil lubricates because it is extremely oily.

13
Coordinating and Subordinating Ideas

Sentences that demonstrate clear thought show a distinction between main ideas and subordinate ideas. A pleasing style will include a variety of sentences. Variety comes by using different forms and elements to spare readers the tedium of constant repetition (see 16). No matter how varied you make your sentences, always be sure to keep readers on track by making a distinction between your major statements and the subordinate elements that support those statements. Your readers should have a sense of smooth flow as they move from one sentence to the next. Improper coordination or subordination can interrupt that flow and can make your readers struggle to understand your thought.

Improper Coordination

The children played happily and the cars were parked along the street and they were generally old.

[The flow of thought in these sentences is difficult to find. Are we learning about cars or about streets or about children? But when we reorganize our thoughts, we can subordinate some ideas to the main statement we want to make.]

Revised

The children played happily in the street among the old parked cars.

[Now it is clear that the major statement the writer wishes to make is this: "The children played happily in the street." The adverbial phrase *among the old parked cars* modifies the verb *played* and helps make the major statement more vivid.]

Sometimes the confusions caused by improper sentence coordination are more complicated.

Improper Coordination

In the fields the cattle grazed placidly, and we heard nothing but the soft hum of insects and the singing of birds, and for the moment we were safe from pursuit.

[The writer is trying to use words to capture a vivid scene. But the triple compound sentence prepares us to believe that all these statements have a close relation to one another. Were we safe from pursuit *because* the cattle were grazing and *because* we heard nothing but the soft hum of insects and the singing of birds? The writer apparently meant something else.]

Revised

CO 13A

In the fields the cattle grazed placidly, and we heard nothing but the soft hum of insects and the singing of birds. For the moment we were safe from pursuit.

[Separating the last independent clause from the first two eliminates the sense that the thoughts expressed in all three are closely related. The first two clauses describe the scene; the last one, now an independent sentence, describes something slightly different—our safety.]

Always be sure that the elements you join with various coordinating devices do indeed have equal status in the statements you wish to make. Separate or subordinate elements that are not equal.

13A Give equal ideas equal value by proper coordination.

You can establish equality between parts of a sentence by using coordinating conjunctions or suitable punctuation or both.

1 Coordinate words, phrases, or clauses, giving them equal emphasis to expand sentence ideas.

The conjunction *and* always calls for equal emphasis on the elements that it joins.

The bear ate the food in camp.

The bear *and* her cubs ate the food in camp.

[In the first sentence, the subject is *bear.* It acts through the verb *ate* to make a statement. In the second sentence, the coordinating conjunction *and* makes a compound subject of the noun *bear* and the noun *cubs* so that both of them act equally through the verb.]

In the following sentences, notice how the conjunction *and* joins equal elements.

The bear *and* her cubs ate the food in camp *and* destroyed our tent.

At the end of our climb, we were hot *and* tired.

He drank only coffee, tea, *and* milk for a week.

She ran the marathon swiftly *and* tirelessly.

After reading her book *and* thinking about her arguments, I decided she was right.

When *and* is used to join unequal elements, confusion results.

His favorite pastimes were reading, walking, *and* he liked to ice-skate in winter.

[In this sentence the words *reading* and *walking* prepare us to find a similar word after *and,* a word used as a gerund such as *skating* or *singing* or *thinking.* Instead, we find not another gerund but an independent clause, and we feel that something has been left out. We can amend the sentence in a couple of ways.]

His favorite pastimes were reading, walking, and ice skating.

His favorite pastimes were reading, walking, and bicycling in the summer, and he liked to ice-skate in winter.

A comma can sometimes replace the *and* in a series:

He zigzagged, fell, rolled, ran into my waiting hand.

—E. B. White

[The comma after *rolled* coordinates the verbs in the sentence without the use of *and.*]

Wistfully, admiringly, the old voice added, "It's snug in here, upon my word!"

—Katherine Mansfield

[Mansfield could have said, "Wistfully *and* admiringly," but she chose to eliminate the *and* and to use a comma instead. Even so, *wistfully* and *admiringly* are equal adverbs in the sentence.]

The conjunction *or* also joins equal sentence elements. It is not as common as *and.*

He could go by bus *or* by train.

They knew that they must work out their differences over money *or* else get a divorce.

Many convicted criminals have suffered neglect *or* abuse *or* both from their parents.

Confusion can arise when *or* joins unequal elements.

They could see a movie, a play, *or* talk all night.

[We feel that something is missing in such a sentence, and we hestitate and go back over it to see if we have not read it correctly.]

They could see a movie or a play, *or* they could talk all night.

co 13A

2 Coordinate thoughts you wish to stress equally by joining short, consecutive sentences.

With careful use, coordination can establish clear relations among equal elements in a sentence. Devices for coordination may make your prose more vivid.

They hesitate, and they regret, and sometimes they petition; but they do nothing in earnest and with effect.

—HENRY DAVID THOREAU

[Written as short, consecutive sentences, Thoreau's statement would not stress the interrelations in the original.]

They hesitate. They regret. Sometimes they petition. They do nothing in earnest. They do nothing with effect.

When you use *and, but, or, for, nor, yet,* or *so* to connect independent clauses and thus coordinate related statements of equal importance, use a comma. (See 24A.)

To act is to be committed, and to be committed is to be in danger.

—JAMES BALDWIN

I buried my head under the quilts, but my aunt heard me.

—LANGSTON HUGHES

[In both these sentences, two related statements are joined by a coordinating conjunction that gives each statement importance to the other.]

You can also use a semicolon to connect related statements that are equally important.

Autonomy is the declaration and affirmation of the self; sex is one of its expressions.

—NANCY FRIDAY

[Here the semicolon coordinates two independent clauses, giving them equal status without the help of a coordinating conjunction.]

Sometimes both a semicolon and a coordinating conjunction introduce an independent clause (see 25A).

> The hands of the man who sawed the wood left red marks on the billets; and the forehead of the woman who nursed the baby was stained with the stain of the old rag she wound around her head again.
>
> —CHARLES DICKENS

[Here both the semicolon and the coordinating conjunction *and* serve to join two independent clauses.]

Exercise 13.1 Rewrite the following sentences to provide proper coordination of elements. You may want to write two sentences instead of one for some of the examples.

1. He loved to shave in the morning because he liked the softness of shaving cream, the clean feel of the razor on his cheek, the smell of his after-shave, and he liked his shower, too.
2. Dickens wrote a lot about poverty, hopelessness, and he also wrote about evil, wealthy men.
3. Police officers in the movies often seem hard, cynical, and yet they are still shown as being honest.
4. Truck drivers in this country complained bitterly about the 55-mile-an-hour speed limit, the price of diesel fuel, and many of them refused to slow down.
5. Our friends would eat out on Saturday night, go to a movie, visit with each other, or they would consider the evening wasted.

13B Give major ideas the emphasis they should have by subordinating minor ideas.

Subordination helps focus attention on major ideas. In many sentences, some ideas depend on others. For example, one condition may cause another; one event may come before another; one observation may explain another. Subordination establishes the dependence of one idea on another by shifting emphasis away from supporting elements so that major statements become clear.

1 Distinguish major words, phrases, or clauses from less important ones; subordinate the less important to the more important so that your readers can tell the difference.

In the following sentences, readers have trouble discerning the statements that carry the major line of thought that the writer wants to pursue.

Columbus discovered the New World in 1492. He made his voyage in three ships. They were tiny and frail. He did not believe that the world was flat. Neither did any other educated person in his time. The Greeks had taught that the world was round. On a round world, a sailor might head west and eventually get to lands other people had found by sailing east. Columbus never believed he had discovered a new world. Columbus wanted to find a new route to China and other lands in Asia. Others had reached those lands. They had sailed around the southern tip of Africa to get there. Columbus thought the world was much smaller than it is. He thought he could get to Asia in about a month of sailing. Suppose America had not been in the way. He would have had a voyage of three or four months. He did not find the East Indies or China or Japan. America was in the way. It is a good thing America was in the way. Columbus might have sailed his three ships into an enormous ocean. His sailors might have starved to death.

sub
13B

[The sentences in this passage are all clear. But they create confusion in the minds of readers because they do not show proper subordination. Thought does not move smoothly from one sentence to another.]

In the following revised version, proper subordination makes the main line of the text easier to track.

With three tiny ships, Columbus discovered the New World in 1492, although he never understood just what he had done. Neither he nor any other educated person in his time believed that the world was flat; from the time of the Greeks, people had believed that the world was round and that by sailing west, a ship might arrive in Asia without having to sail around the tip of Africa. Because Columbus thought the world was much smaller than it is, he expected to find the East Indies, China, or Japan. He found America instead, and if this continent had not been in the way, he might have sailed his crews to starvation in an enormous ocean.

[Much more is involved in this revision than a simple combining of sentences, but combining sentences helps. The writer has put down a series of short and seemingly disconnected sentences in a first draft. Then in the second draft he has thought about the main ideas he wants to present, and he has subordinated some lesser ideas to these main statements.]

The appropriate placement of words and phrases in a sentence helps subordinate ideas clearly. Sometimes writers rely on key words to state the precise relations between major and minor ideas. These key words, often called **subordinators** (see 3B, section 5), help to build subordinate clauses. Commas also may set off subordinate sections from a part they modify, especially when some subordinated element opens the sentence (see 24B).

For subordinate sections that show:	Use one of these subordinators:	Example
place	where	*Where the road forks,* you will find a service station.
condition	as, as if, unless, provided, since, although, if	*Unless the governor intervenes,* they will die in the gas chamber.
cause or purpose	since, because, as long as, in order that, so that, that	*Because they are helpless,* children often become the innocent victims of violence caused by others.
time	after, as, whenever, while, as soon as, when, before, until, once, since	*When President Kennedy announced the "quarantine" against Cuba,* many of us expected war.
manner	how	He taught me *how to throw a curve.*
concession	although, even though, even if, even when, though	*Although she was sometimes discouraged,* she never quit.

sub 13B

The placement of a subordinator in relation to the clause it introduces may affect the meaning of a sentence.

She did not eat *because she was angry.*
[In this sentence, her anger kept her from eating.]

She was angry *because she did not eat.*
[In this sentence, her anger was caused by her not eating.]

When the police arrived, the burglars fled.
[In this sentence, the arrival of the police caused the burglars to flee.]

When the burglars fled, the police arrived.
[In this sentence, the burglars were already gone when the police got there. The sentence may imply that the police did not do their duty.]

After he completed a spectacular pass, we cheered the quarterback.
[This sentence implies that the completed pass caused the cheers.]

After we cheered the quarterback, he completed a spectacular pass.
[This sentence implies that the cheers caused the completed pass.]

Relative pronouns—who, whom, that, which, what, whoever, whomever, whose—also signal subordinate elements in a sentence. Notice how the use of these subordinators speeds up the pace of the prose and makes the line of thought more clear.

Without Subordinators

My cousin does my taxes every year. He is an accountant. He helps me with many suggestions. These suggestions allow me to take several deductions. These deductions reduce my tax bill considerably.

With Subordinators

My cousin, who is an accountant, helps me with many suggestions that allow me to take several deductions that reduce my tax bill considerably.

Without Subordinators

Many amateur pilots are flying ultralight aircraft. The ultralight aircraft were developed from the hang glider. Somebody decided to attach a small motor to a hang glider. Ultralight aircraft are hardly more than a tubular frame, a simple motor, and flimsy wings and a tail. The ultralight reduces flight to the essentials.

With Subordinators

Many amateur pilots are flying ultralight aircraft, which were developed when somebody decided to attach a small motor to a hang glider. Because they are hardly more than a tubular frame, a simple motor, and flimsy wings and a tail, ultralight aircraft reduce flight to the essentials.

Clauses, phrases, and single words can all be subordinate units in a sentence, highlighting the major assertion of the sentence while establishing other levels of emphasis. As you rethink your first drafts, be sure to have clearly in mind the main thoughts you want to convey. Subordinate other thoughts to support those main thoughts.

2 Join a series of short sentences or a string of inexactly coordinated clauses by using embedding techniques.

As we have seen, short sentences are easy to understand, but the effect of several of them coming one after another is monotonous, even if they are all perfectly clear and grammatical. Short sentences may also be confusing because they make it hard for readers to pick out the main line of thought in the prose. You can connect ideas by using various subordinators, and you can also use embedding techniques.

Sentences Without Embedded Elements

She was sad. She did not look back. She mounted the seawall. She was bowed by her burden of failure and sorrow and self-contempt.

Sentence with Embedded Elements

Sadly, without looking back, she mounted the seawall, bowed by her burden of failure and sorrow and self-contempt.

—CONSTANCE HOLME

[Several of the sentences in the first version have been reduced to modifiers in the second version. We say that the ideas expressed in the several sentences in the first version have been *embedded* in the second.]

Sentences Without Embedded Elements

We can turn poetry toward biology. We can suggest a closer relationship between them. This is following in a long line of similar suggestions. Other disciplines made those suggestions.

sub 13B

Sentence with Embedded Elements

To turn poetry toward biology and to suggest a closer relationship between them is only to follow in a long line of similar suggestions made by other disciplines.

—ELIZABETH SEWELL

[Several separate sentences in the first version have been changed to embedded elements in the second version.]

Sentences Without Embedded Elements

That stick has an explosive charge. The coyote tugs at it. It shoots some cyanide into the mouth of the coyote.

Sentence with Embedded Elements

That stick has an explosive charge which shoots some cyanide into the mouth of the coyote who tugs at it.

—JOHN LAME DEER

Sentences Without Embedded Elements

The White Star liner *Titanic* was the largest ship the world had ever known. The *Titanic* sailed from Southampton on her maiden voyage to New York on April 10, 1912.

Sentence with Embedded Elements

The White Star liner *Titanic,* largest ship the world had ever known, sailed from Southampton on her maiden voyage to New York on April 10, 1912.

—HANSON W. BALDWIN

Sentences Without Embedded Elements

She was falling asleep. Her head was bowed over the child. She was still aware of a strange, wakeful happiness.

Sentence with Embedded Elements

> Even as she was falling asleep, head bowed over the child, she was still aware of a strange, wakeful happiness.
>
> —KATHERINE ANNE PORTER

By varying techniques, you can embed several enriching thoughts within one base sentence, transforming a whole group of ideas into a statement in which unstressed elements modify main ideas precisely. By using coordination along with subordination, you can expand your options for embedding and transforming sentences.

sub 13B

> The fissions generate heat, and in a power reactor this heat produces steam, which drives electric turbines.
>
> —JEREMY BERNSTEIN

[The comma and the conjunction *and* connect two independent clauses through coordination; the comma and the relative pronoun *which* subordinate an idea by means of a relative clause. The prepositional phrase *in a power reactor* embeds a subordinate idea too.]

> Equality with whites will not solve the problems of either whites or Negroes if it means equality in a world society stricken by poverty and in a universe doomed to extinction by war.
>
> —MARTIN LUTHER KING, JR.

[The conjunctions *either . . . or* coordinate two objects of the preposition *of*; the conjunction *and* coordinates two prepositional phrases. A subordinate clause begins at the word *if.* Participial phrases—*stricken by poverty* and *doomed to extinction by war*—embed ideas. All seven prepositional phrases serve subordinating functions as well.]

Exercise 13.2 Using the techniques of subordination illustrated in 13B, sections 1 and 2, revise the following sets of sentences. Make any necessary changes to create logical, correct sentences.

1. Bilingual education is expanding in many schools. It is designed for children. The native language of these children is not English. It may be Spanish. It may be some other language.
2. This room is large. The acoustics are bad. Speak into the microphone. Otherwise no one can hear you in the back.
3. Henry James began *The Portrait of a Lady* in the spring of 1879. He wrote parts of the preface more than twenty-five years later. The novel has been one of his most enduring works. It is still in print.
4. A uniform can symbolize a worker's status. Status often means power. People see authority in some uniforms.
5. I read the same want ads over and over. I was looking for a job as secretary. I wanted to do word processing. Finally I found an ad. It wanted someone to do word processing and to act as a secretary.

6. Computers were very large only a decade ago. Few people used them for word processing. The small computer changed all that. Now many homes have small computers. Young people are learning computer literacy. They are writing college papers on computers. Often they own their computers themselves.
7. She wanted to study engineering. She had been discouraged from such study. Her parents did not believe engineering was a good profession for a woman. She loved her parents. She knew they were wrong. She decided to major in engineering in college. She told her parents she was majoring in home economics. She was not really telling a lie. She wanted to design new engineering techniques. These would make home building much more economical.

3 Avoid using so many subordinate structures — clauses or phrases — that you obscure the main statement of a sentence.

Although subordinating elements of a sentence help clarify your main statement, you can do too much of a good thing. Too much subordination may distract your readers and confuse your main statement.

Less Clear

He was a stamp collector of considerable zeal who bought stamps at the post office on the day they were issued and fixed them with care in large books which had leather bindings, loving them not for themselves but for the enormous price that he hoped to gain from them in the passage of years when they had increased in value.

More Clear

He was a zealous stamp collector who bought new stamps on the day of issue and fixed them carefully in large, leatherbound books. He did not love them for themselves. Rather he prized them for the enormous price that he hoped to gain from them after many years when they had increased in value.

Less Clear

An unexpected wave that rose high above the sandy shore that was crowded with people who were sunbathing carried three individuals who were sleeping on the sand out to sea whence they were rescued by the Coast Guard.

More Clear

An unexpected wave, rising high above the crowded beach, carried three sleeping people out to sea. They were rescued by the Coast Guard.

Less Clear

A person who votes for candidates who make promises that are impossible to keep when those candidates are elected is an individual who lacks mature political judgment.

More Clear

People who vote for candidates making impossible promises lack mature political judgment.

Exercise 13.3 Revise this passage by combining sentences through subordination and coordination.

sub 13B

(**1**) Abused children learn poorly. (**2**) They feel unloved. (**3**) They feel stupid. (**4**) They may listen to a question. (**5**) They may even be able to answer it. (**6**) But they give up right away. (**7**) It is easier for them to say "I don't know" than to respond. (**8**) Such an answer suits their feelings of worthlessness. (**9**) Some abused children deliberately avoid answering questions. (**10**) They turn away from any question. (**11**) They purposely disobey instructions. (**12**) They seem to want negative results from teachers. (**13**) It is difficult to teach these children anything.

Exercise 13.4 Revise the following sentences to eliminate excessive subordination. You will have to write at least two sentences for each one in the examples. One point of this exercise is to get you in the habit of clarifying the major statements in sentences.

1. The Paul Newman movies, which nearly always end with an upbeat final scene, have beguiled Americans for years, during which time many movies have been either somber or else nonsensical, causing many adults to quit going to movies at all.
2. The new sun creams, which contain various sun-blocking chemicals, help protect against skin cancer, long a hazard to people who spend much time in the sun, and against aging, which seems to be at least partly a consequence of the ultraviolet rays of the sun.
3. Literacy should mean not only the ability to read and write, which is an essential skill in our culture, but also the ability, which is very much appreciated by academics, businesspeople, and professionals, to talk about many topics with intelligence—which may be another way of saying that true literacy embraces curiosity and the love of learning.
4. When books began to be printed in the fifteenth century, often considered the high point of the Renaissance, many people out of a form of snobbery refused to have printed books in their libraries, much as some people refuse today to allow paperbacks on their shelves, and in consequence printers tried to make printed books look as much like manuscripts as possible so that those books today are difficult to read even when we know the language they are written in, since often the type looks like handwriting.

14
Parallelism

Parallel constructions in sentences bind related thoughts together and give them more force.

In parallel constructions a grammatical form is repeated in a carefully balanced way. The elements in a parallel construction are equal or nearly equal in grammatical structure and importance. Parallel constructions are useful in making lists, in joining similar ideas, and in building emphasis. When three or more parallel elements are present, the structures are connected by commas and by a coordinating conjunction such as *and, but, or,* or *yet.*

The simplest parallel structure is the series:

She loved to read *magazines* and *newspapers.*

She loved to read *books, magazines,* and *newspapers.*

[The series of nouns joined by the conjunction *and* provides a list of words telling what she liked to read.]

They *laughed, sang,* and *danced* all night long.

[The series of verbs joined by the conjunction *and* tells what the subject did during the night.]

At Gettysburg in 1863, Abraham Lincoln said that the Civil War was being fought to make sure that government *of the people, by the people,* and *for the people* might not perish from the earth.

[Here prepositional phrases are joined in a parallel construction.]

He *did the dishes, ran the vacuum, put out the garbage,* and *walked the dog.*

[A compound predicate, here with four verbs, is placed in parallel form. Each element in the series includes a transitive verb and a noun that serves as a direct object.]

He runs marathons, and *she runs* sprints, but *they train* together.

[A series of independent clauses, each with an active verb, makes a parallel form.]

Many athletes live *to hear* the roar of the crowd, *to feel* the love of multitudes, and *to enjoy* the attentions of reporters.

[A series of infinitive phrases makes a parallel structure.]

She walked home, *smelling* the aroma of wood fires, *seeing* the decorated streets, and *feeling* the festive air of the holidays.

[A series of participial phrases at the end of the predicate modifies the subject, *she*.]

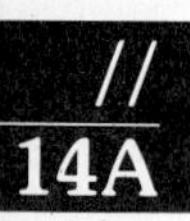

14A Use parallelism to make comparisons and contrasts.

Parallelism helps make comparisons and contrasts more emphatic.

Weak

She preferred *to buy* a house rather than *renting* one.

[The contrasting elements *to buy* and *renting* are not parallel; *to buy* is an infinitive, and *renting* is a participle.]

Better

She preferred *to buy* a house rather than *to rent* one.

[The two infinitives are parallel.]

Better

She preferred *buying* a house to *renting* one.

[The two participles make a parallel structure.]

Weak

The new library was larger than the old one, more beautiful than any other building on campus, and *it cost too much money.*

[The parallel form breaks down in the final, italicized clause. The first two elements, *larger* and *more beautiful,* are comparative adjectives, and readers expect another comparative adjective to follow them.]

Parallel

The new library was *larger* than the old one, *more beautiful* than any other building on campus, and *more expensive* to build than anyone had imagined.

[The revision includes the comparative adjective *more expensive.*]

14B Use parallel forms for coordinating elements like *both . . . and, either . . . or, neither . . . nor, not only . . . but also,* and *whether . . . or.*

Pairs like these, often called correlatives, always indicate a choice or a balance between equal elements. Because the equality is important to the sense of the sentences where these elements appear, it should be expressed in the parallel form that makes it stand out.

Weak

Most men who fought in the Civil War were *neither heroic nor were they cowardly.*

[The adjective *heroic* does not balance the clause *nor were they cowardly.*]

Better

Most men who fought in the Civil War were *neither heroic nor cowardly.*

[The contrasting adjectives *heroic* and *cowardly* are equal grammatically, emphasizing the equality indicated by the words *neither* and *nor.*]

Weak

The parking lot for commuters was *both small* and *it was crowded.*

[The adjective *small* does not balance the clause *it was crowded.*]

Better

The parking lot for commuters was *both small and crowded.*

[The two adjectives give equally important descriptions of the parking lot.]

The magazine was not only *the first thing he read in the morning* but also *the last thing he looked at before bed.*

[The parallelism is maintained by an adjective clause modifying the noun *thing* in each element.]

Our economic future depends on whether we *love automobiles* or *leave them.*

[The parallel forms are the verb *love* with its direct object *automobiles* and the verb *leave* with its direct object *them.* They imply an equal choice.]

14C Use parallelism in making lists and outlines.

Weak

Americans now rely on the automobile because:

1. Cities are sprawling, public transport is poor.
2. Prestige.
3. The cheapness of gasoline for so long.

4. Parking lots often provided for employees and students by businesses and schools.
5. General convenience.
6. Shopping centers made for automobiles.

[In this list, the meaning will be much clearer if every numbered item completes a sentence begun by the lead thought *Americans now rely on the automobile because.* The clarity will be further increased if every numbered item is parallel with every other item.]

Parallel

Americans now rely on the automobile because:

1. Cities are sprawling and public transport is poor.
2. The automobile bestows prestige on its owners.
3. Gasoline was cheap for a very long time.
4. Businesses and schools generally provide parking lots for employees and students.
5. Automobiles are convenient.
6. Shopping centers can be reached only by automobile.

[Each of these numbered items begins with a noun or nouns introducing a clause. Each item could complete the heading by making a complete sentence.]

14D You may emphasize parallelism by repeating important words introducing parallel elements.

Without a Repeated Infinitive Marker

They thought it was better *to* agree than quarrel.

With a Repeated Infinitive Marker

They thought it was better *to* agree than *to* quarrel.

[The infinitive marker *to* is repeated before *agree* and *quarrel* to emphasize the parallelism.]

Without a Repeated Preposition

They searched for the lost keys *in* the house, yard, and street.

With a Repeated Preposition

They searched for the lost keys *in* the house, *in* the yard, and *in* the street.

[The repetition of the preposition *in* emphasizes the parallel form and helps call attention to the difficulty of the search.]

Without a Repeated Article

For the handicapped, getting an education is often *a* tribulation, necessity, and victory.

With a Repeated Article

For the handicapped, getting an education is often *a* tribulation, *a* necessity, and *a* victory.

[Repetition of the article *a* before each noun stresses the parallel form.]

Without a Repeated Connective

I decided to leave when I realized *that* I had offended him, he was angry, and my apology would do no good.

With a Repeated Connective

I decided to leave when I realized *that* I had offended him, *that* he was angry, and *that* my apology would do no good.

[The repetition of the connective *that* emphasizes the parallelism of these three dependent noun clauses.]

Note that the sentences *without* the repeated elements in these examples are correct and parallel. But repetition of an element is a choice you have to add a certain kind of emphasis to your sentences. You do not always have to make that choice, but from time to time, using repetition will strengthen your style.

Exercise 14.1 In the following sentences, underline the parallel elements.

1. The game was long, slow, and boring.
2. They met her at the airport, welcomed her to the city, and took her to lunch.
3. Commuting students are often older, more experienced, and more disciplined than residential students.
4. The prime minister declared that her policies were sound, that her people supported her, but that the newspapers had lied about her.
5. In the morning they got up early and cleaned up the house together, and in the afternoon he went to his job, and she went to hers.

Exercise 14.2 Rewrite the following sentences to make clear parallel constructions. If a sentence contains a good parallel construction as it stands, put a check by the number.

1. The American people have always loved to read newspaper stories about murder, scandals, and how to make money.
2. The children of divorced parents are often pressured to enter the quarrel, take sides, but they usually think that both parents are being unreasonable.
3. Wilfred Owen wrote poetry from the trenches in World War I, poetry that told how horrible the war was, mocking the old, pious patriotism, expressing the suffering of wounded men.

4. The sun is high, the sky is blue, and the birds sing in the trees.
5. Presidential primaries are often neither rational, and they are not democratic either.
6. The electric typewriter is either unplugged or somebody has dropped it on the floor and damaged it.
7. Many people in America are unhappy because of jobs not leading anywhere.
8. She is not a good writer, and neither is her speaking.

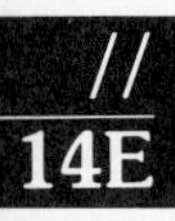

Exercise 14.3 Revise the following sentences to repeat introductory words before parallel forms to make the parallelism more striking.

1. The new ultralight aircraft can land on a sandbar, back lot, or small street.
2. She promised to help out in the day or night.
3. They piled their books on the sofa, tables, and beds.
4. She made three promises—that she would try the machine out, write up a report about it, and tell her friends if she liked it.
5. The railroad tracks passed through a tunnel and then over a river and highway.

14E If you begin a clause with *and which, and that, and who,* or *and whom,* be sure that it follows a clause that begins with *which, that, who,* or *whom.*

Faulty

The peach tree, with its sugary fruit and which was not known in the Middle Ages, seems to have developed from the almond.

[The *and* must join two equal grammatical elements. But here it tries to join the prepositional phrase *with its sugary fruit* to the dependent clause *which was not known in the Middle Ages.*]

Parallel

The peach tree, which has a sugary fruit and which was not known in the Middle Ages, seems to have developed from the almond.

[Now the *and* joins two dependent clauses, each introduced by *which.*]

Faulty

Thelonious Monk, with his deft fingers and who recorded for decades, was one of the great jazz pianists.

[The *and* tries to join the prepositional phrase *with his deft fingers* to the dependent clause *who recorded for decades.*]

Parallel

Thelonious Monk, with his deft fingers and his decades of recording, was one of the great jazz pianists.

[Here the *and* successfully joins the two objects of the preposition *with*—*fingers* and *decades.*]

Faulty

Walt Whitman, influenced by Emerson and whom multitudes loved, was the first great American poet to praise cities in his verse.

[The *and* tries to join the phrase *influenced by Emerson* to the clause *whom multitudes loved.*]

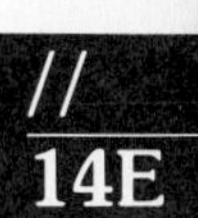

Parallel

Walt Whitman, whom Emerson influenced and whom multitudes loved, was the first great American poet to praise cities in his verse.

[The *and* joins two clauses, *whom Emerson influenced* and *whom multitudes loved.*]

Parallel

Walt Whitman, whom Emerson influenced and multitudes loved, was the first great American poet to praise cities in his verse.

[Here the second *whom* has been dropped, but the parallelism is maintained between *Emerson influenced* and *multitudes loved.*]

Exercise 14.4 Revise the following sentences as necessary to make good parallel constructions.

1. The movie *Gone with the Wind,* filmed in Technicolor and which cost millions of dollars to make, was the first talking movie about the Civil War to be a success at the box office.
2. Television, the great rival to the movies and which movie people hated at first, was not allowed to show the Academy Awards until 1952.
3. General Douglas MacArthur, American leader against Japan in World War II, maker of the Japanese Constitution afterward, and who was fired by President Harry Truman during the Korean war, wanted to become President.
4. She hoped to win her first marathon, the one she entered at Boston and which led over a hilly course.
5. He brought home a new car, large, fire-engine red, expensive, and which he could not afford.

15
Emphasis

When you arrange information carefully in a sentence, you can emphasize your most important ideas and can put less emphasis on less important ideas.

In most declarative sentences, the subject comes first, followed by a predicate that makes a statement about the subject. This form gives readers the feeling that the subject and the statement made about the subject are of equal importance. In very simple sentences, this balance between subject and predicate is easy to see and feel.

Mark *is swimming.*

[The subject, *Mark,* and the verb phrase, *is swimming,* are equally important to the sense of the sentence.]

More complicated sentences can also show balance.

The vast internal migration of the early 1940's *has continued, in a somewhat lower key, in the postwar period.*

—WILLIAM MANCHESTER

[A subject is set down, and a statement is made about it; readers do not feel any special emphasis on either the subject or the predicate. They both seem equally important.]

But sometimes the balance of a sentence may tip heavily to one side or another. In the following example, an enormous weight of emphasis is placed on the subject, but the predicate is so light that it is disappointing.

The battered trees, bending in the screaming winds of the storm, their branches ripped away by the gale, their leaves blowing like a green haze through the driving rain, *were diseased anyway.*

[The subject is full of drama and movement, but the predicate is limp and disappointing.]

If you are going to load a lot of dramatic elements at the beginning of a sentence, you must have a predicate strong enough to carry such a strong subject.

> The sight of the bodies in the water, the strain of the long trip in from the transport ships, and now the ominous nearness of the flat sands and the dunes of Utah Beach *jerked men out of their lethargy.*
>
> —CORNELIUS RYAN

emph 15A

15A Learn to emphasize your main point by using a periodic sentence.

A **periodic sentence** is a sentence that has a strong word or phrase at the end, just before the period. The complete meaning is apparent only when you come to the last few words of the sentence. Study the following periodic sentences:

> If asked to name the central quality in Faulkner's work, one is likely to give the quick answer "Imagination."
>
> —MALCOLM COWLEY
>
> It was always a great affair, the Misses Morkan's annual dance.
>
> —JAMES JOYCE
>
> It was the kind of party where everyone knew everyone else, except no one knew men.
>
> —LINDA BIRD FRANCKE

Sometimes a periodic sentence ends with a striking thought rather than with a striking word.

> The original Hopalong Cassidy was created by Clarence E. Mulford, a Brooklyn marriage-license clerk who at the time had never even seen the West.
>
> —JAMES HORWITZ

[The striking thought occurs at the end of the sentence, where we learn that the hero of so many books and movies about the West was created by a man who had never been there.]

When you have several facts that you want to convey in a sentence, it is nearly always a good idea to put the more important ones toward the end to give a sense of building to a climax that will be memorable.

Loose

John Muir, the naturalist who was more responsible than any other single person for establishing Yosemite National Park, took long, solitary walks and let his beard grow long and tangled.

[The most important fact in this sentence is not John Muir's long and tangled beard but his part in establishing Yosemite National Park—the detail that should come last, making a periodic sentence.]

Revised

John Muir, a naturalist who took long, solitary walks and let his beard grow long and tangled, was more responsible than any other person for establishing Yosemite National Park.

emph
15B

Often when you write your first draft, you may simply jot down a list of events or facts that you can combine to make periodic sentences in later drafts.

First Draft

At last, the hang glider settled softly and safely to earth. Its daring pilot had lunged into space from the cliff above. The cliff was three thousand feet above the valley floor. He knew that if he touched the face of the cliff, he would plunge to his death. He caught the morning winds and drifted down.

[The most important fact in these sentences is that the hang-glider pilot landed safely after a daring flight. Here is a revision to make a periodic sentence.]

Revised

The daring pilot of the hang glider lunged into space from the cliff three thousand feet above the valley floor, caught the morning winds, and drifted down, knowing that to touch the face of the cliff was to plunge to his death, at last coming softly and safely to earth.

15B Do not undermine your sentences by ending them with weak or parenthetical expressions.

Weak

Young people in 1946 and 1947 turned from the horrors of World War II to a love affair with the jukebox, however.

Better

Young people in 1946 and 1947, however, turned from the horrors of World War II to a love affair with the jukebox.

[The reader learns of the contradiction early in the sentence when *however* is placed after the subject.]

Weak

The huge demonstrations in Washington against the Vietnamese war in the 1960s may not have been supported by a majority of the American people, nevertheless.

Better

Nevertheless, the huge demonstrations in Washington against the Vietnamese war in the 1960s may not have been supported by a majority of the American people.

[*Nevertheless* at the beginning of the sentence states a contradiction with something that has been said before and allows the sentence to end on a strong note.]

Exercise 15.1 Rewrite the sentences below to make periodic sentences. Don't be afraid to delete some words and phrases or to invent others that capture the central idea.

1. Adlai Stevenson, laboring against the awesome power of Dwight Eisenhower's smile, lost the presidential elections of 1952 and 1956, as everyone knows.
2. Fiction writers do not often talk very well to interviewers about how they write, so Malcolm Cowley says.
3. The inspector found the body in the kitchen. When she had arrived on the scene, the house was locked and silent. She had the officers break down the door.
4. The gravity of the sun did bend lightwaves passing nearby from distant stars, as experiments during a solar eclipse proved.

15C Write cumulative sentences by adding modifying elements to the predicates of independent or dependent clauses.

In a **cumulative sentence,** several free modifiers or absolutes are added to the end of the predicate, thus bringing new layers of meaning to the basic assertion of the clause.

Free modifiers follow the word they modify, and quite often they are participial phrases that follow a verb and modify the subject. The free modifiers in the following sentences are in italics.

> The motorcycle spun out of control, *leaving the highway, plunging down the ravine, crashing through a fence, coming to rest at last on its side.*
>
> The ocean beat against the shore in long swells, *roaring above the sound of the wind, threatening the tiny houses, slamming against the great rocks on the beach.*

Absolutes (see 3C, pages 129–136) include both a noun and a participle. They may be placed at the end of a sentence to add texture and meaning to the whole. The absolutes in the following sentences are in italics.

> He crossed the finish line in record time, *his lungs nearly bursting with his effort.*
>
> The barn burned, *the flames rising two hundred feet into the night sky.*

Sometimes an absolute uses a noun with an unwritten or understood participle of the verb *to be.*

emph 15C

> She walked into the room, her face bright and cheerful.

[The sentence may be understood in this way: "She walked into the room, her face *being* bright and cheerful."]

A cumulative sentence may use absolutes or free modifiers or both. In contrast, a noncumulative sentence completes its thought with a subject complement, a direct object, or an adverb or adverbial phrase. The sentence below concludes its thought with an adverbial phrase.

> The house stood silently *on the hill.*

But the sentence can be revised so that it completes its thought with absolutes and free modifiers:

> The house stood silently on the hill, baking in the hot sunshine, its broken windows gaping open to the ragged fields, its roof collapsing, its rotting doors hanging open, its glory departed.

[The participial phrase *baking in the hot sunshine* is a free modifier modifying *house;* the phrases *its broken windows gaping open to the ragged fields, its roof collapsing, its rotting doors hanging open,* and *its glory departed* are all absolutes.]

Study the following cumulative sentences, and see how elements added to the end of the predicate help accumulate force.

> He emptied them thoroughly, *unhurried, his face completely cold, masklike almost.*
>
> —WILLIAM FAULKNER

[The phrases in italics add an accumulating force to the sentence.]

> Another characteristic was that once a Veragua had caught and gored a man or a horse he would not leave him but would attack again and again, *seeming to want to destroy his victim entirely.*
>
> —ERNEST HEMINGWAY

[The participial phrase *seeming to want to destroy his victim entirely* is a free modifier, describing a breed of bull called a Veragua that is the subject of the sentence. The modifying phrase comes at the end of the sentence.]

Exercise 15.2 Combine the following sentences to make cumulative sentences.

emph 15D

Example:

He sat at the typewriter. His teacup was at his left. The wind was blowing outside. The clock was ticking over the fireplace. His mind was unable to think of a beginning for the paper due at 9:00 A.M. the next day.

He sat at the typewriter, his teacup at his left, the clock ticking over the fireplace, the wind blowing outside.

1. She studied the map of the block. She was thinking of the fine old buildings that would have to be torn down. She was thinking of her own creation that would take their place. Her ideas were rushing in her head like a flood.
2. He got down from the train and looked around. He saw the courthouse. He saw the city square. It was vacant at this hour of the morning.
3. She saw him. He was sitting in a rocking chair. He was holding a large, black book. It was his family Bible.

Exercise 15.3 Look around the room where you are sitting, and write three cumulative sentences that describe some of the things you see.

15D Give emphasis to the actor or agent in your sentences by using the active rather than the passive voice.

In the active voice, the subject of the sentence performs the action of the verb; in the passive voice, the subject of the sentence is acted upon (see 7E).

Weak Passive

His decision not to run for reelection to the presidency in 1968 was announced on television on March 31 of that year by Lyndon Johnson.

Stronger Active

On March 31, 1968, President Lyndon Johnson announced on television that he would not run for reelection in the fall.

You can use the passive to build a dramatic periodic sentence in which the agent remains a surprise until the end. But such a sentence is valuable only if the surprise is worthwhile, as it may be in a humorous sentence:

The burglar alarms were set clanging, the police were brought running with drawn guns, and the customers in the bank were sent flying out the doors by a signal set off in the vault by a lost puppy.

emph 15E

You cannot use such a device often, and you must be sure that the surprise is real. Readers are likely to feel annoyed by writers who try to surprise them with the obvious:

Macbeth was written by the most brilliant of English playwrights, the Sweet Swan of Avon, the man whose work millions have known and loved, William Shakespeare.

As a rule, use the passive voice only when the actor or agent in the sentence is much less important to your statement than the recipient of the action.

Estes Kefauver *was elected* to the Senate in 1948.

She *was taken* to the hospital last night.

15E Occasionally give emphasis by repeating key words or phrases in several consecutive clauses or sentences.

Let every nation know, whether it wishes us well or ill, that we shall pay *any* price, bear *any* burdens, meet *any* hardship, support *any* friend, oppose *any* foe to assure the survival and the success of liberty.

—John F. Kennedy

[President Kennedy intended the word *any* to pound home his message to the American people and the world.]

Such repetition is effective when used only occasionally to make an emphatic argument against important doubts. It can easily be overdone.

15F Give special emphasis to ideas by writing a very short sentence to follow several long ones.

> The real objection to capital punishment doesn't lie against the actual extermination of the condemned, but against our brutal American habit of putting it off so long. After all, every one of us must die soon or late, and a murderer, it must be assumed, is one who makes that sad fact the cornerstone of his metaphysic. But it is one thing to die, and quite another thing to lie for long months and even years under the shadow of death. *No sane man would choose such a finish.*
>
> —H. L. Mencken

emph 15F

Exercise 15.4 Write a short paragraph in which you repeat a key word several times. You can write about anything you want, but it will probably help to assume that your paragraph is part of a controversial argument.

> Example:
>
> Many protest nuclear energy, and they may be right. But they are wrong when they turn to coal as an alternative source of fuel. Coal is a destroyer. Coal kills the land where it is mined and the men who mine it. Coal dirties the air and blackens our cities. Coal smothers the delicate smells and strews a black dust over the green land. Coal eats at our skin and corrupts our lungs.

Exercise 15.5 Rewrite the following sentences to give emphasis to the elements you think are most important or most dramatic. You may change or delete words and phrases as long as you keep the central idea. Try to find several ways of dealing with each sentence.

1. The college library was locked up by the head librarian, G. W. Cranshaw, who said he got tired of seeing all those careless and sweaty students handling the books.
2. How strongly we believe in something, especially when it is something we think we ought to believe and maybe don't but won't admit it, and somebody comes and asks us if we believe it, is not measured well by statistics.
3. Now swimmers can buy little floats with bright colors on the top and clamps on the bottom under the water, and they can swim out to sea and take off their bathing suits and clamp them with the clamps and go skinny dipping if they want to.
4. An artificial climate has been made by central air-conditioning and central heating, and we are used to it now and cannot think of being without it, although we may have to get along without it someday.
5. Only a few fiction writers have also been good poets because the crafts are different, and not many people can manage both, although Edgar Allan Poe, Thomas Hardy, William Faulkner, and James Joyce have all done their best.

16

Variety

Sentence variety is the spice of lively writing, and you should strive to write sentences varied enough to hold your readers' attention throughout your paper.

16A Vary the patterns and the lengths of your sentences to keep your readers alert and involved.

If you repeat any sentence pattern too often, you will bore your readers, so it is a good idea to learn and practice variations in the basic writing pattern. The basic pattern in modern English writing is *subject + predicate* (see 3A, section 2).

Subject. ↓ Predicate. ↓

My father and my stepmother left on the noon plane to Atlanta.

The most common variation on this basic pattern is to begin with some kind of adverbial opener:

Adverbial Phrase
By the late afternoon, they will be at home.

Adverbial Clause
Because they live so far away, we see them only once or twice a year.

Simple Adverb
Tomorrow they will telephone.

Another variation is to begin a sentence with a participle or a participial phrase that serves as an adjective.

Participle

Smiling, he walked confidently into the room.

Participial Phrase

Stunned by the stock market crash, many brokers committed suicide.

Sentences also can open with an infinitive phrase or a coordinating conjunction.

Infinitive Phrase

To protect my mother, I'd made up stories of a secret marriage that for some strange reason never got known.

—SHERWOOD ANDERSON

Coordinating Conjunction

But, say you, it is a question of interest, and if you make it your interest, you have the right to enslave another. Very well. *And* if he can make it his interest, he has the right to enslave you.

—ABRAHAM LINCOLN

The repetition of the common pattern *subject* + *predicate* is less monotonous than the repetition of the other patterns, but it grows tiresome if it is combined with choppy, disconnected sentences. In the first passage below, the sentences all begin with the subject; they are all about the same length; and they are all short. They are clear and understandable, but notice the improvement in the second passage, where the combined and embedded elements create a pleasing variety in both length and sentence structure.

Repetitious

He dived quickly into the sea. He peered through his mask. The watery world turned darker. A school of fish went by. The distant light glittered on their bodies. He stopped swimming. He waited. He thought the fish might be chased by a shark. He satisfied himself that there was no shark. He continued down. He heard only one sound. That was his breathing apparatus. It made a bubbling noise in operation.

Improved

He dived quickly into the sea, peering through his mask at a watery world that turned darker as he went down. A school of fish went by, the distant light glittering on their bodies, and he stopped swimming and waited a moment to see if the fish might be chased by a shark. Satisfying himself that there was no shark, he continued down. The only sound he heard was the bubbling noise of his breathing apparatus.

(The improved version combines thoughts and reduces the number of sentences in the passage. The repetition of the pronoun *he* is also reduced and the sentence patterns are more varied and interesting.)

16B Ask an occasional rhetorical question.

var 16B

A rhetorical question heightens attention by suddenly requiring the reader to participate more actively in your prose. A rhetorical question allows you to give an answer as the writer does in the following example:

> The movie is called *Rock 'n Roll High School,* and for anyone not into punk, it has only one conceivable point of interest: Can Van Patten act as well as he hits a tennis ball? The answer is no, which is not to say that he isn't a promising young actor. It's just that as a tennis player he is a good deal more than fine.
>
> —*Sports Illustrated*

Sometimes writers ask a question or even a series of questions without giving an answer because to them the answer is obvious.

> Is not marriage an open question, when it is alleged, from the beginning of the world, that such as are in the institution wish to get out; and such as are out wish to get in?
>
> —RALPH WALDO EMERSON

You may ask questions that you know will be asked by your opponents in argument. You can then answer them in ways that support your side. You also can gain an advantage in the argument by raising the difficult questions in a way that helps your cause. Study the following passage with its questions posed, on behalf of his opponents, by Martin Luther King, Jr. It is from his "Letter from Birmingham Jail."

> One may well ask: "How can you advocate breaking some laws and obeying others?" The answer lies in the fact that there are two types of laws: just and unjust. I would be the first to advocate obeying just laws. One has not only a legal but a moral responsibility to obey just laws. Conversely, one has a moral responsibility to disobey unjust laws. I would agree with St. Augustine that "an unjust law is no law at all."
>
> Now, what is the difference between the two? How does one determine whether a law is just or unjust? A just law is a man-made code that squares with the moral law or the law of God. An unjust law is a code that is out of harmony with the moral law. To put it in the terms of St.

Thomas Aquinas: An unjust law is a human law that is not rooted in eternal and natural law. Any law that uplifts human personality is just. Any law that degrades personality is unjust. All segregation statutes are unjust because segregation distorts the soul and damages the personality.

Avoid beginning an essay by asking broad rhetorical questions that might better be phrased as sharp thesis statements. Inexperienced writers use this device so often that it loses its effect quickly. "Why should we study *Huckleberry Finn*?" "How did TVA begin?" "Was Alger Hiss guilty as charged?" Readers may suspect that the writer of such broad questions will not take the trouble to think of a better opening. It is usually better to save your rhetorical questions for an occasional paragraph that comes in the body of a paper after the subject has been introduced in some other way.

16C Use an exclamation on rare occasions for special effects.

Occasionally an exclamation helps you vary a series of declarative sentences:

> Clearly, even if there were a limit on the length of sentences to twenty words, it would not be possible to characterize any individual's knowledge of English by claiming that he carried around a list of all its sentences in his head! But there is in fact no limit to the length of a sentence. A sentence twenty-one words in length can be made longer by adding another modifier or a subordinate of some kind—and so on.
>
> —HELEN S. CAIRNS and CHARLES E. CAIRNS

16D Invert the subject and the verb occasionally.

For variety you can put the verb before the subject. This is another device that should be used only rarely.

> Beyond is another country.
>
> —ROBERT M. PIRSIG

> From high above in the swirl of raging wind and snow came a frightening, wonderful, mysterious sound.
>
> —MARK HELPRIN

Exercise 16.1 Revise the following sets of simple sentences to form two coherent paragraphs made up of sentences that are varied in style and in length. You may change or add words but not facts. Look for places where you can subordinate one idea to another, both to reduce the number of words and to create a pleasing style.

Experiment. Rearrange some sentences to make the verb come before the subject. Convert a sentence into a question, and either begin an answer or point your reader toward an answer. Compare your versions with the work of others in your class.

Set 1

1. Bluegrass music was popular in the rural south before World War II.
2. Radio and recordings have made it popular everywhere.
3. It features hand-held instruments.
4. These include the banjo, the guitar, the fiddle, the mandolin, and sometimes the dulcimer and the bass fiddle.
5. Bluegrass does not use drums.
6. Bluegrass songs are in the tradition of the mountain ballad and the Protestant hymn.
7. It began as the music of poor southern American mountaineers.
8. They had to make their own entertainment.
9. Bluegrass songs are about love affairs gone wrong.
10. Sometimes they speak about the fear of hell.
11. Sometimes they describe conversion experiences.
12. Sometimes they express the yearning of the soul for heaven.
13. Bluegrass bands never use electrified instruments.

Set 2

1. D. W. Griffith was the first great American filmmaker.
2. He made the shot the most important element in filmmaking.
3. Others had made the scene the most important element.
4. He combined shots into scenes.
5. He understood the importance of cutting and composition.
6. He combined scenes into sequences.
7. He combined sequences into plots.
8. He began as an actor.
9. He made five dollars a day.
10. He became a director in 1908.
11. He made 150 films between 1908 and 1913.
12. He had the chance to experiment.
13. Others wanted to photograph the whole human figure.
14. These other film directors thought people wanted whole figures.
15. Griffith used the close-up shot.
16. The close-up shot provided emotions.
17. He made his actors stop making extreme gestures.
18. He tried to make actors seem like real people.

16E Occasionally use free modifiers and absolutes at the end of a sentence to achieve variety (see 15C).

A free modifier, you have learned, is a participle or participial phrase occurring at the end of a clause and modifying the subject.

The plane climbed slowly, *fighting for altitude.*
[The participial phrase *fighting for altitude* is a free modifier describing the subject, *plane.*]

We walked home, *delighting in the autumn colors.*
[The participial phrase *delighting in the autumn colors* modifies the subject, *we.*]

var
16E

An absolute, to review, consists of a noun combined with a participle and usually comes at the end of a clause. Absolutes modify the entire clause where they appear.

The plane climbed slowly, *its engines shrieking.*
[The phrase in italics is an absolute. The noun *engines* is joined to the participle *shrieking.*]

We walked home, *our eyes delighting in the autumn colors and our hearts singing.*
[Two absolutes come at the end of this sentence. The noun *eyes* combines with the participle *delighting* to make the first one, and the noun *hearts* combines with the participle *singing* to make the second one.]

Free modifiers and absolutes allow variety. Writers who use them can combine thoughts that might otherwise have to be expressed by simple sentences. We could say this:

The cows grazed in the field. They made the day seem tranquil.

But by using a free modifier we can say this:

The cows grazed in the field, making the day seem tranquil.

We could say this:

She gathered up her portfolio. Her hands moved slowly and precisely.

But with an absolute we can say this:

She gathered up her portfolio, her hands moving slowly and precisely.

You can combine absolutes and free modifiers to write fairly long sentences that do not become confusing.

> The car moved slowly up the dirt road, wheezing, banging, lurching along, the rust showing through its thin paint, its windshield cracked, its engine smoking.

Exercise 16.2 Combine the following sentence groups to make free modifiers and absolutes.

var
16E

1. The bookshelf stood in the corner. It was overburdened with books. Its paint was worn off.
2. The computer hummed on my desk. Its green monitor was flashing at me in a friendly way.
3. He had stayed at home all his life. He had taken care of his family's farm.
4. The full moon rose over the graveyard. Its face looked ghostly. It frightened me.

PART FOUR
Using Words Effectively

17
Appropriate Diction

In writing, you always should use language that is appropriate to your subject by choosing words that state your meaning exactly and that convey a clear sense of it to your readers. You should avoid a writing style that is too informal or chatty, but you also must beware of stiffness and pomposity.

To get a sense of appropriate language, you should be as honest as you can be, and you should read as much as you can. Being honest means that you do not try to persuade readers by proclaiming passionate emotions that you do not feel or by assuming an authority that you do not have. An understated language that does not draw undue attention to itself is almost always the best voice for communicating ideas. A highly colored language often sends unwanted messages to readers, telling them that you believe you are superior to them or that you are cute or that you are interesting because of the feelings you have rather than because of the information you communicate. If you do feel highly emotional about an issue, it is much more effective to tell your readers the information that stirs your emotions than to tell them that you have the feelings. For example, if you object strongly to some practice like killing baby seals for their fur, you may win readers over by giving them a simple, factual narrative of how seal hunts are carried out. Understate your own feelings, but give all the details that create these feelings if you want to be persuasive. You will not win anybody if you use a shouting, insulting language that simply gives vent to your emotions. That is probably the least effective way of creating these emotions in your readers. For example, a student conducting interviews wrote this sentence in her paper:

> As absurd as all the responses to my previous interviews were, none approached the repulsiveness of my last one.

She would have done much better to report what her interviewees had said so that her readers could judge whether the statements were "absurd" and whether they exhibited "repulsiveness."

The best way to gain a sense of appropriate language is to read as much as you can. Whether you are preparing to write about literature or natural science or history, take some time to read what writers who know the subject have written. Try to use their tone as a model for your own style. Strive to be serious and to be taken seriously, but do not get so serious that you become humorless and stiff. Take the attitude that you want your readers to learn something from you and to appreciate the way you convey information. Your readers should be able to enjoy your writing unless your topic itself is depressing or painful. But even then, your writing should be so clear that it creates sympathetic feelings in your readers to match the subject of your essay.

Some writers work hard to display themselves as vital, interesting people, truly excited about their subject and up to date in their use of language. Unfortunately, their strained efforts at informality often make them sound pretentious, self-conscious, and excessively emotional, as if they would rather be cute than correct:

d

> Now I want to tell you about this real, cool cat, David Farragut, see? At the time I'm getting ready to tell you about, he'd been out there on the deep blue sea for the U.S. Navy for more than fifty long years. When he was just a little kid, he was hauling powder up to the guns of a boat they called the *Essex* back there when we licked the living daylights out of the Brits in the War of 1812. And you know what the old geezer did every time he had a birthday? He did a flip! That's right! He told one of his junior officers that he wouldn't think he was old until he couldn't do that any more. I wonder if he ever did get that old! Must have, since he's dead now! (Ha! Ha!) Well, when the big rip came in 1861, he was settled down there in ole Virginie, in Norfolk by the sea, and he told those Johnny Rebs in his hometown that they were going to catch the devil—that's exactly what he said—before it was all over. Then he split and got himself north to fight for Old Glory. So there he is when we get down to this part of his tale, getting ready to put the evil eye on ole New Orleans, piling all his boats into the river, and getting ready to ram his fleet right smack into the city.

Almost as bad as the slangy, overinformal prose above is this stiff, dead version:

> David Glasgow Farragut had served his country loyally in the United States Navy for over fifty years, more than half a century. As an extremely young sailor, scarcely more than a boy, he had fulfilled the acutely dangerous task of carrying highly explosive gunpowder from the storage magazines below decks to the cannon stationed on the deck of a ship called the *Essex* of the frigate class, a ship well known in the heroic annals of the American navy. At the time of the outbreak of hostilities in

the Civil War, Farragut possessed the strength and vitality of a much younger man, qualities which he exhibited each and every year by doing a handspring on his birthday, much to the astonishment of his younger subordinates, who, it may be assumed, expected actions of a more dignified nature from their commander! He told one of these subordinates one time that he would not suppose himself to be truly growing old until he found himself entirely unable to do such a handspring on his natal day. When the tragic conflict began its bloody pageant across the American stage, he had been dwelling in the city of Norfolk in the state of Virginia, and he delivered himself of a stern verbal warning to those neighbors of his in this important port who believed in withdrawing their allegiance to the Union with its capital in Washington in the District of Columbia. "You fellows will catch the Devil before you get through with this business" was his somewhat brusque and perhaps ungallant but altogether sincere remark to these secessionists, as they were called at that time. He thereupon closed down his house, which we may suppose was a fine one, befitting his long service in the country's military, and departed for the northern climes, where he affirmed his undeviating and eternal loyalty to the government in Washington and resumed his proper position in that floating part of the military establishment destined to carry the war into the Atlantic frontier of the United States. Now he was the supreme commander of the naval fleet of fighting ships that had been sent down from the north to fight against and if possible capture the important port city of New Orleans, "Queen of the Mississippi," and he was undertaking the expedition of small, heavy ships and gunboats up into the river that led in the direction of the city.

Before readers get very far into either of these versions, they start having trouble. Here is Bruce Catton's version in his book *This Hallowed Ground:*

> Farragut had been in the navy for more than half a century—had served as a very juvenile powder monkey on the famous frigate *Essex* when she cruised the Pacific in the War of 1812, and was still spry enough for a midshipman. He had a habit of turning a handspring on every birthday and told an amazed junior that he would not think he was growing old until he found himself unable to do it. He had been living in Norfolk, Virginia, when the war started; had warned his secessionist fellow townsmen, "You fellows will catch the Devil before you get through with this business," and then had closed his house and gone north to stick with the old flag. Now he was in command of the fleet that had been appointed to attack New Orleans, and he was getting heavy sloops and gunboats up into the river.

Catton's diction is informal without being stuffy or chatty. He does not use slang, although he does use the informal expression "powder monkey" because it was common in Farragut's time. He does not weigh his prose down

d

with unnecessary explanations or dreary qualifications. He treats his material seriously, but he adds the humorous information that Farragut turned a handspring on his birthday every year. Catton does not intrude himself into his narrative; he does not tell us what he thinks about everything he says. He gives us information and lets us make up our own minds. We can see that he likes Farragut, that he even admires him. But we can perceive Catton's emotions only by what he chooses to tell us about his subject. He does not say, "David Farragut was an extremely admirable man because of what he did when the Civil War broke out." Catton tells us what we need to know, and he leaves us to make up our own minds about whether the people he describes are good or bad and whether their actions are admirable or not.

You should use a similar discretion. When you write, choose a tone that will not interfere with what you want your reader to know. Catton's style is an example of a common and attractive tone in American prose today. In general, it is a good tone to imitate because it is simple and straightforward and unemotional.

d 17A

You should always choose the tone and the diction that fit your subject. You should not use a breezy, informal tone for a paper on cancer or for an essay on famine in Africa. And you should not use a sober, humorless tone in writing about the World Series or the Super Bowl.

17A Use slang sparingly and only when it is appropriate to the subject and the tone you choose for your essay.

Inappropriate

In *Heart of Darkness,* we hear a lot about a dude named Kurtz, but we don't see the guy much.

Revised

In *Heart of Darkness,* Marlow, the narrator, talks almost continually about Kurtz, but we see Kurtz himself only at the end.

Inappropriate

When Thomas More saw how Henry VIII was going, he might have run off to France to save his hide, but he stayed on and got his head chopped off for his trouble.

Revised

When he saw the direction of Henry's mind, Thomas More might have fled to France to save himself, but he stayed on until he was imprisoned and put to death.

[In both inappropriate examples above, the use of slang and informal diction contradicts the seriousness of each topic.]

Some slang terms are always entering the mainstream of the language, and many American journalists assume a breezy, informal tone. But even these journalists do not fill their prose with slang. Instead, they use slang occasionally to fit a special mood that they are trying to convey.

> But Boston is also a city that historically has pricked the social conscience of many well-heeled undergraduates.
>
> —HOWARD HUSOCK, *The New York Times Magazine*

[The writer of a more formal essay would probably not use the term *well-heeled.*]

> Minutes before the camera's ruby light flashed on, cable TV's garrulous impresario was already well into his inaugural address before a gathering of Atlanta VIPs.
>
> —*Time*

[TV as an abbreviation for "television" is so common now that it is not considered slang and can be used even in formal writing; VIP for "Very Important Person" would probably still be considered too slangy for formal writing.]

d
17A

> Many wisecracky lines are assigned to the spinster, and Joan Pape, when given a chance, delivers them well.
>
> —*The New Yorker*

[The word *wisecracky* is an arresting coinage that many would consider slang, unsuitable for a formal subject. But it is at home in a theater review.]

> Harvey Shapiro is a plump, middle-aged Cherry Hill business man who's been married to the same woman for 26 years. They have two kids.
>
> —*Philadelphia Magazine*

[In informal writing, the word *kids* is appropriate. But no historian would write this sentence in a scholarly article: "Henry VIII had only one kid by his first marriage who survived into adulthood."]

You must use slang if it is part of a direct quotation. There the prose is not yours but that of your source, and you must quote that source exactly if you are using quotation marks.

> Postell said that there is very little illness among students right now, adding, "If you've got a lot of sickness, you've got a lot of people sicking out."

[The term *sicking out* is slang for pretending illness to evade some responsibility—like taking an exam on time. *Sicking out* is a catchy phrase, but it would be glaringly out of place in a term paper about religion: "Bishop John Fisher did not wish to attend the Parliament; so he sicked out and refused to come."]

17B Avoid writing in dialect.

Some inexperienced writers try to use dialect to show the ethnic or regional origins of people, but dialect is difficult to express in writing. Inexperienced writers frequently get it wrong and may appear to be laughing at the people they are writing about.

Dialect

> "Ah'm a-goin' raght over thar," she said, "an if'n you'd go along, hit'ud be a big hep, and Ah'd be much obleeged."

Revised

> "I'm going right over there," she said with a strong Appalachian accent, "and if you'd go along, it'd be a big help, and I'd be much obliged."

d
17C

17C Avoid jargon that inflates language and that makes your thoughts seem more complicated than they really are.

Jargon is a language that uses ordinary English words in ways that are unfamiliar to most people. Sometimes jargon enables people with specialized interests to talk with each other. For example, people who use computers talk to each other in a language nearly incomprehensible to people who know nothing about computers. Computer users speak of "booting a disk" and of making "hard copies" and of "accessing the program." These words communicate very well to the vast number of computer users in our country, and they turn up in computer magazines. "Input is a snap, since the entire program is menu driven (see Figure 2), and Help messages will flash on the screen if you don't understand the significance of an assumption (see Figure 3)." That sentence, from *PC Magazine,* is nonsense to the rest of us because it uses a special jargon with words like "input" and "program" and "Help messages."

Such jargon has its place in both speaking and writing. All too often, though, writers use jargon to make simple thoughts seem complicated and to imply that they have special knowledge that is superior to that of outsiders. Experienced readers see jargon as a false front, and they rarely take it seriously. Consider this paragraph written by an academic author:

> Romantic love is characterized by a preoccupation with a deliberately restricted set of perceived characteristics in the love object which are viewed as a means to some ideal ends. In the process of selecting the set of perceived characteristics and the process of determining the ideal ends, there is also a systematic failure to assess the accuracy of the perceived characteristics and the feasibility of achieving the ideal ends given the selected set of means and other pre-existing ends.

The paragraph means something like the following:

> People in love see only what they want to see in the beloved. They want to believe in an ideal, so they do not question the accuracy of what they see or ask themselves if the ideal they imagine can be attained.

[Notice the wordiness of the original, especially in expressions like *perceived characteristics* and *love object* and in the repetition of words like *ends.* We read that "Romantic love is characterized by . . . characteristics." Throughout the passage, the writer uses the passive voice, which is often a signal of jargon.]

When you think you may be writing in unnecessary jargon, break your sentences down into simple core assertions, keeping subjects close to verbs, limiting modifiers, removing repetitions. Write the simplest sentences that will still keep the meaning you want to convey. See if you can make them so direct that any literate person can understand them.

17D Do not use obsolete and foreign words and technical terms unless you are sure that they are appropriate to your audience.

1 Avoid obsolete or archaic words and expressions that confuse your reader or misstate your meaning.

Obsolete

> In Anthony Trollope's novel *Barchester Towers,* Slope insists on making love to Eleanor Bold in a carriage, despite her efforts to resist his advances.

[In Trollope's day, *to make love* meant to announce one's love to someone and to propose marriage, and Trollope uses the phrase in that sense in all his novels—as did all nineteenth-century English novelists. A scholar of literature might inadvertently fall into using Trollope's phrases today, thus confusing readers to whom the phrase *make love* means something else.]

Obsolete

> It was clear ere she left that the problems had not been resolved.

[The word *ere* is used frequently in early modern English to mean *"before,"* but it seems archaic now and may confuse modern American readers.]

But if you know your readers have read a piece of literature containing obsolete language, you may use it, sometimes humorously, when you write about the piece:

Anyone who hits on an interpretation of Hamlet's character and ponders it for a while is likely to find his resolution sicklied o'er with the pale cast of thought. No single interpretation seems adequate.

[The line *resolution sicklied o'er with the pale cast of thought* comes from a famous speech by Hamlet. The writer assumes that readers know both the play and the line and therefore uses the line, although it involves archaic language. Note that you do not place a well-known literary allusion in quotation marks when you are not referring to the quotation itself and when you are clearly not claiming to have originated the line yourself.]

2 Use foreign words only when they are necessary.

It is pretentious to use foreign expressions when English will do.

d
17D

Pretentious

He used foreign expressions to show how superior he was to the *hoi polloi* because he had discovered *par hasard* that some of the beautiful people were deeply impressed by words they could not understand.

Better

He used foreign expressions to show how superior he was to ordinary people because he had discovered by chance that some of the beautiful people were deeply impressed by words they could not understand.

Pretentious

Her collection of exotic clamshells was her only *raison d'être.*

Better

Her collection of exotic clamshells was her only reason for living.

Pretentious

Sarah's *Weltanschauung* extended no further than her daily whims.

Better

Sarah's view of the world extended no further than her daily whims.

3 Avoid using technical terms unless you are writing for an audience that understands what these terms mean.

The advice that applies to jargon (see 17C) applies here. Sometimes technical terms work well when they are used for a specialized audience that understands them. But technical terms thrown into a paper for a general audience often seem pompous, and they can only confuse the average reader.

Pompous

Baxter felt a pang of existential anxiety when he contemplated his English exam.

Better

Baxter worried about his English exam when he thought about it.

[The words *existential* and *existentialist* have a philosophical meaning understood by students of modern intellectual thought. They should not be used indiscriminately as synonyms for *personal* or *thoughtful.*]

Correct

The potential audience for the existentialists consists of those who feel that, when they ask for bread, the most competent English-speaking philosophers offer them a stone.

—WALTER KAUFMANN

[The philosopher Walter Kaufmann uses the term *existentialists* to describe a group of thinkers. He does not use it as a casual term for any kind of anxiety.]

Exercise 17.1 Rewrite the following sentences to change language that might be inappropriate in a formal paper. Try to keep the meaning of each sentence. To do so, you will need to consider what we mean when we use some common slang words—words that are often emotional but inexact.

1. Told by the British that he must die, Nathan Hale made a laid-back reply: "I regret that I have but one life to give for my country."
2. When the ump called nine consecutive strikes on three batters, Manager Billy Martin got his back up.
3. When the Germans were presented with the Treaty of Versailles in 1919, they really got sore.
4. Maybe the concert of the Boston Symphony Orchestra will be so wicked that the audience will fork over megabucks to go with the flow.
5. John Foster Dulles, Eisenhower's first Secretary of State, was a shrewd old geezer who saw red whenever the Commies did some dirt.
6. Some people think that if Marie Antoinette had not been so stuck up, the French mobs might not have cut her head off in the revolution, but maybe the Frenchies were so riled up over everything in general that they would have beheaded her if she had been as pure as Julie Andrews.
7. In the history of fashion, men's clothing was much more spiffy than women's until the nineteenth century.
8. The President promised to go to Moscow anon.
9. Mr. Thomas B. Cartwright, official flack for the State Department, told a press conference that the United States and China were boogying along toward lasting peace between the two countries.
10. Leonard Bernstein was top dog for the New York Philharmonic Orchestra for many years, although now and then he was accused of show-boating.

Exercise 17.2 Discuss in class the kinds of papers where the following expressions or words might be appropriate. Compose sentences using them.

1. rip-off
2. freaky
3. bull session
4. on the lam
5. hang out
6. hobo
7. team player
8. loner
9. flying high
10. narc

Exercise 17.3 Rewrite the following sentences to eliminate foreign words or stilted expressions. You may need to look up the foreign words or stilted expressions in your desk dictionary. Don't try to translate the foreign words literally; try rather to put their meaning into fresh, idiomatic English.

d
17E

1. The freshmen thought that the *summum bonum* of college life was to own a convertible.
2. Max said that if his roommate kept on smoking cigars in bed at night, it would be a *casus belli.*
3. The mail carrier made her quotidian march *lentemente* from domicile to domicile, wearing her official blue culottes and dropping off little missives in the postal receptacles while phoebus showered the sidewalks with his lethal darts and myriads of canines kept up their iterant ululations.
4. A common multidimensional learning problem for students of the typewriter and the violin is the dexterity factor, for in both cases erroneous application of the fingers has the end result of a negative production response.
5. A sophomore is a kind of *tertium quid* between freshmen and upper-class students.
6. The professor tried to find a *via media* between unceasing research and talking to students all day long in her office.

17E Use idioms according to standard practice.

Idioms are habitual ways of saying things, and when we violate them, we cause readers to stumble. All languages have their own idioms. The French say, "How many years does he have?" while we say, "How old is he?" The Germans say of something they do not understand, "That comes to me like Spanish." We say, "That's Greek to me." Spanish speakers say, "What hour is it?" We say, "What time is it?" The French say, "What do you have?" We say, "What's wrong with you?" The French also say, "I have heat," and we say, "I'm hot." The modern Greeks say, "It's going to make heat today." We say, "It's going to be hot today." Americans in the rural, mountainous South say, "What do you say?" Other Americans say, "Hello," or "How are you?" or "Hi" or "Howdy."

Idioms cannot usually be translated from one language to another, and they sometimes cannot be transferred from one region to another within a country. If you say in French to a Frenchman, "I'm going to eat a hot dog with mustard," he will probably be appalled at your taste for puppies. If you ask a mountain southerner in the United States for a poke, he will hand you a paper bag; if you ask a New Yorker, he may hit you in the mouth.

Teachers often write *id* (for incorrect idiom) in the margin of a paper when the student has mangled some standard English word or phrase. If you write, "The South was angry against Lincoln," your teacher may write *id* at *against* because we commonly say that we are *angry with* someone or *angry at* someone, not angry *against* the person. The same is true of the phrase *different from*. We say, "Fred is *different from* his older brother," not, "Fred is *different than* his older brother." When you disagree with a friend, you say, "I *differed with* her about the interpretation of the news," meaning that you had discussed the news and argued about it. But if you say, "He *differed from* me because he wore tweed pajamas," you are only noting how you and someone else are different without saying whether you have ever discussed the matter. We do not say, "She *laughed on* the joke"; we say, "She *laughed at* the joke."

d 17E

From these examples, you can see that idioms often involve prepositions and that getting an idiom right is often a matter of using a preposition correctly. You know that there is a big difference between these two sentences: "He made off with the money." "He made up with his friend." There is also a big difference between these two sentences: "He bet on the horses every week." "He bet at a window at the racetrack." Sometimes we use the improper idiom by using the wrong preposition. We should not say, "He stayed *to* Boston last Sunday afternoon." We should say rather, "He stayed *in* Boston last Sunday afternoon." Sometimes we use a preposition when none is necessary. We should not say, "We will meet *up with* him in Denver." We should say only, "We will meet him in Denver."

Sometimes idiom refers to diction—how we use some words. We do not say, "On July 1, 1863, the Union Army of the Potomac and the Confederate Army of Northern Virginia *affronted* each other at Gettysburg." We do not mean that these two armies merely offended each other; we mean something stronger, and the idiomatic usage would be this: "On July 1, 1863, the Union Army of the Potomac and the Confederate Army of Northern Virginia *confronted* each other at Gettysburg." It is not idiomatic to say, "*Previous to* the game, the band performed on the field." We say, "*Before* the game, the band performed on the field."

Idiom refers to custom, and no book can give you all the ways idioms may be misused. Neither can a book give you a set of rules that will enable you to get idioms right all the time. Inexperienced writers most often have trouble with idioms when they use unfamiliar words or expressions and do not know how to put them together the way experienced writers use them. We learn idioms one at a time, and we remember them as we grow in experience with language and as we use them in our writing and speaking.

Exercise 17.4 Rewrite the following sentences to correct mistakes in idiom. Don't be afraid to make a mistake. Remember that idiom is very difficult because it often has no logic. It is a reflection of customary speech patterns, and custom often refuses to obey logicial rules. You may wish to consult a dictionary that includes examples of how words are used. The dictionary examples will help you understand the idioms in question.

Example: Jack was angry against Leo.

Correct idiom: Jack was angry with Leo.

1. We celebrate Labor Day at the first Monday after the first Sunday in September.
2. Lyndon Johnson became President on November 1963.
3. My mother introduced me with her friend.
4. Previous to the meeting, we agreed to talk only an hour before adjourning.
5. Newton's general principle states that all bodies have a force of gravity proportionate with their mass.
6. Jazz music has been traditionally centered around the experience of black musicians playing in small groups.
7. He deaned the faculty for ten years and then returned to teaching because he wanted to make something of himself.
8. The sun arose that morning at six o'clock.
9. They promised to meet up with our group on the trail.
10. Computers promise to us much more efficiency than typewriters could ever give.
11. She loved to stay to home and read in the evening.
12. A sailboat race is different than a car race in how the racers start.
13. She had a good relationship to him.
14. His date was still not ready, and he had to wait on her in the dorm.
15. Bernadette was quite impatient of his behavior as she wondered where he was at.

17F Choose words with connotations you wish to convey.

The definition of words is complicated because words have both primary and secondary meanings. These secondary meanings are the impressions or *connotations* the words convey, connotations that allow some words to work in some contexts and not in others. The connotations of words are like the clothing we wear for special occasions. As the occasions differ, so do our clothes. A man who steps out of his house in a tuxedo is probably not going to the barn to milk the cows. A woman who emerges wearing a business suit and carrying a briefcase is probably not on her way to a job as a welder. The man might sometimes milk and the woman weld, but they would do these jobs in different clothes.

Similarly, ideas may be expressed in words that wear slightly different clothes to do different jobs. You can say that your friend Murdock *evaded* the requirement that everyone learn how to swim before graduation, or you can say that he *flouted* it, or you can say that he *escaped* it. Either way we know that Murdock did not learn how to swim and that he did not obey the rule. But if he *evaded* the rule, he slipped away from it; he was sly; he got around the requirement by some quiet and perhaps devious or clever way. If he *flouted* the requirement, he may have announced publicly and arrogantly that he did not intend to observe the requirement and that for all he cared, the administration could withhold his diploma if it wanted to. If he *escaped* the requirement, something may have happened accidentally to make the college forget to enforce the rule for him.

You can say that your boss *requested* that you come to a meeting on Thursday morning or that she *demanded* to see you as soon as you came in. The word *request* is a polite, perhaps neutral term, but when your boss starts making *demands,* you may be in trouble.

d 17F

If you say that the audience was *hypnotized* by a speech, you imply that the speaker was so good that the audience forgot everything else except what the speaker was saying and believed everything; but if you say that a speech *put the audience to sleep,* you mean that the speech was a bore.

You may say that your parents *ignored* your request for money, implying a deliberate act of will on their part; but if they *neglected* your request, they may simply have put it off or forgotten about it.

If you say that someone is *unsympathetic* toward your views, you mean that she may have considered them but that she is not inclined to accept them. But if she is *intolerant* of your opinions, she probably does not want to hear them or talk to you about them or perhaps even be friendly toward you when you express them.

If you say that a shortstop was *confused,* you may mean that when a hard ground ball was hit to him with a man on first, he thought there were two outs when there was only one and in his confusion did not throw to second fast enough to get the double play. But if you say that he was *dazed,* you may mean that he was hit on the head by a line drive and that he could not tell whether he was in the ballpark or a bathtub.

Studying the connotations of words can be enjoyable, but beginning writers often have trouble with connotations. The best remedies are to note how experienced writers use different words and to study the dictionary for the use of **synonyms**—words having similar meanings but different connotations.

Exercise 17.5 Write sentences that use the following words correctly. You may use several of the words in one sentence if you can do so gracefully.

1. ambitious, greedy
2. successful, enterprising
3. proud, arrogant, haughty
4. hit, smash, collide
5. drink, guzzle, sip
6. eat, gobble, pick at

18

Imagery and Figurative Language

You can enliven your writing with imagery, that is, by creating word pictures for the reader. Using concrete nouns and verbs that appeal to the senses, you can change an abstract idea into something vivid and specific. If you write, "The trees were affected by the bad weather," you do not give your readers much to picture in their minds. But if you write, "The small pines shook in the wind," the concrete nouns *pine* and *wind* and the concrete verb *shook* create an image.

Figurative language helps you build images. A figure states or implies a comparison between your subject and something else. If you write "The small pines shook in the wind," you are being literal. If you write "The small pines trembled with fear like children scolded by the wind," you are being figurative. The figure compares the trees to frightened young children and the wind to a person scolding them. Our language is rich in figures because they help us express ideas more clearly and succinctly than we otherwise could.

18A Use nouns and verbs that convey clear, concrete images or that report action.

Avoid nouns and passive verbs that merely report the existence of something but do not report that something happens. Examine this paragraph:

> Often the positions people take on energy are an index to how they stand on other issues. Conservatives, liberals, and radicals tend to group their causes, and if you tell me where you think we ought to get our energy, I can probably tell you what you think about what we ought to eat and how we ought to spend our time. But nearly everybody on every side of every current issue agrees that we should use solar energy.

[This paragraph contains no errors in grammar, and it is fairly clear. But its prose style does not engage our attention, and when we finish reading it, we have a hard time remembering it. Words like *conservative, liberal,* and *radi-*

cal are so vague that we don't know what they mean unless the writer explains them—something few writers do who use these terms. A concept that sounds concrete, like *solar energy,* conveys many meanings to different people, and we don't know which meaning the writer intends.]

Now study this version (italics added):

> Every source of energy seems to have become a political issue. Tell me whether you think the path to a happy future lies with *solar heating* or with *nuclear furnaces,* tell me how you feel about *oil shale* and *coal* and *corn-fed gasohol,* and I'll tell you where you stand on *welfare reform, environmental policy, vegetarianism, busing, backpacking,* and *abortion.* But there is one kind of energy that attracts a diverse following: *photovoltaics,* the art of converting *sunlight* into *electricity.*
>
> —TRACY KIDDER

[Look at all the nouns in italics that call up concrete images in this paragraph. At the end we know just what aspect of solar energy—photovoltaics—the writer is talking about. He uses a technical term and immediately defines it.]

fig 18A

Now study this paragraph:

> In the 1930s, color started being used for movies, first in cartoons. Walt Disney was a pioneer in this field and made several short cartoons before he expanded the technique to make the first feature-length animation, *Snow White and the Seven Dwarfs,* which was very popular.

[This paragraph has some concrete details, including the name of the movie *Snow White and the Seven Dwarfs.* But compared with the following one, it is still vague and general.]

> Color was coming in, but only in cartoons was it really successful. The *Silly Symphonies,* animating *flowers, birds, bees,* and *animals,* mocking well-loved pieces of classical *music,* using the freedom of *design* and *line* and *color* to create funny, moving, dramatic, and sometimes terrifying *effects,* are probably *Walt Disney's masterpieces. Mickey Mouse,* the dog *Pluto,* the *three little pigs* were added to, and often borrowed from the world's *folk-lore. "Who's Afraid of the Big, Bad Wolf?"* took on a special meaning from the threats in *Hitler's speeches.* As for *Snow White and the Seven Dwarfs,* a reputedly hard-boiled and widely syndicated *American columnist, Westbrook Pegler,* thought it "the happiest thing that has happened in this world since the *Armistice."*
>
> —ALAN JENKINS

[Notice all the concrete details set in italics, and notice the quotation at the end, which gives a special force to the whole.]

Exercise 18.1 Read the following short paragraphs and discuss the number of concrete details with your class.

> In the smallest of these huts lived old Berl, a man in his eighties, and his wife, who was called Berlcha (wife of Berl). Old Berl was one of the Jews who had been driven from their villages in Russia and had settled in Poland. In Lentshin, they mocked the mistakes he made while praying aloud. He spoke with a sharp "r." He was short, broad-shouldered, and he had a small white beard, and summer and winter he wore a sheepskin hat, a padded cotton jacket, and stout boots. He walked slowly, shuffling his feet. He had a half acre of field, a cow, a goat, and chickens.
>
> —Isaac Bashevis Singer

fig 18B

> The police broke down the front door and found the hall impassable, then they hoisted a ladder to a second-story window. Behind it Homer was lying on the floor in a bathrobe; he had starved to death. Langley had disappeared. After some delay, the police broke into the basement, chopped a hole in the roof, and began throwing junk out of the house, top and bottom.
>
> —Malcolm Cowley

18B Use metaphors and similes to make your prose more vivid, but be sure that these devices are appropriate to your subject, your tone, and your audience.

Similes and metaphors make comparisons to convey a vivid impression. **Similes** use the word *like* or *as*.

> My love is *like* a red, red rose.
>
> —Robert Burns

> Tom Birch is as brisk *as* a bee in conversation.
>
> —Samuel Johnson

> Mortality weighs heavily upon me *like* an unwilling sleep.
>
> —John Keats

Sometimes in modern journalism, similes are especially striking because they are unexpected.

> He sat in the Speaker's vast office, his huge 260-lb. torso looking like a giant plum pudding, his long white hair falling over his blue eyes.
> —*Time* (on Congressman Tip O'Neill, Speaker of the House of Representatives)

Metaphors, implied comparisons, speak of things or of actions as if they were something other than what they are. Because of its compression, a metaphor may have stronger force than a simile.

> The dice are the gods of the backgammon wars.
>
> —E. J. KAHN, JR.

> Marcel Duchamp once referred to dealers as "lice on the backs of artists"—useful and necessary lice, he added, but lice all the same.
>
> —*The New Yorker*

> As their first-quarter earnings painfully show, the nations' airlines are in a sickening dive.
>
> —*Business Week*

> At least half of all writers, major or minor, have suffered from writing blocks—from inner resistance to dragging oneself, hour after hour, to the bar of self-judgment, and forcing oneself, before it, to confront that most intimidating of objects to any writer: the blank page waiting to be filled.
>
> —WALTER JACKSON BATE

When similes and metaphors work, they enliven writing. But when they are bad, they are embarrassing and often confusing as well. The general rule is that you should not use a simile or metaphor if you have any doubt about it.

The following extended simile goes wrong because it repeats the same idea again and again like someone telling a bad joke and having to repeat the punch line. Remember that comparisons work only when they clarify an important point or teach us something we need to know. This simile does not teach us anything about William Faulkner's short story "A Rose for Emily," which the writer is trying to address.

> Miss Emily Grierson's house was like hell itself. First of all, it was in Mississippi, where it gets hot in summer—just like hell. Second, it was dark and gloomy—just like hell. And third, all sorts of horrible things happened there—just like hell. Miss Emily lived out her existence there and never could escape, and her only real companion was a dead man. Nobody wanted to visit her. People who get into hell have only the dead for companions, and they never can get out, and no one wants to go there for a visit.

Yet the writer could make a short simile, leaving an impression that is striking but not tediously prolonged. A good simile or metaphor—like a good joke—makes its point quickly and sharply.

The stunning, macabre end of Faulkner's story "A Rose for Emily" fills us with both horror and pity—*as if* we had unexpectedly opened a door into hell and found roasting there someone whom we had always thought a little foolish and inferior.

Some extended similes or metaphors may be effective if they are executed with a light touch. But extended comparisons can easily become thin and pointless. Some people, for example, might admire the following extended simile, while others might find it strained. The author is arguing that a new analogy is needed to make teachers aware of the demands of their profession.

Getting through college is a lot like driving a car in heavy traffic. Just as the good driver must know her destination, the college student must know what she wants to get out of her education. And just as the good driver must be aware of all the other cars in the street, the college student must be aware of other students and be willing to give them a piece of the road. As in driving, a little competition may be essential, but too much competition can kill. The good driver must concentrate on what she is doing, and so must the college student. But at the same time, the driver and the student should be relaxed and confident. Too much tension in either case can provoke a serious accident.

In short, similes and metaphors are natural to human thinking, and they enliven prose. But you should use them with caution.

Exercise 18.2 Complete the simile that will describe each of the following actions or objects. Try to avoid any similes that you have heard before. Add as many words as you need.

Example
The snow was as white as __________.
The snow was as white as <u>sugar</u>.

1. My mother was as angry as ____________________.
2. The biscuits were as light and fluffy as ____________________.
3. The coin gleamed in his hand like ____________________.
4. My flower garden was as wild as ____________________.
5. Our football team was as inept as a group of ____________________.
6. My summer job was as boring as ____________________.
7. The music sounded like ____________________.
8. The sky was as blue as ____________________.
9. Learning to operate the computer was as difficult as ____________________.
10. The rain pounded against the glass like ____________________.

Exercise 18.3 Take the current issue of a magazine such as *Time, Sports Illustrated, Rolling Stone, Popular Mechanics,* or anything else you enjoy reading, and find at least five metaphors and similes.

Exercise 18.4 Write a descriptive paragraph on each of the following subjects, using a simile and a metaphor in each.

Example: A violent thunderstorm

The wind sprang up at four o'clock. We heard the first blast shake through the trees, and after it came the rain, blown against our windows like a clatter of stones. The thunder crashed overhead, and the lightning sent its sharp fingers ripping through the sky. Tova, our beagle pup, cowered under the table and whimpered softly, her brown eyes pleading with us to make it all stop so she could go back to sleep again and dream of beefsteaks and cats. But the storm went on, a great wild animal shrieking across our town, and we sat by the windows in silence and watched the rain roar down.

1. A sunny dawn in the spring
2. A child learning that her parents will be divorced
3. The announcement that your father has won a beauty contest
4. Deciding to buy a new car
5. Realizing suddenly that you have a friend who is an alcoholic
6. Something you are proud of having done

18C Avoid using worn-out expressions and clichés.

A **cliché** is an overworked expression. The moment we read the first word or two of a cliché, we know how it will end. If someone says "She was as mad as a __________," we expect the sentence to be completed by the words *wet hen* or *hornet.* If someone says "My biscuits were as light as __________," we expect the sentence to be completed by *a feather.* If someone says "His prose is as heavy as __________," we expect the sentence to end with *lead.*

Some of these expressions once had power to evoke an image or strong feelings in the minds of people who heard them. For example, in the days of wagons and muddy roads, when people on the way to market got stuck in the mire, someone *put his shoulder to the wheel.* Unafraid of exerting himself or getting dirty, he got the wagon moving again. When someone then wrote that the way to succeed in business was *to put your shoulder to the wheel,* readers could visualize the scene and think, "Yes! That is how to succeed—by hard, patient effort." But nobody can put his shoulder to the wheel when a car gets stuck in the mud. We have heard this expression so often that our minds are dead to it even when we understand what it means, and it no longer creates a vivid picture in our minds.

Other expressions create a similar deadness. We hear that we must understand *the cold, hard facts,* and we don't think of the facts as icy or hard; they are simply unpleasant. We hear that something is *an integral part* of something else, and the moment we hear the word *integral,* we know that *part* is sure to follow. We don't stop to wonder why the writer or speaker does not use another expression. If he is describing the *integral part,* won't his description tell us how necessary the part is to the whole? Do we need the word *integral?* When journalists write about the weather, why do they always talk about *weather conditions?* Why don't they tell us about *weather?*

Look over the following clichés, and think of others not on the list. Avoid them when you speak or write.

abreast of the times
acid test
add insult to injury
agony of suspense
beat a hasty retreat
better half
beyond the shadow of a doubt
blind as a bat
blue as the sky
bolt from the blue
brave as a lion
brown as a nut
brutal murder
bustling cities
calm, cool, and collected
cold, hard facts
come to grips with
cool as a cucumber
crazy as a loon
dead as a doornail
deaf as a post
deep, dark secret
depths of despair
diabolical skill
distaff side
doomed to disappointment
drunk as a lord
every dog has his day
face the music
fair sex
few and far between
fire-engine red
flat as a pancake
gild the lily
green with envy
heave a sigh of relief
heavy as lead
hit the nail on the head
in this day and age
ladder of success
last but not least
little lady
live from hand to mouth
livid with rage
nose to the grindstone
one hundred and ten percent
the other side of the coin
paint the town red
pale as a ghost
pass the buck
poor but honest
poor but proud
pretty as a picture
primrose path
proud possessor of
quick as a flash
quiet as a church-mouse
reigns supreme
right as rain
rise and shine
rise to the occasion
sadder but wiser
sharp as a tack
shoulder to the wheel
sink or swim
smart as a whip
sneaking suspicion
sober as a judge
straight and narrow
tempest in a teapot
tired but happy
tried and true
ugly as sin
undercurrent of excitement
walk the line
wax eloquent
white as a ghost
white as a sheet
worth its weight in gold

You may sometimes achieve a new effect with a cliché by changing the words:

Scott Hamilton is a good wind who blows us no ill.

—LEONARD FEATHER

[The cliché is *It's an ill wind that blows no good.* Here the author turns it around to make a clever comment on a tenor saxophone player.]

You may try your hand at inverting clichés. But usually the best thing to do with a cliché is to rephrase it as simply as you can in plain language.

Cliché: When John turned his papers in three weeks late, he had to *face the music.*

Better: When John turned his papers in three weeks late, he had to take the consequences.

Cliché: Harvey *kept his nose to the grindstone.*

Better: Harvey gave close and unceasing attention to his work.

fig 18C

Exercise 18.5 Rewrite the following sentences, eliminating the clichés. You may want to substitute the simple, literal meaning of a cliché. Or you may be able to create a fresh and lively expression to replace a cliché. Be adventurous. Try to think up some similes or metaphors that convey the meaning of a cliché without repeating its tiresome words.

1. Although he had worked like a dog all week long, the conductor seemed as cool as a cucumber and as fresh as a daisy when he mounted the podium and raised his baton to his orchestra.
2. The letter announcing the prize came to her like a bolt fom the blue, making her friends green with envy, while she herself felt worth her weight in gold.
3. Bollinger believed that he had a right to be president of the university, since he had paid his dues as a lower functionary for years, sometimes feeling in the depths of despair over the way people treated him like a dog, believing often that he was doomed to disappointment in life, but determined to put his shoulder to the wheel.
4. The bustling cities of the Renaissance had their share of brutal murders, for men believed that they had to be as brave as lions whenever anyone got under their skin.

Exercise 18.6 Write a paragraph about any subject that you and your teacher agree on. Count the number of details that carry an image and make you see something in your mind. Use metaphors, similes, or simple narration, but include lots of concrete details.

19 Including Needed Words

Be sure to include all the words that are necessary to make your sentences clear and complete.

19A Include all the necessary parts of verbs.

Many forms of the verb require more than one word to make clear English sense. Be sure you include all the words necessary to make a correct verb phrase.

1 Include necessary helpers.

In some dialects of English, past participles serve as **finite verbs,** that is, verbs that report the action of subjects and that control predicates. Correct written English requires helping verbs with these participial forms.

Nonstandard: He *writing* about the beehives.

Standard: He *is writing* about the beehives.

Nonstandard: I *seen* what he *done.*

Standard: I *have seen* what he *has done.*

Nonstandard: She *taken* a minute to rest.

Standard: She *has taken* a minute to rest.

If you have trouble with the principal parts of verbs, see 7A, and study your dictionary when you are in doubt about correct forms.

2 Do not leave out part of a compound verb when the tense of one part of the verb varies from the tense of the other part.

Incomplete: Caldwell has long and always will be sympathetic to those who think jogging is boring.

Complete: Caldwell has long *been* and always will be sympathetic to those who think jogging is boring.

19B Include the subordinating conjunction *that* when you need it for clarity (see 14E).

Unclear: He sent the message canoes were unable to navigate the Platte River.

Clear: He sent the message *that* canoes were unable to navigate the Platte River.

Sometimes *that* can be omitted, especially in short sentences with a simple subordinate clause:

Loretta Lynn sang songs women love.

You could say, "Loretta Lynn sang songs *that* women love," but in a sentence as short as this one, the *that* is unnecessary. But often—especially in longer sentences—the omission of *that* makes readers stumble.

Exercise 19.1 Check the following sentences for missing words. Add words where they are needed. Place a check mark by the numbers of the sentences that are clear and grammatical as they stand.

1. He told the staff men and women deserve equal pensions.
2. He taken the car to a junkyard and found many people in suits now go to junkyards to get parts for old cars they want to keep running a few more years.
3. I been here now for thirty years and never seen so little rain.
4. Air travel getting so expensive only the rich and people on business able to afford it now.
5. She told her daughter driving across the country and staying in motels were much more expensive than flying.
6. I have always and will continue to keep the promises I made when I was running for office.
7. Many outstanding athletes in college plead poverty and hardship so they can be eligible for the pro draft before their senior year.
8. He had and always will be taken for an easy mark.

9. They seen the wreck by the time they came to tell the police investigating it was a hit-and-run accident.
10. The little boy working hard getting the tricycle up the hill.

19C Include necessary articles, prepositions, and pronouns.

1 Include the articles that are necessary for idiomatic expressions.

Not Idiomatic: All people in the room had quit smoking.

Idiomatic: All *the* people in the room had quit smoking.

Not Idiomatic: Dog that bites should be kept on leash.

Idiomatic: *A* dog that bites should be kept on *a* leash.

∧ 19C

2 Include the article when the sentence clearly refers to the specific rather than to the general.

He gave me *the* books he liked best.

[Omission of the article *the* would make the sentence awkward. Because the subordinate clause *he liked best* tells us of specific books, we need the article *the* to balance the clause.]

3 Include prepositions as they are needed.

Not Idiomatic: This type dog is noted for its affection.

Idiomatic: This type *of* dog is noted for its affection.

Not Idiomatic: He did not like taking or giving to the fund.

Idiomatic: He did not like taking *from* or giving to the fund.

[Each participle requires a different preposition here; *taking* requires *from,* but *giving* requires *to.*]

Not Idiomatic: He loved her for her intelligence, for her beauty, and her money.

Idiomatic: He loved her for her intelligence, for her beauty, and *for* her money.

[In formal writing, the preposition *for* is required to make all the parts of this parallel construction grammatically equal.]

4 Include the pronouns that are necessary to complete your meaning.

Not Idiomatic: The parachutist jumped with the red chute, fell into the lake.

Idiomatic: The parachutist *who* jumped with the red chute fell into the lake.

[Perhaps the writer of the first sentence tried for a special effect, but the sentence is confusing. The addition of the pronoun *who* after *parachutist* helps.]

5 Include all the words that are necessary to make comparisons clear.

∧ 19C

Include a possessive form when you are comparing possessions.

Unclear: Plato's philosophy is easier to read than Aristotle.

[The possessive in the first term of the comparison requires a possessive in the second term.]

Clear: Plato's philosophy is easier to read than *that of* Aristotle.

Clear: Plato's philosophy is easier to read than Aristotle's.

Use *other* and *else* to show that people or things belong to a group with which they are being compared.

Unclear: Professor Koonig wrote more books than anyone in the department.

[Was Professor Koonig not a member of the department, too? He did not write more books than he himself wrote.]

Better: Professor Koonig wrote more books than anyone *else* in the department.

Unclear: Professor Koonig's account of how he put a tribe of cannibals to sleep by reading to them from his collected works was longer than any book I have read.

[Was Professor Koonig's account written as a book? If so, the writer of this sentence confuses things, since in effect, the sentence means that Professor Koonig's book is longer than Professor Koonig's book.]

Clear: Professor Koonig's account of how he put a tribe of cannibals to sleep by reading to them from his collected works was longer than any *other* book I have read.

Use the word *as* twice when you use it to compare people or things.

Incomplete: His temper was mild as milk.

Complete: His temper was *as* mild as milk.

Avoid the vague comparison implied in the word *that* used as a weak synonym for *very.*

Incomplete: Professor Koonig was not *that* dull.
[How dull? People who use *that* in this way never tell us. They assume that we have some idea of complete dullness, and they want to assure us that Professor Koonig was not as dull as that unstated standard.]

Complete: Professor Koonig was not *very* dull.
[Although *very* is an extremely weak adverb, it is still stronger than a *that* which does not refer to anything.]

^ 19C

When you are tempted to use *that* as a vague comparative, think of something concrete and lively, and use the comparative form *as . . . as* instead of *that.* Or use *so . . . that* and a clause.

> Professor Koonig was not *as* dull *as* some cows I have known.
>
> Professor Koonig was *so* dull *that* he could make flowers droop from the first word of a lecture.

Be sure that your comparisons are always complete. If you have just said, "Professor Koonig is dull," you can say immediately afterward, "Professor Donovan is more interesting." But you cannot say in isolation, "Professor Donovan is more interesting." You need to name who or what forms the rest of the comparison. You may say, "Professor Donovan is more interesting than Professor Koonig."

Exercise 19.2 Add words as they are needed in the following sentences. If a sentence is correct as it stands, put a check by the number.

1. She was happy as I have ever seen anyone when she graduated from West Point.
2. He took the car in to have the transmission replaced, the body painted, and seats covered.
3. This type grass seed does not do that well in shade.
4. The car I drove to the beach was worse than any car I have ever driven.
5. Pete Rose was not that fast, but he always played hard as a boy even when he was forty years old.
6. He had always and will continue to play well because of his hard work.
7. The night was more clear.

20 Avoiding Wordiness

If you can eliminate words that add only dead weight to your prose, you can make every word count. Tight, economical, meaning-laden sentences that flow easily and directly seldom appear in first drafts. Even famous authors must rewrite their sentences to make their thoughts more clear and less wordy.

Avoiding wordiness does not mean that you must write in short, choppy sentences or that you must reduce your prose to its bare bones. It does mean that every word should add something significant to your thought, because words that add nothing will obscure your meaning and will bore your readers.

20A Edit carefully, eliminating unnecessary words.

The following paragraph, a response to an assignment requiring an explanation of *expository writing,* is a good first draft, but it is entirely too wordy. The writer, correctly, tried to put down thoughts as fast as they came to mind, without pausing to edit the piece. Then she edited the first draft to eliminate wordiness, without rewriting anything:

~~Briefly,~~ E expository writing ~~is the kind of writing that~~ develops an idea. It is not ~~quite the same as~~ narration, which tells a story, though ~~you and I both know that~~ narratives may contain ~~many~~ ideas. But that is not their main purpose. If I tell you that last night I ~~was eating~~ in a restaurant ~~and~~ found a pearl in my oysters, that is narration. ~~And~~ expository writing ~~is~~ does not ~~the kind of writing that~~ describes something, though descriptions may include ~~several of the most~~ important ideas ~~that a writer considers significant.~~ If I describe ~~how~~ the campus ~~looks~~ under a deep, ~~thick, white~~ snow and ~~describe~~ the way people wade through the snow and leave tracks, ~~on its pure and immaculate surface,~~ ~~then~~ that is description. But if I ~~go to the theater and~~ see a play and ~~come home and~~ write ~~down~~ an interpretation of it, ~~then~~ I am doing expository writing even if part of the exposition is to describe the action of the play itself. And if I ~~go on and~~ talk about the ~~aforesaid~~ snow, ~~that I have talked about falling on the campus~~ and if I tell ~~the story about~~ how the history department ~~got out in it and~~ started ~~aggressively and energetically~~ throwing snowballs at the dean, and if I ~~then go on and~~ try to explain why historians on this campus are ~~at this point in time and always have been~~ bellicose, ~~then~~ I am combining description, narration, and expository writing. ~~But the main thing I want you to~~ be conscious of ~~is~~ how you should classify the kinds of writing that are likely to go on in a single piece ~~of writing~~, and ~~you've simply got to~~ remember that it is not ~~an example of~~ expository writing unless it ~~is writing about~~ expound~~ing~~ an idea.

wdy
20A

Here are some questions the writer asked herself while editing the first draft:

1. Since snow is never anything but white when it first falls, do I have to say that it is white?
2. Are members of the history department throwing snowballs at the dean indoors?
3. As for "aggressively and energetically," do people throw snowballs any other way? Again, don't state the obvious.

The revised paragraph still needs more editing. Consider this puzzling sentence: "If I describe the campus under a deep snow and the way people wade through the snow and leave tracks, that is description." The sentence says that to describe is description—defining a word by itself. It is like saying, "To build something is to make a building." And do you have to see a play to write an interpretation of it, as the next sentence implies? The more you look, the more you see that even this draft is a little wordy, a little fuzzy. So the writer has to edit again, this time rewriting some of the sentences and changing some of the words. Remember that she is trying to preserve everything essential in the paragraph, and she is also trying to write concisely without sounding like a primer.

After making further changes, the writer produced this paragraph:

Expository writing develops ideas; narrations tell stories; descriptions tell how things look. If I tell you that last night in a restaurant I found a pearl in my oysters, I am narrating. If I write of a deep snow on campus and how people wade through it and leave tracks, I am describing. But if I interpret a play, I am writing exposition, even if part of my essay describes the action of the play itself. And if I describe snow, and tell how the history department threw snowballs at the dean, and try to explain why historians at this university are bellicose, I am combining description, narration, and exposition. Remember that all three kinds of writing may appear in a single piece, but only expository writing interprets an idea.

The writer has recast the paragraph itself, as well as several sentences, and she has found more ways to shorten sentences too. She has presented her definitions in the beginning as quickly as possible, and by using three short, independent clauses connected with semicolons, she has saved many words. The paragraph now begins with expository writing and ends with it. No one will misunderstand the purpose of the piece—to define expository writing by comparing it with other kinds of prose. You may think of other revisions, but this third draft achieves a short, clear paragraph while saying everything important that was in the first version.

As you revise for wordiness you should look out for redundant words and phrases, the unnecessary repetitions that slip easily into first drafts. Conscious, deliberate repetition can help you emphasize ideas (see 15E); but meaningless repetition makes only flabby sentences. You should avoid redundant constructions like the following.

Redundant

The candidate repeated the answer again.

Improved

The candidate repeated the answer.

[The verb repeated means "to say again." The adverb adds nothing here.]

Redundant

He expressed a number of clever expressions much to the audience's delight.

Improved

He delighted the audience with his clever expressions.

[Repeating the root *express* is careless; the revision makes the point without distracting the reader with the repetition.]

Redundant

The exam was very trying, and I kept trying to finish on time without making too many errors.

Improved

The exam was very difficult, and I kept trying to finish on time without making too many errors.

[The word *trying* used twice, each with a different meaning, jars readers. The improved sentence eliminates the needless repetition.]

Redundant

In the movie *Apocalypse Now* there were several dull parts that I found boring.

Improved

I found several boring parts in the movie *Apocalypse Now.*

[Both "dull" and "boring" say the same thing. The writer of the improved sentences has removed the redundancy.]

Exercise 20.1 Edit the following paragraphs, and make them more concise.

I am going to tell you how much fun and profit there is in it for you to build your own house. If you have the time and a little energy and common sense, then you can build your very own house, save a ton of money, and have lots and lots of fun as you build your house. When it's all done and your house is standing there, built by you and maybe some members of your family, you will be proud of it, really proud.

wdy 20A

Most of us, including probably you and me, usually think there is some kind of strange, secret mystery to the occult art of carpentry, but building things with wood is not a mystery at all. It takes lots and lots of care and lots and lots of hard work, but just about anybody can do it.

Now what do we mean by *care?* Well friends, we mean attention to detail. Among those many details that ought to have a lot of attention are making sure the joints in the wood fit together tightly, driving nails carefully so you don't leave those ugly and unnecessary and thoroughly disgusting hammer marks around the heads of your nails, hanging your doors so they are straight and true, being absolutely and completely and carefully exact in your measurements, sawing your planks exactly and precisely and unwaveringly along the marks you make with a pencil or some other writing implement, perhaps even with a sharp nail and sometimes with your fingernail. All these things are a part of care.

Exercise 20.2 Explain the redundancies in the following examples.

1. at three A.M. in the morning
2. in modern times in the twentieth century today
3. return to the old neighborhood again
4. in my opinion, I think
5. the autobiography of her life
6. resultant effect of the report
7. quite tiny in size
8. the surrounding environment
9. unemployed workers now out of work
10. rectangular in shape

20B Eliminate common phrases that take up space and burden your style without adding anything to your meaning.

When we speak, we often use phrases that serve as "waiting words"—they let us keep talking while we wait to think of something more to say. These waiting words often creep into our writing, where they take up valuable room without doing any work. Common waiting words include *like, you know, sort of, kind of, what I mean is, so to speak, in other words,* and *in the final analysis.*

Other common phrases are cumbersome, roundabout, habitual ways of saying something when we only need a word or two. And some of them are junk—words we can get rid of altogether without losing any of our real meaning.

Study the following examples and their recommended substitutions.

wdy 20B

at the present time in the present circumstances at this point in time at this moment in this day and age	Use *now* or *today* or *nowadays.*
at that point in time in those days in that period	Use *then.*
in many cases	Use *often.*
in some cases	Use *sometimes.*
in exceptional cases	Use *rarely.*
in most cases	Use *most.*
consider as, consider as being I consider study as being necessary to success	Use: I consider study necessary to success.
despite the fact that regardless of the fact that	Use *although.*
due to the fact that for the purpose of by virtue of the fact that the reason is because	Use *because.*
in a position to, in order to	Use *can.*
in the area of	Use *near* or *in.*

in the event that in the event of in case of	Use *if* with a verb.

In the event that fire breaks out, leave the files behind.
If fire breaks out, leave the files behind.

in terms of
[Should usually be revised out of your prose.]
The new curriculum was designed in terms of student needs and faculty ability.
The new curriculum considers both student needs and faculty ability.
The new curriculum was designed to match faculty ability with student needs.

in the final analysis	Use *finally,* or drop the phrase entirely.
in no uncertain terms	Drop the phrase, or use *firmly* or *clearly.*
in the nature of things of that nature	Use *like* or *things like that.*
refer back	Use only *refer.*
He is of a complex character. She is of a generous nature. The car was of a green color.	Use: He is complex. Use: She is generous. Use: The car was green.
The weather conditions are bad. Traffic conditions are congested.	Use: The weather is bad. Use: Traffic is congested.

Exercise 20.3 Edit the following paragraphs to eliminate unnecessary words and phrases. You may find some words and phrases that are not on the list above. Think hard about each sentence to see if you can eliminate padding and wordiness.

Due to the fact that at this point in time we have an energy crisis of a severe nature, we need to devote ourselves to a good rethinking of the academic calendar. At the present time, schools in the area of the United States begin in September and end in May or June. The reason is because schools once upon a time used to begin right after the harvest in societies of an agricultural character. But by virtue of the fact that buildings must be heated in the wintertime, schools in the cold regions of the earth are now paying out millions of dollars for fuel bills—money that might do much more good if it were put into faculty salaries, student scholarships, the library fund, the athletic program, or things of these kinds and of that nature. A solution to the problem may be of a simple nature: make the academic calendar according to the weather conditions prevailing in the different areas where the schools happen to be located.

In the southern United States, where it is in the nature of winters to be mild, schools could continue in many cases to go on operating just as they always have. To cool buildings in the summer would cost more in such regions than heating them in the wintertime. But in the northern areas, the academic year could begin in March and end early in November, providing in many cases for the great fuel economies that could be thereby effected.

20C Combine sentences to avoid wordiness.

wdy
20C

Combining sentences, along with editing, will pull your thoughts together and make your writing clearer and more readable. Combining also gives variety to your prose (see 13 and 16).

Read these choppy declarative sentences:

> The flashlight illuminated the rest of the chamber. It was square. Carter christened it the Treasury. It contained chests. It contained caskets. It contained tall boxes. The boxes were black. They were thin. They were ominous. They were closed and sealed. They were standing against all sides of the room. Several dozen boats were on top of the boxes. The room looked as if somehow it was supposed to be the surface of the Nile itself. A flotilla was ready to sail. Some boats were simple little vessels. They were like sampans. Others were full-fledged sailboats. They had complex rigging. Their sails were furled. They looked as if one had only to give a command. Then a crew of a hundred or more would prepare them for their voyage.

Early in the composing process, when you first jot down your ideas, such sentences would play a valuable role in the formation of your essay. But combining some short sentences and subordinating some ideas to others will make this passage much more concise—and much more elegant (see 13A, section 2, and 13B, section 1).

> The flashlight illuminated the rest of the square chamber, which Carter christened the Treasury. Chests, caskets, and tall, thin, ominous-looking black boxes, closed and sealed, were standing against all sides of the room. And on top of them were several dozen boats, as if the room were somehow the surface of the Nile itself, with a flotilla ready to set sail. Some were simple little vessels like sampans, others full-fledged sailboats with complex rigging and sails furled, looking as if one had only to give

the command and a crew of a hundred or more would prepare them for their voyage.

—THOMAS HOVING

Exercise 20.4

1. Combine the sentences in the following paragraph as economically as you can.

    Before the invention of the motorcar, this was a rural land. Geography dominated. Geography determined where and how we would live. Geography determined where and how we would travel. But then everything changed. The automobile spread communities. It merged them. It ended their distinctiveness. It brought the motel. It brought the fast-food chains. It brought the suburbs and the death of the inner city. It changed courting practices. It took young men and women from front-porch swings. It rolled them down lovers' lanes. It took them by lapping lakes in private and dark backseats. In some ways it added to American democracy. Gasoline was 20 cents a gallon. Factory workers packed their lemonade and their bologna sandwiches. They packed their hampers and their suitcases. They left hot factory neighborhoods in Detroit, Cleveland, Chicago, Milwaukee. They drove north to the woods, islands, and lakes of northern Michigan, Wisconsin, and Minnesota.

wdy
20C

2. Now check what you have done by comparing your revision with the original.

    Before the invention of the motorcar, this was a rural land. Geography dominated, determining where and how we would live, where and how we would travel. But then everything changed. The automobile spread communities, merged them, ended their distinctiveness. It brought the motel, the fast-food chains, the suburbs and the death of the inner city. It changed courting practices, taking young men and women from front-porch swings and rolling them down lovers' lanes, by lapping lakes, in private and dark back seats. In some ways it added to American democracy: with gasoline at 20 cents a gallon, factory workers packed their lemonade and bologna sandwiches, their hampers and suitcases and left hot factory neighborhoods in Detroit, Cleveland, Chicago, Milwaukee and drove north to the woods, islands, and lakes of northern Michigan, Wisconsin, and Minnesota.

—WILLIAM SERRIN

20D Do not inflate simple thoughts with jargon-ridden, overblown language (see 17C).

Inflated

Owning a gun for protection could be a consequence of several other factors. It could be the logical extension of a general home defense orientation. One mode of behavior for individuals who are vulnerable to crime is to increase their personal security, which leads them to a general home defense orientation and the acquisition of a gun.

Better

Some people buy guns to defend their homes, especially when they feel threatened by crime.

Inflated

Lucinda Childs' early development as a choreographer in the 1960s paralleled the rise of minimalist art. And while her work is extremely complex in its patterning and ordering, this complexity is grounded in the permutations of simplicity expressed in a few steps and their repetition.

Better

Lucinda Childs' early choreography in the 1960s developed alongside the work of the minimalist painters. Although she created complex patterns and sequences, she uses only a few simple steps repeated with slight changes.

Exercise 20.5 Edit the following sentences to make them more concise and clear. You may want to make two sentences where the writers have written one. Discuss your results with the class. Use the dictionary when you must.

1. A total site signage program is being studied, and if the study analysis dictates to relocate the stop sign, it will be done as a part of the total signage program and not as a result of your suggestion.
2. Dissatisfaction over the lack of responsiveness and accountability of decision makers is itself a primary source of the recent precipitous decline in confidence and trust that citizens hold for the national government.
3. Many theories of gaze interaction assume that a stare is physiologically arousing and that this arousal accounts in part for the efficacy of eye contact as a communication channel.
4. We were not micromanaging Grenada intelligencewise until about that time frame.

21 Avoiding Sexist Language

In recent years, feminist writers have called attention to the ways language can imply that women are inferior to men or that women must behave in certain ways to be socially acceptable. Distinctions of this sort are called **sexist.** Thoughtful writers try to avoid sexist language because they know that such language is offensive to many readers.

21A Avoid sexist labels and clichés that condescend to women or that imply that women are inferior to men or different from men in intelligence, morals, the careers they can choose, or the talents they possess.

Many cliché labels for women imply that there is one "right" way for women to behave and many "wrong" ways. Consider the implications of such cliché words as *lady* or *ladies, the distaff side, the weaker sex, the fair sex, the better half, girl* or *girls, gals, broads, dames, working wives, working mothers,* and *housewives.*

All such terms imply that women have a special, expected role in society. For example, to call a woman *ladylike* implies that she is polite and cooperative but unwilling to assert herself as men are expected to do in a competitive society.

While some people consider *ladylike* a compliment, others reject the implied suggestion that women must behave like ladies if they are to be acceptable people. Careful writers keep such distinctions in mind and avoid any clichés and labels that might turn women into stereotypes.

1 Do not refer to women as if they were appendages to men.

Not: Lily Roundtree, wife of used-car dealer John T. Roundtree, has been cited by the *New England Journal of Medicine* for isolating a rare virus that may be responsible for Legionnaires' disease.

But: Dr. Lily Roundtree of Brookhaven Laboratories has been cited by the *New England Journal of Medicine* for isolating a rare virus that may be responsible for Legionnaires' disease.

[Lily Roundtree is obviously a distinguished medical researcher. To identify her by reference to her husband is to imply that only her marriage makes her worthy of notice.]

2 Avoid identifying a woman by referring to her children.

Not: Molly Burdine, mother of six, will represent Sourmash State University at the national meeting of the American Association of University Professors to be held in Washington in June.

sxl
21B

But: Molly Burdine, professor of government, will represent Sourmash State University at the national meeting of the American Association of University Professors to be held in Washington in June.

[If Professor Burdine's children figure in your paper, you can mention them later—but would you mention the children if Professor Burdine were a man?]

21B Whenever possible, revise sentences to avoid using the pronouns *he, him, his,* and *himself* as indefinite personal pronouns.

A satisfactory way to avoid masculine singular pronouns is to use the plural forms:

Singular

Every student who signed up for the class had to pay *his* fee in advance and to pledge *himself* to attend every session.

Plural

Students who signed up for the class had to pay *their* fees in advance and to pledge *themselves* to attend every session.

Often you can avoid the masculine pronouns by revising the sentence to eliminate the pronouns altogether.

Every student who signed up for the class had to pay the fee in advance and to pledge to attend every session.

21C In general, avoid cumbersome constructions such as *his or her, his/her,* or *s/he.*

On occasion, it may be perfectly natural to use *he or she* or *his or her.*

> The student who spray-painted the insulting graffiti on the blackboard last night may have thought that he or she was being original and bold, but it was a cowardly act.

[Nobody knows who committed the vandalism; the culprit could have been male or female.]

Such usage generally is cumbersome, though, and it becomes unbearable when it is repeated several times in a paragraph.

> Each student in the psychology class was to pick up a different book according to his or her interests, to read the book overnight and do without his or her normal sleep, to write a short summary of what he or she had read the next morning, and then to see if he or she dreamed about the book on the following night.

Some writers now alternate *he* and *she, him* and *her,* using one gender in one paragraph and the other gender the next time a singular pronoun is called for. This alternative can become distracting, too. Many speakers and some writers use a plural pronoun to refer to an impersonal singular antecedent: "The *person* who left *their* suitcase on the bus can call for it at the office." However, such usage is regarded as nonstandard by most writers and editors.

Some writers use the neuter impersonal pronoun *one* to avoid the masculine pronoun: "The American dream has always been that if one is willing to work, one can succeed in life."

Most professional writers and editors still use the masculine pronoun to refer to an impersonal, singular antecedent: "The American dream has always held that if anybody was willing to work, he could get ahead in life."

21D Avoid artificial coinages that are cumbersome to read and to write.

Many English words ending in *-man* have traditionally applied to both men and women who occupy the positions the words describe: *freshman, chairman, councilman, fellow man, sportsman, workman, policeman, fireman, repairman, statesman,* and *salesman* are among these words.

The new awareness of sexist distinctions in language has led many writers and editors to substitute *-person* for *-man* in such words. Unfortunately, the result is often clumsy and hard to say. The best course seems to be to choose synonyms that use neither *-person* nor *-man.* The *newsman* can become a *reporter* or a *journalist* or a *writer.* The *chairman* can become the *chair,* the *weatherman* the *weather forecaster* or the *weather reporter* or the *meteorologist,* the *freshman* the *first-year student,* the *policeman* the *police officer,* and so forth.

Exercise 21.1 Rewrite the following sentences to eliminate sexist language.

1. An ambassador must learn the customs of the country where he is stationed. He should also learn the language.
2. When machinery breaks down in the home, we must grit our teeth and call the repairman, knowing that he will charge too much money and that we may have to call him again soon.
3. Any country musician worth his guitar knows that true bluegrass music does not use drums. He would also not use an electric guitar.
4. Every organizational man knows the value of pleasing the boss. The boss may be a fool or a beast, but he is still the boss.
5. Anybody who goes to college knows that he has to work hard to earn good grades and that his grades do not always show how much he has learned.

Exercise 21.2 Write synonyms for these words that use masculine beginnings or endings. (Avoid using *-person* as a substitute.)

1. policeman
2. fireman
3. newspaperboy
4. mailman
5. mankind
6. sportsman
7. repairman
8. congressman

22
Using Dictionaries and the Thesaurus

A good dictionary is an essential tool for every writer. You should consult your dictionary every time you have the slightest doubt about the spelling, meaning, proper use, pronunciation, or syllabication of a word.

22A Learn about the most useful dictionaries for the college writer.

Desk Dictionaries

Buy at least one hardbound, abridged dictionary that you can keep comfortably on your desk and use frequently. Paperback dictionaries are handy because they can be carried easily, but they have fewer words than you will need as a college writer, and they fall apart quickly.

A standard desk dictionary contains 140,000 to 170,000 entries. It may include drawings as well. Illustrations are useful because they can show something that otherwise cannot be defined easily.

The following desk dictionaries are all useful for the college student:

***The American Heritage Dictionary of the English Language*, 2d College ed. (Boston: Houghton Mifflin, 1982).**

This dictionary has more than 200,000 entries, including biographical and geographic listings set alphabetically in the body of the work among the other words and expressions.

Most words in English have more than one meaning. The *American Heritage Dictionary* lists definitions in numeric order, beginning with the primary meaning suggested by the etymology or source of the word. The first listing is usually the most common definition of the word. The dictionary proceeds through other senses that are progressively more abstract or less common.

For example, the first meaning of the word *shuffle* is "to drag (the feet) along the floor or ground while walking or dancing; to scuffle." This meaning is closest to the Low German *schueffeln,* from which "shuffle" comes, a word meaning "to walk clumsily, shuffle cards." The second meaning given by the dictionary is "to move (something) from one place to another." The third meaning is "to mix together in a disordered, haphazard fashion."

A valuable feature of this dictionary is the usage note appended to many definitions. The usage notes reflect the opinions of a panel of professional writers, editors, and speakers on what they consider good or bad usage of troublesome words. As the editors of the dictionary recognize, many writers and speakers disagree among themselves about how some words should be used. The usage notes help show these divisions of opinion and allow users of the dictionary to make up their minds in an informed way.

di/th
22A

***Webster's Ninth New Collegiate Dictionary* (Springfield, Mass.: Merriam-Webster, 1983).**

The word *Webster's* is not under copyright, and anybody can put out a "Webster's dictionary," supposedly based on Noah Webster's first dictionary of American English, published shortly after the American Revolution. But the Merriam-Webster dictionary is the most popular and authoritative dictionary bearing the Webster name. It is based on *Webster's Third New International Dictionary,* generally regarded as the standard one-volume unabridged dictionary in English.

Biographical and geographic entries are placed in appendixes, leaving the body of the dictionary for general words. The dictionary has about 160,000 entries and is by far the richest of all the dictionaries in vocabulary from the sciences. It lists the meanings of words in the historical order in which the words came into use. For example, the first meaning given for the word *prevent* is "to be in readiness for," a meaning labeled "archaic" to show that this meaning is rarely used now. Exemplary sentences from well-known writers illustrate usage, and an occasional usage note will offer guidance in the choice of a meaning for a word. In general, the editors view usage rules rather loosely. For example, they approve of the word *hopefully* as a synonym for "it is hoped," and they take a casual attitude toward the distinction most careful writers make between *imply* and *infer.*

***The Random House College Dictionary of the English Language* (New York: Random House, 1980).**

This dictionary has 170,000 entries, a great number of them geographic and biographical. It is rich in scientific vocabulary and in entries that contain more than one word. The typeface is small, and there are few drawings. It does not contain nearly as many examples of usage as the Merriam-Webster and the American Heritage dictionaries, and the examples it does include are not from well-known writers.

Unabridged Dictionaries

In theory, an unabridged dictionary should include every word in the language. In practice, such inclusiveness is impossible. The English language is too rich, and it changes too often to be contained in any one work. A couple of unabridged dictionaries come close to the ideal, and college writers should learn about them and should continue to use them long after college.

***Webster's Third New International Dictionary of the English Language* (Springfield, Mass.: G. and C. Merriam, 1976).**

This enormous volume is housed in the reference room of any respectable library, usually on a lectern in a prominent place. When it first appeared in 1961, purists greeted it with howls of outrage, and a few people burned it in protest. The dictionary included *ain't* and other words not regarded as standard English, and some people thought that it was not so much a dictionary as a symbol of the decay of the language. Critics objected to the editors' philosophy that a dictionary should include words used by a substantial part of the population, even if those words are not regarded as "literate" by more educated people. The dictionary also takes a casual attitude toward usages of certain standard words. For example, it accepts as a meaning for *disinterested* this definition: "not interested." But most literate people define *disinterested* as "impartial" or "unbiased" and believe that a judge can be *interested* in a case but *disinterested* in making a decision about it. The *Third New International Dictionary,* in the opinion of many authorities, can lead inexperienced writers astray because it does not warn them that certain usages are unacceptably casual or confusing.

***The Oxford English Dictionary,* 13 vols. (Oxford, England: Oxford Univ. Press, completed 1933).**

Four supplements are planned. Volume 1, A–G, appeared in 1972; Volume 2, H–N, appeared in 1976; Volume 3, O–S, appeared in 1982; the last volume should appear in 1985. The original thirteen volumes have been available since 1971 in a photographically reduced two-volume edition printed on opaque paper, easily read with the strong magnifying glass furnished with the set.

Indisputably the greatest dictionary of the English language, this work traces each word from its first known appearance in writing to the present. Each variety of meaning is illustrated by sentences drawn from writers in the period when the word was so used. Variations appear in the citations from century to century. The thirteen original volumes include no words that might have offended proper Victorians, but the modern supplements include all such words.

Despite its great reputation, the *Oxford English Dictionary* is more valuable for the literary historian than for the general college writer.

Other Useful Dictionaries

Many highly specialized dictionaries may be found in the reference room of any good library—medical dictionaries; dictionaries of legal terms; dictionaries of philosophy, sociology, engineering, and other disciplines; dictionaries of slang, of word origins, of famous quotations. These dictionaries may often help you write an essay, and you should always browse through them when you are pondering a topic. Your reference librarian can help you locate the dictionaries that will be most helpful.

Here are some dictionaries that might prove especially interesting or helpful in your general writing.

Dictionaries of Slang

Partridge, Eric. *Dictionary of Slang and Unconventional English.* 7th ed. New York: Macmillan, 1970.

Wentworth, Harold, and Stuart Berg Flexner. *Dictionary of American Slang.* 2d ed. New York: Thomas Y. Crowell, 1975.

General English Usage

These dictionaries answer questions that all writers ask now and then about the appropriate use of words. As we noted earlier, many dictionaries will not tell you which of the various definitions is more acceptable than another. But a dictionary of usage will give advice. If you don't know whether to use *like* or *as* or whether to use *infer* or *imply* or whether you should split an infinitive or whether to use *slow* as an adverb, a dictionary of usage will give you helpful advice and will offer alternatives. The three leading dictionaries of usage are the following:

Follett, Wilson. *Modern American Usage.* Ed. Jacques Barzun. New York: Hill and Wang, 1966.

Fowler, H. W. *A Dictionary of Modern English Usage,* 2d ed., revised and edited by Sir Ernest Gowers. Oxford and New York: Oxford Univ. Press, 1965.

Morris, William, and Mary Morris. *Harper Dictionary of Contemporary Usage.* New York: Harper and Row, 1975.

22B Learn how to read the entries in a standard desk dictionary.

All dictionaries contain guides that help readers use them. In these guides, usually located in the front, you will find the meanings of the abbreviations used in the entries, and you will also find a list of the special cautions dictionaries use for words that the editors consider *slang, vulgar, informal, nonstan-*

dard, or something else worthy of notation. When you use a dictionary for the first time, study these instructions carefully. They usually contain sample entries that will help you get the most from the time you spend consulting the dictionary.

Here is part of a column of words as they are entered in the *American Heritage Dictionary,* 2d College edition. Study it and the following suggestions to see the various things you can learn from a good desk dictionary.

com·pare (kəm-pâr′) *v.* **-pared, -paring, -pares.** —*tr.* **1.** To represent as similar, equal, or analogous; liken. Used with *to.* See Usage note below. **2.** *Abbr.* **cf., cp.** To examine in order to note the similarities or differences of. Used with *with.* See Usage note below. **3.** *Grammar.* To form the positive, comparative, or superlative degrees of (an adjective or adverb). —*intr.* **1.** To be worthy of comparison; be considered as similar. Used with *with.* See Usage note below. **2.** To vie; compete. —**compare notes.** To exchange impressions. —*n.* Comparison. Usually used in the phrase *beyond* or *without compare.* [Middle English *comparen,* from Old French *comparer,* from Latin *comparāre,* to pair, match, from *compar,* like, equal : *com-,* mutually + *pār,* equal (see **pere-** in Appendix*).] —**com·par′er** *n.*

Usage: In formal usage, *compare to* is the only acceptable form when *compare* means representing as similar or likening, according to 71 per cent of the Usage Panel: *compare a voice to thunder.* In such comparisons the similarities are often metaphorical rather than real; the things compared are of fundamentally unlike orders, and a general likeness is intended rather than a detailed accounting. *Compare with* is the only acceptable form in the sense of examining in order to note similarities or differences, according to 70 per cent of the Panel: *compare Shelley's poetry with Wordsworth's.* Here the things compared are of like kinds, and specific resemblances and differences are examined in detail. Informally, *to* and *with* are often used interchangeably in the foregoing examples. In formal usage, only *compare with* is acceptable when *compare* intransitively means being worthy of comparison, according to 94 per cent of the Panel: *Promises do not compare with deeds.* In such constructions, *compare to* is infrequent, even in informal usage.

com·par·i·son (kəm-păr′ə-sən) *n.* **1.** A comparing or being compared; a statement or estimate of similarities and differences. **2.** The quality of being capable or worthy of being compared; similarity; likeness. **3.** *Grammar.* The modification or inflection of an adjective or adverb to denote the three degrees (positive, comparative, and superlative). [Middle English *comparisoun,* from Old French *comparaison,* from Latin *comparātiō,* from *comparāre,* COMPARE.]

com·part (kəm-pärt′) *tr.v.* **-parted, -parting, -parts.** To divide into compartments or parts; partition; subdivide. [Italian *compartire,* from Late Latin *compartīrī,* to divide, share with : *com-,* with + *partīrī,* to share, from *pars* (stem *part-*), a part (see **pere-** in Appendix*).]

com·part·ment (kəm-pärt′mənt) *n. Abbr.* **compt.** **1.** One of the parts or spaces into which an area is subdivided. **2.** Any separate room, section, or chamber: *a storage compartment.*

com·part·men·tal·ize (kŏm′pärt-mĕn′təl-īz′, kəm-pärt′-) *tr.v.* **-ized, -izing, -izes.** To divide or partition into compartments or categories.

com·pass (kŭm′pəs, kŏm′-) *n.* **1. a.** A device used to determine geographical direction, usually consisting of a magnetic needle or needles horizontally mounted or suspended and free to pivot until aligned with the magnetic field of the earth. **b.** Any other device for determining geographical direction, such as a **radio compass** or a **gyrocompass** *(both of which see).* **2.** *Sometimes plural.* A V-shaped device for drawing circles or circular arcs, consisting of a pair of rigid, end-hinged, and continuously separable arms, one of which is equipped with a pen or pencil and the other with a sharp point providing a central anchor or pivot about which the drawing arm is turned. **3.** An enclosing line or boundary; circumference; girth. **4.** An enclosed space or area. **5.** A range or scope; extent. **6.** *Music.* The range of a voice or instrument; register. —*tr.v.* **compassed, -passing, -passes.** **1.** To go around; make a circuit of; circle. **2.** To surround; en-

di/th
22B

Spelling, Syllabication, and Pronunciation

Entries in a dictionary are listed in alphabetic order according to standard spelling. In this dictionary, the verb *compare* is entered as **com·pare.** The dot divides the word into two syllables. To break a word at the end of a line, always divide it between the syllables (see 28G). Never break a syllable. Phonetic symbols in parentheses show the correct pronunciation; explanations of these symbols appear across the bottom of the pages in this dictionary. In the word *compare,* the second syllable receives the greater stress when you pronounce the word correctly. You say "comPARE." In this dictionary, the syllable that receives the primary stress is given an accent mark at the end like this: ′. Down the column in this section of the dictionary, you find the word *compartmentalize.* It is pronounced with the heaviest stress on the syllable *men,* and it has a secondary stress on the syllables *com* and *ize.* The syllable with the heaviest stress has the darkest accent mark; the syllables with the secondary stress receive lighter accent marks. Other dictionaries use a simple apostrophe to show accents. Study the accent marks in whatever dictionary you use.

Parts of Speech and Various Forms

The symbol *v.* immediately after the pronunciation tells you that *compare* is most frequently used as a verb. The *-pared* shows the simple past and the past participle forms. If the past participle differed from the simple past, both forms would be included. (Look at the verb *drink* in your dictionary; you will see the forms *drank* and *drunk.*) The *-paring* gives you the present participle form and shows that you drop the final *e* in *compare* before you add the *-ing.* The *-pares* tells you the third-person singular form of the verb so that you know to write "She compares."

The symbol —*tr.* shows that the verb is used transitively. That is, the verb *compare* can be used to take a direct object. A little further down in the entry the symbol —*intr.* shows that *compare* is also used as an intransitive verb, one that does not take a direct object. The symbol —*n.* still further along in the entry shows that *compare* is occasionally used as a noun, and to illustrate this usage, the dictionary gives the phrases *beyond* or *without compare.* The form *comparer* in boldface at the end of the main entry shows that by adding the simple suffix *-er,* we can get the noun meaning "one who compares."

Definitions

The several meanings of the word are arranged according to the parts of speech that the word plays in different contexts. Meanings used in special contexts are often noted by editors. For example, for the verb *compare,* the editors of the dictionary note that in grammar the word has a special and technical meaning, which they indicate by putting *Grammar* in italics. The editors will also note in italics whether a word or a particular meaning of a word is *nonstandard, informal, slang, vulgar, archaic, rare, poetic, regional,* or *foreign.* For example, the *American Heritage Dictionary* gives the word *e'en* meaning "evening" but notes that it is *poetic* so that you would not use it in an essay unless you were quoting from a poem.

Word Origins

At the end of nearly every entry in this column is an etymology—a brief history of the word, usually beginning with its entry into English and tracing its forms from there to the present. We see that *compare* came from *comparen* in Middle English, the English in use during Chaucer's time, in the fourteenth century. *Comparen* came from the French word *comparer,* used by the Normans, who introduced a wealth of French words into Anglo-Saxon speech. *Comparer* came from the Latin verb *comparare;* Latin was the language of the Roman West, and French evolved from it.

A study of word origins often helps you understand what words mean. But always remember that in a living language like ours, words are in flux, and some words have changed drastically from their original meanings.

Usage

The usage note in the *American Heritage Dictionary* is appended to some main entries in the dictionary. The only usage note in this column explains some things about the verb *compare.* Here we see the dictionary's panel of experts divided over *compare with* and *compare to.* Since the majority of the Usage panel holds that *compare with* is the more acceptable idiom for comparisons of similarities and differences, you would be well advised to follow the lead of those experts. If you were comparing geometry and trigonometry, for instance, you would note many ways in which they were alike and many ways in which they were different; so you would compare geometry *with* trigonometry.

But if your comparison were entirely with differences or entirely with similarities, you would use *compare to.* If you write "Compared to Paul, Margaret is kind and generous," you are talking only about a difference, not about both similarities and differences. You mean that Paul is not as kind and generous as Margaret. Again, the idiom is *compare to.*

Exercise 22.1 Which of the following words can be used as verbs? What cautions does your desk dictionary offer about using them? Indicate with a T or an I whether a verb is transitive or intransitive. Put a TI before verbs that can be used both transitively and intransitively.

1. total
2. outside
3. fritter
4. freeze
5. consider
6. victory
7. hipster
8. radio
9. slop
10. postulate
11. land
12. paper
13. grind
14. language
15. rap
16. water
17. help
18. into
19. cool
20. sullenly

Exercise 22.2 Write out your own short definition for each of the following words, noting the part or parts of speech that you think each word may serve. If you can, discuss the words with the class. Then check your definitions with those in a standard desk dictionary. If you don't know a word, try to guess what it means before you look it up in the dictionary.

1. effete
2. jejune
3. jangle
4. parameter
5. pestilent
6. nomenclature
7. manufacture
8. relationship
9. mucus
10. buckboard
11. buttress
12. sprocket
13. habiliment
14. media
15. digital
16. agenda
17. poignant
18. masterful
19. infer
20. dark horse

Exercise 22.3 Look up the etymologies of the following words in your desk dictionary. Discuss with the class how the origins of a word help you understand its modern meaning.

di/th 22B

1. gynecologist
2. gymnasium
3. geology
4. manufacture
5. center
6. dimension
7. populist
8. democracy
9. helicopter
10. muck
11. harlequin
12. courage
13. shrewd
14. physics
15. theology

Synonyms and Antonyms

Here is the entry from the *American Heritage Dictionary,* 2d College edition, for the word *include.* Study the *synonyms.* Note that the editors explain the slightly different sense that each of these synonyms conveys. If you study the synonyms in your dictionary, you will develop a greater understanding of what the words connote. That is, you will develop a sense for the extended meanings that words carry around with them.

> **in·clude** (ĭn-klōōd′) *tr.v.* **-cluded, -cluding, -cludes. 1.** To have as a part or member; be made up of, at least in part; contain. **2.** To contain as a minor or secondary element; imply. **3.** To cause to be a part of something; consider with or put into a group, class, or total. [Middle English *includen,* from Latin *inclūdere,* to shut in : *in-,* in + *claudere,* to close (see **klēu-** in Appendix*).] **—in·clud′a·ble, in·clud′i·ble** *adj.*
> ***Synonyms:*** *include, comprise, comprehend, embrace, involve.* These verbs mean to take in or contain one or more things as part of something larger. *Include* and *comprise* both take as their objects things or persons that are constituent parts. *Comprise* usually implies that all of the components are stated: *The track meet comprises 15 events* (that is, consists of or is composed of). *Include* can be so used, but, like the remaining terms, more often implies an incomplete listing: *The meet includes among its high points a return match between leading sprinters. Comprehend* and *embrace* usually refer to the taking in of intangibles as part of a broader subject: *Law and order comprehend much more than exercise of police power. A person's tastes in reading need not embrace every subject fashionable at the moment. Involve* usually suggests the relationship of a thing that is a logical consequence or required condition of something more inclusive: *A heavy scholastic schedule involves extra effort.*

Antonyms have an opposite or nearly opposite meaning from the dictionary definition of any given word. The antonym of *large* would be *small.* The antonym of *young* would be *old.* Antonyms are generally less useful to writers than synonyms, and many dictionaries do not include them.

Exercise 22.4 Look up both words in each pair of synonyms, and write sentences using each to show that you understand the connotation of the word.

Example: mournful/lugubrious

The funeral procession made its *mournful* way to the graveyard under the dripping trees and threatening skies.

He tired of the *lugubrious* outpourings of her insincere grief.

1. walk/ramble
2. ask/demand
3. urbane/suave
4. mercenary/pecuniary
5. rebut/refute
6. decline/reject
7. bright/gaudy
8. cheap/tawdry
9. reporter/informer
10. ideal/visionary
11. optimistic/utopian
12. plan/scheme

Geographic and Biographical Entries

The handy size of a standard desk dictionary limits the information that each entry can include. But you can find the correct spellings of important place names, the official names of countries with their areas and populations, and the names of capitals. Biographical entries give the birth and death years and enough information about the person to justify a listing in the dictionary.

22C Use a thesaurus with caution.

A **thesaurus** (the word means "treasury" or "collection" in Latin) is a dictionary of synonyms, usually without definitions. Three standard thesauruses are available:

Roget's International Thesaurus. 4th ed. New York: Thomas Y. Crowell, 1977.

The Synonym Finder. Ed. J. I. Rodale. Emmaus, Pa.: Rodale Press, 1978.

Webster's Collegiate Thesaurus. Springfield, Mass.: Merriam-Webster, 1976.

All three thesauruses give many synonyms for each listed word, and the words are indexed in the back of the book. Pocket thesauruses arranged in dictionary form are available but are limited in their number of entries and, hence, in their usefulness. The index entry for *walk* in *Roget's Thesaurus* shows that the noun synonyms may be located under entries for *sphere, slow motion, ramble, gait, circuit, sphere of work, path,* and *arena.* Verb synonyms can be found under entries for *go slow* and *travel. Walk* as a noun is listed with *leisurely gait, snail's* or *tortoise's pace, creep, crawl, saunter, stroll, slouch, shuffle, shamble,* and several more.

A thesaurus does not define words. Thus it is most useful for someone who already knows the definitions of the words and merely wants to be reminded of synonyms that may add color or more precision to a piece of prose. Thesauruses have misled many inexperienced writers by encouraging them to use a word without understanding its connotations (see 17F). The effects may be either laughable or seriously misleading.

di/th
22C

For example, if you wanted to find just the right word for the colorless quality of a twilight just fading into complete darkness, you might look under "colorlessness" in *Roget's Thesaurus* and discover the adjective "ghastly." You might write, "Just before the darkness fell, the light under the trees in the forest turned ghastly." One of the meanings of *ghastly* is "with a ghostlike pallor," and "pallor" led Roget's editors to put "ghastly" among the adjectives of colorlessness. But the connotations of *ghastly* all relate to death, to horror, to dread, or to something equally terrible. So the sense of the word *ghastly* in the sentence above is that something about the light under the trees in the forest was horrible. If you were writing a murder mystery or a ghost story, the word might be the one you would want to use. But if you were describing the peaceful appearance of the woods on a pleasant spring evening, your meaning would go completely awry.

Again, use the thesaurus with extreme caution. If you do not fully understand a synonym that you are about to use in your own writing, look it up in a good dictionary to be sure it is just the word you want to use.

The thesaurus can also be dangerous to a writer tempted to use a fancy style. Most of the time the simple word is much more efficient and forceful than the complicated word in expressing meaning and in creating a good effect. If you use the thesaurus too often, even correctly, you risk creating stiff and pretentious prose.

Exercise 22.5 Find five synonyms for the word *excitement* in a thesaurus. Write a sentence for each of the synonyms, using the words correctly. Use a desk dictionary if you need to check on the connotations of a word.

PART FIVE
Punctuation

23
End Marks

In English as in most other languages, the system of end marks gives writers a means for separating sentences and for indicating other special operations.

23A Use a period after a sentence that makes a statement, that gives a mild command or makes a mild request, or that asks a question indirectly.

Statements (Declarative sentences)

Soap melts in the bathtub.

Every year Americans buy more bicycles than cars.

The building burned down last night.

Mild Commands (Imperative sentences without strong emotion, often sentences that make a mild request)

Please go with me to the lecture.

Consider your opponent's views carefully when you are making an argument.

Lend me the car, and I'll do the shopping.

[Commands showing strong emotion require exclamation points; see 23C.]

Take the money and run!

Indirect Questions

People wonder why they have to pay such high taxes.

She asked me where I had gone to college.

They demanded to know who was responsible for the killings.

He wanted to know how I had come to that conclusion.

[The words *why, where, who,* and *how* in these sentences ask questions indirectly.]

Direct questions require question marks (see 23B).
For the use of the ellipsis marks, see 28F.

23B Use a question mark after a direct question but not after an indirect question.

Who wrote *One of Ours*? [direct question]

She wanted to know who wrote *One of Ours.* [indirect question]

If a question ends with a quoted question, one question mark serves for both the question in the main clause and the question that is quoted.

?
23B

What did Juliet mean when she cried, "Oh Romeo, Romeo! Wherefore art thou Romeo?"

If a quoted question comes in a sentence that makes a statement, place a question mark before the last quotation mark for the quoted question, and put a period at the end of the sentence.

"What was Henry Ford's greatest contribution to the industrial revolution in America?" he asked.

"What did the President know and when did he know it?" became the great question of the Watergate hearings.

Occasionally a question mark changes a statement into a question.

You expect me to believe a story like that?

He drove my car into your living room?

To give emphasis to parts of a series of questions, you can use question marks to separate them into fragments.

And what will we leave behind us when we are long dead? Temples? Amphora? Sunken treasure?

—Marya Mannes

To express uncertainty about a word or a date, you may use a question mark. In such usage the question mark means that no one can be sure if the date or word is true. You should never use such question marks merely to show that you have not bothered to look up the information.

> Napoleon Bonaparte's brother-in-law, Joachim Murat (1767?–1815), was King of Naples for seven years.

23C Use exclamation marks sparingly to emphasize strong emotion.

To convey surprise, outbursts, shock, or some other strong emotion, use exclamation marks.

> The land of the free! This is the land of the free! Why, if I say anything that displeases them, the free mob will lynch me, and that's my freedom.
>
> —D. H. LAWRENCE

> Moon, rise! Wind, hit the trees, blow up the leaves! Up, now, run! Tricks! Treats! Gangway!
>
> —RAY BRADBURY

! 23C

Avoid using too many exclamation marks. If you use exclamation marks too frequently, you will dull the sensitivity of your readers to them, and they will not respond with the excitement that an exclamation mark is supposed to call up. For mild statements, use some other marks of punctuation.

> "Ah, what a beautiful morning," she said, throwing the windows open onto the new day.

[A comma rather than an exclamation mark is used after *morning*.]

> Socrates said, "Know thyself."

[A period is used after *thyself* rather than an exclamation mark.]

Exercise 23.1 Use periods, question marks, and exclamation marks where they are required in the sentences below.

1. He wanted to know if Mr. Kuhns worked for UNESCO or for the FBI
2. "Was it you," she asked, "who painted that wall purple"
3. What did he mean when he asked me, "Is your car an antique"
4. Stolen The money was stolen Right before our eyes, somebody snatched my purse and ran off with it
5. "Help me" he said "I want to learn how to dance"
6. "Isn't the true folk instrument the dulcimer" she asked

7. You expect me to believe that computers can think
8. Pick up the papers Don't you think it's fair for each of us to try to keep this room clean
9. She asked if the theft of credit cards has become a major crime in this country
10. "Where will it end" he asked

Exercise 23.2 Compare the effects of different punctuation marks on the sentences in each pair below. Discuss your reponses in class. Imagine situations when you might have used each version of each sentence.

1. a. You don't have to tell me.
   b. You don't have to tell me!
   c. You don't have to tell me?
2. a. You mowed the lawn!
   b. You mowed the lawn?
   c. You mowed the lawn.
3. a. What will you contribute, your time, your talent, or your money?
   b. What will you contribute? Your time? Your talent? Your money?

24 Commas

When you speak, you may pause to emphasize certain elements of a sentence or to catch your breath. Commas show these pauses within written sentences. Commas also set off sentence elements, clarify the relations of some sentence elements to others, and serve in standard ways for dates, addresses, and other conventions.

Notice how commas take the place of spoken emphasis in the following sentences. Without the commas, you might have to read each of these sentences a couple of times to perceive the correct meaning.

> We are, counting the nonvoting delegates, fifty strong.
>
> Although his first name was Abraham, Lincoln had little religious training and never joined a church.

24A Use commas to set off independent clauses joined by the common coordinating conjunctions.

> No one voted in the election, and the White House stood empty for four years.

[A comma is used before the coordinating conjunction *and,* which introduces an independent clause.]

> He was an all-American quarterback, but no pro team drafted him.

[A comma is used before the coordinating conjunction *but,* which introduces an independent clause.]

> The art majors could paint portraits, or they could paint houses.

[The comma is used before the coordinating conjunction *or,* which introduces the independent clause *they could paint houses.*]

> Many Americans did not at first understand jazz, nor did they enjoy listening to it.

The rock singer did not like to stand with his back to the audience, for then he had to face the music.

The mechanic liked to be different, so he wore a tuxedo when he changed the oil.

Many people don't understand punctuation, yet they use it anyway.

Note that many writers and editors still prefer to use a semicolon rather than a comma before *so* and *yet.*

Printing has made language much less flexible than it once was; *so* the common rules of English grammar will probably not change soon again.

Nearly all of us think we write well; *yet* we all complain about the poor writing of others.

Note, too, that some writers do not separate short independent clauses with a comma.

He stayed at home and she went to work.

But it is always more clear to put the comma in such sentences.

He stayed at home, and she went to work.

24B Use commas after long introductory phrases and clauses to keep these elements distinct from the core assertion of your sentences.

Although short introductory word groups do not require commas to set them off from the rest of the sentence, commas always make long introductory phrases and clauses easier to read and to understand.

After he had been in the hot tub for three hours, the fire department had to revive him.

When dieting to lose fifty pounds, people should take the advice of a doctor.

Because of many complicated and somewhat bizarre reasons, I could not hand my paper in on time.

These short opening phrases do not have to be set off by commas:

Leaving the game I drifted along with the happy crowd.

After her death he felt lonely and sad for years.

In the street he met his friend Dr. Johnson.

A few writers omit the comma even after long opening phrases in their sentences.

In a letter sent by courier to Richmond that same day he went more fully into this and other matters bearing on the issue.

—SHELBY FOOTE

Despite the occasional exception in the way writers use commas, you will make your sentences consistently more clear if you set off long introductory phrases with commas.

You should always put a comma after an introductory subordinate clause (see 13B, section 1).

When we came out, we were not on the busiest Chinatown street but on a side street across from the park.

—MAXINE HONG KINGSTON

Although the struggle and competition for national or international power may not be explained wholly and simply as analogous to the power drive in personal relations, the personal may provide significant insight into the political.

—KENNETH B. CLARK

Commas often set off introductory adverbs, especially transitional adverbs like *therefore, also, however, nevertheless,* and *thus.* Normally it is better to rewrite sentences with one-word adverbial openers so that the adverb comes later on.

However, Mr. Smith finally made justice triumph in Washington—at least in the movie.

Therefore, we should enjoy youth while we can and worry less about the future and its responsibilities.

Nevertheless, we should do nothing in youth that might injure others and leave us with sad memories of our own wrongs.

Also, pitchers are subject to shoulder and elbow injuries.

These sentences may be revised so that they open in a different way.

But Mr. Smith finally made justice triumph in Washington—at least in the movie.

[The *however* that originally began this sentence has been changed to the shorter conjunction *but.*]

We should, therefore, enjoy youth while we can and worry less about the future and its responsibilities.

[*Therefore* here has been moved to a later position in the sentence.]

We should nevertheless do nothing in youth that might injure others and leave us with sad memories of our own wrongs.

[The *nevertheless* has been moved to a later position in the sentence.]

Pitchers are also subject to shoulder and elbow injuries.

[The *also* is moved to another position.]

The reason for not beginning a sentence with these transitional adverbs is that they are often weaker than another kind of beginning. The subject of a sentence, for example, is usually more vivid than a transitional adverb; if that is so, it is better to begin the sentence with the subject.

Other kinds of one-word adverbs regularly begin sentences, and they are frequently not set off by commas.

Yesterday I resolved to stop worrying about things I could not help.

[*Yesterday,* the adverb that begins this sentence, is not set off by a comma.]

24C Use commas to set off absolutes.

Absolutes, you have learned, are phrases that combine a noun with a present or past participle and that serve to modify the entire sentence (see 3C, section 1). They usually appear at the beginning of the sentence or clause of which they are a part, but they may also come in the middle or at the end.

The bridge being built, the British set out to destroy it.

[The absolute phrase, in italics, modifies the clause *the British set out to destroy it.*]

The snake slithered through the tall grass, the sunlight shining now and then on its green skin, its forked tongue feeling its way, its body bending like a ribbon.

[Three absolutes end this sentence. Each is set off by a comma.]

24D Use commas to set off participial modifiers at the end of a sentence.

Participial phrases modifying the subject may come at the end of a sentence. They are set off by commas.

They toiled all night on the engine, grinding and adjusting the valves, polishing the cylinders, cleaning the pistons, replacing the rings, installing a new fuel pump, putting in new spark plugs and points.

[This sentence ends with a succession of participial modifiers, each modifying the subject *they* and each set off by a comma.]

24E Use commas whenever you need to separate elements of a sentence that may cause confusion if you do not separate them.

Unclear: Every time John raced small boys could leave him behind.

Clear: Every time John raced, small boys could leave him behind.

Unclear: No matter what he did to win her love was impossible.

Clear: No matter what he did, to win her love was impossible.

Exercise 24.1 Put commas wherever they are needed in the following sentences.

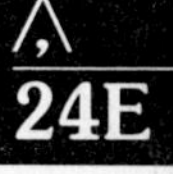

1. Many young people want to write fiction but they do not see that any kind of writing is an art.
2. The plane having left we had to take the bus to New York.
3. Although you need to know grammar exercises in grammar alone will not help you write well unless you also read.
4. Nevertheless Greek wine has become popular in America among non-Greeks and it is often sold in restaurants that do not specialize in Greek food.
5. You can read books or you can live forever in your own small world believing that your ignorance is bliss not knowing how ignorant you are supposing that people are all like you.
6. Strictly speaking there are no rules of grammar but there are conventions that most educated people use and you can violate these conventions only at the cost of making things hard on your readers and making your readers believe that you are ignorant.
7. Pay something if you can but if you cannot go in and enjoy the art anyway.
8. After he had watched television all night long his eyes turned to egg white and his brain became glue.
9. Economic circumstances being what they are a Ph.D. degree is not much help in getting a job.
10. Running hard now she begin passing others in the race feeling her second wind feeling strength come back to muscles she had thought ready to die

gaining confidence as she lunged forward hearing the cheers of the crowd seeing the finish line coming to meet her.

11. Turning their backs on the medieval scholars in the Renaissance tried to recapture the classical age of Greece and Rome.
12. Serving the rich and the famous cooks can become rich and famous themselves if they develop some new and popular dishes.

24F Use commas to set off nonrestrictive clauses and phrases.

Nonrestrictive clauses and phrases can be lifted out of the sentences where they appear without changing the primary meaning of the sentences. The commas that set off a nonrestrictive clause or phrase announce that these words provide additional information for the main assertion of the sentence.

> My dog Lady, who treed a cat last week, treed the mail carrier this morning.

[The nonrestrictive clause *who treed a cat last week* adds information, but the primary assertion of the sentence would be complete without it.]

> On this bright summer day, a day smelling of flowers and radiant with sunshine and cooled by soft winds, my wife and I celebrated our thirtieth wedding anniversary.

[The appositive phrase *a day smelling of flowers and radiant with sunshine and cooled by soft winds* is set off by commas, since it is nonrestrictive. It adds information to the primary assertion of the sentence, but it could be removed without damaging the fundamental meaning.]

Setting off a phrase or a clause with commas can often change the meaning of a sentence.

> The commencement speaker, who was a sleep therapist, spoke for three hours.

[The commas make the clause nonrestrictive. There was only one commencement speaker, and that speaker happened to be a sleep therapist. The clause could be removed without damaging the primary assertion of the sentence.]

> The commencement speaker who was a sleep therapist spoke for three hours.

[The absence of commas makes us think that there must have been several commencement speakers. The writer must, in some special way, single out the one who spoke for three hours. By calling the speaker a sleep therapist, the writer says that although there were several speakers, there was only one who was a sleep therapist, and that person was the one who spoke for three hours.]

Exercise 24.2 Use commas to set off nonrestrictive clauses and phrases in the following sentences. In some you have a choice. You can make the clause or phrase restrictive by not setting it off with commas. In such cases, discuss the changes in meaning so that you may be clear as to what they are and why they occur. At times you must rely on simple common sense to tell you whether to make the clause restrictive or nonrestrictive.

1. The chain saw which had a two-cycle engine gave him a sense of immense power as he took it in his hand and walked into the woods filled with oaks and maples.
2. Fly-fishing a difficult and sometimes dangerous sport requires much more skill than fishing with worms from a boat on a still lake.
3. The McCormick reaper which was invented by Cyrus Hall McCormick vastly increased wheat production in the nineteenth century.
4. Farmers who are by profession often isolated and independent have never been drawn in large groups to communism, but they have been attracted by fraternal organizations that have helped them meet together to satisfy social and economic needs.
5. Bats flying mammals found all over the world probably seem odious to many people because they look like mice that fly.
6. Kit Carson who was illiterate became famous in the mid-nineteenth century as a guide and fighting man and made many friends among important people who ran the national government in Washington.
7. Edith Cavell an English nurse in Belgium was shot in 1915 by the Germans as a spy after she helped many British, French, and Belgian soldiers escape from German-occupied Belgium into neutral Holland.

24G Use commas to separate items in a series.

A **series** is a set of nouns, pronouns, adjectives, adverbs, phrases, or clauses that are joined to each other by commas and—usually—a coordinating conjunction.

A Series of Nouns

In 1940, when he became the prime minister, Winston Churchill told the English people that he had nothing to offer them but blood, toil, tears, and sweat.

A Series of Pronouns

He, she, and I all graduated from high school in the same class.

A Series of Adjectives
My teacher's notes were old, yellow, and worn.

A Series of Adverbs
The three outlaws walked slowly, silently, and cautiously into the Sunday school.

A Series of Phrases
The university raised fees, reduced maintenance, fired assistant professors, turned down the heat, and still went bankrupt.

A Series of Clauses
The traffic was heavy, the parking lot was full, and I was late.

24H As a general rule, use commas to separate two or more adjectives before a noun or a pronoun.

The so-called "rednecks" of the South have been unforgettably evoked by Flannery O'Connor in her hard, tough, shrewd, unnerving stories.
—ROBERT COLES

But warfare for the Kiowas was preeminently a matter of disposition rather than of survival, and they never understood the grim, unrelenting advance of the U.S. Cavalry.
—N. SCOTT MOMADAY

Note that many writers do not use commas to mark off some adjectives that appear before nouns and pronouns, adjectives so closely related to what they modify that the whole phrase seems to stand as one unit.

A good test for whether or not you need a comma is to put a mental *and* between the adjectives. If the *and* fits easily between the adjectives, you may use a comma instead of the *and.* If it seems clumsy to use *and,* you should omit the comma. In the sentence above by Momaday, you could easily say, "They never understood the grim *and* unrelenting advance of the U.S. Cavalry." Because the *and* goes in so easily, you know to use a comma. But see how clumsy it would be to insert *and* between the adjectives in italics below:

Six thin green pines stood against the evening sky.

Adjectives that usually do not require the dividing comma when they appear in a series before nouns and pronouns are those that mention color, size, age, location, or number. But if you mention several different colors or sizes or numbers before your nouns, you should separate the adjectives with commas:

On the last day convertibles were made, the auto assembly line turned out a hundred green, gold, blue, black, silver, and red soft-topped cars.

[The *and* test works here too. You could write of the green *and* gold *and* blue *and* black *and* silver *and* red cars. Where you can say *and,* you may use a comma.]

24I Use commas to set off parenthetical words and phrases, including the sources of indirect quotations.

To be sure, Johnson was boring.

The class, however, should not have booed him.

It was, one student said, a moment of impolite truth.

The students, nevertheless, refused to apologize.

24J Use a comma with quotation marks to set off a direct quotation from the clause that names the source of the quotation.

When the source comes before the quotation, the comma goes before the quotation marks, not within them.

She said, "I'm sorry, but all sections are full."

When the quotation comes before the source, the comma goes before the last quotation mark.

"But I have to have this course to graduate," he said.

Often a direct quotation will surround the clause that gives the source. When that happens, the same rules apply: the comma before the source goes before the final quotation mark, and the comma after the source goes before the opening quotation mark.

"A rule is a rule," she said sweetly, "and you will just have to postpone your graduation."

A comma is not used if some other punctuation mark is used within the quotation marks.

"Do you believe in grades?" he asked.

"Believe in them!" she cried. "I've had them."

[A comma after the question mark or the exclamation point would be incorrect.]

24K Use the comma in direct address.

I'll say this to you, John, and I sincerely mean it.

Ethel, please bring me the soap.

[The writer uses the names of the people addressed in these sentences.]

Exercise 24.3 Place commas where they belong in the following sentences.

1. The old gray mare is not the superb creature she used to be says the old song.
2. Three happy young children came to the door shouting "Trick or Treat!"
3. The hospital smelled of wax linen and iodine.
4. She righted the boat ran up the sail grabbed the rudder and flew before the wind.
5. The storm broke suddenly and furiously the lightning crashed from a black sky and the cattle ran off into the dark.
6. "North Dakota is sky prairie wheat and hospitality" she said. "You must go there Charles. You will never see colors so pure land so vast or cities more manageable and clean."
7. The poor the speaker said commit far more violent crimes than do members of the middle class and the saddest thing he thought is that poor people are most likely to kill or maim members of their own families.
8. To be sure violent crime is not limited to the poor.
9. Nevertheless he said the frustrations of poverty often come to the boiling point in assault robbery and murder.
10. He spoke energetically sadly and eloquently.

24L Use commas to substitute for words in a sentence.

Commas may frequently take the place of the conjunction *and,* and in some constructions, they can take the place of other words as well.

The comma can take the place of *and* in a compound verb.

Power staggers forward, then falls facedown into the dust.

—PHILIP CAPUTO

[Instead of *and* after *forward,* a comma connects *staggers* and *falls,* the compound verb.]

The comma can also take the place of *and* in a series.

The joke was stale, flat, vulgar.

In sentences that express a contrast, the comma can stand for several words.

Lincoln was impressive, not handsome.

[Compare: Lincoln was impressive. He was not handsome. The writer of the sentence above leaves out *He was* and substitutes a comma.]

She said that her automobile was big, bright, and powerful, not economical.

[Compare: She said that her automobile was big, bright, and powerful. She did not say that it was economical.]

24M Use the comma occasionally to give special emphasis to words and phrases, even when the comma is not grammatically necessary.

It seems impossible to get a saint, or a philosopher, or a scientist, to stick to this simple truth.

—D. H. LAWRENCE

[The commas after *saint,* and *philosopher,* and *scientist* draw attention to the separate items in the series. The series would be correct without the commas.]

He found hamlets of three decaying houses with the corrugated iron of their roofs grinding and clanking in a hot wind, and not a tree for miles.

—WILLIAM GOLDING

[The comma after *wind* indicates a slight pause for emphasis before the final phrase *and not a tree for miles,* which gives a striking end to the sentence.]

24N Use commas according to standard practice for places and addresses.

In Cleveland, Ohio, the river sometimes catches fire.

[The comma is used to separate the city, *Cleveland,* from its state, *Ohio.* Another comma comes after *Ohio* to set off the state from the rest of the sentence.]

BUT:

He said he would come to Cleveland the next time he wanted a drink of fire water.

[When *Cleveland* is used by itself in the sentence without its state, it is not set off by commas.]

Commas set off parts of an address both in sentences and in addresses placed on letters and envelopes:

He lived at 1400 Crabgrass Lane, Suburbia, New York.

My address is:

63 Oceanside Drive, Apartment 3

Knoxville, TN 37916

[Note that in the address as it would appear on an envelope, a comma does not go at the end of any line, and it does not go between the abbreviation of the state name and the zip code.]

24O Use commas in dates when the month, day, and year are included.

On June 6, 1944, a British and American force invaded France.

British writers and, increasingly, many Americans use a form of the date that does not require a comma.

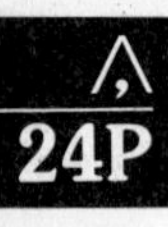

She graduated from college on 5 June 1980.

24P Put a comma before the coordinating conjunction in a series.

Human institutions such as marriage, law, and government do not just happen somehow.

—S. I. Hayakawa

[The comma after *law* helps set *law* apart from *government.*]

Some writers, especially British writers and writers for American newspapers and magazines, do not put a comma before the coordinating conjunction in a series.

Seldom can civil war have been accompanied by so little ill-feeling, so little deliberate cruelty and so much readiness to forgive and forget.

—Mary Clive

[The comma is omitted after the word *cruelty,* the second noun in a series.]

You should use a comma after each item in a series, including the item before the coordinating conjunction.

Exercise 24.4 Use commas correctly in the sentences below.

1. The speaker was rude pompous tiresome.
2. She purchased eggs rolls and butter from a small corner store in Cincinnati Ohio.
3. I shall be thirty on April 7 1987.
4. Dugan takes the motorbike Grady the sedan.
5. Water flows over the rocks then plunges fifty feet to a pond.

24Q Avoid faulty or needless commas.

A comma should not separate a subject from its verb or a verb from its object or complement unless the comma is needed to set off an intervening nonrestrictive clause or phrase.

Faulty

John, sold his pet cat to the laboratory.

[The comma improperly separates the subject, *John,* from the verb, *sold.*]

John sold his pet, cat to the laboratory.

[The comma improperly separates the direct object, *pet,* from the objective complement, *cat.*]

Correct

John, who never liked his cat anyway, sold him to the laboratory.

[The intervening nonrestrictive clause modifies *John* and is set off by commas.]

Prepositional phrases that serve as adjectives are not set off by commas from the noun or pronoun that they modify.

Faulty

The best part, of the meal, is coffee.

[The prepositional phrase *of the meal* serves as an adjective modifying the noun *part.* It should not be set off by commas.]

Correct

The best part of the meal is coffee.

Prepositional phrases that serve as adverbs are not set off from the rest of the sentence by commas.

Faulty

He swam, with the current, rather than against it.

[The prepositional phrase *with the current* serves as an adverb modifying the verb *swam.* It should not be set off by commas.]

Correct

He swam with the current rather than against it.

The phrases in a series of prepositional phrases will be set off from each other by commas according to the normal rules for items in a series.

Lincoln expressed his hope that the suffering of the American Civil War would guarantee that government of the people, by the people, and for the people should not perish from the earth.

[The prepositional phrases *of the people, by the people,* and *for the people* are items in a series, and they are set off from each other by commas. Note, however, that the first phrase in the series—*of the people*—is not set off by a comma from the noun *government,* which is modified by that phrase and the other phrases.]

Do not divide a compound verb with a comma if the elements of the verb are joined by a coordinating conjunction unless the parts of the verb make a series.

Faulty

He ran, and walked twenty miles.

[In a compound verb of only two parts, *ran* and *walked,* a comma should not divide the parts.]

Correct

He ran and walked twenty miles.

If the parts of a compound verb form a series, commas set off the parts of the verb.

He ran, walked, and crawled twenty miles.

Do not use a comma after the last item in a series unless the series concludes a clause or a phrase that is set off by commas.

He loved books, flowers, and people and spent much of his time with all of them.

[The series is not part of a clause or phrase set off by commas. Hence, a comma after *people* would be incorrect.]

Three "scourges of modern life," as Roberts calls the automobile, the telephone, and the polyester shirt, were unknown little more than a century ago.

[The series is part of a nonrestrictive clause, and nonrestrictive clauses are set off by commas. The last word in the series, *shirt,* is the last word of the clause; so it is followed by a comma.]

Avoid commas with quotation marks when the effect of the commas would be to create a false parenthesis.

Faulty

A song called, "Faded Love," made Bob Wills famous.

[The commas make the title "Faded Love" seem like a parenthesis, but a parenthesis may be removed from a sentence without damage to the grammar of the sentence. If the title "Faded Love" were removed from this sentence, the grammar and the sense would be damaged. Hence the title should not be set off by commas.]

Correct

A song called "Faded Love" made Bob Wills famous.

Faulty

The so-called, Buckley Amendment, made some professors fear to write honest letters of recommendation.

[Try to remove the title Buckley Amendment from the sentence; the sentence will be nonsense.]

Correct

The so-called Buckley Amendment made some professors fear to write honest letters of recommendation.

Do not use commas to set off dependent adverbial clauses that come at the end of a sentence. In practice this rule means that you should not use commas before words such as *because, when, since, while, as, neither,* and *either.*

Faulty

He looked forward every year to June, because he always made a long bike trip as soon as school was out.

[The comma before *because* incorrectly sets off an adverbial clause.]

Correct

He looked forward every year to June because he always made a long bike trip as soon as school was out.

BUT:

Because he always made a long bike trip as soon as school was out, he looked forward every year to June.

[When the adverbial clause comes at the beginning of a sentence, it is set off by a comma. See 24B.]

Faulty

She searched for the familiar sights of home, while the plane dipped low toward the runway.

[The comma after *home* incorrectly sets off an adverbial clause at the end of the sentence.]

Exercise 24.5 Eliminate the unnecessary commas in the following sentences. Be careful! Some of the commas belong where they are. If a sentence is correct as it is written, put a check by it.

1. According to reports coming out of Russia, life there for the average man and woman, in the large cities, is one long round, of corruption, lines, and alcoholism.
2. Democracy, has often been called inefficient, and divisive, since it encourages political argument, and diversity of opinions about art, morals, education, religion, and many other important parts, of life.
3. Thousands of people crowded along the banks of the river, swarmed on the bridges, and cheered their favorites, as the boats in the race swept by.
4. The chill air of autumn, the falling leaves, the weak sunshine all told us that winter was not far away.
5. Mr. Giacometti, opened the doors of his establishment promptly at eight in the morning.
6. The apartment she rented in Omaha, was not far from the railroad museum.
7. It is sometimes not easy to tell, when you have drunk too much beer to drive safely.
8. Since divorce has become as common as it is in American society, more and more children are growing without the company, of a mother or a father.
9. Many people, just starting careers in business and government, are afraid to express their true opinions, because they are afraid, they may damage their chances for promotion.
10. Central heating in private homes, was once considered a luxury, and with the rising cost of fuel, we may return to those days, since more and more people heat only one or two rooms, and leave the rest of the house cold.

25 Semicolons

The semicolon is a stronger mark of punctuation than the comma, and it can be used to join sentence elements that cannot be joined by a comma alone. Semicolons can join certain independent clauses and set off elements within a series when there are commas within the elements.

25A Use a semicolon to join independent clauses, either with or without the help of a coordinating conjunction.

> Silence is deep as eternity; speech is shallow as time.
>
> —THOMAS CARLYLE

> Before 8000 BC wheat was not the luxuriant plant it is today; it was merely one of many wild grasses that spread throughout the Middle East.
>
> —JACOB BRONOWSKI

[In each example, two clauses are closely related to each other—one of the reasons for using the semicolon. Each writer could have separated them with a period, but he chose the semicolon to stress the relation of ideas in the clauses.]

> In the first draft I had Bigger going smack to the electric chair; but I felt that two murders were enough for one novel.
>
> —RICHARD WRIGHT

[The writer could have placed a comma where he put the semicolon, but the semicolon adds emphasis to the second independent clause.]

> He stayed up all night to study for the exam; he opened the exam booklet to begin and fainted.

[His staying up all night long is the implied cause for his fainting just as he began the exam. The semicolon emphasizes the cause-and-effect relation by closely joining the two clauses.]

25B Use a semicolon to join main clauses separated by a conjunctive adverb.

Conjunctive adverbs such as *nevertheless, moreover, then,* and *consequently* are not coordinating conjunctions and cannot join independent clauses (see 4E). Even a comma placed before them cannot give them the grammatical strength to link clauses.

Incorrect

He had biked 112 miles in ten hours, nevertheless, he now had to do a marathon.

Corrected with a Semicolon

He had biked 112 miles in ten hours; nevertheless, he now had to do a marathon.

[A semicolon is necessary before the conjunctive adverb *nevertheless* to join the two clauses properly.]

;/ 25B

Exercise 25.1 Review the following sentences for the proper use of semicolons. If a sentence is correct as it stands, place a check beside it. Supply semicolons where they are needed. Eliminate semicolons that are incorrectly used.

1. She was unable to keep the appointment; since she was delayed in traffic; because of the wreck.
2. The sun is our most potent source of energy, nevertheless, research in harnessing solar power has gone slowly.
3. The United States and Canada have relatively few varieties of poisonous snakes; but the climate is warm enough to allow many such snakes to flourish should they be accidentally introduced.
4. Western movies once showed hostile Indians attacking covered wagons drawn up in circles on the plains; although no such attack ever occurred in fact.
5. Videocassette recorders allow many people to rent movies on tape and to play them at home through their television sets moreover, the rental fee for the tape is much less than it would cost a family to see a movie in a theater.
6. Nuclear war is a horror that no one wants to imagine; yet imagining it may help us prevent it.
7. November is a month that is much abused and often unfairly so; true, the leaves fall, and cold weather begins; but November gives us three holidays —Election Day, Veterans Day, and Thanksgiving.

25C Use a semicolon to separate elements in a series when some of those elements contain commas.

They are aware of sunrise, noon and sunset; of the full moon and the new; of equinox and solstice; of spring and summer, autumn and winter.

—ALDOUS HUXLEY

[Two of the four elements in the series contain commas; separating the elements with semicolons prevents confusion.]

Confusing Series

The committee included Dr. Curtis Youngblood, the county medical examiner, Robert Collingwood, the director of the bureau's criminal division, and Darcy Coolidge, the chief of police.

[Readers of this passage would have trouble deciding how many people they were reading about.]

Series with Semicolons

The committee included Dr. Curtis Youngblood, the county medical examiner; Robert Collingwood, the director of the bureau's criminal division; and Darcy Coolidge, the chief of police.

[Now the semicolons show clearly that the name of each man is followed by his title, which serves to identify him. We are clearly dealing with three men and not five or six.]

25D Use a semicolon to separate elements in elliptical constructions, where words left out are clearly understood.

In America, traffic problems are caused by cars; in China, by bicycles.

[We understand that the words left out would make the sentence read like this: "In America, traffic problems are caused by cars; in China, traffic problems are caused by bicycles." The semicolon is used as if the missing words were present in the sentence.]

25E Use semicolons to separate elements in reference notes when those notes contain other punctuation marks.

The assignment will be to read Leviticus 21:1–20; Joshua 5:3–6; and Isaiah 55:1–10.

Exercise 25.2 For each set below, write a single sentence using semicolons correctly. Make reference to all the people and identify them by their jobs.

1. Dr. Mary A. Carter is a professor of history. Mr. Glenn G. Swenson is a football coach. Dean Sylvia Paoli was the moderator of the discussion. Dr. Carter and Mr. Swenson debated the place of intercollegiate athletics in education.
2. Ronald Martin is a designer of computers. Elizabeth Ingersol is an architect. Joseph Greenberg is a science teacher in Bradford High School. The three of them led a discussion on the future of home computers in business and in education.

Exercise 25.3 Punctuate the following sentences correctly.

1. Some were satisfied others disgruntled.
2. He needed seven hours of sleep a night she only five.
3. Cancer is more feared heart disease more fatal.
4. In her room there were three pictures in mine one in his none.

Exercise 25.4 Explain the use of the semicolon in each sentence below.

1. It was not in anger she had forsaken him; it was in simple submission to hard reality, to the stern logic of love.

   —HENRY JAMES
2. Her presence brought memories of such things as Bourbon roses, rubies and tropical midnight; her moods recalled lotus-eaters and the march in "Athalie"; her motions, the ebb and flow of the sea; her voice, the viola.

   —THOMAS HARDY
3. The expansion that derives from city import replacing consists specifically of five forms of growth: abruptly enlarged city markets for new and different imports, consisting largely of goods from rural areas and of innovations being produced in other cities; abruptly increased numbers and kinds of jobs in the import-replacing city; new uses of technology, particularly to increase rural productivity; increased transplants of city work into non-urban locations as older, expanding enterprises are crowded out; and the growth of city capital.

   —JANE JACOBS

26
Apostrophes

We use apostrophes to show possession, to indicate omitted letters in words written as contractions, and to form special plurals.

26A Use an apostrophe to show possession of nouns and of indefinite pronouns. (See 3B, section 3.)

To indicate ownership—or, in special cases, to show that an entity has a particular attribute, quality, value, or feature—writers can often choose among different forms of the possessive case (see p. 115):

Children's toys could mean:	*Everybody's* dreams could mean:
toys *of children*	dreams *of everybody*
toys *for children*	dreams *for everybody*
toys *belonging to children*	dreams *everybody has*
toys *owned by children*	dreams *belonging to everybody*
toys *that children own*	

Most writers would use the first form above without spelling out one of the full phrases. Without words such as *of, for, belonging to,* and *owned by,* only the apostrophe plus *s* ('s) conveys the intended sense of possession. Writers often use possessive forms even when the concept of possession seems uncertain. In the examples above, *everybody* does not possess *dreams* in the same way that *children* possess *toys.* Also, accepted usage requires apostrophes with concepts of duration and of monetary value:

An *hour's* wait   Two *minutes'* work

A *dime's* worth   Five *dollars'* worth

[In these phrases, despite the required possessive forms, *hours* and *dollars* do not really possess anything.]

Showing possession correctly with apostrophes usually requires two essential elements. Someone or something is the possessor, and someone or something is being possessed. The person or entity that possesses something takes an apostrophe, either along with an *-s* or alone if the word already ends in *-s*.

The person or entity being possessed usually appears just after the word with the apostrophe:

	Possessor	**Thing, attribute, quality, value, or feature possessed**
the woman's shovel	woman's	shovel
a child's bright smile	child's	bright smile
Juanita's son	Juanita's	son
the robbers' clever plan	robbers'	clever plan
five dollars' worth	dollars'	worth
everyone's plans	everyone's	plans
babies' books	babies'	books

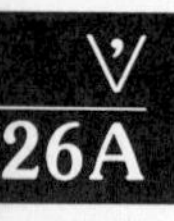

In some instances, the thing possessed precedes the possessor:

The motorcycle is the student's.

Is the tractor Jan Stewart's?

[The student possesses the motorcycle; Jan Stewart possesses the tractor; and the possessive forms (the nouns ending in *-'s*) come after the objects possessed.]

In other cases, the sentence may not name the thing possessed, but its identity is clearly understood by the reader.

I saw your cousin at Nicki's.

[The object possessed, Nicki's *house* or *place,* is implied.]

Sometimes we indicate possession by using both the *of* form and an apostrophe plus *s* or a personal possessive pronoun.

a friend of Rocco's

[Both *Rocco's* and *of* carry the possessive here: *Rocco* is the possessor; *friend* is the entity possessed.]

this dress of Mother's

that child of his

1 Distinguish between plural forms and possessive forms.

Most nouns require *-s* endings to show the plural form: boy/boy*s*; girl/girl*s*; teacher/teacher*s*; song/song*s*. Possessive forms require the apostrophe plus *s* ('s) ending: boy/boy's; girl/girl's; teacher/teacher's. The possessive form and the plural form are not interchangeable; yet errors involving a confusion of the two often occur.

Incorrect	**Correct**
The teacher's asked the girl's and boy's for attention.	The teachers asked the girls and boys for attention.

An apostrophe plus *s* at the end of a word makes that word the possessor of something. In the incorrect sentence above, the teacher, the girl, and the boy possess nothing.

Apostrophes occasionally signal plurals, but only in very special cases (see 26C).

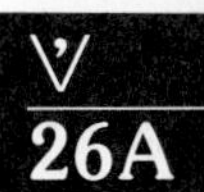

Exercise 26.1 Identify each word in the following list as plural or possessive; then use each word correctly in a sentence.

1. a. women	**b.** women's	**c.** woman's
2. a. man's	**b.** men's	**c.** men
3. a. child's	**b.** children	**c.** children's
4. a. cats	**b.** cat's	**c.** cats'
5. a. professor's	**b.** professors	**c.** professors'

Exercise 26.2 In each of the following sentences, underline the word that shows possession and put an X above the word that names the entity possessed. (The entity possessed may be understood but not named.)

1. Plucking feathers on turkeys is not everyone's idea of a good job.
2. If the responsibility is the mayor's, then our citizens' group should push her to act.
3. At Mario's, the waiters serve with elegance; the diner's pleasure is the staff's only concern.
4. She brought me six dollars' worth of flour.
5. They went on a week's vacation together.
6. Gloria's smile welcomes students to the Writing Center.

2 To form a possessive, add an apostrophe plus *s* to a noun or pronoun not already ending in *-s*, whether it is singular or plural.

Noun/pronoun		As a possessive
baby	singular	a baby's smile
men	plural	the men's club
Wanda	singular	Wanda's sundae
hour	singular	an hour's time
anyone	singular	anyone's idea
children	plural	the children's papers

3 Add only an apostrophe (') to words already ending in *-s*, whether those words are singular or plural.

word (-s ending)		Word used as a possessive
babies	plural	the babies' smiles
Luis	singular	Luis' ring
companies	plural	the companies' employees
Dickens	singular	Dickens' novels
hours	plural	three hours' time

Many writers add both an apostrophe and a final *s* to one-syllable singular nouns already ending in *-s*, especially if the word following the possessive begins with a vowel sound.

Keats's *a*rt, James's *a*dventure

However, the addition of the apostrophe alone is increasingly acceptable.

Note that proper names of geographic locations, associations, organizations, and so forth, sometimes exclude apostrophes:

Kings Point, Veterans Highway

4 For hyphenated words and compound words and word groups, add an apostrophe plus *s* to the last word only.

my father-in-law's job

the editor-in-chief's responsibilities

the union leader's supporters

5 To express joint ownership by two or more people, use the possessive form for the last name only; to express individual ownership, use the possessive form for each name.

Felicia and Elias' house

[The two own the house together.]

McGraw-Hill's book catalog

Felicia's and Elias' houses

[Each one owns a house; notice that *houses* is plural.]

the city's and the state's finances

Exercise 26.3 Change each word in parentheses into the correct possessive form by adding an apostrophe or an apostrophe plus *s*. A word may require a plural form before you change it to a possessive.

Example: The two (woman) <u>women's</u> cars blocked the driveway.

1. (Mr. Cass) __________ contribution to the primaries brought praise from the (governor) __________ reelection committee.
2. The (assistant editor) __________ idea was to run three (student) __________ biographies in each issue.
3. The (Lady) __________ Auxiliary League drew hundreds to its Fourth of July picnic; (everyone) __________ praise meant that the tradition would continue next year.
4. In (Dickens) __________ novel *Great Expectations,* (Pip) __________ adventures hold every (reader) __________ attention.

Exercise 26.4 Change the structures that show ownership to possessive forms that use apostrophes.

Example: The announcement of the Secretary of State
The Secretary of State's announcement

1. the car of Kim and Thai
2. a business belonging to my brother-in-law
3. the houses of Mr. Garcia and Mr. Youngblood
4. the smile of Doris
5. the value of three dollars
6. a term of six months

26B Use an apostrophe to indicate letters or numbers left out of contractions, or letters omitted from words to show regional pronunciation.

In a contraction—a shortened word or group of words formed by omitting some letters or sounds—use an apostrophe in place of the omissions.

it's (for *it is* or *it has*)
weren't (for *were not*)
here's (for *here is*)
comin' (for *coming*)

Sometimes we abbreviate the numbers of years, using the apostrophe. For example, we say, "The '50s were a decade of relative calm; the '60s were much more turbulent." But it is usually better to spell these digits out when they refer to years. "Many claim that the fifties were much more turbulent than we remember and that the sixties only continued trends begun a decade earlier."

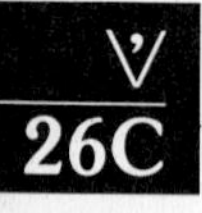

26C Use an apostrophe plus s ('s) to show plurals of letters, numbers, and words stressed as words rather than for the meaning they convey.

Committee has two *m*'s, two *t*'s, and two *e*'s.

[The letters are italicized, but not the final 's. See 32C.]

There are twelve *no*'s in the first paragraph.

He makes his 2's look like 5's.

The 1980's brought renewed efforts at energy conservation.

When no confusion results, it is equally acceptable to eliminate the apostrophe in these plurals.

1980's OR 1980s

2s and 3s

Bs, Cs, and Ds [But to prevent confusion with the word *as*, write the plural of *A* as *A's*.]

26D To show possession for personal and relative pronouns and for the pronoun *it*, use the special possessive forms, which never require apostrophes (my/mine, your/yours, his, her/hers, our/ours, their/theirs, whose, and its).

His cooking won a prize.

Its fur was shedding.

They knew *our* secret.

Is he a friend of *yours?*

The rake is *hers.*

When an apostrophe appears with an *s* in a pronoun, the apostrophe probably marks omissions in a contraction.

It's too hot. [It's = It + is]

Who's there? [Who's = Who + is]

If you're awake, please call. [you're = you + are]

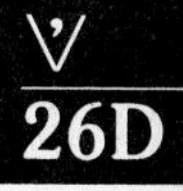

Exercise 26.5 Correct any words in italics either by removing incorrectly used apostrophes or by adding apostrophes where they belong. Some words are correct and require no change.

1. *Iris* cat lost *its* way, but one *neighbors* boys helped her find it.
2. There *wasnt* enough attention placed on writing *skills'* in college English curricula in the *60s.*
3. In the word *occurrence,* the two *c*s and two *r*s confuse many grade school *students'.*
4. If the *ideas'* are *hers', it's* wise to give her credit for them.
5. Many *childrens parents'* bought those *dolls* before the *companies* recalled them at the *governments* request.

27
Quotation Marks

Quotation marks (“ ”) always work in pairs. They are used to enclose words, phrases, and sentences that are quoted directly. Titles of short works like poems, articles, songs, and short stories, when cited with other words, also require quotation marks, as do some words and phrases that you wish to use in a special sense.

27A Use quotation marks to enclose direct quotations

In a *direct quotation* you repeat the exact words of a speaker or of a text. Direct quotations from written material may be whole sentences or significant words or phrases taken from other sentences.

> James Baldwin wrote of his experience of whites during his childhood, “The only white people who came to our house were welfare workers and bill collectors.”
>
> James Baldwin wrote that the only white visitors he saw in his home as a child were “welfare workers and bill collectors.”
>
> The “only” whites who visited Baldwin’s childhood home, he wrote much later on, came to distribute welfare or to collect bills.

The following diagrams will help you see how direct quotations are used and punctuated in sentences.

Sentence: Quoted Words First

Quotation mark. Capital letter.

“The first thing that strikes one about Plath’s journals is what

End quotation mark. End mark.

they leave out,” writes Katha Pollitt in *The Atlantic.*

Comma inside quote. Small letter.

Sentence: Quoted Words Last

Comma.
Small letter. Capital letter.

In *The Atlantic* Katha Pollitt writes, "The first thing that

Quotation marks.

strikes one about Plath's journals is what they leave out."

End mark inside quote.

Sentence: Quoted Words Interrupted

Quotation mark.
Quotation mark. Comma inside quote.
Capital letter. Small letter.

"The first thing that strikes one about Plath's journals," writes

Quotation mark. End mark inside quote.

Katha Pollitt in *The Atlantic*, "is what they leave out."

Comma. Small letter. Quotation mark.

In writing dialogue, use quotation marks to enclose everything a speaker says. When one person continues speaking, use quotation marks again if the person's quoted sentence is interrupted.

"I don't know what you're talking about," he said. "I did listen to everything you told me."

"You listened," she said, "but you did not try to understand."

In an *indirect quotation,* you paraphrase. That is, you express in your own words the meaning of someone else's words. Indirect quotations do not require quotation marks.

Direct Quotation

Casey said, "What I like best about driving the locomotive is blowing the whistle."

Indirect Quotation

Casey confessed that he enjoyed blowing the whistle more than anything else he did as a locomotive engineer.

Direct Quotation

Odette asked me, "May I please borrow your chain saw?"

Indirect Quotation

Odette asked if she could borrow my chain saw.

When you quote more than five lines, type them double-spaced and set every line off by a five-space indentation from the left margin. Triple-space above and below the quotation. *Be sure that you indent every line in a block quotation.*

Block quotations are *not* set off by quotation marks. If the block includes a direct quotation, however, use quotation marks as they are found in the text. The example that follows shows you how to do this.

> Some of the most interesting pages in Schorske's book describe how Sigmund Freud arrived at psychoanalysis and the interpretation of dreams and so made a revolution in our understanding of how the mind works. But as Schorske points out, the young Freud's first passion was not the working of the mind but classical archeology:
>
> > He consumed with avidity Jakob Burckhardt's newly published *History of Greek Culture,* so rich in materials on primitive myth and religion. He read with envy the biography of Heinrich Schliemann, who fulfilled a childhood wish by his discovery of Troy. Freud began the famous collection of ancient artifacts which were soon to grace his office in the Berggasse. And he cultivated a new friendship in the Viennese professional elite—especially rare in those days of withdrawal—with Emanuel Loewy, a professor of archeology. "He keeps me up till three o'clock in the morning," Freud wrote appreciatively to Fliess. "He tells me about Rome."
>
> —CARL SCHORSKE

[Note the quotation marks for material quoted within the block quotation.]

” 27A

Use block quotations sparingly. They cut down on the readability of your papers. When you are tempted to use long block quotations, try to paraphrase the material, and include it in your text, giving proper credit to your sources (see 33F).

Short quotations from poetry may be run into your text, much like any other short quotation. Line breaks are usually shown with a slash.

> In the nineteenth century Wordsworth gave language to the weary acquisitiveness of our modern age: "The world is too much with us; late and soon,/Getting and spending, we lay waste our powers:/Little we see in nature that is ours."

Longer verse quotations are indented block-style like long quotations from prose. If you cannot get an entire line of poetry on a single line of your typescript, you may put the end of the line under your typed line near the right margin of your paper.

Ah, what can ever be more stately and admirable to me
than mast-hemmed Manhattan?
River and sunset and scalop-edg'd waves of flood tide?
The sea-gulls oscillating their bodies, the hay-boat in the twilight,
and the belated lighter?
What gods can exceed those that clasp me by the hand, and with voices
I love call me promptly and loudly by my nighest name
as I approach?
—WALT WHITMAN

In American practice, a pair of single quotation marks (made with the apostrophe on the typewriter) is used to set off quotations within quotations.

What happened when the faculty demanded an investigation of dishonest recruiting practices in the athletic department? The president of the university said, "I know you're saying to me, 'We want an honest football team.' But I'm telling you this: 'I want a winning football team.' "

British practice with quotation marks differs from American practice. Commonwealth countries usually enclose direct quotations within single quotation marks and use double marks to enclose quotations within quotations. Because many English books are now being reproduced photographically in America, you may see both systems. In your own writing, use the American system.

27B Learn the conventional use of other punctuation with quotation marks.

A comma or period coming at the end of a quotation is always set before the last quotation mark. A question mark is set before the last quotation mark if the quotation itself asks a question. Punctuation marks that come before the quoted material are not included within quotation marks.

"The worst movie I've ever seen is *Jaws,*" he said.

"How can you say that?" she asked. "I loved *Jaws.*"

"How can I say that?" he said. "I'll tell you how I can say that; I can say that because I saw it eight times!"

She said, "I think *Jaws II* is even worse."

"Yes," he replied, "I agree. I saw it only four times."

Standard American practice is to place the period or the exclamation point before the final quotation mark even when the quotation is only one or two words long. The question mark is placed after the last quotation mark if the quoted material is not itself in the form of a question.

> He had what he called his "special reasons."
>
> Why did he name his car "Buck"?
>
> "Because," she said, "people pass it all the time."

Standard American practice is to put colons and semicolons after the final quotation mark.

> "I think the jokes in this book are terrible"; she made the remark at the top of her voice, and since I wrote the book, I was hurt.
>
> Dean Wilcox cited the items he called his "daily delights": a free parking place for his scooter at the faculty club, a special table in the club itself, and friends to laugh with after a day's work.

Exercise 27.1 Punctuate correctly the following sentences. Some sentences require no additional punctuation.

1. I want you to write a book Ted told me one night.
2. He said Give me a manuscript, and I'll get it published
3. She told me that she would rather play tennis than eat
4. He said to his friend I bought the car on credit
5. The wind is rising she shouted Make the boats secure The hurricane is coming
6. They told me that the finance company would repossess my typewriter tomorrow, but I said It doesn't matter at all since I'm going to finish my novel tonight
7. These were what Mark called his showcase talents: friendliness, intelligence, good looks, and humility
8. We asked our secretary to account for the absence of the treasurer, and these were his exact words I'm afraid she's run off with all our money since she called me last night and said Jack, I don't think the club can ever forgive me But who knows Jack said Maybe she only meant that she had lost the account book

27C Use quotation marks for titles of essays or chapters or other sections that occur within books or periodicals.

> "How to Die: The Example of Samuel Johnson" is the title of a recent article in *The Sewanee Review.*

The chapter was called "Another Question of Location."

Note that the titles of songs and short poems are usually put in quotation marks. Titles of long poems are put in italics. In manuscripts, titles of long poems are underlined (see 32A).

Robert Herrick wrote the poem "Upon Julia's Clothes."

George Gordon Noel, Lord Byron, wrote *Childe Harold's Pilgrimage.*

27D Use quotation marks to show that someone else has used a word or phrase in a special way, one that you or the general public may not use or agree with completely.

The "workers' paradise" of Stalinist Russia turned out to be a combination of slums, shortages, secret police, and slave-labor camps.

George had the "privilege" of working his way through school by cleaning bathrooms.

Quotation marks can let your readers know that a group or a person you are writing about uses words in a special sense.

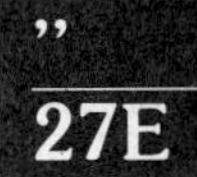

For them, getting "saved" is clearly only the first step.
—FRANCES FITZGERALD

The "core curriculum" has now been in effect for several years.

27E Avoid apologetic quotation marks.

Experienced writers rarely enclose slang or clichés in quotation marks, but inexperienced writers sometimes do so as if to show that such words or expressions do not belong in their writing. They believe that they are somehow excused if they show readers that they know better. In fact, such quotation marks only mark you as inexperienced and do not contribute to good prose.

People in California are "laid back."

You can accomplish great things only if you "keep your nose to the grindstone."

I thought he was "cute."

When you are tempted to use apologetic quotation marks, take time to think of a better way of expressing yourself.

People in California pride themselves in living for pleasure without taking anything too seriously.

You can accomplish great things only if you pay attention to what you are doing.

I thought he was attractive.

Exercise 27.2 In some of the following sentences, quotation marks are incorrectly used. Correct any incorrect usages, and put a check by those sentences where the quotation marks are used in the right way.

1. "Traditional Principles of Rhetoric" is the title of a chapter in Kenneth Burke's book *A Rhetoric of Motives.*
2. "Gee whiz," he said, "I coud rap with you all night long."
3. When I waited to do my term paper until the night before it was due, I was really "up the creek without a paddle."
4. "Sweet Baby James" is the title of a song James Taylor sings.
5. I wanted to know if I could bring the "kids" to the party.
6. She was "put off" by my reaction to her paper.
7. "To His Coy Mistress" is a celebrated poem by Andrew Marvell.
8. Most "utopian" communities emphasize rigid conformity, hard work, and puritanical ethics.
9. "Lochinvar" is a rousing poem by Sir Walter Scott.
10. The word "trees" can be both a noun and a verb.
11. Most of the students here are "laid back" and "cool," but some of them are "nerds."

28
Other Marks of Punctuation

28A Use the dash to set off words, phrases, and sometimes whole sentences so that they receive special emphasis.

Think of the dash as a very strong pause intended to give a special emphasis to what follows—and sometimes to what comes immediately before.

> A Wisconsin man traveling on horseback had the lower parts of his boots—brand-new ones, be it noted—eaten by wolves, but managed to save his toes.
>
> —RICHARD ERDOES

> I think this is the most extraordinary collection of human talent, of human knowledge, that has ever been gathered at the White House—with the possible exception of when Thomas Jefferson dined alone.
>
> —JOHN F. KENNEDY

On the typewriter the dash is made with *two* unspaced hyphens, and there is no space between the dash and the words on each side of it. Handwritten and typeset dashes are single, unbroken lines about as wide as a capital M.

```
Beer, cheese, and brevity--these are the marks of
a good study session in the dorm.
```

Often the dash is used to set off nouns placed for special emphasis at the beginning of a sentence and then summarized by a pronoun after the dash, as you see in the sentence above. The dash can sometimes set off an independent clause within a sentence. In such sentences, the content of the set-off independent clause is not essential to the main assertion of the sentence. It is added information.

Grant had three divisions in line—reinforcements came up the Cumberland in transports, just behind Andrew Foote's gunboats—and he had them strung out in a long semicircle facing the Confederate trenches.

—BRUCE CATTON

[The pair of dashes sets off the independent clause starting with the word *reinforcements* and ending with the word *gunboats.* The main sentence can stand without this inserted clause, which adds interesting but nonessential information.]

Remember that overuse of the dash can distract your readers. You should use the dash only for special emphasis; if you try to emphasize everything, your readers will find the tactic tedious.

28B Use the colon to link independent clauses, to introduce direct quotations and lists, and to set off words and phrases at the end of a sentence. Use the colon also as standard punctuation for Bible verses and for other specialized forms.

: 28B

The colon links independent clauses when you want to emphasize the clause that follows the colon:

Women in Switzerland have an overwhelming political disadvantage: they cannot vote.

[Some writers might use a semicolon here instead of the colon. But the colon indicates that the second clause is an explanation of the first, a statement that makes the first clause more explicit and clear.]

You can use a colon to introduce a direct quotation:

"Don't speak of it," she said in a reciting voice and choosing her words sadly and carefully: "It was a stroke."

—V. S. PRITCHETT

[The colon before *It was a stroke* emphasizes the close relation between the two quotations and the long clause between them.]

Later she recalled the hours Faulkner spent helping her to recover hope: "He kept me alive," she said.

—DAVID MINTER

[A colon is more formal than a comma. The use of the colon before this direct quotation separates the independent clauses. The quotation amplifies the first clause.]

To introduce block quotations, you should use a colon:

> Dickens had a contempt for lazy people. His heroes and his heroines are always industrious, always active, always in motion. His worst characters are those who pretend to do honest labor and don't, or those who lie about, waiting for others to wait on them. Here is the way he introduces Mrs. Witterly in *Nicholas Nickleby:*
>
> > The lady had an air of sweet insipidity, and a face of engaging paleness; there was a faded look about her, and about the furniture, and about the house altogether. She was reclining on the sofa in such a very unstudied attitude that she might have been taken for an actress all ready for the first scene in a ballet, and only waiting for the drop curtain to go up.

Colons also serve to introduce itemized lists:

> During its first four years the Virginia venture had failed to meet three basic needs: political stability, economic prosperity, and peaceful Indian relations.
>
> —ALDEN T. VAUGHAN

[The words *three basic needs* imply itemization, and the colon precedes the listing that follows.]

: 28B

The colon *cannot* be used to introduce a simple series.

Incorrect

> During its first four years the Virginia venture had failed to meet: political stability, economic prosperity, and peaceful Indian relations.

[The colon cannot interrupt an independent clause or a sentence. The colon used before a list must follow an independent clause. If you replace the colon with a period and eliminate the following list, the sentence should still make grammatical sense.]

Correct

> During its first four years the Virginia venture had failed to meet three basic needs.

[The list, including the words *political stability, economic prosperity, and peaceful Indian relations,* has been eliminated. The remaining sentence is grammatically complete.]

Note that some writers still follow the old custom of capitalizing the first letter of the first word after a colon if a complete sentence follows the colon.

He is kind: Innumerable unknowns in dire need have received financial help from Sinatra.

—Isobel Silden

But most writers capitalize the first letter in the word following the colon only when they are writing titles. (A proper noun is, of course, capitalized wherever it appears. See 30B.)

Doing Without: Meeting the Energy Crisis in the 1980s

Colons intervene between Bible chapters and verses:

Young writers should take Proverbs 12:1 as a motto.

To indicate the time of day, use a colon between the hour and the minutes:

He woke up at 6:30 in the morning.

Colons follow salutations in business letters:

Dear Mr. Bush:

28C Use parentheses to set off information that breaks the flow of your thought within a sentence or a paragraph.

Parentheses enclose material that is not as important as material set off by commas or dashes.

The first money you get for a book will probably be your advance; as a rule, half of that is paid when you sign your contract (or as soon thereafter as the legal department and the accounting department fill out the appropriate forms), and the other half comes due when you deliver a satisfactory manuscript.

—Judith Applebaum and Nancy Evans

At another barrier a seaman held back Kathy Gilnagh, Kate Mullins, and Kate Murphy. (On the *Titanic* everyone seemed to be named Katherine.)

—Walter Lord

Note that when parentheses enclose a whole sentence, a period comes after the sentence but before the final parenthesis, as in the example above. A sentence that appears within parentheses *within a sentence* is neither capitalized nor closed with a period.

John Henry (he was the man with the forty-pound hammer) was a hero to miners fearing the loss of their jobs to machines.

But a question mark or an exclamation point may follow a parenthetical sentence within a sentence.

John Henry (did he really swing a forty-pound hammer?) was a hero to miners fearing the loss of their jobs to machines.

John Henry (he swung a forty-pound hammer!) was a hero to miners fearing the loss of their jobs to machines.

Parentheses are used to enclose many numbers within a text. In some forms of annotation (see 33K), parentheses enclose page numbers of a book referred to throughout the paper.

Stevens writes that the demands of their offices turn the best university presidents into machines (43).

Carmichael says that the argument Stevens makes is nonsense because (1) university presidents don't work as well as machines, (2) university presidents don't do any real work at all, and (3) universities would be better off if they were run by faculty committees.

Note that forcing readers to wade through many parenthetical numbers is usually distracting. In the example above, the numbers within parentheses could be left out, and the statements could be set off by commas, making the passage more readable.

28D Use brackets to set off material within quoted matter that is not part of the quotation.

Samuel Eliot Morison has written, "This passage has attracted a good deal of scorn to the Florentine mariner [Verrazzano], but without justice."

[In this sentence, a writer is quoting Morison. But the sentence from Morison does not include the name of the "Florentine mariner." The writer adds the name—Verrazzano—but places it in brackets so readers will know the identity of the mariner Morison is talking about.]

Sometimes material in brackets provides an explanation or a correction for something that is quoted.

Vasco da Gama's man wrote in 1487, "The body of the church [it was not a church but a Hindu shrine] is as large as a monastery."

[The brackets in this example correct a mistake made by one of the early sailors who went to India with Vasco da Gama. The material within the brackets comes from the writer of the essay, who has quoted the report made by a member of da Gama's crew. If that material were in parentheses, readers might think that it was in the original source, and they would be confused.]

Brackets are also used when you must change a quotation slightly to make it fit the style or grammar of your own sentence.

A Source to Be Quoted

I went back to the country and farmed a crop of tobacco with my dad that next year. For all the work I put in I didn't make half as much as I'd been making at the factory, so, after market closed, I wandered back to town and started looking for another job.

—ANN BANKS

The Source Quoted in a Paper

[ ]
28D

Jim Wells came off the farm to work in a cigarette factory in North Carolina during the depression. He was fired because he hit a foreman who mistreated him, and, he said, "I went back to the country and farmed a crop of tobacco with my dad that next year [but] I didn't make half as much as I'd been making at the factory." The only thing he could do was to go back to the city and look for another job.

[The bracketed word *but* eliminates the need for an ellipsis (three spaced periods), although several words, *For all the work I put in,* have been cut out of the quotation. The brackets show that the writer has changed the quotation to fit the style of the paper that uses the material.]

Brackets may enclose the word *sic* after a piece of correctly quoted information that a reader might believe had slipped into the text erroneously.

The dean said, "Those kids is [*sic*] going to get kicked out of school for saying I don't know no [*sic*] grammar."

[The *sic* in brackets shows that the dean did, in fact, make these errors in grammar.]

Brackets are frequently used, as they are in this book, to enclose editorial notes, page numbers, or other information inserted in a text. In formal essays they should be used sparingly.

28E As a rule, use the slash only to divide lines of poetry written as a quotation within a sentence (see 27A).

Sophocles wrote of the uncertainty of human knowledge: "No man can judge that rough unknown or trust in second sight/For wisdom changes hands among the wise."

Occasionally the slash is used to show that something happened over a couple of calendar years.

The book sold well in 1976/77.

But it is usually better to write this:

The book sold well in 1976 and 1977.

The slash is sometimes used nowadays to substitute for the conjunction *or.*

The course was offered credit/noncredit.

The winner will be chosen by lot, and he/she will drive a new car home.

Most writers, however, consider such usage awkward. It is usually better to rephrase the sentence.

Students who took the course received no grades. If they satisfied the requirements, they got credit; if they did not, they received no penalty.

The winner, to be chosen by lot, will drive a new car home.

[For more on he/she, his/her, see Chapter 21, "Avoiding Sexist Language."]

28F Use three spaced periods, called an *ellipsis,* to show that words have been omitted from quotations.

To shorten a passage you are quoting, you may choose to leave out some words in the quotation. To show readers that you have left out some words, use ellipsis marks.

Quotation
"In the nineteenth century, railroads, lacing their way across continents, reaching into the heart of every major city in Europe and America, and bringing a new romance to travel, added to the unity of nations and fueled the nationalist fires already set burning by the French Revolution and the wars of Napoleon."

Quotation Used with Ellipsis Marks

> In his account of nineteenth-century society, Wilkins credited railroad building with increasing nationalism when he wrote that "railroads . . . added to the unity of nations and fueled the nationalist fires already set burning by the French Revolution and the wars of Napoleon."

[The ellipsis shows that the second writer has left some words out of the original source.]

Most writers do not use ellipsis marks to indicate that words have been left out at the beginning or the end of a quotation. Academic writers occasionally use ellipsis marks to show omissions at the beginning or at the end of quotations, but such usage is rare. The primary function of the ellipsis is to show that something has been left out of the middle of a quotation.

Ellipsis marks may be used at the end of a sentence if you mean to leave a thought hanging, either in your own prose or in something you are quoting. Such a usage suggests that you are not sure how the thought might be ended.

In the following passage, the writer—Dick Gregory—reports some thoughts he was having as a child.

> Oh God, I'm scared. I wish I could die right now with the feeling I have because I know Momma's going to make me mad and I'm going to make her mad, and me and Presley's gonna fight. . . .
>
> "Richard, you get in here and put your coat on. Get in here or I'll whip you."

[Gregory is saying that the consequences of all this are so unpredictable that he cannot even try to state them. Therefore, he ends his sentence with ellipsis marks.]

You should always use ellipsis marks honestly. That is, you should never distort a writer's meaning by leaving out words in the material you quote. The ellipsis should serve *only* as a means of shortening a quotation, never as a device for changing its fundamental meaning or for creating emphasis where none exists in the original.

Exercise 28.1

1. Write three sentences using the dash and three using parentheses. What difference, if any, do you find in the effects of using the two punctuation marks?
2. Go to the periodical reading room of your library, and look at *Time, Newsweek, Sports Illustrated, Popular Mechanics,* or *The New York*

Times Magazine. Find sentences that use parentheses and sentences that use the dash. Copy as many of them down as you can find. What can you say about how these punctuation marks are used?

3. Write a paragraph in which you quote something and insert material within brackets in the quotation. Explain to your class what you have done.

Exercise 28.2 Explain the use of the punctuation marks in color in each of the following examples. Is the punctuation appropriate to the meaning? What other punctuation might serve as an alternative?

1. An air-cooled engine requires no antifreeze in winter (an advantage), but it must be fairly small for the cooling to work (a disadvantage).
2. Diesel engines are fuel-efficient and durable—but they are expensive to manufacture.
3. The Ford Motor Company paid workers five dollars a day (people said Henry Ford was undermining capitalism by paying so much) to build the Model T on assembly lines before World War I.
4. The rotary gasoline engine (the first popular model sold in the United States was the Japanese Mazda) was smooth, quiet, and durable, but it burned 15 percent more fuel than conventional engines—a reason for its swift demise.
5. Mechanical automobile brakes operated with springs, levers, and the physical strength of the driver—a strength that might not be sufficient to stop a car hurtling down the highway at forty miles per hour.
6. A high administration official said today, "All we can do now [to decrease the consumption of oil in the United States] is to let prices rise until it hurts to fill a gas tank."
7. Mr. Hatch told reporters, "When you see an antique car rolling down the interstate, it looks like a lot of fun [but] you are in fact looking at lethal danger."
8. Leslie Fiedler wrote, "The novel proper could not be launched until . . . the Seducer and the Pure Maiden were brought face to face in a ritual combat designed to end in marriage or death; the form and its mythology were born together, in the works of Samuel Richardson."

- 28G

28G Use the hyphen to divide a word at the end of a line only when such division is absolutely necessary. (See 29E for the use of hyphens to form compound words.)

Try to avoid breaking words at the ends of lines because such divisions slow your readers down. Never divide the last word on a page. Leave yourself wide margins and you will rarely have to divide a word.

When you must break a word, put a hyphen at the end of the first line only, and not at the start of the next line. Although the general rule is to divide words only between syllables, not every word can be divided according to this rule. If you are unsure about how to break a word into syllables, consult your dictionary (see 22B, section 1). The following pointers will help you to divide words correctly.

1. Never divide one-syllable words.

Incorrect

None of us at the dean's luncheon thought that the dean would arrive in tattered jeans and a torn undershirt.

Correct

None of us at the dean's luncheon thought that the dean would
arrive in tattered jeans and a torn undershirt.

None of us at the dean's luncheon thought that the dean
would arrive in tattered jeans and a torn undershirt.

[The one-syllable word *would* has no natural break and cannot be divided. Fit the word in on the end of the first line, or write the entire word at the beginning of the second line.]

- 28G

2. Never divide a word if the division leaves only one letter at the end of a line or only one or two letters at the beginning of a line. Avoid breaking words like *hap·py, could·n't, read·er, o·pen, light·ly, hat·ed,* and so on.

Incorrect

Naomi Lee Fong, who graduates today, never felt so happy in her life.

Correct

Naomi Lee Fong, who graduates today, never felt so happy
in her life.

Naomi Lee Fong, who graduates today, never felt so
happy in her life.

3. Divide compound words into the words that make them up, or at the hyphen if the word contains a hyphen. Compound words like *hardworking, rattlesnake, bookcases,* and *paperwork* should be broken only between the words that form them: *hard-working, rattle-snake, book-cases, paper-work.* Compound words that already have hyphens, like *brother-in-law, self-denial, ex-convict,* and *anti-Semitic,* are broken after the hyphens only.

Incorrect

She loves being a detective, but she hates the paperwork.

Correct

She loves being a detective but she hates the paperwork.

Incorrect

I gave my old fishing rod to my brother-in-law, and he will sell it at his yard sale.

Correct

I gave my old fishing rod to my brother-
in-law, and he will sell it at his yard sale.

4. When two consonants come between vowels in a word you are dividing, make the split between the two consonants. Do not split the two consonants if the division does not reflect pronunciation. In the following words, for example, make the split where the dot appears:

   ter·ror   run·ning
   shel·ter   bril·liant

   However in a word like *respire,* you would have to divide the word after the prefix *re* and not between the *s* and the *p*, because the word is pronounced *re·spire* and not *res·pire.*

5. Avoid confusing word divisions. Sometimes part of a divided word forms a shorter word that can mislead your reader. In such cases, write the complete word or break the word where it will not cause confusion. The following examples show some misleading divisions and some possible alternatives.

Divisions to avoid	**Possible alternatives**
a-toll	atoll
at-tire	attire
bar-row	barrow
fat-uous	fatuous
his-torian	histor-ian
im-pugn	impugn
jew-elry	jewel-ry
mud-dled	muddled
pig-mentation	pigmen-tation, pigmenta-tion

- 28G

PART SIX
Mechanics

29 Spelling

Spelling is one of the chief signs of literacy. If you misspell words, your readers may understand you, but they will be less likely to take your thoughts seriously.

Teachers sometimes ignore misspellings, and even when they mark them, they may not count off for them. After all, your teacher has several months to get to know you and your work, and over a long period, misspelling may seem less important than the good things you do in a class and in your writing.

But in the public world of business and the professions, the people you write to are often in a hurry; they may not know you; and they have to read and judge your work quickly. If you misspell several words in a letter of application for a job, your reader may assume that you are a careless person or that you do not take your application seriously. There may be dozens of candidates for the same opening, and an application with misspellings gives the reader an excuse to reject it quickly. If you are writing a memo to your boss or to a committee, misspelled words in your memo may give the impression that your thoughts are as slapdash as your writing. In short, frequent or even occasional misspellings in your writing can make people believe that you are careless or ignorant, and if that happens, you will have to work twice as hard to make them take you and your thoughts seriously.

Here are some rules to help you toward better spelling. The rest of this chapter on spelling will expand on these rules and will give you some tips to make following them easier.

1. Make yourself realize the importance of good spelling, and resolve to spell correctly.
2. Write down in a notebook all the words you misspell. Writing the word over and over again when you realize you have made a mistake will help fix the correct spelling in your mind and in your fingers. Good spelling is a habit of both mind and hand.

3. Try to group your errors. Misspellings often fall into patterns—errors with prefixes, with suffixes, with plurals, and so on.
4. Pronounce words carefully. Many people misspell words because they pronounce them incorrectly.
5. Learn the rules that generally hold for spelling, and learn the exceptions to those rules. Most of the rules have only a few exceptions, and by learning these words, you will make the rules themselves stick better in your mind.
6. Proofread your writing carefully. Misspellings creep into the prose of the best of writers when they are in a hurry, when they are thinking ahead to their next thought as they write something down, or when they do not wish to break their train of thought to look up a troublesome word.
7. Use your dictionary frequently when you proofread your work. Whenever you doubt the correctness of a word you have spelled, look it up. Writing continually and using a dictionary continually are two excellent ways to become a good speller.

29A Read and pronounce words carefully.

Some common words are frequently misspelled because people misread them or mispronounce them. Of course, pronunciations vary from region to region, and no list can include all mispronunciations that lead to spelling trouble. But if you study the following list, you can train your eye and your ear to spot the parts of common words that often cause spelling errors.

accident**al**ly	**NOT**	acciden**tl**y
ari**thm**etic	**NOT**	arith**e**metic
athletics	**NOT**	ath**e**letics
can**di**date	**NOT**	ca**nni**date
cor**por**ation	**NOT**	co**per**ation
disas**tr**ous	**NOT**	disas**ter**ous
dro**wned**	**NOT**	drownede**d**
every**y**body	**NOT**	**ever**body
every**y**thing	**NOT**	**ever**thing
Feb**ru**ary	**NOT**	Feb**u**ary
gen**eral**ly	**NOT**	**genr**ally or gen**erly**
gover**n**ment	**NOT**	gover**m**ent

hei**ght**	**NOT**	heigh**th**
hun**dr**eds	**NOT**	hun**der**eds
irr**el**evant	**NOT**	irr**eve**lant
la**bora**tory	**NOT**	la**bra**tory or la**ber**tory
li**br**ary	**NOT**	li**berry**
light**n**ing	**NOT**	ligh**ten**ing
lit**era**ture	**NOT**	**litra**ture or li**ter**ture
ma**the**matics	**NOT**	ma**thm**atics
mischiev**ous**	**NOT**	mischiev**i**ous
op**tim**ist	**NOT**	op**tom**ist
peremptory	**NOT**	**pre**emptory
performance	**NOT**	**pre**formance
perspiration	**NOT**	**pres**peration
prescription	**NOT**	**per**scription
production	**NOT**	**per**duction
pro**gram**	**NOT**	pro**grum**
pub**licly**	**NOT**	publi**cal**ly
rep**re**sent	**NOT**	re**per**sent
stren**gth**	**NOT**	stren**th**
stu**d**ious	**NOT**	stud**jous**
temper**a**ture	**NOT**	tem**per**ture, tem**pra**ture, or tem**perchoor**
won**drous**	**NOT**	won**der**ous

sp 29A

Be especially careful of those words that sound nearly alike but have different meanings and different spellings. (See also the Glossary of Usage.)

Affect/Effect

The new museum would *affect* our plans for acquiring new paintings. ["to influence," a verb]

His speech did not have the *effect* he hoped for; the audience hated it. ["a result, a consequence," usually a noun, although it can also be a verb meaning "to cause"]

Capital/Capitol

The *capital* of Kansas is Topeka.
[The location of the seat of government]

The legislature meets in the *capitol* building, which is located on a hill overlooking the city.

Waist/Waste

His *waist* was the same size as it was when he was in the army twenty years ago.

Some villages in the third world could live comfortably on the *waste* thrown out after an average weekend in a college dining hall.

Some common plurals may be misspelled because they are mispronounced. This misspelling is especially common in the plurals of words ending in *ist* or *est.* The plural of *scientist* is *scientists.* The final combination *ts* sounds like the *tz* in *Ritz* or the *ts* in *fights.* Because this *ts* is difficult for some people to pronounce, they often leave it off, thinking almost unconsciously that the *s* sound in *ist* or *est* is sufficient to make the plural. But the plural of such words always requires a final *s.* So remember:

The plural of *humanist* is *humanists.*

The plural of *nest* is *nests.*

The plural of *socialist* is *socialists.*

The plural of *biologist* is *biologists.*

The plural of *racist* is *racists.*

Other words having a difficult *s* sound in the final syllable sometimes trouble writers forming the plural, but the rule is the same: the final *s* is necessary to make the noun plural.

disc/discs, rasp/rasps, desk/desks

Since words like these are much less common, they give much less trouble than words ending in *est* and *ist.*

29B Learn as many principles of spelling as you can, and always use a dictionary when in doubt.

Some principles of English spelling are so generally true that learning them will help you be a better speller.

1 Consider the previous letter and the sound of the word when you are deciding between the combinations *ei* and *ie*.

When these letters sound like the *ee* in *see,* usually place the *i* before *e* except after *c.*

believe, relieve, grief, chief, yield, wield
receive, deceive, ceiling, conceit

But there are exceptions:

species, seize, caffeine, codeine

When the sound is like *ay* in *bay* or *May,* the spelling is nearly always *ei.*

neigh, feign, neighbor

As for most other words with different sounds, memorize the spelling:

stein, weird, pietism, sierra, pierce, pier, pie, pied, fiery, sieve, foreign, height, forfeit

Exercise 29.1 Some of the following are misspelled. Spell them correctly. Put a check by each word in the list that is spelled correctly.

1. freindly	**7.** ceiling
2. weight	**8.** height
3. sieve	**9.** frieghten
4. beleif	**10.** wierd
5. beir	**11.** conceited
6. believing	**12.** concievable

sp
29B

Exercise 29.2 Fill in the blanks in the following words with *ei* or *ie* to make the words correct. Tell why you make your choices.

1. s ____ zure	**7.** d ____ gn	**13.** s ____ ge
2. rec ____ pt	**8.** hyg ____ ne	**14.** conc ____ t
3. perc ____ vable	**9.** th ____ f	**15.** dec ____ t
4. b ____ ge	**10.** fr ____ ze	**16.** perc ____ ve
5. r ____ n	**11.** l ____ n	**17.** conc ____ ve
6. v ____ n	**12.** p ____ ce	

2 Before the suffix -*ing*, nearly always drop a final silent *e* from the root word.

force/forcing, surprise/surprising, manage/managing, hope/hoping, scare/scaring, come/coming, pave/paving, become/becoming, fume/fuming

There are only a few exceptions to this rule:

dye/dyeing [To avoid confusion with *dying.*]
age/ageing [But *aging* is becoming common.]
shoe/shoeing [To avoid mispronunciation and confusion with *showing.*]
hoe/hoeing [To avoid mispronunciation.]

3 A final, silent *e* on a root word is always dropped before the suffix *-ible.*

force/forcible

4 Though the silent *e* of the root is usually dropped before the ending *-able,* the *e* is retained often enough to make this principle uncertain. It is best to memorize the words.

Drop *e* and add *-able:*

observe/observable, advise/advisable, move/movable (sometimes moveable), argue/arguable, debate/debatable

Do not drop the *e* when adding *-able*:

manage/manageable, peace/peaceable, notice/noticeable, change/changeable, embrace/embraceable

5 Keep the final *y* on the root word or change it to *i* according to the nature of the root and the nature of the suffix.

Keep a final *y* on the root word when adding *-ing:*

study/studying, rally/rallying, enjoy/enjoying, cry/crying, ready/readying, steady/steadying, lay/laying

When a final *y* follows a consonant in the root word, change the *y* to *i* before adding an ending other than *-ing.*

merry—merriment, merriest, merrier
happy—happier, happiness, happiest
rally—rallies, rallied, rallier
supply—supplier, supplies, supplied
pity—pitiless, pitiable, pitiful

mercy—merciful, merciless

kingly—kingliness

ugly—uglier, ugliest, ugliness

When a final *y* follows a vowel in the root word, keep the *y* when adding an *s* to make the plural of a noun or the third person singular of a verb.

valley/valleys, defray/defrays, delay/delays, dismay/dismays, enjoy/enjoys, toy/toys, ploy/ploys

The past tense of verbs ending in a final *y* preceded by a vowel is usually made by keeping the final *y* and by adding the suffix *-ed*.

play/played, dismay/dismayed, enjoy/enjoyed

But there are important exceptions:

pay/paid, say/said, lay/laid

Exercise 29.3 Add the suffix indicated for each of the following words. Be sure to change the spelling of the root word when such a change is appropriate.

1. advance + ing
2. highboy + s
3. learn + able
4. horrify + ing
5. quote + able
6. sally + s
7. sense + ible
8. pray + ed
9. quality + s
10. solicit + ing
11. fancy + ful
12. construct + ed
13. tally + ing
14. digress + ing

6 Spell correctly words formed by adding a suffix that begins with a vowel to a root that ends with a consonant. These suffixes are *-ing, -er, -est, -ed, -ence, -ance, -ible, -able,* and *-ened.*

With most words of one syllable ending in a consonant immediately preceded by a vowel, double the final consonant.

grip/gripping, quip/quipped, stun/stunning, quit/quitting, plan/planned, sad/saddest, scar/scarring

If the root word ends with two consecutive consonants or with a consonant preceded by two consecutive vowels, do not double the final consonant before suffixes that begin with vowels.

tight/tighter, stoop/stooping, straight/straightest, sing/singer, strait/straitened, deep/deepened, creep/creeping, crawl/crawler

If the root word has more than one syllable, and if the accent of the root falls on the last syllable, usually double the final consonant.

occur/occurrence, refer/referred, rebut/rebutting, concur/concurring

But if the final consonant of the root is preceded by a consonant or by two consecutive vowels, *or* if the accent shifts from the final syllable of the root when the suffix is added, don't double the final consonant.

depart/departing [There are two final consonants in the root.]

refer/reference [The accent shifts from the last syllable of the root when the suffix is added.]

repair/repairing [The final consonant of the root is preceded by two consecutive vowels.]

ferment/fermenting [The root ends with two consecutive consonants.]

This rule sounds so complicated that you may think it better to memorize the spelling of all these words rather than to memorize the rule. But give the rule a try; it does work!

7 Add most standard prefixes without changing the spelling of the prefix or the root word. Before root words beginning with vowels, prefixes ending in vowels sometimes have a hyphen added, although the hyphen is tending to disappear in such forms (see 29E, section 4).

appear/disappear

eminent/preeminent

operate/cooperate

usual/unusual

create/procreate

create/re-create [to create again]

creation/recreation [recreation meaning to refresh oneself by doing something for the pleasure of it]

satisfy/dissatisfy

Exercise 29.4 Use the rules you have learned to add the indicated suffixes to the root words below. Explain why you change some roots to add the suffix and why you leave other roots unchanged. The exercise will help you most if you discuss your choices with other members of the class.

1. attend + ance
2. din + ed
3. strip + ing
4. dine + ing
5. mar + ed
6. despair + ed
7. bob + ing
8. accept + ance
9. dip + er
10. map + ing
11. submit + ing
12. reckon + ed
13. detest + able
14. soon + est
15. omit + ed
16. silly + est
17. depend + ence
18. prefer + ing
19. mad + est
20. star + ing
21. confer + ence
22. hop + ed
23. disdain + ed
24. drown + ing
25. pretend + ed

29C Learn the spelling of the regular and irregular forms of the plural.

1 With most nouns, form the plural simply by adding *s*:

grove/groves, boat/boats, cobra/cobras, bank/banks, scientist/scientists, moralist/moralists, gripe/gripes, gasp/gasps, disc/discs

The plurals of acronyms are formed by adding *s* to the acronym:

It can be said that there have been two *FBIs*—the one before the death of J. Edgar Hoover and the one that came later on.

Most nations believe that they cannot do without their *KGBs* and their *CIAs*.

sp 29C

The plurals of years are formed by adding *s*:

The *1890s* were popularly called "The Gay Nineties" because of the extravagant pleasures of the rich during that decade.

[Occasionally writers use an apostrophe plus *s* ('s) to make the plurals of acronyms, numbers, and dates. See 26C.]

2 When the singular of a noun ends in *s*, *x*, *ch*, or *sh*, add *es* to form the plural:

kiss/kisses, Marx/the Marxes, Mr. Jones/the Joneses, church/churches, dish/dishes

A few words ending in a vowel and an *x* may change when the plural is formed.

appendix/appendices, index/indices, vortex/vortices

But increasingly writers are making the plurals of these words simply by adding *es*:

appendixes, indexes, vortexes

3 If a noun ends in a *y* preceded by a consonant, change the *y* to *i* and add *es* to form the plural; if the final *y* is preceded by a vowel, keep the *y* and add an *s* to make the plural.

beauty/beauties, sally/sallies, glory/glories, city/cities, country/countries, destiny/destinies, crudity/crudities, ray/rays, boy/boys, joy/joys, valley/valleys

4 With nouns that end in *o* in the singular, form the plural by adding *s* or *es*.

Fortunately, nouns that end in *o* in the singular are so rare that you can memorize the plural forms of each without much trouble.

hero/heroes, solo/solos, tomato/tomatoes, tyro/tyros, potato/potatoes, hypo/hypos, flamingo/flamingos or flamingoes, piano/pianos

5 With some nouns ending in *f*, change the final *f* to a *v* and add *es* to make the plural. With some nouns ending in an *f* and a silent *e*, also change the *f* to a *v*.

leaf/leaves, hoof/hooves, beef/beeves, life/lives, wife/wives, self/selves

Here again modern practice favors the simpler form of making plurals, merely adding a final *s* to some of these words:

hoof/hoofs, beef/beefs

6 With many hyphenated words that begin with a noun, form the plural by adding *s* or *es* to the first noun:

mother-in-law/mothers-in-law, father-in-law/fathers-in-law, court-martial/courts-martial

7 Memorize irregular plurals of nouns.

Some nouns have irregular plurals that correspond to no rules and that must be memorized individually. Fortunately, most of these nouns are such familiar everyday words that the irregular plurals are not difficult.

child/children, man/men, woman/women, tooth/teeth

8 Drop the singular ending *-um* or *-on* and add the plural *-a* to form the plural for many words that come from Greek or Latin.

addendum/addenda, criterion/criteria, datum/data, medium/media, phenomenon/phenomena

Some editors and writers now use *data* as a singular, but the preferred practice is still to insist that *data* should take a plural verb: "The data *are* clear on this point; the pass/fail course has become outdated by events."

Like *data,* the word *media* should always be in the plural.

On the other hand, the word *agenda* is now fully accepted as a singular form.

A few English words with Latin roots ending in *us* have plural forms made by changing the *us* to *i*.

alumnus/alumni, tumulus/tumuli, cumulus/cumuli, hippopotamus/hippopotami or hippopotamuses, calculus/calculi, cirrus/cirri

Even fewer words with Latin roots ending in *a* have plural forms made by changing the *a* to *ae*:

alumna/alumnae

sp 29C

Exercise 29.5 Form the plural for each of the following words. Check yourself by the dictionary when you have finished. (See Chapter 22 for a discussion of how to use the dictionary.)

1. mess
2. harp
3. disco
4. arch
5. potato
6. hello
7. dodo
8. grief
9. fish
10. buffalo
11. elegy
12. harpy
13. phlox
14. rest
15. flamingo
16. handful
17. day
18. valley
19. father-in-law
20. sheep
21. cow
22. garnish
23. harpist
24. rabbi
25. prophecy
26. symposium
27. rasp
28. fascist
29. scientist
30. musicologist
31. rest
32. risk
33. critic
34. soprano
35. locus

29D Use spelling lists to help improve your spelling.

The following lists of words misspelled in student papers were compiled a few years ago by New York State. In the examination of over 31,000 misspelled words gathered by English teachers throughout the country, it was found that the following 407 words were misspelled more frequently than others. These words are arranged below in descending order of difficulty. Study the lists carefully. It will help if you have someone read the words aloud to you and if you try to spell them without looking at them.

I. Words and Word Groups Misspelled 100 Times or More.

believe
belief

benefit
benefited
beneficial

choose
chose
choice

definite
definitely
definition
define

description
describe

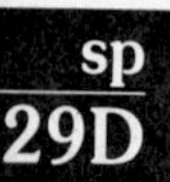

environment

exist
existence
existent

its
it's

lose
losing

necessary
unnecessary

occasion

occur
occurred
occurring
occurrence

perform
performance

personal
personnel

precede

principle
principal

privilege

professor
profession

receive
receiving

referring

separate
separation

similar

success
succeed
succession

than
then

their
they're
there

too
two
to

write
writing
writer

II. Words and Word Groups Misspelled 50 to 99 Times.

accommodate

achieve
achievement

acquire

affect
affective

all right*

among

analyze
analysis

apparent

argument
arguing

began
begin
beginner
beginning

* Although the spelling *alright* is also accepted by some dictionaries, it is listed as nonstandard usage by others. Many college teachers regard *alright* as a misspelling.

busy
business

category

comparative
conscience
conscientious

conscious

consistent
consistency

control
controlled
controlling

controversy
controversial

criticism
criticize

decision
decided

disastrous

embarrass

equipped
equipment

excellent
excellence

experience

explanation

fascinate

forty
fourth

grammar
grammatically

height

imagine
imaginary
imagination

immediate
immediately

intelligence
intelligent

interest

interpretation
interpret

led

loneliness
lonely

marriage

Negro
Negroes

noticeable
noticing

origin
original

passed
past

possess
possession

prefer
preferred

prejudice

prevalent

probably

proceed
procedure

prominent

psychology
psychoanalysis
psychopathic
psychosomatic

pursue

realize
really

repetition

rhythm

sense

shining

studying

surprise

thorough

tries
tried

useful
useless
using

varies
various

weather
whether

sp
29D

III. Words and Word Groups Misspelled 40 to 49 Times.

accept
acceptance
acceptable
accepting

accident
accidentally

acquaint
acquaintance

across

aggressive

appear
appearance

article

athlete
athletic

attended
attendant
attendance

challenge

character
characteristic
characterized

coming

convenience
convenient

difference
different

disappoint

discipline
disciple

dominant
predominant

effect

exaggerate

foreign
foreigners

fundamental
fundamentally

government
governor

hero
heroine
heroic
heroes

humor
humorist
humorous

hypocrisy
hypocrite

incident
incidentally

independent
independence

liveliest
livelihood
liveliness
lives

mere

operate

opinion

opportunity

paid

particular

philosophy

planned

pleasant

possible

practical

prepare

quantity

quiet

recommend

ridicule
ridiculous

speech

sponsor

summary
summed

suppose

technique

transferred

unusual
usually

villain

woman

sp
29D

IV. Words and Word Groups Misspelled 30 to 39 Times.

advice
advise

approach
approaches

author
authority
authoritative

basis
basically

before

careless
careful

carrying
carried

carries
carrier

conceive
conceivable

condemn

consider
considerably

continuous

curiosity
curious

dependent

desirability
desire

efficient
efficiency

entertain

extremely

familiar

finally

friendliness
friend

fulfill

further

happiness

hindrance

influential
influence
knowledge
laboratory
maintenance
ninety
oppose
opponent
optimism
parallel
permanent

permit
physical
piece
propaganda
propagate
relieve
religion
response
satire
significance
suppress

temperament
therefore
together
undoubtedly
weird
where
whose
you're

V. Words and Word Groups Misspelled 20 to 29 Times.

accompanying
accompanies
accompanied
accompaniment
accomplish
accustom
actually
actuality
actual
adolescence
adolescent
against
amateur
amount
appreciate
appreciation
approximate
arouse
arousing
attack
attitude
boundary

Britain
Britannica
capitalism
certain
capital
certainly
chief
clothes
completely
counselor
counsel
council
curriculum
dealt
despair
disease
divide
divine
especially
excitable
exercise

expense
experiment
fallacy
fantasy
fantasies
favorite
fictitious
field
financier
financially
forward
guarantee
guaranteed
guidance
guiding
hear
here
huge
hungry
hungrily
hunger

sp 29D

ignorance
ignorant

indispensable

intellect

interfere
interference

interrupt

involve

irrelevant

laborer
laboriously
labor

laid

later

leisure
leisurely

length
lengthening

license

likeness
likely
likelihood

luxury

magazine

magnificent
magnificence

maneuver

mathematics

meant

mechanics

medicine
medical

medieval
miniature

mischief

moral
morale
morally

narrative

naturally

noble

obstacle

omit

peace

perceive

persistent

persuade

pertain

phase

playwright

politician
political

primitive

regard

relative

remember

reminisce

represent

roommate

sacrifice

safety

satisfy
satisfied

scene

schedule

seize

sentence

sergeant

several

shepherd

simply
simple

sophomore

source

story
stories

straight

strength

strict

substantial

subtle

suspense

symbol

synonymous

tendency

themselves
them

theory
theories

those

thought

tragedy

tremendous

vacuum

view

whole

yield

29E Use hyphens to form compound words and to avoid confusion.

1 Join two nouns with a hyphen to make one compound word.

Often in modern American English, two nouns are joined with a hyphen to make one compound word. Scientists speak of a *kilogram-meter* as a measure of force, while personnel managers speak of a *clerk-typist,* an employee who does general office work plus typing. The hyphen lets us know that the two nouns work together as one.

As new compound nouns come into general use, their hyphens often disappear. The nouns come to be written as one word, such as *thundershower, firelight, firefight,* and *housefly.*

2 Use a hyphen to link adjectives with nouns to make compound words.

Adjectives can be linked with nouns to make compound words. The compound word may be an adjective or a noun. To form the word *accident-prone,* an adjective, the noun *accident* is linked with the adjective *prone.* We say, "He was accident-prone," meaning that he seemed to have a knack for having accidents. To form the word *free-lancer,* a noun, the noun *lancer* is linked with the adjective *free.* We say, "She once worked for *The Daily Planet,* but she quit to become a *free-lancer* writing for various publications."

sp
29E

3 Use a hyphen to join modifiers when the absence of the hyphen might cause confusion.

Hyphens often help us sort out modifiers that come before the word they modify. If we say, "He was a hard running back," we might mean that he was hard and that he was also a running back. If we say, "He was a hard-running back," we mean that he ran hard. If we say, "She was a quick thinking person," we might mean that she was quick and that she was also thinking. If we say, "She was a quick-thinking person," we mean that she thought rapidly.

Notice that the hyphenated words in these examples employ adverbs *(hard, quick)* that do not end in *-ly.* When adverbs end in *-ly,* they do not require a hyphen if they modify an adjective that in turn modifies a noun.

They explored the *newly discovered* territories.
They endured his *clumsily arrogant* bragging.

Modifiers that are hyphenated when they are placed *before* the word they modify are usually not hyphenated when they are placed *after* the word they modify.

He was a crisis-and-confrontation politician.
His politics were a mix of crisis and confrontation.

It was a bad-mannered reply.
The reply was bad mannered.

4 Use hyphens to attach prefixes to certain words.

A hyphen often joins a prefix and a capitalized word.

un-American, pre-Columbian, anti-Semitic

In a few words the prefix is attached with a hyphen even though the main word is not capitalized.

ex-husband, all-conference

The prefix *self-* is usually joined to a word with a hyphen.

self-interest, self-control, self-centered

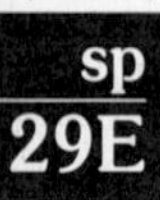

Some national names that are joined to make an adjective are hyphenated.

the Franco-Prussian war, the Sino-Japanese agreement, a Mexican-American heritage

Some numbers are hyphenated.

three-fourths of a gallon, twenty-five

Exercise 29.6 Rewrite the following sentences to correct misspellings. Hyphenate words when necessary.

1. He beleived that the badly damaged plane could land safly.
2. The love them today leave them tomorrow philosophy is probly on the decline becaus people now unnerstan it's hypocricy.
3. His nervous laff was a hinderence to his carreer.

4. She remained an optomist though her experence told her that optomist often have trouble acommodating themselves to a pityless city.

6. He had a tendancy to miss classes as a sophmore, and his teachers were bad mannered enough to take attendence.

7. The presperation broke out all over my face when I thot that all my laber had been in vain because I had mispelled so many words.

30 Capitalization

Capital letters give readers signals about sentence patterns, names, titles, and pronouns. Most rules for capitalization have been fixed by custom, but some of those rules are more flexible than others. A standard dictionary is a good guide to those names that should be capitalized. Names that should always be capitalized are entered with capitals; all others are entered in lowercase, or small letters. (Remember that when we speak of capitalizing a word, we mean only that the first letter in the word is capitalized; all other letters in the word appear in lowercase.)

30A Capitalize the first word of every sentence.

The capital letter at the beginning of a sentence is an essential signal to the reader that a new unit of thought is about to begin. The capital letter at the beginning of a sentence goes with the punctuation mark at the end of the previous sentence to make reading easier.

> The coming of the robot to the modern assembly line has raised both problems and possibilities. Because robots greatly reduce human error, the products they manufacture are of a much more uniform quality. But because they reduce human employment, robots risk eliminating part of the market for which their products are destined.

In sentence fragments used for special effects, capitalize the first word.

> But aside from good hair grooming, they are oblivious to everything but each other. Everybody gives them a once-over. Disgusting! Amusing! How touching!
>
> —Tom Wolfe

[The three sentence fragments, used for special effect, begin with capitals.]

Why did she lie under oath on the witness stand to defend her husband? Because she knew he was innocent? No, because she knew he was guilty.

[An immediate answer to a rhetorical question is often phrased as a fragment. Here, the two fragments represent answers to the question asked in the first sentence.]

Some writers who ask a series of questions by using fragments do not capitalize the first word of each fragment.

How many individuals can we count in society? how many actions? how many opinions?

—RALPH WALDO EMERSON

[The first question is a complete sentence; the next two are fragments and are not capitalized.]

The more common practice is to capitalize the first word in each fragment that answers a question.

And what are the fundamentals? Reading? Writing? Of course not!

—SLOAN WILSON

Most writers do not capitalize the first word of an independent clause immediately following a colon:

If a person suffer much from sea-sickness, let him weigh it heavily in the balance. I speak from experience: it is no trifling evil, cured in a week.

—CHARLES DARWIN

cap
30B

But sometimes writers do capitalize the first word after a colon:

The answer is another question: How many days must go by before millions of people notice they are not eating?

—*The New York Times*

The first word in an independent clause following a semicolon is never capitalized unless it is a proper noun (see 30B below).

All in all, however, outside support counted for little; the men of the village did the work themselves.

—OSCAR HANDLIN

30B Capitalize proper nouns and their abbreviations.

Proper nouns are the names of specific people, places, or things, names that set off the individual from the species. Proper nouns include names like *Jane* (instead of the common noun *person*), *France* (instead of the common noun *country*), and *Empire State Building* (instead of the common noun *building*).

The following are all proper nouns.

Names and Nicknames of People

Wolfgang Amadeus Mozart, Ernest Hemingway, Jim Ed Rice, Dwight Evans, John F. Kennedy, Stonewall Jackson, U. S. Grant, Gore Vidal, Joan Didion, the North Carolina Tarheels

Names of Places

France, the U.S.A., the U.S.S.R., Tennessee, the Panama Canal, Back Bay, the Mississippi Delta, the North Shore, the Irunia Restaurant, the Sierra Nevada, the Great Lakes

Official Names of Organizations

Phi Beta Kappa, the U.S. Department of Defense, The Authors' Guild of America, the University of Notre Dame, Cumberland College, Ford Motor Company, the Roman Catholic Church, the American Red Cross, the Boy Scouts of America, the NCAA, the NAACP

Days of the Week, Months, Special Days

Monday, July, Veterans Day, Christmas, Labor Day, Halloween, Yom Kippur, Earth Day, Pearl Harbor Day

Ethnic Groups, Nationalities, and Their Languages

Jews, Greeks, Chinese, Americans, Arabs, Turks; Hebrew, Greek, Chinese, English, Arabic, Turkish

[NOTE: The words *blacks* and *whites* generally are not capitalized when they are used to refer to ethnic groups, but many writers use individual choice in this matter. The older and now less favored word *Negro* is capitalized.]

Members of Religious Bodies and Their Sacred Books and Names

Christians, Baptists, Holy Bible, God, Allah, Hindus, Jesus Christ, Holy Spirit, the Koran, the Torah, Pentecostals, Christian Scientists

[Note that many religious terms such as *sacraments, altar, priests, rabbi, preacher,* and *holy water* are not capitalized. The word *Bible* is sometimes not capitalized in both English and American practice, and it is never capitalized when it is used as a metaphor for an essential book, as in this sentence: "His book *Winning at Stud Poker* was for many years the *bible* of gamblers."

Sometimes words not ordinarily capitalized do take capitals when they are used as parts of proper names. We say, "My *aunt* is arriving this afternoon." But we say, "My *Aunt Lou* tells fantastic stories that I think she makes up." We say, "I have to go to the *bank* before we can leave." But we say, "The

Cambridge Bank is on the corner." We say, "I graduated from *high school* in 1951," but we say, "I went to *Lenoir City High School.*"

Pronoun references to a deity worshiped by people in the present are sometimes capitalized, although some writers use capitals only to prevent confusion.

Allah, so Muslims believe, sent Mohammed to deliver *His* word to the world.

God helped Abraham carry out *His* law.

[In each of the sentences above, the capitalization of the pronoun *His* helps avoid confusion. If the pronoun were not capitalized, readers might not be able to tell if the *word* in the first sentence referred to Allah or Mohammed, or if the *law* in the second sentence was God's law or Abraham's law.]

God acts for *his* own purposes and according to *his* own wisdom.

[In this sentence the pronoun *his* is not capitalized, since no confusion is involved. You may choose to capitalize the pronoun if you wish.]

Pronoun references to deities no longer worshiped are not capitalized.

Jupiter was the Roman god of thunder and lightning, and *he* led a tempestuous love life that often got *him* into deep trouble with *his* wife Juno.

Names like *Mother, Father, Cousin, Brother,* and *Sister* may replace proper names in some kinds of speech and writing. If you intend to refer to a specific individual, capitalize the word.

I still miss *Mother,* although she has been dead for over a decade.

He supposed that his *Uncle* would come to his aid again as he had so many times in the past.

But most of the time these words are not capitalized, since they do not replace a proper name. Whether you capitalize such words depends on your intention.

I asked my *mother* to wake me at 5:00 A.M.

[The word *mother* is not being used as a substitute for a proper name. It is being used in the more general way to denote a relation. It is not capitalized.]

Some titles that may be capitalized before a proper name are often not capitalized when they are used after the name.

Everyone knew that *Governor* Grover Cleveland of New York was the most likely candidate for the Democratic nomination.

[The title *Governor* before the name of Grover Cleveland is capitalized.]

The most likely candidate for the Democratic nomination was Grover Cleveland, *governor* of the state of New York.

[The title written after the name is not capitalized.]

Writers and editors do not agree on the capitalization of some titles. The title *President of the United States,* or the *President* (meaning the President of the United States), is almost always capitalized. But practice varies for other titles. Some writers say, "I will speak to the *Governor* about your wish to give him a new Cadillac for his personal use." Others say, "The *governor* of this state received a new Cadillac last week from an old political friend and business associate." Most writers say, "The *president* of this university has seventeen honorary degrees." Others will say, "The *President* of this university would rather have a winning football team than seventeen honorary degrees."

In general, editors and writers are tending to capitalize less, but it is still important to be consistent. If you write "the *P*resident of the *U*niversity," you should also write "the *C*hair of the *H*istory *D*epartment." If you write "the *p*resident of the *u*niversity," you should also write "the *c*hair of the *h*istory *d*epartment." And, of course, if you say "the *P*resident of the *U*niversity" in one place, you must capitalize in the same way whenever you write "the *P*resident of the *U*niversity."

cap 30B

When proper names describe or identify common nouns, those nouns that follow are generally not capitalized.

Sanka brand, Russian history, French fries, Pennsylvania-Dutch shoofly pie, English literature

[The words *brand, history, fries, shoofly pie,* and *literature* are not capitalized because they are not considered part of the proper names they follow.]

Use capitals for abbreviations made from capitalized words or for words formed from the initial letters of words in a proper name. (These words are called acronyms. See section 31E.)

WAC, FBI, NOW, UNESCO, U.S.A., ANZAC, NCAA, SWAT

Abbreviations used as parts of proper names usually take capitals.

T. S. Eliot; Sammy Davis, Jr.; George Sheehan, M.D.

Words derived from capitalized words generally keep the capitals of the original words.

Reaganomics, Miltonic, Hollywoodiana

30C Capitalize the first and last words of the title of any piece of writing and of any work of art or architecture. Do not capitalize the articles (*a, an,* and *the*) or prepositions and conjunctions of fewer than five letters unless they begin the title. Capitalize the first word after a colon or semicolon in a title.

Pride and Prejudice

The Taming of the Shrew

the *Spirit of St. Louis*

the *Titanic*

the *Mona Lisa*

"Beating the Market: How to Get Rich on Stocks"

On Old Age

Two Years Before the Mast

[Note that the preposition *Before* in this last title is capitalized. The general rule is that a preposition or conjunction of five letters or more is capitalized.]

cap 30D

30D Capitalize the first word of spoken dialogue included within quotation marks.

"You're going to kill us both!" she shouted.

"Calm down," he shouted back. "I spent just thirty minutes learning to drive this motorcycle, and we're already doing a hundred miles an hour."

"Help!" she said.

Indirect quotations and questions require no capitals for words attributed to a speaker or writer.

She said that jazz was one of the many contributions of blacks to world culture.

He asked me which I liked better, bluegrass music, without drums and electrically amplified instruments, or the more modern country music that is closely akin to soft rock.

Many authors in earlier centuries of the English language and some writers today—especially poets—have used capitals in eccentric ways. If you are quoting a text directly, reproduce the capitalization used in the source whether or not it is correct by today's standards.

> Sun and moon run together in one of Pyramus's speeches, "Sweet Moon, I thank thee for thy sunny Beams."
>
> —ELIZABETH SEWELL

30E Use capitals consistently when you have a reason for doing so, but avoid unnecessary capitals.

Some inexperienced writers are tempted to use capitals for emphasis, and they capitalize too much. Unnecessary capitals may confuse readers or irritate them. In modern prose the tendency is to use lowercase whenever possible.

> The Department of Agriculture and the Department of the Interior have often had conflicts because of overlapping jurisdictions. Both departments have responsibility for the American land. The secretary in charge of each department usually wants to increase his own power. The congress must sometimes step in and arbitrate the disputes between the two. But a strong Secretary of Agriculture or a greedy Secretary of the Interior can quickly undo any compromise made between the departments.

cap 30E

[In this paragraph, the nouns *department, departments,* and *secretary* are not capitalized when they appear as nouns that are not part of a complete title. Some writers today might have capitalized the word *congress.* But the tendency now is to capitalize as little as possible, and most writers and editors would prefer the version shown here.]

A Reference Chart for Capitals

Consult this chart for ready reference about capitalization. Designed for quick reference, the boxes highlight appropriate uses for capitals; the color numbers refer to the appropriate sections in the text.

Sentence Conventions 30A, 30D

After periods, the pronoun **I,** quotations, colons
 They laughed. **T**he child grinned.
 When **I** finally spoke, **I** whispered.
 She said, "**L**et me check your blood pressure."
 This is clear: **T**he (OR the) lake is unfit for swimming.

BUT
They laughed; the child grinned.
Did she ask who arrived?
He said that fear can blind judgments.

People 30B

General George Patton
Justice Thurgood Marshall
D. K. Rivera, M.D.
Chancellor Joseph Murphy
The Governor (OR governor) waved to the crowd.
Uncle Kwok; hearing Uncle (OR uncle) speak
BUT
the general, the judge, a doctor, the chancellor, a governor, my uncle

---

Geographic Locations 30B

Zimbabwe, Rhodesia
Pike's Peak
Tennessee
Main Street
Lake Placid
BUT
a new country, a historical mountain, this state, the street, a lake

---

Areas, Regions, Directions 30B

the Middle East
a Northerner
Northwest Territory
in the South
BUT
an eastern route, turn south, the territory

Historical Events, Names, Movements, and Writings 30B, 30C

World War II
the Louisiana Purchase
Modernism
the Bill of Rights
Moby Dick
"To Autumn"
BUT
a war, a bill, a philosophy, a document, amendments, laws, a novel, that event, the book

---

Institutions, Groups, and Organizations 30B

Democratic Party
Boston Red Sox
the High School of Music and Art
University of Maryland
the Knights of Columbus
Bank Leumi
McGraw-Hill Book Company
USN
BUT
political party, team, a high school, this university, the organization, our bank, the company, the navy

Academic Subjects 30B

English, Chinese, Indian religions
Mathematics 13
BUT
language, theology, mathematics, psychology, history, senior class

Religion, Race, Nationality, Sacred Things 30B

Judaism, Catholics
Old Testament
Almighty God
Allah
Caucasian, Negro, black or Black
Pakistani
BUT
my religion, a race of people

Days, Months, Holidays 30B

Tuesday
June
Labor Day
BUT
tomorrow, this month, spring, summer, fall, winter

Plants, Animals, Games, Illnesses 30B

African violet, Queen Anne's lace
Siamese cat
Monopoly
Addison's anemia
BUT
elm tree, rose, kiwi, baseball, measles, pneumonia

Exercise 30.1 Follow the directions in each item below, and write full-sentence responses. Observe the conventions of proper capitalization.

1. Name the professor in your school whose lectures you find most interesting.
2. Name the city and state (or city and country) where you were born.
3. Name a supermarket where you or your family members buy groceries.
4. What is your favorite season of the year?
5. In what direction must you walk or ride to get to campus?
6. In what region of the country did you grow up?
7. What two academic subjects do you enjoy most?
8. Name a book you enjoyed reading recently.
9. What is your favorite TV show?
10. Name your favorite holiday.
11. What is your favorite flower?
12. What was the name of your high school? (Use the words *high school* immediately after the name of the institution.)

Exercise 30.2 Fill in the correct capital or lowercase letters in the blanks below. Explain your choices.

1. ____hen ____overnor Blankenship stood on the steps of the state ____apitol ____uilding and said to the ____resident of the ____nited ____tates, "____he states in the ____outh need more of the ____overnment's support," my neighbors on Main ____treet applauded wildly.
2. ____t the ____an ____iego ____oo last summer, I disliked the ____onkeys and the ____pes because they looked so much like little men and women in a cage, but I was fascinated by the reptile house, where I saw the ____frican ____ock ____ython as well as the ____ndian ____obras and the ____oa ____onstrictor.
3. ____ake ____ociology 320, a ____ourse in the ____ociology of ____eligion, where you learn to understand some of the strengths of ____rotestantism, ____udaism, and ____oman ____atholicism.

cap
30E

Exercise 30.3 Rewrite the following sentences, using capital and lowercase letters correctly.

1. during Summer i like to visit the Ski Resorts in vermont, where few visitors disturb my meditations among the Fir Trees and the Maples that dot the Landscape.
2. when I was a child, thanksgiving day was one of the best holidays, not only because the family always got together for a huge dinner but also because thanksgiving came on thursday, and at Belmont high school, we were given both thursday and friday off.

3. in your sophomore course in english literature next fall, you may read at least one novel by daniel defoe, whose book *robinson crusoe* is sometimes called the first true novel in the english language.
4. when we had our accident, we were taken to memorial hospital on greeley parkway, where a doctor named thomas babington examined us and told us there was nothing wrong with us. later, when i discovered that i had a fractured skull and that my brother had a broken leg, we sued the hospital, but the hospital claimed that dr. babington was only visiting the emergency room that day and was not an employee of memorial hospital at all.

31 Numbers and Abbreviations

Variations in the style of different authors and in the demands of different editors make it difficult to fix rules for figures and abbreviations. In some newspapers and some magazines the use of figures to express numbers may be common. In books, figures and abbreviations are less common, at least in the body of a text. In footnotes, bibliographies, scientific or technical reports, letters, charts, tables, and graphs, figures and abbreviations must be used no matter what the publication.

You should use figures sparingly for numbers in standard essays, and you should use abbreviations for words only when convention allows.

31A In general, use words instead of figures for numbers that take only one or two words to spell out, and use figures instead of words for numbers that require three or more words to spell out.

When spelling numbers out takes a great deal of space, use figures, even in the body of an essay.

six cartons **BUT** 181 cartons

twenty-four dollars **BUT** $23.88

forty thousand children **BUT** 39,658 children

If you must begin a sentence with a number, you should usually spell the number out.

Not 450 motorcycles jammed the parking lot.

But Four hundred and fifty motorcycles jammed the parking lot. [Here the number is spelled out because it begins the sentence.]

Motorcycles—450 of them—jammed the parking lot.

[*Motorcycles* begins the sentence, and the number, written in figures, follows as an appositive.]

31B Use figures for numbers in prose that gives a lot of statistical or quantitative information. Use figures for dates, times of day, and addresses.

In writing about some subjects, you may use numbers so frequently that to avoid confusion you should write the numbers as figures.

> The original plan for the house called for a dining room that would be 18 × 25 and a living room that would be 30 × 34 with plate-glass windows at each end. The wall of the dining room was to include one enormous window measuring 16 × 5, to be set in the wall 1.5 feet above the floor.

Dates that include the year usually appear as figures, but some writers prefer to spell them out.

October 9, 1893	The ninth of October, 1893
9 October 1893	October ninth (NOT October 9th)
the 1960s	the nineteen-sixties
1929–1930	from 1929 to 1930

n/ab 31B

The time of day followed by the abbreviation A.M. or P.M. is always expressed in figures.

6:00 A.M., 6 A.M., 8:15 P.M.
six o'clock in the morning
a quarter past eight in the evening

Street and highway numbers almost always appear as figures except when a house number and the number of a street come together in an address. Then one of the numbers is written out.

1 Park Avenue	850 Fifteenth Street
Apartment 6J	
Interstate 80	
State Highway 2	

31C In formal essay writing, spell out most words rather than abbreviate them.

1 Common titles such as *Mister* and *Doctor* are abbreviated even in formal prose.

Other abbreviations may cut down readability, since a general audience may be unfamiliar with them or may not recognize them at all. But in some technical writing such as memos or reports intended for a limited audience, you may use abbreviations that are standard to that audience.

Not Dr. Ruth Smith and SOL Dean Th. Luciano discussed the std. rules about hab. corp. proceedings in the pol. cts. as they might apply to studs. arrested on DWI charges in the commercial dist. alg. Mass. Ave.

But Dr. Ruth Smith and School of Law Dean Thomas Luciano discussed the standard rules about habeas corpus proceedings in the police courts as they might apply to students arrested on charges of driving while intoxicated in the commercial district along Massachusetts Avenue.

[Readers may decipher the abbreviations of the first sentence, but the second sentence is much clearer and easier to read, even to those who know all the abbreviations in the first example.]

> President Jaworski said that the college should eliminate at least fifty full-time-equivalent positions. He said that for each FTE eliminated, an across-the-board raise of one hundred dollars would be possible for the remaining faculty.

n/ab
31C

[Here the abbreviation *FTE* is acceptable, since the audience for whom this report is meant would be familiar with it. It is even more acceptable because it is explained in the first sentence.]

If you use the name of an agency or an organization frequently in an essay or a report, you may abbreviate it to make the repetition less tedious. You are always safe if you write out the name of the agency or the organization the first time you use it and abbreviate it afterward. You may give the abbreviation in parentheses immediately after you mention the name the first time.

> The Student Nonviolent Coordinating Committee (SNCC) began earnest and often dangerous work in Mississippi and other parts of the South during the summer of 1964. SNCC was far to the left of other civil rights organizations, and its leaders often mocked the "conservativism"

of Dr. Martin Luther King, Jr. SNCC quickly burned itself out and disappeared, but some scholars now give the organization much credit for some of the progress made in civil rights during those hard years.

2 Spell out the names of countries, cities, boroughs, and states and the words *Avenue, Boulevard, Highway, Street, River,* and *Mountains* and words like them used as parts of proper names when they appear in the body of your prose.

The Catskill Mountains (NOT *Mts.*) of New York (NOT *N.Y.*) flank the Hudson River (NOT *Riv.*) to the west.

Veterans Highway (NOT *Vets H'wy*) crosses Deer Park Avenue (NOT *Ave.*)

3 Spell out the names of months and days of the week; spell out people's names.

Not In Sept. and Oct. Chas. visits the botanical gardens every Sun.

But In September and October Charles visits the botanical gardens every Sunday.

4 Avoid using the ampersand as a symbol for the conjunction *and* unless the ampersand is part of an official name or title.

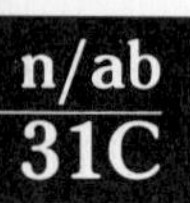

Loneliness and (NOT *&*) poverty often accompany old age.

The A & P is one of the oldest supermarket chains in America.

The stock index published by Standard & Poors is one of the most important economic documents in America.

[In the last two examples, the ampersand is part of an official name.]

5 Spell out the words *pages, chapter, volume,* and *edition,* the names of courses of study, and words such as *company, brothers,* and *incorporated* except as they may appear in official titles.

Not In Ch. 16 several pp. present new developments in open-heart surgery.

But In Chapter 16, several pages present new developments in open-heart surgery.

Remember that you may use abbreviations for *page, chapter,* and *edition* in footnotes, endnotes, and bibliographical references (see 33C and 33K).

Use the abbreviation *Inc., Corp., Co.,* or *Bros.* only when it is part of the official title of a company.

Not His bros. formed a toy co. called Kidstuff, Inc., and later changed the name to Goldstein Bros.

But His brothers formed a toy company called Kidstuff, Inc., and later changed the name to Goldstein Bros.

6 Avoid the use of *etc.*

It is almost always better to name the items you intend to blanket under the abbreviation *etc.* than to use the abbreviation as a catchall. If you don't want to make a long list, use *and so on, and so forth, for example,* or *such as.*

Not This garden is good for planting lettuce, broccoli, spinach, etc.

But This garden is good for planting lettuce, broccoli, spinach, radishes, onions, and other cool-weather vegetables.

Or This garden is good for planting cool-weather vegetables—broccoli and spinach, for example.

Or This garden is good for planting vegetables such as lettuce and broccoli.

When you do use *etc.*, do not put the conjunction *and* before it. The abbreviation *etc.* stands for the Latin *et cetera,* or *et caetera,* which means "and the rest," so the *and* is included in the abbreviation itself. To add the English word is redundant. And note the spelling of the abbreviation: in *etc.* the *t* comes before the *c*, not after it.

31D Use abbreviations for familiar titles that may stand before or after a person's name.

Some commonly abbreviated titles always go before the person's name. These include *Mr., Mrs., Ms., Dr., St., the Rev., the Hon., Sen., Rep.,* and *Fr.*

Fr. Louis joined our monastery twenty years ago.

Mrs. Jean Bascom designed the brick walkway in front of our building.

Dr. Epstein and Dr. Goodson consulted on the operation.

The Rev. Dr. Karl Barth visited Gettysburg, Pennsylvania, shortly before he died.

[Note that the abbreviation *Rev.* for *Reverend* should always be preceded by the article *the.*]

Many women now prefer to use the title *Ms.* instead of *Miss* or *Mrs.* (see Chapter 21). Strictly speaking, *Ms.* is not an abbreviation, since it does not stand for a word. But it is used in the same way *Mr.* and *Mrs.* are used—before a name. The title *Miss* is not an abbreviation, so it is not followed with a period. It, too, should precede the name.

Some abbreviations are always used after a proper name. Usually these indicate academic or professional degrees or honors. Note that a comma is placed between the name and the abbreviation and that a space follows the comma.

Kai-Y Hsu, Ph.D.
Maria Tiante, M.D.
Elaine Leff, C.P.A., LL.D.
Michael Bartlett, Esq.

Spell out most titles used without proper names:

Not Mr. Carew asked if she had seen the Dr.

But Mr. Carew asked if she had seen the doctor.

Notice that when an abbreviation ends a sentence, the period at the end of the abbreviation itself will serve as the period of the sentence. If a question mark or an exclamation point ends the sentence, you must place such a punctuation mark *after* the period in the abbreviation:

When he was in the seventh grade, we called him "Stinky," but now he is William Percival Abernathy, Ph.D.!

Is it true that he now wants to be called Stanley Martin, Esq.?

31E Abbreviate the names of agencies, groups, people, places, or objects commonly referred to by capitalized initials.

Some of these abbreviations use periods; others do not. Follow standard practice, and consult a dictionary if you have any doubts.

CIA OR C.I.A.
JFK OR J.F.K.
U.S. government OR US government
Washington, D.C. OR Washington, DC

Many government agencies known by their acronyms are regularly referred to with abbreviations, especially in publications where they are frequently mentioned. Often the abbreviations of these agencies are so well known that they do not require any explanation.

The FBI entered the case immediately, since under the Lindbergh Act kidnapping is a federal crime.

Both the Secretary of Defense and high officials in NASA worry about Russian military technology in space.

31F Abbreviate words typically used with times, dates, and figures.

6 P.M. OR 6:00 P.M.

9:45 AM OR 9:45 A.M.

498 B.C.

A.D. 1066

6000 rpm

[Note that in common practice, the abbreviation *A.D.* is written before the number indicating the year, and the abbreviation *B.C.* is written after the year number.]

n/ab 31G

31G Translate most Latin abbreviations into English in the body of your writing. Old systems of documentation do use Latin abbreviations in footnotes, endnotes, bibliographies, or parenthetical comments.

cf. should be "compare"

e.g. should be "for example"

et al. should be "and others"

etc. should be "and so on," "and so forth," or "and the rest"

ibid. should be "in the same place"

i.e. should be "that is"

vs. should be "versus"

Although new documentation systems for research papers use a minimum of abbreviations, you may come across these abbreviations in your own reading. A list of the most familiar of these appears on page 515.

Exercise 31.1 Rewrite the following paragraphs, using numbers and abbreviations properly.

1936 was the year he moved to our town and set himself up as a doctor. He hung out the sign on his front porch saying, "Dr. Ezra Muscatel, M.D." His house was over on 2nd. Ave. next to the warehouse owned by the Ledbetter bros., & Doctor Muscatel used to sit out on the porch overlooking the ave. & stare at the mts. in the distance on the border between Tenn. and N.C.

Mister Ledbetter went to him first, with a stomachache in the early A.M., & Doctor Muscatel gave him 8 or 9 little pills that made him feel good right away, & after that people started going to Doctor Muscatel with stomachaches, headaches, rheumatism, etc. He was the only dr. in town who would make house calls. You could call him up at six PM, & he would come to your house & give you some pills, and etc., & you would feel better. He would come to your house to deliver a baby at three A.M. in the morning. He did not charge much money, & he was always serious about things. He listened to people and nodded his head when they told him their symptoms and never looked like one of those drs. that want to run off after 5 or 6 mins. with a patient. He sat there, looking sober and concerned, & afterward he would scribble something on his prescription pad & tell you to get it filled at the drugstore, & he would go shuffling off as if he was still thinking about you and what was wrong with you.

FDR was President of the U.S.A. back then, & we had a lot of people coming & going in our little town. One of them saw the old dr. one morning on Main St. and recognized him & began telling everybody that dr. Muscatel was an ex-con who had served thirty years in the Tenn. prison for manslaughter & that he had never finished high sch.

32
Italics

To set off certain words and phrases from regular type, printers use *italics,* a typeface in which the characters slant to the right. Since most typewriters lack an italic face, and since it is impossible to make italics in handwriting, writers preparing manuscripts underline those words that a printer would place in italics.

Handwritten

Katharine Hepburn gives one of her best performances in The African Queen.

Typed

Katharine Hepburn gives one of her best performances in The African Queen.

Printed

Katharine Hepburn gives one of her best performances in *The African Queen.*

32A To indicate italics, underline in your manuscript the titles of books, magazines, journals, newspapers, plays, films, works of art, long poems, pamphlets, and musical works.

Joan Didion, a former editor of Vogue and The National Review, received glowing reviews in The New York Times for her novel A Book of Common Prayer.

In most titles, *a*, *an*, or *the* as a first word is capitalized and underlined. If titles of newspapers and magazines include the name of a city, you may decide whether to underline that name. You may write "the Los Angeles Times" or "The Los Angeles Times." Writers often do not underline or use italics for the initial *the* in the title of a periodical. But no hard-and-fast rule exists here. In most titles other than those of periodicals, *a*, *an*, or *the* as a first word is usually italicized and capitalized.

> Picasso's *Guernica* captures the anguish and despair of violence.
>
> Plays by Shakespeare provide details and story lines for Verdi's opera *Falstaff*, the musical comedy *Kiss Me Kate* by Cole Porter, and Franco Zeffirelli's film drama *Romeo and Juliet*.
>
> Edwin Newman's book *A Civil Tongue* is an amusing essay on modern language.
>
> This book is entitled *The McGraw-Hill College Handbook.*

[If you were writing any of these italicized words in your own paper, you would underline them.]

Some publishers of newspapers, books, and magazines have special rules for the use of italics. They often use quotation marks either to save money in setting type or to conform to their preferred format. Usually such publishers give a style manual to their writers to ensure consistent styling. *The New Yorker,* for example, italicizes newspaper titles but places the titles of books, musical works, films, and plays in quotation marks. Most newspapers use quotation marks where formal writing requires italics.

> Nelson Gidding did the adaptation of the Shirley Jackson novel "The Haunting of Hill House."
>
> —*The New Yorker*
>
> On our way, dodging snowflakes, we picked up the Sunday *Times* to see what had happened to the world.
>
> —*The New Yorker*
>
> As readers of "Crazy in Berlin" and "Little Big Man" ought to know, you can never tell what to expect from a novel by Thomas Berger.
>
> —CHRISTOPHER LEHMANN-HAUPT (in *The New York Times*)

However, quotation marks usually mark off only the titles of short works—essays, newspaper and magazine articles and columns, short stories, television and radio programs, short poems, songs, chapters or other subdivisions in books, and unpublished dissertations and theses (see 27C).

> Willa Cather's "A Wagner Matinee" appears in a collection of her stories called *The Troll Garden.*

[The title of the story requires quotation marks; the title of the book in which it appears, italics.]

Note that in referring to the Bible or other sacred books like the Koran, to court cases, or to government documents, you use neither italics nor quotation marks.

> The Book of Ecclesiastes provides some of the most haunting phrases in the Bible.
>
> In Brown vs. Topeka Board of Education, the United States Supreme Court handed down a far-reaching interpretation of the Constitution.

Do not underline the titles you give to your papers when you write them on the title page. When the titles of books appear on the jacket, the binding, or the title page, they are not italicized. The titles of articles are not italicized when they appear in the title position in a journal or a book.

32B Underline (to indicate italics for) foreign words and phrases not commonly regarded as part of English.

> They are wise to remember, however, one thing. He is Sinatra. The boss. *Il Padrone.*
>
> —GAY TALESE
>
> *Chota hasari*—the little breakfast—consists of a cup of tea at five-thirty or six in the morning, with possibly some fruit or toast served with it. At eleven or at midday a heavier meal is eaten, *chapatis*—thin unleavened wheat cakes—and curry, with *dal*—a kind of lentil soup—and curds and sweets of some sort.
>
> —SANTHA RAMA RAU
>
> Memphis, in fact, was definitely the mecca, yardstick and *summum bonum.*
>
> —TERRY SOUTHERN

ital 32B

Many originally foreign words have become so common in English that everyone accepts them as part of the English language, and they require no underlining or italics—words like rigor mortis (Latin), pasta (Italian), sombrero (Spanish), bête noire (French), and festschrift (German). In the sentence by Terry Southern above, a city in Saudi Arabia—Mecca—has given its name as a common noun meaning any place where large numbers of people go to have some exalting experience.

Some foreign words are still borderline, and some writers would underline them while others would not—words like *ex nihilo* (Latin for "from nothing"), *imprimatur* (Latin for "Let it be printed"), and *Weltanschauung* (German for "world view"). Often the preference of the writer or the need for a special effect dictates the decision to underline or not.

Dictionaries offer some help. By labeling as *French* a phrase like *mise-en-scène,* for example, a dictionary guides your decision to underline. Some dictionaries have special sections labeled "Foreign Words." Others italicize foreign words when they appear. But writers must use their own judgment about the borderline words. Here it is good to consider your audience and to try to imagine the expectations that readers may bring to your work.

32C Use underlining (to indicate italics) to call attention to words or phrases you wish to stress as words rather than for the meaning they convey.

> The use of the word *glide* at the end of the last stanza is effective and gives just the amount of emphasis required at the end of the poem.
>
> —CLEANTH BROOKS and ROBERT PENN WARREN

> And if the word *integration* means anything, this is what it means: that we, with love, shall force our brothers to see themselves as they are, to cease fleeing from reality and begin changing it.
>
> —JAMES BALDWIN

Letters or numbers stressed as words also require underlining to show italics.

> The word *bookkeeper* has three sets of double letters: double *o*, double *k*, and double *e*.

ital 32D

Some writers will use quotation marks to show that words are being spoken of as words.

> When I was in graduate school in the late fifties, "criticism" was still a fighting word.
>
> —GERALD GRAFF

32D Underline (to indicate italics for) the names of ships, trains, and air or space vehicles.

> I packed my valise, and took passage on an ancient tub called the *Paul Jones* for New Orleans.
>
> —MARK TWAIN

> Lindbergh had flown his tiny plane, *The Spirit of St. Louis,* from San Diego to New York, with one stop at St. Louis, in the elapsed time of twenty-one hours, clipping five hours from the transcontinental record.
>
> —WILLIAM L. SHIRER

32E Use underlining only occasionally for emphasis.

Reserve italics to show stress only occasionally. Too many words italicized to show emphasis in your writing will fatigue your readers; their eyes may leap over the underlined or italicized words—the very opposite effect from what you intended. Too much emphasis may mean no emphasis at all.

Weak

You don't *mean* that your *teacher* told the whole *class* that *he* did not know the answer *himself!*

Revised

It was your teacher, then, who astonished the class by not knowing the answer?

[The new sentence through language and structure (and without italics) shows the surprise that the first sentence shows weakly with so many italicized words.]

For special effects, an occasional word in italics helps you emphasize a point:

> That advertisers exploit women's subordination rather than cause it can be clearly seen now that *male* fashions and toiletries have become big business.
>
> —ELLEN WILLIS

> It now seems clear that we are not going to improve instruction by finding *the* method or methods that are good for all peoples.
>
> —K. PATRICIA CROSS

ital 32E

In written dialogue, writers may use italics to emphasize words to show the rhythms of speech used by characters.

> The lady, however, regarded it very placidly. "I shouldn't have gone if she *had* asked me."
>
> —HENRY JAMES

> As they turned to him, Blackburn said: "Can *you* give *me* a few minutes, Dr. Howe?" His eyes sparkled at the little audacity he had committed, the slightly impudent play with hierarchy.
>
> —LIONEL TRILLING

Exercise 32.1 Underline any words or phrases that require italics in the following sentences.

1. An advertisement in the San Diego Evening Tribune announced a cruise on the Queen Elizabeth II, but after I read Katherine Anne Porter's novel Ship of Fools, a vacation on the sea did not interest me.

2. Time reported that Da Vinci's painting The Last Supper had deteriorated seriously from pollution and neglect.
3. The word hopefully is common nowadays, but many people who take writing seriously object to it because they think the words I hope or we hope or it is hoped usually express the meaning more clearly.
4. By the time the police discovered the body, rigor mortis had set in, and Inspector Michaelson told reporters from the Times and the Globe that death had taken place about twelve hours before.
5. Russell Baker's column Observer appears in the New York Times several days a week.

Exercise 32.2 Rewrite the following sentences to eliminate excessive emphasis. You may change the wording—eliminating some words and adding others. You may also change the order of the sentences as you see fit.

1. Mr.Watt promised that this was *absolutely* the last time that he or *any other* member of his department would even *mention* digging a coal mine in Yellowstone National Park.
2. Who could *possibly* have known that the landing gear *was* defective and that the pilot was *drunk?*
3. The crew of the space shuttle *firmly* believed that the *engineering problems of the flight were less serious than the psychological problems of living so close together under such a demanding* routine.
4. *Anyone* desiring to change sections *must* file a form with the registrar *before* Friday afternoon.

PART SEVEN
Special Writing Tasks

33 Writing a Research Paper

Research papers, also called library papers, grow out of a careful investigation of documents and other materials in the library. Because it is a formal composition, a research paper must be more than just a summary of what you have read about a given topic. A research paper presents a thesis that you have developed by reading and thinking about your topic and your sources; using careful documentation, it cites evidence to make your thesis plausible to readers.

To help you see how to develop a research paper from start to finish, this chapter offers two papers, one on a topic from literature and one on a topic from science. Good research and writing techniques apply to any subject, of course. But examining two different papers and seeing how they were developed will help you to expand your thinking about research papers. You can also compare parenthetical documentation with endnotes and see how diagrams and other visual techniques can help to clarify your final presentation. The conventions of writing about research vary from discipline to discipline. The more you know about these conventions, the easier it will be for you to investigate sources and present your findings for different courses of study.

Thinking through a research paper is much like thinking through any other written composition, even though research papers differ in content and format from other kinds of papers. If you follow the planning guidelines set forth in this chapter, you can produce a successful research paper.

33A Choose a subject that interests you, and develop a limited topic by doing prewriting exercises and using the library and by discussing the topic with friends or your instructor.

Select a general subject that fits your own interests and your instructor's assignment. Think about various specific topics within that general subject; then discuss them with people you know. Try brainstorming, jotting ideas down in an informal list, asking yourself questions about your subject, writing nonstop, or developing a subject tree (see 1A).

Prewriting exercises will help you to explore what you already know about the subject and to identify areas that you would like to know more about. See, for example, how two different kinds of prewriting techniques—a subject tree and nonstop writing—have helped two writers narrow down a large subject to more limited topics:

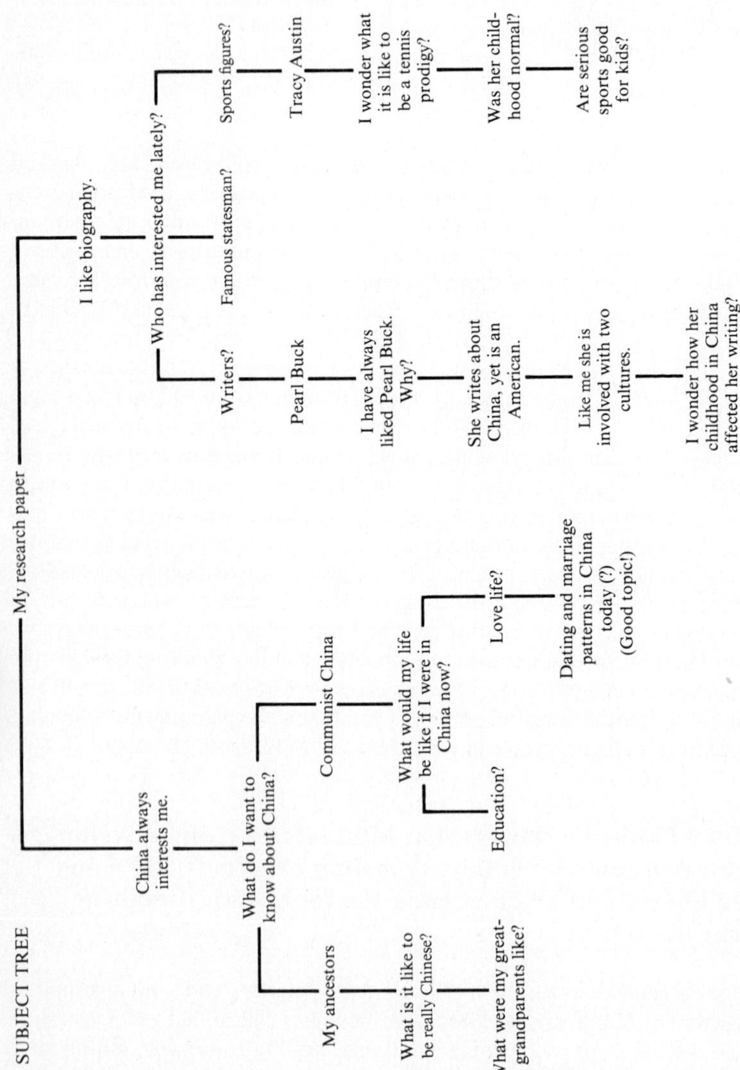

33A

Nonstop Writing

So, I have to do a research paper. About what? Wow! I haven't done a research paper really ever except for half-way jobs in high school. What interests me? Astronomy. I have always loved astronomy. I remember when I used to look at the moon through dad's big binoculars. You could see the craters. Always gave me an eerie feeling. I remember the first time I saw a satellite. Thought it was a star, but it kept moving. Then I thought it was an airplane, but it was going too fast and didn't blink like airplane lights do. Funny that you don't hear much about satellites these days. How many out there now? What are they used for? Television. Telephones. Maybe I could write a paper on something about satellites. My teacher will probably say that is still too broad. Let's see. What else interests me in astronomy? Two ideas—black holes and the new things our space probes found out about Jupiter and Saturn. Black holes fascinate me. I saw a movie about them several years ago. What a great name—kind of like a cosmic Bermuda Triangle. Get too close to one in your space ship and you are swallowed up! I don't really know what a black hole is. Something about space being curved? I think that scientists say that nothing can escape from a black hole, not even light. If no light can escape, how do you see them or know they are there? That would be a good topic—searching for black holes. Another topic is Jupiter or Saturn. From the news I guess those pictures from the space probe really baffle scientists. Those spokes on Saturn's rings. I think that a moon or something has a volcano or something. That would be another good paper—what new problems we have discovered as a result of the space probes. The more I think about it, the more topics start pouring in. Comets, life on other worlds, all sorts of things. Well, time's up.

Once you have a preliminary idea for your research paper, you should browse through the library, checking the card catalog, general reference books, and periodical indexes to see what other people have written on your topic. Preliminary reading in books and magazines helps you to decide on the suitability of your topic and to limit and sharpen its focus. Also, this early exploring of books and magazines will help you to plan the development of your topic and to organize your later research successfully.

How narrow a topic must you choose? Answers to that question depend upon your interests, the nature of the assignment, the required length of the paper, the number and the quality of available library materials, and the time you have to do your assignment. But try to narrow your topic as much as possible, because narrow topics allow you to use enough specific examples and details to keep readers interested in your writing. Note how prewriting exercises and preliminary library research have helped these students to narrow their topics through progressive stages until they have promising starting points for their papers.

Astronomy

Current questions about the universe

↓

Black holes

↓

How black holes might be located in space

↓

Various techniques used in the search for black holes

Biography

The life of a writer

↓

Pearl Buck's life

↓

Pearl Buck's early life in China

↓

How Pearl Buck's early experiences in China inspired her interest in writing

As you pursue your research, you may discover that your topic needs further limiting. Carefully limiting your topic will help you to exclude many fruitless areas before you investigate them. For instance, the writer of the paper on Pearl Buck (see pages 536–551) would have wasted time researching Buck's later travels, her later life in China, or the rise and fall of her reputation among critics.

When you are satisfied that you have a workable limited topic, talk about it with your instructor or with friends before you begin your research in depth. At this point, discussions with people you trust can help you test your ideas and can lead to important reshaping that may save time and hard work later on.

*__Exercise 33.1__ Choose three of the general subjects below, and limit each subject to produce at least one topic suitable for a research paper. (You may wish to choose one of these narrowed-down topics for your own library paper. Exercises marked with an asterisk (*) in this chapter—that is, Exercises 33.1, 33.3, 33.4, 33.5, 33.6, 33.8, 33.11, 33.12, 33.16, and 33.17—are designed to help you with your own research project.)

1. famous Hispanic Americans
2. mental illness
3. Martin Luther King, Jr.
4. drugs in America
5. kindergarten
6. rock music
7. women political leaders
8. the history of the theater
9. cowboys
10. Shakespeare's sonnets
11. sports
12. Ibsen's plays
13. energy conservation
14. mythology
15. computers
16. mass transportation
17. space travel
18. genetic engineering
19. illegal aliens
20. television advertising

33B Learn about the various libraries available to you and the types of help they offer.

If your college has only one library, that may simplify your life, but it may also limit your resources. Most large universities have several specialized libraries scattered across the campus. Your school may have both an undergraduate library and a graduate or a main library, and it may have a science library and various other special collections. Many cities have large public libraries, and in some cities that have several colleges, students in one school can often use the libraries of all the others.

The concept of the library is changing rapidly because new technologies to preserve information are competing with books and periodicals for shelf space. Many libraries collect microfilm or microfiche, phonograph records, movie films, audio- and videotapes, and photographs. In the microfilm or microfiche collection, you will find books and papers that do not appear in the library's collection of printed and manuscript materials. You may find newspapers and periodicals from all over the world. Audiotapes may include oral history, the recorded reminiscences of people who lived through important events or helped to shape them. Videotapes may include popular films and programs that have appeared on public television, covering anything from scientific studies to productions of Shakespeare's plays. If you choose to write about one of these plays, for example, you may be able to watch a performance of it in your library's viewing room.

Once you have chosen your topic and have put an initial limit on it, you should talk with a reference librarian, who can tell you what resources are available for your research. Librarians enjoy helping people, and you can save time if you let them help you. Most librarians know not only the resources available in their own libraries but also those you can consult elsewhere in the region. Ask for help at the very beginning. And as you write, ask for help whenever you need it.

33C As you do your research, copy down in standard form the required data about any research materials you may want to include in your list of works cited.

You should provide a list of works cited for readers of your research paper. A **list of works cited** is the alphabetical list of books, articles, and other sources (like films, interviews, or dramatic productions) that you consulted in doing your research. All the citations in your paper will be keyed to this list of research materials. (If you use print materials only, your list will be called a *bibliography*.) Although you are far from developing your final list of works cited at this early stage of your research, you should master the style you will use. As you take notes for your early drafts (see 33F), be careful to record your sources, noting full publishing data in the form you will use when you prepare the final draft of your paper. This habit accomplishes two valuable goals. First, it assures you that all your notes are accurately and fully documented. Second, it saves you the trouble of going back to your reference materials to copy down data for your list of works cited after you have finished your research.

Because academic disciplines vary in the precise forms they require for documentation, you must follow carefully the specific format that your instructor requests. The entries in this section (and in section 33K) follow the style recommended by the Modern Language Association (MLA) in its 1984 *MLA Handbook for Writers of Research Papers.* Your instructor may require the documentation style recommended in The University of Chicago Press's *The Chicago Manual of Style,* in Kate L. Turabian's *Manual for Writers of Term Papers, Theses, and Dissertations,* or in the *Publication Manual of the American Psychological Association* (APA). Many other style manuals are available.

No matter which style you follow, remember to record all the information you will need to prepare a final list of works cited. (Most researchers find it helpful to prepare bibliography cards: see 33D, section 1.)

The following models show you how to document the usual kinds of sources for your research. If you cite some special sources (cartoons, computer programs, musical compositions, and works of art, for example), you should consult the *MLA Handbook* or some other comprehensive guide to documentation for the correct format.

Books and Reference Works

Model Entry in a List of Works Cited: A Book with One Author

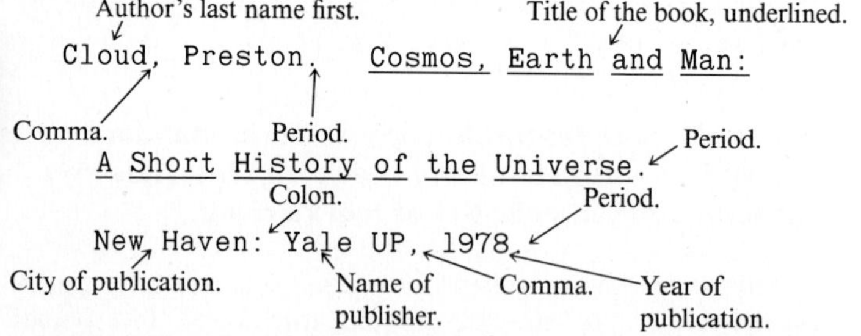

33C

[The periods set off three major divisions in the bibliographic entry: the author's name, the title, and the publishing data. *Yale UP* is the short form for *Yale University Press,* the publisher's full name. The short form usually is acceptable, but follow your instructor's advice. If the entry requires more than one line, indent the second line and all other lines five spaces.]

Sometimes other facts than simply the author, title, and publishing information are required, as in the following sample:

McCray, Curtis L. ''Kaptain Kronkite: The Myth of the Eternal Frame.'' Television: The Critical View. Ed. Horace Newcomb. 2nd ed. New York: Oxford UP, 1979. 319-33.

McCray is the author of an essay in the second edition of a book edited by Newcomb. Newcomb collected a number of essays and prepared them for printing, hence his designation as editor (Ed.) of the book. The book is in its second edition (2nd ed.), which means that one earlier version exists but that the researcher used the more recent book.

An anthology

Wolfe, Don M., ed. American Scene: New Voices. New York: Lyle Stewart, 1963.

[The abbreviation *ed.* says that Wolfe is the editor of this collection. If the author is a compiler (of a bibliography, for example) or a translator, use *comp.* or *trans.* after the name.]

A book by two or more authors

Morford, Mark P. O., and Robert J. Lenardon. Classical Mythology. New York: Longman, 1971.

Morgan, Clifford T., and Richard A. King. Introduction to Psychology, 2d ed. New York: McGraw-Hill, 1961.

[Note that only the first author's name is inverted.]

33C

Morgan, Clifford T., Richard A. King, and Nancy M. Robinson. Introduction to Psychology. 6th ed. New York: McGraw-Hill, 1979.

[The abbreviation *ed.* here stands for *edition.* An arabic number (with an appropriate suffix to show that the number is ordinal) indicates the edition number.]

Baugh, Albert C., et al. A Literary History of England. New York: Appleton, 1948.

[The abbreviation *et al.* is short for the Latin *et alii,* meaning "and others"; with more than three authors et al. replaces the names of all authors but the first, whose name is inverted as usual.]

Two or more books by the same author

Brooks, Cleanth. Fundamentals of Good Writing: A Handbook of Modern Rhetoric. New York: Harcourt, 1950.
---. The Hidden God: Studies in Hemingway, Faulkner, Yeats, Eliot, and Warren. New Haven: Yale UP, 1963.
Brooks, Cleanth, and Robert Penn Warren, eds. Understanding Poetry. 3rd ed. New York: Holt, 1960.
Farrington, Benjamin. Aristotle: Founder of Scientific Philosophy. New York: Praeger, 1969.
---. The Philosophy of Francis Bacon. Chicago: U of Chicago P, 1964.

[When you list more than one book by the same author, give the author's name in the first entry only. For each succeeding entry, instead of the author's name type three hyphens and a period, then skip a space and type the title. The hyphens always stand for the author's name exactly as it appears in the entry that comes directly before. (Brooks' name is repeated in the third entry because hyphens would have referred to his name only; in *Understanding Poetry* he is one of two authors.) If the author is an editor, a complier, or a translator, use a comma after the hyphens and write in the correct abbreviation —*ed., comp.,* or *trans.*—before the title. Of course, all works listed for the same author appear alphabetically by title.]

A book with corporate authorship

Commission on the Humanities. The Humanities in American Life: Report of the Commission on the Humanities. Berkeley: U of California P, 1980.

A book with no author's name on the title page

Greece: 1974. Athens: National Tourist Organization of Greece, 1973.

[The entry begins with the title; on the list of works cited, alphabetize the entry by the first word other than an article.]

A selection from an anthology

Sewell, Elizabeth. ''Bacon, Vico, Coleridge, and the Poetic Method.'' In Giambattista Vico: An International Symposium. Ed. Giorgio Tagliacozzo and Hayden V. White. Baltimore: Johns Hopkins P, 1969. 125-36.

[Page numbers indicate where the essay being cited appears in the longer work.]

A preface, an introduction, a foreword, or an afterword

Blackmur, Richard P. Introduction. The Art of the Novel: Critical Prefaces. By Henry James. New York: Scribner's, 1962. vii-xxxix.

Fowles, John. Preface. Islands. By Fowles. Boston: Little, Brown, 1978. 1-2.

[The name of the writer of the preface, introduction, foreword, or afterword begins the entry, followed by the name of the part you are citing. Quotation marks or underlining is unnecessary. When the writer of the piece differs from the author of the book, use the word *By* after the title and cite the author's full name, first name first. If the writer of the piece is the same person who wrote the book, use only the last name after the word *By*. In the first entry, Blackmur wrote the introduction; James wrote the prefaces. In the second entry, the writer of the preface is also the author of the book.]

A work in more than one volume

Browne, Thomas. The Works of Sir Thomas Browne. Ed. Geoffrey Keynes. 4 vols. London: Faber, 1928.

Browne, Thomas. The Works of Sir Thomas Browne. Ed. Geoffrey Keynes. 4 vols. London: Faber, 1928. Vol. 2.

[The first entry says that the work is in four volumes and that the researcher used them all. The second entry says that only the second volume was used.]

An edited book

Buck, Pearl. China as I See It. Ed. Theodore F. Harris. New York: John Day, 1970.

[Harris prepared this work of Buck's for publication. The entry indicates that citations in the text of the paper are to Buck's writing. If the citations are to the editor (his introductory comments, for example), his name would begin the entry; see the entry for Blackmur above.]

A translation

Maffei, Paolo. Beyond the Moon. Trans. D. J. K. O'Connell. Cambridge: MIT Press, 1978.

[Note that the 1984 MLA style of referencing does not include the abbreviation for the state after the city. If your citations are to the translator's comments, and not to the translation itself, use the translator's name to begin the entry; see the entry for Blackmur above.]

A republished book

Knowles, John. A Separate Peace. 1959. New York: Bantam, 1966.

[The original edition appeared in 1959; the writer of the paper used the edition republished by Bantam in 1966.]

Reference books

''Kindergarten.'' Encyclopaedia Britannica. 1974 ed.

[Material from a well-known reference work does not require full publication data, but you should note the year of publication. The title in quotation marks is the entry word for the topic in the encyclopedia. The title appears first in such an entry because the information under the subject is unsigned. That is, the author's name does not accompany the article.]

Moore, Norman. ''Hodgkin, Thomas, M.D.'' Dictionary of National Biography. 1908.

Naylor, John Henry. ''Peninsular War.'' Encyclopaedia Britannica. 1974 ed.

[For a signed article in an encyclopedia, include the author's name. Sometimes only initials appear after the article; in that case check the list of initials in the index or in some other volume of the encyclopedia to find out the author's full name.]

Pamphlets, bulletins, and public documents

33C

United States. Congressional Budget Office. Proposition 13: Its Impact on the Nation's Economy, Federal Revenues, and Federal Expenditures. Washington: GPO, 1978.

National Academy of Sciences. Committee on Water, Division of Earth Sciences. Alternatives in Water Management. National Research Council Publication No. 1408. Washington: National Academy of Sciences, 1969.

[For a work by a government the name of the government comes first, then the name of the agency.]

A work in a series

Swimming Medicine IV. International Series on Sports Sciences 6. Baltimore: University Park Press, 1978.

[Neither underlined nor in quotation marks, the name of the series appears after the title of the book.]

Journals, Magazines, and Newspapers

Model Entry in a List of Works Cited: An Article in a Journal with Pages Numbered Continuously Throughout the Annual Volume

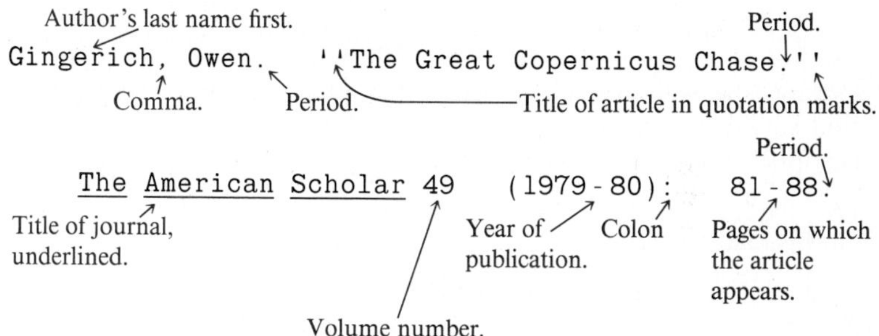

[The author's name, the title, and the publishing data are the main divisions in the entry for a journal article, too. Note the titles both of the article and of the journal in which the work appears.]

An article in a journal that numbers pages separately in each issue of an annual volume

Jewell, Walter. ''The Contribution of Administrative Leadership to Academic Excellence.'' WPA: Writing Program Administration 3.3 (1980): 9-13.

[If each issue in a volume is numbered, include the issue number in the citation. A period separates the volume number from the issue number. If the journal uses only issue numbers, treat them like volume numbers.]

33C

An article in a monthly or bimonthly magazine

Gebelle, Thomas R. ''The Central Parsec of the Galaxy.'' Scientific American July 1979: 60-70.

An article in a weekly or biweekly magazine

Pringle, James. ''A Black Hole in the Center of M 87?'' Nature 3 Aug. 1978: 419-20.

An unsigned article in a magazine

''Astronomers Hear from a Black Hole.'' New Scientist 14 July 1979: 23.

An article in a daily newspaper

Clark, F. Atherton. ''Metric Lengths Make Computation Easier.'' San Antonio Express 31 July 1978: A13.

[For the readers' convenience in locating the article, the section designation appears along with the page reference. If an edition is named on the masthead, specify the edition (*natl. ed.* or *late ed.,* for example) after the date. Use a comma between the date and the edition.]

Special Works

Unpublished dissertations and theses

Eisenberg, Nora. ''The Far Side of Language: The Search for Expression in the Novels of Virginia Woolf.'' Diss. Columbia U, 1977.

Book reviews

Fleming, Peter J. ''Nobel Lady.'' Rev. of Pearl S. Buck: A Biography, by T. F. Harris. Catholic World Dec. 1969: 138-39.

Recordings

33C

Verdi, Giuseppe. La Traviata. With Joan Sutherland, Luciano Pavarotti, and Matteo Manuguerra. Cond. Richard Bonynge, National Philharmonic Orchestra and London Opera Chorus. London Records, LDR-73002, 1981.

Plays and concerts

Brown, Arvin, dir. American Buffalo. By David Mamet. With Al Pacino. Circle in the Square Downtown Theatre, New York. 14 Aug. 1981.

Thomas, Michael Tilson, cond. American Symphony Orchestra Concert. Carnegie Hall, New York. 15 Feb. 1981.

Films and television programs

Redford, Robert, dir. Ordinary People. With Donald Sutherland, Mary Tyler Moore, and Timothy Hutton. Paramount, 1980.

The Mother. Writ. Paddy Chayevsky. Dir. Delbert Mann. Philco Television Playhouse. NBC, 4 Apr. 1954.

Interviews

Sills, Beverly. Telephone interview. 6 Dec. 1981.

For instructions on how to prepare a final bibliography to include in your paper, see 33M, section 1.

Exercise 33.2 Using the models in 33C, write correct entries for the following sources to be included in a list of works cited. (You may not need all the data that appear in each group.)

1. Margaret M. Bryant's book *English in the Law Courts,* published in New York by Columbia University Press in 1930.
2. Volume one of the two-volume edition of *Joseph Conrad: Life and Letters* edited by G. Jean-Aubry and published in 1927 by Doubleday in Garden City, New York.
3. An essay, "From Madcap Prince to King," written by Elsa Sjoberg and published in the winter of 1969 in Volume 20 of *Shakespeare Quarterly.* The essay appears on pages 11 through 16; the journal is published by The Shakespeare Association of America.
4. Bruno Bettelheim and Karen Zelan's "Why Children Don't Like to Read," which appeared on pages 25 to 31 in volume 248, number 5 (November 1981) of the *Atlantic,* an illustrated monthly magazine published in Boston by The Atlantic Monthly Company.
5. *Writing in the Arts and Sciences,* a 1981 textbook published by Winthrop Publishers, Inc., in Cambridge, Massachusetts. The authors, in the order that appears on the title page, are Elaine Maimon, Gerald L. Belcher, Gail W. Hearn, Barbara F. Nodine, and Finbarr W. O'Connor.
6. An article by Leo Seligsohn called "A Simple Service for Harry Chapin," in *Newsday,* a Garden City, New York, newspaper. The article appeared on Wednesday, July 22, 1981, on page 3.

7. The 20th Century Fox film of 1981, *The Empire Strikes Back,* directed by Irving Kershner and starring Mark Hamill, Harrison Ford, and Carrie Fisher.
8. The fifth edition of the nine-volume *Grove's Dictionary of Music and Musicians,* published in 1954 by St. Martin's Press in New York City.
9. Rolfe Humphries' translation of Ovid's *Metamorphoses* published in London in 1957 by John Calder.
10. Henry Sambrooke Leigh's poem "The Twins" in *A Century of Humorous Verse: 1850–1950* edited by Roger Lancelyn Green and published in London by J. M. Dent and sons. The poem appears on page 96.

33D Find out what has been written about your subject and make a preliminary bibliography by using the card catalog, indexes to periodicals, reference books, and other sources.

1 Use the card catalog in your library.

The card catalog contains a 3 × 5 card, issued by the Library of Congress upon the publication of a book, for every volume in your library except those published many decades ago. These cards are arranged alphabetically in file drawers, which usually are located near the circulation desk. In some large schools with several libraries, you will find a card catalog in each. You may also find a union catalog in the main library listing all the holdings of the school's libraries, including the locations of the books.

In most libraries, every book is listed on at least three cards: a *subject* card, a *title* card, and an *author* card. If it covers several subjects, the same book may be listed on several subject cards.

As soon as you pick your topic, find the subject section of the card catalog, and list the books related to your topic. You will probably notice that some authors seem to be experts in the field you are exploring. They may have written other books and articles worth your time, even though these titles were not listed on the subject cards that you inspected during your preliminary research. Look them up in the author cards.

Even at this early stage, you should list each promising source on a separate 3 × 5 bibliography card. If you make good bibliography cards from the start, you will be able to find your sources quickly later on. You will also have all the data you need to prepare the list of works cited for your final paper.

Subject Card

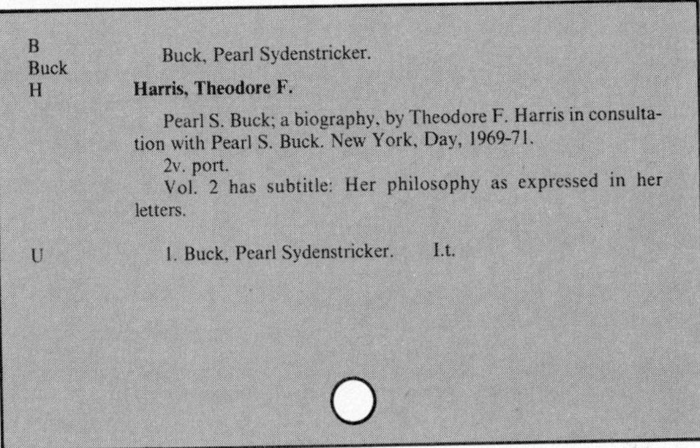

B
Buck
H

Buck, Pearl Sydenstricker.

Harris, Theodore F.

Pearl S. Buck; a biography, by Theodore F. Harris in consultation with Pearl S. Buck. New York, Day, 1969-71.

2v. port.

Vol. 2 has subtitle: Her philosophy as expressed in her letters.

U

1. Buck, Pearl Sydenstricker. I.t.

Title Card

B
Buck
H

Pearl S. Buck.

Harris, Theodore F.

Pearl S. Buck; a biography, by Theodore F. Harris in consultation with Pearl S. Buck. New York, Day, 1969-71.

2v. port.

Vol. 2 has subtitle: Her philosophy as expressed in her letters.

U

1. Buck, Pearl Sydenstricker. I.t.

Author Card

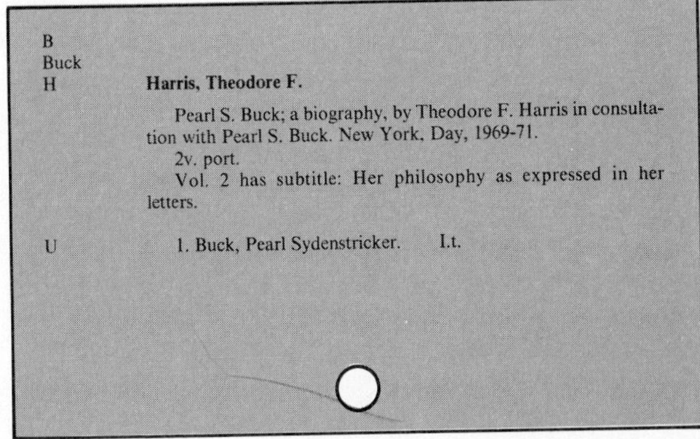

B
Buck
H

Harris, Theodore F.

Pearl S. Buck; a biography, by Theodore F. Harris in consultation with Pearl S. Buck. New York, Day, 1969-71.

2v. port.

Vol. 2 has subtitle: Her philosophy as expressed in her letters.

U

1. Buck, Pearl Sydenstricker. I.t.

33D

Sample Bibliography Card

Harris, Theodore F. Pearl
S. Buck : A Biography. 2 vols.
New York : Day, 1969-71.
B
B 9223 H

[The bibliographic information appears in the correct format on this student's bibliography card. However, all information must be checked against the title page in the book.]

Always include the call number at the bottom of your card. You must have this number, whether you search for the book in the stacks or fill out a slip asking someone to find the book for you. Most libraries use the Library of Congress system to catalog their books, but whatever system a library uses will be displayed on charts near the card catalog and the circulation desk.

If you can go into the stacks in your library, check the shelves near the books you have found in the card catalog. Often, you will find books nearby that have some relation to your topic. Look through them, and if they seem useful, jot down the titles on bibliography cards so that you can go back to them.

Most of the sources you will use for a brief research paper will be *secondary,* although you should try to use *primary* sources wherever possible. *Primary* sources include works of literature, such as novels and poems; historical documents, such as diaries, letters, journals, speeches, and autobiographies; and interviews, private conversations, observations, and experiments. *Secondary* sources analyze and comment on other source material. The student writing about Pearl Buck could use as a primary source one of Buck's novels or any of her other printed works; as secondary sources, the student could use books or articles written *about* Buck or her novels.

2 Use indexes to periodicals.

Your reference librarian can show you several general indexes to periodical literature where you can look up journal articles pertaining to your topic. A good index usually lists articles by year of publication, under various subject headings; some indexes list by authors as well.

Make bibliography cards for any articles that you think might pertain to your subject. Follow the formats for periodical articles set down on pages 477 to 479.

The periodical indexes have their own notation systems, and most of these do not match the formats for documentation required in your research papers. Unless you copy down data in the correct format on your bibliography cards, you may have trouble developing appropriate citations in your paper. You must usually check the article itself for information missing from the entry in the index—the author's first name, for example. Because index entries also include information not required in footnotes or endnotes, it is unwise to use an index entry as a model for your bibliography card.

The Readers' Guide to Periodical Literature, 1900–.
The Readers' Guide is the best-known general guide to many popular periodicals. It is issued regularly (about every month) in paper covers throughout the year, and annual volumes appear in hard covers, fully indexed. Entries in *The Readers' Guide* are arranged by subject and by author. There is a helpful page of suggestions about how to use each volume, as well as a key to all abbreviations used in the index.

Sample subject and author entries from the August 1982 issue appear below. Marginal notations explain the parts of the entries.

Subject entry

Subject heading.
Name of article.
Volume number.
Pages on which article appears.

Black holes (Astronomy)
The black heart of the Milky Way. L. J. Robinson. il Sky Telesc 64:133-5 Ag '82
The black hole in earth's backyard. P. Huyghe. il Sci Dig 90:12-14 S '82
The central engine. J. R. Schendel. il Astronomy 10:12-13 N '82
Cosmological crocodiles. G. Sweetnam. Sci Dig 90:85 Jl '82
Exploring the naked singularity [excerpt from The edge of infinity] P. Davies. il Sci Dig 90:30-2 My '82
A hole in the Milky Way. M. M. Waldrop. il Science 216:838-9 My 21 '82

Author's name.
Article has illustrations.
Date of issue.

33D

Author entry

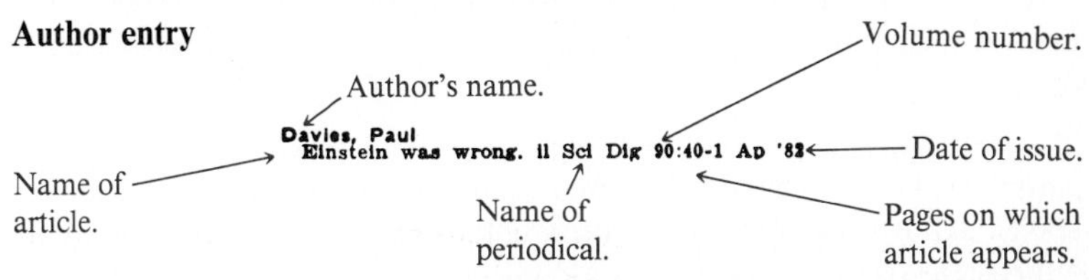
Davies, Paul
Einstein was wrong. il Sci Dig 90:40-1 Ap '82

Other Indexes

Humanities Index, 1974–.

Arranged by author and subject, the *Humanities Index* includes entries from more than 250 periodicals in archaeology, classics, language, literature, history, philosophy, religion, performing arts, and folklore. Book reviews appear in a separate section at the end.

Social Sciences Index, 1974–.

This index covers periodicals in the fields of anthropology, criminology, economics, law, political science, psychology, and sociology, among other areas of interest to social scientists. Here, too, a separate section of book reviews appears in each issue.

From 1965 to 1974, the *Humanities Index* and the *Social Sciences Index* were published as the *Social Sciences and Humanities Index.* From 1907 to 1965 the name of the combined index was the *International Index.*

New York Times Index, 1913–.

This is an indispensable index to researchers in history, government, the arts, sports, and other subjects of interest. Including all stories that have appeared in *The New York Times,* the *New York Times Index* gives the date of each story, the page and column number of the paper, and an abstract of the entry. Cross references are numerous.

The British Humanities Index, 1962–.

This British version of *The Readers' Guide* indexes periodicals published in Great Britain and has a much broader range than its American counterpart because it includes scholarly and professional journals. It succeeds the *Subject Index to Periodicals* published by the Library Association.

Access, 1975–.

This index bills itself as "the supplementary index to periodicals," meaning that it indexes periodicals not included in *The Readers' Guide* and other general indexes. Even so, *Access* limits itself to the kind of periodical that you might find in a large magazine store.

America: History and Life, 1964–.

An especially useful index for the research writer investigating any topic dealing with American (including Canadian) history and culture, *America* includes not only citations to the articles but also abstracts. An **abstract** summarizes the article, usually in a short paragraph, without criticizing it. Because this summary tells you much more than the title, it may save you lots of time.

Psychological Abstracts, 1927–.

Abstracts of thousands of articles in psychology published every year appear here, making this volume an excellent tool for any topic with a psychological dimension.

Public Affairs Information Service Bulletin (P.A.I.S.), 1915–. Listing articles by subject, this volume is a rich resource for almost any topic dealing with politics, economics, international relations, city planning, or other aspects of social or political life.

Many other indexes to periodical literature deal with specialized fields and include citations from highly specialized journals. Some articles may help you in the later stages of your research, after you have summarized the information about your topic and have developed a general idea of what you want to say about it. Among the specialized indexes are the following:

Applied Science and Technology Index, 1913–

Art Index, 1929–

Arts and Humanities Citation Index, 1978–

Biography Index, 1947–

Biological and Agricultural Index, 1964–

Business Periodicals Index, 1953–

Current Index to Journals in Education, 1969–

Education Index, 1929–

Essay and General Literature Index, 1900–

Film Literature Index, 1973–

Index to U.S. Government Periodicals, 1974–

Music Index, 1949–

Social Sciences Citation Index, 1973–

Be sure to ask for help from your reference librarian, who will guide you to other indexes for topics dealing with other special fields.

Most periodicals publish an annual index of their own. When you work in a special field, consult the indexes of journals published in the field for articles that will be useful for your research.

Anyone who does a research paper in literature, for example, should consult the various publications of the Modern Language Association (MLA), especially its annual *Bibliography.* Here is an entry from the 1968 MLA *Bibliography:*

Buck. 10754. Thompson, Dody W. "Pearl Buck." [F 79]: 85–110.

The [F 79] refers you to the front of the volume, to the section titled "Festschriften and other analyzed collections." (A **Festschrift** is a collection of articles, usually dedicated to an esteemed scholar.) Festschrift 79 is listed in the following way:

French, Warren G., and Walter E. Kidd, eds. *American Winners of the Nobel Literary Prize.* With Intro. and Bibliog. Notes. Norman: University of Oklahoma Press.

[You can look this book up by title in the card catalog. The article on Pearl Buck appears on pages 85 to 110.]

3 Use standard reference books such as encyclopedias and dictionaries.

You must do much more than merely repeat information out of encyclopedias and dictionaries when you write a research paper. But it is always a good idea to use such reference works for background information and, perhaps, for inspiration in thinking of other ways to explore your topic. The reference room of your library has several encyclopedias. Here are a few standard works you may wish to consult.

Multivolume Encyclopedias

Collier's Encyclopedia

Encyclopaedia Britannica

Encyclopedia Americana

[These encyclopedias also publish yearbooks that try to keep up with general knowledge in various disciplines as it develops each year.]

Single-Volume Encyclopedia

The New Columbia Desk Encyclopedia

[The type is small, but the amount of information in this volume is staggering.]

33D

Many disciplines have encyclopedias of their own, and your reference librarian can help you find them. Here are a few that may prove especially useful for research papers.

American History

Dictionary of American History, 8 vols.

Art

Encyclopedia of World Art, 15 vols.

The McGraw-Hill Dictionary of Art

Canadian History and Culture

Encyclopedia Canadiana, 10 vols.

Classical Civilization

The Oxford Classical Dictionary, 2d ed.

Film

The International Encyclopedia of Film

The New York Times Film Reviews, 1913–

Music

Harvard Dictionary of Music

The New Grove Dictionary of Music and Musicians, 20 vols.

Religion

Encyclopaedia Judaica, 16 vols.

Encyclopaedia of Religion and Ethics, 13 vols.

The Golden Bough: A Study in Magic and Religion, edited by Sir James G. Frazer, 13 vols.

New Catholic Encyclopedia, 15 vols.

The Oxford Dictionary of the Christian Church

Science and Technology

The McGraw-Hill Encyclopedia of Science and Technology, 15 vols.

Social Sciences

International Encyclopedia of the Social Sciences, 19 vols.

Literature

When you write research papers for literature courses, you have a large body of research materials to draw from, including several outstanding works.

The Oxford Companion to American Literature, 4th edition, edited by James D. Hart, offers biographies of American writers and summaries of literary works written in English by Americans. This volume pays little attention to literature not written by U.S. authors, and it ignores Latin American writers.

33D

The Oxford Companion to English Literature, 4th edition, edited by Sir Paul Harvey, presents biographies of British writers and summaries of their important works; it also gives writers' biographies and plot summaries from European literature considered influential in Britain and America.

The Oxford History of English Literature comes in twelve volumes, each covering a period of literature and written by a distinguished specialist in that field.

The Year's Work in English Studies, published in London annually since 1920, contains graceful, well-written summaries of books and articles published each year in the entire field of English literature.

Contemporary Authors, 1962–, is a large, multivolume series giving short biographies and publication information for twentieth-century writers.

Contemporary Literary Criticism, 1976–, is another large, multivolume series. It presents excerpts from reviews written by prominent critics of contemporary literature. The series has recently expanded to include film criticism.

The Harvard Guide to Contemporary American Writing, edited by Daniel Hoffman, 1979, surveys the most prominent recent American writers.

4 Use the bibliographies and notes in the works you consult to help you with your own research.

Look carefully at the scholarly books and articles you consult to find useful bibliographies and footnotes. References to other books and articles often lead to new and useful sources of information.

***Exercise 33.3** For any topic you narrowed down in Exercise 33.1 (page 470), make a list of five indexes that you might use to help you to locate articles in periodicals. Use the reference section of your library.

***Exercise 33.4** For any topic you narrowed down in Exercise 33.1, develop at least ten bibliography cards for books, periodicals, and other sources. Be sure to follow either the format suggested by your instructor or the format described in 33C as you copy down the required data.

33E Develop your thinking on your topic by exploring a few sources; then form a tentative thesis and develop a rough plan.

33E

After prewriting and after limiting your topic, explore some of your resources for information about it. Your purpose in reading at this stage is to develop your ideas about the topic. You will find that you do have ideas, and you can develop them. Doing research is more than simply gathering information—it is developing something of your own to say about what you have read. Don't worry about the number of people who have written about your topic before you. Some careful thought about your resources at this stage and as you continue your research will stimulate original ideas on your topic.

As your thoughts take shape, put together a tentative thesis (see 1F) and a rough plan. Both of these will help you concentrate on the topic you expect to develop in your paper. Your preliminary thesis should state your central idea and your special view of it. Your tentative plan and your thesis will guide the rest of your research and will help you to eliminate from your reading list books and articles that you cannot use.

The tentative thesis statements and the rough plans that follow might well have guided the writers of the papers on pages 522 and 536.

Plan: Write about the search for black holes

Tentative thesis: The search for black holes presents complex problems for astronomers today.

1. Definition
2. History of the idea
3. Early search
4. Pulsars
5. Binary stars
6. Current search

Plan: Write about Pearl Buck's life in China

Tentative thesis: Pearl Buck's unusual early childhood in China inspired her interest in writing.

1. Condition of Buck's childhood
2. What she learned and who taught her as a child
3. What she thought about reading and writing

These preparatory steps bring the topic into focus for note-taking and for real outlining. Of course, as you continue to read, you will make many changes, both in the thesis and in the rough plan.

***Exercise 33.5** Do some preliminary reading to shape your ideas about the topic that you chose in Exercise 33.1. Then, develop a tentative thesis and a rough plan to guide your research.

33F Read your sources with care, and take careful notes.

Whether you summarize, paraphrase, or copy quotations, always distinguish your own comments from the words and thoughts of your sources.

Write your notes on 3 × 5 cards, putting only one idea on each card. Limiting your notes in this way will make it easier for you to organize your materials later (see 33G). Some students prefer larger index cards, but big cards make it tempting to copy down more information and more quotations than you need. Quote directly on your note cards only if you think you may use the quotation in your paper. It is wise to summarize or to paraphrase many of your sources. Summarizing and paraphrasing force you to absorb the thoughts of your source and to express them in your own words rather than merely repeat them.

A formal **summary** is a sharply condensed version of your original source, in your own words. The summary of an essay usually states the thesis briefly and gives the most important points in the argument. A summary rarely cites evidence that supports the thesis; it limits itself to the main conclusions.

A **paraphrase** is a much fuller summary; it may cite some of the evidence and use some of the words in the original source. A good paraphrase follows the line of reasoning in the original source, and the sequence of ideas as well. In both paraphrases and summaries, you must acknowledge your sources.

If you have a book lying on your desk, do not waste time copying down a long quotation or writing a paraphrase or a summary on a note card. Instead, make a signal card. On a **signal card,** you note the page numbers where the information appears and record your thoughts about how a quotation might be used in your paper. Of course, you can't keep library books forever; so when you write signal cards, you should be ready to write your paper.

If you think you may not have the book handy when you do write, copy down the material you need, either as a direct quotation or as a paraphrase. Because copying long direct quotations by hand leads to errors, you must proofread such copied passages with great care.

Copying machines are available in most libraries, and you can copy a page or two from a book or a periodical. (Such copying is strictly regulated by federal copyright laws, and your library may have regulations about the use of copying machines.) Remember that copying the source on a machine is no substitute for reading it. If you are going to use the source in your paper, you must read it carefully and make it part of your own thinking.

Often, when you are taking notes, ideas about what you are summarizing, paraphrasing, or copying will occur to you. Be sure your notes distinguish your words and ideas from those of your source. In your paper you will have to identify the sources of all the ideas you have borrowed. If you do not make clear in your notes just whose ideas are whose, you may find yourself committing plagiarism (see 33L). Use parentheses, asterisks, arrows, or some other means to identify your own thoughts in your notes.

Below is an excerpt on black holes from page 37 of Preston Cloud's *Cosmos, Earth and Man: A Short History of the Universe* (New Haven: Yale UP, 1978). Various types of note cards prepared from the excerpt follow it. Note that the writer has identified the source at the top of each card in an abbreviated form. (Full bibliographic data will appear on the writer's bibliography cards; see 33D, section 1.)

Source
As early as 1798 the French astronomer and mathematician Pierre Simon de Laplace suggested that, if a star were dense and massive

enough, the velocity required for gravitational escape from its surface would be greater than the speed of light and that it would, therefore, be invisible. Even neutron stars cannot support a load greater than two or three solar masses. A more massive star must collapse until, consistent with relativity theory, light cannot escape and the condition visualized by Laplace is fulfilled. Such objects, assuming they exist, have been appropriately called *black holes.* A black hole may be thought of as a region in space of such fantastically high density that nothing ever leaves it. Volume at its center shrinks toward zero and density approaches infinity. Its ancestral star has essentially vanished from the visible universe—although, when quantum effects are taken into account, it appears that black holes actually do emit small amounts of radiation.

Quotation Card

Cloud, Cosmos . . ., p. 37

"A black hole may be thought of as a region in space of such fantastically high density that nothing ever leaves it. Volume at its center shrinks toward zero and density approaches infinity."
→ Compare definition with definition in Thorne and elsewhere. Definitions are very similar. No dispute on terms?

[The exact words of the source are in quotation marks; the quotation is not extensive and is one the researcher might want to use to define black holes. An arrow distinguishes the writer's thought from that of the source.]

Summary Card

Cloud, Cosmos . . ., p. 37

Black holes confirm 1798 ideas advanced by French mathematician/astronomer Laplace. Very dense stars with high mass prevent escape of light and are invisible. Black holes: high-density places in space where nothing can escape.

[This summary highlights the major points in the passage that pertain to the writer's concerns and interests. Note all the details omitted from the source.]

Paraphrase Card

Cloud, *Cosmos* . . ., p. 37
French astronomer-mathematician Laplace in 1798 believed that if a star had a high enough mass and density, it would be invisible, because the velocity of light would be less than the velocity needed to break loose from the pull of gravity on the star. A massive star "must collapse until, consistent with relativity theory, light cannot escape." Black holes are in spots of space "of such fantastically high density" that escape is impossible.
→ Gravity always increases as density increases? Check.

[Here the notes closely follow the line of reasoning of the original, although the writer has used his own words to restate the point. The few words in quotation marks are exact words from the source, which may be useful to support an idea in the research paper. Again, the writer uses an arrow to set off his own thought from the ideas in the original.]

* **Exercise 33.6** Take notes as you read and consult the various sources you have selected for your research. Use the note cards on pages 491 to 492 as models.

33G

33G Read and organize your notes carefully, and use them to help you focus your ideas and develop your plan.

Your early thesis statement and rough plan will guide your reading and note-taking and will shape your thoughts about the topic. Your thoughts, in turn, will suggest changes in your thesis and plan. Don't worry if your thesis and plan change many times as you develop your outline, rough drafts, and final draft for the paper. Following a preliminary plan too rigidly keeps you from making the major changes in emphasis and organization that later reading and thinking often suggest.

If you have done your research carefully, you will have many note cards on which you have collected quotations, paraphrases, statistical information, and other data from your sources. Only one idea should appear on each card. Now you have to read your notes over carefully and organize them so that you can develop your paper.

In reading through your note cards, you should find that your material falls naturally into subject groups. The headings in your rough plan were, of course, your guide for taking and organizing notes from the beginning. By now you have probably clustered related data from various sources around the general headings in this plan. Yet as you reread your note cards, you will think of new major headings that bear on your topic and discover some old main headings that do not. You will also think of subheadings that flesh out the main headings.

At this point, you are ready to expand your rough outline further, to prepare a formal outline, or to write a first draft. First, collect all your note cards, put them in order, and number them consecutively. Now you can prepare a summary guide that tells you, by number, where each note card fits into your plan. Here are excerpts from the summary guide developed for the paper on Pearl Buck:

Topic Summary Guide

Headings	**Note cards**
Conditions of Buck's childhood	3, 14, 15, 16
What she learned as a child	1, 8, 9
Buck's education in Chinese language and culture	10, 11, 12, 13
Buck's education in English	4, 5, 22, 23, 31
Her feelings about America	6, 7, 24
Her determination to be a writer	40, 45

This kind of guide to your note cards helps you arrange them according to tentative headings. And because the cards are numbered and each card includes the author's name and the title of the book or the article, you can keep track of your sources as you go along.

This system of organization allows you to experiment. You can group and regroup related data and ideas and shift the order of subject groups around before you make any final decisions about your plan. This experimentation also can help you to develop your plan by suggesting more effective headings and subheadings.

You also may find it useful to think on paper about your topic in its current state. The following excerpt from several pages of notes shows how the writer of the paper on black holes began focusing his ideas and shaping the essay. These notes are experiments—attempts to build a design that will help the writer decide exactly what should be in the paper and what should not.

Writing notes like these will help you develop your information into a paper. Notice that there are questions, sentence fragments, thoughts that don't lead anywhere. All these are part of that initial shaping that eventually makes a paper.

Notes on Black Holes

Topic: The search for black holes

Should of course define what black holes are. Definition will help explain why the search for them is worth a paper. Black holes are compressed objects, containing trillions and trillions of tons of matter in the volume of a pinhead or less. How can anybody imagine that! Jastrow says our intuitions tell us such objects cannot exist. But intuition told people the world was flat. Maybe they do exist.

Black holes are collapsed stars. Not just any star. Has to have a mass of at least three times the mass of the sun before gravity strong enough to make a black hole. Before a star collapses, energy from nuclear burning balances the gravity and holds the star in being. Like our sun. But as the star burns out its nuclear fuel, it begins to shrink. As star grows smaller, gravity grows greater, star shrinks more, until it disappears within itself.

Concept of black holes especially hard to grasp because we all grow up with Newton's idea of the universe as a great, silent machine, turning and turning. Newton's universe has no end; went on forever, at least mathematically. Had no beginning either. But the black hole idea means that it all ends in such compression that the elements themselves disappear. Atoms squeezed together in an undifferentiated mass. There goes Shakespeare! Nothing survives.

Religious people say this mathematical picture not necessarily true. God could intervene. God might have other plans. But can't treat that in a paper. Just say black holes are the end of the universe as we know it. Maybe don't even need to go into such things. Paper supposed to be nine or ten pages. Can't begin to cover everything!

Discuss discovery of pulsars. Pulsars only about ten miles across. They spin in space, throwing off radio waves from the friction of the atoms compressed in them. Jastrow says pulsars like the beam of light from a lighthouse. As the pulsar spins, it throws a pulse of radio waves toward earth. Can be picked up by radio telescopes. Should I explain radio telescopes? No, just say they are huge radio receivers that can be turned to different parts of the sky.

From the brief plan on page 489 and from the notes he developed in investigating the topic "black holes," the writer prepared this expanded plan.

Topic: The Search for Black Holes

Thesis: Astronomers are finding it almost impossible to discover and investigate black holes.

1. Definition of black holes
—Schwarzschild's theory
—Oppenheimer's move from theory to reality
—Problems of detection presented by the nature of black holes
2. The beginning of the search for black holes
—Why people did not search for them for a long time
—Discovery of a turbulent universe in the sixties
  a. The end of Newton's calm assumptions
  b. Possibility that people did not look for black holes because they did not want to prove such a bleak theory
—Discovery of pulsars, or neutron stars
—Relation of the compressed pulsar to the black hole
3. Russian work on black holes
—Idea that a black hole and a bright star might exist in a binary relationship
—Method of their search
  a. Examination of star catalogs for stars with unusual patterns
  b. X-ray emissions from stars
4. Continuation of the search among binaries
—*Uhuru* satellite and detection of x-rays
—V861 Sco
5. The search for black holes at the center of galaxies
—Qualities of galactic centers
—How phenomena may be explained by positing a black hole
—Galaxy M 87
6. Reinterpretation of existing data
—Cassiopeia A
—Qualities that need to be explained
—Iosef Shklovsky's theories
7. Conclusion

With an expanded plan like this, you can prepare a draft of the paper. You have a format, a fairly clear idea of what you want to say, and a collection of evidence to support your generalizations. But as you write, some things are bound to change. The plan may need to be simplified, or you may find it necessary to leave some things out. (It is always good to have more information than you can possibly use in your paper.) You may also realize that diagrams or charts would help to clarify some points that are hard to describe in words.

Exercise 33.7 Compare the rough plan on the topic "black holes" (page 489) with the later plan for the topic (pages 494–495), and be prepared to discuss similarities and differences.

* **Exercise 33.8** Continue reading about your topic. Using the rough plan you formulated in Exercise 33.5, develop a more detailed plan.

33H Write a formal outline if one is required or is useful at this stage, and revise your thesis if necessary.

1 Write a formal outline.

Your instructor may require a formal outline, or you may find that one is useful in your efforts to refine your plan. A formal outline gives you an orderly visual scheme of your ideas, with supporting points subordinated to controlling ones. As you set down these ideas, use roman numerals for the most important points, capital letters for the next most important points, arabic numbers for supporting points under lettered points, and lowercase letters for the smallest items you include in the outline. Further subordination is possible, but you will rarely need to use all four degrees. For most papers, two or three degrees of subordination will do. The scheme looks like this:

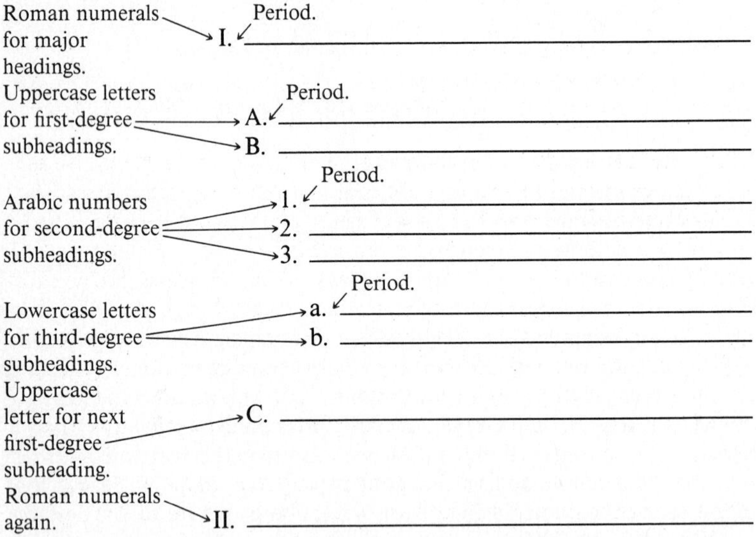

Once you have grouped large related ideas in your notes, label them with accurate, mutually exclusive, logically arranged headings. Follow your rough plan in doing this. But at this stage it is more important to concentrate on making your headings sufficient in number and breadth to cover the topic properly.

33H

As you look over these headings, some changes in organization may occur to you. Make whatever changes you need to shape your ideas, and then fill in supporting information under each major heading. Watch for and delete any overlap or repetition of ideas. The purpose of making a formal outline is to lay out your argument as clearly and as simply as possible.

All outlines follow the same format, but you can write them up in different ways. In a *topic outline,* you write out your points as brief capsules of meaning. They must communicate an idea, of course, but they need not appear in full sentences. In a *sentence outline,* each point appears as a complete grammatical statement, with a subject and a predicate. The sentence outline requires more effort because it asks you not only to name what you are going to talk about but also to summarize what you are going to say about it. For this reason, a sentence outline may be more productive, but a topic outline can be just as helpful if you think it through just as carefully.

Two rules govern the construction of every formal outline, whether topic or sentence:

1. *Every entry requiring division must be divided into at least two parts.* Division must produce two or more parts. When you divide a topic, you must have two or more subheadings under it. If you can come up with only one subpart, incorporate it into the main heading; it belongs there. In short, a *I* requires a *II*; an *A* requires a *B*; a *1* requires a *2*; an *a* requires a *b*.
2. *Main headings must be parallel in form to each other, and subheadings under each main heading must be parallel in form to each other.*

These rules will help you to construct a clear and useful outline of your paper. But remember that you should never be bound to your outline as you write. Feel free to pull out of the air the thoughts that come to all writers, ideas they did not have in mind when they planned their work. In fact, you may very well prepare the formal outline *after* you write the paper. Every essay that works has a logic and structure that can be outlined; so you should be able to outline your essay once you have completed it. Then the outline will help you see that you have constructed a logical and clear piece of prose, that you have put everything in its proper place, and that you have developed a thesis in a thoughtful and attractive series of paragraphs leading to a conclusion.

33H

The topic outline on page 523 and the sentence outline on pages 537–538 show you the skeletons of the sample research papers on pages 522–535 and 536–551. Study them carefully, and use them as models for correct form and style.

Exercise 33.9 Discuss the strengths and weaknesses in the following outline for a paper. Look especially at the relation of the thesis to the points on the outline; at the appropriateness and parallelism of main headings and subordinate points; and at the form of the outline, including divisions and the use of numbers and letters.

OUTLINE

Thesis: A study of liberal arts and sciences is valuable for students seeking careers in business.

I. Exclusion of liberal arts and science courses from business curricula
- **A.** Need for specialized business courses for job training

II. An understanding of people
- **A.** Value of psychology and sociology
  - **1.** In a study of personality and group dynamics
- **B.** Value of natural sciences in seeing problems and in stating and in finding solutions to them
- **C.** Insights into human character from literature
  - **1.** Complete personality studies from fiction
  - **2.** Opportunities to share thoughts of pressured characters

III. Recognition by businesses today of capabilities developing from employees' varied educational backgrounds
- **A.** Strong qualities of character
- **B.** Ability to deal with future technologies

IV. Transmission of humanity's cherished values

Exercise 33.10 Compare and contrast the formal topic outline for the black holes paper (page 523) with the earlier expanded plan (pages 494–495). What additions or deletions do you notice?

33H

* **Exercise 33.11** As your instructor directs, prepare a formal outline for your research paper. Use a *topic* or a *sentence* outline according to your instructor's wishes.

2 Make any necessary revisions in your thesis.

After studying your plan or outline and the notes that you now have in order, you should reevaluate your thesis in the light of what your reading has revealed about the topic. For the research papers that begin on pages 522 and 536, notice the evolution of the thesis sentences.

Tentative thesis	Revised thesis (1)	Revised thesis (2)
Pearl Buck's unusual early childhood in China inspired her interest in writing.	Pearl Buck's life in China and what she learned there were major influences on her life and her writing.	Pearl Buck's youth in China and what she learned as a child about America and the West provided the subject matter and influenced the style of her later writing.
The search for black holes presents complex problems for astronomers today.	Astronomers are finding it very difficult to discover and investigate black holes.	Although the search for black holes goes on, they are by definition almost impossible to find.

As you prepare your drafts and revise them, you may find that your thesis sentence needs to be further revised as well. Neither sentence under "Revised Thesis (2)" appears in the final drafts of the research papers you will see in 33N.

*** Exercise 33.12** Study your notes, and make revisions in your thesis sentence as required.

33I Write the first draft of your paper, integrating research materials thoughtfully with your own writing and acknowledging all sources.

Using your rough plan or your formal outline and your note cards, write a rough draft of your research paper. Stay relaxed as you write. This is not your final copy, and the point is not to say everything perfectly but simply to flesh out what you have to say. Once you have your paragraphs drafted, use them to adjust and to refine your rough plan or your formal outline.

At this stage you will have a rough draft but a nearly final outline. Your outline should now be a trusted guide to your next draft, although as new ideas come to you in the process of creating that draft, you may need to refine the outline still further. Throughout the writing process, the outline enables you to check the logic of your progress from one point to the next. Also, the outline helps you check the accuracy and the consistency of your argument.

As you write your draft, you will be drawing upon what you wrote on your note cards from your readings. Integrating source material into your own writing takes thought and care. Suppose you wanted to use material from the source below in your research paper:

Source

> The new group of readers was a large one, the largest in history, and it grew steadily on into the nineteenth century until it had established publishing as the first mass-production industry in the world; but its members were imperfectly educated, progressively less well educated, some would argue, the larger their number grew. Before the rise of the bourgeoisie, literacy was not considered something valuable in itself, but merely one of a desirable set of skills, values, and traditions. When a man learned to read at all, he acquired, with the mechanical art of spelling out words, certain standards; but with the final victories of the new class, literacy became a political demand and a sign of status, like suffrage or the right to carry weapons.
>
> —LESLIE FIEDLER

One option is to quote the source exactly. Depending on your purpose, you could quote a sentence or two to make your point, or you could present a longer quotation in block form, perhaps reproducing the entire paragraph above. Either way, you must separate your ideas from those of your source. At the same time, you should blend your own words with the words of the writer you are quoting to produce a smooth and pleasing sentence. In 33K you will learn the mechanics of documenting your sources in a variety of citation systems. Here we are concentrating on how to make smoother connections between your prose and the prose of your source.

Quotation from Source

```
The success of the novel as a literary form
relates to the growth of the middle class in the
nineteenth century and to the new value placed on
literacy. ''Before the rise of the bourgeoisie,''
Fiedler says, ''literacy was not considered
something valuable in itself.'' Later on, ''with
the final victories of the new class, literacy
became a political demand and a sign of status,
like suffrage or the right to carry weapons'' (40-41).
```

33I

[The quotation, starting with the word *before,* follows smoothly from the first sentence, which is the point that the writer wants to support with expert testimony. The tags *Fiedler says* and *later on* help the writer to integrate the quoted passages with her own writing. Full documentation appears in the list of works cited. (See 33C and 33K, section 1.)]

Quotation from Source

Fiedler writes in <u>Love and Death in the American Novel</u> that the novel succeeded because it reached a growing middle-class audience:

```
   The new group of readers was a large one, the
   largest in history . . . but its members were
```

imperfectly educated. . . . Before the rise of the bourgeoisie, literacy was not considered something valuable in itself, but merely one of a desirable set of skills, values, and traditions. When a man learned to read at all, he acquired, with the mechanical art of spelling out words, certain standards; but with the final victories of the new class, literacy became a political demand and a sign of status, like suffrage or the right to carry weapons. (40-41)

[The block form sets off a long quotation from the source. The quotation supports the point that the writer makes in the introductory sentence. Notice how the ellipses shorten the quoted paragraph (see 28F).]

Instead of quoting, you may choose to summarize or to paraphrase. Here, too, you must acknowledge the source of your ideas.

Summary

Fiedler points out that the new bourgeoisie looked upon literacy as a status symbol of great value (40-41).

Paraphrase

According to Fiedler, the new middle-class audience of readers looked at literacy in a new light. Previously, literacy was just one of many ''skills, values, and traditions'' that people wanted and was not itself of special value. However, as the bourgeoisie asserted itself, the right to read and write became ''a political demand and a sign of status'' (40-41).

[In the paraphrase, which follows the original line of reasoning more closely than the summary, the writer uses quotation marks around the phrases from the original.]

You must use your judgment about when to use quotation marks for individual words or for brief phrases borrowed from another source. Notice that the words *literacy* and *bourgeoisie* both appear in the original by Fiedler, but in the summary and the paraphrase, these words are not enclosed within quotation marks. A good general rule is that when you use three or more consecutive words from another source, you need quotation marks. Sometimes common sense will tell you that you need not use quotation marks, but the rule is a good one to keep in mind. It will make you think about what you are doing and will help you avoid the unconscious plagiarism that can get you into just as much trouble as the deliberate act (see 33L).

You are bound to have questions as you write your draft. Is your thesis as clear as you mean it to be? Do your ideas follow from each other logically? Do the quotations and paraphrases you have used support your points? At this stage, ask someone to read your draft before you go on. Perhaps your instructor will read it or will arrange for the class members to read each other's papers. If not, ask your roommate, some other trusted friend, or a family member. Nothing can help so much now as another pair of eyes.

Make a list of the questions you want to ask about your paper. Listen carefully to your reader's responses to those questions and to any advice your reader offers. Before you prepare another draft, consider what your reader has said, and if necessary, address your reader's concerns as you revise.

33J Once you have prepared an acceptable revised draft, edit it carefully for clarity of language and ideas and for conciseness.

Take the time to polish your expression and to check paragraph and sentence structure, grammar, spelling, and mechanics. Also, check the accuracy of quotations, paraphrases, and summaries. Avoid plagiarism by citing your sources clearly and consistently (see 33I and 33L).

33K Cite your sources in the text of your essay, or in endnotes or in footnotes that are clear and consistent in form.

When you cite your sources, you provide documentation for the materials you used in your paper. Each time you borrow someone's words or ideas you must tell your readers. You can use either internal documentation or footnotes (or endnotes) to indicate your source of information.

The 1984 MLA guidelines recommend a simple system of in-text documentation that eliminates footnotes and endnotes for citation purposes. This system uses footnotes and endnotes only for peripheral explanations, comments, evaluations, and biographical data. The MLA recommends that documentations in the text include only the bare essentials. With a comprehensive bibliography or list of works cited at the end of the paper, readers can easily find full documentation.

Because footnotes and endnotes are also widely used for documentation, you should know how to use these systems as well.

1 Use parenthetical references to document your sources directly in your text.

In the MLA system of internal documentation, all citations are integrated directly into the text, in the form of parenthetical references. Each citation must include:

1. The author's last name.
2. The location of the material you borrowed. Usually the page numbers alone are enough; in a multivolume source, give the volume number as well. For literary works, you may want to give the act, scene, line, chapter, book, or stanza.

Remember: Complete bibliographic information must appear in the list of works cited at the end of the paper (see 33C).

Model Internal Documentation

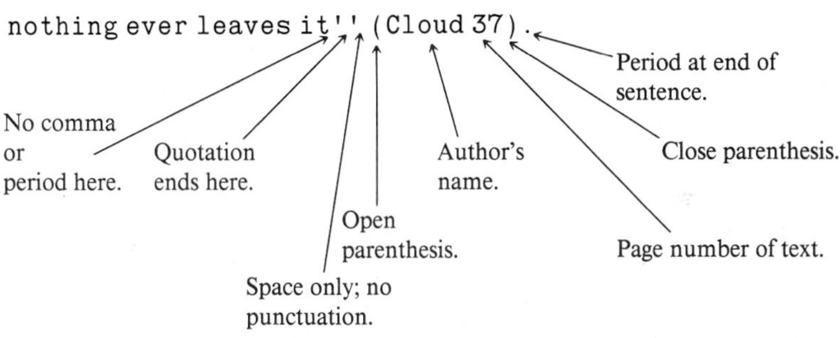

33K

The complete entry for Cloud's book in the list of works cited appears on page 535. (For the full source from which the model internal documentation is taken, see pages 491–492.)

The key to successful parenthetical documentation is your complete list of works cited at the end of the paper. Every reference you make in your text must correspond to an entry on that list. Information you provide in the parenthetical documentation must match the information on your list of works cited.

Try to be concise and unobtrusive with your parenthetical references. Place them where pauses occur naturally in your sentences and as close as possible to the information you are identifying.

What you include in parentheses and what you include in the accompanying text will reflect your individual style as a writer. Feel free to experiment with different formats for references, remembering that what you include in your text determines what you include in the parenthetical documentation. If you use the author's name in a sentence, do not put that name in parentheses. If you do not name the author in your sentence, name him or her in parentheses.

No one can show all the stylistic possibilities for internal documentation, but the following examples illustrate the simplest options. Wherever possible, these examples correspond to examples presented in 33C (preparing entries for the list of works cited) and 33K, section 3 (preparing footnotes and endnotes).

Parts of Single Volume Books or Articles

Cloud defines a black hole as ''a region in space of such fantastically high density that nothing ever leaves it'' (37).

A black hole, as Cloud points out, ''may be thought of as a region in space of such fantastically high density that nothing ever leaves it'' (37).

The density of a black hole is so high that anything inside it is trapped forever (Cloud 37).

[The first two examples provide documentation that cites the author's name in the text. The third example is a paraphrase taken from Cloud; because the author's name does not appear in the sentence, the writer includes it in the parenthetical reference.]

This definition of black holes is one with which Cloud would agree (37).

One scientist describes the shrinking of the volume in a black hole to zero (Cloud 37).

It may be true that black holes are definable (Cloud 37), but many still find it difficult to believe that they exist.

Gingerich introduces the issue thoughtfully (81-82).

Coleridge compels us ''to recognize the nullity of those habitual processes which we call thinking . . .'' (Sewell 131).

A switch to the metric system will make arithmetic computations simpler than in the past (Atherton 13).

To cite an entire work rather than a part of it, name the author in your text and avoid a parenthetical reference:

Cloud provides a detailed explanation of the phenomenon of black holes.

Morford and Lenardon have published an interesting collection of Greek and Roman myths.

Morgan, King, and Robinson have provided a basic text for beginning students of psychology.

Baugh et al. trace the growth and development of English literature from the Middle Ages to the twentieth century.

[The three citations directly above are all for books with more than one author.]

Al Pacino's performance in American Buffalo surprised the drama critics.

In his debut as a director, with the film Ordinary People Robert Redford drew upon his skills as an actor of long standing.

Multivolume Works

Sir Thomas Browne's Pseudodoxia Epidemica was ''no hasty compilation, but was the product of many years of patient thought, reading, observation, and experiment'' (2: vii).

[The number before the colon in parentheses refers to the volume; the number after the colon refers to the page number. (The vii tells you that the quotation comes from the preface; pagination in the preface or other front matter in a book is generally in lowercase roman numbers.)]

Modern readers may be mystified by the range of classical allusions in the Pseudodoxia Epidemica (Browne, vol. 2).

[This parenthetical reference is to an entire volume of a multivolume work and not to any particular part of that volume. Here, you use a comma to separate the author's name from the volume and you use the abbreviation for volume.]

Works Cited by Title Only

A recent report suggests that keen interest in black holes is continuing in the scientific community (''Astronomers'').

[For parenthetical references to a work that appears in the list of works cited by title only, use a shortened version of the title. Omit the page number if the article is brief; otherwise include the page number after the title.]

Works by a Corporate Author

The Modern Language Association points out that the research paper '' is a carefully constructed presentation of an idea--or a series of ideas--that relies on other sources for clarification and verification'' (2), but many students merely present a collection of other people's ideas and opinions without supporting a hypothesis.

[The reference is to the *MLA Handbook for Writers of Research Papers.*]

Two or More Works by the Same Author

Bacon condemned Plato as ''an obstacle to science'' (Farrington, Francis Bacon 35).

Farrington points out that Aristotle's father Nicomachus, a physician, probably trained his son in medicine (Aristotle 15).

[The title, or shortened form of it, is necessary in the parenthetical reference to a work by an author who appears more than once on your list of works cited. A comma follows the author's name if you use it in the parenthetical reference. If you put the author's name in the text, give only the title and the page reference, as in the second example above. Two of Farrington's books, *The Philosophy of Francis Bacon* and *Aristotle: Founder of Scientific Philosophy,* would appear on the list of works cited in this case. See 33C for how to list more than one work by the same author on your list of works cited.]

Literary Works

In the opening sentence of Lord Jim, Conrad shows us the physical power of his hero (3; ch. 1).

Marlowe says about Brown that what set him apart from other scoundrels ''was the arrogant temper of his misdeeds and a vehement scorn for mankind at large and for his victims in particular'' (Conrad 352-53; ch. 38).

[For classical literary works in several editions, readers find it useful to have more than just page numbers in a reference. Chapter, book, or act and scene numbers make it easier to find materials in any copy of a novel or play. In the parenthetical reference, cite the page number first, then use a semicolon, and then give any other useful information, such as chapter, book, or act and scene numbers. Use accepted abbreviations.]

More Than One Work in a Single Reference

In 1978 and 1979 a number of popular scientific journals reported on the phenomenon of black holes (Cebelle; Pringle 419; ''Astronomers'').

[Use semicolons to separate works when you cite more than one in a single parenthetical reference. Because a reference that is too long will distract your readers, you may want to use a footnote to cite multiple sources.]

Indirect Sources

Wolfe was upset at an anonymous criticism of his play The Mountains. He told his teacher at Harvard, George Pierce Baker, that ''if I knew who wrote that, I would no longer be responsible for my actions'' (qtd. in Turnball 54).

[You should take material from original sources whenever you can. But when the original is unavailable and you have only an indirect source (for example, a published account of someone's spoken comments) use the abbreviation "qtd. in" in your parenthetical reference, right before your citation. Your list of works cited would include a reference like this:

Turnball, Andrew. Thomas Wolfe. New York: Scribner's, 1967.

You might choose to document your original source in a footnote or an endnote; see 33K, section 3.]

Footnotes or Endnotes with Parenthetical Documentation

Karl Schwarzschild, a German astronomer, first formulated the idea of a black hole in 1916. He argued that such an object could exist if we assume that light is affected by the force of gravity (''Schwarzschild'').[1]

[1] In 1798 the French mathematician and astronomer Pierre Simon de Laplace hinted at the possibility of phenomena like black holes, but he never used the term. See Cloud 37.

[When you use parenthetical references in your research paper, footnotes or endnotes can provide additional comments on the text, bibliographical information for several sources, or evaluative comments on those sources. In the above example, the writer cites in the text the source of his information and uses the note to explain information that does not belong in the text itself. In addition, he offers a further citation, a reference to Cloud's book.]

2 Other systems of parenthetical documentation

The Author-Date System

Scientists generally agree that a black hole is ''a region in space of such fantastically high density that nothing ever leaves it'' (Cloud 1978).

[In the author-date system, popular in the social and physical sciences, the parenthetical reference includes the date of publication after the author's name. (Any information cited in the text itself would not appear in the parenthetical reference.) To assist the reader in finding bibliographical data easily, the format for the entry in the list of works cited requires that the year of publication come immediately after the author's name. Thus, in such a system, the book by Cloud would be listed in this way:

Cloud, Preston. 1978. Cosmos, Earth and Man: A Short History of the Universe. New Haven: Yale UP.

If you have more than one work by an author in any given year, use a lowercase letter to distinguish them (1978a, 1978b). The lowercase letter would appear in the internal citation and in the list of works cited.]

The Number System

This definition of black holes is one with which Cloud would agree (2, 37).

[The number system requires arabic numbers for each entry in the list of works cited; these numbers appear in the parenthetical citation, too. A comma separates the number of the entry from the relevant page number, and the entry number is often underlined as you see above. With such a system, references included in the list of works cited may be arranged in any useful order, such as the order in which the writer cites the references in the text.]

33K

Full Publication Data in Parenthetical References

Cloud describes the shrinking of the volume in a black hole to zero. (Cosmos, Earth and Man: A Short History of the Universe [New Haven: Yale UP, 1978] 37).

[If you are required to give full parenthetical citation, use square brackets to replace the parentheses you would ordinarily use around city, publisher, and date. Full publication information in parenthetical references is rare; it distracts readers from the text and does not provide for a list of works cited that readers always find useful. Occasionally, however, you will see this system in a bibliographic study or in a work that cites only a few references.]

3 Use footnotes or endnotes to document your sources.

Many researchers use a system of notes to document their sources accurately. In such a system, notes provide full publishing information, but they may also provide useful data, commentaries, or detailed explanations of points made in the text. As an example of this secondary use of notes, see note 5, page 549, in the paper on Pearl Buck.

Footnotes appear at page bottoms, numbered consecutively throughout the paper. Endnotes, which are easier to set up because you number them consecutively and put them at the end of an essay, often appear in both student papers and scholarly works. But many readers—especially academic readers—still prefer to see the documentation of a source in a footnote, at the bottom of the page where the source is used.

Annotation must be clear and consistent. Your notes should make it easy for your reader to locate your sources, and they should be patterned consistently to avoid confusion. The following notes (based on the *MLA Handbook*) show you the most common style used in academic publications. Each note corresponds to an entry in 33C. For each source, therefore, you can compare the format for a footnote (or an endnote) with the format for an entry in the list of works cited.

Books and Reference Works

Model Footnote Entry: A Book with One Author

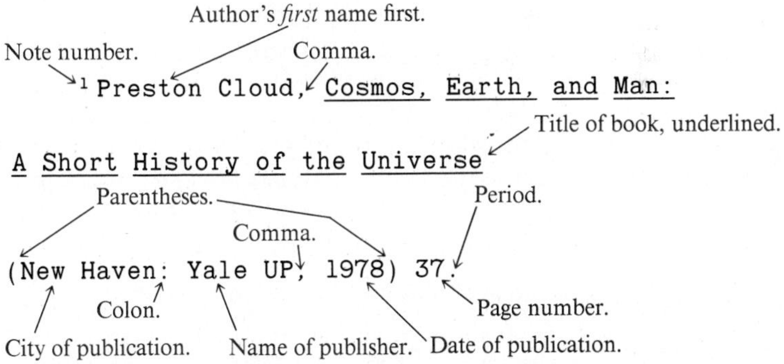

Author's *first* name first.

Note number. Comma.

     1 Preston Cloud, <u>Cosmos, Earth, and Man:</u>

Title of book, underlined.

<u>A Short History of the Universe</u>

Parentheses. Period.

Comma.

(New Haven: Yale UP, 1978) 37.

Colon. Page number.

City of publication. Name of publisher. Date of publication.

[Commas separate the major divisions in a note reference to a book: the author's name, the title and the publishing data, and the page number. Parentheses set off the publishing data from the rest of the reference, and, as in bibliographic entries, you can always use the short form of the publisher's name. A period completes the entry. Raised a half space above the line, the number of each note comes after a five-space indentation.]

33K

An anthology

[2] Don M. Wolfe, ed., American Scene: New Voices (New York: Lyle Stuart, 1963) xi-xii.

A book by two or more authors

[3] Mark P. O. Morford and Robert J. Lenardon, Classical Mythology (New York: Longman, 1971) 153-54.

[4] Clifford T. Morgan and Richard A. King, Introduction to Psychology 2d ed. (New York: McGraw-Hill, 1961) 10.

[5] Albert C. Baugh et al., A Literary History of England (New York: Appleton, 1948) 307.

[6] Clifford T. Morgan, Richard A. King, and Nancy M. Robinson, Introduction to Psychology, 6th ed. (New York: McGraw-Hill, 1979) 296.

A book with corporate authorship

[7] Modern Language Association, MLA Handbook for Writers of Research Papers, Theses, and Dissertations (New York: MLA, 1977) 138-39.

A book with no author's name on the title page

[8] Greece: 1974. (Athens: National Tourist Organization of Greece, 1973) 141.

A selection from an anthology

[9] Elizabeth Sewell, ''Bacon, Vico, Coleridge, and the Poetic Method,'' in Giambattista Vico: An International Symposium, ed. Giorgio Tagliacozzo and Hayden V. White (Baltimore: Johns Hopkins P, 1969) 127-28.

33K

A preface, an introduction, a foreword, or an afterword

[10] Richard P. Blackmur, introduction, The Art of the Novel: Critical Prefaces, by Henry James (New York: Scribner's, 1962) xvii.

A work in more than one volume

[11] Thomas Browne, The Works of Sir Thomas Browne, ed. Geoffrey Keynes, 4 vols. (London: Faber, 1928) 2: 7.

[The number *2* refers to the second volume. A colon and a space after it separate the volume number from the page number, here page *7*. If you wanted to cite the entire volume, you would write *vol. 2* right after the space following the final parenthesis. A period would complete the entry.]

An edited book

[12] Pearl Buck, China as I See It, ed. Theodore F. Harris (New York: John Day, 1970) 15.

A translation

[13] Paolo Maffei, Beyond the Moon, trans. D. J. K. O'Connell (Cambridge: MIT Press, 1978) 19.

A republished book

[14] John Knowles, A Separate Peace (1959; New York: Bantam, 1966) 66.

A work in a series

[15] Swimming Medicine IV, International Series on Sports Sciences 6 (Baltimore: University Park Press, 1978) 416.

Selections from reference books

[16] ''Kindergarten,'' Encyclopaedia Britannica, 1974 ed.

[17] Norman Moore, ''Hodgkin, Thomas, M.D.,'' Dictionary of National Biography (1908).

[18] John Henry Naylor, ''Peninsular War,'' Encyclopaedia Britannica, 1974 ed.

Pamphlets, bulletins, and public documents

[19] United States, Congressional Budget Office, Proposition 13: Its Impact on the Nation's Economy, Federal Revenues, and Federal Expenditures (Washington: GPO, 1978) 7-8.

[20] National Academy of Sciences, Committee on Water, Division of Earth Sciences, Alternatives in Water Management, National Research Council Publication No. 1408 (Washington: National Academy of Sciences, 1969) 3.

Model Footnote Entry: An Article in a Journal with Pages Numbered Continuously Throughout the Annual Volume

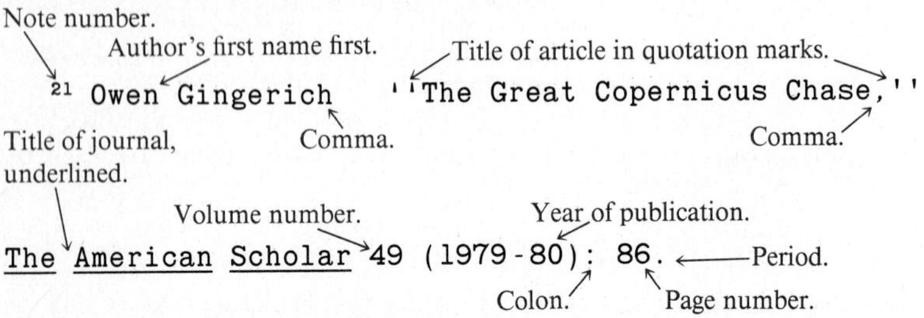

Note number.
Author's first name first.
Title of article in quotation marks.

[21] Owen Gingerich, ''The Great Copernicus Chase,''

Title of journal, underlined.
Comma.
Comma.

Volume number.
Year of publication.

The American Scholar 49 (1979-80): 86. ← Period.

Colon.
Page number.

[As in the reference to a book, commas separate the main elements here.]

An article in a journal that numbers pages separately in each issue of an annual volume

[22] Walter Jewell, ''The Contribution of Administrative Leadership to Academic Excellence,'' WPA: Writing Program Administration 3.3 (1980): 9-13.

An article in a monthly or bimonthly periodical

[23] Thomas R. Gebelle, ''The Central Parsec of the Galaxy,'' Scientific American July 1979: 69.

33K

An article in a weekly magazine

[24] James Pringle, ''A Black Hole in the Center of M 87?'' Nature 3 Aug. 1978: 419.

[The question mark at the end of the title makes a comma unnecessary.]

An unsigned article in a magazine

[25] ''Astronomers Hear from a Black Hole,'' New Scientist 14 July 1979: 23.

An article in a daily newspaper

[26] Atherton F. Clark, ''Metric Lengths Make Computation Easier,'' San Antonio Express 31 July 1978: A13.

Special Works

Unpublished dissertations and theses

[27] Nora Eisenberg, ''The Far Side of Language: The Search for Expression in the Novels of Virginia Woolf,'' diss., Columbia U, 1977, 29-30.

Book reviews

[28] Peter J. Fleming, ''Nobel Lady,'' rev. of Pearl S. Buck: A Biography, by T. F. Harris, Catholic World Dec. 1969: 139.

Recordings

[29] Giuseppe Verdi, La Traviata, with Joan Sutherland, Luciano Pavarotti, and Matteo Manuguerra, cond. Richard Bonynge, National Philharmonic Orch. and London Opera Chorus, London Records, LDR-73002, 1981.

Plays and concerts

[30] Arvin Brown, dir., American Buffalo, by David Mamet, with Al Pacino, Circle in the Square Downtown Theatre, New York, 14 Aug. 1981.

[31] Michael Tilson Thomas, cond., American Symphony Orch. Concert, Carnegie Hall, New York, 15 Feb. 1981.

Films and television (or radio) programs

[32] Robert Redford, dir., Ordinary People, with Donald Sutherland, Mary Tyler Moore, and Timothy Hutton, Paramount, 1980.

[33] The Mother, writ. Paddy Chayevsky, dir. Delbert Mann, Philco Television Playhouse, NBC, 4 Apr. 1954.

Interviews

[34] Telephone interview with Beverly Sills, director of the New York City Opera, 6 Dec. 1981.

Later References to the Same Source

Once you provide full publishing data in a note, you can use a shortened form of citation in each later reference to your source. Generally, these references include only the author's last name and the page number. Although the *MLA Handbook* (1977) discourages the use of the Latin abbreviation *ibid.* for *ibidem,* meaning "in the same place," the form still persists in academic writing. The samples below of first and later citations show both styles.

[1] Irvin Block, The Lives of Pearl Buck (New York: Crowell, 1973) 6.

[2] Peter J. Fleming, ''Nobel Lady,'' rev. of Pearl S. Buck: A Biography, by T. F. Harris, Catholic World Dec. 1969: 139.

[3] Block 15.

[4] Block.

[5] Fleming 139.

[Notes 1 and 2 give all the data required as well for the sources in notes 3 and 5, respectively. Therefore, the shortened form appears in notes 3 and 5, with only the author's last name and the page number in each. Since the reference in note 4 is to the same page as the page in note 3, the author's last name alone is enough.]

[1] Irvin Block, The Lives of Pearl Buck (New York: Crowell, 1973) 6.

[2] Ibid. 15.

[3] Peter J. Fleming, ''Nobel Lady,'' rev. of Pearl S. Buck: A Biography, by T. F. Harris, Catholic World Dec. 1969: 139.

[4] Ibid.

[5] Block 6.

[*Ibid.* indicates that the citation appears in exactly the same source as in the preceding note. Capitalize *ibid.* as the first word of the sentence, in the note, and always use a period after the abbreviation. In note 2, the reference is to the same book named in note 1, although the page number is different. Note 3 introduces a new citation. *Ibid.* in note 4, therefore, refers only to the source named in 3; because the page number is the same in both, no reference to pages is required in note 4.]

When you use two or more sources by the same author, the author's name alone in later references would be unclear. Avoid confusion by using a shortened form of the title along with the author's name, but be sure that readers can recognize the source easily.

[15] William Labov, ''The Study of Language in Its Social Context,'' Studium Generale 23 (1970): 68.

[16] William Labov, The Study of Nonstandard English (Urbana: NCTE, 1970) 16.

[17] Labov, ''The study of Language'' 33.

[18] Labov, Nonstandard English 18.

[Notes 17 and 18 refer to different sources by the same author. A shortened form of the title identifies the source more specifically than the name alone.]

Abbreviations

As noted before, the Modern Language Association recommends that writers avoid using Latin abbreviations, which at one time were standard in research papers. You will encounter abbreviations often in your reading, however, and you should know what they mean. The following list includes familiar abbreviations for bibliographic citations, along with some of the short forms of Latin terms that you may encounter.

anon.	anonymous
bk., bks.	books(s)
c., ca.	circa ("about"), used with approximate dates
cf.	compare
ch., chs.	chapter(s)
col., cols.	column(s)
diss.	dissertation
ed., eds.	edition(s) or editor(s)
et al.	et alii ("and others")
ff.	and the following pages, as in: *pp. 85ff.*
ibid.	ibidem ("in the same place")
illus.	illustrated by, illustrator, illustration(s)
l., ll.	line(s)
loc. cit.	loco citato ("in the place cited")
ms, mss	manuscript(s)
n., nn.	note(s), as in p. 24, n. 2
n.d.	no date (of publication)
no., nos.	number(s)
n. pag.	no pagination
n.p.	no place (of publication) or no publisher
op. cit.	opere citato ("in the work cited")
p., pp.	page(s)
pt., pts.	part, parts
passim	throughout
q.v.	quod vide ("which see")
rev.	revision, revised, revised by; or review, reviewed by
rpt.	reprint, reprinted
sec., secs.	section, sections
trans.	translator, translated by, translation
univ.	university
vol., vols.	volume(s)

Placement of Footnotes and Endnotes

Number your notes consecutively throughout the paper, starting with 1. Do not use asterisks or other symbols instead of numbers. In the text, type the arabic number of the note a half space above the line after all punctuation (except a dash). Note numbers always come in a logical place after a quotation or a paraphrase, and they should not distract the reader by breaking up a thought unit. Keep your notes as unobtrusive as possible.

The MLA recommends that you use endnotes for research papers that require notes, unless you receive other instructions. Type endnotes on a separate page (or pages) after your last page of text. Use double spacing throughout the endnotes. Leave a one-inch space on top of the first page, then type the word *Notes.* Double space beneath it before you type the first note of your paper. Here, too, place note numbers half a space above the line. Continue numbering the pages of endnotes as consecutive pages of your text. Thus, if your last page of text is page 10, the first page of endnotes will be page 11. The sample research paper on Pearl Buck (536–551) shows endnotes.

If you use footnotes, leave enough space to type them at the bottom of each page. Leave four blank lines between the last line of your text and the first footnote. Indent five spaces before typing the note number (again raised above the line), and leave one space after it. Only the first line of each note is indented; all other lines are flush with the left margin. Use single spacing between the lines in each note. Use double spacing between the notes themselves.

Exercise 33.13 Select a passage from a magazine article or a book, and incorporate elements from it into your own writing by following the directions below. Use appropriate citations. Clip out the passage or make a copy of it to show your teacher.

1. Write a brief summary of the passage as part of a paragraph that might appear in a draft of your paper.
2. Write a short paragraph in which you quote a few lines exactly from the passage.
3. Write a short paragraph in which you paraphrase the passage.

Exercise 33.14 Write a sentence that summarizes, paraphrases, or quotes a portion of each selection below. Within your sentence, provide documentation for the source. Use the new MLA guidelines; do not use footnotes or endnotes. Give full documentation for a list of works cited.

1. "When Shakespeare came to London from Stratford-on-Avon, the new poetry, which was to crown the last decades of the sixteenth century and the beginning of the seventeenth, was already established. Its arrival had been announced in 1579 by the publication of Spenser's *The Shepherd's Calendar.*" (The selection is from *Shakespeare's Songs and Poems,* edited by Edward Hubler. The quotation is from pages xii–xiii. The book was published in 1959 by McGraw-Hill in New York.)
2. "Every summer, one of the nation's longest-running and most hotly contested photo competitions takes place at the offices of Sierra Club Books in San Francisco. Between 50,000 and 100,000 color transparencies are submitted for publication in the four Wilderness calendars, and the flood of entries keeps a small army of freelance photo editors and clerks busy from July to November." (The selection is from an article called "Wilderness Pin-Ups by Sierra Club" by Catherine Kouts in *Publishers Weekly,* volume 225, number 17, April 27, 1984, page 41.)

Exercise 33.15 Write footnotes or endnotes according to the following instructions.

1. In note 1 cite pages 28 to 29 in Sidney Verba and Norman H. Nie's 1972 book *Participation in America,* published in New York by Harper and Row.
2. In note 2 cite page 1 of an article called "Joint Project with University Aims at Revitalizing High School" by Beverly T. Watkins in *The Chronicle of Higher Education* dated May 16, 1984. *The Chronicle* is a weekly newspaper.
3. In note 3 cite page 8, column 2 of the same article.
4. In note 4 cite the Verba and Nie book again, page 40.
5. In note 5 cite the Verba and Nie book again, same page as in note 4.

33L Credit all your sources to avoid plagiarism.

When we learn, we always borrow. But we also always presume that having borrowed learning from others, we can make something out of it that is our own. When you borrow something and use it in your own writing, you must leave no doubt in your reader's mind as to what you have borrowed. If you are conscious of your debts and try to show them, you will not commit plagiarism.

Plagiarism occurs whenever you present words or ideas taken from another person as if they were your own. The easiest way to avoid plagiarism is always to use quotation marks when you quote directly from a source, and always to acknowledge a source in your text or in a footnote (or an endnote) when you borrow or even allude to someone else's ideas and language, even though you may not have used that person's exact words.

If you fail to follow these rules for borrowing from other writers, you may commit plagiarism. The most obvious plagiarism is *simply copying,* either word for word or with a few words added or shifted around. Anyone who compares the source and the copy can recognize plagiarism instantly.

Another form of plagiarism, called **mosaic plagiarism,** may result when a well-meaning, uninformed writer takes bad notes or when a dishonest one deliberately attempts to deceive readers. Here the words are not copied entirely from the source. The writer may add words or sentences or even whole paragraphs. But anyone who reads the source and the plagiarism can tell that the latter entirely depends on the former:

Source

> A territory is an area of space, whether of water or earth or air, which an animal or group of animals defends as an exclusive preserve. The word is also used to describe the inward compulsion in animate beings to possess and defend such a space. A territorial species of animals, therefore, is one in which all males, and sometimes females too, bear an inherent drive to gain and defend an exclusive property.
>
> In most but not all territorial species, defense is directed only against fellow members of the kind. A squirrel does not regard a mouse as a trespasser. In most but not all territorial species—not in chameleons, for example—the female is sexually unresponsive to an unpropertied male. As a general pattern of behavior, in territorial species the competition between males which we formerly believed was one for the possession of females is in truth for possession of property.
>
> —ROBERT ARDREY

33L

Mosaic Plagiarism

> Territory may be defined as an area of space, water, earth, or air, which animals defend as an exclusive preserve. The word *territory* also describes the inner compulsion in living beings to own and defend such a space. In a territorial species, males and some females are driven to gain and defend their exclusive property against fellow members of the species. The female of most territorial animals is not responsive sexually to a male without property, and the competition between males that we once believed was for the possession of females is really for possession of property.

[Anyone can see that this paragraph depends entirely on the original. Some words have been changed or added, and many phrases have been altered, but the second passage is out-and-out plagiarism.]

Plagiarism is the most serious offense that a writer can commit. The prose we write ourselves is our property. Writing and thinking are so individual that when we write something in a striking way or express a new idea, we have produced something that always belongs to us. Plagiarism is a theft from the mind. It is also foolish. Plagiarism is almost always discovered, and the professional writer who plagiarizes may never get anything published again. The student who plagiarizes can expect a failing grade on the paper, and in almost all schools for the whole course. In many schools plagiarism is an honors-code violation and grounds for expulsion.

How can you avoid plagiarism? The following suggestions will help.

Avoiding Plagiarism: Some Pointers

1. Study the subject you are writing on until you believe that you have something of your own to say about it. The more you think about your research, the more you will realize that you do have ideas of your own and that your opinions are worthy of being expressed. As you study, think, and write, you can come up with good ideas, and you won't have to copy the work of others.

2. Always keep your own notes and comments about a subject separate from the things you copy from other sources. Students sometimes commit accidental plagiarism because their note-taking fails to distinguish between what is their own and what they have copied.

   Read 33F on note-taking again. You may choose a different way of keeping your words separate from those of your sources. You could write your comments in a different color or keep them in a separate notebook or draw a circle around them or indicate them with an arrow. Whatever you do, do something! If you can see at a glance that some ideas came out of your own head and some from your sources, you'll avoid plagiarism.

3. Always acknowledge your sources. Here is how the writer of the mosaic plagiarism on page 518 could have avoided it by acknowledging the source of those thoughts, Robert Ardrey:

   Ardrey defines territory as an area "whether of water or earth or air" that animals see as theirs exclusively and which they are driven by an "inward compulsion" to defend against members of their own species. A female in a territorial species is "sexually unresponsive to an unpropertied male." Ardrey believes that males do not compete for females. Instead, "the competition . . . is in truth for possession of property" (3).

[This is a paraphrase that gives Ardrey credit for his points. Quotation marks enclose phrases and a clause taken directly from the original. The page number in parentheses shows exactly where in Ardrey's work these ideas appear. Full documentation would appear in the list of works cited.]

4. Always use quotation marks when you are quoting directly, even if you choose to quote only a short phrase or clause.
5. Even when you are not quoting directly from a source, always be sure to attribute striking ideas to the person who first thought of them. Let your readers know the source of any novel ideas you use in your own paper, and you will be both honest and courteous.
6. You need not attribute information that is common knowledge. If you say that World War II ended in 1945, you do not have to footnote your statement, since it is common knowledge. But if you do not know whether information is common knowledge or not, you should consult your teacher or an expert in the field.

33M Prepare the final version of your research paper in acceptable form. Follow standard manuscript preparation requirements.

Most instructors ask that you type long papers, and you should follow the guidelines for manuscript preparation carefully (see 1K). Handwritten research papers are hard to produce neatly because of their length and are difficult to read. If, with your instructor's permission, you choose to handwrite your final copy, take special pains to produce a neat, clear manuscript.

Final copy for a research paper or a term paper usually includes, in this order:

1. A title page. The *MLA Handbook* suggests that the author's name, the class, the date, and so on, should appear on the first page of the paper, an inch down from the top and an inch from the right. The title is centered, four spaces above the text of the paper. But when formal outlines are required, many instructors prefer a title page. (See page 522 for a sample.)
2. A formal outline.
3. The body of the essay.
4. Endnotes. (If your instructor requires footnotes, place them at the bottoms of pages. If you use parenthetical documentation, endnotes or footnotes will be minimal.)
5. The list of works cited.

Number all your pages consecutively in the upper right-hand corner, starting with page 1 of your text. Some writers type their last name before the page number in case pages are misplaced. Do not use a period, hyphen, or the word *page* (or the abbreviation *p.*) with the page number. Remember that endnotes and the list of works cited do count in the total pagination of your paper.

1 Prepare a final list of works cited.

Your list of works cited, placed at the end of your paper, must include all the materials you used. If you used print materials only, call your list a "Bibliography." A list that also includes materials consulted but not cited is entitled "Works Consulted." For a sample of "Works Cited," see page 535; for a sample of "Works Consulted," see page 551.

Guidelines for Preparing a List of Works Cited

1. Set up your list on a separate page at the end of your paper.
2. Type the title ("Works Cited," or "Works Consulted," or "Bibliography") about one inch from the top of the page, and double space before you type the first entry.
3. Arrange all your entries alphabetically according to the author's last name, but do not number them. The author's last name goes first, then the first and middle names.
4. See page 474 for listing two or more books by the same author.
5. List all entries without authors alphabetically according to the first important word in the title.
6. Do not separate books from periodicals. Strict alphabetical order guides the arrangement of entries. (For advanced research projects, writers sometimes separate primary from secondary sources.)
7. Start the first line of each entry at the left margin. Indent five spaces all the other lines within each entry. Double-space within entries and between them.

33N Examine sample research papers.

The two research papers that follow illustrate the many suggestions made in this chapter and demonstrate some of the options available to a researcher in different subject areas. Examine these sample research papers, and use them as models whenever you encounter problems in setting up research papers of your own.

***Exercise 33.17** After reading the sample papers and following the guidelines set forth in 33M, prepare the final copy of your research paper. Observe any requirements made by your instructor. Include a list of works cited.

The Search for Black Holes

by

Richard Lanier

English 101, Section 6

Nov. 7, 1983

33N

Outline

Thesis: Although the search for black holes goes on, they are, by definition, almost impossible to find.

I. Black holes vs. ordinary stars
   A. Definition of black holes
   B. Contrary forces on ordinary stars
      1. Expansion from nuclear burning
      2. Compression from gravity
   C. Theory of black hole formation
      1. Crush of atoms
      2. Lack of light

II. Beginnings in the search for black holes
   A. Problems in finding them
      1. Their invisibility
      2. Their infinitesimal size
      3. Their place in theories of the universe
   B. Discovery of pulsars, or neutron stars

III. Russian work on black holes
   A. Idea of binary relationship
   B. Method of search
      1. Examination of star catalogs
      2. Theory of stars' x-ray emission

IV. Continuation of search among binaries
   A. _Uhuru_ satellite and x-ray detection
   B. X-ray star called V861 Sco
   C. Doubts from inadequate instruments

V. The continuing hunt for black holes

The Search for Black Holes

One of the most talked-about scientific concepts to emerge during the past two decades is the black hole. Astronomers are scanning the skies with all their amazing technology, accumulating evidence for the existence of black holes. The trouble is that if black holes do exist, they are by definition almost impossible to find.

What is a black hole? In theory it is a burned-out, enormous star that has collapsed. Its atoms have become so squeezed together that what is left of the star is almost infinitely dense. When density increases, so does gravity. In the black hole, the density is so great and the gravity of the object is so powerful that even light cannot escape from it.

In an ordinary ''healthy'' star like our sun, two contrary forces balance each other. One force is the expansion caused by nuclear burning pushing out toward the surface of the star. The other force is the star's own gravity, which tends to compress the star into a ball. It is much the same effect as the one we have observed with water floating in space when our astronauts have journeyed into weightlessness. Water squeezes itself into a ball, but the ball does not weigh enough to crush the atoms that it contains.

A diagram may help show the forces acting on a star like our sun.

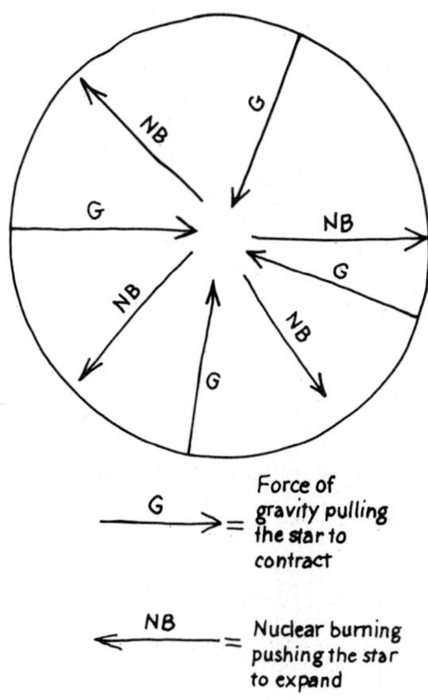

33N

All stars go through a complicated life cycle. The theory of black holes is based on the belief that eventually the force of gravity within the star becomes much stronger than the expanding force generated by the nuclear reaction in the star. The star literally burns itself out, and when its fuel is exhausted, it begins to shrink. If the star is large enough--at least three times larger than our sun--it contains so much mass that its gravity begins to crush its atoms. All atoms have a great deal of space in them--much more space than substance. Gravity squeezes the space out, making them more and more dense and, of course, reducing the circumference of the star.

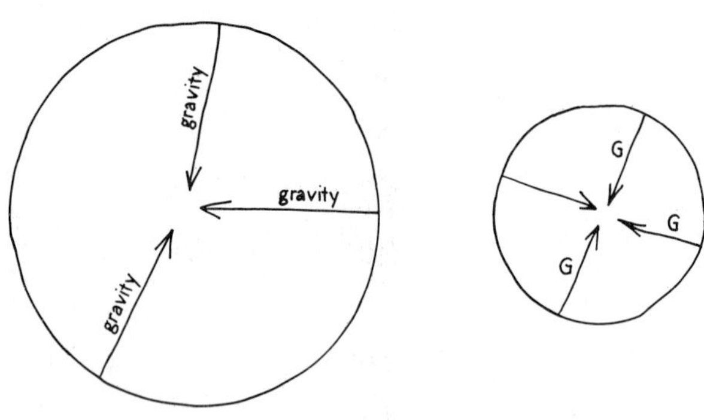

This crushing of atoms releases energy that might take the form of light. But scientists who believe in black holes think that the gravity of the crushed star is so great that no light can escape from it. Robert Jastrow sums up the process in the following passage, where he compares rays of light to a ball thrown up from the earth and returning because of the pull of gravity:

> But if the core of the collapsing star is squeezed into a very small volume, the force of gravity on its surface is very great. Suppose the core is squeezed down to a radius of a few miles. At that point,

> the mass is so compact that the force of gravity at the surface is billions of times stronger than the force of gravity at the surface of the sun. The tug of that enormous force prevents the rays of light from leaving the surface of the star; like the ball thrown upward from the earth, they are pulled back and cannot escape to space. All the light within the star is now trapped by gravity. From this moment on, the star is invisible. It is _a black hole in space_. (65)

This amazing theory has developed slowly. Karl Schwarzschild, a German astronomer, first formulated the idea of the black hole in 1916. He argued that such an object _could_ exist if we assume that light is affected by the force of gravity (''Schwarzschild'').[1]

In 1939, J. Robert Oppenheimer--later to become famous for his role in creating the atom bomb--and his student Hartland Snyder suggested that a black hole might result from the collapse of enormous, massive stars several times larger than our own sun. Their idea moved black holes from the realm of pure

[1] In 1798 the French mathematician and astronomer Pierre Simon de Laplace hinted at the possibility of phenomena like black holes, but he never used the term. See Cloud 37.

theory into real possibility (Dupree and Hartman 30). But how could black holes be found?

The most obvious problem is that black holes cannot be seen. No light can escape from them--an almost total barrier to observing them directly.

Not only are black holes invisible; they also may be tiny, even smaller than objects we can see with a powerful microscope. Jastrow writes:

> The star's volume becomes smaller and smaller; from a globe with a two-mile radius it shrinks to the size of a pinhead, then to the size of a microbe, and still shrinking, passes into the realm of distances smaller than any ever probed by man. At all times the star's mass of a thousand trillion trillion tons remains packed into the shrinking volume. But intuition tells us that such an object cannot exist. At some point the collapse must be halted. Yet, according to all the laws of twentieth-century physics, no force, no matter how powerful, can stop the collapse. (65)

Until the mid-1960s, few astronomers cared to undertake the detection of black holes. In fact, the idea of black holes challenged the concept of a calm, orderly universe, a concept inherited from Newton that guided the development of space theory for many years. As Kip S. Thorne has observed, ''Objects such as black holes . . . were too bizarre to fit naturally into our tranquil universe'' (67). But in the 1960s, scientists began to discover that the universe was much more turbulent than they had dreamed. In 1967 an astronomy student at Cambridge University in England discovered pulsars, which were soon recognized to be neutron stars. These were stars that had collapsed until the protons, the positively charged particles in atoms, and electrons, which are negatively charged particles, had been forced together to form neutrons, or electrically neutral particles (Thorne 66-67).

The inner space of the atoms in these neutron stars had been so reduced that the stars were only ten miles in diameter, far too small to be seen with optical telescopes. But they gave off powerful radio waves, the product of intense radiation created as the compressed atoms in the neutron stars collided with each other. (Because they pulsate with radio waves, these stars are called ''pulsars.'') Since a neutron star is spinning rapidly, it flings radio waves off into space as it whirls in orbit so that ''the stream of radiation from its surface sweeps through space like the light from a revolving lighthouse beacon. If the earth happens to lie in the path of the rotating beam, it will receive a sharp burst of radiation once in every turn of the pulsar'' (Jastrow 63). Neutron stars exhibited the massive atomic collapse long theorized for dying stars. Their discovery made many astronomers think that black holes might also exist.

If black holes do exist, it seems logical to try to find them by studying their possible influence on nearby objects. Even before pulsars were discovered, two Russian astrophysicists had hit on the idea of examining binary stars as a way to discover black holes. Binary stars (double stars that revolve around each other) are numerous in the universe. Astronomers discovered long ago that in many binaries a bright star is joined to a dark one, one presumed dead; thus the bright star appears to wink as the dark star comes between it and the earth in the extremely rapid rotation typical of such bodies.

Could a bright star be joined in a binary combination with a black hole? The black hole would be too small to make the bright star wink. But it might show its presence by the tremendous gravitational pull it should exert on the bright star, a pull that could be detected by the sophisticated means astronomers use to measure the movement of light in space. If they could find a bright star with a peculiarly vibrating light, they might have a binary pair that includes a black hole.

As early as 1964, two Russians, Y. B. Zel'dovich and O. K. Guseynov, began looking through lists of stars compiled by astronomers over the years together with a record of the kind of light the stars give off. They searched for any records that might show the fluctuating light that might be caused by the gravitational pull of a nearby black hole. In the end, Thorne reports, the two Russians located five such stars (67).

Astronomers made another assumption: if a black hole was near a visible star, the black hole must be pulling that star's gas into itself. This action is illustrated by the following diagram, with the black hole enlarged in scale compared with the visible star.

In theory, the stellar gas must be falling into the black hole at a speed approaching the speed of

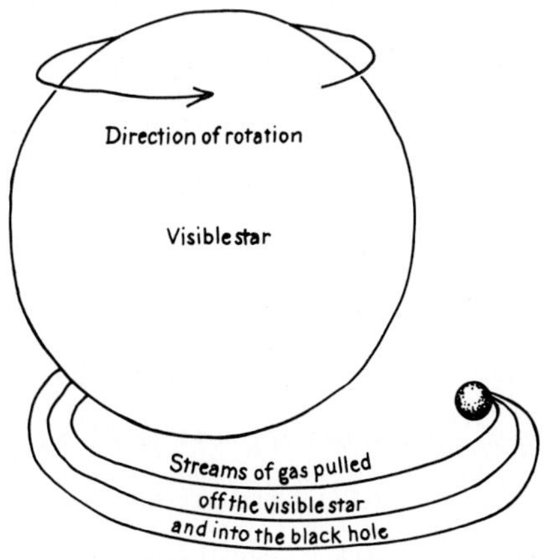

33N

light, 186,000 miles per second (Dupree and Hartman 30). When the molecules of gas moving at such a terrific speed collide with each other and with the surface of the black hole itself, enormous quantities of x-rays should be generated. So a star with an apparent wobble in space, having no detectable companion such as a pulsar and yet giving off huge quantities of x-rays, might be a star paired with a black hole.

But because the earth's atmosphere absorbs x-rays, the search for such x-ray-emitting stars could only be reliably conducted in space, and the hypothesis could not be tested until a satellite with an x-ray telescope had been launched into orbit.

In 1970, the United States and Italy jointly launched such a satellite, the Uhuru, and analysis of the data from this satellite showed that the best case for a black hole among the five stars the Russians had found is one called Cygnus X-1. (Stars are named for the constellations where they are found and according to a system of grid marks set on standard photographs of each segment of the sky.) The mass of the unseen companion pulling on Cygnus X-1 is estimated to be eight times that of the sun. This mass is easily large enough to have the gravitational pull that could produce a black hole. Some astrophysicists have concluded that the unseen companion is indeed a black hole (Thorne 69-70).

Another recently discovered x-ray star thought to be part of a binary pair is called V861 Sco. The object appears to be connected to a dark companion, and it is curious because it generates a large, luminous ultraviolet flare. William Oegerle and Ronald S. Polidan of Princeton University were struck by this flare. Derek Thomson reported on their findings in Science News:

> From the optical properties of V861 Sco, they could determine an orbital period of seven days. They figure that the mass of the primary star is between 20 and 50 times that of the sun. The unseen companion is between 7.5 and 13 solar masses. That rules out a neutron star or a white dwarf. [White dwarfs are stars that have shrunk to a few thousand miles across, thus having enormous density but giving off an intense, white light.] Either ought to have much less mass. It is possible in theory to link the ultraviolet flare with an X-ray flare. X-ray flares are seen in these X-ray binaries, and they are explained by changes in the gas flow between the two objects. So it all looks good provided V861 Sco really is the X-ray source. (25)

Thomson means that there is some slight chance that the x-rays detected by Oegerle and Polidan are coming

33N

from behind V861 Sco, from some more distant point in space.

There always seems to be another possible explanation for phenomena that might be caused by black holes. White dwarfs, those collapsing stars that still give off light although their mass is so great that a teaspoon of it would weigh ten tons (Jastrow 58), can draw gas from neighboring stars and produce x-rays. But so can neutron stars, and some astronomers are doubtful that their instruments are yet sensitive enough to tell the difference between these bodies and black holes (Dupree and Hartman 13). Some astronomers, like David Layzer at Harvard, are still extremely doubtful that black holes even exist.

But still the search goes on, and hardly a month goes by without the publication of an article in some scientific journal about yet another test for black holes. As a commentator on the television program Nova recently observed, human beings seem to have an unquenchable curiosity both about the way life begins and about the way the universe will end. If the universe does end in a black hole, the prospect is, appropriately enough, ultimately black. But no matter how bleak the prospect may be, the development of new technology, including much more sensitive instruments, is bound to mean that the quest for these strange objects will continue.

Works Cited

Cloud, Preston. Cosmos, Earth and Man: A Short History of the Universe. New Haven: Yale UP, 1978.

Dupree, Andrea K., and Lee Hartman. ''Hunting for Black Holes.'' Natural History Oct. 1979: 30-37.

Jastrow, Robert. Red Giants and White Dwarfs. New York: Warner Books, 1979.

Layzer, David. Personal interview. 25 Sept. 1983.

Nova. PBS television, 18 Sept. 1983.

''Schwarzschild, Karl.'' Encyclopaedia Britannica. 1974 ed.

Thomson, Derek. ''V861 Sco's UV Flare.'' Science News 14 July 1979: 25.

Thorne, Kip S. ''The Search for Black Holes.'' Cosmology ± 1. San Francisco: Freeman, 1977, 66-70.

Pearl Buck's Two Cultures

by

Helen Tong

English 101, Section 5

Mr. M. Lewis

April 7, 1985

33N

Outline

Thesis: Pearl Buck's youth in China and what she learned about America and the West provided the subject matter and influenced the style of her later writing.

I. She developed impressions about the two cultures early in her life.
   A. She learned from experience that adults in China indulged small children.
   B. The stories about China that she loved to hear as a child built impressions that she would draw upon later in her writing.
   C. The great writers she read as a young girl stimulated her desire to become a novelist.

II. Buck's formal education shows her experiences in two cultures at the same time.
   A. Although she read and wrote English easily, Buck had learned to speak Chinese first.
   B. As a child, she had lessons each day in both Chinese and English.
   C. At Miss Jewell's School for Western children she learned about some of the evils in Asian life.
   D. Although her parents taught her to consider an idealized America as her home, she never felt like an outsider in China.

III. Buck's writing often demonstrates a mixture of Eastern and Western cultures.

   A. Her publishers disapproved of her efforts to copy from writers before her although Chinese stylists endorsed this technique.

   B. Three novels, _East Wind: West Wind_, _The Good Earth_, and _The Three Daughters of Madam Liang_, show both traditional Chinese values and modern American values.

   C. A biography of Buck's mother shows a contrast between the two worlds.

IV. Buck lived in two worlds, and although she may not have felt finally at home in either, she gave Americans a view of the Chinese people based upon her own experiences in both worlds.

Pearl Buck's Two Cultures

Any reader of Pearl Sydenstricker Buck must come away from her novels, stories, biographies, and essays with a great respect for her ability to see things through both Eastern and Western eyes. Although she ''generally kept her work on American and Chinese subject matter separated,''[1] social, cultural, and intellectual values of the two worlds underlie most of her writing. Born in Hillsboro, West Virginia, but raised in China, she grew up in fact in those two worlds. The first was the world of America, which she had left as a child of a few months but about which she learned from her parents. The second was the world of China, where she lived for the first eighteen years of her life, before she came to America to study, and then again for many years as an adult. But more than anything else, it was the early years of Eastern and Western influences that laid the foundation for Buck's career as a writer, affecting significantly both the substance and the form of her work.

Early in her childhood she developed ideas and impressions about the two cultures. Certainly, China had played an important part in Buck's life. She writes:

> Born in my own country, the United States of America, of pre-Revolutionary ancestry, it was China who nurtured me. My first conscious memories are of her people and her landscapes. They formed my childhood world, they shaped my adolescent years, they brought me to my maturity.[2]

Buck's ''childhood world'' was a pleasant one, surrounded by indulgent adults. From Chinese servants she learned of the ways a child's whims were honored, for in China adults always indulged children. No one ever tried to stop their tantrums, and babies were picked up when they cried and were always carried around. Buck wrote that ''the Chinese child is not told or taught that he is wicked. . . . If he wants to scream, his elders bear it patiently, because he is a child and because they believe it is bad for anyone to bottle up anger.''[3] In the Sydenstricker household the Chinese servants spoiled the young child excessively. When her parents punished her, the servants begged for pardon on her behalf. They always took her side against discipline. Buck had only to look sad and a servant secretly would do a task that had been intended as a punishment for the child or would reward her with comforting sweets and toys.[4] When Wang Lung indulges his sons so often in <u>The Good Earth</u>, surely Buck is reflecting in her novel those moments of indulgence she herself experienced as a child.

As a young girl, she was fascinated by stories. She was engrossed by the lives of the people around her and listened hour after hour to anyone who would talk to her. In particular, she listened to the wonderful stories told by Wang Amah, the old Chinese nurse who had cared for her since she was three months old. This old nurse, who taught Buck to speak Chinese, also told her China's many legends and tales about religion that made her marvel. Buck recalls the Buddhist stories of gods and hell, as well as the Taoist tales ''of devils and fairies, and of the many spirits that live in tree and stone and cloud, and of the dragons in the storm and wind.''[5] Buck was a curious child, plaguing everyone with questions that sometimes became ''too intimate and personal.''[6] The people she met and their stories not only helped to develop the imagination of an alert, intelligent child but also, when she grew up, provided her with a considerable amount of material for her novels. From the story she tells of her own youth it is clear that many of her childhood acquaintances became characters in her books.''[7]

Before she was ten, Buck was determined to become a novelist. ''One longs to make what one loves,'' she wrote, ''and above all I loved to hear stories about people.''[8] In addition to listening to stories, she read incessantly, frequently about the Western world because she was eager to learn more about it. Whatever money she earned or received as gifts she spent for books. And although few American books ever reached China, her parents had many good collections of English writers: Dickens, Thackeray, George Eliot, Walter Scott, the English poets, and Shakespeare were among the writers of her youth in China.[9] Dickens impressed her greatly, and she later acknowledged his contribution to her writing.[10] Perhaps more than all these, however, it was the King James Bible that she enjoyed reading most in English, and Buck noted the similarities between the Bible and older Chinese writing and the importance of both these influences on her life: ''Since I was deprived of conversation in English with other children my own age, I suppose that these two classics of literature must have had some effect on my writing.''[11]

Perhaps Buck's experience with two cultures at the same time best shows up in her formal education, which was in both English and Chinese.

She spoke to her parents in English, and she read and wrote English sooner than Chinese because her mother taught her in English and insisted on good English usage and frequent exercises in writing. As a result, Buck developed ''a feeling for words and an ability to express ideas in a clear, pointed manner.''[12] Yet she did learn to speak Chinese before she learned English, and, as she points out, Chinese was her primary language in her childhood and had a lasting influence on her writing: ''The first curls of my tongue and lips were made about Chinese vowels and consonants, and my first sentences were in Chinese idioms. . . . When I am writing about Chinese people the story spins itself in my mind entirely in Chinese and I literally translate it as I go.''[13] She had formal instruction in the Chinese language from a Confucian tutor, Mr. Kung. At daily lessons with him she learned more than reading and writing in Chinese: ''I learned the first axiom of human life, and it is that every event has had its cause, and nothing, not the least wind that blows, is accident or causeless.''[14] These were peculiar and difficult days for Buck: in the mornings she ''sat over American schoolbooks'' and learned from her mother, and in the afternoons she ''studied under the wholly different tutelage of Mr. Kung.''[15] Buck says that as a result of these learning conditions she became ''mentally bifocal.''[16] However, despite what she notes as a strange education, Buck's early learning was painless and happy.

Even during the restless years of learning later

on in Shanghai at Miss Jewell's School for Western boys and girls, Buck absorbed much about China that would contribute to her writing, although she admits to little interest in formal instruction then. Compelled frequently by Miss Jewell to visit the Door of Hope, a home for Chinese slave girls rescued from their cruel mistresses, Pearl Buck at the age of seventeen saw different and more dreadful features of Asian life than she had seen before. Stories she heard of beatings with whips and of punishments with live coals or pipes and cigarettes disturbed her deeply. ''Many a night,'' she wrote, ''I woke up in my little room at Miss Jewell's School to ponder over the stories these young girls told me and I wept to think there could be such evil in the world.''[17]

China was the real world of Buck's youth; but her own country, America, remained a kind of fantasy. Everything in the white land was foreign to her. Her parents were her sole source of learning about her birthplace as Buck grew old enough to ask questions. She declared that ''My parents conveniently forgot all the less admirable aspects of their country, and while I was a child they regaled me with memories of quiet village streets, large houses set far back in trees and lawns.''[18] Consequently, Buck got the notion of incredible perfection in America and was always taught to call America ''home.'' But unlike her parents, she did not really consider herself a foreigner in her Chinese world. There she was Chinese: she spoke Chinese, behaved like a Chinese, and ate as the Chinese ate. She was not a foreigner, either in her own opinion or in the estimation of her Chinese friends. Not until 1910, when she entered Randolph-Macon Woman's College in Lynchburg, Virginia, did she realize that she would have to separate her two identities to some degree, and it was then that she began to dress and to speak in a more Western manner.[19] As late as 1932, however (Buck was forty years old then), she wrote of the mixed heritage that was so much a part of her: ''By birth and ancestry I am American, by choice and belief I am a Christian, but by the years of my life, by sympathy and feeling, I am Chinese.''[20]

Although experiences in the two cultures contributed to much of Buck's originality as a writer, they did cause some problems for her when she started her career in America. Chinese writers thought it was good style to borrow phrases and diction from great writers before them, and Buck aimed for similar results in her English writing. When she prepared her first book of fiction, East Wind: West Wind, the publisher insisted, however, that she revise the manuscript to remove ''the large number of clichés and hackneyed phrases''[21] she had deliberately included from books she had read in English!

Her writing frequently showed a mixture of Eastern and Western influences. In East Wind: West Wind a young Chinese couple struggles to deal with the attack on Chinese traditions by modern Western influences, and ''From this division of allegiance comes the basic conflict of the story.''[22] In the Pulitzer-prize winner, The Good Earth, a novel exclusively about China and the Chinese, Buck also portrayed important American values. One critic says that this novel stresses ''the old American belief in hard work, thrift, ceaseless enterprise, and the value of living close to the land.''[23]

One of Buck's last novels, The Three Daughters of Madame Liang, draws heavily upon the attractions and drawbacks of America and China. Madame Liang owns a restaurant in Shanghai under communist rule, but she lives in a magnificent house that she bought from American friends forced to leave China forever. Proud of China, yet drawn by America, Madame Liang sends her daughters to school in the United States. In those daughters' lives Buck shows the tragic conflicts between Western and Eastern values and loyalties. Finally, in a biography of her mother,

Buck draws upon a keen sense of the contrasts between the two worlds to present an image of this West Virginia woman living in China, a woman whose nature in so many ways symbolized those contrasts:

> Strange figure there in that American garden she has made in the dark heart of a Chinese city! She could pass for none other than an American, although the foreign sun has burned her skin browner than is its nature. . . .
>
> It is she who has planted American flowers there, wallflowers and bachelor's buttons and hollyhocks against the enclosing brick wall of the compound. . . . Over the ugly, angular lines of the mission house she has persuaded a Virginia creeper to climb, and it has covered two sides already.[24]

Buck was in the curious position of existing ''In one world and not of it, and belonging to another world and yet not of it.''[25] Her background and her experience gave her ''a two-sided view of every situation,''[26] but not without complications. Theodore Harris, a biographer who knew Buck well, says:

> Though her early memories are of China, she was an alien in that land and a stranger to the land of her birth. I have

33N

> thought many times that perhaps it is this beginning that partly explains the deep sadness that often comes over her face in repose. . . . Could it stem from a Chinese heart and mind living in a body with Western appearance and American heritage? Could her basic loneliness originate from the fact she is not at home with either side of herself?[27]

Certainly, China was a very important side of her. Reading her work, one can feel the respect she had for that country. And her writing, influenced by both the culture of her birthplace and that of her childhood, told a piece of the truth about China. She tried through her books to help the American people to understand and to accept the Chinese people and their ways.

Notes

[1] Paul A. Doyle, Pearl S. Buck (New York: Twayne, 1951) 134.

[2] Pearl S. Buck, China As I See It, ed. Theodore F. Harris (New York: John Day, 1970) xi.

[3] Buck 69.

[4] Pearl S. Buck, My Several Worlds (New York: John Day, 1954) 10-11.

[5] Theodore F. Harris, Pearl S. Buck: A Biography, 2 vols. (New York: John Day, 1969-71): 33. Buck's father, Absalom Sydenstricker, also told her many strange and exciting stories based on his travels as a missionary. See Doyle 23.

[6] Buck, My Several Worlds 62.

[7] P. J. Fleming, ''Nobel Lady,'' rev. of Pearl S. Buck: A Biography, by T. F. Harris, Catholic World Dec. 1969: 138.

[8] Buck, My Several Worlds 75.

[9] Buck, My Several Worlds 62-63.

[10] Pearl S. Buck, ''A Debt to Dickens,'' Saturday Review of Literature 4 Apr. 1936: 11.

[11] S. J. Woolf, ''Pearl Buck Finds That East and West Do Meet,'' New York Times 20 Nov. 1938: (7)4.

[12] Doyle 24.

[13] Harris 2: 224-25.

[14] Buck, My Several Worlds 52.

[15] Buck, My Several Worlds 51-52.

[16] Buck, My Several Worlds 52.

[17] Buck, My Several Worlds 70. This awareness of evil, she points out, made her resolve to fight it fiercely throughout her life by helping the victims of cruelty.

[18] Buck, My Several Worlds 5.

[19] Doyle 225.

[20] Harris 2: 297.

[21] Doyle 30.

[22] Doyle 30.

[23] James D. Hart, The Popular Book (New York: Oxford UP, 1950) 253.

[24] Pearl S. Buck, The Exile (New York: Reynal and Hitchcock, 1936) 10.

[25] Buck, My Several Worlds 51.

[26] Doyle 21.

[27] Harris 1: 30.

Works Consulted

Bentley, Phyllis. ''The Art of Pearl S. Buck.'' English Journal 24 (1935): 791-800.

Buck, Pearl S. China As I See It. Ed. Theodore F. Harris. New York: John Day, 1970.

---. ''A Debt to Dickens.'' Saturday Review of Literature 4 Apr. 1936: 11, 20, 25.

---. East Wind: West Wind. New York: John Day, 1930.

---. The Exile. New York: Reynal and Hitchcock, 1936.

---. The Good Earth. New York: John Day, 1931.

---. My Several Worlds. New York: John Day, 1954.

---. The Three Daughters of Madame Liang. New York: John Day, 1969.

Doyle, Paul A. Pearl S. Buck. New York: Twayne, 1951.

Fleming, Peter J. ''Nobel Lady.'' Rev. of Pearl S. Buck: A Biography, by T. F. Harris. Catholic World Dec. 1969: 138-39.

Harris, Theodore F. Pearl S. Buck: A Biography. 2 vols. New York: John Day, 1969-71.

Hart, James D. The Popular Book. New York: Oxford UP, 1950.

Snow, Helen F. ''Pearl S. Buck, 1892-1973.'' New Republic 24 Mar. 1973: 28-29.

Woolf, S. J. ''Pearl Buck Finds That East and West Do Meet.'' New York Times, 20 Nov. 1938, sec. 7: 4, 19.

34
Business Writing

Whenever you send out a business letter, a job application, or a résumé, you can expect to be judged on the form of what you have written as well as on the content. If you misspell words, type over errors without erasing them, or leave smudges and stains on what you send out, you can expect your readers to conclude that you are sloppy and careless in all your work. If you do not use the standard forms of business writing, your readers will assume that you do not know how to use them. If you do not communicate information in a clear and structured way, your readers will be likely to see you as disorganized. But if your business correspondence is written clearly, directly, and neatly, your business audience will be inclined to pay serious attention to you.

34A Write letters according to accepted business standards.

Formats for business letters vary, but a simple, acceptable presentation uses a modified-block style, single-spaced. In the scheme for the letter below, notice how all the lines (except those in the heading and in the closing) are flush with—that is, full out to—the left margin. Note, too, the correct layout on the page, as well as the spacing and the punctuation. (For ease of reference and discussion, the various parts of the letter are identified by names and numbers.)

Always type business letters and résumés on unlined, sturdy bond paper, usually 8½ × 11 inches, and use standard envelopes, 4 × 9½ inches. (You may choose to use smaller envelopes—3½ × 6½ inches—but be sure that your letters are folded to fit neatly within the envelopes.) Take special care to produce neat, clean copy that is error-free, and double-check your spelling. Many prospective employers immediately eliminate candidates whose résumés or letters include even one or two misspellings. Often so many people

Parts of a Business Letter

(1) Heading. Street address ____________

City, state, and zip code ______, ______ ______ (Comma.)

Date ______, ______ (Comma.)

space (3–4 lines)

______ Name

______ Title

______ Company (2) Inside address.

______ Street address

______, ______ ______ City, state, and zip code (Comma.)

space (2 lines)

______: (Colon.) (3) Salutation.

space (2 lines)

______

______

______ (4) Body.

space (2 lines)

______

______

______

______

space (2 lines)

______

______

space (2 lines)

Complimentary close ______, (Comma.)

space (4 lines)

(5) Closing. Signature ______

Typed name ______

34A

apply for the same jobs that employers must find a quick way of cutting down a long list of applicants. General sloppiness or misspelled words provide a quick excuse for discarding an application.

1 Give your full mailing address and the date in the heading.

A comma separates the city from the state and the day of the month from the year; no other punctuation appears. Write out all entries fully (see 31C, section 2). Paragraphs appear in block form; that is, they are not indented. With letterhead stationery, write the date a few lines above the office address and flush with the left or right margin, or else center the date below the address.

College Division McGraw-Hill Book Company

1221 Avenue of the Americas
New York, New York 10020
Telephone 212/ 512-6317

October 3, 1985

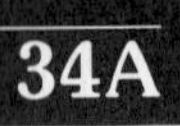

2 Give the full name, title, and address of the person to whom you are sending the letter.

Three or four lines below the date, type the inside address so that it matches the form of the heading. Avoid abbreviations (see 31C, section 2). The addressee's title may appear on the same line as the addressee's name, on the same line as the name of the company, or on a separate line.

Mr. David Delaney, Registrar
Nantaskette Community College

Mr. David Delaney
Registrar, Nantaskette Community College

Mr. David Delaney
Registrar
Nantaskette Community College

3 Use an appropriate salutation.

The salutation, always followed by a colon, greets the addressee. It is placed flush with the left margin, below the inside address, and it is separated from the inside address by a double space.

Use the addressee's surname in the salutation. Styles vary and change with time, but these examples offer a range of salutations acceptable to most people.

Dear Mr. Spanos:

Dear Messrs. Smith and Dale: [*Messrs.* is the abbreviated plural for *Mister* and also for *Monsieur.*]

Dear Dr. Majeski:

Dear Ms. DeQuarto:

Dear Mrs. Hao:

Dear Mmes. Cohen and Grey: [*Mmes.* is the abbreviated plural for *Madame* and is used in the rare instances that *Mrs.* requires a plural.]

Dear Miss Williams:

To avoid unnecessary reference to marital status, many writers favor *Ms.* as a title for women (see 31D). This usage has won wide acceptability, and many women in business prefer it for its neutrality. However, *Miss* and *Mrs.* still do appear, and you should use one of these forms of address if you know that the person you are addressing prefers it. (One way to learn this preference is to see how that person has signed any letters written to you or to see how the name is listed in the posting for a job.) Use the first name alone only if you know the addressee well as a friend.

In writing to business organizations or to someone whose name you do not know, use one of the following salutations:

Dear Registrar: [Title of the person]

Dear American Express: [Name of the organization]

Dear Sir or Madam:

Dear Sir: [If you know that the recipient is a man]

Dear Madam: [If you know that the recipient is a woman]

Gentlemen: [If you know that everyone is male in the group you are addressing]

Dear Colleagues:

To whom it may concern:

A good dictionary will provide correct forms for addresses and salutations in the special cases of elected government officials, religious leaders, military personnel, and so on.

4 Plan the body of your letter so that it will achieve your goals.

You must plan your letters carefully to achieve your purpose in writing. Good letters are clear, concise, concrete, and complete, giving accurate and sufficient information precisely and without complication or error. Courtesy is essential, but you should not appear to grovel toward your addressee. The letter should reflect your personality while maintaining a serious tone appropriate to your purpose in writing.

Many people suppose that a good business letter must be bland and impersonal. Do not fall into this false belief. Letters should be interesting—but take care to write naturally and to avoid extremes. Do not get entangled in stilted, overblown, or wordy constructions, and beware of a breezy informality that tells readers that you do not take your topic or them seriously.

Unnatural I want to take this opportunity to inform you of the fact that I was most seriously interested in the announcement of the accounting job you advertised last week.

Too Informal Your accounting job sounds like a real grabber. Count me in.

Better I would like to apply for the accounting job you announced in *The Times-Standard* on November 15.

34A

With the modified-block form, lines are flush with the left margin. Do not indent the first line of paragraphs; double-space between them, and single-space from line to line within them. Although content dictates the number of paragraphs your letter requires, try to be brief. Your readers probably do not want to read more than one page; they certainly do not want to read anything unnecessary. For ease and speed of reading, your paragraphs in business letters should be shorter than those you use in other forms of writing.

5 In the closing, include the complimentary close, your handwritten signature, and your typed name (and title if appropriate).

Letters usually close with one of the endings below. A capital letter always starts the first word of the *complimentary close;* a comma always follows the complimentary close.

Yours truly,	Sincerely,
Very truly yours,	Sincerely yours,
Yours very truly,	Yours sincerely,
Cordially,	Cordially yours,
Respectfully,	Respectfully yours,
Regards,	Best regards,

The *signature* appears in a four-line space between the complimentary close and the *typed name* of the writer. Most writers avoid adding a professional title (such as attorney-at-law) or a degree (such as Ph.D.) after their typed name. However, to indicate their official capacity, writers who have a business title sometimes use it.

Sincerely yours,	Yours truly,
Carolyn Garfield Marketing Manager	Tremont T. Blast Dean of the Faculty

34B Address envelopes clearly and completely, following postal guidelines.

Address envelopes to include all essential information required for postal delivery. The address centered on the envelope is the same as the inside address; the return address in the upper left of the envelope includes the sender's name and address. Write out all words according to standard practice (see 31C, section 2), except for official post office abbreviations for names of states.

```
Julie Holden
3200 Lake View Drive
State College, PA 16801

          Ms. Delores Smith
          Personnel Manager
          Farm Journal, Inc.
          230 West Washington Square
          Philadelphia, PA 19105
```

Fold $8\frac{1}{2} \times 11$ stationery in thirds so that it fits a standard $4 \times 9\frac{1}{2}$ envelope. Fold the bottom third up, then the top third down, leaving about a quarter inch between the top edge of the paper and the bottom fold so that your recipient can open the letter easily. For smaller business envelopes, fold standard paper in half from the bottom up; then fold the paper in thirds, left side first, right side over left.

34C To apply for a job, write a letter that catches the reader's attention.

Among the scores of responses a personnel director receives after a job is advertised, your letter must stand out if you are to receive the consideration you want.

A job application letter usually accompanies a full résumé, which gives the applicant's educational background, work experience, and other interests. Thus the purpose of the letter is to convince your reader that you can bring special talents to the position. You should make your own letters as specific and as vigorous as you can. Don't be satisfied with telling your reader, "I have had much valuable experience that will help me in this job." Tell what that experience has been in clear, concrete language. Avoid commonplace endings such as "Thank you for your consideration" or "Thank you for your time." An effort to arrange an interview will help establish your seriousness of purpose.

The following sample letter is an example of a forceful and concise job application letter. Note that each paragraph serves a specific function. The first states the writer's purpose in sending the letter. The second describes how the writer's background would help her to do well in the job she is applying for. The third paragraph explains how the writer's education has prepared her for this job, and the last paragraph asks for an interview. Everything is to the point.

34D Prepare a standard résumé that accurately presents your education, your work experience, your interests, and other pertinent personal data.

Formats for résumés differ (some are discursive, while others are brief outlines), but all include the information potential employers need to know about their workers. As the sample shows, you should type your résumé and lay it out attractively. Because a brief résumé helps a prospective employer evaluate your record quickly, you should try to keep your presentation to a

R.D. 2, Box 9
Manheim, PA 17545
February 22, 1982

Ms. Dolores Smith
Personnel Manager
Farm Journal, Inc.
230 West Washington Square
Philadelphia, PA 19105

Dear Ms. Smith:

My four years of education at The Pennsylvania State University and my twenty years' experience as a farmer's daughter have given me the knowledge and background necessary to become a good editorial assistant with Farm Journal, Inc.

Like many of your readers, I was born and raised on a farm. I have planted corn, mowed hay with a tractor, delivered calves, and built fences. I share with your readers an appreciation of farm life and an understanding of many of the problems of the independent farmer.

As you will see on my résumé, I am graduating from the university in June with a bachelor of arts degree and a double major in English and sociology. I have studied the problems of writing, editing, and producing a magazine. In my classes, I have practiced and refined my knowledge of writing and editing. Now I would like to apply what I have learned. For you.

I will be in Philadelphia for a week starting March 15. If we could arrange for an interview on the morning of March 16, I would be most grateful. I will call you before that day to see if it is convenient for you.

I look forward very much to meeting you.

Sincerely,

Julie Holden

Julie Holden

Encl.

page unless you have extensive qualifications that you feel you must describe. Do not inflate your résumé with unnecessary details in an effort to make it seem more impressive than it really is. If you are just starting a career, no one will expect you to be rich in experience and skills.

Personal Data

Give your name, current address, home address (if it is different from your current address), zip codes, and telephone number with the area code. Mention any special abilities such as fluency with languages other than English or experience in using business machines or computers.

Career Objective

Express your interest in a specific kind of position by stating your immediate and perhaps also your long-range objectives realistically.

Education

List the schools you attended, beginning with high school. Start with your most recent school and work backward. Give your dates of attendance and the degrees you received, and include any honors or awards you won, your major, and any courses you think qualify you especially for the job you are seeking.

Experience

List the jobs you have held, the dates of your employment, the names of your supervisors, and a brief description of your duties. Again, start with the most recent job and work backward.

Special Interests

To reveal details about yourself as an individual, you may wish to include information about hobbies, about membership in clubs and organizations, about volunteer work, or about any special talents you have. Be sure to mention any interests that might be useful in the job you are applying for.

References

Give the names, addresses, and telephone numbers of people who will attest to your character and skill as a student and a worker. (Be sure to ask permission from anyone you list as a reference, and be sure to select people who will write or speak strongly in your behalf.) People you use as references should write directly to your prospective employer. You may send letters that you have received in the past, commending you for your work, and sometimes you may send letters of recommendation that you have solicited yourself from various people. But some employers tend to disregard such letters, preferring instead those written directly to the employer on your behalf.

Résumé

JULIE HOLDEN

Campus Address	Home Address
8200 Beaver Avenue	R.D. 2, Box 9
State College, PA 16801	Manheim, PA 17545
Phone: (814) 998-0004	Phone: (717) 777-7888

Career Objective
A position of responsibility on the editorial staff of a magazine or publishing firm.

Education

1974-1978	The Pennsylvania State University, bachelor of arts in English (June 1978). Grade point average: 3.25 of 4.0. Honors: Dean's List. Major courses: Article Writing, News Writing and Reporting, Techniques of Fiction, Technical Writing, Advanced Technical Writing and Editing, Magazine Journalism, Problems of Style, Nonfiction Writing; also, in my area of knowledge --Sociology, Rural Social Psychology, Intergroup Relations, and Rural Community Services.
1971-1974	Central High School, Manheim, Pennsylvania Academic diploma (1974).

Experience

Summers of 1976 and 1977	Employed as a clerical assistant at Central High School under the supervision of Mr. Horace K. Williams, Manheim, Pennsylvania. Duties included microfilming confidential permanent records, typing, and filing.
Summers of 1974 and 1975	Worked as a farmhand on the Schwarzmuller Dairy Farm under the supervision of Mr. Robert Wilkes, Manheim, Pennsylvania. Duties included field work (operating tractors and implements) and barn work (feeding and cleaning).
Special Interests	Painting, photography, gardening, macramé.

References

Professor Bernard Krimm
Department of English
The Pennsylvania State University
University Park, PA 16802
Phone: (814) 987-4994

Professor Carolyn Eckhardt
Department of English
The Pennsylvania State University
University Park, PA 16802
Phone: (814) 987-2268

Mr. Horace K. Williams
Guidance Counselor
Central High School
Manheim, PA 17545
Phone: (717) 998-8768

35 Study Techniques

Develop your study skills by applying techniques for improving your comprehension and retention of what you read. Learn to take useful notes when you read and when you listen to lectures. Studying is an active, continual process that requires planning, repetition, and *writing* to help you remember and use newly acquired information.

35A First, plan a reasonable study schedule.

Examine your week's activities, and develop a realistic plan for studying. Consider all the demands on your time—eating, sleeping, attending classes, doing homework, exercising, socializing, commuting, watching TV—and set aside time for regular studying. Some students make a weekly chart of their activities so that it's easier to keep track of their hours. If you do block in regular activities and study time on a calendar, leave a number of free periods so that you have time for relaxing and for making adjustments. When exams or special projects come up, for example, you'll need blocks of time over several days, even weeks, to complete your work on time. Try to avoid cramming for tests, because the stress it produces prevents deep learning and memory. If you must cram, try to outline the major points you need to cover and concentrate on learning the central ideas and facts.

35B Learn and retain information by reading actively.

You can improve your ability to learn and retain material by approaching your reading with a clear plan and by taking various kinds of notes.

1 Survey your text before you read it carefully.

Surveying—looking at the text for information without reading every word—gives you an outline of the material so that you can focus on what you are about to read. When you survey a book, look for chapter titles and subtitles, headings and subheadings, charts, graphs, illustrations, and words in boldface or italics. Skim the opening and closing paragraphs of a chapter or of chapter sections. Surveying like this can give you the sense of a book very quickly.

2 Write out questions in advance so that you can read with a purpose.

Once you have looked quickly through the reading material, jot down some questions about it. Writing will help make things stick in your mind, and your written questions will provide a good short review. It is always better to write your own questions about a text you are reading, but if questions do appear at the end of a chapter, consider them carefully before you read. Then let them guide your reading.

Keeping specific questions in mind as you read will get you actively involved in the material at hand. Your reading then has a purpose: you are trying to find answers to your questions.

3 Take notes on your reading.

Take notes on what you read. Learn how to make summaries. When you read, try to summarize every paragraph by composing a simple, short sentence. Be ruthless in cutting out the nonessential, and put the author's thoughts into your own words. Don't try to duplicate the style of the book or article you are reading. Putting somebody else's ideas into your own words is a good way of making sure that you truly know those ideas.

Many students underline as they read. Underlining has several disadvantages. Obviously, you cannot underline in a library book; so if you underline material, you will have to own the book. Underlining is also a passive way of learning; it is merely a signpost to tell you that something here is worth remembering. But often, when students come back to passages they have underlined, they cannot remember why they put those lines down in the first place. Often, too, they underline too much, and too much emphasis becomes boring and confusing. Underlining is never as effective as writing down a short summary sentence for each paragraph. Writing a summary sentence ensures that you will reconsider the thoughts in the book, translate them into your own words, and put them on paper.

4 Look up your reading topic in some reference books.

You can also aid your memory by looking for the same information or closely related information in another source. Your teacher may require you to buy one or more books for the course, and you should read these books and make notes about them. But it is also an excellent idea to check information mentioned in your reading by looking things up in some of the many reference books available in the library. Try an encyclopedia, various dictionaries, and other reference books your librarian may help you find. (Many of these reference books are listed in 33D, section 3, of this handbook.) When you read the same information several times, presented in slightly different ways, you will find that each source has some details that the others do not have. This seeking of variety in your learning will provide wonderful help to the mind in remembering. If you have taken careful summary notes on the various things you have read, your memory will be all the more strengthened.

5 Learn to analyze what you read by asking questions about it.

Another skill required in study is the ability to analyze, to tell what things mean, to discover how they fit with other things you know. Here again, writing will help you to study. Many writing teachers advise students to keep a notebook in which they can jot down their notes from sources on one page and then jot down their thoughts about those notes on a facing page. If you ask yourself questions about the things you put down, you will develop your analytical powers. Pay attention to your own feelings. Do you like a book? Make yourself set down reasons why you like it. Do you dislike a book? Again, write down the reasons for your preference. Whether you feel interested, bored, repelled, or excited, ask yourself what there is in the book (or movie or whatever else you may be studying) that rouses such feelings. Then write your reasons down. Don't think that you have to like a work of literature or art or a study in history merely because someone else does. But you should be able to justify your opinions, not merely to others but to yourself. And as you get into the habit of writing out these justifications, you will find your analytical ability improving steadily.

6 Look up unfamiliar words, practice using them, and build them into your vocabulary.

With the aid of a dictionary (see 22B, sections 1 to 3), keep a record of new words; write them on index cards or in a notebook. Include correct spelling, pronunciation clues, clear definitions that you write yourself, and a phrase or a sentence using the word properly. Arrange the words in related groups to help yourself study (business words, economics words, psychology words, literature words, and so on). Incorporate new words in your speaking and your writing vocabulary. Here is an example of a word written down for further study.

```
                puerile (PYOO ar il)
juvenile in a bad sense. People who are puerile
are not just children; they are childish. He was
puerile when he refused to let her name appear
before his on the program for the play.
```

7 Review your notes and your reading assignments.

Immediately after you finish reading, and at convenient intervals thereafter, look over whatever questions, notes, summaries, or outlines you have created from your reading. Don't try to read every word of the original material in the book or article every time you review. Skim over it. You will learn better from many rapid readings than from one or two slow readings. Skimming will help you get the shape of the material in your mind, and as you study your own notes, you will recall many of the supporting details.

Use your written work to help you complete your assignments. It often helps if you close your book, put away your notes, and try to jot down from memory a rough outline of what you are studying. The more different ways you can write about material you are learning, the more effectively you will learn it.

35C Learn to write useful notes on your lectures, and compare notes with your classmates.

Taking good notes during a lecture is a skill that requires practice. Some students tape-record lectures so they can listen again to what the teacher has said. But even if you have a tape recorder and the teacher is willing to be recorded, writing can still help you understand and remember the lecture.

Never try to write down everything you hear in the lecture as it is going on. Unless you know shorthand, you cannot write as fast as a person speaks, and while you are struggling to get a sentence down, the lecturer will have gone on to another point. In your haste, you may garble both what has been said and what is being said.

Your best bet is to write down words, phrases, and short sentences. Use these jottings to stimulate your memory later on. As soon as possible after the lecture is over, take your notes to a quiet place and try to write down as much of the lecture as you can remember. If you do this regularly, you probably will find yourself remembering more and more of each successive lecture.

Once you have written up your notes, compare what you have with the notes taken by another member of the class. If four or five of you get together to share your notes, you will each acquire an amazingly complete set, and in your discussions of gaps and confusions, you will further your learning.

35D Take breaks.

Don't try to sit for hours without a break, writing notes about your reading or your lectures. Get up every forty-five minutes or so and walk around the room and stretch. Then sit back down quickly and go to work again. Taking a break will relax your body and perhaps stimulate your mind to some new thought that you can use when you start studying again.

36 Writing the Essay Examination

Most college courses require students to write a midterm and a final examination and perhaps other exams as well. The pressure of time during an examination makes this kind of writing especially challenging, but essay examinations call for the same skills demanded by other kinds of writing. Therefore, you should use writing to help you prepare to take an examination. Writing can be one of your most effective tools for learning both from what is said in class and from what you read outside of class, and if you practice your writing as you learn, you may find that the exam itself is almost easy.

36A Review all your notes.

If you have taken useful notes on lectures and assigned readings, preparing for your exam should not be overwhelming (see 35B and 35C). Read what you have written in the margins of your text and in your notebooks. Underline key words and phrases. Develop outlines. Your goal should be to highlight the major concepts and details that the exam is likely to cover.

36B Write out in advance any questions that you think your teacher might ask in the examination.

Imagine that you are the teacher giving an examination on material covered in class and in assigned readings. Write out the questions that you would give in your teacher's place. Merely writing those questions down helps you organize your mind to answer them, and you will often be surprised at how close you can come to the questions that appear on the examination. If you have paid attention to what your teacher has said in class, and if you have read the material outside of class carefully, and if you have made good notes on the lectures and the readings, you will have a clear idea of what the teacher thinks is important.

36C Read each examination question carefully, and briefly outline your response before you start to write.

Once the fateful hour comes and you have the exam before you, you should take several steps. First, read the entire examination carefully and spend a minute or two thinking about it. You may find that a later question will remind you of information that will be useful in an earlier question. Be sure you understand exactly what each question is asking you to write. A great many students go wrong on exams because they read the questions hastily and misunderstand them.

Next, take a moment to review the first question several times, until you are sure you have it right. Then jot down a few words to help guide your answer. You can write short phrases or short sentences. They will provide a brief outline for you to use in developing your answer, and they will nearly always stimulate your mind to think more clearly about the question. The two or three minutes you spend reading the question clearly and writing down words to help you answer it will save you much time in the actual writing of the exam. Suppose you have a question like this:

> What were the major causes of the First World War? Which of these causes do you think was most important in the conflict that broke out in the summer of 1914? Justify your opinion.

As you read the question carefully, you see that it is really two questions. The first one requires you to name several causes of the First World War. The second part of the question requires you to make a choice among the various causes that you have named—and then to give reasons for your answer.

Once you understand the question, you are ready to start jotting down a few words and phrases to help guide your answer. You begin by asking yourself who took part in the war as it developed in the summer of 1914—information you should remember readily if you have taken careful notes from your lectures and your reading. You remember that Germany and Austria-Hungary stood on one side and that against those two powers stood Serbia, Russia, Belgium, France, and Great Britain. You might write those countries down. Then you write phrases like these:

Russia vs. Austria-Hungary in the Balkans/Sarajevo
Germany vs. France and England; Alsace-Lorraine/naval race
Germany vs. Russia; Germans fear Russians; Schlieffen Plan
Neutral Belgium in the way of German army
Most important cause: German fear of Russia

From these quickly jotted notes, you are then able to start writing.

36D When you write your answer give concrete details that justify the opinions you express.

Many responses to essay questions are so vague and general that teachers wonder whether the students who wrote them know anything or not. A good examination answer mentions names, dates, facts, specific details, and other concrete data. A good examination answer also carries an argument and makes a point—just as any other good piece of writing does.

A good beginning for the essay question about World War I might read something like this:

> In the summer of 1914, Europe was an arena of peoples who hated each other. The Germans hated the English because the English had a great empire, making the Germans feel cheated out of an empire of their own. The English hated the Germans because, since 1896, the Germans had been building a huge navy under the goading of the German Kaiser, Wilhelm II. The British believed that this German navy was to be used against them, and when the Kaiser sided with Britain's enemies in the Boer War, the British people saw their darkest suspicions confirmed.
>
> The French hated the Germans because the Germans had annexed the French territories of Alsace and Lorraine after the Franco-Prussian War of 1870–1871; the French wanted their land back and spoke continually of "revenge." The Germans heard that talk about revenge and hated the French for not adjusting to the new reality of Europe, which in the German view meant German domination of the Continent.

[The writer establishes the theory that national hatreds were a major cause of World War I by giving specific reasons for each country's hatred of another country, including appropriate names and dates.]

36E Read over your response, and make any necessary changes and additions.

Once you have written your response, take a moment to read it over. Though you cannot rewrite it, you can often improve your response by making minor corrections and additions. Look for ways to strengthen general statements by making them more specific. Simply adding a name, a date, or a factual detail may transform a vague claim into a specific reference that will demonstrate your knowledge of the subject.

Vague Though others flew before them, the Wright brothers are credited as the first to fly.

Specific Because their powered flights of December 17, 1903, were recorded by witnesses and photographs, the Wright brothers are credited as the first to fly.

appendix A
Writing with Word Processors

Many users of this book will be writing papers with the aid of computers and word processing programs. If you use such programs, you will eliminate much of the painful physical labor of writing. You will still have to work hard and think deeply to write well; no computer can think for you or tell you what you ought to say on a given subject for a given audience. But the computer, a good word processing program, and a printer will make some of your choices easier. In particular, computers can make revision easier, and as we have said often in different ways in this book, revision is the heart of writing.

Here are several hints for effective use of word processing programs.

1. At the end of every working session on the computer, print out your work. In the jargon of computer users, printed material is *hard copy.* The magnetic disks used in small computers are extremely sensitive. They can be ruined if you place them too close to any source of magnetism, such as the speakers in a stereo. One powerful source of magnetism is the video screen on most personal computers, and if you put disks on top of the screen or lean them against it, you may ruin them. Once a disk is ruined, the data you have put on it—a research paper, for example—is gone forever. If you have a printed copy of your work, you may suffer the inconvenience of having to type it over again—but at least you have your work.
2. When possible, make back-up disks to duplicate your work so that if you ruin one disk, you have another to fall back on. On most personal computers, you can easily copy a disk after you finish a working session. If you have two disks containing the same data, you are much less likely to lose your work. Even with two disks, your safest procedure is to print out a copy of what you have done. If you are using a mainframe computer, you should frequently file your data to the buffer. *Filing to buffer* means that you press keys that put your work on a tape in the mainframe. Once the work is on tape, the computer can crash because of an electrical surge or a failure of current or some other reason, and you can still retrieve your work.

3. When you have printed out a copy of your work, go over it carefully. It is helpful to sit down with a pencil and make any changes in your work that you may wish. Then you can take the printed copy back to your keyboard, call up your work on the screen of the terminal, and type in the changes you have made.
4. Keep your successive drafts. You may decide that you want to return to an earlier version of a sentence or a paragraph.
5. If you think that you have used some stylistic mannerism too frequently, let the computer count the times you have used the mannerism so you can decide whether you should revise it away. For example, if you think that you have used the expression *It is to be hoped* too frequently, let the computer search for those words (in computer jargon such a line of words is called a *string*). Then you can decide whether you have used the expression too often.
6. Printers come in two sorts. *Dot matrix* printers make characters out of combinations of tiny dots; the dots are pressed on the paper, and the effect is like the appearance of the lights in a scoreboard that create different letters and numbers within a square. *Letter-quality* printers provide a type that looks like that of an excellent electric typewriter. Dot matrix printers are more common. They are cheaper and much faster than letter-quality printers; they are also usually more reliable. But many dot matrix printers provide characters that are difficult to read. If you use a dot matrix printer, be sure that it makes letters with true descenders. That is, the g, p, q, and y should have tails that come below the baseline of the rest of the type. If you are in doubt about the quality of the typeface produced by the printer you use, take a sample of its work to your teacher and ask whether it is acceptable.

   Be sure the ribbon on your printer is new enough to provide a dark print. The ribbons on dot matrix printers wear out rapidly, and a faint, scarcely legible type in dot matrix can make life even more difficult for a hard-pressed teacher.
7. Paper for a computer printer is usually fed into the printer on a continuous roll. A perforated strip of paper on each side allows a tractor feed to roll the paper into the printer so that there is no wrinkling up or twisting on the roller. When you hand in your paper, be sure to separate the sheets from one another. Also, tear off the tractor strips on the sides so that you hand in sheets of paper 8½ by 11 inches. Teachers will become justifiably annoyed if they have to separate your individual sheets and put your work together. You should do that job for them. Computer paper is notoriously poor in quality, but nearly all computer printers will accept ordinary white bond paper. You must feed bond paper into the printer one sheet at a time. However, the speed of the printer is much faster than that of a good typist, so feeding sheets one at a time is not much of a problem.
8. When you format a document, be sure that headings do not appear as

the last line of a page. When you prepare the computer to paginate, you must tell it how many lines to put on a page. If you are going to double-space on an $8\frac{1}{2} \times 11$ sheet of paper, you will usually have twenty-seven lines on a page. When you tell the computer to paginate, it counts the number of lines you have specified and moves to the next page. Sometimes you may have a heading that will turn up as the twenty-seventh line. The material that the heading introduces will begin on the next page. This arrangement can be disconcerting to readers, and it makes your work look sloppy. With a little practice, you can learn to insert blank lines to make the computer move your heading to the top of the next page, where it belongs.

9. Don't overuse the variety of types your computer may offer you. With some letter-quality printers, the temptation is great to use as many of the available typefaces as possible, but in general, you should avoid eccentric types. Never turn in papers written in a script or gothic typeface. Use an easy-to-read typeface that will allow your teacher to concentrate on what you are saying.

By all means learn to use computers and word processing programs before you leave college. The computer is rapidly becoming a standard medium of communication. Word processing programs enable you to make sweeping revisions or small changes in your work with relative ease. They are fun to use, and they often give people a sense of control over their writing which they lacked when they were trying to do everything with a pencil or a typewriter.

Word processing programs come with manuals written in various degrees of difficulty. Study the manual before you sit down to work at your computer. When the manual is not clear, ask for advice from someone who has experience with the computer and the program that you are using.

Wp

appendix B
A Sampler of Prose for Imitation

One way to make your writing style more flexible is to imitate the work of various authors whom you discover. The following sentences illustrate many writing styles, and the notes that follow each example describe the techniques that make the examples effective. To exercise your own talents, practice writing about subjects familiar to you by imitating the examples that follow. Follow each model as closely as you can. When you read a sentence that begins with an adverbial clause or with a prepositional phrase, begin your own sentence in the same way. If the model sentence contains a simile or a series of verbs or an absolute phrase, your sentence should include these elements, too. Don't worry if you find the process awkward at first; it will quickly become easier and more rewarding with practice, and you will discover that your own writing style will grow more flexible as you gain confidence in doing different things.

1. A half moon, dusky-gold, was sinking behind the black sycamore tree.

—D. H. Lawrence

[The hyphenated adjective "dusky-gold" is an appositive that adds information about the noun preceding it—"moon." Most of the time, we put adjectives before the nouns they modify, or else we connect them to those nouns with linking verbs. Making an adjective an appositive compresses details and gives us an alternative to a string of adjectives before the nouns.]

2. Around the Muslim's restaurant, I met some of the converts, all of them neatly dressed and almost embarrassingly polite.

—Malcom X

[The adjectival phrase at the end of this sentence, "all of them neatly dressed and almost embarrassingly polite," modifies the noun "converts." Putting the adjective phrase after the noun it modifies keeps the action of the sentence clear and provides a pleasing variety.]

3. But every night the fraternal lounge was open, under the skies, in the salt air, out near the beach, and the party was on, and one and all braved the palmetto bugs and the No See'um bugs and celebrated the fact that they were on the scene where this great Cold War adventure was taking place. Naturally nothing gave the party quite so much magic as the presence of an astronaut.

—TOM WOLFE

[The first sentence gets its power from the rhythmic repetition of phrases and clauses, set off by commas and the conjunction "and." The sentence goes on and on, just like the endless round of parties it describes. The shorter, simpler sentence that follows also gains emphasis by contrast.]

4. From a distance, quite faint though quite clear, he can hear the sonorous waves of massed voices from the church: a sound at once austere and rich, abject and proud, swelling and falling in the quiet summer darkness like a harmonic tide.

—WILLIAM FAULKNER

[This sentence gains its power by a series of **antitheses,** thoughts that at first may seem contradictory. But they are not contradictory here because the author tells us they will go together. We usually suppose that *faint* sounds are unclear; Faulkner tells us that these sounds are both faint *and* clear. We think of something *austere* as being *poor,* but Faulkner captures the paradox of singers in church singing an *austere* hymn with *rich* voices. The hymn expresses a humility that sounds *abject,* but the voices themselves are *proud.* And the sound is both *swelling* and *falling.* Antithesis can be a powerful prose model because it is unexpected and yet believable. Notice also the use of the present tense, which sometimes can make action seem more immediate, and the images of the ocean that add another dimension to the description of the music.]

5. His words leap across rivers and mountains, but his thoughts are still only six inches long.

—E. B. WHITE

[Again, we have antithesis. White speaks of someone with great oratorical skill, someone who speaks with great power. But the thoughts behind the words are weak. So White gives us two metaphors—words *leaping* over rivers and mountains like a giant, but thoughts that are only six inches long like some kind of worm.]

style

6. Never in the field of human conflict was so much owed by so many to so few.

—WINSTON CHURCHILL

[This famous short sentence has three rhetorical features. It is an **inverted sentence;** that is, the verb "was" comes before the subject "much." The sentence also has a repeated word "so," which carries the thought along vigorously. And it also uses antithesis; "so much" and "so many" are in dramatic antithesis to "so few." Notice that like most inverted sentences, this one begins with an adverb. Churchill was writing of the debt that all the

British people owed to a few hundred Royal Air Force pilots, who defeated the German air force during the Battle of Britain early in World War II.]

7. He threw his affectation of detachment to the winds, moved his shoulders slightly, very slightly, made a step nearer to the couch, and looked down on her with an expression of amused courtesy.

—JOSEPH CONRAD

[The sentence gives a sense of continuous motion by using a compound verb that expresses four different actions—"threw," "moved," "made," and "looked." In fact, the subject barely moves, and so the sentence emphasizes his swiftly changing feelings rather than his physical actions.]

8. Hating anything in the way of ill-natured gossip ourselves, we are always grateful to those who do it for us and do it well.

—"SAKI" (H. H. MUNRO)

[This is an **ironic sentence,** one that expresses a meaning different from the literal meaning of the words. The author tells us, in an opening participial phrase, that we hate bad gossip. But then he tells us that we like people who do our gossiping for us. Therefore we must not *really* hate gossip. The participial phrase that opens this sentence compresses thought and makes the irony break on us with the suddenness of the punch line of a joke.]

9. The rolling period, the stately epithet, the noun rich in poetic associations, the subordinate clauses that give the sentence weight and magnificence, the grandeur like that of wave following wave in the open sea: there is no doubt that in all this there is something inspiring.

—W. SOMERSET MAUGHAM

[Five successive nouns, each accompanied by modifiers, come rolling toward us in just the oceanic style that Maugham is describing. They illustrate his point about style perfectly, but they are only phrases. The sentence actually begins after the colon with an adverb—"there." Maugham builds up our expectations by showing us how this rolling, stately style works before he pauses to give his opinion about it.]

10. Like a skeleton, a sentence is a piece of construction.

—JACQUES BARZUN and HENRY F. GRAFF

[The sentence begins with a striking simile and then twists the expectations that the simile gives us. We expect something "like a skeleton" to be ghostlike or horrible, but our expectations are abruptly transformed and we find ourselves being led off in a surprising direction. This sentence embodies surprise in a very few words, and the surprise makes us chuckle.]

11. He was always coming back—back from Korea, back from a broken collarbone, a shattered elbow, a bruised heel, back from drastic bouts of flu and ptomaine poisoning.

—JOHN UPDIKE

[Updike is writing about Ted Williams, the great outfielder for the Boston

Red Sox. The pattern of repetition in the sentence, emphasized by the repeated use of the word "back" and supported by specific details, echoes and enhances Updike's statement about Williams's persistence.]

12. Behind Wilson's speeches were thought and profound belief and ideas which pierced through to men's hearts, aroused minds, and awakened hopes.

—BARBARA TUCHMAN

[Notice the triple compound verb in the clause "which pierced through to men's hearts, aroused minds, and awakened hopes." A triple compound verb gives the subject three related actions and helps speed up the pace of the sentence.]

13. His mind had one compartment for right and one for wrong, but no middle chamber where the two could commingle.

—HOWARD K. BEALE, quoted in MICHAEL L. BENEDICT

[This sentence uses a metaphor to describe the mind of Andrew Johnson, President of the United States after the assassination of Abraham Lincoln. The metaphor of two compartments shows how Johnson looked at people and issues; they were either altogether right or altogether wrong. A mind does not have physical compartments, of course, but imagining that it does helps us see the rigid quality of Johnson's character.]

14. In the streets, in the cars, in the subways, I was always seeking, ceaselessly seeking for eyes, a face, the flash of a smile that would be light in my darkness.

—ANZIA YEZIERSKA

[Notice the extraordinary amount of repetition packed into this short sentence. The three opening prepositional phrases, each starting with "in," the repeated verb "seeking," the three objects, "eyes," "face," and "flash," the six commas that break up the sentence into tiny, hesitant fragments—everything in the sentence emphasizes the constant and desperate nature of the search.]

15. Frenham, his face still hidden, did not stir.

—EDITH WHARTON

[This sentence uses an absolute phrase, "his face still hidden," to compress action and pick up the pace. An absolute phrase always uses a noun and a participle, but notice here that the participle is understood rather than expressed—"his face [being] still hidden."]

style

16. The moments were numbered; the strife was finished; the vision was closed.

—THOMAS DE QUINCEY

[Three independent clauses are joined by semicolons. Each clause uses the past tense of the verb *to be* in a verb phrase with a past participle. The three clauses produce a form of parallelism that gives a sense of inevitable progression to the final word, *closed.*]

17. Most timekeeping relies upon counting a regular series of events: the alternations of day and night, the swings of a pendulum or a balance wheel, the vibrations of a quartz crystal, and so on.

—NIGEL CALDER

[The main clause of this sentence makes a statement and illustrates it by a series of phrases following the colon. Calder could have used a dash instead of the colon.]

18. Behind the bush where I was hiding I came upon various relics of the earlier fighting—a pile of empty cartridge-cases, a leather cap with a bullet-hole in it, and a red flag, obviously one of our own.

—GEORGE ORWELL

[Here we have a statement followed by a dash and a series of illustrative details. Orwell could have used a colon instead of the dash—as Calder does in the example above. But he chose the dash instead.]

A Glossary of Usage

It is almost always best to use words and expressions in their traditional meanings. Although the meanings of words often change through the years, clear communication is enhanced when these changes take place slowly and the meanings of words are kept as constant as possible. The following words and expressions are often misused, or used in nontraditional ways. Studying this list will help you to improve your vocabulary and to develop a sense of precision about the use of words.

Accept/Except
Accept is a verb meaning "to receive willingly."
Please *accept* my apologies.
Except is a preposition meaning "but."
Everyone *except* Carlos saw the film.

Advice/Advise
Advice is a noun; *advise* is a verb. The c in *advice* is pronounced like the c in *certain;* the s in *advise* is pronounced like the last s in *surprise.*

Affect/Effect
The verb *affect* means "to impress, to move, to change."
The noun *effect* means "result."
The verb *effect* means "to make, to accomplish."
The noun *affect,* meaning a feeling or an emotion, is used in psychology.
Inflation *affects* our sense of security.
Inflation is one of the many *effects* of war.
Inflation has *effected* many changes in how we spend money.
To study *affect,* psychologists probe the unconscious.

Ain't
This is an eighteenth-century contraction that has become a sign of illiteracy and ignorance; it should not be used in formal writing or speech.

All/All of; More/More of; Some/Some of

Except before some pronouns, the *of* in these constructions can usually be eliminated.

All of us wish you well. [The pronoun *us* requires the *of* before it here.]
All France rejoiced.
Some students cut class.

All right/Alright

The spelling *alright* is becoming more common, but most educated readers still think it is incorrect.

I told him it was *all right* to miss class tomorrow.

All together/Altogether

All together expresses unity or common location; *altogether* means "completely," often in a tone of ironic understatement.

At the Imitators-of-Elvis national competition, it was *altogether* startling to see a swarm of untalented, loud young men with their rhinestones, their dyed and greased hair, and their pretensions, gathered *all together* on a single stage.

Allusion/Illusion

Allusion means an indirect reference to something; *illusion* means a fantasy that may be confused with reality.

He wrote to her of an "empty house," an *allusion* to their abandoned love affair.
They nourished the *illusion* that they could learn to write well without working hard.

Almost/Most

Almost, an adverb, means "nearly"; *most,* an adjective, means "the greater part of." Do not use *most* when you mean almost.

He wrote her about *almost* [NOT most] everything he did.
He told her about *most* things he did.

Among/Between

Between is usually said to express a relation of two nouns; *among* is supposed to express a relation involving more than two:

The distance *between* Boston and Knoxville is a thousand miles.
The desire to quit smoking is common *among* people who have smoked for a long time.

us/gl

But throughout the history of English, *between* has sometimes been used for more than two nouns. It often has the sense of "within":

He covered the space *between* the four corners of his yard with concrete.

Between is sometimes used for more than two when each noun is considered individually:

The treaty that was signed was *between* the United States, Israel, and Egypt. [Each country signed the treaty individually.]

Between usually expresses a more precise relation, and *among* is more general, but no rule completely satisfies everyone.

Amount/Number

Things measured in *amounts* usually cannot be thought of as having any individual identity; things measured in *numbers* usually can be sorted out and counted separately.

The *amount* of oil left underground in America is a matter of dispute.

But the *number* of oil companies losing money is tiny.

The word *number* often makes for wordiness in a sentence and may be eliminated by a little revision.

CLUMSY: A large number of people booed the band.
BETTER: Many people booed the band.

Anxious/Eager

Careful writers distinguish between these two words when they are used to describe one's feelings about something that is going to happen. *Anxious* means fearful; *eager* signals strong interest or desire.

I am *anxious* when I visit the doctor.

I am *eager* to get out of the hospital.

Any more/Anymore

Anymore is an adverb. *Any more* may be an adjective and a pronoun as in the sentence "I can't stand any more." Or it can be an adverb and an adjective as in the sentence "I don't want any more peanut butter."

Anymore is always used after a negation: "I don't enjoy dancing *anymore.*" *Anymore* should not be used *before* the negation in a sentence.

Anyone/Any one; Anybody/Any body; Everyone/Every one; Everybody/Every body

Observe the difference between the indefinite pronouns *anyone, anybody, everyone,* and *everybody* and the noun *body* modified by the adjectives *any* and *every.*

Anybody can make a mistake.

A good murder mystery accounts for *every body* that turns up in the story.

The Scots always thought that *any one* of them was worth three of the enemy.

Anyone can see that this book is complicated.

Apt/Liable/Likely

Careful writers will distinguish between these three words.

Apt means that someone has a special talent for doing something: "The President is always *apt* to explain away his failures."

Liable means having legal responsibility: "If my singing breaks your chandelier, I am *liable* for damages."
Likely conveys a general expectation or consequence: "People who picnic in the woods are *likely* to get poison ivy."

As

Careful writers do not use *as* as a synonym for *since, when, while,* or *because.*

> UNCLEAR: I told him that he should visit Alcatraz *as* he was going to San Francisco.
> BETTER: I told him that he should visit Alcatraz *since* he was going to San Francisco.

> UNCLEAR: *As* I complained about the meal, the cook said he didn't like to eat there himself.
> BETTER: *When* I complained about the meal, the cook said he didn't like to eat there himself.

> UNCLEAR: *As* American Indians fought as individuals and not in organized groups, no wagon train in the history of the West ever had to circle up and fight off a mass attack by an Indian tribe.
> BETTER: *Because* American Indians fought as individuals and not in organized groups, no wagon train in the history of the West ever had to circle up and fight off a mass attack by an Indian tribe.

As/Like

In formal writing, avoid the use of *like* as a conjunction. Although this usage is becoming more common even among the educated, it still irritates so many people that you would be wise to avoid it.

> NOT: He sneezed *like* he had a cold.
> BUT: He sneezed *as if* he had a cold.

Like is perfectly acceptable as a comparative preposition.

> He rode his horse *like* a cavalry soldier.
> The peas were *like* bullets.
> At the closing bell, the children scattered from the school *like* leaves before the wind.

It is unnecessary to substitute *as* for *like* any time *like* is followed by a noun unless the noun is the subject of a dependent clause.

> She enjoyed tropical fruits *like* pineapples, bananas, oranges, and mangoes.
> They did the assignments uncomplainingly, *as* they would have done nothing, uncomplainingly, if I had assigned them nothing.

Some authorities on writing claim that you should use *like* when you are making comparisons between one thing and one or more other things and that you should use *such as* when you name a class of things and then name several things belonging to that class.

He had a voice *like* thunder.

She enjoyed tropical fruits *such as* pineapples, bananas, oranges, and mangoes.

There is nothing wrong with making such a distinction, but many writers ignore it.

At

Avoid the use of *at* as a false particle to complete the notion of *where.*

Where is Carmichael?

NOT: Where is Carmichael *at?*

Awful/Awfully

Careful writers use *awful* and *awfully* only when they mean to convey emotions of terror or wonder.

The vampire flew out the window with an *awful* shriek.

Careful writers avoid the use of *awful* and *awfully* when they mean *very* or *extremely.*

NOT: It was an *awfully* good meal.

NOT: It's *awful* that you have a cold.

A while/Awhile

A while is an article and a noun:

Many authors are unable to write anything else for *a while* after they publish their first novel.

Awhile is an adverb:

Stay *awhile* with me.

Because

Avoid expressions like this one: "*The reason is because* I don't have the time."

Write: "The reason is that I don't have the time."

Being as/Being that

These terms should not be used as synonyms for *since* or *because.*

NOT: *Being as* the mountain was there, we had to climb it.

BUT: *Because* the mountain was there, we had to climb it.

Beside/Besides

us/gl

Beside means "next to" or "apart from."

The ski slope was *beside* the lodge.

She was *beside* herself with joy.

Besides means "in addition to" or "except for."

Besides a bicycle, he needed a tent and a pack.

Better

Avoid using *better* in expressions of quantity.

Crossing the continent by train took more than [NOT better than] four days.

But that/But what

Avoid writing these phrases when you mean *that* in expressions of doubt.

NOT: I have no doubt *but that* you can learn to write well.
BUT: I have no doubt *that* you can learn to write well.

NOT: I doubt *but what* any country music singer and writer has ever had the genius of Hank Williams.
BUT: I doubt *that* any country music singer and writer has ever had the genius of Hank Williams.

Can't hardly

This is a double negative that is ungrammatical and self-contradictory.

NOT: I can't hardly understand algebra.
BUT: I can hardly understand algebra.
OR: I can't understand algebra.

Case/Instance/Line

These words are often used in expressions that can be revised, made more clear, or shortened.

NOT: In Murdock's case, I had to decide if he was telling the truth.
BUT: I had to decide if Murdock was telling the truth.

NOT: In that instance, Murdock lied.
BUT: Murdock lied.
OR: Murdock lied then, but he told the truth the rest of the time.

NOT: Along that line, Murdock lied.
BUT: Murdock lied when he said he was allergic to cats.
[In many sentences, the use of *in that instance* or *along that line* or some other similar phrase keeps writers from being specific and keeps their prose from being lively.]

Censor/Censure

To *censor* is to keep a part of all of a piece of writing, a film, or some other form of communication from getting to the public. To *censure* is to scold or condemn someone for doing something wrong. Sometimes the censure is a formal act; sometimes it is a personal expression.

The Argentine government *censors* newspapers.

The House of Representatives *censured* Congressman Larsonee for stealing from the Post Office.

Compare with/Compare to

When you wish to stress either the similarities or the dissimilarities between two things, use *compare to;* when you wish to stress both similarities and differences, use *compare with.*

She compared his singing to the croaking of a wounded frog.

[She thought that nearly everything about his singing was like the croaking of a wounded frog.]
Compared to cigarette smoking, smoking a pipe is much safer.
[No effort is made to sort out the similarities and the dissimilarities between smoking a pipe and smoking cigarettes. The dissimilarity is stressed.]
He compared Omaha with San Francisco.
[The use of *compared with* means that he found some things alike in Omaha and San Francisco and some things that were not alike and that he mentioned both the similarities and the dissimilarities.]

Complement/Compliment

A *complement* is something added to something else to complete it.

He insists that sauerkraut is a perfect *complement* to hot dogs.

A *compliment* is an approving remark.

She received many *compliments* because she made a memorable speech.

Complimentary is an adjective referring to something freely given, as approval or a favor.

All veterans received *complimentary* tickets.
His remarks were *complimentary.*

Contact

Many writers and editors frown on the use of *contact* as a verb because it is weak, imprecise, and overused in common speech. You should not *contact* all the members of your club who have not paid their dues; you should *call, write, threaten,* or *speak to* them.

Convince/Persuade

Convince usually means to win someone over by means of argument; *convince* should always take *that* with a clause.

The experiment *convinced* him *that* light was subject to gravity.

Persuade means to move to some form of action or change by argument or by some other means. *Persuade* is often followed by *to.*

I *persuaded* him *to* buy stock in the company.
Careful writers usually do not write, "I persuaded him that it was so." They say rather, "I convinced him that it was so."

us/gl

Could of/Should of/Would of

These are ungrammatical forms of *could have, should have,* and *would have.* Avoid them and use the proper forms.

Different from/Different than

The idiom is *different from.* Careful writers avoid *different than.*

The east coast of Florida is *different from* the west coast.

Differ from/Differ with

Differ from expresses a lack of similarity; *differ with* expresses disagreement.

The ancient Greeks differed less from the Persians than we often think.
Aristotle differed with Plato on some important issues in philosophy.

Disinterested/Uninterested
To be *disinterested* means to be *impartial.* A disinterested party in a dispute has no selfish reason to favor one side over another.

We expect members of a jury to be *disinterested.*

To be *uninterested* means to have no concern about something, to pay no attention, to be bored.

Most people nowadays are *uninterested* in philosophy.

Don't/Doesn't
Don't can only be a contraction for *do not. Doesn't* is the contraction for *does not.*

You *don't* know what you're talking about.
He *doesn't* either.

Some American speakers say *he don't* and *she don't.* But such usage is non-standard and should be avoided.

Due to/Because
Due to is an overworked, wordy, and often confusing expression when it is used to show cause.

WORDY: Due to the fact that I was hungry, I ate too much.
BETTER: Because I was hungry, I ate too much.

Most writers accept the causative use of *due to* in short phrases.

His failure was *due to* laziness.

Such constructions can be vague and confusing. Whose laziness? His or someone else's? The sentence does not tell us. We may assume that it is his laziness. But what about a sentence like this one: Their divorce was due to infidelity. Whose infidelity, his or hers? Or were both partners unfaithful? Such sentences that are changed to include an agent are almost always clearer and more vigorous.

He failed because he was lazy.
His unfaithfulness to her caused their divorce.

A good rule of thumb is to use *due to* only in expressions of time in infinitive constructions.

The plane is *due to* arrive at five o'clock.

Each and every
Use one or the other but not both:

Every cow came in at feeding time.
Each bale has to be put in the barn loft.

Eager/Anxious
See Anxious/Eager.

us/gl

Either . . . or/Neither . . . nor
Both are always singular, and as subjects, they take singular verbs.

> *Neither* Kant *nor* Hegel enjoys much popularity today.
> When things get calm, *either* he *or* she starts a fight.

Either has an intensive use that *neither* does not, and when it is used as an intensive, *either* is always negative.

> She told him she wouldn't go *either.*

Eminent/Imminent/Immanent.
Eminent means "exalted," "celebrated," "well known."

> The *eminent* Victorians were often melancholy and disturbed.

Imminent means "about to happen" or "about to come."

> In August 1939, war was *imminent.*

Immanent refers to something invisible spread everywhere through the visible world.

> Medieval Christians believed that God's power was *immanent* through the universe.

Enthused/Enthusiastic
Most writers and editors prefer the word *enthusiastic.*

> The Secretary of the Interior was *enthusiastic* [NOT enthused] about the plans to build a high-rise condominium in Yosemite National Park.

Etc.
This is a Latin abbreviation for *et cetera,* meaning "and others" or "and other things." Since the *and* is included in the abbreviation, you should not write "and etc." In a series, a comma comes before *etc.* just as it would come before the coordinating conjunction that closes the series.
CAUTION: Inexperienced writers often overuse *etc.* It should seldom be used because it is vague and often implies more knowledge than the writer may have.

Everyone/Every one
See Anyone/Any one.

Except/Accept
See Accept/Except.

Expect
Avoid the use of *expect* as a synonym for *suppose* or *presume.*

> I *suppose* [NOT expect] that he lost money on the horses.

Farther/Further
Farther is used for geographic distances.

> Ten miles *farther* on is a hotel.

Further means "in addition" when geography is not involved.

He said *further* that he was annoyed with the play, the actors, and the stage.

The Department of State hired a new public relations expert so that *further* disasters could be more carefully explained to the press.

Fewer/Less

See Amount/Number.

Fewer is the adjective for groups or collections whose parts can be counted individually; *less* is used for things in bulk not commonly considered collections of individual entities.

There were *fewer* people at commencement this year.

There is *less* substance to your argument than you think.

Flaunt/Flout

Flaunt means to wave, to show publicly. It connotes a delight tinged with pride and even arrogance.

He *flaunted* his wealth by wearing overalls lined with mink.

Flout means to scorn or to defy, especially in a public way without seeming to care for the consequences.

He *flouted* the traffic laws by speeding, driving on the wrong side of the road, and running through a red light.

The suffragettes often *flouted* all the conventions accepted by women in their day, cutting their hair, wearing shorter dresses, and smoking cigarettes in public.

Former/Latter

These words can only refer to one of two persons or things—in sequence, named first, named last.

John saw *Star Wars* and *The Empire Strikes Back.* He liked the former better than the latter.

If you are speaking of three or more things, use *first* and *last.*

Guy's closest friends were Paul, Curtis, and Ricco. The first was Greek, the second was English, and the third was Italian.

CAUTION: All these terms can be confusing, and it is usually better not to use them.

John saw *Star Wars* and *The Empire Strikes Back.* He liked *Star Wars* better.

Get

Get is one of the most flexible verbs in English. But in formal writing, you should avoid some of its more colloquial uses, as in *get with it, get it all together, get-up-and-go, get it, get me,* and *that gets me.*

Good/Well

Good is an adjective; *well* is an adverb except when it refers to good health in which case it is an adjective. Avoid confusing them.

I felt *good* after the doctor told me that I looked *well.*
[Both *good* and *well* are adjectives in this sentence.]
She did *well* on the exam.
[*Well* is an adverb.]
He hit the that ball real *good.*
[Here, *good* tries to masquerade incorrectly as an adverb.]

Half/Half a/A half of
Write *half, a half,* or *half a,* but not *a half a* or *a half of* or *half of.*
Half the baseball players went out on strike.
Half a loaf is better than none unless you are on a diet.
I want *a half* dozen eggs to throw at the candidate.

Hanged/Hung
People are *hanged* by the neck until dead. Pictures and all other things that can be suspended are *hung.*

Hopefully
Since the 1960s, *hopefully* has come into common use as an adverb modifying an entire sentence. Usually, adverbs modify only verbs, adjectives, or other adverbs, although there are exceptions to this practice. Many careful writers and speakers object to *hopefully* as a modifier of an entire sentence because it does not tell who has the hope, it is usually uneconomical, and it may be confusing.
Hopefully Franklin will play poker tonight.
[Does this sentence mean that Franklin will play poker with hope in his heart? Who has the hope, Franklin or the other players who hope to win his money? Or perhaps the hope is held by someone who yearns for Franklin to be out of the house this evening.]
I hope Franklin is going to play poker tonight.
Franklin *hopes* to play poker tonight.
All his gambling friends *hope* that Franklin will play poker with them tonight.
[In these sentences, the source of the hope is identified, confusion is eliminated, and economy is preserved.]

us/gl

If . . . then
Avoid the common redundancy that results when you use these words in tandem.
REDUNDANT: *If* I get my license, *then* I can drive a cab.
BETTER: If I get my license, I can drive a cab.
BETTER: Once I get my license, I can drive a cab.

Imply/Infer
To imply means to suggest something without stating it directly; to *infer* means to draw a conclusion from evidence.

By pouring hot coffee on his head, she *implied* that he should stop singing.

When she dozed off in the middle of his declaration of love for her, he *inferred* that she was not going to marry him.

In/In to/Into

In refers to a location inside something.

Charles kept a snake *in* his room.

In to refers to motion with a purpose.

The dorm supervisor came *in to* kill it.

Into refers to movement from outside to inside or from separation to contact.

The snake escaped by crawling *into* the drain.

The supervisor ran *into* the wall, and Charles got *into* trouble.

Incredible/Incredulous

The *incredible* cannot be believed; the *incredulous* do not believe. Stories are *incredible;* people are *incredulous.*

Avoid using *incredible* and *incredibly* so loosely that your reader can tell that you were too lazy to think of a more precise and more vivid word. The writers of the following senseless sentences did not heed this advice:

I had an *incredible* time at the sociology department party.

She is just an *incredible* teacher, but I still got *incredibly* bad grades.

Individual/Person

Avoid the use of *individual* as a pompous synonym for *person,* and avoid using *individuals* when *people* will do. *Individual* as either a noun or an adjective should be used only to show a contrast between a person or a single entity and the group. Even then, *person* or one of its cognates may often be used.

The Bill of Rights guarantees *individual* liberties.

OR: The Bill of Rights guarantees *personal* liberties.

The speech was directed to every *person* in the square.

BUT: One of the oldest political questions is the relation between the *individual* and society.

It is a good idea for writers to discipline themselves not to use *individual* as a noun.

us/gl

Inside of/Outside of

The *of* is unnecessary.

He was *inside* the house watching the pro football game on television.

She was *outside* the house mowing the lawn.

Irregardless

This is a nonstandard form of *regardless.* The construction *irregardless* is a double negative, since both the prefix *ir-* and the suffix *-less* are negatives.

It's/Its

It's is commonly the contraction for *it is;* sometimes it is a contraction for *it has. Its* is a possessive pronoun.

It's clear that *its* paint is peeling. *It's* often been said that English grammar is difficult.

Kind/Kinds

Kind is a singular form and must take singular verbs and modifiers.

This kind of house *is* easy to build.

These kinds are better than those kinds.

Kind, sort, and *type* are often overused in writing. Always try to do without them unless the classification they imply is necessary.

AWKWARD: She was a happy kind of person.

BETTER: She was a happy person.

Lie/Lay

Lie means to recline; *lay* means to place.

I am going to *lie* down to sleep.

He said he would *lay* the clothes carefully on the bed.

Part of the confusion in the way we use *lie* and *lay* comes because the principal parts of the verbs are confusing. Study the following sentences:

I often *lie* awake at night. [present]

He *lay* on his stomach for a long time and listened intently. [past]

He had *lain* there for an hour before he heard the horses. [past participle]

He will *lay* the bricks in a straight line. [present]

She *laid* her book on the steps and left it there. [past]

He had *laid* away money for years to prepare for his retirement. [past participle]

Literally

Literally shows that an expression often used in a figurative way is to be taken as true in the sentence where *literally* appears.

Literally thousands of people gathered for the funeral.

[The writer knows that *thousands* is sometimes used to mean merely "a great crowd." He wants people to know that if they counted the crowd at the funeral, they would number thousands.]

Literally is often incorrectly used as an intensive adverb. Avoid this usage, which can make you sound misleading or even ridiculous.

He *literally* scared Grandpa to death.

[He did something so frightening that Grandpa fell over and died.]

His blood *literally* boiled.

[The use of *literally* means that his blood rose to 212 degrees Fahrenheit and bubbled.]

Her eyes *literally* flashed fire.

[This is an extremely dubious statement.]

Maybe/May be
Maybe is an adverb; *may be* is a verb.

Maybe he can get a summer job selling dictionaries.

That *may be* a problem because he doesn't know how to use one.

Moral/Morale
The noun *moral* means "lesson," especially a lesson about morals or one that is supposed to grant a general wisdom about life. It is most commonly used in the idiom *the moral of the story.*

The noun *morale* means "attitude" or "mental condition."

Morale dropped sharply among the students in the class when they discovered that they would be penalized for misspelling words.

More important/More importantly
The correct idiom is *more important,* not *more importantly.*

More important, if Jackson had not won the battle of New Orleans, the city might have remained in British hands.

[The phrase is elliptical: What is *more important* is that Jackson did win the battle, and the Mississippi River became a highway from the center of the United States to the Gulf.]

Myself (Himself, Herself, etc.)
All the pronouns ending with *-self* are best used as reflexives that intensify the stress on the noun or pronoun that serves as the antecedent.

"I cleaned the stables *myself,*" Hercules said.

[He wanted to stress that he did the job without delegating it and without having help from anyone.]

Standing in the doorway was Count Dracula *himself* with a silver goblet in his hand.

We *ourselves* have often been guilty of the same fault.

Although in casual speech some people use the *-self* pronouns instead of ordinary pronouns, you should always avoid nonstandard usages like the following:

NONSTANDARD: The quarrel was between him and *myself.*
STANDARD: The quarrel was between him and me.

NONSTANDARD: John and *myself* shoed the horses.
STANDARD: John and I shoed the horses.

Sometimes when you are unsure of whether to use *I, me, she, her, he,* or *him* after a verb, you may be tempted to substitute one of the reflexive pronouns, which sounds safer: "The guest list included Roxie Jones and myself." But such usage is wrong, and you should avoid it.

Nohow/Nowheres
These are nonstandard for *anyway, in no way, in any way, in any place,* and *in no place.*
Don't use these words in writing.

Of/Have
See Could of/Should of/Would of.

Off of
Omit the *of.*

NOT: He knocked the hide *off of* the ball.
BUT: He knocked the hide *off* the ball.

Parameter
Parameter is most properly a mathematical term, especially one used in computer science. It is often misused as a synonym for *perimeter,* or *limit,* especially in the plural.

NONSTANDARD: The *parameters* of his biography of Theodore Roosevelt were set by Roosevelt's birth and death.
STANDARD: The limits of his biography of Theodore Roosevelt were set by Roosevelt's birth and death.

Parameter can be used correctly in speaking of computers:

The *parameters* were set to give the standard deviation from many different distributions.

Parameter can sometimes be used correctly outside of mathematics to mean some constant whose value varies, allowing us to measure other variables by it:

Religion has been one of the *parameters* of life for as long as human beings have been on this planet, allowing us to observe how it affects the relation between family and society.

The word is so technical, however, that you can easily avoid it in general writing.

Plus
In formal writing, avoid using *plus* as a substitute for *and.*

NONSTANDARD: He had to walk the dog, wash the dishes, and take out the garbage, *plus* he had to write a book.
STANDARD: He had to walk the dog, wash the dishes, take out the garbage, and write his book.

Practicable/Practical
Practicable is an adjective applied to things that can be done.

A tunnel under the English Channel is *practicable,* given today's machinery and engineering skills.

Practical means "sensible."

The English don't think such a tunnel is *practical* because they think of the English Channel as their first line of defense.

Previous to/Prior to
Avoid using these wordy and somewhat pompous substitutes for *before.*

Principal/Principle
Principal is an adjective meaning first in importance or a noun referring to the highest office in an organization. *Principle* is a noun referring to a standard for life, thought, or morals, or else the underlying unity that joins distinct phenomena.

The *principal* objection to our school's *principal* is that he had no *principles.*

Real/Really
Avoid the use of *real* when you mean *very.*

The cake was *very* [NOT real] good.

It is grammatically correct to use *really* for the adverb *very,* but *really* is overworked nowadays and should be given a rest, especially because it rarely adds anything worthwhile to a sentence. The overuse of *really* makes you sound insincere, as if you were trying to convince somebody of something without having any evidence at your command. Any time you see a *really,* you are likely to think, "Really?"

Reason is because
Don't use this redundant expression.
The reason he fell on the ice is that [NOT because] he cannot skate.

Relation/Relationship
A short while ago *relationship* was most commonly used for *blood kin.* Now it has almost replaced *relation. Relationship* is called a *long variant* of *relation* by H. W. Fowler, a great authority on the English language. It says nothing that *relation* does not say, but often writers use it because it lets them imagine that they are saying much more than they are.

Respective
The word is almost always unnecessary in constructions like the following, and you can usually leave it out.

Charles and Robert brought in their *respective* assignments.
[Unless we are told otherwise, we would not expect Charles to bring in Robert's assignment or Robert to bring in Charles's assignment.]

us/gl

Set/Sit
Set is usually a transitive verb, taking a direct object. Its principal parts are *set, set,* and *set.*

DiMaggio *set* the standard of excellence in fielding.

It is occasionally intransitive.

The concrete took a while to *set.*

Sit is always intransitive; it never takes a direct object except in the idiom *he sits his horse,* meaning that he sits *on* his horse—so some would argue that *horse* is not a true direct object. The principal parts of *sit* are *sit, sat,* and *sat.*

The dog *sat* on command.

Shall/Will

Not long ago, *shall* was the standard first-person future of the verb *to be* when a simple statement of fact was intended; *will* was the future for the second and third person. But to say *I will, you shall, she shall,* or *they shall* implied a special determination to accomplish something.

I *shall* be forty-eight on my next birthday.

I *will* eat these cursed beets because they are good for me.

Now the distinction is blurred in the United States, although it is still observed in Britain. Most writers use *will* as the ordinary future tense for the first person.

We *will* come to New York next week.

Shall is still used in a few emphatic constructions in the second and third person.

They *shall* not pass.

You may take my life, but you *shall* not rob me of my dignity.

Some

Avoid the use of the adjective *some* in place of the adverb *somewhat.*

He felt *somewhat* [NOT some] better after a good night's sleep.

Somewheres

Don't use this nonstandard form for *somewhere.*

Sure

Avoid confusing the adjective *sure* with the adverb *surely.*

The hat she wore on the streetcar was *surely* [NOT sure] bizarre.

Sure and/Sure to

Sure and is often used colloquially:

Be *sure and* get to the wedding on time.

In formal writing, *sure to* is preferred:

Be *sure to* get to the wedding on time.

That/Which

A few writers use *that* as a restrictive pronoun to introduce restrictive clauses and *which* to introduce nonrestrictive clauses.

The bull *that* escaped ran through my china shop, *which* was located on the square.

Though such a distinction might be useful if generally adopted, it has never been so widely observed or respected that it can be considered a rule of grammar. The distinction offers no help for restrictive and nonrestrictive phrases or for *who* and *whom* clauses, which can be restrictive or nonrestrictive. The best rule is to set off the nonrestrictive elements with commas and to avoid setting off restrictive elements with commas.

Their/There/They're
Their is a possessive pronoun:
  They gave *their* lives.
There is an adverb of place:
  She was standing *there.*
They're is a contraction for *they are:*
  They're reading more poetry than they once did.

This here/These here/That there/Them there
Avoid these nonstandard forms.

Try and/Try to
Use *try to.*
  Try to understand.

Use/Utilize
Utilize seldom says more than *use,* and simpler is almost always better.
We must learn how to *use* [NOT utilize] computers.

Wait for/Wait on
People *wait on* tables or customers; they *wait for* those who are late. Don't say, "Wait on me at the bus stop"; say, "Wait for me."

Which/Who/Whose
Which is used for things, *who* and *whose* for people.
  The plane, *which* was late, brought the team home from California.
  My lost fountain pen was found by a man *who* had never seen one before, *whose* whole life had been spent with ballpoints.
But *whose* is increasingly being used for things in constructions where *of which* would be awkward.
  The cathedral, *whose* towers could be seen from miles away, seemed to shelter its city.
Some writers, however, would insist on this form:
  The cathedral, the towers of which could be seen from miles away, seemed to shelter its city.

A Glossary of Grammatical Terms

Absolute Phrase
A phrase made up of a noun and a participle, extending the statement made by the sentence but not modifying any particular element in the sentence.

The sun rose at six o'clock, *its red light throwing long shadows in the forest.*

When the participle is some form of the verb *to be,* it is often omitted.

He flung the ball from center field, *his throw* [being] *like a bullet.*

Absolutes are common in modern English style; they allow compression of action and provide variety in sentences.

Abstract Noun
A noun that does not call up a concrete memory involving sensual experience. Examples of abstract nouns are *relation, idea, thought, strength, matter, friendship, experience,* and *enmity.* An abstract noun refers to some quality *abstracted,* or drawn, from many different experiences, and it may be used to name many different kinds of experiences. In writing you should always be sure that abstract nouns do not dominate your prose. Abstract nouns require the help of concrete nouns if they are to make sense.

Acronym
A noun made of the initials of an organization and sometimes pronounceable as if it were a word. Common acronyms in recent history include FBI (Federal Bureau of Investigation), CREEP (Committee to Re-elect the President), SNCC (Student Non-Violent Co-ordinating Committee), and HEW (Department of Health, Education and Welfare). The forms of acronyms usually do not change, but the possessive case and the plural are formed in the same way as for other nouns.

SNCC's first leader was Bob Moses.

Active Voice
The voice of a verb used to report that the subject does something.

The guitar player *sang* tenor.

The active voice always makes a stronger sentence than the passive voice. (See *Passive Voice.*)

Adjectival

Refers to any word or group of words (a phrase or a clause) that can be used as an adjective to modify a noun or pronoun. In the following examples, the adjectival words are in italics:

my book, *your* picture, *his* anger, *her* success

She painted the house *next door.*

The computer table *in the corner* belonged to me.

Writers *who cannot spell* often choose the wrong word.

Adjective

Any word that modifies a noun or pronoun by describing some quality.

The *red* coat; the *blue* book

Adjectives can come before or after a noun:

The roof of the *old red* barn collapsed.

The barn—*old, weather-beaten,* and *abandoned*—finally collapsed in the last snow.

Adjectives can also come after a verb when they modify the subject. In this position they are *predicate adjectives.*

The barn was *red.*

Adjectives often have special forms in comparisons:

Her car is *big.*

Jack's car is *bigger.*

My car is the *biggest* of all, and I can't afford to drive it.

She bought an *expensive* meal at the Ritz.

She bought a *more expensive* meal at the Algonquin.

But she bought her *most expensive* meal at Tommy's Lunch, since it gave her food poisoning, putting her in the hospital for a week.

Adjective Clause

A clause used to modify a noun or pronoun.

The car *that I drove then* appears in these old snapshots.

Adjective Phrase

A phrase such as a prepositional phrase that modifies a noun or pronoun.

He came to the end *of the road.*

Adverb

A word used commonly to modify a verb, an adjective, or another adverb. Increasingly in modern English, adverbs are being used to modify whole sentences, though here the effect may be confusing.

They left *yesterday.*

The sun was *insufferably* hot.

The *more frequently* used room deteriorated *more seriously.*

Happily, the car hit the wall before it could hit me.

Adverbs tell us *when, where, why,* or *how.*

Adverb Clause

A clause that acts as an adverb, usually modifying a verb in another clause but sometimes modifying an adjective or another adverb. Adverb clauses often begin with subordinators like *when, because, although, since, if, whether, after,* and *before.*

After he lost at Gettysburg, Lee knew he could not invade the North again.

We often think that women's fashions in the nineteenth century were dull *because we see them only in black-and-white photographs.*

Adverbial

A word sometimes used to describe phrases and clauses that act as adverbs. Sometimes nouns are pressed into service as adverbials.

Many Americans go to church *Sundays.*

We plan to go *home* for Thanksgiving.

Adverb Phrase

Any phrase used as an adverb. The most common adverb phrase is the prepositional phrase.

You may find me *at home* this evening.

We groped around *in the dark.*

Agreement Between Pronouns and Antecedents

A matching in number and gender between pronouns and the nouns to which they refer.

Most *Americans* pay too little attention to *their* bodies.

Emma Bovary hated *her* dull life in *her* little town.

Flaubert created in her *his* greatest character.

Agreement Between Subjects and Verbs

A matching in number between subjects and verbs. A singular subject must take a singular verb; a plural subject must take a plural verb.

The *general* over all the armies *was* Eisenhower.

The *horses run* nearly every day at Suffolk Downs.

The greatest trouble in agreement between subjects and verbs usually comes in the third person singular, made by adding *s* or *es* to the dictionary form of the verb.

She dances with grace and strength.

He yearns to return to the South.

The common contractions *don't* and *doesn't* give particular difficulty. Remember that *doesn't* is used in the third person singular in the present tense; *don't* is used in all other forms of the present tense:

It *doesn't* matter now.
They *don't* believe us.
She *doesn't* live here any more.

Appositive

A noun or noun phrase that identifies another noun or pronoun, usually by naming it again in different words. Appositives usually come after the nouns they identify.

This is my brother *John.*
They loved Chinese food—*tofu, rice, and sweet-and-sour sauces.*
Clarence Penn, *the children's leader at the YMCA,* loved to lead hikes.

Notice that the appositives have the same relation to the rest of the sentence as the nouns they identify. You can leave out either the appositive or the noun identified by the appositive and have a grammatically complete sentence:

The children's leader at the YMCA loved to lead hikes.

Article

The *indefinite articles* are *a* and *an*; the *definite* article is *the.* Articles (sometimes called *determiners*) set off a noun or noun substitute in a sentence or phrase.

Auxiliary Verb

A verb used to help form the proper tense of another verb in a clause. Common auxiliary verbs are *am, is, are, was, be, been, were, have, has, had, shall, will, may, might, can, would, should, must,* and *ought.*

He *had been* sleeping before the earthquake hit.
Rock music *must* have some strange power over children.
They *have* invited Norman to the party, but he *has* not yet accepted.

Case

An inflected form of a noun or pronoun that shows a grammatical relation to some other part of the sentence. English has only three cases: the nominative (or the subjective), the possessive, and the objective. Only pronouns change their form from the nominative in both the possessive and the objective case. Nouns commonly change their form only in the possessive.

To form the possessive of a singular noun, add *'s*. For nouns ending in *s*, add only an apostrophe.

Erasmus/Erasmus's, Dick/Dick's, Germany/Germany's

Some pronouns have different forms for all three cases.

Nominative	Possessive	Objective
I	my/mine	me
who	whose	whom
we	our/ours	them
they	their/theirs	them
he	his	him

gt/gl

Some pronouns have only two forms.

Nominative	Possessive	Objective
you	your	you
it	its	it
she	her/hers	her

Clause
A group of words that includes a subject and a predicate. An independent clause may stand alone as a sentence; a dependent clause acts as a noun, an adjective, or an adverb for some element of another clause. Independent clauses are sometimes called *main clauses;* dependent clauses are sometimes called *subordinate clauses.*

He thought his book was a failure *because it lost money.*

The independent clause (beginning with "He thought") can stand alone as a sentence; the dependent clause (in italics) acts as an adverb modifying the verb *was* in the independent clause.

Collective Noun
A noun naming a group of people or things. In American English it is usually considered a grammatical singular.

The *team* was upset because of the penalty.
The *government* is the plaintiff in the case.
The *majority* is opposed to the measure.

Comma Splice/Comma Fault
The misuse of a comma to join two independent clauses without the help of a coordinating conjunction.
The comma splice can be mended either by using a coordinating conjunction or by replacing the comma with a semicolon.

COMMA SPLICE: They gathered the wood, she built the fire.
REVISED: They gathered the wood; she built the fire.
REVISED: They gathered the wood, and she built the fire.

Common Noun
A noun that is not specific enough to be capitalized within a sentence. Common nouns are words like *desk, typewriter, chair, aircraft, automobile, glue, cow,* and *football.*

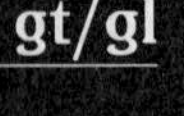

Comparative Degree (See *comparison.*)

Comparison
Adjectives and adverbs can make comparisons. They indicate degrees with different inflected forms.
The positive degree is the form that makes no comparison: *swift, quickly.*
The comparative degree compares no more than two things: a *swifter* boat, runs *more quickly.* The comparative degree is formed by adding *-er* to the

modifier or by using the word *more* before the uninflected form of the modifier.

The superlative degree compares three or more things: the *swiftest* boat, runs most quickly. The superlative degree is formed by adding *-est* to the modifier or by using the word *most* before the uninflected form of the modifier.

Complement

A word or group of words that extends the meaning of some other element in a clause.

A subjective complement usually follows the verb but adds something to the meaning of the subject. Subjective complements can be predicate nominatives or predicate adjectives:

> PREDICATE NOMINATIVE: Her work was her *life.* [The noun *life* defines the subject, *work.*]
>
> PREDICATE ADJECTIVE: Her work was *difficult.* [The adjective *difficult* modifies the subject, *work.*]

Both the predicate nominative and the predicate adjective are subjective complements.

An objective complement follows immediately after the direct object of a verb or another object in the sentence and extends or provides the meaning of the object.

> I wrote a letter to my sister *Nancy.* [*Nancy* is the complement of the object of the preposition, *sister.*]
>
> The university named her *president* last week. [*President* is the complement of the direct object, *her.*]

Complete Predicate (See *predicate.*)

Complete Subject (See *subject.*)

Complex Sentence

A sentence with an independent clause and at least one dependent clause.

> If you want to write well, you must work hard.

Compound Sentence

A sentence with at least two independent clauses joined by a comma and a coordinating conjunction or by a semicolon or a colon.

> We faced strong opposition, but we won.
>
> She washed the clothes; he did the dishes.
>
> Their point was this: men and women should receive equal pay for equal work.

Compound-Complex Sentence

A sentence that has at least two independent clauses and at least one dependent clause.

> The Russians declared war on Germany, and the Germans invaded

Belgium, because a Serbian nationalist killed an Austrian prince far down in the Balkans.

Conjugation
A listing of the various forms of a verb to show tense, person, number, voice, and mood.

Conjunctions
Words that join elements of sentences to one another. The coordinating conjunctions are *and, but, or, nor, for,* and sometimes *so* and *yet.* The coordinating conjunctions can join independent clauses. *And* is the most frequently used coordinating conjunction, and it can be used to join many different elements in a sentence, but all the elements joined by *and* must be grammatically equal. That is, you should not write a sentence like this one: "The house was large, old, and it had not been painted in years." You should make the elements joined by *and* equal as in this revision: "The house was large, old, and weather-beaten."

Some conjunctions are called *subordinators* because they mark a dependent clause to come. Examples of subordinators are *although, after, because, when,* and *before.* Some relative pronouns such as *that* and *which* act as conjunctions and introduce dependent clauses.

Some adverbs have a conjunctive sense, linking two clauses or sentences. These adverbs are words such as *however, nevertheless, moreover, indeed, in fact,* and *as a result.* These conjunctive adverbs are not strong enough to join two clauses without the help of a strong punctuation mark such as the semicolon as in this sentence: "The sea voyage was long and difficult; however, Darwin seemed to enjoy it." Conjunctive adverbs may be used to begin a sentence, indicating a strong relation between that sentence and the one immediately before it:

> Another war is not inevitable. Indeed, nothing in human life is inevitable except death.

Connotation and Denotation
The *connotation* of a word is the traditional collection of associations that surround its use. If I say, "I *demand* an answer," the connotation is much less friendly than if I say, "I *request* an answer." If I say, "The orchestra *slogged through* Beethoven's Sixth Symphony," the impression is much less flattering to the orchestra than if I say, "The orchestra *marched* through Beethoven's Sixth."

gt/gl

The *denotation* of a word is the strict, dictionary definition. It is often difficult to separate connotation and denotation.

Contraction
A combination of two words with the help of an apostrophe. Contractions include forms such as *doesn't* for *does not, can't* for *cannot,* and *won't* for *will not.* Contractions are common in informal speech and writing; they are

generally not used in formal writing. You may find contractions in a magazine article; you will probably not find them in a history book.

Coordinating Conjunction (See *conjunction.*)

Coordination
A grammatical structure that joins sentence elements so that they are of equal importance.

They flew, but we drove.

The bird tumbled from its perch and did a flip.

Correlatives
Pairs of words that connect sentence elements. Common correlatives are *either . . . or, neither . . . nor, not only . . . but also, both . . . and,* and *whether . . . or.*

Dangling Modifier
An adjectival element, usually but not always at the beginning of a sentence, which does not correctly modify the grammatical subject.

DANGLING MODIFIER: *Crushed by the debt on her credit cards,* it was difficult for her to understand that she was making $40,000 a year and was still broke.

REVISED: Crushed by the debt on her credit cards, she could hardly understand that she was making $40,000 a year and that she was still broke.

Declarative Sentence
A sentence that makes a statement rather than gives a command or asks a question. Some writers define a *declarative sentence* as a sentence that begins with the subject followed by a verb without any intervening phrases or clauses.

Declension
A table of all the forms of a noun or pronoun, showing the various cases. In English, a declension would include the forms of the nominative, the possessive, and the objective in the singular and the plural.

Degree (See *comparison.*)

Demonstrative Adjective
An adjective like *these, those, this,* or *that* which points out a noun or noun substitute.

gt/gl

Demonstrative Pronoun (See *pronoun.*)

Denotation (See *connotation.*)

Dependent Clause (See *clause.*)

Determiner (See *article.*)

Diagramming
A pictorial method of showing relationships among various grammatical parts of a sentence.

Direct and Indirect Quotation
In a *direct quotation,* the exact words of a source are given within quotation marks.

> DIRECT QUOTATION: The chair of the board said today, "I will not permit that no-good turkey of a president to dictate to this corporation."
> In an *indirect quotation,* the sense of what has been said is given in a paraphrase; the exact words of the source are not used.
> INDIRECT QUOTATION: The chair of the board declared that he would not allow the president to tell the corporation what to do.

An indirect quotation is not enclosed within quotation marks.

Direct Object (See *object.*)

Double Negative
A substandard construction that makes a negative statement by using two negative forms. A double negative can be a single word such as the nonstandard *irregardless,* a word that has a negative form, *ir-*, at the beginning and another negative form, *-less,* at the end. A double negative is more commonly two negative words, as in this nonstandard sentence: "I *don't* have *no* reason to go there." To correct the sentence, remove one of the negatives, as in this version: "I *don't* have a reason to go there," or in this one: "I have *no* reason to go there." A common double negative is the phrase *can't hardly,* as in the sentence "I *can't hardly* do that assignment." The phrase should read, "I *can hardly* do that assignment."

Ellipsis
An omission from within a direct quotation, marked off by three dots made with the period on the typewriter. You should mark an ellipsis by making a space after the last word you quote; setting a period after the space; making another space, another period, another space, a third period, and another space; and then typing the first word of the quotation beyond the omitted material.
A sentence from David McCullough's *Mornings on Horseback:*

> He must bide his time, maintain perfect decorum and silence, and so passive a role did not sit at all well with him.

The sentence quoted with an ellipsis:

> "He must bide his time, . . . and so passive a role did not sit at all well with him," McCullough said.

Notice that the comma after *time* is included before the ellipsis marks.

Elliptical Elements
Phrases or clauses that we understand although some words have been left out.

[what is] *More important,* we learned to write well.
They are older *than she* [is old].
We enjoyed France more than [we enjoyed] *Switzerland.*

Expletive
The use of *there, here,* or *it* followed by a form of *to be.*

We saw that *there were* feathers beneath the fence.
"*Here are* footsteps in the mud!" she exclaimed.
It was only Lucinda the cat who had torn a pillow to shreds.

When *it* is used as an expletive, this pronoun is the grammatical subject of a clause, the *it* having no antecedent.

It is said that his grandfather did time in prison.
It was all a mystery, and we were baffled.

Finite Verb
A verb with a tense that reports action done in the past, present, or future. A subject must control a finite verb to make a clause. Nonfinite verbs are verbal forms without time in themselves, forms like *infinitives, participles,* and *gerunds.*

Fragment (See *sentence fragment.*)

Free Modifier
A modifier, usually in the form of the present or past participle, serving as an adjective modifying the subject but appearing after the verb. Free modifiers may be multiplied almost infinitely without confusing the sentence:

Hank Williams began his country music career as a young boy in Alabama, *playing* nightclubs called blood buckets, *writing* songs in cars between engagements, *drinking* too much whiskey, *making* his way painfully to the Grand Ole Opry and national fame.

Fused Sentence (See *run-on sentence.*)

Future Perfect Tense (See *tense.*)

Future Tense (See *tense.*)

Gender
Nouns and pronouns can have a masculine, feminine, or neuter *gender,* the name given to sexual reference in grammar. Many writers now make a special effort to use nouns that do not specify gender when both males and females may be included in the name: *police officer* rather than *policeman, chair* or *chairperson* rather than *chairman, flight attendant* rather than *stewardess.*

Genitive Case
Another name for possessive case. (See *case.*)

Gerund
A verbal (a nonfinite verb) in the form of the present participle (with the ending *-ing*). It is used as a noun.

Bicycling is my favorite exercise.

Helping Verb (See *auxiliary verb.*)

Idiom
A word or expression that conveys a meaning established by custom and usage rather than by the literal definition. According to American English idiom, *making out* with someone is different from *making up* with that same person. If you say you are *burned out* at your job, you are saying something different from what you mean if you say you are *burned up* with your boss.

Imperative Mood (See *mood.*)

Indefinite Pronoun
A pronoun (like *anybody* or *everyone*) that does not require an antecedent noun or pronoun, although it may refer to a noun or pronoun that comes after it in a sentence or a paragraph. (See *pronoun.*)

Independent Clause (See *clause.*)

Indicative Mood (See *mood.*)

Indirect Object (See *object.*)

Indirect Quotation (See *direct quotation.*)

Infinitive
A verbal (nonfinite verb) in the form of the simple present and usually marked by the infinitive marker *to.* Infinitives can be used as nouns or adjectives or adverbs.

NOUN: *To die* may not be the worst thing one can do.

ADJECTIVE: She believed she had many books *to write.*

ADVERB: Most Americans are willing *to work.*

Sometimes the infinitive appears in a sentence without the infinitive marker *to.*

She can *do* anything. [You can write, "She is able *to do* anything."]

gt/gl

Inflections
The changes in nouns, pronouns, verbs, adjectives, and adverbs to make these words serve various functions in sentences. The inflections of nouns and pronouns are called *declensions,* the inflections of verbs are called *conjugations,* and the inflections of adverbs and adjectives are called *comparisons.* (See *declension, conjugation,* and *comparative degree.*)

Intensifiers
Adjectives and adverbs that supposedly add emphasis to the words they

modify. They are often unnecessary. Some common intensifiers are *very, really, absolutely, definitely,* and *too.* When you are tempted to use an intensifier, you should always ask yourself if you need it. Too many intensifiers will make readers think that you shout all the time.

Interrogative Pronoun (See *pronoun.*)

Intensive Pronoun (See *pronoun.*)

Interjection
A part of speech usually somewhat disconnected from the sentence where it appears and used to express sudden or strong feeling.

Ouch! That hurts!
Hey! You can't do that to me!

Intransitive Verb
A verb that reports an act or a state of the subject without taking a direct object.

Jack *ran* all the way home.

Intransitive verbs that join a subject with a subject complement are called *linking verbs.*

He *was* sick all that week.
She *had been* an architect in Missouri.

Inverted Object
A direct object that comes before the subject in a sentence:

Whiskey he drank by the barrel.

Inverted Sentence
A sentence where the subject comes after the verb. The most common inverted sentences begin with the adverb *there:*

There is something in what you say.

But other inverted sentences sometimes occur in English:

Ding, ding, ding went the bell.
Far, far away sounded the trumpets against the hills.

Irregular Verb
Sometimes called a *strong verb,* a verb whose simple past and past participle are not formed with the addition of the suffix *-ed.* Irregular verbs are verbs such as come/came/come; think/thought/thought; and sit/sat/sat.

Linking Verb
A verb that joins a subject to its complement. The most common linking verbs are forms of the verb *to be,* but all the verbs of sense are also linking verbs, so you should follow them with an adjective form:

I felt bad because he disliked my play.
The spring rain smelled good.

Main Clause (See *clause.*)

Misplaced Modifier
A modifier that is misplaced in the sentence so that it modifies the wrong thing.

> Mrs. Hotchkiss, who loved Indian customs, served the Thanksgiving turkey in a sari and sandals.

Modifier
Any word or group of words used as an adjective or adverb to qualify another word or group of words. Modifiers help set off elements from other elements in a class. The *red* truck is set off from trucks that are not red, and the horse *in the field* is set off from horses not in the field.

Mood
The form of a verb that shows whether the writer or speaker thinks the action reported is true, false, or desirable.
The *indicative mood* reports actions that the writer assumes to be true:

> Cat books now *crowd* the best-seller list.

The *subjunctive mood* reports actions that the writer assumes are not true:

> If I *were* rich, I would do nothing but farm.

The subjunctive mood can report actions or states that may not be true but that the writer thinks are desirable:

> Let justice roll down like waters and righteousness as a mighty stream.

The *imperative mood* is a form of the subjunctive, expressing a command or a request for an action that the writer or speaker thinks is desirable:

> *Get* out of here!
>
> *Bring* the books with you when you come.

Nominative Case (See *case.*)

Nonrestrictive Modifier
A clause or phrase that adds to the description of the word it modifies without being essential to the core assertion of the sentence. Nonrestrictive modifiers are usually set off by commas from the word they modify.

> Faulkner, *who never finished college,* became one of America's greatest writers.
>
> He ran toward the sound of the train, *stumbling in the tall grass, laughing, longing to see the locomotive and the engineer.*
>
> The DC-3, *one of the most durable aircraft ever built,* still flies the skies in some parts of the world.

gt/gl

Noun
Nouns are names of persons, places, things, ideas, actions, etc. Any word can be a noun if in a given context it can have a name. A sure test for a noun is whether it can have one of the articles—*a, an,* or *the*—placed before it. The plurals of nouns are usually formed with the addition of *s* or *es*, but there are

exceptions: sheep/*sheep,* child/*children,* and man/*men,* for example. *Common nouns* name things according to a general class: *desk, street, tractor, welder,* and so on. *Proper nouns* name specific people, places, or things and are spelled with initial capital lettes: *Italy, the Department of Agriculture,* and *Abraham Lincoln,* for example. *Abstract nouns* name entities that lack any specific associations with sense experience: *friendship, ambition, relationship, haste, details. Concrete nouns* name entities that we may recall from our own sense experience —*wood, house, computer, cigar, highway, truck stop, bulldozer. Collective nouns* name groups—*team, crew, church, synagogue, audience, department.* The categories of nouns may overlap. The collective noun *community* is also an abstract noun, since the idea of community is abstracted from how we see people acting together. *George Washington* is a proper noun, since the name refers to a specific person and is capitalized; but it is also a concrete noun, since the man George Washington was a person whom we can identify by his picture and by works that have been written about him.

Noun Clause
A dependent clause used as a noun.

They told me *where we would meet in Athens.*

[The clause in italics is a noun, acting as the direct object of the verb *told.*]

Number
The form of a noun, verb, pronoun, or demonstrative adjective that indicates singular or plural.

Object
A noun or noun substitute that receives the action reported by a verb, a preposition, or a verbal. (Verbals are infinitives, participles, and gerunds.) Objects usually but not always come after the element that conveys action to them. A direct object receives the action of a verb (or a verbal) and generally follows the verb in a sentence.

Politicians must raise *money* to be elected. [direct object]

An indirect object is a noun or pronoun placed before a direct object and used to show for whom or to whom the action is conveyed by the verb.

He promised *me* a hot cup of coffee. [indirect object]

Infinitives and verbals may take objects too.

We hoped to give her the *victory.* [object of an infinitive]

Pushing *the couch,* she injured her back. [object of a verbal]

Prepositions always take objects.

They swam across the *river* together. [object of a preposition]

Object Complement
A word or group of words appearing after an object in a sentence and further defining that object.

Jesse James rode with his brother *Frank.*
No one swims across the river *Styx.*
They called the storm a *hurricane.*

Objective Case
Properly speaking, we say that any noun or noun substitute is in the objective case when it is a direct object, an indirect object, or the object of a preposition or verbal. (See *case.*)

Ordinal Numbers
Numbers such as *first, second,* and *third,* distinguished from the cardinal numbers—*one, two, three,* etc.

Parenthetical Element
An element not essential to the main assertion of the sentence. If a parenthetical element represents a large interruption of the flow of a sentence, that element is usually placed within parentheses or dashes.

Herbert Hoover detested Franklin Roosevelt (Hoover would scarcely speak to him during Roosevelt's inaugural in 1932) and went on denouncing the New Deal for years.

He disliked the country—its loneliness appalled him—and refused to visit it, even to ski or picnic or hike.

Nonrestrictive modifiers are sometimes called parenthetical, since they can be removed without making the main assertion of the sentence unintelligible. Some words and expressions such as *incidentally* and *to be sure* are also considered parenthetical.

Participial Phrase (See *phrase.*)

Participle (See *present participle* and *past participle.*)

Parts of Speech
The names given to words to describe the role they play in communication. The eight parts of speech are noun, pronoun, verb, adjective, adverb, preposition, conjunction, and interjection.

Passive Voice
The form of a verb phrase that causes the subject of a clause to be acted upon. The passive is always made with some form of the verb *to be* and a past participle.

Lincoln *was elected* President in 1860.
The houses on the hill *were* all *built* alike.

(See *voice* and *active voice.*)

Past Participle
The third principal part of verbs, the form of a verb used with the auxiliaries *have* and *had.* It usually ends in *ed,* but irregular verbs have different endings. The past participle finds common use as an adjective:

The hymn, *sung* by the mighty choir, rolled out into the night.

Their *worn* faces showed the futility of their effort.

The past participle, used with some form of the verb *to be,* is necessary to the passive voice:

Jefferson Davis *was captured* while trying to escape to South America.

Person

The form of a pronoun that tells whether someone or something speaks (I, me, we, our), is spoken to (you, your), or is spoken about (he, she, it, their, them).

Verbs also change to show person in some tenses, especially in the third person singular.

First person: *I cry* (or *we cry*) at sad movies.

Second person: *You cry* at sad movies.

Third person: *He cries* (or *they cry*) at sad movies.

Personal Pronoun

A pronoun that refers to a person, such as *I, you, he, she, who, whom,* or *they.* (*See* Pronoun.)

Phrase

A group of related words. It has neither subject nor predicate, and it serves as a part of speech in a sentence.

Verb phrase: We *are toiling* in the vineyard. [verb]

Prepositional phrase: We must work *until sunset.* [adverb]

Participial phrase: *Leaping the fence,* the horse carried me swiftly to safety in the woods. [adjective]

Infinitive phrase: Lyndon Johnson yearned *to be somebody important.*

Gerund phrase: *Walking the dog* was his own exercise. [noun]

Absolute phrase: The car crashed through the house, *the front wheels coming to rest on the living room sofa.*

Positive Degree (See *comparison.*)

Possessive Case

The form of a noun or pronoun that indicates possession or a special relation. Some pronouns can only indicate possession—*my, mine, our, ours, your, yours, their.* The possessive of nouns (singular or plural) and some pronouns is formed by adding an apostrophe (') and an *s* at the end—*anybody's, everyone's, Gertrude's, Hubert's, women's* bank, *children's* toys. The possessive of nouns ending in *s* (singular or plural) is generally formed by adding only an apostrophe—*James', Erasmus'*, the *class'* responsibility, the *states'* governors. Some writers prefer to add '*s* even to those nouns that end in *s* in the singular—James'*s*, Erasmus'*s*. (See *case.*)

Predicate

Everything in a clause or sentence besides the subject and its immediate adjectives. The predicate declares something about the subject. The *complete predicate* comprises everything in the sentence but the subject cluster; the *simple predicate* comprises only the verb or verb phrase.

The art of the late twentieth century [subject cluster]
has departed [verb phrase; simple predicate]
from all the rules that supposedly guided both painting and sculpture for centuries.
[The complete predicate, including the simple predicate, is in italics.]

Predicate Adjective
An adjective, coming after a verb and modifying the subject.

She was *dignified.*

(See *complement.*)

Predicate Noun
A noun coming after the verb and helping to identify the subject of the sentence.

Ms. Smythe was an *architect.*

(See *complement.*)

Prefix
A letter or a group of letters, often derived from Latin or Greek, added to the beginning of a word to form another word. Common prefixes are *dis-, ir-, un-,* and *a-,* implying some kind of negation, as in the words *disbelief, irreplaceable, unreliable,* and *asymmetrical; ad-* means something added or joined to something else, as in *admixture.*

Preposition
A word, usually short, that does not change its form and that, by joining with a noun object, helps bring the strength of the noun into the sentence to act as an adjective or adverb. Common prepositions are *about, above, across, after, against, outside, toward,* and *within.* A preposition and its object, the noun (or noun substitute), make a prepositional phrase, and the prepositional phrase almost always serves as an adjective or an adverb in the sentence where it is found.

Prepositional Phrase (See *phrase.*)

gt/gl

Present Participle
The form of a verb that ends with *ing.* With the aid of auxiliary verbs, the present participle forms the progressive of the various verb tenses. Standing by itself, the present participle can be an adjective or an adverb.

ADJECTIVES: *Staggering* and *shouting,* he protested his innocence.
ADVERB: They went *singing* through the streets at Christmas.

Present Perfect Tense (See *tense.*)

Present Stem
For all English verbs except *to be,* the present stem is the form used with the

personal pronoun *I* in the present tense (I go, I stop). It is also the form of the infinitive (to go, to stop). For regular verbs, the simple past is formed by adding *ed* or *d* to the present stem, and the present participle is formed by adding *ing* to the present stem. If the present stem ends in *e*, that letter is almost always dropped before *ing* is added. Dictionaries list words in alphabetical order according to the spelling of the present stem; so the present stem is sometimes called the *dictionary form* of the verb.

Present Tense (See *tense.*)

Principal Parts of a Verb
The present stem, the simple past, and the past participle of a verb. The various tenses of verbs are formed from their principal parts.

    Present stem: smile, do
    Simple past: smiled, did
    Past participle: smiled, done

(See *tense.*)

Progressive Tense (See *tense.*)

Pronoun
A word used in place of a noun. Many pronouns have an antecedent that comes before them either in the sentence where they are found or in an earlier sentence. But some pronouns such as *I, you, we, anybody,* and *everyone* may lack a formal antecedent, and sometimes the noun to which a pronoun refers may follow the pronoun in the text. Pronouns are generally classified in the following ways:

Personal: I, you, we, they, he, she, our
Relative: who, whom, which, that
Interrogative: who? which? what?
Demonstrative: this, that, these, those
Indefinite: anybody, anyone, everyone, everybody
Reciprocal: each other, one another
Reflexive: myself, yourself, oneself
Intensive: myself, yourself, oneself

The difference between reflexive and intensive pronouns depends on how they are used in a sentence. Their forms are the same. If the subject is in the same person as the pronoun and acts on it, the pronoun is reflexive, as in the sentence *I did all the damage to myself.* But if the pronoun serves to make a statement much more emphatic than it would be without the pronoun, we say that it is intensive, as in this sentence: *I said it myself.*

Proper Noun (See *noun.*)

Reciprocal Pronoun (See *pronoun.*)

Reflexive Pronoun (See *pronoun.*)

Regular Verb
A verb whose simple past and past participle are both formed with the addition of *ed* to the present stem: play/played/played. (See *irregular verb.*)

Relative Pronoun (See *pronoun.*)

Restrictive Element
A modifying element that cannot be removed from a sentence without confusing the sense of the main assertion.

> The bicycle *that I rode to the coast* had eighteen speeds.
> [You are not talking about just any bicycle; you are talking about the one *that I rode to the coast.* So the clause is restrictive.]
> The man *in the gray suit and white hat* held the gun.
> [The phrase *in the gray suit and white hat* provides an essential bit of information about the subject, *man;* so the phrase is a restrictive element: not just any man, but the man in the gray suit and the white hat.]

Rhetorical Question
A question asked so that the writer or speaker may provide an answer or may demonstrate to the audience that the answer is obvious.

> How long are we going to let a government of the people be the chief destroyer of the people's land?
> How can we explain the seeming shift between Thomas More's early humanism and his later fury toward the Protestants?

The rhetorical question is often a convenient device for getting into a subject or for shifting emphasis within an essay, but you should not overuse it

Run-on Sentence
Two independent clauses run together with no punctuation to separate them.

> FUSED SENTENCE: Scientists, grammarians, and artists are all alike in one respect they depend on the work of others like themselves.
> REVISED: Scientists, grammarians, and artists are all alike in one respect: they depend on the work of others like themselves.

Sentence
A statement, question, or command made by creating a grammatical union between a subject and a predicate. The subject must be a noun or noun substitute, and the predicate must include a finite verb. The subject controls the verb, and the subject and the verb must agree with each other in number. In sentences that are not commands, the predicate makes a statement about the subject. In questions, the statement is made in the form of an inquiry that asks to know if the statement is true.

> The personal computer *will soon become as common in the American home as the sofa in the living room.*
> [The predicate, in italics, makes a statement about the subject, *The personal computer.*]

Will the personal computer soon become as common in the American home as the sofa in the living room?
[The question asks whether the statement made by the predicate is true.]

Sentence Fragment
A group of words that begins with a capital letter and ends with a closing mark of punctuation, so that at first glance it looks like a sentence, but does not include a subject in grammatical union with a predicate.
Correct a sentence fragment by giving it a subject or predicate (or both, when necessary) or by adding it to the sentence that comes directly before or after, if the revision is logical.

SENTENCE FRAGMENTS (in italics)

The telephone dropped. *Onto the floor.*
Working at her desk. She suffered terribly.
Dr. Leyton introduced the visiting surgeon. *Who spoke formally without looking up from her notes.*

CORRECTED SENTENCES

The telephone dropped. It fell to the floor.
Working at her desk, she suffered terribly.
Dr. Leyton introduced the visiting surgeon, who spoke formally without looking up from her notes.

Simple Predicate (See *predicate.*)

Simple Sentence
A sentence with only one clause. Some simple sentences are not very simple.

Catherine arrived in England in 1501 and immediately encountered the English hatred of foreigners, a hatred shown in the scorn heaped on her retainers, in the bitter stinginess of her royal father-in-law Henry VII, and in the indifference of those around her to her comfort and even to her dignity.

Simple Subject (See *subject.*)

Squinting Modifier
A modifier so confusingly located that readers are not sure whether it modifies the element before it or the one after it.

The speech he was giving *slowly* put the audience to sleep.
[Was he giving the speech slowly, or was the audience slowly going to sleep?]

Subject
The noun or noun substitute about which the predicate of a clause or sentence makes its statement. The *simple subject* is the noun or noun substitute;

the *complete subject,* or the *subject cluster,* includes all the immediate modifiers of the subject.

> *The absurd and angry group that assembled in a beer hall in Munich that night in 1923* were to create, a decade later, the most bloody revolution in German history.
> [The simple subject in the sentence above is the noun *group.* The complete subject, or subject cluster, includes all the modifying elements gathered immediately around the simple subject, including the adjective clause *that assembled in a beer hall in Munich that night in 1923.*]

Subject Complement (See *complement.*)

Subjective Case (See *case.*)

Subjunctive Mood
The mood of the verb that indicates the writer's doubts about the truth of the statement made in the sentence.

> If we *were* in Athens now, we could see the sun shining on the Acropolis. [We are not in Greece; the verb *were* is in the present subjunctive.]
> I fear lest we *be* too optimistic about the outcome. [We may not be too optimistic, but the writer fears that we may be so.]

Subordinate Clause (See *clause.*)

Subordinating Conjunction (See *conjunction.*)

Subordination
The act of placing some elements in sentences in a dependent relation with others so that readers can follow the flow of discourse, knowing what is more important and what is less important. So-called choppy sentences are usually sentences without adequate subordination.

> The hunters walked for miles.
> They did not know where they were going.
> They had never been in these woods before.
> Although the hunters walked for miles, they did not know where they were going, since they had never been in these woods before.

Suffix
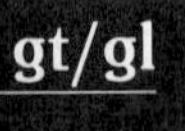

An ending that changes the meaning of the word to which it is attached. The suffixes in the following words are in italics:

> care/care*less,* delight/delight*ful,* boys/boy*s,* visual/visual*ize*

Superlative Degree (See *comparison.*)

Syntax
The part of grammar that considers the relations between sentences and between parts of sentences. In English syntax, the subject usually comes before the verb; prepositional phrases include a preposition and a noun or

noun substitute that acts as the object of the preposition; and clauses serve as nouns, adjectives, or adverbs.

Tense

The form of a verb that indicates time, whether present, past, or future. The *simple tenses* include the present, the past, and the future.

Present: I *speak,* she *laughs*
Past: I *spoke,* she *laughed*
Future: I *shall* (or *will*) *speak,* she *will laugh*

The *perfect tenses* indicate time previous to the simple tenses. Perfected tenses are formed with the past participle and an auxiliary verb *have* or *had.*

Present perfect: I *have spoken,* she *has spoken*
Past perfect: I *had spoken,* she *had spoken*
Future perfect: I *shall have spoken,* she *will have spoken*

The progressive tense indicates continuing action. It is formed with the present participle and a form of the verb *to be* as auxiliary.

I *am speaking.*
She *was speaking.*
They *had been speaking.*

Transitive Verb

A verb that conveys action from a subject to a direct object. (See *verb.*)

Verb

A word that reports an action or a condition; a word that makes an assertion. *Main verbs* combine with *auxiliary verbs* to form the various tenses. *Intransitive verbs* report that the subject acts or exists in a certain condition; these verbs do not take a direct object. *Transitive verbs* carry action from the subject to an object. Sometimes the same verb can be either transitive or intransitive, depending on its use in the sentence.

Jackson *smoked.* [intransitive]
Jackson *smoked* a pipe. [transitive, since *pipe* is a direct object]
Linking verbs join a subject with a complement, either a noun or an adjective. (See *linking verb.*)

Verbal

A nonfinite form of a verb, that is, a form that does not express tense. Verbals are gerunds, participles, and infinitives. A verbal cannot make an assertion about a subject by itself, though it can do so with a helping verb or with another verb phrase. (See *gerund, infinitive,* and *past participle.*)

gt/gl

Verb Complement

A direct or indirect object. (See *object.*)

Verb Phrase

A main verb and its helpers, or auxiliary verbs. A verb phrase gives a complete statement of tense.

I *am helping* with the project.
He *had been seen* in the vicinity.

Voice

The active or passive form of a verb. In the active voice, the subject acts through the verb; in the passive, the verb asserts that some action is done to the subject.

ACTIVE VOICE: Cecil Cooper *hit* the ball out of the park.
PASSIVE VOICE: A ball was hit out of the park by Cecil Cooper.

Word Order

The order of words in an English sentence. Most English sentences begin with the subject, but many English sentences begin with an adverb or an adverbial. Relatively few English sentences begin with participles or conjunctions. The subject usually comes before the verb. The direct object usually comes after the verb. An indirect object always comes between the verb and the direct object. Most adjectives come immediately before or after the noun or noun substitute they modify. Predicate adjectives modify the subject of a clause but come after the verb. Adverbs may be separated by several words from the word or phrase they modify.

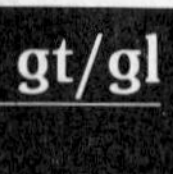

Acknowledgments

Note: Text quotations have been excerpted from the following works.

Adler, Mortimer J., and Van Doren, Charles. *How to Read a Book.* Copyright © 1940, 1967 by Mortimer J. Adler. Copyright © 1972 by Mortimer J. Adler and Charles Van Doren. Reprinted by permission of Simon & Schuster, Inc.

American Heritage Dictionary of the English Language. Copyright © 1971 by Houghton Mifflin Company. Reprinted by permission.

Bereiter, Carl. "Genetics and Educability: Education Implications of the Jensen Debate," in *Disadvantaged Child. Compensatory Education: A National Debate,* vol. 3, edited by Jerome Hellmuth. Brunner Mazel, publisher. Reprinted by permission.

Bird, Caroline. *The Crowding Syndrome: Learning to Live with Too Much and Too Many.* David McKay, publisher. Copyright © 1972. Used by permission of the author.

Bouton, Katherine. "The Norseman Cometh," *The New York Times Magazine,* 9/28/80. Copyright © 1980 by The New York Times Company. Reprinted by permission.

Brody, Jane E. "The Evidence Builds Against Marijuana," *New York Times,* 5/21/80. Copyright © 1980 by The New York Times Company. Reprinted by permission.

Brown, Claude. *Manchild in the Promised Land. Copyright* © 1965 by Claude Brown. Reprinted with permission of Macmillan Publishing Company.

Buck, Pearl S. *China as I See It,* ed. T. F. Harris. Copyright © 1970 by The Pearl S. Buck Foundation. *The Exile* (John Day Company). Copyright 1936 by Pearl S. Buck; renewed by Pearl S. Buck. By permission of Harper & Row, Publishers, Inc., and Harold Ober Associates. *My Several Worlds.* Copyright © 1954 by John Day Company. Reprinted by permission of Harper & Row, Publishers, Inc.

Burke, James. *Connections.* Used by permission of Little, Brown and Company.

Cairns, Helen S., and Charles E. *Psycholinguistics: A Cognitive View of Language.* Copyright © 1976. Used by permission of CBS College Publishing.

Cantwell, Mary. *The New York Times,* 9/11/80. Copyright © 1980 by The New York Times Company. Reprinted by permission.

Carson, Rachel. "A Fable for Tomorrow," from *Silent Spring* by Rachel Carson. Copyright © 1962 by Rachel L. Carson. Reprinted by permission of Houghton Mifflin Company and of Frances Collin, Literary Executor.

Charlton, Linda. Interview with Michael Fitzgerald, *The New York Times,* 2/17/80. Copyright © by The New York Times Company. Reprinted by permission.

Chute, Marchette. *Shakespeare of London.* Used by permission of E. P. Dutton.

Cloud, Preston. *Cosmos, Earth and Man: A Short History of the Universe.* Copyright © 1978. Used by permission of Yale University Press.

Cowley, Malcolm. *The View from 80.* Copyright © 1976, 1978. 1980 by Malcolm Cowley. Reprinted by permission of Viking Penguin, Inc.

Dary, David. *Cowboy Culture.* Used by permission of Alfred A. Knopf, Inc.

Didion, Joan. "Some Dreamers of the Golden Dream," from *Slouching towards Bethlehem* by Joan Didion. Copyright © 1966, 1968 by Joan Didion. Reprinted by permission of Farrer, Straus & Giroux, Inc., and of Wallace & Sheil Agency, Inc.

Doyle, Paul A. *Pearl S. Buck.* Copyright 1951 by Twayne, Inc. Used by permission of G. K. Hall and Company.

Epstein, Joseph. *Ambition.* Used by permission of the author. "Dandies Askew," *The American Scholar,* vol. 48, Winter 1978–79. Copyright © 1979 by the United Chapters of Phi Beta Kappa. By permission of the publishers.

Fantel, Hans. Copyright © 1981 by The New York Times Company. Reprinted by permission.

Fiedler, Leslie. *Love and Death in the American Novel.* Copyright © 1966 by Leslie Fielder. Reprinted with permission of Stein & Day Publishers.

Fowles, John. *Daniel Martin.* Used by permission of Little, Brown and Company.

Gore, Rick. "An Age-Old Challenge Grows," *National Geographic,* November 1979.

Gregory, Dick. *Nigger: An Autobiography.* Used by permission of E. P. Dutton.

Guth, Hans. *English for a New Generation.* Used by permission of McGraw-Hill Book Company.

Harris, Theodore F. *Pearl Buck: A Biography,* vol. 1. Copyright © 1969 by The John Day Company, Inc.

Horwitz, James. *They Went That-a-Way.* Used by permission of E. P. Dutton and of the author.

Jacobs, Jane. *Cities and the Wealth of Nations.* Used by permission of Random House, Inc.

Jastrow, Robert. *Red Giants and White Dwarfs.* Used by permission of the author.

Jenkins, Alan. *The Thirties.* Copyright © 1976 by Alan Jenkins. Reprinted with permission of Stein & Day Publishers, and William Heineman Ltd.

Jones, LeRoi. *Home: Social Essays (1966)* by LeRoi Jones. Copyright © 1966 by LeRoi Jones. By permission of William Morrow & Company.

Jong, Erica. *Fear of Flying* by Erica Jong. Copyright © 1973 by Erica Mann Jong. Reprinted by permission of Holt, Rinehart and Winston, Publishers.

Kendall, Henry. "Second Strike." Reprinted by permission of *The Bulletin of the Atomic Scientists,* a magazine of science and public affairs. Copyright © 1979 by the Educational Foundation for Nuclear Science, Chicago, IL 60637.

Kidder, Tracy. *The Soul of a New Machine.* Used by permission of The Atlantic Monthly Press and Little, Brown and Company.

King, Martin Luther, Jr. "Letter from Birmingham Jail" from *Why We Can't Wait.* Copyright © 1963, 1964 by Martin Luther King, Jr. Reprinted by permission of Harper & Row, Publishers, Inc., and Joan Daves.

Kingston, Maxine Hong. *The Woman Warrior: Memoirs of a Girlhood among Ghosts.* Used by permission of Alfred A. Knopf, Inc.

Kisselgoff, Anna. "Cunningham's Followers," *The New York Times,* 4/5/81. Copyright © 1981 by The New York Times Company. Reprinted by permission.

Kuh, Katherine. *Breakup: The Core of Modern Art.* Used by permission of Little, Brown and Company.

Lorenz, Konrad Z. *King Solomon's Ring.* Used by permission of Harper & Row, Publishers, Inc.

Mannes, Marya. *More in Anger.* Used by permission of the author.

Mariana, Paul. *William Carlos Williams.* Used by permission of McGraw-Hill Book Company.

Maugham, W. Somerset. *The Summing Up.* Reprinted by permission of the Executors of the Estate of W. Somerset Maugham and William Heineman Ltd.

Morgan, Clifford T., King, Richard A., and Robinson, Nancy M. *Introduction to Psychology,* 6th ed. Used by permission of McGraw-Hill Cook Company.

Newsweek. Excerpts from 9/8/80 and 9/22/80. Copyright © 1980 by Newsweek, Inc. All rights reserved. Reprinted by permission.

Orwell, George. *Homage to Catalonia.* Copyright 1952, 1980 by Sonia Brownell Orwell. Reprinted by permission of Harcourt Brace Jovanovich, Inc.; the estate of the late Sonia Brownell Orwell; and Martin Secker & Warburg, Ltd., "Shooting an Elephant" from *Shooting an Elephant and Other Stories* by George Orwell. Copyright 1950 by Sonia Brownell Orwell; renewed 1978 by Sonia Pitt-Rivers. Reprinted by permission of Harcourt Brace Jovanovich, Inc.,; the estate of the late Sonia Brownell Orwell; and Martin Secker & Warburg, Ltd.

Parkinson, C. Northcote. *Parkinson's Law.* Copyright © 1957 by C. Northcote Parkinson. Reprinted by permission of Houghton Mifflin Company and of John Murray (Publishers) Ltd.

Plath, Sylvia. "Daddy" from *Ariel,* by Sylvia Plath, and *The Collected Poems of Sylvia Plath,* edited by Ted Hughes. Copyright © 1963, 1965 by Ted Hughes. Reprinted by permission of Harper & Row, Publishers, Inc., New York, and Faber & Faber, London.

Pollock, Thomas Clark. Frequently misspelled words. Used by permission of Thomas Clark Pollock.

Popular Mechanics. "How to Protect Your Home from Thieves," January 1982. Copyright © 1982 by The Hearst Corportion. All rights reserved.

Readers' Guide to Periodical Literature. Copyright © 1982 by The H. W. Wilson Company. Material reproduced by the publisher.

Rodriguez, Richard. *Hunger of Memory: The Education of Richard Rodriguez.* Copyright © 1981 by Richard Rodriguez. Reprinted by permission of David R. Godine, Publisher, Boston.

Roget's International Thesaurus, 4th ed., revised by Robert L. Chapman (Thomas Y. Crowell Company). Copyright © 1977 by Harper & Row, Publishers, Inc. Reprinted by permission of Harper & Row, Publishers, Inc.

Rosenblatt, Roger. "The Staff Ate My Homework." Copyright © 1982 by Time Inc. All rights reserved. Reprinted by permission from *Time.*

Roueché, Berton. *What's Left.* Used by permission of Little, Brown and Company.

Sale, Kirkpatrick. *Human Scale.* Used by permission of Martin Secker & Warburg, Ltd.

Serrin, Willilam. "Detroit Strikes Back," *New York Times Magazine,* 9/14/80. Copyright © 1980 by The New York Times Company. Reprinted by permission.

Singer, Isaac Bashevis. "The Son of America," from *A Crown of Feathers* by Isaac Bashevis Singer. Copyright © 1970, 1971, 1972, 1973 by Isaac Bashevis Singer. Reprinted by permission of Farrar, Straus & Giroux, Inc.; the author; and Jonathan Cape, Ltd. Originally published in *The New Yorker.*

Stewart, George R. *The California Trail.* Copyright © 1962 George R. Stewart. Reprinted by permission of University of Nebraska Press.

Symons, Allene. "Booksellers and Publishers Speak Out on Credit Hold." Excerpted from the October 22, 1982, issue of *Publishers Weekly,* published by R. R. Bowker Company, a Xerox company. Copyright © 1982 by Xerox Corporation.

Thomas, Lewis. *The Medusa and the Snail.* Copyright © 1977 by Lewis Thomas. Originally appeared in the *New England Journal of Medicine.* Reprinted by permission of Viking Penguin, Inc.

Thomson, Derek. "V861 Sco's UV Flare," *Science News,* 7/14/79. Reprinted with permission from *Science News,* the weekly newsmagazine of science, copyright © 1979 by Science Service, Inc.

Toth, Susan Allen. *Blooming.* Used by permission of Little, Brown and Company.

Webster's Ninth New Collegiate Dictionary. Copyright © 1984 by Merriam-Webster, Inc., publisher of the Merriam-Webster® Dictionaries. Used by permission.

Webster's Third New International Dictionary. Copyright © 1981 by Merriam-Webster, Inc., publisher of the Merriam-Webster® Dictionaries. Used by permission.

Whissen, Thomas. *A Way with Words: A Guide for Writers.* Copyright © 1982 by Oxford University Press, Inc. Reprinted by permission.

White, E. B. "Death of a Pig," from *Essays of E. B. White.* Copyright 1947, 1975 by E. B. White, Reprinted by permission of Harper & Row, Publishers, Inc.

White, Timothy. "Slaves to the Empire," *Rolling Stone,* 7/24/80. Straight Arrow Publishers, Inc., Copyright © 1980. All rights reserved. Reprinted by permission.

Wilson, Cynthia, and Gelman, Eric, "Why Women Are Depressed," *Newsweek,* 9/8/80. Copyright © 1980 by Newsweek, Inc. All rights reserved. Reprinted by permission.

Wright, John W. *American Almanac of Jobs and Salaries.* Avon Books, 1982. Used by permission of The Balkin Agency.

Index

Page numbers in *italic* indicate glossary entries.

Chapter Plan and Guide to Symbols